COMPARATIVE POLITICS

Our other books by the same author

1. Contemporary Political Theory
2. International Relations and Politics
   (Diplomatic History between Two World Wars)
3. International Relations and Politics
   (Theoretical Perspective in the Post-Cold War Era)
4. Great Radical Humanist—M. N. Roy
5. The Constitution of India—A Politico-Legal Study

(Hindi Translations)

1. तुलनात्मक राजनीति
2. समकालीन राजनीतिक सिद्धान्त
3. आधुनिक राजनीति विज्ञान के सिद्धान्त
4. अन्तर्राष्ट्रीय सम्बन्ध व राजनीति (उत्तर-शीत युद्ध काल में सैद्धान्तिक परिप्रेक्ष्य)

Edited Books

1. Indian Freedom Movement and Thought (1919-29)
   by Dr. Lal Bahadur
2. Indian Freedom Movement and Thought (1929-47)
   by Dr. R.C. Gupta
3. Struggle for Pakistan (1906-47)
   by Dr. Lal Bahadur
4. Introduction to International Relations
   by Pierre-Marie Martin
5. Introduction to the Methods of Social Sciences
   by Jean Louis Loubet del Bayle

COMPARATIVE POLITICS

J.C. Johari
M.A., L.L.B., Ph.D.

STERLING

STERLING PUBLISHERS (P) LTD.
Regd. Office: A1/256 Safdarjung Enclave, New Delhi-110029.
Cin: U22110DL1964PTC211907
Mobile: +91 120-6251823
e-mail: mail@sterlingpublishers.in
www.sterlingpublishers.in

Comparative Politics

ISBN 978 81 207 5758 5
First Edition, 1972
Second Revised Edition, 1976
Third Revised and Enlarged Edition, 1982
Fourth Revised and Enlarged Edition, 2011
Reprint 2012, 2013, 2014, 2015, 2016, 2017, 2018, 2019, 2020, 2021, 2022, 2023, 2024, 2025, 2026

Printed in India

Printed and Published by Sterling Publishers Pvt. Ltd.,
Plot No. 13, Ecotech-III, Greater Noida - 201306, Uttar Pradesh, India

Preface to the Fourth Edition

I feel pleasure in placing this edition in the hands of its readers. In view of many significant developments in the field of comparative politics. I have suitably revised, retouched and enlarged its chapters. A chapter on 'Democracy' has been appended at the end. I hope it shall win the appreciation of the readers and thereby my labour shall be suitably rewarded. I am thankful to my publisher (Shri S.K. Ghai) for bringing it out in a new and attractive format.

November, 2010

— *J.C. Johari*

Preface to the Third Edition

Several important developments have occurred in the field of comparative politics ever since the second edition of this book was placed in the hands of its readers some six years back. A fairly larger number of 'western' writers have come forward with their new approaches, strategies, techniques, theories and the like to understand and explain, what they term, 'political reality'. I have carefully taken note of all such developments and, with this view, all chapters have now been thoroughly revised and suitably enlarged. Besides, two chapters—one on Major Approaches and the other on Party Politics—have been added. Themes of political elites, oligarchy, bureaucracy, and military rule have been developed into full chapters. The text has been arranged in two parts. While Part I includes chapters on different approaches, techniques, strategies, theories and the like, Part II covers a detailed study of formal and informal institutions and supra as well as infra-structures of a political system. It has been done to meet the long-felt requirements of students offering this course at the degree and post-graduate levels or preparing for various competitive examinations.

I am sure that this edition will be well received at the hands of its readers and thus my labours be suitably rewarded. I am highly thankful to a good number of my esteemed friends who have been conveying their critical comments to me from time to time in the light of which necessary alterations and improvements have been made in this edition. If still something remains to be done, I crave the indulgence of my readers and, once again, express my desire to count on their gracious co-operation.

— *J.C. Johari*

Preface to the Second Edition

The subject of Comparative Politics is becoming popular owing to the utilisation of more and more sophisticated tools for understanding and explaining, what is termed, political reality. Inter-disciplinary focus on the themes of political significance has been, by and large, responsible for expanding the frontiers of Political Science in the direction of an empirical study of several uncultivated regions hitherto considered as 'non-state areas'. The result is that traditional approaches to the study of politics resting primarily on the foundations of history, ethics and law are being replaced by new approaches drawing inspiration from the disciplines of Sociology, Economics and Psychology. The trend, is towards taking the study of politics to the level of a scientific enquiry into the phenomenon of power.

The first edition of this book was very well received by the readers. It encouraged me to bring out a complete text-book so that the requirements of students and teachers engaged in the study of this subject at the degree and post-graduate levels could be fulfilled in a satisfactory manner. Perhaps all the important topics included in the syllabi of various Indian universities have been covered in this thoroughly revised and enlarged edition. Proper care has been taken to present the subject-matter in an interesting and intelligible manner. I hope that my readers will find this book worthwhile and oblige me by sending their suggestions in the light of which necessary changes may be made in the next edition or print of this books.

I shall be failing in my duty if I do not record my gratitude to my friends like Dr J.S. Bains and Dr R.B. Jain of Delhi University and Prof. Frank Thakurdas (President, Indian Political Science Association, 1975), my meetings with whom have always been a source of inspiration and guidance. I like to record my thanks to my teacher Dr. R.K. Awasthi (Head of the Political Science Department and Director, Centre of Behavioural Studies and Research at Vikram University, Ujjain), who invited me to deliver a few lectures on this subject about two years ago. Likewise, I owe much to my friend Dr K.L. Kamal (Pol. Sc. Dept., Rajasthan University, Jaipur) who engaged me for delivering a series of lectures on this subject to his students assembled in Delhi for contact programmes.

I am thankful to the authorities of the National Book Trust, India, who included this book in their programme and subsidised its publication.

— J.C. Johari

Preface to the First Edition

The study of comparative politics is erroneously taken by some writers subscribing to the 'old order' as an all-encompassing affair for the reason that it, to a considerable extent, makes the traditional study of comparative government redundant by extending its frontiers beyond the scope of some major contemporary political systems of the western world. The motivating idea behind it is that the study of political organisation, instead of remaining confined to the superstructures of governmental departments of certain developed countries, should be widened towards a systematic analysis of problems and issues relating to the struggle for power at different levels in as many countries of the world as possible.

It is true that such a way of looking at things would result in the making of more and more studies in the sphere of 'non-state' institutions and forces operating in different countries of the world—western and non-western or developed and developing—even causing gaps and deficiencies and thereby making it quite difficult for the coming generation of political scientists to lay down principles of universal applicability. And yet it is hoped that most of the gaps would be filled and deficiencies removed by the new generation of writers having increasing interest in extending and improving their studies in this direction. It would be worthwhile to suggest that the study of comparative politics should be made with this point in view that its end is not merely the acquisition of more and more knowledge of the 'political' institutions and forces of some selected countries of the world, it is, in addition to that, significantly connected with knowledge of the empirical world of 'political' man and his 'power oriented' associational life.

In the end, I may say that the various topics included in this book are based on the findings and observations of many eminent western writers to whom I express my sense of gratitude. I hope that it will cater well to the requirements of those engaged in the study of this subject at the degree and post-graduate levels and thereby my labours be suitably rewarded.

—***J.C. Johari***

That which entitles it to be called scientific is that it reaches general conclusions by tracing similar results to similar causes, eliminating those disturbing influences which, present in one country and absent in another, make the results in the examined cases different in some points, while similar in others. When by this method of comparison the differences between the working of democratic government in one country and another have been noted, the local or special conditions, physical or racial or economic, will be examined so as to determine whether it is in them that the source of these differences is to be found. If not in them, then we must turn to the institutions and try to discover which of those that exist in popular governments have worked best. . . . When allowance has been made for the different conditions under which each acts, it will be possible to pronounce, upon the balance of considerations, which form offers the best prospect of success. After the differences between one popular government and another have been accounted for, the points of similarity which remain will be what one may call democratic human nature, viz., the normal or permanent habits and tendencies of citizens in a democracy and of a democratic community as a whole.

—Lord James Bryce
Modern Democracies (London: Macmillan, 1921)
Vol. I, p. 18.

Contents

Preface to the Fourth Edition v
Preface to the Third Edition v
Preface to the Second Edition vi
Preface to the First Edition vii
List of Tables, Charts and Illustrations xiv

PART I: APPROACHES AND THEORIES

1. **Comparative Politics** 3
   - Comparative Politics: Meaning, Nature and Scope: Emergence of the 'New Science of Politics'
   - Growth of Comparative Politics: From Unsophisticated to Increasingly Sophisticated Directions
   - Comparative Politics and Comparative Government: Case of Identities and Similarities in Basic Implications
   - Comparative Method in Comparative Politics: An Instrument for Making Comparisons in Search for Theory-Building and Testing in Political Science
   - Critical Appraisal: Problems and Prospects of Scientific Analysis in Comparative Politics

2. **Major Approaches** 19
   - Meaning and Nature of 'Approach': Similarity and Distinction with Related Themes
   - Traditional Approaches: Emphasis on Value-Laden Study of Politics
     (i) Philosophical Approach
     (ii) Historical Approach
     (iii) Institutional Approach
     (iv) Legal Approach
   - Modern Approaches: Emphasis on Fact-Laden Study of Politics
     (i) Sociological Approach
     (ii) Psychological Approach
     (iii) Economic Approach
     (iv) Quantitative Approach
     (v) Systems Approach
     (vi) Simulation Approach
     (vii) Behavioural Approach
     (viii) Marxian Approach
   - Enmeshment of Traditional and Modern Approaches: David Apter's Illustration of Certain Leading Themes
   - Concluding Observations

3. **Systems Analysis** 38
   - Systems Analysis in Political Science: Growth and Implications
   - General Systems Theory: Certain Concepts and Their Implications
   - General Systems Theory and its Application to Political Analysis
   - Systems Analysis of David Easton: 'A New Enquiry into the State of Political Science'
   - Critical Appraisal

4. **Political System** 52
   - Political System: Implications and Nature
   - Properties and Characteristics of the Political System: Analysis of Gabriel A. Almond
   - Variables of a Political System: Fourfold Analysis of Beer and Ulam
   - Functional Aspects of the Political System: A Configuration—Model of Structures and Functions:
     Analyses of Easton, Mitchell, Almond, Blondel, and Apter
   - Structure and Culture of a Political System: Doctrine of Capability as Enunciated by Almond and Powell
   - Critical Appraisal

5. **Structural-Functional Analysis** 71
   - Structural-Functional Analysis: Subtle Implications and Basic Assumptions
   - Functional Analysis: Varieties and Frameworks
   - Structural-Functionalism in Political Sociology: Analyses of Levy, Merton and Parsons
   - Structural-Functionalism in Political Science: Analyses of Easton, Mitchell, Apter, Almond and Kaplan
   - Critical Appraisal

6. **Input-Output Analysis** 93
   - Input-Output Analysis: Implications and General Characteristics
   - Input-Output Analysis in Comparative Politics: Interpretations of David Easton and Gabriel A. Almond
   - Key Concepts: Inputs, Outputs, Feedbacks and Capabilities
   - Critical Appraisal

7. **Political Communication** 105
   - Political Communication: Nature and Meaning of the Approach: Clarification of Basic Concepts
   - Functional Aspects of the Approach: Political Communication as a Variable for the Comparative Study of Political Systems
   - Quantification of Political Communication: Study of Social Cohesion and Change
   - Exponents of the Communication Approach: Neuropolitics of Karl Deutsch
   - Critical Appraisal

8. **Political Simulation** 119
   - Game Theory
   - Decision-Making Approach
   - Critical Appraisal

9. **Political Development** 135
   - Political Development: Meaning, Diversity of Definitions and Pye's 'Development Syndrome'
   - Concept of Political Development: Some Definitional Problems and Requirements of a New Theory
   - Political Development: A Synthesised Version of its Multi-Faceted Implications and Dimensions: The Issue of Problems and Crises
   - Marxian Model of Political Development
   - Political Development: Model of Stages and Search for an Approach
   - Political Under-Development and Dependency Theory
   - Critical Appraisal

10. **Political Modernisation** 161
    - Political Modernisation: Comprehensive Implications and Dimensions
    - Stages of Political Modernisation: Apter's Paradigm of the Developing Countries
    - Political Modernisation and Social Change
    - Political Modernisation and Political Systems
    - Critical Appraisal

11. **Political Socialisation** 174
    - Political Socialisation: Nature and Essential Implications
    - Development of Political Socialisation: Case of Open Versus Closed Societies

- Major Agents of Political Socialisation
- Critical Appraisal

12. Political Culture 185
- Political Culture: Meaning and Components: Concept of Secularisation
- Political Culture and the Issue of Political Stability and Change
- Ideology and Political Culture: Phenomenon of a Well-Defined Admixture of Political Values
- Political Culture and Political Systems: Morphological Analyses of Almond and Finer
- Critical Appraisal

13. Political Ideology 201
- Political Ideology: Meaning, Nature and Characteristics
- Political Ideology and Political Power; Varieties and Functional Aspect of the Action-Related Values in Politics
- Ideologies and the Nature of Political Power: Elitism Versus Marxism
- Ideologies and Party System: Transformation in Social Structure and Decline of Ideological Controversy
- Critical Appraisal

14. Constitutionalism 214
- Meaning of Constitutionalism: Concepts of 'Constitution' and 'Constitutional Government'
- Development of Constitutionalism: An Historical Process of the Rise of Constitutional State
- Varying Concepts of Constitutionalism: 'Liberal' Versus 'Socialist' Interpretations: Case of 'Developing' Countries
- Liberal Concept of Constitutionalism
- Socialist Concept of Constitutionalism
- Concept of Constitutionalism in Developing Countries
- Problems and Prospects of Constitutionalism
- Latest Perspective

15. Federalism 232
- Federal System: Meaning and Dynamic Implications
- Essential Conditions for the Successful Organisation of Federal Government
- Unitarian Federalism
- Co-operative Federalism
- Inter-governmentalism and International Federalism
- Critical Appraisal

PART II: POLITICAL INSTITUTIONS AND STRUCTURES

16. Party Politics 249
- Party Politics: Momentous Importance of the Subject in Recent Times
- Broad Functional Dimension of Party Politics. The Concept of Linkage
- Meaning and Nature of a Political Party: Liberal Versus Marxist Interpretations
- Horizontal and Vertical Elements of a Political Party: Duverger's Thesis on its Organisation and Membership: Case of Interior and Exterior Parties
- Leadership and Its Autocratic Tendency: Michels' Iron Law of Oligarchy
- Critical Appraisal

17. Party System 266
- Nature and Essential Implications
- Determinants and Functions of a Political Party
- A Typological Illustration: Recent Paradigm of Sartori—Single-Party System, Bi-Party System, Multi-Party System
- Party Systems: 'Western' and 'Non-Western' Paradigms
- Operational Dimensions of Party System: Peculiar Case of the Communist Party
- Critical Appraisal

18. Presure Group Politics 288
- Pressure Group Politics: Significance of a New Area of Study
- Political Parties and Pressure Groups: Inter-Action and Inter-Penetration
- Pressure Groups and Electoral Process: Recruitment of Legislators
- Pressure Groups and Rule-Making Department: Influencing the Process of Legislation
- Pressure Groups and Rule-Implementation Department: Influencing the Political Executive
- Pressure Groups and Bureaucracy: Influencing the Permanent Civil Servants
- Pressure Groups and Judiciary: Influencing the Adjudicators
- Pressure Groups and Public Opinion: Influencing the Mass Media
- Determinants of Pressure Group Politics
- Critical Appraisal

19. Pressure Groups 310
- Group Theory: Meaning, Nature and Functional Dimension
- Pressure Groups: Meaning and Nature
- Existence and Articulation of Pressure Group Politics
- Critical Appraisal

20. Techniques of Pressure Politics 325
- Lobbying
- Strike
- Bandh
- Gherao

21. Typology of States 338
- Liberal-Democratic State
- Totalitarian State
- Autocratic State
- Corporatist and Neo-Corporatist State
- State in the Third World Countries
- Welfare State

22. Rule-Making Department 360
- Legislature: Meaning and Functions
- Emergency Role of Legislatures: A Modern Interpretation
- Modern Legislature: A Typological Illustration
- Delegated Legislation
- Committee System
- Decline of Legislature

23. Representation 385
- Meaning, Nature and Typological Illustrations
- Representation and Responsiveness: Role of Representative and Doctrine of the Legislative Mandate
- Varieties of Representation– Territorial Representation, Proportional Representation, Minority Representation, Functional Representation, Concluding Observations
- Critical Appraisal

24. Rule-Application Department 401
- Executive: Meanings and Varieties
- Functions of the Executive
- Parliamentary Government: Classical English Model
- Cabinet Government: Recent English Model
- Prime-Ministerial Government: Latest English and Indian Models
- Presidential Government: Models of USA, Brazil and South Africa
- Quasi-Presidential Government: The French and Russian Models
- Chancellor Government: The German Model
- Council Government: The Swiss Model
- Critical Appraisal

25. Rule-Adjudication Department 419
- Judiciary: Meaning and Nature of Law and Political Process
- Recruitment and Functions of Judges
- Judicial Review
- Critical Appraisal

26. Separation of Powers 432
- Meaning: Classical and Modern Interpretations
- Main Exponents: Montesquieu's Classic Contribution for the Protection of Individual Liberty
- Separation of Powers in the United States: Application of the Doctrine with the System of Checks and Balances
- Critical Appraisal

27. Political Elites 439
- Theory of Political Elites: Nature and Essential Implications
- Different Approaches: Kroese's Theory of Fulfilment of a Specific Mission by the Elites
- Leading Elite Theorists
- Elite Theory and Different Political Systems
- Critical Appraisal

28. Oligarchy 452
- Nature and Essential Implications: Its Distinction with Elite Rule
- Operational Dimension
- 'Iron Law of Oligarchy': Empirical Justification of Minority Rule
- Critical Appraisal

29. Bureaucracy 458
- Concept of Bureaucracy: Liberal and Marxist Interpretations
- Bureaucracy: Nature and Essential Implications of the System
- Theories of Bureaucracy
- Organisation of Bureaucracy
- Functions and Role
- The Power Concept: Elitism and Bureaucracy
- Bureaucracy and Military: Similarities and Differences in the Assumption of Power
- Varieties of Bureaucratic Hold: Direct and Indirect, Democractic and Autocratic
- Bureaucracy as a Pressure Group in Its Own Right
- Politicisation of Bureaucracy: Debate on Neutrality Versus Commitment of Public Services
- Bureaucracy and the Third World Perspective
- Controlling Bureaucracy
- Critical Appraisal

30. Military Rule 480
- Types of Military Rule: Search for Legitimacy and Distinction with Authoritarian Regimes
- Forms of Military Intervention
- Causes of Military Intervention
- Levels of Military Intervention
- Critical Appraisal

31. Democracy 491
- Meaning and Forms
- Case of Developed Countries: 'First Wave of Democracy'
- Case of Developing Countries: 'Second Wave of Democracy'
- Post - Communist States: 'Third Wave of Democracy'
- Critical Appraisal

Bibliography 513

Index 518

List of Tables, Charts and Illustrations

		Pages
1.	Some Important Statements about Old Comparative Politics	5
2.	Some Important Statements about New Comparative Politics	12
3.	Some Important Statements about Uses of Comparative Method	16
4.	Reasons for Studying Comparative Government	17
5.	Shortcomings of Traditional Approaches	23
6.	Apter's Paradigm of Main Approaches	36
7.	Substantive Nature of General Systems	43
8.	A Dynamic Response Model of a Political System	47
9.	Some Statements about Political System	56
10.	Models of Easton's Political System	61
11.	Models of Mitchell's Political System	62
12.	Almond's Model of Political System	63
13.	Blondel's Model of Political System	65
14.	Apter's Model of Political System	66
15.	Structural-Functional Model of Parsons	78
16.	Some Important Statements about Structural-Functionalism	80
17.	Parsonian Model	82
18.	Structural-Functional Imperatives and Requisites of Marion Levy Jr. Dahrendorf and Apter	84
19.	Some Critical Observations about Structural-Functionalism	90
20.	Some Important Statements about Input-Output Analysis	96
21.	Almond's Model of Input-Output Analysis	100
22.	Deutsch's Model of Political Communication	116
23.	Type, Forms and Characteristics Defining the Forms of Conflict in Game Theory	121
24.	SBS Model of Decision-Making Cluster	132
25.	Indices of Political Development and Decay	142
26.	Variables of Political Development and Decay	152
27.	Wallerstein's Illustration	156
28.	Critical Comments of Chilcote on Political Development and Under-Development	158
29.	Rustow and Ward on Characteristics of Modern Polity	168
30.	Huntington on Characteristics of the Modernisation Process	168
31.	Political Modernisation and Social and Political Systems	171
32.	Some Important Statements about Political Socialisation	176
33.	Lasswell's Common Set of Categories	182

34. Some Important Statements about Political Culture 186
35. Almond's Morphological Illustration of Political Culture and Political System 194
36. Some Important Statements about Ideology 208
37. End of Ideology—Ideologisation versus De-ideologisation 210
38. Some Important Statements about Constitutionalism 215
39. Friedrich's Paradigm 216
40. Heywood's Analysis of Federal System 238
41. Some Important Statements about Federalism 243
42. Some Definitional Statements about a Political Party 254
43. Party Systems 272
44. Sartori's Classification of Party Systems 278
45. Lijphart on three kinds of Party Systems 279
46. Apter's Model of Party-State Relationships and Its Characteristics 280
47. Functions of Political Parties 285
48. Merits and Demerits of Party System 286
49. Interest Group Systems and their Characteristic Features 292
50. Determinants of Pressure Group Politics 305
51. Almond's Classification of Pressure Groups 317
52. Heywood's Analysis of Pressure Groups and their Merits and Demerits 322
53. Liberal Democracy, Totalitarianism and Authoritarianism 343
54. Corporatism and Neo-Corporatism 349
55. Functions and Role of a Legislator: Price's Paradigm of a Senator 366
56. Some Important Statements about Representation 400
57. Kinds of Executive 403
58. Vital Political Powers of the French President 414
59. Separation of Powers: Checks and Balances 436
60. Some Important Statements about Separation of Powers 438
61. Finer's Model of Political Elites 442
62. Political Elite Theorists 445
63. Statements about Iron Law of Oligarchy 456
64. Some Important Statements about Military Rule 483
65. Two Methods of Controlling Military 483
66. Levels and Methods of Military Intervention 487
67. Finer's Paradigm of Political Culture and Military Intervention 489
68. Some Important Statements about Democracy 492
69. Salient Features of Liberal Democracy 493
70. Salient Features of Radical or Social Democracy 493
71. Some Important Terms relating to Democracy 494
72. Huntington on Three Waves of Democracy 495
73. Essential Features of Democracy 498
74. Features of a Post-Communist State 498
75. Dahrendorf on the Dilemma of Three Clocks 499
76. Types of Democracy in the Third World 501

77. Commonwealth of Independent States: Democratic Features of the Minsk Agreement (1991) 503
78. Some Important Statements about Socialist Democracy 504
79. Communist Regimes in the 1980s 506
80. Main Features of a Communist State 506
81. Some Important Definitional Statements about Democracy 507
82. Synonyms for Semi-Democracy 508
83. Varieties of Democracy 509
84. Some Important Statements about Democracy and Democratisation 511

PART I

APPROACHES AND THEORIES

Whether we are thinking of a body politic as a whole or face-to-face situation, we are considering 'arenas' in which "participants" are striving to accomplish their purposes by influencing 'outcomes'. The purposes are directed towards 'preferred events' ('values' and 'interpretations' of values in terms of 'institutional practices'). Participants are seeking to maximise power and other values by influencing outcomes. They use the values at their disposal as 'base values' according to strategies.

—Harold D. Lasswell[1]

Now the problem is to identify the general perspectives associated with other disciplines – the vantage points from which events are viewed. Our concern is with the kinds of data that are considered and the kinds of concepts that are employed. The assumption is that the approaches of the other disciplines might in some cases be useful in handling political questions.

—Vernon Van Dyke[2]

Political Science has been unable to evolve a central model that could serve as a reasonably stable point of departure into political inquiry....Modern political science resembles a Gothic cathedral, built over many many centuries, with its turrets, spires, balconies, nooks, and crannies.

—Heinz Eulau[3]

---

1. See Lasswell: "Current Studies of the Decision Process: Automation versus Creativity" in *Western Political Quarterly,* Vol. 8 (Sept, 1955), pp. 81-82.
2. V.V. Dyke: *Political Science: A Philosophical Analysis* (Stanford: Stanford Univ. Press, 1962), p. 122.
3. Eulau: "Political Science" in B.F. Hoselitz (ed.): *A Reader's Guide to the Social Sciences* (New York, 1959) p. 92.

1

Comparative Politics

> More recently, modern social science also has increased our powers to observe and compare systematically this empirical world of facts around us and to subject many of these facts and processes to quantitative measurement and logical and mathematical analysis. At the same time, the behavioural sciences have given us a good deal of new and partly verified information as to how people think, feel, perceive, and act, individually and in groups.
>
> **—Karl Deutsch[1]**

The subject of comparative politics virtually constitutes a study in the direction of the 'expanding horizon of political science' wherein we seem to have emerged from the 'plains of doubts and darkness' to a 'higher plateau' to see what our passionate endeavours, particularly of the skeptical decade of the 1950's and the 'determined decade' of the 1960's, "have produced, in which the earlier high points of the discipline have lost some of their erstwhile importance or at least are now seen in a new light, and those whose significance suffered by neglect, have emerged in our perspective and awareness in the vale of political knowledge, which contains both rushing torrents *(i.e.,* political process as a whole) as well as limped pools *(i.e.,* speculative political thought)".[2] What has played the role of a motivating force in this important direction is the quest to study 'political reality' by means of new techniques and approaches in a way so that the entire area of 'politics' may be covered. As a result, not a study of the 'government' but of the 'governments' has become the central concern that implies the taking of 'decision' whether "in the United Nations, or in a parish council, in a trade union or in a papal conclave, in a board room or in a tribe."[3] Comparative politics has appeared as a subject of momentous significance on account of this vital reason that a great deal of experimentation "is now going on with new approaches, new definitions, new research tools. Perhaps the main reason for the present intellectual ferment is a widespread feeling of disappointment and dissatisfaction with the traditional descriptive approach to the subject."[4]

Comparative Politics: Meaning, Nature and Scope: Emergence of the 'New Science of Politics'

Politics is a continuous, timeless, ever-changing and universal activity having its key manifestation in the making of a decision to face and solve a 'predicament'. It "flows from a special kind of activity, a form of human

1. Karl Deutsch : "Nation and World" in Ithiel de Sola Pool (ed.) : *Contemporary Political Science : Towards Empirical Theory* (New York : McGraw Hill Co, 1967), p. 207.
2. Frank Thakurdas : "The Expanding Frontier of Political Science" in *Indian Journal of Political Science,* Vol XXXIV, No. 4, 1973, p. 397.
3. Jean Blondel: *An Introduction to Comparative Government* (London : Wieden-field and Nicolson, 1969), p. 1.
4. Bernard E. Brown : *New Directions in Comparative Politics* (Bombay : Asia Pub, 1962), p. 1.

behaviour."[5] It refers to the making or taking of a decision in which some political action is involved. It is a different thing that political scientists define and interpret the term 'political action' in their own ways that ascribes to them the title of being a conservative, or a traditionalist, or a modernist. It is for this reason that while Oakeshott defines political activity as "an activity in which human beings, related to one another as members of a civil association, think and speak about the arrangements and the conditions of their association from the point of view of their desirability, make proposals about changes in these arrangements and conditions, try to persuade others of the desirability of the proposed changes and act in such a manner as to promote the changes"; David Easton treats it as an action for the 'authoritative allocation of values'; Harold Lasswell and Robert Dahl describe it as 'a special case in the exercise of power'; and Jean Blondel lays emphasis on the point of 'decision taking'. However, a fine interpretation of the term 'political activity' is thus given by Oakeshott who says: "In political activity, then, men sail a boundless and bottomless sea; there is neither harbour for shelter nor floor for anchorage; neither starting place nor appointed destination. The enterprise is to keep afloat on an even keel; the sea is both friend and enemy."[6]

In the field of comparative politics, the term 'politics' has three connotations—political activity, political process and political power. As already pointed out, political activity consists of the efforts by which conditions of conflicts are created and resolved in a way pertaining to the interests of the people, as far as possible, who play their part in the 'struggle for power'. The reduction of tensions or the resolution of conflicts naturally takes place through the operation of permanent mechanisms of tension reduction as well as, from time to time, by the introduction of further 'reserve' mechanisms designed to reduce the amount of tensions and conflicts in emergencies. If politics means the authoritative allocation of 'values', some measure of conflict is bound to arise between 'values' as desired by the people and 'values' as held by the men in power. Thus arise conflicts that demand their solution and what leads to efforts in this regard constitutes political activity. It is the government that "has to solve these conflicts by whatever means are at its disposal, the only limitation being that in so doing it must prevent the break-up of the polity. Politics ceases where secession, and indeed civil war begins, as, at that point, there is no longer an authoritative allocation of values, but two sides allocating their values differently"[7]. It should, however, not be inferred from this statement that there is nothing like political activity during the days of civil war or some revolutionary upheaval, it simply means that as such an eventuality "constitutes a high point of tension in the life of a community, the role of political action must consist of preventing the community from reaching such a point."[8]

Politics not only connotes 'political activity', it also implies a 'train of activities', *i.e.*, efforts directed towards creating the conditions of tension and having their resolution until the point of 'spontaneous unanimity' is achieved.[9] Political activity emanates from a situation of 'predicament'—a form of human behaviour in which the interests of persons, more than one, clash or interact for the purpose of having an allocation of binding values in their respective favours. The moment a voice is raised in a group or a community of people for a common rule or policy on any issue whatsoever, a predicament is created in the sense that even to decide against the demand requires to take a

5. Samuel E. Finer : *Comparative Government* (London : Allen Lane, Penguin Press, 1970). p. 7.
6. Michael Oakeshott: *Political Education* (Cambridge, 1952), p. 15.
7. Blondel, *op. cit.*, p. 7.
8. *ibid.*
9. Finer, *op. cit.*, p. 11.

Some Important Statements about Old Comparative Politics

The term 'comparative politics' refers to a subject matter, a field of specialty within the academic study of politics (that is, political science), and a method of approach to the study of politics. The subject matter of comparative politics is the domestic politics of countries or peoples.

—Mark Kesselman, Joel Krieger and W.A. Joseph
Comparative Politics at the Crossroads, p. 4.

Within political science, comparative politics is a sub-field that compares this struggle across countries. By studying a wide variety of countries, comparativists hope to shed light on the countries under study as well as on our own political systems.

— Patrick O'Neil
Essentials of Comparative Politics, p. 3.

Comparative politics is the study of political systems, not as isolated cases but through generalisations and comparisons.

— G.A. Almond, G.B. Powell, Jr., Kaare Strom and R.J. Dalton
Comparative Politics Today - A World View, p. 11.

Comparative government usually refers to the study of institutions and functions of countries or nation-states in Europe with attention to their executives, legislatures and judiciaries as well as such supplementary organisations as political parties and pressure groups. Comparative politics, in contrast, studies a broader range of political activity organisations, not directly related to national government for example, tribes, communities, associations, and unions.

—R.H. Chilcote
Theories of Comparative Politics, p. 3.

decision. The matter does not stop here. Further problem arises when the members of a group or a community advocate mutually exclusive policies. The result is clash of interests and the stage of resolution of conflicts can be achieved either by peaceful means of reasoning, persuasion, adjustments, diplomacy or compromise or by the violent means of force and coercion. While, in the former case, competing agents may come piecemeal to abandon a part of their demands in order to have a mutually acceptable solution, in the latter case, the policy of one section may, wholly or largely, prevail over the desires of another. The former position may be called the state of 'spontaneous unanimity', the latter as imposed consensus. The common point is that political activity stops at the point of 'political rest.' "So, just as a situation of political rest does not start up any political activity, it also closes down a cycle of political activity."[10]

Political process is an extension of the sense of political activity. Here the case of all those agencies figures in which have their role in the decision-making process. The study of politics is thus broadened so as to include even 'non-state' agencies. A study of the way groups and associations operate shows that they are not free from the trends of struggle for power; they have their internal'governments' to deal with their internal conflicts and tensions. What is particularly important for our purpose is that

10. *ibid.* As Prof. Vernon Van Dyke says: "To sum up, politics can be defined as (1) an activity occurring within and among groups, (2) which operate on the basis of desires that are to some extent shared, (3) an essential feature of the activity being a struggle of actors, (4) to achieve their desires, (5) on questions of group policy, group organisation, group leadership, or the regulation of inter-group relationships, (6) against the opposition of others with conflicting desires. More briefly, politics may be defined as a struggle among actors pursuing conflicting desires on public issues." *Political Science : A Philosophical Analysis* (Stanford: Stanford Univ. Press, 1962), p. 134.

these 'non-state' associations influence the government of the country for the sake of protecting and promoting their specific interests. Thus, there occurs a very sharp process of interaction between the groups *inter se* and between the groups and the government of the country. Finer is right in saying that clearly a private association's hope of success in its competition with other groups is maximised if the full power of the state, as mediated through the government, is put behind it. And so it is that, once such competition takes place within the framework of the state, what would otherwise have to be a private and intermittent struggle of one group against another now becomes a public competition with other groups, either to get the government to espouse its policy and enforce it, or else to go forward and become the government. And the set of procedures whereby the private associations existing in a state seek to influence the government, or participate in policy formation by the government or become the government, is the 'political process'.[11]

Since comparative politics includes all that comes within the scope of political activity and political process, it is said to 'drown' the national governments "among the whole universe of 'partial governments' which exist in any community."[12] It is needed that the study of the government (as an element of the state) should be made *vis-a-vis* the 'governments' of non-state associations that operate in a way so as to influence the government of the country and also be influenced by it in some way or another. As Blondel says: "Government is the machinery by which values are allocated, if necessary by using compulsion: what is, therefore, important is to examine the three stages of the operation by which these values are allocated. Firstly, we must see the way in which the values come to be formulated and government is made aware of them. Secondly, we must see how the machinery of government 'digests' and transforms these values into decisions applicable to the whole community. Thirdly, we must see how these decisions come to be implemented down the level of governmental command. The whole operation of government thus takes the form of a two-way operation, or, perhaps more appropriately, of a machine which receives signals and transforms these signals into others."[13]

Finally, the scope of comparative politics includes the subject of 'political power'. The term 'power' has been defined by different writers in different ways. For instance, while Carl J. Friedrich describes it as 'a certain kind of human relationship',[14] Tawney regards it as 'the capacity of an individual, or a group of individuals, to modify the conduct of other individuals or groups in the manner in which he desires.[15] Referring to the role of power in the matter of decision-making, Lasswell says: "The making of decision is an interpersonal process: the policies which other persons are to pursue are what is decided upon. Power as participation in the making of decisions is an interpersonal relation."[16] Politics thus connotes a special case in the exercise of power—an exercise in the attempt to change the conduct of others in one's own direction.[17] To define the term precisely, one can say that power "is taken to denote the whole spectrum of those external influences that, by being brought to bear upon an individual, can make him move in a required direction."[18]

---

11. Finer, *op. cit.,* pp. 25-26.
12. Blondel, *op. cit.,* p. 3.
13. *ibid.,* p. 6.
14. Friedrich : *Constitutional Government and Democracy* (New York : Harper, 1937), pp. 12-14.
15. R.H. Tawney : *Equality* (New York : Harcourt Brace, 1931), p. 230.
16. Harold D. Lasswell and Abraham Kaplan : *Power and Society : A Framework for Political Enquiry* (New Haven Conn. : Yale University Press, 1950), p. 75.
17. Finer, *op. cit.,* p. 13.
18. *ibid.*

It is the study of the subject of politics from the standpoint of 'power' that has widened the scope of comparative politics so as to include a study of the infra-structure of the political systems. It is on account of this that politics "cannot be studied properly without identifying the ruling class, or the governing and non-governing elites, and measuring their respective roles. Politics also functions, by and large, within groups, though as we have seen earlier, however important in themselves the group may be, neither the individual nor the society can be left out."[19] The subject of 'authority' becomes the handmaid of power. The rulers in a democratic system try to justify their authority by means of having the title of 'consensus', those of a totalitarian system resort to the naked use of power for achieving the superficial title of legitimacy. Thus, it becomes a celebrated principle of comparative politics: "Where consensus is weak, coercion tends to be strong, and *vice versa.*"[20]

It is on account of these important connotations that the term 'politics' has come to have its peculiar definition in the realm of comparative politics. Here politics has been made free from the shackles of normative dimensions and restated in empirical terms. The result is that it is not merely a study of the state and government, it is a study of the 'exercise of power'. As Curtis says: "Politics is organised dispute about power and its use, involving choice among competing values, ideas, persons, interests and demands. The study of politics is concerned with the description and analysis of the .manner in which power is obtained, exercised, and controlled, the purpose for which it is used, the manner in which decisions are made, the factors which influence the making of those decisions, and the context in which those decisions take place."[21]

Growth of Comparative Politics: From Unsophisticated to Increasingly Sophisticated Directions

The study of comparative politics became highly significant in the 1950's when a good number of leading American political scientists sought to 'transform the field of politics' by taking the study of this subject 'from foreign to comparative political phenomenon' and 'from the study of the governments to the study of the political systems'.[22] In broad terms, the transformation which "has taken place has been from a field which would most appropriately be labelled 'foreign governments' to one which might most adequately be called comparative political systems."[23] However, the historical development of this subject may be roughly put into three phases – unsophisticated, sophisticated, and increasingly sophisticated.[24]

The contributions made to the study of politics by great figures like Aristotle, Machiavelli, de Tocqueville, Bryce, Ostrogorski and Weber belong to the first phase who simply utilised the comparative method for the primary purpose of understanding better the working of the political organisations. These writers employed, what was called, the comparative method that "aimed through the study of existing polities or those which had existed in the past to assemble a definite body of material from which the investigator by selection, comparison, and elimination may discover the ideal types and progressive forces of political history."[25] John Stuart Mill undertook to show

19. S.P. Varma : *Modern Political Theory* (Delhi : Vikas, 1975), p. 267.
20. Finer, *op. cit.*, p. 36.
21. Michael Curtis : *Comparative Government and Politics : An Introductory Essay in Political Science* (New York : Harper & Row, 1968), p. 1.
22. David M. Wood : "Comparative Government and Politics" in Stephen L. Wasby: *Political Science: The Discipline and Its Dimensions : An Introduction* (Calcutta : Scientific Book Agency, 1970), p. 486.
23. *ibid.*
24. G.K. Roberts : "Comparative Politics Today" in *Government and Opposition,* London, Vol. 7, No. 1, Winter, 1972, p. 38.
25. J.W. Garner: *Political Science and Government* (Calcutta : World Press, 1952 p. 23.

that the comparative method "may assume several forms, the 'most perfect' of which is the process of difference by which two polities, identical in every particular except one, are compared with a view to discovering the effect of the differing factor."[26] Lord James Bryce preferred comparative method and designated it as scientific by adding: "That which entitles it to be called scientific is that it reaches general conclusions by tracing similar results to similar causes, eliminating those disturbing influences which, present in one country and absent in another, make the results in the examined cases different in some points while similar in others."[27]

The contributions of some important recent writers like Samuel H. Beer, M. Hass, Bernard Ulam and Roy C. Macridis may be included in the second phase who made use of the comparative method with a good amount of self-consciousness and also with a deliberate mood to present a more useful study of different political institutions. As a matter of fact, the writers belonging to this category, unlike political thinkers and writers belonging to the first, applied the instruments of institutional comparisons in a quite rigorous manner to present a better (in the sense of realistic) study of the governments what they desired to address as 'political systems'. This may be called the 'sophisticated' phase in the growth of the subject of comparative politics inasmuch as these writers "were concerned with the various strategies of comparison: area studies, configurative approach, institutional and functional comparisons, a problem-based orientation, and with various methodological problems: conceptualisation, the establishment of agreed categories for comparison, validity as a problem, cross-cultural difficulties and the availability of data."[28]

The contributions of David Easton, Gabriel A. Almond, James C. Coleman, Karl Deutsch, G.B. Powell, Harold Lasswell, Robert A. Dahl, Edward Shils, Harry Eckstein, David Apter, Lucian W. Pye, Sidney Verba, Myron Weiner and a host of others may be included in the final phase. It may rightly be described as the mark of an increasingly sophisticated phase in the growth of comparative politics. The writers belonging to this phase have made use of inter-related set of concepts for the sake of presenting their contributions on the basis of comparative analyses, though they have provided a specialised vocabulary in their own ways. As Roberts says: "If Easton talks of inputs, outputs, demands, gatekeepers, supports and stresses, environment, feedback, values, critical ranges and political authorities; Almond offers a set of input and output functions; Deutsch borrows a cybernetic language which applies to political systems the concept of feedback of various types—autonomy, memory, load, lag, lead and gain, receptors, communication, selective screening of information and so on. Almond's aim of 'universality' sums up the purpose for the choice of such languages—they are sufficiently general to be applicable to any political unit, regardless of size, period, degree of development or other factors."[29]

The subject of comparative politics as developed, in the latest phase, has these main characteristics:

1. ***Analytical and Empirical Investigation:*** The analytical-cum- empirical method adopted by the writers belonging to the latest phase "has definitely enlarged the field of our enquiry as it has cleared up the mist in which many helpful distinctions within the framework of political studies lay obscured."[30] Eckstein has referred to the late decades of the nineteenth century as a period

26. *ibid.,* p. 24.
27. James Bryce : *Modern Democracies,* Vol, I, p. 18.
28. Roberts, *op. cit.,* p. 43.
29. *ibid.,* p. 44.
30. Frank Thakurdas, *op. cit.,* p. 405.

in which Political Science, influenced by a 'primitive positivism' "effected a divorce between its normative and its descriptive concerns."[31] He further says that in the realm of 'comparative government', more and more writers "turned from a concern for the evaluation of governmental forms to a pure description. By and large they retained the analytical categories developed by their predecessors, but began to shape their meanings to fit descriptive rather than normative purposes. Thus, for example, a pure ideal-type democracy, while it continued to be a tool employed in normative political theory, no longer had utility for specialists in comparative government, and the definition of democracy was loosened to permit inclusion of a congeries of actual governmental forms and socio-political conditions."[32]

2. ***Study of the Infrastructure:*** The study of comparative politics is not confined to the formal structures of government as was the trend with the traditional political scientists. Here a student is concerned 'with inquiry into matters of public concern, with the behaviour and acts that may concern a society as a totality or which may ultimately be resolved by the exercise of legitimate coercion."[33] Instead of remaining concerned with the formal structures of government alone, he "has to be concerned with crystallised patterns of behaviour, with 'practices' since these are parts of the living structures of government."[34] If instead of 'government' the term 'political system' is used, naturally it becomes a part of the entire social system and the 'input-output' process includes all those forces of the 'environment' that have their effect on the decision-making process. Thus, the role of political parties and pressure groups, for example, becomes as significant as the role of legislatures and executives in the study of modern political systems. As Blondel says: "Structures of government exist; they have to exist because this is the way in which tension is reduced and delayed and thereby tension decreases and the polity is maintained. But structures change gradually and in a complex fashion. Thus, if we are to understand how governmental systems operate, we have to note that the 'law' (in the general sense of the rule of procedure) is an indispensable element of the life of governmental systems; it makes political life possible and maintains politics."[35]

3. ***Emphasis on the Study of Developing Societies:*** What has added more to the significance of the study of comparative politics is the emphasis of more writers on the 'politics of the developing areas'. It has occurred as a result of the realisation that the subject of comparative politics must include all governments along with their infra-structures that "exist in the contemporary world and, where possible, references to governments throughout time."[36] The study of comparative government is no longer a study of the selected European or American governments; it is as much a study of developed western governments as those of the developing political systems of the poor and backward countries of the Afro-Asian and Latin American world.

However, what is of striking importance in this regard is that more and more attention is being paid to the study of the politics of developing societies both for

31. See Harry Eckstein: "A Perspective on Comparative Politics, Past and Present" in Eckstein and Apter (eds.) : *Comparative Politics : A Reader* (New York : Free Press of Glencoe, 1963), pp. 9-11.
32. David M. Wood, *op. cit.*, p. 487.
33. Curtis, *op. cit.*, p. 2.
34. Blondel, *op. cit.*, p. 11.
35. *ibid.*
36. *ibid.*, p. 5.

the reason of making this a subject of universal study and for building theories and models so that the 'system of democracy' prevailing in these countries could be saved from being subverted by the forces opposed to it. As Wood says: "One could not help being aware of the fact that there existed in the recent political experiences of dozens of countries a veritable laboratory in which to test propositions about the way governmental systems behave under stress and the factors which bring about changes in political forms. What was more, there were appearing on the scene or waiting close by in the wings dozens more of the formerly colonial countries of Asia and Africa, for which political institutions were being carved out with or without concern for the well-catalogued experiences of their older brethren. Political scientists were worried about the preservation of democracy as the dominant form of government in the world or simply about the best way of assuring that the newly emerging fragile systems would have the best opportunity for stable development. They found ample reason to build theory to help find answers to the problems immediately at hand, because they found themselves woefully bereft of a body of theory upon which to draw for adequate leverage over the question of how to provide new nations with stable democracy."[37]

4. ***Focus on Inter-Disciplinary Approach*:** What has really enriched the field of comparative politics and, at the same time, made it a 'complex subject' is the focus on inter-disciplinary study. Writers have made more and more use of tools that they have borrowed from the disciplines of sociology, psychology, economics, anthropology and even from natural sciences like biology. For instance, systems analysis with its two derivatives in the form of structural-functional and input-output approches owes its origin to the discipline of biology that has been borrowed by the leading American political scientists like David Easton from sociologists like Robert Merton and Talcott Parsons. The result is that comparative politics has come to have much that makes it look like political sociology and political psychology. A study of new topics like political development, political modernisation, political socialisation, political acculturation, political change, political leadership and the like shows that now political science has become the "application of sociological and psychological analysis to the study of the behaviour of government and other political structures."[38] A modern political scientist interested in the subject of political development "has learned that he cannot treat this topic without looking for the conditions of social mobilisation; men cannot become citizens in political sense without changing their values and personality orientations."[39] A well-known writer in the field of comparative politics has thus pointed out that classical political theory "is more a political sociology and psychology and a normative political theory than a theory of political process. What goes on inside the black box of the political system and its consequences are inferred from the ways in which the social structure is represented in it."[40] It is certainly on account of the adoption of this interdisciplinary approach by the writers on comparative politics that the subject of political science is said to have "undergone a revolution of sorts."[41]

37. Wood, *op. cit.*, p. 489.
38. S.M. Lipset: "Introduction" in his (ed.): *Politics and the Social Sciences* (New York : Wiley, 1969), p. xvii.
39. *ibid.*, p. xiii.
40. Gabriel A. Almond : "Political Theory and Political Science" in Ithiel de Sola Pool, *op. cit.*, p. 5.
41. See William C. Mitchell: "The Shape of Political Theory to Come : From Political Sociology to Political Economy" in Lipset (ed.), *op. cit.*, p. 101.

5. ***Value-Free Political Theory:*** Finally, the subject of political science has lost its normative aspect and assumed empirical dimensions in the sphere of comparative politics. The result is that value-free political theory has replaced value-laden political theory. The concern of the students of comparative politics is not with the things as they ought to be in their ideal forms; it is with what they are. There is hardly any place for the rules of history or ethics in the subject of comparative politics as the entire field has been covered by the rules of sociology, psychology and economics. There is thus hardly any place for a man like Leo Strauss in the field of comparative politics who, while sticking to the traditions of Plato and Aristotle, contends that political theory cannot eschew 'values' and thus a value-free political science is impossible.[42] It should, however, be made clear that the use of the term 'values' by Easton (when he defines politics as 'the authoritative allocation of values') or of 'value system' by Almond (when he identifies it with a system of ideas and beliefs) has an empirical, and not a normative, connotation. We may say that the term value is used by the writers on comparative politics in the sense of a 'price' or 'worth' that a thing gets after it is recognised by the policy-makers. There is no value in a thing unless it is allocated by those who are in authority. Political science, thus, becomes *inter alia* a study of the distribution by persons in authority of things which are valued, or the attribution by such persons of value to things, or the deciding by such persons of disputes relating to things which are valued.[43]

In fact, the study of comparative politics in its latest form includes significant contributions of those recent writers who have broadened the scope of this subject by taking into their areas of study more and more countries of the world, particularly of the Afro-Asian and Latin-American regions better known as the'world of developing areas'. These writers, in a way, have paid their sincere heed to the counsel of Lord James Bryce who once said that 'the time seems to have arrived when the 'actualities' of government in its various forms should be investigated."[44] The eminent writers on comparative politics have not only endorsed but also improved upon the observation of James T. Shotwell that as "we pass from France to Italy, Switzerland, Germany and USSR, there is no common thread, no criterion of why these particular countries were selected and no examination of the factors that account for similarities and diversities."[45]

"Politics is the struggle for power in any organisation, and comparative politics is the study of this struggle around the world."[46] Most of the states of the world are engaged in activities of their development in social, economic and political spheres. Non-state institutions are also playing their role in this regard that naturally strengthens the case of a civil society in 'non-western' countries.[47] The

42. See Leo Strauss : "What is Political Philosophy?" in Gould and Thursby (eds.): *Contemporary Political Thought* (New York: Holt, Rinehart and Winston, 1969), p. 46.
43. Morton R. Davies and Vaughan A. Lewis : *Models of Political Systems* (Delhi: Vikas, 1971), p. 54.
44. See Roy C. Macridis : "A Survey of the Field of Comparative Government" in Jean Blondel (ed.) : *Comparative Government* (London : Macmillan, 1969), p. 4.
45. *ibid.*, p. 7.
46. Patrick O'Neil: *Essentials of Comparative Politics* (New York: W.W. Norton and Company, 2004), p. 20.
47. By 'Civil Society" is meant" a society in which people are involved in social and political interactions free of state control or regulation. . . . . participation in associational or institutional groups socialises individuals into the types of political skills and cooperative relations that are a part of well functioning society. People learn how to organise, how to express their interests, and how to work with others to achieve common goals. They also learn the important lessons that the political process itself is as important as the immediate results. Thus, a system of active associational groups can lessen the development of anomie or non-associational activity." G.A. Almond, G.B. Powell, Jr., Kaare Strom and R.J. Dalton: *Comparative Politics Today: A World View* (Singapore: Pearson Education, 2001), p. 68.

Some Important Statements about New Comparative Politics

Careful studies that deal comparatively with the cultures and the ideologies, the historical development and the whole complex of forces that seek final expression politically would lead not only to a better understanding of the countries of the world with which we must deal, but should likewise enable us to understand ourselves better.

—**Pendleton Herring**

In general, then developmentalism led to the comparison of societies with widely different social and political institutions and cultural practices. The central hypotheses were drawn from how 'modern' institutions evolved in the west; the shift from theocratic to secular; from status to contract; pre-capitalist to capitalist; static to evolutionary notions of societal change, organic and mechanical solidarity; traditional to legal-rational authority; *Gesellschaft* and *Gemeinschaft;* and for those of a more radical persuasion, transformation from pre-capitalism to bourgeois democracy and the prospects of socialism.

—**David E. Apter**

In the 1970s and 1980s, comparative politics became defined largely by ideological and methodological debates. Left and right accused each other of bias and distortion while advocates of quantitative and qualitative methods argued over how to structure and use research. Yet even as these debates raged among scholars, new global debates were taking shape that would shake the foundations of comparative politics once again. The first major development was rapid industrialisation in Asia. . . . A second major event was the collapse of communism in the Soviet Union and Eastern Europe. A third and related development was what has come to be known as the 'third wave' of democracy.

—**Patrick O'Neil**

We are living in extraordinary times. Since the mid-1980s, politics throughout the world has been rocked by dramatic and unpredictable developments. . . . Beyond the unforgettable images captured in front-page news photos, these developments mark a fundamental political crossroads for our world.

—**Mark Kesselman, Joel Krieger and W.A. Joseph**

result is growing interaction between state and non-state actors that provides a kind of interesting material to the study of comparative politics in present times, particularly after the disintegration of the socialist world what Fukuyama calls the 'end of history'. Thus, the study of comparative politics has become widespread and highly diversified. Apter prefers to rechristen it as 'new comparative politics'. It has its emphasis on growth and development and thus involves within itself the trends of decolonisation and democratisation having their manifestation particularly in the 'undeveloped' or 'under-developed' parts of the world. Politics " is no longer Euro-centred; it is more concerned with how to build democracy in countries in which it is not indigenous."[48] Apter calls it 'neo-institutionalism' that "combines older institutionalist concerns with developmentalism."[49]

Comparative Politics and Comparative Government: Case of Identities and Similarities in Basic Implications

Although the two terms 'comparative politics' and 'comparative government' are used loosely and interchangeably, there is a point of distinction between the two. While the latter

48. David E. Apter: "Comparative Politics, Old and New" in R.E. Goodin and Hans-Dieter Klingemann (eds.): *A New Handbook of Political Science* (London: Oxford University Press, 1996), p. 381.
49. *ibid.*, p. 386.

covers a comparative study of different political systems with special emphasis on their institutions and functions, the former has a broader scope so as to cover all that comes within the purview of the former and, in addition to that, all else that may be designated as the study of 'non-state' politics. In other words, the scope of comparative politics is wider than that of comparative government despite the fact that the search for making comparisons is central to the study of both. The concern of a student of comparative politics does not end with the study of rule-making, rule-implementing and rule-adjudicating departments of the political systems or even with the study of some extra-constitutional agencies (like political parties and pressure groups) having their immediate connection, visible or invisible, with the principal departments of state activity. In addition to all this, he goes ahead to deal, though in a particular way, with even those subjects hitherto considered as falling within the range of economics, sociology, psychology and anthropology. As Sidney Verba concisely suggests—"look beyond description to more theoretically relevant problems; look beyond the formal institutions of government to political processes and political functions; and look beyond the countries of Western Europe to the new nations of Asia, Africa and Latin America."[50]

The meaning and nature of comparative politics as distinguished from that of the comparative government is well brought out by Curtis in these words: "Comparative politics is concerned with significant regularities, similarities and differences in the working of political institutions and in political behaviour. Meaningful analysis requires explanatory hypotheses, the testing of sentiments, categories and classification by the collection of empirical data, observation, experimentation if at all possible; and the use of research techniques such as sampling, and communications data to increase knowledge."[51] Curtis, however, makes it quite obvious that the inquiry into similarities and differences is not a search for certainty or predictability, nor does it start from the premise that what is not 'scientific' is not knowledge. Systems classification and categories are always tentative: they cannot claim finality. Politics cannot be reduced to a series of involuntary and automatic responses to stimuli. Sometimes, the most significant political phenomena are those changes in the mood of the times that are impossible to quantify.[52]

From the above, it infers that the term 'comparative politics' should be preferred to the term 'comparative government', as the scope of the former is wider and more comprehensive to include all the essential characteristics that we have discussed in the preceding section. One may, however, agree with the observation of Blondel that the term 'comparative government' has two aspects— horizontal and vertical—and this term may be identified with 'comparative politics' if both the aspects are taken into account. Vertical comparison is a comparative study of the state *vis-a-vis* other associations and groups that have their 'political character' and cast their impact upon the functioning of a political system; horizontal comparison is a comparative study of the state *vis-a-vis* other national governments. Blondel may be justified to some extent in saying that comparative government becomes comparative politics when both the vertical and horizontal aspects of comparisons are taken into account that lead to this definition: "Comparative government can thus be defined in a preliminary fashion as the study of patterns of national governments in the contemporary world."[53]

Though one may, or may not, fully agree with the view of Blondel, it may, nevertheless,

50. Sidney Verba : "Some Dilemmas in Comparative Research" in *World Politics,* Vol. XX, No. 1, 1967-68, p. 111.
51. Curtis, *op. cit.,* p. 5.
52. *ibid.*
53. Blondel, *op. cit.,* pp. 5-6.

be added that it is always safer to use the title 'comparative politics' in perference to 'comparative government'. Perhaps, it is for this reason that Edward Freeman makes an attempt to bring out a distinction between the two in these words: "By comparative government I mean the comparative study of political institutions, of forms of government. And, under the name of comparative politics, I wish to point out and bring together many analogies which are to be seen between the political institutions of times and countries most remote from one another... We are concerned with the essential likeness of institutions and we must never allow incidental traits of unlikeness to keep us away from seeing essential likeness."[54]

It may, however, be added with a word of caution that, comparative politics, though concerned with significant regularities, similarities and differences in the sphere of political institutions and human behaviours, the work of comparison should neither be done half-heartedly to ignore much that is really useful, nor should it be taken to the extremes of over-simplification making the whole study vulgar and implausible. We should be guided by the counsel of Roberts that any lesser conception of comparative politics "tends to lack either clear identity or criteria of selection and exclusion."[55] We should also pay heed to the warning of Eckstein and Apter that "too broad a conception of comparative politics would widen it to encompass political science."[56]

Comparative Method in Comparative Politics: An Instrument for Making Comparisons in Search for Theory-Building and Testing in Political Science

The subject of comparative politics is necessarily concerned with the study of political systems for the obvious reason that here comparative method is used in a special sense—a sense that covers both macro and micro aspects or, as Blondel says, vertical and horizontal dimensions of political systems. It should be pointed out again that here comparative method is not used in the same manner as it was done by classical writers on political science like Aristotle, Machiavelli and Montesquieu; rather, in the sphere of comparative politics, it is used for a particular reason and also in a particular sense. As Wood says: "The only reason for including the term comparative in the designation of the field is to emphasise that the responsibility which the field has to the discipline of political science is to treat the political systems existing in the world as units for comparison in the general quest of theory-building and testing in political science."[57]

As applied to the field of comparative politics, the comparative method has three essential characteristics :[58]

1. ***Definition of Conceptual Units:*** The units which we compare in the field of comparative politics "are conceptual units in the sense that they are the objects of the definitions to which the real phenomena we say are comparing more or less conform."[59] The business of a student of comparative politics does not end with the making of similarities and differences between two governmental systems; he has to deal with the macro units, *i.e.,* the entire political systems which perform functions for large and complex societies. It is needed that, apart from looking at the three formal structures of a political organisation like legislature, executive and judiciary, he should also study the role of legislators, behaviour of the voters, operational form of the political parties and pressure groups, etc. In other words, a student of comparative

54. Cited in Gunnar Heckscher : *The Study of Comparative Government and Politics* (London : George Allen and Unwin, 1960), p. 68.
55. Roberts, *op. cit.,* p. 39.
56. Eckstein and Apter, *op. cit.,* p. vi.
57. Wood, *op. cit.,* p. 494.
58. *ibid.,* pp. 494-99.
59. *ibid.,* p. 495.

politics is concerned with the 'units of lesser scope' that constitute the infra-structure of a political system. It is a different thing that, while making a definition of the political system, he may take some and ignore other aspects as per his area of concern. As such in the field of comparative politics, one should feel concerned with the conceptual units and proceed ahead in the direction of making comparisons on the basis of definitions that he has made. Thus, a writer on comparative politics studies the 'units of lesser scope' as elements within the context of a national political system and that he "is interested in them only in so far as they help him to characterise the system as a whole."[60]

2. ***Classifications :*** Taxonomy occupies a very important place in the field of comparative politics on account of this fact that it facilitates the making of broad general judgments as to the characteristics of a very complex phenomenon. The work of theory-building and testing conclusions becomes easier when a student of comparative politics draws tables and charts to categorise different political systems on the basis of divisions of powers (between federal and unitary systems), or relationship between the executive and legislative departments (between parliamentary and presidential systems), or liberties of the people (between democratic and totalitarian systems), etc. What is especially noticeable at this stage is that a student of comparative politics widens his scope of study so as to make typological illustrations on the basis of the 'units of lesser scope' that helps him in presenting a better and more plausible explanation of the varieties of political phenomena. Realising that the problem of presenting a classification of modern political systems is to establish categories that 'are neither so numerous as to make comparisons impossible, nor so few as to make contrasts impossible'.[61] Finer, in his own way, says; "What differentiates one system of government from another are: (a) how far the mass of the public are involved in or excluded from this governing process—this is the participation-exclusion dimension; (b) how far the mass of the public obey their rulers out of commitment or how far out of fear—what may be called the coercion-persuasion dimension; and (c) how far the arrangements are designed to cause the rulers to reflect the actual and current values of the mass of the public or how far they may disregard these for the sake of continuity and future values — what may be called the order-representativeness dimension."[62]

3. ***Hypothesis Formulation and Testing :*** The work of making comparisons should be done in a way that hypotheses are formulated and then tested so that the requirement of verifiability and applicability is fulfilled. By taking political system as the basic unit of his study, a student of comparative politics is necessarily concerned with the question as to how political systems operate. A host of questions that haunt his attention are: What determines the degree to which political systems will be responsive to popular demands? What determines the degree to which the outputs of a system will be sufficient to meet the threats of external pressure or domestic crisis? What determines the degree of support which the system will receive and extract from the populace, whether in the form of voting, tax paying or personal service in times of crisis? What determines the degree of institutional stability within the system? What determines the level of internal

60. *ibid.,* p. 496.
61. S.E. Finer, *op. cit.,* p. 39.
62. *ibid.,* p. 40.

Some Important Statements about Uses of Comparative Method

Without comparisons to make, the mind does not know how to proceed.

—Alexis de Tocqueville

Comparison is fundamental to all human thought. It is the methodological core of the humanistic and scientific method as well. It is the only way we can fully understand our own political system. Comparing the past and present of our nation and comparing our experience with that of other nations deepens our understanding of our own institutions. Examining politics in other societies permits us to see a wide range of political alternatives and illuminates the virtues and shortcomings of our own political life. By taking us beyond our familiar arrangements and assumptions, comparative analysis helps expand our awareness of the possibilities of politics. Comparison is the methodological core of the scientific study of politics.

—G.A. Almond

Explanation, however, requires an exhaustive compilation of data in common categories and the formulation of hypotheses that can be tested. Finally, it aims towards the development of a body of knowledge in the light of which predictions of trends and policy recommendations can be made. In this sense, comparative politics becomes a matrix from which theories emerge and at the same time a laboratory for their testing.

—R.C. Macridis

violence which the system must withstand? What determines the capacity of the system to produce effective leadership to meet the needs of all times?[63] An answer to such important questions has to be sought and offered by a serious student of this subject in a way that the general theory and tested generalisations are brought together into a 'self-contained, internally consistent, but empirically sound body of knowledge'.[64]

In brief, comparative method is the life-breath of the subject of comparative politics and a writer on this subject, whether he likes it or not, "has to examine, account for and, as many would want him to do, find recipes to redress the structure and behaviour of government."[65] There may be different forms of comparisons, but for a student of comparative politics it is required that he should move ahead in a way so that the conceptual units chosen by him are precisely defined and the theories that he has evolved should be empirically verifiable and testable. He should keep it in mind that in an effort to discover general principles, the diversity of conditions and circumstances, such as differences of the temperament and genius of the people, economic and social conditions, moral and legal standards, political training and experience, are not apt to be ignored or minimized.[66]

Critical Appraisal: Problems and Prospects of Scientific Analysis in Comparative Politics

The study of comparative politics is beset with a number of problems that defy the requirements of a scientific analysis. These are:

1. There is the problem of a standard and precise definition of various important concepts and terms. Leading writers on this subject make use of different concepts according to their specialised knowledge, what Sartori calls 'conceptual stretching'. Want of concept construction often hints at

63. See Wood, *op. cit.*, p. 498.
64. *ibid.*, p. 499.
65. Blondel, *op. cit.*, p. 3.
66. See Garner, *op. cit.*, p. 24.

Reasons for Studying Comparative Government

1. It is to find out more about the countries we know least about them.
2. It is to formulate and test hypotheses. Comparison enables us to develop and scrutinise important questions as do plurality electoral systems. Verified hypotheses are valuable not just for their own sake, but because they can then help to account for the particular. Without comparison, we would lack general knowledge of politics and, therefore, reliability to explain particular observations.
3. Generalisations which emerge sometimes have potential for prediction. Sometimes, researchers choose to study specific countries for their productive value.
4. It improves our classification of politics. Classification is a stepping stone on the journey to understanding distinction between democracy and dictatiorship, authority and power, etc.

Rod Hague, Martin Harrop and Shaun Breslin: *Comparative Government and Politics : An Introduction* (London: Macmillan, 1998), pp. 12-13.

the tedious job of making accurate comparisons.

2. Many political terms used in the field of comparative politics not only suffer from ambiguity, they are also used as political rhetorics that creates the fear of neologism.
3. Serious difficulties are encountered in collecting information and data about the political systems and other non-state institutions having their definite connection, whether visible or invisible, with the departments of a political organisation. Several difficulties also arise from the range and character of the background variables, role of norms, institutions and behaviour in governments and cross-cultural studies. There are several important matters that defy accurate measurement and, as such, they are scarcely amenable to precise comparative treatment.
4. Political behaviour is not necessarily conducted on a rational basis or on scientific principles thereby rendering a scientific study more difficult.
5. A value-free political science becomes a source of problem for one who has a normative approach; not only this, even a purely empirical political theory has its own problems when similar terms convey different connotations at the hands of practical theorists. It is for this reason that the so-called systems analysis is taken as 'unsystematic' by those subscribing to the Marxist-Leninist approach, or the term 'development' has its different meanings when we study the views and interpretations of the 'bourgeois' and 'Marxist' writers on this subject.
6. There is the factor of the complexity of political systems and political behaviour. No single factor like love for power or appeal of charisma and the like can serve the purpose of a comparative study of diverse political systems and highly diverse behaviours of the people.
7. The roles that the individuals play in the politics of their country cannot be subjected to uniform rules as evolved by a student of comparative politics. For instance, the rules of behaviour finding their place in the conservative character of the English people cannot apply to the behaviour of the people living in Ghana or Indonesia and *vice versa.*
8. Much of the comparative politics is concerned with the issues of stability and maintenance of a political system perhaps on account of this basic assumption that'power is always conservative'. It is a fact that all political systems undergo change and with it politics can never remain in a changeless situation. The point of

difficulty arises when we find leading theorists virtually ignoring the aspect of change.

9. The adoption of inter-disciplinary approach has so much widened the scope of comparative politics that one is often faced with the difficulty of knowing as to what the subject of comparative politics includes and what it excludes.

These formidable difficulties lead to a very simple and straightforward conclusion that the study of a subject like comparative politics cannot be given a 'scientific' character without having a set of rigorous concept construction. It may also be admitted that this subject misses the character of a scientific study in view of the fact that it lacks tools for comparative inquiry with the help of which statements of universal political truths may be made. Thus, G. Sartori, while commenting on the concept misformation in comparative politics, remarks that no comparative science of politics "is plausible on a global scale unless we can draw on extensive information which is sufficiently precise to be meaningfully compared."[67] To some extent the obsession for having an inter-disciplinary approach, what Colin Leys in a critical vein describes as 'Procrustean' 'involving a phenomenal effort of self-denial', makes the entire study of politics a very 'complex' affair.[68] Not only this, it deprives the subject of politics of its 'autonomous' character and makes it 'a subsidiary, or a satellite of sociology, in that political activity and institutions reflect the nature of society and are determined and patterned to a large extent by divisions within society.' Politics in this sense is to be seen as dependent on forces outside the political system, and as such ceases to have a major role as an independent social science.[69]

However, a correct evaluation should be made from a different standpoint. Such a list of problems that beset the study of comparative politics does not tend to suggest that the study of this subject "is impossible, but it explains why the development of a general theory has proved an arduous task."[70] Undaunted by such problems, even though formidable, recent political scientists have invented certain theories with which political systems may be compared not only on the basis of their structures but also on the lines of their infra-structures in a way as much precise as possible. Blondel makes a very fine observation when he counsels: "Rather than try to define with great precision the 'things' which belong to government and those which do not, it seems much more fruitful to think in terms of lines, or of channels by which the govermental machine is activated and comes to respond. Although we may not always be certain in advance which 'things' will, indeed, constitute these lines, we have a technique, or a frame of reference by which we shall be able to decide concretely in individual instances, whether or not a thing or a problem belongs to the study of government."[71] Irrefutable is the statement of Curtis on this subject that the study of comparative politics "is at the heart of contemporary political science."[72]

---

67. Cited in Roberts, *op. cit.*, p. 48.
68. Colin Leys : "Introduction" in his *Politics and Change in Developing Countries : Studies in the Theory and Practice of Development* (London : Cambridge Univ Press, 1969), p. 8.
69. A.R. Ball: *Modern Politics and Government* (London: Macmillan, 1971), pp. 10-11.
70. Blondel (ed.) : *Comparative Government*, p. xxv.
71. Blondel : *An Introduction to Comparative Government*, p. 6.
72. Curtis, *op. cit.*, p. vi.

2

Major Approaches

> But whatever the approach or the origin of its ideas, we can say that political science as a discipline is concerned with the problem of ends; the goals of the good society; the means of governing in such a manner as to realise the good society, the activities of the ruled (the public), especially political actions personified in voting, public opinion and attitude formation; and the underlying connections between society and government. Its key concern is with power—how it is shared through participation and representation and how it is affected by growth and change.
>
> **—David E Apter**[1]

What really makes the study of comparative politics significant as well as interesting, even perplexing, to a new student of this subject is the use of different approaches, methods and techniques to understand and explain 'political reality'. A host of leading writers on this subject hold divergent points of view and adopt varying ways with the result that different terms like approaches, methods, techniques, models, paradigms, strategies and the like seem to be either inter-related or synonymous. It, therefore leaves a definite impression that in the study of politics, existence and utilisation of several approaches may be discovered. Moreover, while different approaches "have, from time to time, seemed to be predominant, their time has also passed as some other way of going about the study of politics has come to the fore."[2] An attempt to discuss different approaches to the study of politics is called for in view of the fact that the difference between them "has been significant and the heat generated by the partisans of each way battling to prove the supreme virtues of their approach has been great."[3]

Meaning and Nature of 'Approach': Similarity and Distinction with Related Themes

An approach, in simple terms, may be defined as a way of looking at and then explaining a particular phenomenon. The perspective may be broad enough to cover a vast area like world as a whole in the study of politics, or it may be very small embracing just an aspect of local, regional, national or international politics. Besides, it also covers within its fold every other thing related to the collection and selection of evidence followed by an investigation and analysis of a particular hypothesis for an academic purpose. Thus, an approach "consists of criteria of selection—criteria employed in selecting the problems or questions to consider and in selecting the data to bring to bear; it consists of standards governing the inclusion and exclusion of questions and data."[4]

---

1. Apter: *Introduction to Political Analysis* (New Delhi : Prentice-Hall of India, 1978), p. 17.
2. Stephen L. Wasby: *Political Science—The Discipline and Its Dimensions: An Introduction* (Calcutta : Scientific Book Agency, 1970), p. 35.
3. *ibid.*, Michael Curtis is right in holding that an inquiry into comparative politics "has taken many avenues, started from various points, and been influenced by a variety of other disciplines." *Comparative Government and Politics* (New York : Harper & Row, 1968), p. 6.
4. Vernon Van Dyke : *Political Science : A Philosophical Analysis* (Stanford : Stanford Univ Press, 1962), p. 114.

It is for this reason that approaches to the study of politics are so many. As the criteria for selecting the problems and data or questions seeking answers to some questions are determined by the standpoint that a scholar adopts or makes use of, so there may be several approaches. However, when a scholar seeks to channelise his efforts into a presentable form, the same approach leads to the utilisation of a particular method. Approaches and methods, in this way, become closely inter-related themes. The latter becomes the integral counterpart of the former. Thus, Van Dyke observes: "In brief, approaches consist of criteria for selecting problems and relevant data, whereas methods are procedures for getting and utilising data."[5]

However, with a view to bring out a subtle line of distinction between an approach and a method, we may say that the latter is commonly used either to denote epistemological assumptions on which the search for knowledge is based, or the operations and activities that occur in the acquisition and treatment of data.[6] It is the use of varying methods generally borrowed from other social and natural sciences that modern political science looks like moving closer and closer to the domains of other disciplines as economics, psychology, sociology, biology and anthropology. It is all done to fit better the specific problems of data collection and interpretation faced in political studies. As a result of this, political science "seems to some like history or sociology or economics applied to political data."[7] If so conceived, a method may also be called a technique. However, the difference, if any, between the two is that the latter "may be more susceptible to routine, or mechanical application and more highly specialised, depending less (once they are mastered) on imaginative intelligence."[8]

While the term 'approach' may be identified with other related themes like 'method' and 'technique', it is certainly distinguishable from a 'theory'. An approach is closely related to a theory in view of the fact that its very character determines the way of generalisation, explanation, prediction, and prescription—all of which are among the main functions of a theory. But a line of difference between the two may also be drawn. The term 'theory' is so vague that its real meaning is often indeterminable. It may be identified with anything like thought, idea, trend, tendency, conjecture, hypothesis, speculation, explanation, even interpretation, of some kind.[9] Different is the case with an approach that may be defined as the creator or a precursor of a theory. An approach "is transformed into a theory if and when its function extends beyond the selection of problems and data about the subject under study."[10]

With a view to highlight the meaning of different related themes used in the sphere of modern political analysis, Apter defines some of them in the following manner:[11]

1. ***Paradigm :*** It is a framework of ideas that establishes general context of analysis. Fundamentally, paradigms combine a mixture of philosophical assumptions and criteria of valid knowledge. The resulting combinations are sharply distinguished from each other.
2. ***Theory :*** It is a generalised statement summarising the real or supposed actions of a set of variables, whether dependent, or independent, or intervening. Parameters represent the conditions within which

5. *ibid.*
6. *ibid.*
7. Wasby, *op. cit.,* p. 7.
8. Dyke, *op. cit.,* p. 114.
9. Sec M.H. Marx : "The General Nature of Theory Construction" in his *Psychological Theory* (New York, 1951), p. 6.
10. Mahendra Kumar : *Theoretical Aspects of International Politics* (Agra : Shiva Lal, Agarwal and Company, 1981), p. 45.
11. Apter, *op. cit.,* pp. 31-32.

independent variables operate. A theory may be macro or micro dealing with large or small groups or units. Moreover, it may be abstract, or formal or notational, or concrete.

3. *Method :* It is a way of organising a theory for application to data. Thus, methods are known by the name of conceptual schemes. They may be of many types like comparative, configurational, historical, simulative and experimental.
4. *Technique :* It links method to the relevant data. It represents various modes of observation and ways of recording empirical information. As such, techniques vary in appropriateness, sampling, public opinion testing, interviewing, regression analysis, factoring, scaling and testing.
5. *Model :* It is a simplified way of describing relationships. It can be constructed from a paradigm, a theory, a method, a technique. It may be typological, descriptive, formal, mechanical, organismic, biological etc.
6. *Strategy :* It is a peculiar way of applying one or any combination of the above type to a research problem. It is required that quality and integrity should be combined in a strategy. A good strategy fits together problem, theory, methods and techniques in a systematic and coherent way.
7. *Research Design :* It converts strategy into an operational plan for field work or an experiment. It is a prospectus or an outline from which research is carried forward. It is a final stage in professional research preparation.

It may, however, be added at this stage that in the field of comparative politics most of the related themes, as briefly defined above, have become synoymous for the sake of presenting an empirical study of politics. Herein lies the reason of the use of a new methodology in the field of politics. The real purpose is "to adopt new techniques for acquiring knowledge, new criteria for judging the validity of claims to the possession of knowledge, and new analytical tools for refining the meaning of the terms and raising the level of precision and logical inference, all of which were introduced more or less concurrently."[12]

Traditional Approaches: Emphasis on Value-Laden Study of Politics

Approaches to the study of politics may be broadly classified into two categories—normative and empirical. While the former is said to be value-laden, the latter is known for being 'value-neutral'. In other words, while normativism is the hallmark of the former, empiricism is that of the latter. Fact-value relationship is, therefore, the basis of our classification in this regard. On this basis, we may say that while traditional approaches lean to the side of 'values', the latter do the same for 'facts'. The result is that 'fact-value dichotomy' becomes the determining factor. The traditional approaches have a historical-descriptive and prescriptive character with a dominating place for values and goals. Their different varieties may be discussed as under.

1. ***Philosophical Approach :*** The oldest approach to the study of politics is philosophical. It is also known by the name of ethical approach. Here the study of state, government and man as a political being is inextricably mixed with the pursuit of certain goals, morals, truths or high principles supposed to be underlying all knowledge and

12. Eugene Meehan : *The Theory and Method of Political Analysis* (Homewood, Illinois : The Homewood Press, 1965), p. 10. Avery Leiserson says : "The reader will note that the word 'methodology' is assumed to include three kinds of problems : (1) those relating to the personality, motivation or purposes of the researcher—in brief, his orientation; (2) problems of conceptualisation— organising ideas or tools of analytical thought; and (3) problems that are often exclusively denoted by the word 'method'—techniques of collecting, organising and presenting data." Refer to his paper "Problems of Methodology in Political Research" in Heinz Eulau, S.J. Eldersveld and Morris Janowitz (eds.) : *Political Behaviour : A Reader in Theory and Research* (New York ; Free Press of Glencoe. 1956), p. 53.

reality. A study of politics, in this field, assumes a speculative character, because the very word 'philosophical' "refers to thought about thought; a philosophical analysis is an effort to clarify thought about the nature of the subject and about ends and means in studying it. Put more generally, a person who takes a philosophical approach to a subject aims to enhance linguistic clarity and to reduce linguistic confusion; he assumes that the language used in description reflects conceptions of reality, and he wants to make conceptions of reality as clear, consistent, coherent, and helpful as possible. He seeks to influence and guide thinking, and the expression of thought so as to maximise the prospect that the selected aspect of reality (politics) will be made intelligible."[13]

It is for this reason that thinkers and writers subscribing to the philosophical-ethical approach look like advising the rulers and the members of a political community to pursue certain higher ends. Thus, great works of Plato, More, Bacon, Harrington, Rousseau, Kant, Hegel, Green, Bosanquet, Nettleship, Lindsay and Leo Strauss take the study of 'politics to a very high level of abstraction and also try to mix up the system of values with certain high norms of an ideal political system. Here normativism dominates and empiricism as contained in certain classics like those of Aristotle, Machiavelli, Bodin, Hobbes, Locke and Montesquieu looks like integrating the study of politics either with ethics, or with history, or with psychology, or with law respectively just in an effort to present the picture of a best-ordered political community.

The philosophical approach is criticised for being speculative and abstract. It is said that such an approach takes us far away from the world of reality. For this reason, it is accused of being hypothetical. At the hands of Kant and Hegel, it culminates in the exaltation of state to mystical heights. Politics, therefore, becomes like the handmaid of ethics or metaphysics. The case of things as they 'are' is dominated by the case of things as they 'ought to be.' However, great protagonists of such an approach like Leo Strauss and Berlin affirm that values are an indispensable part of political philosophy and they cannot be excluded from the study of politics. He says : "If this directedness becomes explicit, if men make their explicit goal to acquire knowledge of the good life and of the good society, political philosophy emerges."[14]

2. ***Historical Approach :*** The distinguishing feature of this approach is focused on the past or on a selected period of time as well as on a sequence of selected events within a particular phase so as to find out an explanation of what institutions are, and are tending to be, more in the knowledge of what they have been , and how they came to be, what they are than in the analysis of them as they stand."[15] It may also be added that here a scholar treats history as a genetic process—as the study of how man got to be, what man once was and now is."[16] A study of politics with such a point of view also informs him "to look into the role of individual motives, actions, accomplishments, failures and contingencies in historical continuity and change."[17]

---

13. Dyke, *op. cit.*, p. 129. Also see Peter Winch : *The Idea of a Social Science* (New York : Humanities Press, 1958), pp. 5-15.
14. Leo Strauss: "What is Political Philosophy?" in *Journal of Politics*, Vol. XIX, No. 3 (August 1957), pp. 313-68.
15. Sir Fredrick Pollock: *Introduction to the History of the Science of Politics*, p. 126.
16. Louis Gottschalk : "A Professor of History in a Quandary" in *American Historical Review*, Vol. 59 (January 1954), p. 279.
17. *ibid.*

Shortcomings of Traditional Approaches

Focus on Western Political Systems

1. It dealt primarily with a single-culture configuration-Western world.
2. It dealt mainly with representative democratic systems as their aberrations.
3. It prevented a student from dealing systematically with Western as well as non-Western systems.
4. Research was just superficial as it was founded on the study of isolated aspects of the governmental process within specific countries.

Excessively formalistic in its approach

1. The analysis was focused on the formal institutions of government to the detriment of a sophistincated awareness of the informal arrangements of society and of their role in the formation of decisions and the exercise of power.
2. It proved to be relatively insensitive to the non-political determinants of political behaviour and hence to the non-political bases of governmental institutions.
3. Comparison was made in terms of the formal constitutional aspects of Western systems which are not necessarily the most fruitful concepts for a truly comparative study.

Descriptive rather than problem solving nature

1. Except for some studies of proportional representation, emergency legislation and electoral systems, the field was insensitive to hypotheses and their verifications.
2. Even in the purely descriptive approach to political systems, it was relatively insensitive to the methods of cultural anthropology, in which descriptions are fruitfully made in terms of general concepts or integrating hypotheses.
3. Thus, description in comparative government did not readily lend itself to the testing of hypotheses, to the compilation of significant data regarding a single political phenomenon-or class of such phenomenon in a large number of societies.
4. Description without systematic orientation obstructed the discovery of hypotheses regarding uniformities in political behaviour and prevented the formulation, on a comparative basis, of a theory of political dynamics-change, revolution, conditions of stability etc.

Factors accounting for our increasing awareness in this regard

1. The prevalent dissatisfaction with the country-by-country approach in teaching and research. The study of foreign governments is not in any sense of the word comparative study. It results in making superficial similarities and differences between political systems.
2. The need to broaden our approach by including in our study non-Western systems and by attempting to relate the contextual elements of any system with the political process.
3. The growing concern with policy-making and policy implementation. It is probably not untrue to say that research is often related to the broad exigencies of policy-making. Its global requirements have suggested the close inter-relationships of a number of factors that were considered to be separate in the past and have shown the fallacy of compartmentalisation-that is of area studies.
4. Comparative analysis is being increasingly a part and parcel of the growing concern with the scientific approach to politics.

Source: R.C. Macridis: "A Survey of the Study of Comparative Government" in Jean Blondel (ed.): *Comparative Government* (London: Macmillan, 1969), pp. 47-48.

The historical approach stands on the assumption that the stock of political theory comes out of socio-economic crises and the reactions they have on the minds of the great thinkers. Thus, historical evidence has an importance of its own. The conditions of ancient Greece created Plato nnd Aristotle; likewise, the conditions of seventeenth century England produced Hobbes and Locke; the capitalist system of the nineteenth century created Mill and Marx. Obviously, in order to understand political theory, it is equally necessary to understand clearly the time, place and circumstances in which it was evolved. The political philosopher "may not actually take part in the politics of his times, but he is affected by it and, in his own turn, he tries vigorously to affect it."[18] Sabine well takes note of this fact when he observes that all great political theories "are secreted in the interstices of political and social crises."[19]

It may, however, be added at this stage that the historical approach to burning political questions differs in many ways depending upon the range of choice that a scholar adopts for his purpose. If Machiavelli could make use of history for exalting the record of the Romans and thereby exhorting his people to restore the 'glory of Rome', Oakeshott associates it with the trend of conservatism. It is contained in his treatment of politics as the "activity of attending to the general arrangements of a collection of people who, in respect of their common recognition of a manner of attending to its arrangements, compose a single community."[20] That is, a political activity mainly springs neither from instant desires, nor from general principles, but from the existing traditions of behaviour themselves. As he says: "In any generation, even the most revolutionary, the arrangements which are enjoyed always far exceed those which are recognised to stand in need of attention, and those which are being prepared for enjoyment are few in comparison with those which receive amendment; the new is an insignificant proportion of the whole."[21] Again: "What we are learning to understand is a political tradition, a concrete manner of behaviour. And for this reason it is proper that, at the academic level, the study of politics should be an historical study."[22]

The historical approach has certain weaknesses. For instance, as James Bryce says, it is often loaded with superficial resemblances. As such, historical parallels may sometimes be illuminating, but they are also misleading in most of the cases.[23] Likewise, Prof. Ernest Barker holds: "There are many lines—some that suddenly stop, some that turn back, some that cross one another; and one may think rather of the maze of tracks on a wide common than of any broad king's highway."[24] That is, a scholar subscribing to this approach adheres to a particular path of his choice in making use of historical data and then offering his explanation so much so that other important aspects are virtually ignored. It is also possible that he may play with his emotions or prejudices while making use of this approach as we may find in the cases of Machiavelli and Oakeshott.

Nevertheless, the value of the study of political theory in the context of its historical evolution and growth cannot be so lightly dismissed. Works of G.H. Sabine, R.G. Gettell, W.A. Dunning, C.C. Maxey, T.I. Cook, R.J. Carlyle, G.E.G. Catlin, C.E. Vaughan, etc. have an importance of their own. Such an approach has its own usefulness in understanding the

18. S.P. Varma : *Modern Political Theory* (Delhi : Vikas, 1975), p. 8.
19. See G.H. Sabine : "What is Political Theory?" in *Journal of Politics,* Vol. 1, No. 1, (February 1939), pp. 1-16.
20. Michael Oakeshott : "Political Education" in Peter Lasslett (ed.) : *Philosophy, Politics and Society* (New York : Macmillan, 1956), p. 12.
21. *ibid.*
22. *ibid.* Also see Oakeshott : "Rationalism in Politics" in *Cambridge Journal* (November, 1947), pp. 88-90 and Dyke, *op. cit.,* pp. 119-21.
23. Bryce : *Modern Democracies* (London : Macmillan, 1921), Vol I, p. 16.
24. Barker : *Political Thought in England* (London : Oxford Univ Press, 1951), p. 166.

meaning of eminent political thinkers from Plato and Aristotle in ancient to St. Augustine, St. Thomas and Marsiglio in the middle and thereon to Machiavelli, Bodin, Hobbes, Locke, Rousseau, Hegel, Mill, Marx and Laski in the modern ages. If political theory has a universal and respectable character, its reason should be traced in the affirmation that it is rooted in historical traditions.[25]

3. ***Institutional Approach :*** Here a student of politics lays stress on the study of the formal structures of a political organisation like legislature, executive and judiciary. This trend may be discovered in the writings of a very large number of political scientists from Aristotle and Polybius in the ancient to Bryce and Finer in the modern periods. However, the peculiar thing about modern writers is that they also include party system as the 'fourth estate' in the structures of a political system, while contemporary writers like Bentley, Truman, Latham and V.O. Key, Jr. go a step further by including numerous interest groups that constitute the infra-structure of a political system. That is why, institutional approach is also known by the name of structural approach.

The institutional or structural approach may be visualised in the works of several English and American writers. We may refer to the works of Walter Bagehot, F.A. Ogg, W.B. Munro, Herman Finer, H.J. Laski, Richard Neustadt, C.F. Strong, Bernard Crick, James Bryce, Harold Zink, Maurice Duverger and Giovanni Sartori. The striking feature of their works is that the study of politics has been confined to the formal, as well as informal, institutional structures of a political system. Moreover, in order to substantiate conclusions, a comparative study of major governmental systems of certain advanced countries of the West has also been made.

This approach has been criticised for being too narrow. It ignores the role of individuals who constitute and operate the formal, as well as informal, structures and sub-structures of a political system. It is because of this that behavioural approaches have overshadowed the significance of this approach. Another difficulty is that the meaning and range of an institutional system vary with the view of the scholar. "Those who have conceived governmental institutions, offices and agencies have been inclined to teach and write about government accordingly, organisation charts being suggestive of much of what they have done. Under this conception, the study of politics becomes, at the extreme, the study of one narrow, specific fact about another."[26] Finally, the students of this approach "have also tended to ignore international politics. Since for long there were no world institutions analogous to the state or government, there seemed to be nothing in this area for political scientists to talk about."[27]

4. ***Legal Approach :*** Finally, in the realm of traditional approaches, we may refer to the legal or juridical approach. Here the study of politics is mixed up with legal processes and institutions. Themes of law and justice are treated as not mere affairs of jurisprudence, rather political scientists look at state as the maintainer of an effective and equitable system of law and order. Matters relating to the organisation, jurisdiction and independence of judicial institutions, therefore, become an essential concern of a political scientist. Analytical jurists from Cicero in the ancient to Dicey in the modern periods have regarded state as primarily a corporation or a juridical person and, in this way, viewed politics as a science of legal norms having nothing in common with the science of the state as a social

25. Sabine, *op. cit.*
26. Dyke, *op. cit.*, p. 136. Albert Somit and Joseph Tanehaus have attacked the institutional-structural approach as "a routine description and pedestrian analysis of formal political structures and processes based on the more readily accessible official sources and records." *The Development of American Political Science : From Burgess to Behaviouralism* (Boston, 1967), p. 70.
27. *ibid.*, p. 137.

organism. Thus, this approach "treats the state primarily as an organisation for the creation and enforcement of law."[28]

In this context, we may refer to the works of Jean Bodin, Hugo Grotius and Thomas Hobbes of the early modern period who propounded the doctrine of sovereignty. In the system of Hobbes, the head of the state is the highest legal authority and his command is law that must be obeyed either to avoid punishment following its infraction, or to keep the dreadful state of nature away. The works of Bentham, John Austin, Savigny, Sir Henry Maine, and A.V. Dicey may also be referred to in this connection. The result is that the study of politics is integrally bound up with the legal processes of the country and the existence of a harmonious state of liberty and equality is earmarked by the glorious name of the rule of law.

The legal approach, applied to the study of national as well as international politics, stands on the assumption that law prescribes action to be taken in a given contingency and also forbids the same in certain other situations; it even fixes the limits of permissible action. It also emphasises the fact that where the citizens are law-abiding, the knowledge of law provides a very important basis for predictions relating to political behaviour of the people. A distinguished student of this approach like Jellinek advises us to treat organised society not as a mere social or political phenomenon but as an ensemble of public law rights and obligations founded on a system of pure logic or reason. It implies that the state as an organism of growth and development cannot be understood without a consideration of those extra-legal and social forces which lie at the back of the consideration and, for this reason, are responsible for many of its actions and mutual reactions. It may, however, be pointed out that this approach has a very narrow perspective. Law embraces only one aspect of a people's life and, as such, it cannot cover the entire behaviour of the political actors. As the idealists can be criticised for treating state as nothing else but a moral entity, so the analytical jurists commit the mistake of reducing every aspect of a political system to a juridical entity. "Determination of the content of law through legislative power is a political act, ordinarily to be explained on the basis of something other than a legal approach."[29]

The traditional approaches may be said to have four main varieties as discussed above. Their outstanding feature is that value-laden system dominates. Normativism assigns to them a peculiar and distinctive character. As a result of this, political theory is said to have become abstract, hypothetical, speculative, even metaphysical.[30] On the whole, normativism lays stress on the significant discussion. It "looks to the establishment of a moral criterion of political conduct and asks questions about the nature of the state and its ends, the limit of one's obligations to obey the commands, the basis and content of the individual's rights and freedom, the form of good life and so on."[31]

Modern Approaches : Emphasis on Fact-Laden Study of Politics

From the above, it is evident that the study of politics in the context of philosophical, ethical, institutional-structural, historical and legal perspectives cannot assign to it the character of, what modern behaviouralists like David Easton call, a 'pure science'. Thus, normativism should be replaced by empiricism. Modern approaches are, therefore, marked by empirical investigation of the relevant data. They have arisen from the realisation that "a search for fuller integration was not thought of or even hinted at by the political scientists belonging to

28. J.W. Garner : *Political Science and Government* (Calcutta : World Press, 1952), p. 22.
29. Dyke, *op. cit.*, p. 140.
30. J.W.M. Mackenzie : *Politics and Social Science*, pp. 283-87.
31. W.H. Greenleaf : "Theory and Study of Politics" in *British Journal of Political Science*, Vol. 2, (October, 1972), p. 471.

the old order and, for this reason, the positivism of this science was not dreamt as posing a challenge to the already age-worn methods of study and approach."[32] Hence, in this direction, we may refer to the following important approaches:

1. ***Sociological Approach :*** The sociological approach to the study of politics has become very popular now. Eminent writers like R.M. Maclver, David Easton and G.A. Almond subscribing to this approach have taken into recognition the essential fact that ample data is available in the realm of sociology so as to lay down certain empirical rules of political behaviour. They have accepted the view of leading sociologists like Comte, Spencer, Ratzen-hofer, Weber, Parsons, Merton and a host of others that state is more of a social than that of a political institution. That is, social context is necessary for the understanding and explanation of political behaviour of the individuals. It is the social whole in which we may find the individuals having a status and playing a role. The role is determined by certain traits acquired by the individuals. This process of transmission of values from one generation to another is called 'political socialisation.'

Another term which this approach has popularised is 'political culture' that "refers to the totality of what is learned by individuals as members of a society; it is a way of life, a mode of thinking, acting, and feeling."[33] A scrutinised study of the rise and fall of a political system shows that its causes may be traced in the domain of wrong political socialisation whose objective manifestation is the political culture of the people. Thus, sociological approach has its own place in the twin doctrines of political development and political decay. Besides, as society is a network of numerous associations and groups which play their own part in the operation of the politics of a country, this approach automatically suggests an investigation of the study of interest groups that constitute the infra-structure of a political system. As such, sociological approach has many sub-varieties of its own and, for this reason, 'some writers prefer the term 'sociological approaches'.

2. ***Psychological Approach :*** Political Science has moved very close to the discipline of psychology in recent times particularly at the hands of Graham Wallas, Charles Merriam, Harold D. Lasswell, R.A. Dahl and Eric Fromm. In early modern times, Machiavelli and Hobbes stressed the point of security of life and material possessions as a motivating force and held that the desire for it was inseparable from the desire for power. Recently a good number of political scientists have borrowed material from the writings of eminent psychologists like Freud, Jang, Eyesenck and McDougall to lay down certain valid rules of political behaviour. A study of politics has, for this reason, been made so as to display the role of emotions, habits, sentiments, instincts, ego etc. that are the constituent elements of human personality.

The concept of 'power' has, therefore, gained its own importance. A recent writer like Prof. W.A. Robson has frankly treated political science as a study of power. "It is with power in society that political science is primarily concerned—its nature, basis, premises, scope and results....The 'focus of interest' of the political scientists is clear and unambiguous; it centres on the struggle to gain or retain power, to exercise power or influence over others, or to resist that exercise."[34] Likewise, Fredrick M. Watkins says: "The proper scope of political science is not the study of state or of any other specific institutional complex, but the investigation of all associations in so far as they can be known to exemplify the problem of

32. Frank Thakurdas : "The Expanding Frontier of Political Science" in *Indian Journal of Political Science,* Vol. XXXIV, No. 4, 1973, p. 420.
33. Ely Chinoy : *Sociological Perspective* (Garden City : Doubleday, 1954), pp. 10-11.
34. Robson : *The University Teaching of Social Sciences : Political Science* (Paris : UNESCO, 1954), pp. 17-18.

power."[35] Its most succinct interpretation may be seen in the views of Harold Lasswell who identifies the term power with 'influence' and then defines politics as the study of'the "influence and the influential."[36] It is, therefore, known by the name of 'power approach'.

3. ***Economic Approach :*** Matters relating to the production and distribution of goods have an economic character. But as their regulation is done by the state, they are very much involved in the political process. The prominent schools of liberalism, socialism and communism emerge because of the divergent interpretations of the role of the state in regulating economic matters. Eminent political scientists like Mill, Marx, Mitchell, Schumpeter, Friedman and a host of others have written volumes having a relevance of their own in the domain of political economy. However, in this regard the most outstanding name is that of Karl Marx who has built his political theory on the basis of the criticism of the prevailing capitalist system. It is contained in his well-known assumption: "The mode of production of the material means of existence condition the whole process of social, political and intellectual life."[37] So says Engels: "The ultimate cause of all social changes and political revolutions are to be sought not in the minds of men—but in changes in the mode of production and exchange; they are to be sought not in the philosophy but in the economics of the period concerned."[38]

4. ***Quantitative Approach :*** Also known by the name of statistical approach, it stands for the use of numerical data so as to impart exactitude to the process of describing and analysing a political phenomenon. Mere descriptive or prescriptive analysis is not enough. The subscribers to this approach demonstrate their conviction in an old saying that 'there is safety in numbers' and, as such, we may prove scientifically the validity of a proposition by making use of tables, charts, graphs, etc. For instance, a study of electoral behaviour, questions asked by the members and answers given by the ministers in the legislature, organisation, achievements and failures of a government department or of a public undertaking, voting and cross-voting records of a public institution, constructive and destructive aspects of the politics of defection, rise and fall of a political party and the like can be well analysed with the help of quantitative data.

Several important writers and agencies have added to the stock of comparative politics by making use of this approach that, in a real sense, is a methodology. The names of Dr Gallup, Charles Merriam, Harold Gosnell, Paul Lazarsfield and Samuell Lubell in the United States may be referred to in this connection. They have developed sophisticated ways to study the electoral behaviour of the people. Similarly, in Britain, the Nuffield College election surveys have tried to show the votes shared by each party in a general election and its representation in the House of Commons. Men like R.S. Milne and H.C. Mackenzie have produced works by making election surveys of different constituencies. It may, however, be pointed out that this approach need not involve any special thematical expertise. It requires the habit of exposing in numerical terms every generalisation to simple tests relating to the number of people and their way of doing in some political activity. The subscriber is not expected to rely exclusively or heavily on the mathematical data, rather "a happy balance

35. Watkins : *The State as a Concept of Political Science* (New York : Harper, 1934), p. 83.
36. See Lasswell and Kaplan : *Power and Society* (New Haven : Yale Univ. Press, 1950). Easton has also defined political science as "the study of the authoritative allocation of values as it is influenced by the distribution and use of power." *Political System : An Inquiry into the State of Political Science* (New York : Alfred A. Knopf, 1953), p. 146.
37. See Alexander Gray : *The Socialist Tradition* (New York : Longmans, 1946), pp. 302-4.
38. *ibid.*

has to be struck between ignoring statistics and using them to excess."[39]

5. ***Systems Approach*** : This approach has become very popular in recent times. As the very name of this approach suggests, here the focus is on *systems* that are defined as "bounded regions in space-time, involving energy interchange among their parts, which are associated in functional relationships, and with their environments."[40] Borrowing from the discipline of biological sciences, the sociologists like Parsons thought in terms of a social system. From them the idea came to new political scientists like David Easton and G.A. Almond who developed the idea of a political system. The purpose of general systems theory, as it is known, is to reduce multiplication of efforts by integrating all knowledge and treating all systems as inter-related. Not only this, even parts of a system (called sub-systems) should be treated not as separate and isolated units but organic parts of the same system. Thus, the intention is that the theory "should be relevant to many or all kinds of systems, from the smallest subsystems of an atom to the systems composed of galaxies."[41]

In this way, the emphasis is on cross-cultural studies with an inter-disciplinary focus. Every discipline is like the sub-system of a general system. There is a natural system and all natural sciences like physics and chemistry are its sub-systems, though each subsystem is a system in its own place. If so, politics, economics, psychology, ethics etc. are all sub-systems of a social system, though each is a system in its own right. For this reason, we should use new terms like a political system, an economic system, a psychological system, an ethical system and the like. Not only that, since every system has its own structures and sub-structures which function with the help of inputs, withinputs, throughputs, outputs and feedbacks, so two more approaches have emerged as derivatives of the systems approach.

The 'structural-functional approach' lays emphasis on the structures and functions of every part and sub-part of a system and its functional aspect. Functions may be latent or manifest. In case some structure or sub-structure is dysfunctional or malfunctional, it should be repaired or replaced. The 'input-output approach' is a corollary to the same in the sense that here emphasis is laid on certain forces or inputs that come from the 'environment' and play their part in the decision-making process, while decisions taken by the 'men in authority-roles' are called 'outputs'. The 'feedback' process plays its own part in connecting the inputs and outputs with the result that the political system remains like an 'ongoing concern'. Easton calls it 'a flow model of the political system'. One may easily form an impression here that systems theory with its two derivatives in the forms of structural-functional and input-output approaches seeks to make the study of a political system too mechanical. Human beings are not lifeless entities like machines. As such, human behaviour cannot be explained with the laws of mechanics. Thus, Alfred Adler has denounced this approach as "a huge mis-step in the right direction—the direction of systematic empirical analysis."[42]

6. ***Simulation Approach*** : That contemporary political scientists have borrowed much from natural sciences as well as from cybernetics and mathematics may be studied in this direction. Simulation means a study with the help of image-construction or model-building. We may take note of this fact in the study of political communication, decision-making and game theory. The political communication

39. C.V. Nana Rao : *Introduction to Modern Political Analysis* (Meerut : Meenakshi, 1976), p. 71.
40. J.G. Miller : "Towards a General Theory for the Behavioural Sciences" in *American Psychologist*, Vol. 10, (September, 1955), p. 514.
41. Dyke, *op. cit.*, p. 160.
42. *ibid.*, p. 61.

approach, as popularised by Karl Deutsch, lays emphasis on how one part of a system affects another by sending messages or transmitting information with the result that other parts function and, in turn, do the work of sending messages and transmitting information to each other because of the 'feedback' process. Thus, according to this approach, politics and government "appear in essence as processes of steering and co-ordinating human efforts towards the attainment of some set of goals."[43]

Decision-making approach is another variety of the simulation approach. Here a scholar lays focus on the characteristics of decision-makers, on persons or groups who might exercise .influence over the decision-makers though not being in the capacity of taking a decision themselves, on the situations under which a decision is actually taken and the like. Allied with it is the approach of game theory where social scientists, like mathematicians, look like developing a conceptual design that will help the decision-makers to choose a strategy whereby they may make the best possible bargain out of the competing or conflicting situations. Here the simplification "is reflected in such assumptions as following: that there are only a very few alternatives among which to choose; that the criteria of the judgment of all parties (i.e., the ends that each party pursues) are known to all; and that each party is thoroughly rational. Since certain games—e.g., poker—involve simplified decision-making situations, study of the problems has tended to focus on games and the subject has come to be called game theory."[44]

From a critical standpoint, it may be added that, like systems approach, simulation approach also is too mechanistic, even abstract. It tries to simplify the behaviour of real decision-makers by taking them as fully rational beings. Social sciences may not be converted into natural sciences, nor sciences of numbers and cybernetics may help in understanding and explaining entire political reality A mechanical engineer or a mathematician may have a very simplified way of studying his subject, but a social scientist has to take into consideration the complexities of human life that beset all fixed and definite calculations. For instance, decision-makers are living human beings who act rationally in few and irrationally in most of the given situations. As such, decision-making approach or the use of game theory cannot be applied to explain their behaviour in a thoroughly successful measure.

7. ***Behavioural Approach :*** Modern empirical approaches have found their best manifestation in the trend of behaviouralism where a host of leading American writers have laid emphasis on the collection and examination of 'facts' relating to the actual behaviour of man as a social and political being. This approach has emerged on the scene in the midst of a large amount of turmoil and controversy within the profession widely lauded by the protagonists as a 'revolution' in the realm of political science.[45] E. Kirkpatrick, the Executive Director of the American Political Science Association, explained its meaning thus: "Between World War II and the mid-fifties, the term 'political behaviour' represents both an approach and a challenge, an orientation and a reform movement, a type of research and a rallying cry, a 'hurrah' term and a 'boo' term. Debate about behavioural techniques and methods was often accompanied by vituperation; discussions were more often aimed at vanquishing adversaries than at clarifying issues."[46]

---

43. O.R. Young : *Systems of Political Science* (Englewood Cliffs, New Jersey : Prentice Hall, 1968), p. 50.
44. Dyke, *op. cit.*, p. 154.
45. Benjamin E. Lippincott : "Political Theory in the United States" in *Contemporary Political Science* (Paris : UNESCO Pub, 1950), p. 219.
46. Kirkpatrick : "The Impact of Behavioral Approach on Traditional Political Science" in Austin Ranney (ed.) : *Essays on the Behavioural Study of Politics* (Urbana : University of Illinois Press, 1962), p. 11.

Simply stated, the behavioural approach bears the following important characteristics:[47]

(i) It specifies as the unit of object of both the theoretical and empirical analysis the behaviour of persons and social groups rather than events, structures, institutions, or ideologies.

(ii) It seeks to place theory and research in a frame of reference common to that of social psychology, sociology and cultural anthropology.

(iii) It stresses the mutual interdependence of theory and research. Theoretical questions need to be stated in operational terms for purposes of empirical research. And, in turn, empirical findings should have a bearing on the development of political theory.

(iv) It tries to develop rigorous research design and to apply precise methods of analysis to political behaviour problems.

Since David Easton is regarded as the leading light in this direction, we may refer to the 'intellectual fundaments' of this trend, as enumerated by him, in the following manner:[48]

(i) That regularities exist which are discoverable and which can be expressed in generalisations.

(ii) That such generalisations must be testable with reference to human behaviour.

(iii) That means for acquiring and interpreting data cannot be taken for granted; they are problematic and need to be examined self-consciously.

(iv) That measurement and quantification are necessary, but only where such measurement makes sense in terms of other purposes.

(v) That ethical evaluation and empirical explanation should be kept separate.

(vi) That research ought to be systematic; research, untutored by theory may prove trivial and theory unsupportable by data futile.

(vii) That understanding and explanation of political behaviour should precede application of this knowledge.

(viii) That material from the various social sciences should be integrated.

It is true that,as a result of the utilisation of this approach, the scope of political science has widened and the nature of the discipline improved in understanding and explaining 'political reality.' However, it may be criticised on these grounds:

1. It is based upon a false theory of knowledge. It takes facts alone as real. On the contrary, 'universals are as real as facts' and facts can have meaning only in connection with the universals.[49]
2. It is based on a false conception of scientific method. Even after collecting facts and doing their measurement and quantification, the writer cannot free himself from the limitations of subjectivity or his own sense of value-judgment while making some observation on their basis. Thus, fixity and definiteness of a natural science cannot be infused in the discipline of a social science.[50]
3. It circumscribes the scope of political science by advising us to study only those aspects of political life that are amenable to measurement and quantification. In this way, the significance of speculative political theory is sacrificed at the altar of a dry and barren craze of 'mad scientism'.[51]

47. Heinz Eulau, Samuel J. Eldersveld and Morris Janowitz (eds.) : *Political Behaviour : A Reader in Theory and Research,* pp. 3-4.
48. David Easton : "Introduction : The Current Meaning of Behaviouralism" in James C. Charlesworth (ed.) : *Contemporary Political Analysis* (New York : Free Press of Glencoe, 1967), pp. 11-31.
49. Lippincott, *op. cit.,* p. 219.
50. H. J. Morgenthau : *The Decline of Democratic Politics* (Chicago University of Chicago Press, 1962), pp. 26-27.
51. G. Sartori: "From the Sociology of Politics to Political Sociology" in Lipset (ed.), *Politics and the Social Sciences* (New York: Oxford University Press, 1969).

4. Finally, it makes political science a handmaid of sociology by laying down that all political activity and institutions reflect the nature of society and are determined and patterned to a large extent by divisions within society.

By way of clarification, it may, however, be added that leading subscribers to the modern approaches have not repudiated the foundations of their counterparts in toto whose names are well known in the realm of 'traditionalism'. They have only sought to understand the limitations that flowed from the necessarily subjective, descriptive and prescriptive mode of theorising and analysis. For this reason, they have experienced the difficulty of formulating a method of analysis or approach that may be of universal acceptance. Surprisingly, even the arch-priests of behaviouralism realised the shortcomings of their own obsessions and a great figure like David Easton himself veered round to the point that 'mad craze for scientism' should be abandoned. In this way, the era of post-behaviouralism was ushered in that designated the mood and programme of the new dissenters.[52] Reaffirmation of norms and values demonstrated that rigid behaviouralists had conceded to the existence of fact-value dichotomy. In other words, they realised that fact-value distinction had encouraged 'an undesirable foreshortening of vision and a moral insensitivity'[53] and that some sort of reconciliation of facts and values may be possible, if necessary.[54]

8. ***Marxian Approach :*** In this direction, Marxian approach has a place of its own that may be regarded as basically different from both the traditional and the modern approaches in several important respects, though we may discover certain points of resemblance with both as well. The astonishing feature of this approach is that here 'state', being the central theme of political science, is conceived as an inevitable consequence of class contradictions. As such, the system of Marxian dialectics culminates in the justification of a stateless condition of social life that would come into being as the final stage of social development. Moreover, economics dominates the scene so much so that all other disciplines like history, sociology, psychology and ethics become its offshoots. Politics becomes integrally connected with the basic economic structure finding its mainfestation in the forces and relations of production. Thus, it is stressed that in the real world, "economic and political forces and factors are constantly interacting and are extremely hard to disentangle one from the other."[55]

The significance of the Marxian approach is traceable in the fact that its utilisation calls for a deeper scrutiny of the meaning and nature of politics. Instead of keeping the focus of study confined to the formal structure and sub-structure of a political system, it lays emphasis on going at the roots. Thus, it holds that the economic system determines the class structure and as there is a change in the means of production, distribution and exchange, so there is a corresponding change in the relations of the masters and the slaves, the feudal lords and the serfs, the capitalists and the workers—the dominant and the dominated classes. Struggle for power constituting the bedrock of politics should, therefore, be studied in the context of the conflict between two antagonistic classes. This state of contradictions can end only in the establishment of a socialist society. Obviously this approach not only lays stress on the fact of social contradictions, it also discovers their resolution. In this way, it assumes a deterministic character.

52. Dwight Waldo: "Political Science: Tradition, Discipline, Profession, Science, Enterprise" in Fred Greenstein and N.W. Polsby (eds.) : *Political Science: Scope and Theory,* Vol I (California: Addison-Wesley, 1975), pp. 113-14.
53. *ibid.,* p. 114.
54. Thomas Spragens, Jr. : *The Dilemma of Contemporary Political Theory : Towards a Post-Behavioural Science of Politics* (New York: Dunellen, 1973), p. 5.
55. S. Strange : "The Study of Trans-National Relations" in *International Affairs* (London), July. 1952, No. 3, p. 337.

If so, the Marxian approach becomes like an ideology. It stands on a particular set of propositions that are not open to question and that call for a concerted action for the sake of their realisation and implementation so as to change the world and not merely interpret it. It not only exposes the inherent weaknesses and defects of the existing capitalist system, it also informs the exploited and the oppressed class of the workers, peasants and toilers to unite so as to break the chains of slavery and win the whole world. Thus it treats state as an instrument of exploitation and oppression by one class over another and lays down that class character of the state cannot come to an end until the classless society is culminated in the stateless condition of life. As Marx in his *German Ideology* says : "...in a communist society, where nobody has one exclusive sphere of activity, but where each can become accomplished in any branch he wishes, society regulates the general production and thus makes it possible for me to do one thing today and another thing tomorrow, to hunt in the morning, to fish in the afternoon, rear cattle in the evening, criticise after dinner, just as I have a mind, without ever becoming a hunter, fisherman, shepherd or critic."[56]

Since the subject of comparative politics throws special focus on the study of the Third World countries, the Marxian approach endeavours to study the politics of the undeveloped and developing areas in the context of imperialistic exploitation that has for centuries kept a very large number of the Afro-Asian countries in a state of political subjugation and economic exploitation and is still making efforts for the retention of the same in the garb of neo-colonialism. In this way, not the state but the 'class' remains the main actor even in the realm of international politics and the entire class of the workers of the world is informed to break the hold of the imperialist powers, Thus, Lenin calls imperialism the 'final stage of capitalism' and Maurice Dobb says: "Capitalism has grown into a world system of colonial oppression, and of financial stangulation of the overwhelming majority of the population of the world by a handful of 'advanced' countries. And this 'booty' is shared between two or three powerful world marauders aroused to the teeth...who also involve the whole world in their war over the sharing of their booty."[57]

Viewed in this context, a study of the politics of the poor and backward countries of the world should be made in the context of extra-societal forces operating *in* the international environment. Instead of making superficial comparisons between the political processes and institutions of the rich and advanced countries of the world like the United States, Britain and France on the one hand and the newly independent countries of the Third Word like Zaire, Zimbabwe and Combodia on the other, we should study the working of the political system of the poor and backward countries of the world in the light of 'inputs' coming from the environment and the 'outputs' being a result of the same. Thus, Frantz Fanon suggests that the Marxist analysis "should always be stretched everytime we have to do with the colonial power."[58] The reason of the justification of liberation wars going on in the dependent or semi-independent parts of the world and the support of the Marxists for the same should be traced here. It is evident from the statement of Khrushchev : "The communists fully support such just wars and march in the front rank with people's waging liberation struggles."[59]

In this way, the Marxian approach claims itself to be scientific as well as progressive. It rejects the present as oppressive, exploitative and inequilitarian and instead desires a new set up in which exploitation ,and oppression

56. See L.S. Feuer (ed.) : *Marx and Engels* (London, Fontana, 1969), p. 295.
57. Maurice Dobb : "Lenin and Imperialism" in *Marxism Today,* April 1970, pp. 5-6.
58. Fanon : *The Wretched of the Earth* (London: Penguin, 1972), p. 30.
59. Cited in B.D. Wolfe : *An Ideology in Power* (London : George Allen and Unwin, 1969), p. 357.

are replaced by the glorious virtues of co-operation and harmony. Politics is treated as a manifestation of class antagonisms and its end is conceived in the culmination of social development when the phase of class identification and resolution of conflicts would unleash glorious human values. Thus, this approach, that has been empirical so far, assumes a normative character in the end. In short, the whole approach looks like "a theory, which *qua* theory, provides a broad-based vision of society in all stages of development; at its base lies the fundamental importance of production, and from there the economic sub-structure of society and the crucial role of the class."[60]

The Marxian approach may be appreciated for being empirical. The role of economic factors in the operation of politics cannot be lost sight of. If the working of a political system is to be studied and analysed with the help of any modern approach (as structural-functional, input-output, political communication and simulation, political socialisation and acculturation, political development and modernisation etc.), the role of economics in the creation of inputs cannot be ignored. The inputs are so powerful that they have their definite impact on the decisions of the 'men in authority roles'. Similarly, we may not ignore the fact of international economic forces that have an impact of their own on the environment within which the politics of a country, particularly of a poor and backward country, operates. The multinational corporations or transnational agencies have their strength in the domain of economics and their working in the form of neo-imperialism has its definite impact upon the politics of a country as a result of which revolutions and counter revolutions occur in a country like Indonesia, Chile and Iran. However, the weakness of this approach may be seen in its conversion into an ideology. The perspectives of this approach are so rigid that the subscriber has to work within a specified parameter. Elasticity is replaced by rigidity that has a circumvential effect on the scientific study of politics. Thus, this approach is criticised for culminating in the 'pseudo-scientism of degenerated Marxism.'[61]

Enmeshment of Traditional and Modern Approaches : David Apter's Illustration of Certain Leading Themes

From the above, it may be inferred that while normativism—the hallmark of the traditional approaches—stands for a value-laden system, empiricism—the hallmark of modern approaches—does the same for a system loaded with 'facts'. It should, however, be borne in mind that not all traditional approaches have been free from empiricism altogether, nor all modern approaches have discarded the aspect of normativism in entirety. The real difference between the two should be seen not in the abandonment of one of the two elements of fact-value dichotomy, but in giving excessive importance to one at the cost of the other.

Perhaps it is on account of this that major approaches collide as well as synchronise with 'fields', 'themes', 'methodologies' etc. regardless of the fact that the latter may even mesh or intersect with the former. Apter has offered his own scheme without involving himself into the cobweb of either rigid traditionalism or modernism. His argument is that each of the main approaches to the study of politics has its own methodological emphases and subject areas or fields of study in the following manner:[62]

1. ***Political Philosophy*** : It tends to be concerned with the establishment of moral purposes, the ethical basis of the political community and a logic which establishes their priority or validity. The results comprise the field of normative political

60. Tony Thorndike : "The Revolutionary Approach: The Marxist Perspective" in Trevor Taylor (ed.) : *Approaches and Theory in International Relations* (London: Longman. 1978), pp. 61-62.
61. Martin Seliger : *Ideology and Politics* (London: George Allen and Unwin, 1976), p. 257.
62. Apter, *op. cit.*, pp. 12-13.

theory and evolution of the moral basis of the state.

2. ***Institutionalism*** : It assumes such ethical priorities as given and tries to realise them in the mechanism of government. Hence its emphasis is on law and history, both of which describe how appropriate instruments of government evolved. In turn, these provide the base, of course, of American and comparative politics and more specialised subjects like constitutions, bureaucracies, political parties and the like.
3. ***Behaviouralism*** : Ii focuses on both the individual and the aggregate, emphasises experimental methods in group situations, how decisions are made, and organisational aspects affecting action. Courses in the field include methodology, study of public opinion and voting, how opinions form and belief systems are established, political psyschology and theories of political coalitions and games.
4. ***Pluralism*** : It combines both institutional concerns with behavioural ones, is more concerned with how social differentiation and participation broaden the political sphere. The primary emphasis is on modes of democratic participation and their effect on learning and behaviour. Courses of liberal and radical modes of participation, communalism, community power, decentralisation of functions, all become important.
5. ***Structuralism*** : It is concerned with the 'hidden agenda' behind political action, seeks to discover the determinants of behaviour. Hence, its emphasis is on class analysis, role analysis, exchange theory, and Marxist functionalist, or other way of determining the boundaries of political behaviour. Courses include the study of classes, ideologies of change and revolution, stable parties and regimes as 'systems'.
6. ***Developmentalism*** : It emphasises problems of transition, from one type of political system to another, and how innovation occurs, its effects, distribution, who benefits, how imperialism works, problems of instability etc. Courses include studies of new nations, revolutionary transformations, nationalism, and even the impact of the multi-national corporations on 'periphery' countries by 'metropolitan' centres of power.

Despite the fact that the paradigm of Apter allows some room for normativism, it, may be easily found out that the side of empiricism dominates. It may be discovered in his affirmation that "no matter how much we discuss such approaches and emphasis, there can be no substitute for substantive data information. Modern scholars, in his view, develop an aversion to abstract formulations. Extensive knowledge about an area or deep acquaintance with a problem elucidates its complexities and reveals the inadequacies of abstract formulas. Hence, descriptive or intuitive techniques can by no means be ruled out of political science."[63]

Concluding Observations

A detailed study of the major approaches to the study of politics, as contained in the preceding sections, leaves the following important impressions:

1. While several approaches to the study of politics may be broadly grouped into two categories—traditional and modern —a sort of overlapping cannot be lost sight of. It is a different matter that we treat the former as loaded with normativism and the latter with empiricism. The fact stands out that empiricism is available in the classical approaches of great political theorists from Aristotle and Polybius in the ancient to Marx and Tocqueville in the modern ages. Similarly, normativism has not been discarded even by the most prominent figures subscribing to modern approaches.

63. *ibid.*, p. 14.

Apter's Paradigm of Main Approaches

Main Approaches	*Emphases*	*Fields*
Political Philosophy	Logical Analysis, Principles of the Good Society, Moral Basis of Authority	History of Ideas and Political Philosophy
Institutionalism	Legal and Historical Analysis, Descriptive and Comparative Methods, Interest Group Theory	American, Comparative and International Politics, Parties, Constitutions,
Behaviouralism	Experimental Method, Psychological Analysis, Learning, Decision-Making and Organisational Theory	Public Opinion, Voting, Coalitions, Violence, Ideology
Pluralism	Participation Theory, Empirical Methods, Coalition Theory, Maximizing Behaviour	Political Parties, Electoral System, Legislative Behaviour, National Government, Community Power
Structuralism	Exchange Theory, Role Analysis, Class Analysis, Marxian, Functionalist, Linguistic Analysis	Class and Elite, Change and Revolution, Ideology and Social Position, Stability and Integrations
Developmentalism	Theories of Transition, Growth, Causes of Innovation, Instabilities, Political Regimes	Developing Areas, Revolution, Colonialism and Imperialism, New Nations, Nationalism.

Even Marxism has a normative orientation in the end when it conceives of an era of emancipated humanity wedded to the observance of 'glorious human values'. Thus, it may be affirmed that the label of traditionalism is neither a criticism nor a refutation of the patent fact that norms still play an important role in modern political studies although no longer monopolising the avenues of approach.[64]

2. The dichotomy of facts and values should not be given undue importance in belittling the place of values. Nor should it be taken for granted that the value system is all hypothetical or abstract and, for this reason, scientifically untenable. This point should be remembered that the critics of traditional political theory commit a wrong by neglecting the part that the facts play in support of value judgments. It is true that the judgments of value "cannot be *directly* tested by the criterion of accordance with fact, they are susceptible to an *indirect* text of this kind, for they often presuppose beliefs about facts which can be subjected to the text of accordance."[65]
3. Several approaches to the study of politics should not be treated as mutually exclusive. Most of them are inter-related. Not only that, they overlap. For instance, a sociological approach may be psychological in some respects; or a simulation approach may look like a systems approach in some other respects. Most of the elements of different empirical approaches may be discovered in the behavioural approach with the result that some writers have preferred the term behavioural approaches.

64. A.R. Ball: *Modern Politics and Government* (London : Macmillan, 1976), II Ed., p. 10.
65. D.D. Raphael: *Problems of Political Philosophy* (London: Macmillan, 1977), p. 10.

It is correct to say that different categories "do not meet the requirements of logic. They are employed, nevertheless in the belief that they reflect usage and in the belief that it is more significant to comment on usage than to devise an entirely logical classification scheme."[66]

Thus, the point remains that traditional and modern approaches have a relevance of their own in the study of a political phenomenon. The purpose is to understand and explain political reality and, as such, it should not be tried to be achieved in a way that the conclusions become thoroughly abstract or too mechanistic not at all applicable to the life of a living and dynamic people. As we shall see, the great mistake committed by rank empiricists is that they have taken away freshness from the discipline of political science by treating politics like a game of soul-less creatures having no higher aim of life. 'Scientism' is good, but the 'mad craze' for the same, as counselled by David Easton, is bad that should be avoided. Let us not forget the sagacious observation of G.E.G. Catlin that no political theory could be complete without the 'consideration of the ends of action and the discussion of values'. H.R. Greaves is right in holding that "a value-free analysis would prove destructive to political theory."[67]

---

66. Dykc, *op. cit.,* p. 115.
67. Greaves : *Foundations of Political Theory* (London: George Allen and Unwin, 1958), p. 7. Dyke well sums up the whole case in these words: "The final comments on the above taxonomy of approaches to the study of politics may be in order. The first is that, if the classification scheme is sound, all or nearly all approaches actually employed should fit into one or another of the categories; the qualifier on this is that many students of politics are eclectic in their approach, mixing quite different types of data. In many cases, such eclecticism is highly desirable. The second general comment is that no one of the approaches should be regarded as being necessarily and always the best. Students of politics do and should feel free to choose among them, basing their choice on any of a number of considerations; their own personal training and skills, the nature of the general problem that they confront, the audience at which they are aiming, and so on. At the same time, the object should be to develop causal theories that are applicable to all questions concerning the explanation and prediction of events." *op. cit.,* p. 178.

3

Systems Analysis

> The study of politics has fluctuated between two poles ever since men began to think about the nature of the polity. At one end were those who focused on the political institutions as key agencies of social control and social change. They regarded the behaviour of the state, and the intentions of the prince as the most important aspects. Conversely, others stressed how much extra-political factors or conditions affected political events and institutions. In a real sense, these two emphases differed about whether society or the polity is the primary. Since the study of non-political institutions ultimately constituted the content of various social science disciplines, anthropology, sociology, economics and psychology, the issue of the relations between the study of politics and the other social sciences has existed from the start of intellectual interest in such matters.
>
> **—Seymour M. Lipset**[1]

A study of the latest contributions made particularly by recent American writers to the subject of Political Science leaves an impression that it "has undergone a revolution of sorts in the definition of its mission, problems and methods."[2] It is this startling development in this subject that has been designated by Heinz Eulau as 'Behavioural Persuasion' and as 'Epitaph for a Monument to a Successful Protest' by Robert A. Dahl. It is, however, a matter of serious academic debate whether the story of new developments in the sphere of Political Science should be lauded as a revolution or a counter-revolution; it is, nevertheless, certain that it has within its fold much that should be described as a revised version of the traditional political theory; it has also much that may be designated as momentous as the original foes feared, or the doughty band of revolutionists hoped.[3] Systems analysis in social sciences finds a very significant place in this regard that draws its main inspiration from natural sciences flowing through the discipline of sociology inasmuch as it argues that all social phenomena "are part of discernible, regular and internally consistent patterns of behaviour."[4]

Systems Analysis in Political Science: Growth and Implications

The introduction of the systems analysis in social sciences owes its genesis to the realisation of some leading American writers like David Easton, G.A. Almond and Morton A. Kaplan who have reacted against the traditional tendency of rigid compartmentalisation of any discipline belonging to the world of social sciences like economics or politics, psychology

1. Lipset: "Politics and the Social Sciences: Introduction", in his (ed.): *Politics and the Social Sciences* (New York: Wiley, 1966), p. viii.
2. William C. Mitchell: "The Shape of Political Theory to Come: From Political Sociology to Political Economy", *ibid.*, p. 101.
3. *ibid.*
4. Michael Rush and Philip Althoff: *An Introduction to Political Sociology* (London: Nelson, 1971), p. 11.

or sociology, that, in their views, has resulted in nothing else than a reduction of the cross-flows between various sister fields of study. These writers have realised that uni-dimensional studies in social sciences have not only caused duplication, triplication and even multiplication of efforts, but also impeded the patterns of a scientific analysis by creating conditions hostile to the tendency of unification of all knowledge. With this realisation they have veered round to the point that important opportunities would be available to the students of one discipline in case they take the help of analogous disciplines for the study of their analogous problems, as far as possible, in the interest of meaningfully integrating their knowledge of the subject under a scientific investigation and explanation.

These new social scientists, in this direction, have drawn inspiration from the contributions of natural scientists like Ludwig von Bertalanffy who pioneered the movement of unification of all natural sciences. The line shown by this biologist in the third decade of the present century became quite prominent after about a gap of some twenty years. Several important conferences were held in leading American educational institutions to explore the possibilities of scientific research towards a unified theory of human behaviour. However, the setting up of the Society for the Advancement of the General Systems Research in 1956 makes a very important event under whose auspices annual year-books appeared to throw special focus on the areas of general systems theory. The introduction of general systems theory thus became a matter of fashionable study. As Young says: "With such an orientation it was natural that people interested in this movement should begin to search for a body of concepts lending unity or organisation to studies undertaken in a variety of disciplines and making insights and theoretical advances from individual disciplines widely available. The central and guiding notion that they developed in this quest was the concept of *systems,* which has since become the basic conceptual asset of general systems theory."[5]

The word 'system' has been used and defined differently by different writers belonging to different disciplines. Ludwig von Bertalanffy describes system as "a set of elements standing in interaction."[6] Hall and Fagen define system as "a set of objects together with relations between the objects and between their attitudes."[7] Collin Cherry says that a system "is a whole which is compounded of many parts—an ensemble of attitudes."[8] According to Morton A. Kaplan, "A brief and non-technical description of the object of systems analysis would include: the study of a set of interrelated variables, as distinguished from the environment of the set, and of the ways in which this set is maintained under the impact of environmental disturbances."[9]

According to David Apter, we may then restate the characteristics of systems as follows:[10]

1. Systems have boundaries within which there are functional inter-relationships mainly based on some of the communications;
2. Systems are divided into sub-systems, with exchanges existing between the sub-systems (as, for example, between a city and a state, or a state and the national government); and
3. Systems have a capacity for coding—that is, they take informational inputs; are able to learn from inputs, and translate inputs into some kind of output.

5. O. R. Young: *Systems of Political Science* (Prentice Hall, Inc., Englewood Cliffs, New Jersey, 1968), p. 15.
6. Ludwig von Bertallanfy: "General Systems Theory", in *General Systems,* Vol. I, 1956, p. 3.
7. Hall and Fagen: "Definition of a System", *ibid.,* p. 18.
8. Cherry: *On Human Communication* (New York: Wiley, 1961), p. 307.
9. Kaplan: "Systems Theory" in James C. Charlesworth (ed.): *Contemporary Political Analysis* (New York: Free Press, 1967), p. 150.
10. Apter: *Introduction to Political Analysis* (New Delhi: Prentice Hall, 1978), pp. 257-58.

In short, in a system there is a relationship between information and the use of energy. The relationship between coding and the use of energy—outputs—is transformational. The result is a general systems paradigm which can be applied to different system levels, each with its own boundaries: cells, organs, individuals, groups, societies, or whatever. The *general system model,* then, uses energy and information input, control mechanisms, memory banks, checking instruments, and outputs which generate new energy and information.

An examination of various definitions shows that while each one of them "embodies the idea of a group of objects or elements standing in some characteristic structural relationship to one another and interacting on the basis of certain characteristic processes",[11] points of controversy hinge in regard to the problem of empirical operationalisation. Thus, the following points should be kept in mind while dealing with a proper definition of the term 'system' in social sciences:

1. A system is not to be taken as a mere random aggregation of elements; it is composed of elements all at a level of inter-dependence that can be located with some precision both in time and in space. The elements of a system may be either concrete entities or the intellectual constructs of aspects or attributes of concrete entities. While the former makes physical, the latter makes an analytical system. A social scientist is concerned with the latter and not with the former system.[12]
2. A system may have two constructs—homological and interlocking. While the former, also known as *isomorphism,* signifies 'one-to-one correspondence' between objects, in different systems which preserves the relationship between two objects, the latter refers more directly to scale effects and to the vertical or hierarchical association of systems. This line of distinction between the two revolves on the point that whereas systems may differ in terms of size, time, scale and specific substances, they may yet resemble one another closely in regard to certain basic structures and processes and may also have significant subsets of such structures and processes which interlock.[13]
3. A study of systems analysis thus forms a significant part of multi-disciplinary or, more correctly stated, an inter-disciplinary approach. The basic implications of both—the isomorphism and interlocking constructs of a system—"suggest very strongly that there are important concepts and propositions that are meaningful over a significant range of specific systems and that it is possible to develop in conceptual terms a small number of general systems. These notions together with the fundamental concept of systems now form the heart of the campaign aimed at breaking down the compartmentalisation of disciplines and moving towards the unification of science. General systems theory constitutes a record of efforts to elaborate basic principles relevant to a wide range of systems and to develop techniques for applying these principles to the specific and concrete systems of interest to various fields of research."[14]
4. Systems theory in its particular aspects relating to natural sciences like those of physics and biology is fundamentally different from the general theory of all systems where we find serious attempts to conceptualise a framework based on certain hypotheses and concepts that may be roughly applicable to various branches of social sciences. That is, systems theory as applied to the field of natural sciences is not to be taken as a general theory of all

11. Young, *op. cit.,* p. 16.
12. *ibid.*
13. *ibid.,* p. 17.
14. *ibid.*

systems. Even though general systems theory does not make an attempt to distinguish between different types of systems and also to establish a framework within which similarities between systems can be recognised despite differences of subject matter, different kinds of systems require different theories for the sake of furnishing scientific explanations. Moreover, the systems theory is not only different from general systems theory, rather it makes an improvement upon it by sticking to the additional questions of looking into the how and why of efforts that failed or became likely to fail and thus laid down a law that any user of systems theory will have to look for different theories for an explanation of different types of systems. Such a point has its special significance for the student of a social science like politics who, for the sake of a correct application of this theory, would prefer to move away from a general theory to a comparative theory.[15]

5. The use of systems theory in social sciences should be made with certain precautions. As social objectives lack the fixed and definite character of the natural objects, social sciences must likewise avoid extreme particularisation in social and political formulations. That is, we cannot construct models coping faithfully with the particular objects of the real world. What we can do at the most is to draw some points of analogy or to make certain exercises in the direction of resemblances in order to have the character of empirical explanations to our social and political theories. Moreover, we shall be aware of the danger that the more we go ahead in the direction of making our model complex, the more there are the chances of allowing room for the entry of subtle variations either in loop directions or in the rates of the flow. Thus, highly complex models "run the risk of being artifacts. That is, slight variations that we could neither detect nor measure in the real world might – and highly likely world – produce major differences in outcomes and in behaviours. Such highly particularised models lack both generality and relevance to any specific problems of social science."[16]

6. The researcher of a social science should, for this reason, adopt the golden mean or the middle course. He should bank upon the models of a natural science; he should also be aware of the limitations of a social science. What he should do, therefore, is to act like, what Kaplan says, 'a balancer'. Thus, he should make use of the comparative method and thereby stick to the point of saying different things about distinguishable systems rather than the same thing about every system. As Kaplan says: "If the variables that are treated in the comparative systems theories have sufficient importance for selective aspects of the real world behaviour, they should then constitute reasonable first order approximations that are useful for exploring these realities. At this level of generality, the fact that even analogous and counterfactual assumptions are sometimes employed does not contraindicate the validity of the enterprise."[17]

The advocates of systems analysis believe that there are a number of things common to various disciplines and that if only they can be put in an abstract form, a general theory can emerge that might help each discipline to understand its problems better and which each discipline uses as a broad conceptual guideline in its general perspective before it enters into a more detailed research. Obviously, this approach is against far too rigid compartmentalisation of disciplines which "had led to a reduction of cross-flow between

15. Kaplan, *op. cit.*, p. 154.
16. *ibid.*, *p. 156.*
17. *ibid.*

various fields of research, and was obstructing progress in each specific field. This tendency on the part of each discipline to concern itself with specific phenomena and detailed studies in its own field to the exclusion of abstract and general theoretical considerations, while a definite gain in one discipline, could not be of much use in the understanding of similar problems in other discipline, and each discipline had to start from a scratch, and build up its own theoretical concepts, generalisations, and abstractions."[18]

General Systems Theory: Certain Concepts and Their Implications

We have already seen that the idea of systems analysis has been taken over from biology and adopted by certain social scientists to the study of their subject matter so that it assumes the form of an empirical investigation. It is for this reason that systems analysis has its own set of specific concepts that should be understood before grasping its nature. The basic concepts used in the elaboration of the general systems theory may be put into three categories – concepts of descriptive nature or those which can also be used as tools of classificatory variables, concepts that relate to the regulation and maintenance of a system, and concepts that throw light on the forces that bring about change in a system.

1. ***Concepts in the nature of primarily descriptive and classificatory variables :*** In this category we can include concepts that lay down the lines of differences between various kinds of systems like a democratic or open and a non-democratic or closed system, or an organismic and a non-organismic system; we may also refer to concepts that show hierarchical levels like systems and subsystems, orders of interaction and scale of effects; we may also make use of the terms to understand the working of the internal organisations of the systems through the degrees of integration, differentiation, inter-dependence and centralisation; the systems also interact with their environment and that leads to the introduction of the terms like boundaries, inputs and outputs; finally, there may be concepts relating to the various paths that systems follow over time such as state-determinedness and equi-finality.
2. ***Concepts in the nature of regulatory and preservative variables :*** As a matter of fact, this category constitutes the key part of the general systems theory as the real stress of this theory is on the regulation and maintenance of the systems. Thus here we find several important concepts that have their relationship with the forces that play their role in the regulation or maintenace of a system. Here are introduced the notions of stability, equilibrium and homeo-statis. Connected with this are the concepts of feedback and its processes in the forms of repair, reproduction and entropy. Every system must have a state of equilibrium that may be unstable like a ball on a ridge, or static like a ball on the surface, or stable like a ball in a valley.
3. ***Concepts in the nature of forces causing dynamics :*** Change is the law of nature, but this change can be both disruptive and non-disruptive. A non-disruptive change can be brought about through responses to altered conditions of the environment; non-disruptive changes can be either reversible or irreversible. While changes in the reversible directions include adaptation, learning and growth and purposes, goals and teleology, change towards irreversible directions covers disruption, dissolution and breakdown, crises, stresses and strains and overload and decay leading to the application of the law of positive entropy.[19]

A quite large number of conceptual patterns and the propositions built upon them constitute the body of general systems theory. However,

18. S.P. Varma: *Modern Political Theory* (Delhi: Vlkas, 1975), p. 153.
19. See Young, *op. cit.*, pp. 17-18.

Substantive Nature of General Systems

Primarily Descriptive and Classificatory Variables	Regulatory and Preservative Variables	Dynamics
1. Concepts that separate different kinds of systems like open v. closed or organismic v. non-organismic.	1. Stability equilibrium or home-ostatis.	1. Non-disruptive change either through internally generated process or through responses to altered environmental conditions.
2. Concepts concerning hierarchical systems such as sub-systems, orders of interaction	2. Feedback.	2. Change towards reversible level of directions: (i) Adaptation, learning and growth. (ii) Purposes, goals, and teleology.
3. Concepts delineating aspects of the internal organisation of systems such as integration, differentiation, inter-dependence and centralisation.	3. Repair and reproduction.	3. Changes towards irreversible directions: (i) Disruption, dissolution and (ii) Crises, stresses and strains. (iii) Overload and decay leading to the law of positive entropy.
4. Concepts relating to the inter-action of systems with their environments such as boundaries, inputs-outputs, etc.	4. Entropy.	
5. Concepts dealing with various paths which systems may follow over time such as state-determindness and equi-finality.		

two points should be borne in mind in this connection. First, the general systems theory "appears as an integrated and generalised set of concepts, hypotheses and validated propositions with hope of establishing an integrated set of high level theoretical principles dealing with all, or almost all, the significant elements of a small number of inclusive general systems and applicable to important phenomena in a wide range of disciplines. On the other hand, it may be studied, as,a set of techniques and as a framework for systematic process of analysis. In this instance, it is not so much the specific principles and propositions of the theory that are of ultimate interest, rather it is the suggestion that the theory offers for analysing and organising data, the insights derivable from the use of the notion of isomorphism, the richness of the concepts, and the value of framework of systems theory for purposes of coding large amounts of data which are significant."[20]

General Systems Theory and its Application to Political Analysis

It may be asked as to how the principles of the general systems theory, originally developed in the spheres of natural sciences should be applied to the study of politics with certain transformations made first by the anthropologists and then by the sociologists. It is a fact that general systems theory in its extended and well-integrated form "has very rarely been applied to the analysis of political phenomena."[21] The reason for this should be traced in this explanation that the terms of general systems theory are of such a nature that they can be applied with rigour and that deters a social scientist to move ahead with the help of this theory. It is a different thing that the concepts of general systems theory have become quite popular in recent years, even then it cannot be asserted that modern writers on different social sciences can make use of the concept freely and in a well-understood style. Realising this fact fully, Easton observes: "In most cases, it is just a handy notion, popular and apparently simple, to refer to the range of phenomena that in earlier days might have roused a different terminology, such as politics, government and the state."[22]

It is true that the propositions of the systems theory, in particular, are somewhat scattered, it does support a rather impressive analytical super-structure that is made all the more ambitious by the objectives of general systems theory in developing a set of basic principles applicable to a wide range of empirical systems. Undoubtedly, the use of this approach is of great value in sorting out a large quantity of data and in recognising the patterns and uniformities that tie the elements of a system together. Several concepts like those of inputs and outputs, stability and equilibrium, feedback and entropy have become well-accepted terms at the hands of empirical political scientists who deal with the formation and working of political systems in open and closed societies or in advanced and developing countries of the world. It well enables an empirical researcher to analyse how changes take place in the political systems and in what directions of political development or political decay. Thus, a political scientist remains concerned not merely with the growth of integration of a system, he is equally concerned with its disintegration or breakdown. Then, a study in this regard facilitates the course of inter-disciplinary investigation that may bring more useful results for a student of comparative politics. It may be used both for a macro-analysis and a micro-analysis. Finally, apart from being useful for operational research, the systems analysis may be of great benefit for normative or deductive purposes in the sense that we may be able to lay down what remedial steps taken in time may save a system from collapse or disintegration.

---

20. *ibid.*, p. 19.
21. *ibid.*, p. 20.
22. Easton: *A Framework for Political Analysis*, p. 26.

It is on account of these advantages that recent political scientists like David Easton and G.A. Almond have made use of systems analysis in political science and thus contributed much to the literature on empirical political theory. It is due to this that structural-functional and input-output approaches have become so popular that we shall discuss them in separate chapters. Keeping all this in view, it may be said that the concepts developed by the general systems theory "open up new questions and create new dimensions for investigation into the political processes, and several of them can be used to great advantage by political scientists in their own analysis of political phenomena."[23] Likewise, Young says: "The discipline of Political Science is presently at a stage where it can benefit substantially from a consideration of theoretical problems, techniques of conceptualisation, and methods of overcoming various difficulties of analysis in other disciplines, as well as from direct insights that may be wholly or partially transferred to political problems. General systems theory provides excellent channels for maximising the flow of such interchanges even with disciplines that are sometimes considered far removed from political science in abstract terms."[24]

Systems Analysis of David Easton: 'A New Enquiry into the State of Political Science'

The most important name in the list of recent political scientists subscribing to the use of systems analysis is that of David Easton. His monumental work *A Systems Analysis of Political Life* published in 1965 was appreciated by leading writers on contemporary empirical political theory as "providing an original set of concepts for arranging at the level of theory and interpreting political phenomena in a new and helpful way."[25] Following the course of a natural scientist like Stephen Toulmin,[26] he set out to develop a theory that would help to explain behavioural reality inasmuch as political theory is but a symbolic system useful for understanding concrete or empirical political analysis. The empirical political theory of Easton has these salient characteristics:

1. Easton is for a unified theory of politics—a theory capable of explaining the behaviour of both national and international political systems as well as for bringing out their comparisons. He desires that same categories and propositions could be applied to all kinds of political activities whether at the national or international level, and whether for the developed and developing political systems.
2. Easton is concerned with the issue of survival or persistence of the political system. The purpose of an empirical political scientist, according to him, is to study primarily those conditions under which political systems are maintained over a period of time.
3. Easton is critical of the equilibrium analysis that stops at the point of analysing factors that create stability or instability in a political system. His real concern is to deal with the conditions necessary for the existence and continuation of a political system.
4. The purpose of Easton is to study political system in both theoretical and applied perspectives. He is critical of the Lasswellians who look to the applied side of a political system in their study of 'power' and thus ignore the theoretical aspect of

23. S.P. Varma: *Modern Political Theory* (Delhi: Vikas. 1975), p. 161.
24. Young, *op. cit.*, pp. 22-23.
25. Davies and Lewis: *Models of Political System* (Delhi: Vikas, 1971), p. 44.
26. Toulmin has said that the heart of all major discoveries in the physical sciences is the discovery of novel methods of representation and so of fresh techniques by which influences can be drawn—and drawn in ways which fit the phenomenon under investigation, *ibid.*

the subject that is concerned with the study of conditions necessary for the very survival of the political system.

5. Easton rejects the approach of a sociologist like Talcott Parsons who suggest that 'political theory can be analysed in terms of a general theory of social institutions'. Such a view, Easton contends, makes politics a handmaid of sociology. The purpose of Easton is thus to keep the study of politics at an autonomous level, since it is the study of the authoritative allocation of values as it is influenced by the distribution and use of power.

As pointed out above, Easton seeks to study political systems in their abstract or theoretical and as well as concrete or applied aspects. While the former, in his view, may be designated as the 'life process of the system' or a 'conceptual framework' or a 'structural analysis' of a political system, the latter is described by him as the 'persistence of politics'.[27]

In other words, while the former constitues a theoretical study of the conditions under which a conceptual study of the political system can be made, the latter is concerned with the problems as to how political systems manage to persist through time in the face of the inevitable stress which they face. It is a different thing that the concrete aspect overshadows the theoretical one in course as the central question that Easton seeks to answer is not how a particular political system "persists in a given set of circumstances but how political systems generally persist both in a stable environment and a changing world."[28]

The study of political system in its theoretical or conceptual and practical or concrete aspects enables Easton to present a systems analysis in his several important writings[29] whose main features may be given as under:

1. A political system is a set of interactions abstracted from the totality of social behaviour, through which values are allocated for a society.[30] Easton has coined a new definition of the terms like 'politics' and 'political system' by stressing the element of 'authoritative allocation of values'. The word 'authoritative' signifies the decision of those who are in power as only they can make something binding that gives to their decisions the character of being 'authoritative'. It should, however, be noted carefully that while using the term 'values', Easton is not at all concerned with the viewpoints of those who subscribe to the 'value-laden' political theory. He is not an ethicist; he is an empirical political scientist. He even differs from a sociologist like Talcott Parsons as well as from a political sociologist like Gabriel A. Almond who use the term value system in relation to a system of ideas and beliefs. Perhaps, the meaning of Easton may be identified with that of the economists who take 'value' as a token of price or worth. Thus, allocation of 'worth' is made by the decisions of the men in power. In this way, politics becomes the 'authoritative allocation of values' and a political system becomes a set of interactions operating inside the entire social system through which values are allocated for a society. Political Science thus "becomes, *inter alia*, a study of the distribution by persons in authority of things which are valued, or the attribution by such persons of value to things, or the deciding by such persons of

27. Easton: *The Political System* (Calcutta: Scientific Book Agency, 1953), p. 85.
28. Davies and Lewis, *op. cit.*, p. 48.
29. See Easton's *The Political System: An Enquiry into the State of Political Science* (New York: Alfred A. Knopf, 1953); *A Framework for Political Analysis* (Englewood Cliffs, New Jersey : Prentice Hall, 1965); *A Systems Analysis of Political Life* (New York: John Wiley, 1965) and "Systems Analysis: An example of Functionalism" in Gould and Thursby: (eds.) *Contemporary Political Thought* (New York: Holt, Rinehart and Winston, 1969).
30. Easton: *A Framework for Political Analysis,* p. 112.

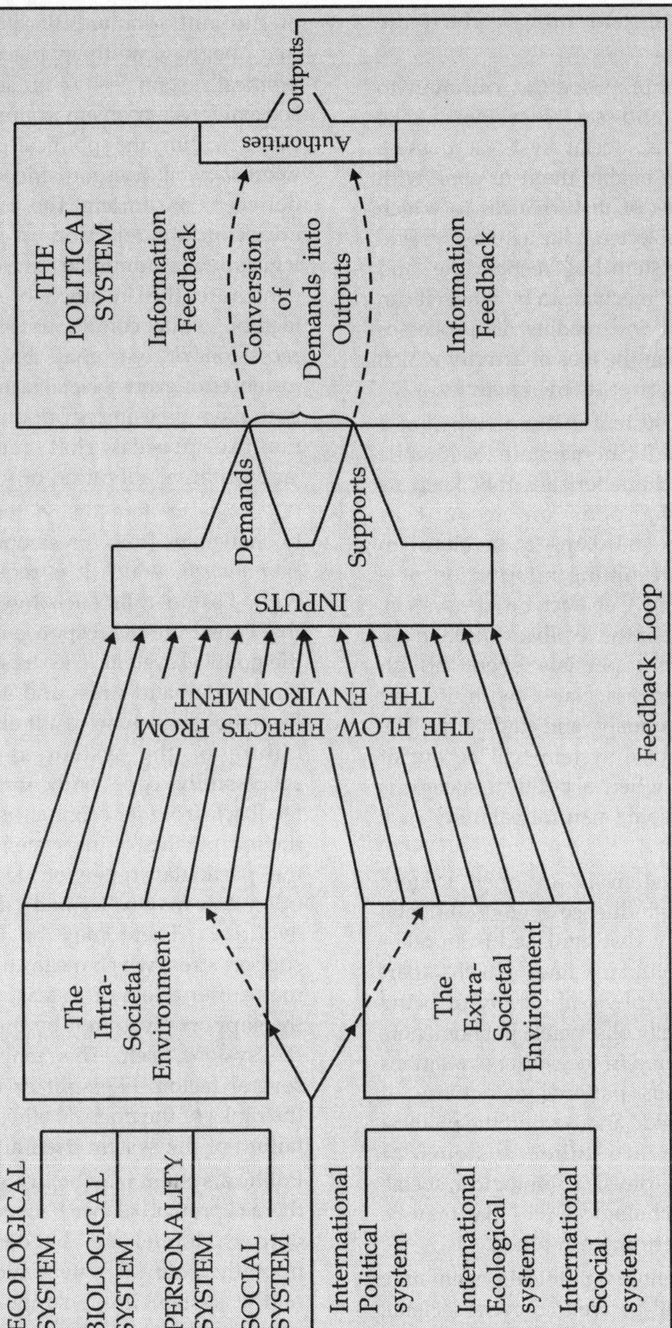

A Dynamic Response Model of a Political System

disputes relating to things which are valued."[31]

2. There are certain properties common to both natural and social systems. Like natural systems, social systems possess properties that enable them to cope with the worst types of disturbances to which they may be subjected. Like a living system, the political system has 'responding' and 'self-regulating' mechanism by which it can change, correct and readjust its processes and structures in the face of activity which threatens to disrupt its own activity.
3. If so, political system is not a static but a dynamic affair. It can maintain itself while retaining the characteristics that keep its identity. It happens on account of 'feedback' mechanism—a mechanism capable of transmitting information of a positive or negative character to the system. It is on account of the feedback mechanism that the system persists even though everything else associated with it may change continuously and radically. The very survival of a system will be out of question only when a political society is destroyed by some natural calamity or a bloody war.
4. A political system is an open system amenable to the influence or environmental factors. It can be distinguished from other systems by boundary lines which, apart from being of a physical variety or being like an empirically observable phenomenon, may be discovered in the nature of relations between various patterns of activity. It means that outside and beyond the political system there are other systems or environments—physical, biological, social, economic, psychological, etc. that may be distinguished from each other.
5. The environment of a political system may be intra-societal as well as extra-societal. That is, the conditions affecting the process of the authoritative allocation of values may be having their place within the political system itself or outside of it. Intra-societal forces of an environment have their place within the political system itself, extra-societal ones outside of it. Clashes between or among the rulers on the adoption or rejection of a particular legislative or administrative measure may constitute the instance of intra-societal factors, while conditions of inflation or recession or war may be cited as the instances of extra-societal factors. However, both have their impact upon the decision-making process that results in the 'authoritative allocation of values'.
6. A political system always remains subject to challenges from forces operating in the *environment,* which it is required to cope with. Easton calls such forces as *stresses* that constitute the response mechanism of the political system. The stresses are of two kinds—demand stress and support stress. Demand stress may result either from the failure of the system as it exists to successfully cope with the information feedback from its original output or from the incapability of the system to deal with the particular range of demands made upon it. It may be termed' 'demand-input overload'. There may be the factor of support stress which means that the system may suffer a loss or at least an erosion of the support given to it by the members of the system itself. This may result from several factors like split or dissension in the ranks of the political elites or structural failure of the system itself and the like.
7. Political system may be in a steady state if there is proper balance between inputs and outputs. Inputs are the demands made upon the political system and the support of the system itself; supports are those processes or structures which give to it the

31. Davies and Lewis, *op. cit.,* p. 54.

capacity to cope with the demands made upon it. Outputs are the results of the processing of demands. There may be *withinputs* also or the demands made by the political elites themselves.

8. A political system lives in a *critical range.* It is possible that the inputs and outputs are properly balanced; it is also possible that the inputs have an overload and the outputs are not there in sufficient measure to save the political system from disintegration or breakdown.
9. The survival of a political system requires certain structural bases that may be in the form of institutional arrangements like electoral machinery and political parties and non-institutional arrangements in the form of political beliefs and attitudes of the people. Both types of structural bases may be termed 'objects of support of the system'.
10. The objects of the support of the political system are three—political community, regime and authorities. The political community means a group of people living together with willingness to cooperate in solving the problems of their political system. The community continues to exist even though the regime and the authorities may change from time to time. The regime or the 'constitutional order' implies written and unwritten rules of the constitution that determine the structure of the political organisation and also the values and norms on which the entire organisation of government is based. Finally, the authorities mean people who are entrusted with the work of allocating values authoritatively. In simple words, they are the rulers who convert the inputs into outputs by taking decisions in response to the impact of environmental conditions.
11. The political system, apart from being a system in itself, consists of sub-systems such as mediating groups that are involved in the decision-making process. There are several organisations and groups that play their part in the political process without having the character of a political organisation. Easton calls them 'para-political systems'.

Easton's definition of the political system is thus a consequence of his subscribing to the systems analysis. Thus, in his view, the political system can be seen basically as input-output mechanism dealing with political decisions and the activities associated with these conditions.[32] As a political scientist first and a political sociologist afterwards, he describes political system as having an autonomous place within the social system. His description of the political system is thus determined by his definition of 'political life'—a set or system of interaction defined by the fact that they are more or less directly related to the authoritative allocation of values for a society[33] and, as such, a political system is a set of interactions abstracted from the totality of social behaviour, through which values are allocated for a society.[34] In his view, after all in its elemental form, a political system is just a means whereby certain kinds of inputs are converted into outputs.[35]

Critical Appraisal

We have seen that the use of systems analysis in political science has come from natural sciences through anthropology and sociology and, in this direction, the works of social anthropologists like Emile Durkheim and sociologists like Robert K. Merton and Talcott Parsons have a significance of their own. A number of significant criticisms have appeared against general systems theory that may further be applied to the subject of systems analysis in the field of political science. Moreover, as David Easton has made remarkable contributions in this sphere, his interpretations may also be subjected to various lines of criticism. First, we

32. *ibid.,* p. 53.
33. Easton: *A Framework for Political Analysis,* p. 74.
34. *ibid.,* p. 50.
35. *ibid.,* p. 112.

shall take up the points that relate to the criticism of the systems analysis in relation to its special application in the discipline of political science. Prof. Young has raised these important points in this regard :

1. There is some controversy about the content of the notion of isomorphism. It is maintained that, actually speaking, there are not many significant isomorphic relationships and that this theory's demands for isomorphisms sometimes "lead to a practice of featuring things into 'boxes' to which they do not belong."[36] There seems to be an obsession on the part of the writers contributing to this theory. It is evident that the conceptual categories of systems theories "lead analysts to force all phenomena into the framework of a system."[37] One may find the proof of such obsession in this 'constructivist' viewpoint of Easton that 'any set of variables selected for description and explanation may be considered a system of behaviour.'
2. It is also said that the systems analysis constitutes an elaborate and abstract conceptual structure that is lacking when it comes to hypotheses and propositions.[38] It cannot be denied that this theory does support a good number of hypotheses and propositions of an abstract nature that cannot be subjected to an empirical investigation. Thus, this theory "throws up certain snags in regard to problems of empirical operationalisation."[39] It is on account of this that "the distinction between open and closed systems sometimes begins to blur, boundaries are difficult to place especially in temporal sequences, and analytic systems must often be separated from tangible political systems."[40]

When we come across the systems analysis of Easton, we find several difficulties in spite of the fact that his analysis appears like a very neat conceptual framework. Three points may be raised in this connection :

1. Easton's definitions of terms like 'politics'and 'political system' based on the ingredient of 'a set of interactions' are so broad that one fails to apply the line of distinction between an abstract and a concrete political system. Sometimes, it appears that Easton is concerned with a concrete political system alone; sometimes it also appears that his concern is with a system in an abstract form as well. A close study of Easton's analysis "makes it very clear that his continuous efforts to move from the abstract to the concrete only lands him into a great deal of confusion."[41] It is, thus, said that while being a critic of Talcott Parsons, Easton reaches very close to him by not thinking of a theory in terms of explanation but in terms of the creation of conceptual frameworks. The result is a highly abstract structure that is logically suspect, conceptually fuzzy and empirically almost useless. Easton's political system turns out to be an abstraction whose relation to empirical politics is virtually impossible to establish. The promise of a conceptual framework with 'high empirical relevance' simply has not been fulfilled.[42]
2. Apart from presenting a 'dichotomy of natural and analytic systems'or giving us a weapon against two ghosts that he helped instal in the house of political science, he looks like "proposing a container, not an actor—he has dissolved the traditional actor in the acid of interaction but has not attempted an aesthetic reconstruction."[43] In

36. Young, *op. cit.*, p. 24.
37. *ibid.*, p. 25.
38. *ibid.*
39. *ibid.*
40. *ibid.*, p. 26.
41. Varma, *op. cit.*, p. 184.
42. Eugene Meehan : *Contemporary Political Thought: A Critical Study* (Homewood, Illinois : The Dorsey Press, 1967), pp. 173-74.
43. Paul F. Kress: "A Critique of Easton's Systems Analysis" in Gould and Thursby, *op. cit.*, pp. 213 and 223.

other words, it may be pointed out that if Easton "has hesitated in identifying his 'political system' with the national system, he has also flinched from looking at the individual, whom he tries to *subject to empirical* observation straight in his eyes. On deeper probe, it appears that Easton "is not interested in the individual at all, nor even in his behaviour except in that it forms a part of an interaction with the behaviour of other individuals. All the time he is looking at the individual from outside, from the point of view of the role he might be playing in the preservation and persistence, or disruption and destruction, of the analytic political system he has in mind."[44]

3. Last, and it flows from the above points as well, that Easton in his serious efforts to move away from the institutional to the behavioural approach, "finds himself hanging somewhere in the middle."[45] The result is that, in the end, Easton "offers us a behavioural complement to Musil's man without qualities—a politics without substance."[46] This critic goes to the length of saying that a theory 'so respectful of facts' should be so lacking in substance and thus presenting to us like an 'empty vision of politics.'[47]

In brief, systems analysis in politics, like general systems theory, "is much too broad a framework for political analysis to take note of the complex psychological aspects of the interaction function. It may not be able to answer questions like what was the scope, depth and weight of power as it was being used. Nor does it help us to understand what strategies and tactics were adopted by those who employed power and influence."[48] Prof. Young understands this point when he critically observes that although systems theory "may be helpful in organising material on human relationship into systemic patterns in such a way that questions concerning pattern maintenance, stability, regulation, and so forth can be posed fruitfully, it does not have as much to offer for studies dealing with the political aspect of such matters as perception, expectation, formation, or cognition."[49]

Despite these points of criticism, it cannot be denied that general systems theory proper has been utilised very little in the social sciences and that it is, therefore, difficult to judge its utility in a definitive manner at this stage. It may be expected that this theory "may achieve a high standing as an approach to political analysis, but it is too early to make any definitive judgments on this question."[50] Even Prof. Paul F. Kress whose primary concern was 'to explore the gross contours of Easton's theory through the prism of other disciplines', concludes his paper with these words of hope: "We should also remain open to the possibility that systems theory of this sort may some day prove capable of ordering political enquiry in a satisfying manner."[51] Or as Spiro says: "...I should have made clear that my evaluation of the utility of systems theory is high—indeed, that I consider systems theory indispensable to political science, in all its branches. Whatever our central focus of enquiry, we can best approach answers to the questions we are asking by conceiving of politics in terms not only systematic but also systemic."[52]

---

44. Varma, *op. cit.*, p. 185
45. *ibid.*, p. 186.
46. Kress, *op. cit.*, p. 223.
47. *ibid.*, p. 226.
48. Varma, *op. cit.*, p. 188.
49. Young, *op. cit.*, p. 24.
50. *ibid.*, p. 26.
51. Kress, *op. cit.*, p. 227.
52. Herbert J. Spiro: "An Evaluation of Systems Theory" in James C. Charlesworth (ed.): *Contemporary Political Analysis* (New York: Free Press, 1967), p. 165.

4

Political System

> It is the thesis of this volume that scientific politics can develop only if the materials of politics are treated in terms of systems of actions. A system of action is a set of variables so related, in contradistinction to its environment, that desirable behavioural regularities characterise the internal relationships of the variables to each other and the external relationships of the set of individual variables to combinations of external variables.
>
> **—Morton A. Kaplan[1]**

A change from the study of the governments to the study of the political systems should be attributed to the shift in the emphasis from that of formal political institutions to that of the real political processes. It has occurred owing to certain developments indigenous to the discipline of political science in which more and more writers have sought to study political system in relation to the role of 'extra-governmental' agencies. Writers on comparative politics have come to hold the view that studies in this field have, to a very large extent, been 'uncomparative' in the sense that the role of environmental factors in the form of 'inputs', that have their definite impact upon the 'output' agencies of every political organisation, has been thoroughly ignored. It has been widely recognised by a good number of seminal theorists like Easton, Almond, Deutsch and Kaplan that structural categories such as courts, legislative bodies, and cabinets, however adequate for an understanding of the realities of certain countries, "are hopelessly unrealistic as guides to the essence of the political realms of other countries. Instead, political scientists have searched for abstract processes and functions which are performed by some structures in all countries, but not necessarily by structures which appear the same or even bear the same labels from one country to another."[2]

Political System : Implications and Nature

The term 'political system' refers to the study of a government in its empirical dimensions and also from a strictly interdisciplinary standpoint. Political system thus becomes 'a set of interrelated variables conceived to be politically relevant and treated as if they could be separated from other variables conceived to be politically relevant, not immediately relevant to politics.'[3] A set of concepts considered to make up a political system is advanced not to help one to understand the government and politics of a particular country but to aid in understanding the government and politics of any country of the world. The idea behind it is that the study of particular countries of particular kinds of structures or processes (known as sub-systems) can be related to this broader conceptual scheme with the hope that

1. Kaplan: *Systems and Process in International Politics* (New York: Wiley, 1957), p. 4.
2. David M. Wood : "Comparative Government and Politics" in Stephen L. Wasby(ed.): *Political Science : The Discipline and Its Dimensions* (Calcutta : Scientific Book Agency, 1970), p. 491.
3. *ibid.*, p. 492.

the work done in one realm "will be compatible with work done in another realm, to the extent that similar definitions are employed and concepts are given similar content by different users."[4] Or, as Beer and Ulam add: "We want a definition that is useful— useful in the sense that it gives us promise of leading us towards a growing body of explanatory theory about human behaviour and useful also in the sense that the behaviour it identifies is not trival, but important to enduring human concerns."[5] It is from such important considerations that the concept of political system has emerged as "a part of the broad way of looking at all social behaviour. From that perspective, the political system is a structure that performs a certain function for a society. In the fewest possible words, that function is to make legitimate policy decisions."[6]

The concept of political system has certainly acquired wide currency for the reason that it "directs attention to the entire scope of political activities within a society, regardless of where in the society such activities may be located."[7] Defining this term. Almond and Powell say: "When we speak of the political system, we include all the interactions which affect the use or threat of use of legitimate physical coercion. The political system includes not only govermental institutions such as legislatures, courts and administrative agencies, but *all structures in their political aspects.* Among these are traditional structures such as kinship ties and caste groupings; and anomic phenomena such as assassinations, riots and demonstrations; as well as formal organisations like parties, interest groups, and media of communications."[8]

The term "political system' is a compound of two words. First, we take up the meaning of the term 'political'. If we "consult the current literature for an adequate definition of the politics and political, we find considerable variety and some help."[9] For instance, Max Weber says that a state "is a human community that (successfully) claims the monopoly of the legitimate use of physical force within a given territory."[10] In order to make his point more clear, Weber further says that the right to use physical force "is ascribed to other institutions or to individuals only to the extent to which the state permits it."[11] A well-known sociologist like Marion Levy, Jr. says that political allocation may be defined "as the distribution of power over and responsibility for the actions of the various members of the concrete structure concerned, involving on the one hand coercive sanctions, of which force is the extreme form in one direction, and, on the other, accountability to the members and in terms of the structure concerned, or to the members of other concrete structures."[12]

Recent political sociologists and political psychologists have offered their own interpretations. For instance, David Easton says that a political system allocates values by means of its policies that are binding on the society by virtue of being authoritative. According to him, a policy "is clearly authoritative when the feeling prevails that it must or ought to be obeyed...that policies, whether formal or effective, are accepted as binding."[13] Lasswell

---

4. *Ibid.*
5. S.H. Beer and A.B. Ulam : *Patterns of Government* (New York : Random House, 1968) 8th Ptg., p. 21.
6. *ibid.*
7. Almond and Powell : *Comparative Politics: A Developmental Approach* (Boston : Little, Brown Co., 1966), p. 17.
8. *ibid.*, p. 18.
9. Almond : "Introduction" in Almond and Coleman (eds.) : *The Politics of the Developing Areas* (Princeton : Princeton Univ Press, I960), p. 5.
10. Max Weber : "Politics as Vocation" in Gerth and Mills (eds.) : *From Max Weber* (London : Routledge and Kegan Paul, 1947), p. 78.
11. *ibid.*
12. Levy : *The Structure of Society* (Princeton : Princeton Univ Press, 1952), p. 469.
13. Easton : *The Political System : An Enquiry into the State of Political Science* (New York : Alfred Knopf, 1953), pp. 130ff.

and Kaplan say: "Power is a special case of the exercise of influence; it is the process of affecting policies of others with the help of (actual or threatened) severe deprivations for non-conformity with the policies intended."[14]

All these definitions, however, suffer from some element of deficiency in one respect or another. For instance, Weber's emphasis on 'the legitimate use of physical force' may not apply to primitive, small and undifferentiated political communities where there is monopoly of power.[15] Marion Levy, Jr. lays emphasis on 'coercive and other sanctions' and also on 'structures' that apply these sanctions without telling us as to what these sanctions are and what are the structures that apply to them. The element of 'severe deprivations', as given in the interpretations of Lasswell and Kaplan, cannot be used as a criterion for distinguishing one political system from another. Likewise, the element of "authoritative allocation of values', as coined by Easton, "does not differentiate political systems from churches, business firms and the like."[16] Despite all this, the interpretations of Weber and Easton, if reconciled together, offer a better and palusible explanation keeping which in view Almond says: "Certainly the comparative politics of modern times must be in a position to handle primitive and traditional systems which are political but are not states in the sense of Weber's definition, as well as transitional and revolutionary systems in which there may be no monopoly of the legitimate use of physical force within a given territory."[17]

Now we refer to the word 'system'. Systems analysis, as elaborately discussed in Chapter 3 views political life as a system of behaviour embedded in the environment to the influences of which the political system itself is exposed and, in turn, reacts. The term 'system' is rigorously defined "to single out from all classes, aggregates, or phenomena those which can satisfy the following criteria:

1. One can specify a set of elements.
2. Among at least some of the elements, one can specify identifiable relations.
3. Certain relations imply others...Dynamics is added (to this definition) by including a time dimension.
4. A certain complex of relations at a given time implies a certain complex (or one of several possible complexes) at a later time. A dynamic theory of a system is, therefore, one which enables us to deduce certain future states from a given present state."[18]

According to Almond, a system "implies the interdependence of parts and a boundary of some kind between it and its environment."[19] The criterion of 'comprehensiveness' "means that when we speak of the political system, we include all the interactions—inputs as well as outputs—which affect the use or the threat of the use of physical coercion."[20] Then, by 'inter-dependence' we mean that a change in one subset of interactions "produces changes in all the other subsets."[21] Finally, by the existence of a 'boundary' in a political system, we mean that there are points where other systems "end and the political system begins."[22] The result is that while the word 'political' signifies an attempt to separate out a certain set of interactions in a society in order to relate it to other sets, by 'system' is meant "attribution to a particular set of properties of these interactions."[23]

14. Harold D. Lasswell and Abraham Kaplan : *Power and Society* (New Haven : Connecticut, 1950). p. 76.
15. See I. Schapera : *Government and Politics in Tribal Societies* (London, 1956), p. 119.
16. Almond, *op. cit., p. 6.*
17. *ibid.,* p. 7.
18. Anatol Rapoport: "Some System Approaches to Political Theory" in David Easton (ed.) : *Varieties of Political Theory,* pp. 129-30.
19. Almond and Powell, *op, cit.,* p. 19.
20. Almond, *op. cit.,* pp. 7-8.
21. *ibid.,* p. 8.
22. *ibid.*
23. *ibid.,* p. 7.

After understanding the meanings of the two terms— 'political' and 'system'—we now come to the state of presenting a precise definition of the 'term political system' as it is understood in the realm of comparative politics. Beer and Ulam describe it as 'a structure that performs a certain function for a society'. It 'includes an arrangement for making decisions'. These decisions have 'legitimacy', because the members of a society accept them as 'being in conformity with their conceptions of authority and purpose.' The political system "produces a certain output for the society: legitimate policy decisions. The goals at which these decisions aim may be precise and programmatic, or only vague and general. They may be accepted readily or reluctantly, by many or by few. But to call them policy decisions is to stress that they do have consequences for the society, and to note their legitimacy is to draw attention to the main characteristics that makes them political. Through the political system goals for the society are defined and carried out by legitimate policy decisions."[24]

A definition of the term 'political system' is thus given by Almond: "What we propose is that the political system is that system of interactions to be found in all independent societies which performs the functions of integration and adaptation (both internally and *vis-a-vis* other societies) by means of the employment, or threat of employment, of more or less legitimate, order-maintaining or transforming system in the society. We use the term 'more or less' to modify legitimacy, because we do not want to exclude from our definition political systems, like the totalitarian ones where the degree of legitimacy may be very much in doubt, revolutionary systems, where the use of legitimacy may be in process of change, or non-Western systems, in which there may be more than one legitimate system in operation."[25]

Properties and Characteristics of the Political System: Analysis of Gabriel A. Almond

What we have discussed above shows that a political system has its own properties and essential characteristics. According to Almond, a political system has three main properties—comprehensiveness, interdependence and boundaries and it has five essential characteristics—universality of political systems, universality of political structures, universality of political functions, multi-functionality of political structures and the culturally mixed character of the political systems. Let us first examine the main properties of the political system which are:

1. ***Comprehensiveness :*** It implies that a political system includes all the interactions—inputs as well as outputs—that affect the use or the threat of the use of physical coercion. Almond is not concerned with the mere structures based on constitutional and legal foundations as parliaments, courts and bureaucracies or with informal organisations like political parties and pressure groups and means of communications; he is rather concerned with all the structures in their political aspects, including undifferentiated structures like kinship and lineage, status and caste groups, religious and cultural bodies, as well as anomic phenomena like violent riots and street demonstrations.[26]
2. ***Interdependence :*** It implies that a change in one subset of interactions (as the enactment of a measure enfranchising the working classes) produces changes in all other subsets as the working of the political parties and pressure groups and the functioning of the legislative and executive departments. For instance, the changes in the technology of communications have

24. Beer and Ulam, *op. cit.,* pp. 21-22.
25. Almond, *op. cit.,* p. 7.
26. *ibid.,* pp. 7-8.

Political System

A political system is a particular type of social system, namely, one involved in the making of authoritative public decisions. To put it slightly differently, the political system is a set of institutions such as parliaments, bureaucracies and courts, that formulate and implement the collective goals of society or of groups within it.

—G.A. Almond

A political system is a term that applies to broad patterns of interaction among state institutions, economic coordination and political culture.

—Mark Kesselman

A political system is a broader term that encompasses not only the mechanism of government, and the institutions of the state, but also the structures and the processes through which these interact with the larger society. A political system is, in effect, a sub-system of the larger social system. It is a 'system' in that there are inter-relationships within a complex whole, and 'political' in that these interrelationships relate to the distribution of power, wealth and resources in society.

—Andrew Heywood

transformed the electoral process, the characteristics of political parties, the legislature and the executive. The concepts of system and interdependence lead us to look for these changes when any specific role changes significantly.[27]

3. ***Existence of Boundaries :*** It implies that there are certain points where the political system ends and other systems begin. The boundaries between society and polity differ from one political system to another but even in the communicational primitive brand, some signalling occurs, making the transition (of an incumbent) from a religious to a political role. Almond cautions that when we "talk about good and bad boundary maintenance, we must use criteria appropriate to the system. In one case diffuseness and intermittency may be appropriate boundary maintenance; in another specialised secular structures are appropriate."[28]

Then, the characteristics of a political system may be said to be five in number:

1. ***Universality of Political Systems :*** It implies that all political systems, whether primitive or modern, or whether developing and developed, have political structures, *i.e.,* they have a legitimate pattern of interaction by means of which internal and external order is maintained. A student of comparative politics is, therefore, concerned with a study of all political systems whether they are European, or American, or Afro-Asian. If this point is examined in greater detail, it may be said that a student of comparative politics should pay greater attention to the political systems of the poor and backward countries inasmuch as they provide abundant material for him that is not available in a study of the developed political systems of the European and American countries. Viewed in this perspective, every political system may be said to have these four characteristics: (i) All political systems have political structures. (ii) The same functions are performed in all political systems, though these functions may be performed with different frequencies in different kinds of structures. (iii) All political structures, no matter how specialised, are multifunctional.

27. *ibid.,* p. 8.
28. *ibid.,* pp. 8-9.

(iv) All political systems are 'mixed' in the cultural sense. There are no 'all-modern' cultures and structures, in the sense of rationality, and no all primitive ones in the sense of traditionality. They differ in the relative dominance of the one as against the other, and in the pattern of mixture of the two composite components.[29]

2. ***Universality of Political Structures :*** All political systems have same structures that perform same functions, though with varying degrees of frequency. The articulative, aggregative, and communicative functions may be performed diffusely within the society or intermittently through the kinship or lineage structure. An adequate analysis of a political system must locate and characterise all of these functions and not simply those performed by the specialised political structures. Indeed, it is this emphasis on the specialised structures of politics which has led to the stereotyped conception of traditional and primitive systems as static systems, since the political structures most likely to be differentiated are executive, legislative and adjudicative structures. The machanics of political choice are there as well, but in the form of intermittent political structures.[30]

3. ***Universality of Political Functions :*** The approach of a student of comparative politics should not be 'structure-bound'; rather it should be 'function-bound'. That is, his area of concern should not be confined to the superficial study of the legislative, executive and judicial departments of a political system. He should also take into account the role of the factors of initiation, communication, authorisation, modification, vetoing, representation, advocacy and interpretation and the like in the study of 'non-state' institutions and agencies like political parties, interest groups, factions, elites, mass media agencies etc. which constitute the infrastructure of a political system. He should look into the questions as how people are recruited to and socialised into political roles and orientations in different political systems. Almond offers a sevenfold classification in the input and output categories. While the input category includes: (i) political socialisation and recruitment, (ii) interest articulation, (iii) interest aggregation, and (iv) political communication; output category includes: (i) rule-making, (ii) rule-application, and (iii) rule-adjudication functions.[31]

4. ***Multifunctionality of Political Structures :*** All political structures, irrespective of the degree of specialisation in point of time or space, are multi-functional. The model of the western political system has over-stressed the functional specificity of political structures, while that of the traditional system has over-emphasised the undifferentiated and diffuse character of political and social structure. Once again, Almond reacts against the tendency of 'limiting case model' of the western systems. A student of comparative politics should appreciate the facts that the courts not only adjudicate, they also legislate; that bureaucracy is one of the most important sources of legislation; that legislative bodies affect both administration and adjudication; that political parties and pressure groups initiate legislation and participate in national administration; that the means of communications represent interests and affect the working of all the three departments of a political organisation. Two important things should, however, be noted in this regard. "First, what is peculiar to modern political systems is a relatively high degree of structural

29. *ibid.*, *p.* 11.
30. *ibid.*, p. 12.
31. *ibid.*, p. 15.

differentiation in the form of the emergence of legislatures, executives, bureaucracies, courts, election systems, political parties, organised interest groups and means of communication with each structure tending to perform a regulatory role for that function within the political system as a whole.'[32] Second, a political system does not eliminate intermittency and traditionality, rather it tends to regulate and control it and, for this reason, it "can penetrate it, regulate it, translate its particularistic and diffuse impacts into the modern political language of interest articulation, public policy and regulation."[33]

5. ***Culturally Mixed Character of Political Systems :*** All political systems are 'mixed' in the cultural sense. Certain kinds of political structures usually considered to be peculiar to the primitive are also found in modern political systems. In other words, it may be said that all political systems have formal and informal structures. No political system is quite modern or western in the same sense as no individual is fully mature or emancipated from the ties and diffuse dependence. As Almond says : "What is useful in these concepts of multi-functionalism, cultural dualism, and political acculturation is that they set aside once and for all the geographic, cultural, and analytical polarisations which have plagued our efforts at social and political comparison. We have been talking of 'modern' and 'pre-modern', 'developed' and 'under-developed', 'industrial' and 'agrarian', 'Western' and 'non-Western', or the Parsonian syndromes of universalism-specificity-achievement-affective neutrality, versus particularism-diffuseness-ascriptive-affectivity. The universe of political systems is less tractable to simple contrasts than we have supposed. We need dualistic models rather than monistic ones, and developmental as well as equilibrium models, if we are to understand differences precisely and grapple effectively with the processes of political change."[34]

Variables of a Political System : Fourfold Analysis of Beer and Ulam

The concept of a political system, as discussed in the preceding section, directs our attention towards the process by which legitimate policy decisions are made in a political community. It implies that the elements of the process must be interdependent. Beer and Ulam, however, warn against the insidious tendency of using such variables that apply only to a few democratic countries of Europe and America. Reference to such institutions as legislatures, executives, political parties, electorate, etc. would not serve the purpose for the simple reason that though these terms are used in every political system, whether developed or developing, or whether democratic or totalitarian, they have different connotations in different political systems. For instance, the meaning of 'party' is fundamentally different from one that we use in the English or American countries. Likewise, the National People's Congress of China can hardly be called a legislature like the English Parliament or American Congress if it means a body of the chosen representatives of the people. It is, therefore, counselled that, in short, the scheme of variables "must be such that it can be found in any political system. Only if it retains its high level of generality can the concept of the political system keep its high degree of usefulness."[35]

Having this important consideration in mind, Beer and Ulam offer a fourfold analysis of the variables that can be found in any political system of the world whether western or non-western, democratic or totalitarian, developed or developing and the like. These are:

---

32. *ibid.*, p. 17.
33. *ibid.*, p. 19.
34. *ibid.*, p. 25.
35. Beer and Ulam, *op. cit.*, p. 28.

1. ***Pattern of Political Culture :*** It refers to the beliefs, convictions and attitudes of the people towards their political system. Just as an individual acts to solve some particular problems and his actions are made against a broad background of his knowledge about and adherence to a set of values, similarly in a political system the basic political attitudes of its members are an important influence on what is done or not done. The people have certain notions about what is worthwhile to spend time and energy on as well as notions of certain ethical limits that they ought not to overstep. They look at the situation in the light of their practical knowledge comparing the immediate obstacles or opportunities facing them with the consequences of a certain line of action for their other objectives. It is this broad background of attitudes that will strongly influence what particular goals they decide to pursue and how they go about working for them. A deeper study of the working of political systems shows that these attitudes condition the interests and goals being pursued, the means that are adopted to reach them and the acceptance or rejection of the decisions by the members of the system. "As cultural background, they will have great bearing upon the fortunes of the political system: whether it is stable or unstable; whether it is capable of orderly and gradual development or is caught in paralysing stalemate; whether the struggle for power is kept within bounds or burst forth in self-destroying excess."[36]
2. ***Pattern of Power :*** It refers to an array of means by which the process and action of decision-making may be influenced. Authority is a form of power. Each group has a base of power and it is from this base that it tries to influence the process of making decisions. Harry Eckstein points out the principal power base of each of various groups within the Labour Party of England – "in the case of the Fabians, brains; in the case of the constituency parties, political activism; in the case of the trade unions, money. Normally, of course, the power base of a group will be a complex of several factors."[37] One should look at the decision-making process that operates in every political system and that acts as a factor on which the working of different systems can be compared. For instance, while the pressure groups use their lobbying tactics that influence the decision-making process of the American Congress, the National People's Congress of China is controlled from outside, the real power resting principally with the higher organs of the Communist Party. A student of comparative politics is, therefore, required to study the working of political system in the light of the struggle for power whether it takes place in the party in power, inside the legislature, or in the administrative departments and the like.
3. ***Pattern of Interest :*** It refers to the set of goals that various individuals or groups pursue for the sake of protecting and promoting their specific interests. Power is sought for the sake of achieving the desired goal; it is also sought for the purpose of realising further objectives. It is for this reason that so many political parties and interest groups operate in a democratic system and their operation cannot be made out of existence in a totalitarian system. We find that the peasants offered resistance to the collectivisation of agriculture in the Soviet Union, or there were desperate struggles inside the communes in China. Interests may be positive or negative, they may be special or general; their role is, nevertheless, important and that should be discovered in a satisfactory answer to such questions as what they hope to achieve and in what ways they desire to change the policy of the government.

---

36. *ibid.*, p. 30.
37. *ibid.*, p. 47.

4. *Pattern of Policy* : As with the interplay of ends and means, interests and power interact to produce certain consequences that may be designated as the pattern of policy. Policy consists of decisions. Any particular policy whether it relates to the collectivisation of farming as in the Soviet Union, or co-operativisation of agriculture as in India emerges from a series of decisions that have a binding character on account of their acceptance by the men in power. A student of comparative politics is concerned with these decisions at each stage and how they affect the next stage of decisions. "The final outcome is the pattern of policy. The decision as a product is not an inert thing. It is part of a further stage of political or social process. So from asking what was decided, we go on to ask what are the consequences of this decision in those further stages. While the patterns of power and interest focus attention on the origins and emergence of decisions, the pattern of policy focuses attention on its content and consequences."[38]

Though every political system has these four variables, they are interdependent in view of the fact that a change in one pattern certainly brings about a change in another. It is a different matter that the change in one pattern may not have a change of equal weight in all patterns of a political system. We may, however, endorse that it is on account of the study of these four variables of a political system that it cannot be treated as an isolated branch of study. A political system becomes a part of the social system and, as such, it cannot be separated from the study of the rest of the society. For instance, the stress on policy leads naturally to the consideration of the consequences of the political system for the society—its functioning for the stability or development of the political community. The four patterns of political culture, power, interest and policy suggest major ways in which some disturbing force may enter the political system. A study of the political in the context of the non-political phenomena, therefore, becomes a matter of study in comparative politics. Such a scheme of analysis has value in that it "continually directs attention to the relations of the political system with the other subsystems of society."[39]

Functional Aspects of the Political System: A Configuration Model of Structures and Functions

The framework of political system, though not truly a model, "provides the theoretical equipment both for looking at political phenomena on a macroscopic level and the setting in which microanalysis can be carried out by providing an opportunity for a political scientist to relate the more specific work which he is doing to the larger political world. The political system idea serves to keep us attuned to the broad implications of political acts and institutions, and to the inter-relatedness of the events rather than to their ideosyncratic or particularistic aspects."[40] In order to understand the truth of this statement, we should look at the functional aspects of the political system that leads towards, what Almond calls, a 'probabilistic theory of politics'. It means that the political system of each country "should be described in reference to a particular configuration of structures and functions in which each element would be 'involved' by performing in part a number of functions."[41]

For this, it shall be worthwhile to discuss, though briefly, the ideas of some eminent writers on this subject:

Analysis of Easton : In this direction, the most outstanding name is that of David Easton

38. *ibid., p. 59.*
39. *ibid.,* p. 31.
40. Stephen L Wasby : *Political Science : The Discipline and Its Dimensions* (Calcutta : Scientific Book Agency, 1970), p. 109.
41. Jean Blondel : *An Introduction to Comparative Government* (London: Weidenfield and Nicolson, 1969), p. 25.

who seems primarily concerned with portraying the relationships between a system and the environment in which it is located. He is interested in directing our attention to the boundary between politics and other aspects of social life and postulate the existence of a close relationship between a system and the environment. He divides the basic components of his model of the political system into 'inputs' consisting of 'demands' and 'supports' and 'outputs' connected by the 'feedback'. The 'support' derives from the satisfaction of the outputs of the system and from more generalised or diffuse support or approval for the system itself. The latter is necessary, because a system's output cannot satisfy everyone. Easton distinguishes between external demands coming from the environment and internal ones emerging from within the system. There are also three subjects of support—*political community* or a 'group that seeks to settle differences or promote decisions through peaceful action in common'; *regime* or the constitutional order including arrangements for the processing of demands and the implementation of decisions; and *government* that undertakes concrete tasks.

The environment in which a political system operates may be put into two parts: (i) intra-societal, i.e., one consisting of systems in a given society other than the political, and (ii) extra-societal or the one including all those systems that lie outside the given society itself. Intra-societal systems include sets of behaviour, attitudes and ideas like the economy, culture, social structures and personalities, the extra-societal systems are functional components of an international society, a 'super system' of which any single society is a part. It is these two classes of systems-the intra-societal and the extra-societal—that comprise the total environment of a political system and it "is from these sources that these influences arise that are of consequence for possible stress on the political system."[42]

Models of Easton's Political System

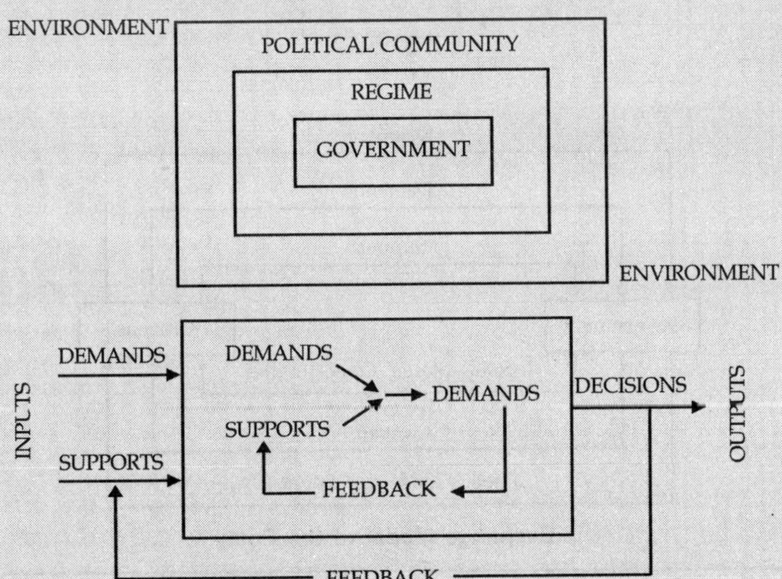

'Black Box Model' of the Polity

42. P K. Ghosh: *Studies in Contemporary Political Theory* (Calcutta : Minerva 1970), p. 119.

A question arises as to how the 'potentially successful conditions' from the environment communicate themselves to the political system. In order to solve this problem, Easton presents his input-output model. While the 'input' means all 'demands' and 'supports' through which 'a wide range of activities in the environment, "can be channelled, mirrored, summarised, and brought to bear upon political life...They are the key indicators of the way in which environmental influences and conditions modify and shape the operations of the political system."[43] 'Outputs' are the decisions of the authorities. Thus, the decisions taken by the legislative, executive and judicial departments may be termed 'political outputs'; moreover, they are 'authoritative' as they are taken by the men in power. In between the 'inputs' and outputs', there is a 'feedback loop' the identification of which helps us to explain the processes through which the system may cope with stress. Through it the system may take advantage of what has been happening by trying to adjust its future behaviour.[44] The 'feedback loop' consists of the production of outputs by the authorities, a response by the members of the society to these outputs, the communication of information about this response to authorities, and finally, possibly succeeding actions by the authorities giving rise to a new round of the same activities. The 'feedback' is thus crucial in determining the capacity of the system to cope with stress.[45]

Models of Mitchell's Political System

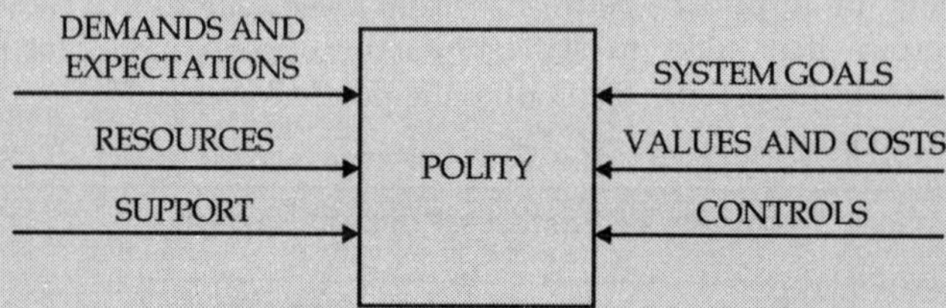

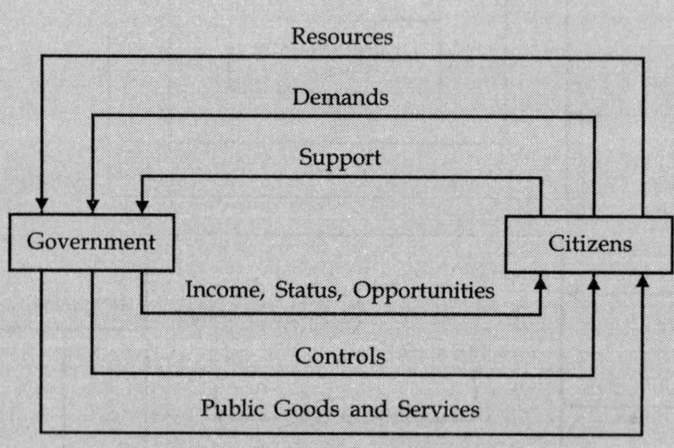

Exchange Model of the Polity

43. Easton : "Categories for the Systems Analysis of Politics" in his (ed.): *Varieties of Political Theory*, p. 151.
44. *ibid.*, *p.* 152.
45. Ghosh, *op. cit.*, p. 121.

Almond's Model of Political System
Political System

Characteristics
1. Comprehensiveness
2. Interdependence
3. Boundaries

Properties
1. Universality of political systems
2. Universality of political structures
3. Universality of political functions
4. Multifunctionality of political structures
5. Culturally mixed character of political systems

Functions

Input
1. Political socialisation and recruitment
2. Interest articulation
   (Organised interest groups)
   (a) Associational
   (b) Non-Associational
   (c) Institutional
   (d) Anomic
3. Interest aggregation
   (a) *Party systems*
      (i) Authoritarian
      (ii) Dominant-authoritarian
      (iii) Competitive
      (iv) Competitive multi-party
   (b) *Performance of aggregative functions*
      (i) Secular or pragmatic bargaining
      (ii) Absolute value-oriented
      (iii) Particularistic or traditional
4. Political communication
   (Variables of comparison)
      (i) Homogeneity of political information
      (ii) Mobility of information
      (iii) Value of information
      (iv) Direction of the flow of information

Output
1. Rule-making
   (a) Prescription
   (b) Termination
2. Rule-application
   (a) Invocation
   (b) Application
3. Rule-adjudication
   (a) Rule-application
   (b) Rule-appraisal

Analysis of Mitchell : What Easton termed the 'black box model' of the political system has been taken over and presented in a new form by other eminent writers on this subject. Mitchell divides 'inputs and outputs' in a way somewhat different from that of Easton indicating that demands and supports donot account for all the system's inputs; expectations (what individual members of the society desire, but short of demands and perhaps not even conscious) and resources, on which the system operates, are also necessary. He also defines the 'outputs' of the system into three categories —goals, values and costs, and controls. "Values in a sense are positive 'outputs' and costs negative ones; what is a value for one person usually involves costs for himself or others. Controls are the ways in which the goals, values and costs are implemented."[46]

It may be commented that while Easton talks in terms of political sociology, Mitchell offers an economic interpretation. While Mitchell's model of a polity shows inter-relationship between demands, expectations, resources and supports on the one side and system goals, values and costs and controls on the other, his 'exchange model of the polity' manifests an inter-relationship between resources, demands and supports, public goods and services on the other. In one of his important writings, Mitchell makes it clear that his purpose is to discuss 'the shape of political theory to come'. As he adds with a word of optimism: "I predict that the new political theory, under the influence of economics, will fill this gap if we do not. They have already made a powerful beginning in welfare economics and in the development of such tools as 'cost benefit analysis', 'systems theory', 'program budgeting' and economic theory more generally."[47]

Analysis of Almond : Almond presents a sevenfold classification of the functional variables in his input-output model that, as he claims, he has developed for the purpose of comparing political systems as whole systems and particularly for comparing the modern and developed political systems with primitive and developing political systems of the 'Third World' countries. He mentions four variables in the input category what he calls as political socialisation and recruitment, interest articulation, interest aggregation, and political communication.

1. The variable of 'political socialisation and recruitment' refers to a sociological analysis of how people are trained to have faith and conviction in political values and how they are inducted into the specialised roles of a political system. Political socialisation is viewed as the end-product of a set of attitudes, cognition, value standards and feelings towards the political system in its various roles and role-incumbents; political recruitment inducts members of the society out of particular subcultures and inducts them into the specialised roles of the political system, trains them in the appropriate skills, provides them with political cognitive maps, values, expectations and effects.
2. 'Interest articulation' refers to the study of interest groups that struggle for the protection and promotion of their specific interests. These groups may be 'institutional' like legislatures, political executives, bureaucracies, churches, etc; or 'non-associational' like kinship and lineage groups, ethnic, religious, regional, status and class groups that act informally and intermittently; 'anomic' that are more or less spontaneous breakthroughs into the political system from the society as riots and demonstrations, and 'associational that are specialised structures of interest articulation like trade unions and business organisations,' etc.
3. 'Interest aggregation' refers to the organisation and role of the political parties. It is the party system that is the distinctively modern structure of political aggregation regulating or giving orders to the performance of the aggregative function by other sub-systems.
4. All input and output functions in a political system are carried out by means of communication what Almond terms 'political communication'.[48]

Almond includes in his output category three variables — rule-making, rule-application and rule-adjudication functions that are

46. Mitchell : *The American Polity* (New York : The Free Press, 1962), p. 6.
47. Mitchell: "The Shape of Political Theory to Come : From Political Sociology to Political Economy" in S.M. Lipset (ed.): *Politics and the Social Sciences* (New York : Wiley, 1972), p. 126.
48. See Almond, *op. eit.,* pp. 26-57.

performed respectively by the legislative, executive and judicial departments of the government. Though Almond nowhere makes a mention of the term 'feedback loop', it is implied in the treatment of such input functions as interest articulation and interest aggregation in relation to the output function of rule-making. Almond's analysis, in this way, "provides a convenient framework for the comparison of different types of political systems. It is significant that, unlike Easton, he also regards the systems analysis of political institutions as a prelude to the building of a 'probabilistic theory' of the polity.[49]

Analysis of Blondel : Disagreeing with both Easton and Almond in a somewhat different way, Blondel gives his own analysis of the 'functions' of the political system. According to him, there arise 'conflicts' in every society and it is the function of the political system to 'digest' them. The political system 'selects' and 'combines' these demands that arise out of the social conflicts. These demands have their impact on the decision-making process. However, the normative aspects should not be ignored as customs, usages, rules of good behaviour that also operate and the decision-makers have to work in the context of these ideals. Thus, a mere empirical analysis is insufficient. Then, outputs are the decisions of the government that can be either natural or imposed. They are natural if they are in accord with the normative values of the society; they are imposed if they pertain to the whims and caprices of the men in power.

Keeping this input-output model in view, Blondel says that the functions or the operations of the political system can be summarised in the following ways:[50]

1. In order to process inputs, the system has to select from among the pressures exercised by structural and circumstantial facts which characterise the community.
2. The selection process is followed by a combination process, both being related to the normative standpoints of the political system and being, therefore, liable to depression or 'increase' as a result of these norms.
3. In order to convert inputs into outputs, the political system goes through two successive phases. The norms of the system are first expressed in the form of *general statements.*
4. These are subsequently applied to *particular* situations.
5. There is, finally, a process of *double-checking* by which norms are directly confronted with individual outputs as this is both an element of the feedback mechanism and a normative demand in human communities.

It is on the basis of this interpretation of the 'structures and functions of a political system' that Blondel comes to offer his paradigm in this form:[51]

	Functions	*Structures*
Monitoring	Selection (articulation)	Groupings (social and economic)
	Combination (aggregation)	Parties
Conversion	General and norms (rule-making)	Assemblies and councils
	Particular decisions (rule-implementation)	Executives, bureaucracies
		Judiciaries
	Particular and norms (rule- adjudication)	

49. Ghosh, *op. cit.,* p. 124.
50. Blondel, *op. cit.,* p. 23.
51. *ibid.,* p. 26.

What emerges from the study of all these analyses is. that each type of structure fulfils one function, only one function and always the same function. An impressionistic evidence shows that this is not the case: interest groups, parties or bureaucracies are involved differently in the political process of a country like the United States; they have a quite different character in a country like China. The principle behind such an analysis is simple and, in a formal manner, could be expressed in the form of the matrix of the structure-function relationship for each country. These matrices could be compared and comparative government would effectively consist of the comparison between these matrices.[52]

Analysis of Apter : David Apter has presented his own analysis of a political system in a way bringing about a marked distinction between their democratic and totalitarian varieties. According to him, a democratic system "responds to crisis variables by trying to mediate between contending groups in order to produce effective policies that can ameliorate the causes of tension. Their success depends in part on the effectiveness of the link between society and government. Government is the dependent variable; society is independent.'[53] It may be thus illustrated:

Inputs				**Outputs**
Social systems	⟶	Government	⟶	Policy decisions

In this model, the social system "comprises a national society. Government responds to societally generated crises as inputs. Since the democratic government model is, above all, an instrument of tension reduction, it responds with instruments that act on society, government, political parties, electoral systems and the like. The ability of governments to resolve crises depends on their relationship to the official system and the quality or appropriateness of policy decisions. Government is cast in the role of a mediator and judge. Its functions are to reduce tensions and to mediate. Its political norms are embodied in law, which serves as a framework for instruments of rule. And the legal framework is itself important to the tension-reducing and mediating activities of government".[54]

Opposed to it is the totalitarian model where the government tries "to deal with institutionalisation, socialisation, and internalisation by mobilising the people. It does not mediate within it. It mobilises the population to this end. Participation which checks the power of elites, in which people establish priorities over their own circumstances, is restricted. The mobilisation of all toward the achievement of certain goals is facilitated in the hope that this will co-ordinate all efforts, unify all objectives, and provide collective power for transforming and transcending the restrictions of society."[55] It may be thus illustrated:

Inputs				**Outputs**
Government	⟶	Policy decisions	⟶	Changes in the social system

52. *ibid.*, p. 25.
53. Apter: *Introduction to Political Analysis*, (New Delhi: Prentice Hall of India, 1978.) p. 431.
54. *ibid.*
55. *ibid.*, pp. 431-32.

In this model, government is the instrument by means of which radical change "is produced in the social system. Defining the purposes and objectives of such change (normative characteristics) establishes new structural characteristics of society."[56]

In short, in a democratic model, rulers become a government and the government is a unit with particular responsibilities for the maintenance and adaptation of society. "The ruled, organised in classes and role networks functional to the exchange process, represent *social systems*. The largest social system is a *society*. Government is the one sub-unit among all others that has a unique responsibility. It exercises a virtual monopoly over the instruments of force, and is the sole legitimate agency for the exercise of public power on behalf of society. The societal-government relationship creates a political system."[57] On the contrary, where there "is centralised power or authority with sacrosanct norms and belief systems, the political system is likely to be monistic and ideological, seeking to create a society for the future. Its emphasis is on the realisation of moral purposes. The party takes over the government. The government transforms the society and achieves the final goal."[58]

Structure and Culture of a Political System: Doctrine of Capability as Enunciated by Almond and Powell

The terms 'structure' and 'culture' have a central importance in an analytical study of the political system. By the term 'structure' we 'mean the observable activities which make up the political system."[59] Let us look at the role of the individuals in the political process, since the role of the actors is integrally connected with the structure of a political system. The individual members of a society perform roles in a variety of social systems as in families, churches, clubs, unions, etc., but the part of their activity that has its connection with the political process is called 'political activity'. In the field of comparative politics, we are concerned with the units which make up all social systems, including political system, that are called *roles*. "It is the particular set of roles that are related to one another as *structures*. Thus, judgeship is a role; a court is a structure of roles."[60] A definite change in the use of vocabulary is not without definite purpose. "The reason we use the terms 'role' and 'structure' rather than 'office' and 'institution' is that we wish to emphasise the actual behaviour of the individuals who are involved in politics, and the actual performance of the particular institutions with which we may be concerned...'Role' and 'structure' refer to the observable behaviour of individuals.'"[61]

Viewed with a developmental approach, it appears that political activities bring about a change in the political system over time. In every political system there occurs the development of transformation that leads to differentiation in roles and structures. By the term 'differentiation' is meant the process whereby roles "change and become more

56. *ibid.;* p. 432.
57. *ibid.,* pp. 432-33.
58. *ibid.,* p. 433. Apter cites Lenin in support of his argument who wrote that the bourgeoisie "encircle the proletariat on every side with a petty bourgeois atmosphere, which impregnates and corrupts the proletariat (externalisation) and causes constant relapses among the proletariat into petty-bourgeois spinelessness, disintegration, individualism and alternative moods of exaltation and dejection (desocialisation). The strictest centralisation and discipline is required in the political party of the proletariat in order to counteract this, in order that the organisational role of the proletariat (and this is its *principal* role) may be fulfilled correctly, successfully and victoriously (institutionalisation). The dictatorship of the proletariat is a persistent struggle—sanguinary and bloodless, violent and peaceful, military and economic, educational and administrative—against the forces and traditions of the old society (enforced resolution of crises.)" *Left-Wing Communism : An Infantile Disorder,* pp. 28-29.
59. Almond and Powell, *op. cit.,* p. 21.
60. *ibid.,*
61. *ibid.,* pp. 21-22.

specialised or autonomous or whereby new types of roles are established or new structures and subsystems emerge or are created. When we speak of role differentiation and structural differentiation, we refer not only to the development of new types of roles and the transformation of the older ones, we refer also to changes which may take place in the relationship between roles, between structures, or between subsystems.''[62]

Apart from studying the structures of a political system, we are also required to study the underlying propensities as well as its actual performance over a given period of time that relates to its psychological dimension and is known by the name of 'political culture'. The political culture "consists of the attitudes, beliefs, values and skills which are current in an entire population, as well as those special propensities and patterns which may be found within separate parts of that population."[63] It is on account of the varying political cultures that while the English people are called conservatives who do not take the matters to the path of violence and struggle for their rights in a peaceful and constitutional manner, the people of a country like France take the matters to the extreme of staging a violent revolution that is construed as a mark of their radical character.

According to Almond and Powell, the analysis of a political system "must consist not only of observation of the actual patterns of behaviour and interaction over a period of time, but also of those subjective propensities located in the political system as a whole and in its various parts. As we learn about the structure and culture of a political system, our capacity to characterise its properties, and to predict and explain its performance is improved."[64] Apart from this, we should also examine the *capabilities* of a political system. It means the way it performs its role as a unit in the environment. When we "speak of the capabilities of a political system, we are looking for an orderly way to describe its over-all performance in its environment".[65]

The capabilities of a political system may be of several varieties as regulative, extractive, distributive and responsive. For instance, a totalitarian system has *regulative* and *extractive* capabilities in the sense that it can well coerce its members in the way it likes. It has *distributive* capability also. It means that it can redistribute resources among its members in a way that is conducive to the principles of socialism. A democratic system is *responsive* as it allows all interests to operate and struggle for the protection and promotion of their specific interests and in it decisions are taken by the role of input agencies. The nature of these capabilities is contained in the operation of the input-output process for the obvious reason that capabilities "are simply the ways of talking about the flows of activity into and out of the political system."[66]

Then, every political system has a *conversion* process that means the reduction of the inputs into outputs. All political systems have this process and a comparison among them can be made with the help of a sixfold morphological illustration: interest articulation, interest aggregation, rule-making, rule-application, rule-adjudication, and political communication. Finally, there is the issue of the *system maintenance and adaptive functions.* As all parts of a machinery must work well and they must be repaired or changed from time to time in order to avoid any dislocation in its working, so in a political system the incumbents of various roles like diplomats, military officers, tax officials, administrators, etc. "must be

62. *ibid.*, p. 22.
63. *ibid.*, p. 23.
64. *ibid.*, p. 24.
65. *ibid.*, p. 28.
66. *ibid.*, p. 29.

recruited to these roles and learn how to perform in them. New roles are created and new personnel broken in."[67]

A scientific study of the classification of political systems of the world, according to Almond and Powell, can be made only on the basis of the capabilities, conversion function and system maintenance and adaptive functions of a political system and the interrelationships among these three kinds or levels of functions. Every political system has its political structure, though it is possible that in some systems one or a few structures perform all political functions. For instance, the leader or a religious head in a primitive political community may perform several functions, while there may be a high degree of differentiation in a country like the United States. It is for this reason that political structures "tend to be multi-functional, although the degrees of multi-functionality depend on many factors."[68]

A comparative study of political systems should be made on the basis of structural differentiations; it should also be made with the help of another criterion—cultural differentiation. One cannot question the fact that important differences do exist in the cultural characteristics of traditional and modern systems, any analysis of modern political systems must take account of the continuing importance of the informal and traditional relationships which shape the attitudes, beliefs, convictions and actions of the individuals. It is for this essential reason that, according to Almond and Powell, all political systems "have mixed political cultures. The most primitive societies have threads of instrumental rationality in their structure and culture. The most modern are permeated by ascriptive, particularistic, and informal relationships and attitudes. They differ in the relative dominance of one against the other and in the pattern of the mixture of these components. Secularisation is a matter of degree and of these rational aspects."[69]

Critical Appraisal

What we have discussed in the preceding sections leaves the following critical impressions:

1. Recent writers on the subject of comparative politics have made use of certain new terms to present a 'scientific' study of the governmental systems of the world. What has inspired them to do so is their "search for a new and coherent way of thinking about and studying politics that is implied in such slogans as the 'behavioural approach".[70] It is for this reason that instead of the term 'state', limited as it is by legal and institutional meanings, we prefer 'political system'; instead of 'powers', which again is a legal concept in connotation, we are beginning to prefer 'functions'; instead of 'offices' (legal again), we prefer 'roles'; instead of 'institutions', which again directs us towards formal norms, 'structures'; instead of 'public opinion' and 'citizenship training', formal and rational meaning, we prefer 'political culture' and 'political socialisation'.[71]

---

67. *ibid.*, p. 29-30.
68. *ibid.*, p. 31.
69. *ibid.*, p. 33. Secularisation is defined as "the process whereby men become increasingly rational, analytical, and empirical in their political action ... The secularisation of culture is the process whereby traditional orientations and attitudes give way to more dynamic decision-making processes involving the gathering of information, the evaluation of information, the laying out of alternative courses of action, the selection of a course of action from among these possible courses, and the means whereby one tests whether or not a given course of action is producing the consequences which were intended." *ibid.*, pp. 24-25.
70. See Almond, *op. cit.*, p. 4.
71. *ibid.*

2. Though the purpose behind the study of modern governmental systems in the name of a comparative study of the political systems cannot be questioned, it may be asserted that the study of the political systems has still remained far from being thoroughly empirical. The study of a political system from the standpoint of an inter-disciplinary focus leaves a big room open for the researchers who, are, as a matter of fact, confronted with the problem of what to include and what to exclude. It is, therefore, rightly pointed out that such a theory "is too broad a framework for a political analysis to take note of the complex psychological aspects of the interaction function. It may not be able to answer questions like what was the scope, depth and weight of power as it was being used. Nor does it help us to understand what strategies and tactics were adopted by those who employed power and influence."[72] A study of modern governments from the viewpoint of systems theory, says O.R. Young, "may be helpful in organising material on human relationship into systemic patterns in such a way that questions concerning pattern maintenance, stability, regulation, and so forth can be posed fruitfully, it does not have as much to offer for studies dealing with the political aspects of such matters as perception, expectation, formation, or cognition."[73]
3. Then, it may also be said that though the study of political system looks like involving questions of stability, equilibrium, survival and adaptation of desirable changes, it cannot be made free from the bias of conservatism and reaction. As in the case of general systems theory so here, we may see that there is much emphasis on the maintenance of the political system and very little stress on change. The idea of change has been carefully couched in the expression of slow, gradual and peaceful change in the political system. The idea of political stability "does not imply absence of change; it means the ability of the system to absorb change without violent upheavals."[74] While referring to the analysis of Almond in respect of his input-output model, it is said that the entire approach is 'culture bound', since it resembles the theory, if not necessarily, the practice of the separation of powers system.[75]

Despite these lines of criticism, we may agree with the optimistic view of many important writers on this subject that by means of the study of the political systems, new vistas have been opened and opportunities afforded to the political scientists to relate the more specific work they are doing to the larger political world. As Wasby says: "Until the systems approach was developed, political scientists studying one area of politics or government had no way in which to place in context the phenomena they were studying or to relate institutions to each other systematically. Not only does the political systems framework encourage political scientists to check for such interrelationships, but also it provides a large-scale map of the political world so that the researcher can see which areas remain unexplored."[76] Its leading exponents hopefully claim that the systems framework "represents a genuinely important step in the direction of 'science' for political science and provides a new paradigm for the discipline".[77]

---

72. Varma: *Modern Political Theory* (Delhi, Vikas, 1975) p. 188.
73. Young: *Systems of Political Science,* (Englewood Cliffs, New Jersey, Prentice Hall, 1968,) p. 24.
74. A.R. Ball, *Modern Politics and Government,* (London: Macmillan, 1971,) p. 263.
75. Blondel, *op. cit.,* p. 20.
76. Wasby, *op. cit.,* p. 109.
77. Gabriel A. Almond: "Political Theory and Political Science" in *American Political Science Review,* Vol. LX, 1966, p. 875.

5

Structural-Functional Analysis

> Regardless of what the individual political scientist may want to do (or not do) with functionalism, he must acknowledge that it is from this 'theory' that we learned of conceptualising the political system as a set of finite, inter-related functions essential to its existence and that the manner in which such functions are performed anywhere in space and time is not necessarily bound to a specific set of institutions (read 'concrete structure').We learned too that it is not merely a formal institution that may represent a 'structure' of the political system but that other analytically interesting and important patterns, such as value systems, economic allocation, attitudes towards innovation, and so on, can also be viewed from a structural-functional vantage point.
>
> **—Joseph la Palombara[1]**

Systems analysis, as it has been borrowed by leading American political scientists from the disciplines of anthropology and sociology, has two important derivatives in the form of structural-functional and input-output analyses also known by the name of approaches. As already pointed out in the preceding chapter, we shall deal with a detailed study of structural-functional analysis here and of input-output analysis in the next chapter in order to have a thorough understanding of the new trends of empirical investigation in the field of comparative politics. In a conceptual and theoretical sense, both analyses or approaches derive from the basic framework of general systems theory as first developed in the field of natural sciences and then adopted by some well-known social anthropologists and empirical sociologists in order to understand, what they call, 'social reality'. The motivating idea behind it, with which a good number of social theorists agree, is that the world is objective and cognisable, no matter the points of disagreement have their source in the forms and methods of cognition and the ways of attaining approximate truths about social reality. What has engaged their attention, in this direction, is that when a social scientist "confronts the complexity of social reality, he must find out logically defensible and empirically verifiable explanations. For this exercise, some social scientists have always remained concerned with the need for a holistic theoretical framework. One such holistic framework is known as 'functionalism'.[2]

Structural-Functional Analysis: Subtle Implications and Basic Assumptions

As an offshoot or a derivative of the systems analysis, the analysis of structural-functionalism "is a means of explaining what political structures perform what basic functions in the political system, and it is a tool of investigation."[3] We must keep this essential

1. Joseph la Palombara: "Parsimony and Empiricism in Comparative Politics : An Anti-Scholastic View" in Holt and Turner (eds.) : *The Methodology of Comparative Research,* (New York: Free Press, 1970,) p. 129.
2. C.P. Bhambhri, "Functionalism in Politics" in *Indian Journal of Political Science,* Delhi, Vol. XXXIV, No. 4, October-December 1973, p. 455.
3. A.R. Ball: *Modern Politics and Government,* (London: Macmillan, 1971,) p. 14.

point in our mind that the very concept of 'political system' in the context of systems analysis "lays stress on the relation of the 'political' to the society. It characterises a certain structure—that is, the arrangements by which legitimate policy decisions are made—but with an eye to its functions in the whole context of social behaviour."[4] Social theorists subscribing to this approach lay emphasis on this point that, indeed, no society "can survive or develop unless it has a political system performing such a function; that is, we might hold that a political system is a functional requisite of a society."[5] "The survival and maintenance of a social system require that society must be having a well-functioning economic system, a legal system, a system of values and so on. In this scheme, the political system "would appear as that sub-system performing the distinctive function of making legitimate policy decisions, or, to use shorter expression, the function of 'goal attainment', for the society of which it is a part."[6]

With a view to understand the implications and nature of the structural-functional analysis, we should look at its basic assumptions and postulates:

1. It takes the society as a single, inter-connected system each element of which performs a specific function. The basic feature of such a system is the interaction of its components for the maintenance of its equilibrium. As Hempel says: "The kind of phenomenon that a functional analysis is involved to explain is typically some recurrent activity or some behaviour pattern in an individual or a group . . . And the principal objective of the analysis is to exhibit the contribution which the behaviour pattern makes to the preservation or development of the individual or the group in which it occurs. Thus, functional analysis seeks to understand a behaviour pattern or a socio-cultural institution in terms of the role it plays in keeping the given system in proper working order and thus maintaining it as a going concern."[7]
2. If society is a system as a whole, it has its parts that are interrelated. A social system has a dominant tendency towards stability that is maintained by virtue of built-in mechanism. If there are deviations or tensions, they are resolved. Thus, change in a social system is not sudden or revolutionary but gradual and adjustive.
3. Underlying the whole social structure there are broad aims and principles that are observed by the members of the society. Thus comes the factor of value consensus with its on-going usefulness even if this was unrecognised by those who were involved in them.[8]

---

4. Samuel H. Beer and Adam B. Ulam: *Patterns of Government*, (New York: Random House, 1968) 8th Printing, p. 22.
5. *ibid.*
6. *ibid.*, p. 23.
7. Carl G. Hempel: "The Logic of Functional Analysis" in Llewellyn Gross (ed.) : *Symposium on Sociological Theory*, p. 278.
8. A.W. Gouldner: *The Coming Crisis of Western Sociology*, (Delhi: Heine-mann, 1971,) p. 123. As Radcliffe Brown says : "The concept of function applied to human societies is based on an analogy between social life and organic life . . . It is through and by the continuity of the functioning that the continuity of the structure is preserved. 'Function' is the contribution which a particular activity makes to the total activity of which it is a part. The function of a particular social usage is the contribution it makes to the total social life as the functioning of the total social system. Such a view implies that a social system (the total social structure of a society together with the totality of social usage in which the structure appears and on which it depends for its continued existence) has a certain kind of unity we may define it as a condition in which all parts of the social system work together with a sufficient degree of harmony or internal consistency, i.e., without producing persistent conflicts which can neither be resolved nor regulated." *Structure and Function in Primitive Society*, (New York: Free Press,) pp. 178-79.

As its very name suggests, the structural-functional analysis revolves around two key concepts—structures and functions. Let us, therefore, study the subtle implications of this approach after studying the key concepts separately before furnishing a definitive definition of this approach.

Concept of Structure : While functions deal with the consequences involving objectives as well as processes of the patterns of actions, structures refer to those arrangements within the system which perform the functions. A single function may be fulfilled by a complex combination of structures, just as any given structural arrangement may perform functions which might have different kinds of consequences for the structure.[9] For instance, a political party is a structure within the political system that performs many functions, including those of communicating the wishes of the electorate to the government, informing the electorate on important political issues and allowing for wider participation by more people in the political system. The party "helps to maintain the system because it performs these tasks, but other structures such as pressure groups or formal institutions of the government may also carry out these functions, and in other political systems may carry out these functions in the absence of political parties."[10]

Concept of Functions : Three basic questions are involved in the concept of functions—what basic functions are discharged in any given system, by what instruments those functions are performed, and under what conditions the performance of these functions is done. Defining this term, Young says: "Functions deal ultimately with objective consequences, but they may be perceived as objectives, processes, or results from various points of view and for various purposes."[11] A better and more precise definition is thus given by Merton: "Functions are those observed consequences which make for the adaptation or readjustment of a given system; and dys-functions those observed consequences which lessen the adaptation or adjustment of the system."[12]

As a model adapted from the natural sciences, functionalism accepts the 'organismic' analogy—that a social or political unit will have certain adaptive qualities—in contrast to a cybernetic or mechanistic analogy. Living organisms inherently possess organismic properties, including the capacity to reproduce themselves, the capacity to perceive and learn, and the capacity to adapt and adjust to new circumstances or changes in the environment.[13] David E. Apter dwells on this interpretation and then affirms that the functional analysis of politics "begins by assuming that these properties which inhere in human beings have their counterparts in communities. Societies reproduce themselves. They perceive and learn. They can, within limits, adapt to problems. Societies also adjust to change by means of collective problem solving. They have a built-in tendency towards integrating collective symbols, language, and the beliefs into the system to assert coherence, just as individuals have a built-in tendency towards speech. So we may say that functionalism begins with *system.* It is not a method of classification, but a system of ingredients."[14]

The structural-functional analysis having its prominent place in the discipline of sociology is based on the 'intellectual fundaments' of the concept of a 'system'. It "is nothing if it is not the analysis of social patterns as parts of larger systems of behaviour and belief. Ultimately, therefore, an understanding of functionalism

---

9. S.P. Varma: *Modern Political Theory,* (Delhi: Vikas, 1975.) p. 163.
10. Ball, *op. cit.,* p. 14.
11. Oran R. Young: *Systems of Political Science* (Englewood Cliffs, New Jersey, Prentice Hall, 1968), p. 29.
12. Robert K. Merton: *Social Theory and Social Structure* (Illinois: Free Press of Glencoe, 1959) II Rev. Ed., p. 51.
13. See R.E. Jones: *The Foundational Analysis of Politics* (London: Routledge and Kegan Paul, 1967.)
14. Apter: *Introduction to Political Analysts* (New Delhi: Prentice Hall of India 1978), p. 394.

in sociology requires an understanding of the resources of the concept of 'system'."[15] As borrowed by theorists belonging to different social sciences, the functionalist approach in all its forms, while studying a given social or political system, is not how a pattern of behaviour may have originated so much as what part it plays in maintaining the system as a whole.[16]

Functional Analysis : Varieties and Frameworks

As it applies to contemporary empirical political science, functionalism "can refer to several rather disparate types of political analysis; there is no broad, distinctive functional approach to analysis which can be contrasted, say to an institutional, or legal approach."[17] According to Merton, from the very beginning, this approach "has been caught up in terminological confusion."[18] And, "too often, a single term has been used to symbolise different concepts, just as the same concept has been symbolised by different terms."[19] Merton refers to various positions in which the term 'function' can be and is made use of.[20] There is a popular usage according to which function refers to some public gathering or festive occasion usually conducted with ceremonial overtones. Second, it becomes equivalent to the term 'occupation', as Max Weber says, that is the mode of specialisation, specification and combination of the functions of an individual so far as it constitutes for him the basis of a continual opportunity for income or for profit.[21] Third, it also refers to the activities assigned to the incumbent of a social status and more particularly to the occupation of an office or political position. Fourth, in the field of mathematics, as first used by Leibniz, it refers to a variable considered in relation to one or more other variables in terms of which it may be expressed or on the value of which its own value depends. Last, in sociology or social anthropology, it is understood to refer to the vital or organic processes considered in respects in which they contribute to the maintenance of the organism.[22]

Functionalist approach has come to political science quite recently and, before looking towards its contributions, we should first clarify the variety of types of analysis that are included in this term. Functionalism thus has two varieties—*eclectical* and *empirical*. Eclectical functionalism means that in analysing some phenomenon a political scientist should be concerned with, among other things, its functions in the sense of purposes served by the phenomenon. Here function is treated as one—and not necessarily a more significant one—among many relevant considerations that together comprise a comprehensive political analysis.[23] In addition to function, an analyst "may be equally concerned with the structure, history, ideology, and other aspects of the phenomena."[24] It may be termed as 'eclectical functionalism' inasmuch as it involves no commitment to a specific or particular set of approach. It makes every social theorist a functionalist who deals with the functions of an institution or a department. Viewed thus, every political scientist is a functionalist, for he deals with the functions of a legislature, or of an executive, or of a judiciary and the like.

---

15. Gouldner: "Reciprocity and Autonomy in Functional Theory" in Gross (ed.), *op. cit.*, p. 241.
16. W.G. Runciman: "Functionalism as a Method in Political Thought" in Gould and Thursby (eds.) : *Contemporary Political Thought* (New York : Holt, Rhinehart and Winston, 1969), p. 188.
17. William Flanigan and Edwin Fogelman: "Functional Analysis" in (New York, Free Press, 1967), p. 72.
18. Merton, *op. cit.*, p. 20.
19. *ibid.*
20. *ibid.*
21. Max Weber: *Theory of Social and Economic Change*, edited and translated into English by Talcott Parsons (London: William Hodge & Co., 1947), p. 230.
22. Ludwig von Bertalanfly: *Modern Theories of Output* (New York: Oxford Univ Press, 1973), pp. 9ff and 14ff.
23. Flanigan and Fogelman, *op. cit.*, p. 72.
24. *ibid.*

What we are concerned with in the field of comparative politics is not eclectic but empirical functionalism or a special type of functionalist approach that takes society as an on-going system having its structures performing definite functions whereby the very system remains in operation. An empirical functionalist is concerned with those functions that are performed in so far as activities satisfy the demands made by the 'actors' of a political system. It is a different thing that the functions may be, as Merton says, *manifest* having obvious or intended purposes and consequences or *latent* having covert and unintended purposes and consequences. The best example of empirical functionalism is found in the work of Merton who, unlike the eclectical functionalists," does not merely consider function as one among a number of equally significant aspects of a political machine, but rather he concentrates upon function as the 'most promising orientation'."[25]

While empirical functionalism is an important subject of sociology, structural-functionalism has an important place in the field of comparative politics. Here we find an analytic framework having three characteristic features—first, an emphasis on the whole system as the units of analysis; second, postulation of particular functions as requisite to the maintenance of the whole system; third, concerns to demonstrate the functional interdependence of diverse structures within the whole system.[26] It can be seen that here functionalism "assumes a theoretical significance potentially far greater than in either eclectic functionalism or empirical functionalism. The premise of structural-functionalism is nothing else than to provide a consistent and integrated theory from which can be derived explanatory hypothesis relevant to all aspects of a political system."[27] It is aptly visualised: "Eclectic functionalists find in functionalism an important additional dimension for their analysis, a dimension which brings the analysis into closer touch with the actual consequences of political activity. Empirical functionalists find in functionalism not simply an additional dimension for their analysis but a central organising concept which serves to illuminate unexpected aspects of important, though limited, political phenomena. Structural-functionalists find in functionalism the promise of a scientific theory of politics and this is certainly the most ambitious claim that has been made for functionalism by political scientists."[28]

It is, therefore, clear that structural-functionalism implies an applied form of empirical functionalism to the study of political phenomenon. While in eclectic functionalism, the concept of functions remains merely one of several equally significant categories and in empirical functionalism functions become the focus for the analysis of a limited range of phenomena, structural-functionalism aims at providing a scientific theory of the political system.[29] It is structural-functionalism that sets out in search of the particular structures that perform requisite functions. It is on account of this that the major descriptive task of structural-functionalism is said "to indicate what structures contribute to the satisfaction of what functionality requisites."[30] As such, structural-functionalism becomes a 'requisite analysis' in an analytic framework that "specifies a set of functions as necessary and sufficient for the persistence of a system."[31]

---

25. *ibid.,* p. 73.
26. *ibid.,* p. 76.
27. *ibid.,* pp. 75-76.
28. *ibid.,* pp. 81-82.
29. *ibid.,* p. 84.
30. Robert Holt: "A Proposed Structural-Functional Framework" in Charlesworth, (ed.) *Contemporary Political Analysis* (New York: Free Press of Glencoe, 1967) p. 86.
31. Flanigan and Fogelman, *op. cit.,* p. 77.

Structural-Functionalism in Political Sociology: Analyses of Levy, Merton and Parsons

Functionalism has its intellectual roots in the writings of social anthropologists like Radcliffe Brown and B. Malinowski that appeared in the early decades of the twentieth century. These eminent scholars 'belonging to the discipline of social anthropology studied pre-literate and tribal societies and functionally justified the role of rituals, magic and religion with special emphasis on their integrative role.' Subsequently, certain sociologists adopted this approach in order to refine their studies. Especially, since the 1950's, a number of political scientists started applying its principles to the study of the themes of comparative politics having their fundamental concern with the phenomenon of system maintenance and regulation. We shall, therefore, first discuss, though briefly, the analyses of political sociologists who adopted this approach and then switch over to the study of this approach in the field of comparative politics.

The name of Marion Levy, Jr. is important in this direction who defined that structural-functional analysis "proceeds from the definition of the unit to the elaboration of its setting."[32] According to him, the basic requisites of structural-functional analysis may be put as under:[33]

1. One must define the unit to be discussed. For these purposes, the unit must be something in terms of which operation (or processes) can or do take place. The choice of unit will depend on the problem to which the analysis is addressed. In this case, the unit chosen is any society for reasons discussed below briefly.
2. One must *discover* (at least by hypothesis) the factors setting the most general limits of possible variations for the type of units chosen. For any human society, the most general limiting factors are human heredity and the non-human environment.
3. One must try to determine what general types of conditions must be met if the unit is to persist as defined within these limits. These conditions are the functional requisites.
4. One must then determine what patterns must be present if operation in terms of them is to result in the production of the functional requisites. These patterns are the structural requisites.

A study of the writings of this well-known sociologist shows that he is primarily concerned with the problem of the survival of the system and he has developed the concept of functional requisites or requirements or conditions of survival necessary for the maintenance of the essential characteristics of the same. The considerations of Marion Levy, Jr. "correspond very closely to the definition of a system and the discussion of its environment and boundary conditions that are the characteristics of analysis under the general systems approach. In addition, both forms of analysis are very much concerned with questions focusing on differences between relevant system levels, the reciprocal influences of various system levels on one another, and the implications of these factors for the levels of generalisation and abstraction at which particular analyses are formulated."[34]

However, the name of Robert K. Merton is more important who, apart from dealing with the data of structural-functionalism "suggested certain new directions to rescue the functionalist

32. Marion Levy, Jr.: *The Structure of Society* (Princeton, New Jersey: Princeton Univ Press, 1952), pp. 36-38.
33. See Levy, Jr.: "Some Aspects of Structural-Functional Analysis and Political Science" in Ronald Young : (ed.) : *Approaches to the Study of Politics* (Evanston, Illinois : Northwestern Univ. Press, 1958), p. 53.
34. Young, *op. cit.*, p. 28.

theory from the critics."[35] According to him, the central orientation of functionalism "is expressed in the practice of interpreting data by establishing their consequences for larger structures in which they are implicated."[36] It is in the study of Merton that we find that it is not merely the use of terms like structures and functions in descriptions of social reality that differentiates functionalism from other approaches, but the special way in which these terms are employed. The unique characteristics of functionalists description may be illustrated by looking at what is one of the most frequently cited examples of a functional analysis, namely, Merton's treatment of the functions of the political machine in a large city. As he says: "The machine fulfils the important social function of humanising and personalising all manner of assistance to those in need and that it serves the function of providing those political privileges (to business) which entail immediate economic gains."[37] It is the particular way what Merton describes reality in terms of structures and the needs (functions) of the system and the manner in which these concepts are used to explain the phenomenon of the political machine that mark as a functionalist description.[38]

Merton's special contribution to the structural-functional approach finds place in his doctrine of functions that may be 'manifest' or 'latent' and that may be in order (functional) or out of order (dysfunctional). While the 'manifest functions' are those whose purposes and consequences are both intended and recognised, the 'latent functions' are those whose purposes and consequences are covert, unintended and recognised. There may be an intermediate pattern also in the nature of unintended but recognised purposes and consequences. He, however, insists that it "is more important for the researcher to recognise latent functions, which are highly complex and difficult to recognise, than manifest functions which are clear and well recognised."[39] Merton's distinction between functions and dysfunctions is based on the issue of the survival and disintegration of the system. Thus, while 'functions' are those observed consequences which make for the adaptation or adjustment of a given system, 'dysfunctions' are those observed consequences which lessen the adaptation or adjustment of the same.[40]

One important point that enhances the reputation of Merton over and above that of Marion Levy Jr. and Talcott Parsons is that he seeks to save the structural-functional approach from the charge of being implicitly conservative and biased towards social change. Thus the name of Merton is distinguished from those of Levy, Jr. and Parsons and associated with those of Almond, Binder, Apter and others who have drawn upon structural-functionalism for the light it could throw on the process of political modernisation in the name of conservatism. As a result of this, structural-functional approach, despite its emphasis upon the conditions for stability or maintenance, "has come to look like not leading necessarily to a defence of the *status quo* or to a disregard for processes of change."[41]

Undoubtedly, the most important name in this direction is that of Talcott Parsons who developed a comprehensive theoretical framework for the study of societies on the

35. Bhambhri, *op. cit.*, p. 460.
36. Merton, *op. cit.*, pp. 46-47.
37. *ibid.*, p. 75.
38. *ibid.*
39. Varma, *op. cit.*, p. 163.
40. Merton, *op. cit.*, p. 105. According to R.K. Merton, the central orientation of functionalism "is expressed in the practice of interpreting data by establishing their consequences for larger structures in which they are implicated." *ibid.*, pp. 46-47.
41. Flanigan and Fogelman, *op. cit.*, p. 79.

basis of structural-functional approach.[42] The contributions of this well-known sociologist relate to the concept of a system, primary subsystems of a society, pattern variables and notion of change. His starting point "is that the parts in a society are to be understood only in the context of the whole." It is the whole which is important, and this whole, according to him, is a system. Parsons' concern is to analyse society and system of functionally inter-related variables, and a system as an ongoing set of recurrent and inter-related social actions.[43] As he says: "The most essential condition of successful dynamic analysis is continual and systematic reference of every problem to the state of the system as a whole... Functional significance in this context is inherently teleological.[44]

A study of Parsons' empirical functionalism shows that he offers a model of his own system with its problems that it has to cope with, and a set of five basic variables or dilemmas that the 'actors' have to confront in any social situation and they have to come to terms with them before arriving at any determinate

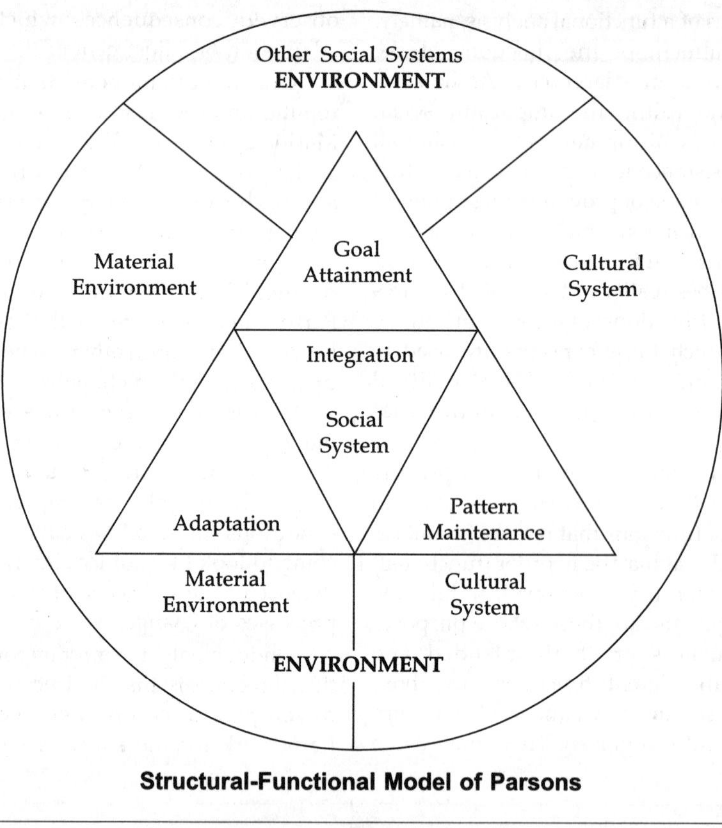

Structural-Functional Model of Parsons

42. The major ideas of Parsons are contained in his *The Structure of Social Action* (1937), *Essays in Sociological Theory—Pure and Applied* (1949), and *The Social System* (1951).
43. Bhambhri, *op. cit.*, p. 460.
44. Parsons : *Essays in Sociological Theory—Pure and Applied* (New York: Free Press of Glencoe, 1949), p. 21. Parsons says : "Thus our conception of the actor's drives is that they are organised in an equilibrating system of relationships to an object world, and that this system, if disturbed, will set in motion forces tending either to restore a previous state of equilibrium or to make subtle a new state. This conception will undermine all our analysis of learning processes and of the operation of the personality as an on-going system." Parsons and Shils : *Towards a General Theory of Action* (Harvard : Harvard Univ Press, 1951), p. 113

orientation. It should, however, he kept in mind that the real concern of Parsons is to study the needs of the system as a whole and its stability that is dependent upon their satisfaction. A system, according to him, is an action framework inasmuch as all human actions occur within it. The individuals are the 'actors' who play their 'roles' in the context of the 'shared values' of the system. What is, therefore, of paramount necessity is that a state of *equilibrium* should be maintained on the basis of the fulfilment of the functional needs of the society relating to four problems—allocation of resources, defining and sustaining the pursuit of certain fundamental goals, maintenance of solidarity, and sustaining the motivations of the actors and of repairing any damage to these arising out of the performance of roles. These four problems are designated by him as:

1. ***Adaptation :*** It means that the capacity of the system to meet the demands of the 'actors' must be increased. It "is concerned with the relationships between the social system and its non-human environment—relationships that lead to the supplying of disposable resources which can be used as means to realise the goals of the system as a whole or the goals of any of its subunits."[45] The processes that are relevant to the satisfaction of the adaptive functional requisites are economic by nature as processes of production and allocation and management of resources.
2. ***Goal Attainment :*** It means the coordinate actions of collectivity and the units to bring about desired relations between the system and its environment to move towards the goal set by the system for itself. The cultural system specifies a set of goals for the social system as a whole that are sets of desired relationship between the system and its environment. The environment that is relevant for goal attainment is complex, including an aspect of the cultural system and the non-human environment, and other societies. As one of the most important goals of the social system at the societal level is the preservation of the society itself, the defence of the realm involves a set of activities that contribute to the satisfaction of the goal attainment functional requisite. In society this function is performed by the state or polity.[46]
3. ***Pattern Maintenance and Tension Management :*** It refers to the upholding of the basic principles of the system with regard to both the value of such patterns and the commitment of the system units to them. Goal attainment is concerned with the cultural components of a system and pattern maintenance with its social components. The role of the family or the household figures in. However, the role of other associations like schools, church, unions, etc. should also be emphasised in this connection. Three major premises are involved here. First, that major values must be passed on from one generation to another and it may be called *acculturation* process. Second, a social control process is concerned with the application of sanctions for violations of the prescriptions of the value system. Third, a tension management process "attempts to prevent the development of situations that increase the probability that large numbers of actors will violate basic norms."[47]
4. ***Integration :*** It is concerned with the adjustment of relations between and among the units of a system for establishing a level of solidarity among them to permit the system to function. It involves an aspect to the socio-control process. As a matter of fact, this functional requisite is basically concerned with the internal problem of co-ordination of differentiated but

45. Holt, *op. cit.,* p. 94.
46. *ibid.,* pp. 93-94.
47. *ibid.,* p. 93.

Some Important Statements about Structuralism–Functionalism

Structuralism can consider politics from the standpoint of changes in the organisation of order. This represents a concern with politics at its broadest. If the method of contradiction is concerned with polarities-conflict versus adaptation, revolution versus bureaucratisation, and democracy versus alienation-the method of equilibrium implies that if needs are not met, a society will die. If certain fundamentals are disregarded or handled inappropriately, society will change.

– David E. Apter

Functionalism can, indeed, be interpreted as a conscious alternative to Marxism. Some of its critics have even wanted to interpret it as a political ideology conditioned by the structure of American capitalism. But leaving aside the separate issue of its historical origins, it is interesting to notice just how far functionalism provides a sort of mirror-image of Marxism. . . . The fact remains, however, that some form of functionalism is the only current alternative to Marxism as the basis for some kind of general theory in political science.

– W.G. Runciman

Functionalism is a method of explaining events or institutions by specifying what they do, that is the function they perform, in a given complex. In political thought functionalism attempts to explain events in a political structure as it operates through time. It asserts that all political activities of a system function to maintain that political system.

– J.A. Gould and V.V. Thursby

interdependent roles. Parsons admits that in every social system there may be some behaviour that is not prohibited by norms but is nevertheless malintegrative. The integrative function is performed both by coercive mechanism (state) and non-coercive mechanisms (social institutions).[48]

Let us now look at the dichotomous variables or basic dilemmas. They may be designated as 'attitudinal dilemmas' also. They are:[49]

1. *Affectivity* : It may also be called affective neutrality By it Parsons means to know whether the actors are interested in accepting immediate gratification, or they want to defer it and instead prefer discipline.
2. *Specificity* : It may be called diffuseness also. It refers to the scope or inclusiveness of the relationship.
3. *Universalism* : It may be called particularism as well. Here the issue is how to judge an object. It may be judged in terms of some universal or general frame of reference or in terms of a particular reference scheme in which ego is personally involved.
4. *Ascription* : It may be called achievement too. The dilemma is whether the primary consideration, in defining a relationship, is given to the ascriptive quality of the object or to some particular complex of performances.
5. *Self-Orientation* : It may also be known as collectivity-orientation. It means whether the relationship is disinterested or self-interested.

The real attempt of Parsons "is to find out how far units are adjusted with the whole, only then system equilibrium is possible."[50] The

48. *ibid.*, pp. 94-95.
49. See Bhambhri, *op. cit.*, p. 459.
50. *ibid.* On this point, Eugene Meehan has observed that though Parsons does make use of Freudian terminology, particularly the adjust mechanism—repression, displacement, projection, reaction formation etc.—but always in a context when order and stability are prime." *Contemporary Political Thought* (Homewood, Illinois : The Dorsey Press, 1967), p. 130.

stability of a system is not possible without a general system of common cultural orientation. The sharing of value orientation is of special importance that makes the study of the attitudinal dilemmas of the actors as essential. One may say that, as a functionalist Parsons does admit the factor of change as the total system "is never at rest, it is always being pushed, prodded and keel-hauled, it is always subject to stresses and strains."[51] But he is for a change that is 'ordered' and, for this reason, gradual and peaceful.[52]

Structural - Functionalism in Political Science: Analyses of Easton, Mitchell, Apter, Almond and Kaplan

By the mid-1960s, the idea of functionalism marked a most striking shift in conceptual emphasis in the world of social sciences. It became a dominant model of inquiry and also a mode of explanation in political science. It was hailed by some important members of the discipline as the best possible approach to the development of the theory in the field of comparative politics. While explaining it, Ernest Nagel says that it may refer to the contribution of some element in a system to the maintenance of system in a given state. The basic principle in functional explanation "is the relation of a particular phenomenon, usually a recurrent pattern of social behaviour, to the system in which the phenomenon occurs..At an absolute minimum, functional explanations require (l) a phenomenon to be explained, (2) a system in which the phenomenon occurs, and (3) a stipulation of the consequences of the phenomenon for the total system."[53]

The method of structural-functionalism was adopted in political science by some leading American writers who came to realise that while analysing some political phenomenon, they should be concerned, among other things, with their functions in the sense of the purposes served by it. It should be pointed out again that here function "is treated as one—and not necessarily a more significant one—among many relevant considerations that together comprise a comprehensive political analysis."[54] It is a different thing that writers have described the meaning of this approach differently. For instance, while Hempel had little difficulty in identifying this approach as 'a special breed', he with others like Brown did distinguish functionalism from other approaches by sticking to the idea of its particular application. A subtle point of distinction between the two should be traced in this fact that while, according to Hempel, it is simply a particularly inconsequential type of explanation,[55] in the view of Brown, it is something different from an explanation on the basis of laws. Apart from some subtle points of distinction, it should be emphasised that structural-functional analysis "is a distinguishable approach primarily because of the selective aspects of social reality that it seeks to describe, explain and predict. It describes social reality largely in terms of structures, processes, mechanism and functions, and these four concepts are of particular importance in the laws and theories that are developed."[56]

If the prime concern of structural-functionalism is with the maintenance of order and the belief says that order depends on a combination of social mechanisms and internalised sentiments as well as consequent emphasis on the process of socialisation and re-socialisation, then David Easton must be regarded as the most consistent and systematic functionalist in the field of political science. It may be visualised in his elaboration of the 'political system' that works with the help of demands and supports constituting 'inputs'

51. Parsons : *The Social System,* p. 482.
52. Bhambhri,. *op. cit.,* p. 459.
53. Meehan, *op.cit.,* pp. 111-13.
54. Flanigan and Fogelman, *op. cit.,* p. 72.
55. Hempel, *op. cit.,* p. 296.
56. Robert R. Brown : *Explanation in Social Science* (Chicago : Aldine, 1963), pp. 109-32.

Parsonian Model

System Problem	*Output*	*Category*	*Input*	*Category*
	Economy: Factors of Production	Polity: Ingredients of Power	Economy: Shares of Income	Polity: Types of Power
1. Pattern Maintenance 2. Goal Attainment 3. Adaptation 4. Integration	1. Land 2. Labour 3. Capital 4. Entrepreneurial Service	1. Political Commitments 2. Contingent Support 3. Facilities of Power 4. Legitimation of Goals	1. Rent 2. Wage 3. Interest 4. Profit	1. Security: Prestige 2. Binding Decisions 3. Control of Facilities 4. Allocation of Prestige

and the decisions of the men in authority roles called 'outputs' with a connecting link called the 'feedback process'. According to him, a situation of stress for a political system develops when the interaction between its essential variables threatens to break down. The three variables mentioned by him are—demands, supports and outputs. Demands and supports (the input variables) must be coming into the system in order that it may not cease to function due to lack of use or attention. However, they "are potential sources of stress and must be maintained at manageable levels. An excess of demand relative to the system's capacity to produce appropriate outputs (i.e., value allocations) will mean an overloading of the system and political immobility. A high level of support for the system is desirable, but, either because of its incapacity to satisfy demands or for extraneous reasons, support may be withdrawn and the system may not be able to sustain itself any longer."[57]

It is obvious that Easton is concerned with the maintenance of a well-going political system. He believes that if political system is a useful conception, then some means of separating it from all other systems must be found. But the difficulty arises when we find that he has not been able to pass safely through the dilemma. A critic says that if he (Easton) "chooses the first horn of the dilemma, his understanding is fatuous; if he chooses the second, a definition of 'political' is essential. The second horn was actually chosen; hence, the validity of the definition of 'political' is a matter of prime concern."[58] Another difficulty arises when we find that, like Parsons, he "does not think of theory in terms of explanation but in terms of the creation of conceptual frameworks. The result is a highly abstract structure that is logically suspect, conceptually fuzzy, and empirically almost useless. Easton's 'political system' turns out to be an abstraction whose relation to empirical politics is virtually impossible to establish. The promise of a conceptual framework with 'high empirical relevance' simply has not been fulfilled. . . The political system which he so busily dissects exists nowhere except in his mind; the closest empirical approximation is probably the sovereign national state. The conceptual inadequacies of the framework prevent Easton from reaching the goal that he sets for himself and, at the same time, inhibit the kind of

57. See David M. Wood : "Comparative Government and Politics" in S.L. Wasby : *Political Science : The Discipline and Its Dimensions : An Introduction* (Calcutta : Scientific Book Agency, 1970), p. 501.
58. Meehan, *op. cit.*, p. 172.

generalised treatment of system in general that might have been carried out."[59]

Mitchell's name deserves mention in this direction. In his work on American political system, he offers four requisite functions that are performed by a polity—authoritative specification of the system goals, authoritatjve mobilisation of resources to implement the goals, integration of the system, and allocation of values and costs.[60] The deep influence of Talcott Parsons on this political scientist can be traced in this fact that polity is defined by him as a sub-system primarily concerned with the mobilisation of resources to meet the goals of the system. The treatment of the state as a 'subsystem' having its primary concern with the mobilisation of resources, as pointed out by Mitchell, takes him very near to Talcott Parsons who treated the factor of the mobilisation of resources as one of the four basic functions of the'system'. What is of special importance about Mitchell is that he "does not limit himself to a consideration of mobilisation of resources to meet systems goals, but rather ranges over all of the functional requisites of the social system, pointing out ways in which political processes contribute to the performance of all the functions.[61]

Focus on the study of new political systems belonging to the developing countries of the Third World has led to the inclusion of some interesting problems relating to the types and forces that have played their part in causing rapid transformations in them. David Apter calls such problems as 'concrete issues' and lays stress on the development of new techniques for their proper study.[62] Thus, he gives us certain new directions in the spheres of systems analysis and structural-functionalism that, apart from making a study of the political system in systemic terms, also deals with the classification and analysis of types of government. In his work on the politics of modernisation, we find that, in fact, the elements of the social system "are analysed mainly for the purpose of understanding the extent to which particular types of governments or systems of authority operate best only in particular kinds of social environment; and how changes in elements, or relations, between the elements of the social system influence changes in governmental systems."[63]

What strikes at the very outset in a study of Apter's political system is that he tries to establish a sort of workable reconciliation between the normative and empirical dimensions of political theory. As he says: "I believe that the politics begins with models that are primarily normative and secondarily empirical."[64] By the very term 'modernisation', he means "a beginning whereby any societal culture allows individuals to develop a critical view of man in his relation to nature and society; then men begin to see life as involving different kinds of choices— personal, social, structural and moral."[65] The choices are made by the government that have implications and consequences for all members of the society and the choices that are made by the government and accepted by the society over a period of time can be said to constitute the moral aims of the society.[66]

A serious student of modern political theory may thus find much in Apter what is known as answers to the questions familiar to the traditional theorists. Though his attention is confined to certain political systems of Africa like Uganda and Ghana, he looks at the culture

---

59. *ibid.*, pp. 173-74. For a balanced critique, see review by P.E. converse of David Easton's *A Framework for Political Analysis* in *American Political Science Review*, Vol. LIX (1965), pp. 1001-2.
60. William C. Mitchell: *The American Polity* (New York : Free Press, 1962)
61. Flanigan and Fogelman, *op. cit.*, p. 78.
62. David Apter : *The Politics of Modernisation* (Chicago : Chicago Univ. Press, 1965).
63. Davies and Lewis : *Models of Political Systems* (Delhi : Vikas, 1971), p. 59.
64. Apter, *op. cit.*, p. x.
65. *ibid.*, pp. 10-11.
66. Davies and Lewis, *op. cit.*, p. 60.

Structural-Functional Imperatives and Requisites

Analysis of Marion Levy. Jr.

Functional Requisites

1. Provision for an adequate physiological relationship to the setting and for sexual recruitment
2. Role of differentiation and role assignment
3. Communication
4. Shared cognitive orientations
5. Shared articulated goals
6. Regulation of the choice of means
7. Regulation of affective expression
8. Adequate socialisation
9. Effective control of disruptive behaviour
10. Adequate institutionalisation

Structural Requisites

1. Structure of role differentiation
2. Structure of solidarity
3. Structure of economic allocation
4. Structure of political allocation
5. Structure of integration and expression

Analysis of Dahrendorf

1. Every society is a relatively persistent, stable structure of elements
2. Every society is a well-integrated structure of elements
3. Every element in a society has a function, i.e., renders a contribution to its maintenance
4. Every functioning social structure is based on a consensus of values among its members.

Analysis of Apter

1. Adaptability—degree of accommodation or ability to see the world realistically
2. Goal gratification—ability to satisfy the needs of the members
3. Integration—mediation between the opposite tensions of the pattern variables
4 Latent pattern maintenance—capacity of a society for self-renewal

of the people that should be described as 'mixed' on account of being a crude hotch-potch of traditionalism and modernism—culture of the white people superimposed over the tribal culture of the black people. Since the dependent countries adopted the political systems of their master countries and since these 'imported systems' could not function well, there arose the basic problem of how the 'political institutional transfer' could be effected in colonial countries. At the same time, it led to the creation of a more serious problem: that of ensuring that change in general is as orderly as possible, taking place in a manner that is in some degree predictable and that of ensuring that the holders of governmental authority succeed each other in a peaceful manner. These problems arise as a result of social and economic changes and, as such, they require their proper solution in the context of social and economic system. The study of the Third World countries naturally engages our attention for the reason that where this mixture of political, economic and other social problems "is perhaps most obvious and so they present, as it were, a laboratory for extensive scientific analysis, if not experiment."[67]

Such a type of study leads Apter to look into the politics of modernisation from the standpoint of a structural-functionalist. First of all, he takes up the subject of modernisation that he regards as a process that occurs predominantly in developing societies where it "may be described as the transposition of certain roles— professional, technical, administrative—and the transposition of institutions supporting those roles—hospitals, schools, universities, bureaucracies."[68] As he adds: "Modernisation is like hurtling through a tunnel at frightening speed without knowing what is at the other end. Fear creates serious political problems."[69] The structural-functionalist approach of Apter assumes the nature of a behavioural interpretation when we find him insisting that as 'roles' are no more than institutionalised forms of behaviour defined by functions, then there needs to be added to structural-functionalism some other form of analysis which deals with the motives underlying behaviour.[70]

Apter's politics of modernisation seeks to study political system in three respects—nature and purpose of the government, types and models of the government, and functions of the government. However, here we are concerned with the aspect of structure and functions. For this reason, we take note of his affirmation that all political systems are characterised by a number of contingent functions. Thus, they must act as (1) the loci of sanctions in a society, (2) the providers of symbols linking a people's past and future, (3) the responsible agents for the orderly arrangement and performance of roles in the system, and (4) the providers of criteria for deciding on membership and participation in the society.[71] Apart from performing these functions, all governments are characterised by 'a structure of authoritative decision-making' and a 'structure of accountability' that may be described as the main institutional requirements of government. Similarly, all governmental systems possess contingent structures which give an indication of the efficiency of the system. These are really 'substructures' of the structural requisites and include mechanisms for political recruitment, rule enforcement and rule delimitation, the allocation and determination of resources and some mechanism through which, at some official level, government registers societal approval of its decisions and policies (a parliament or a central committee for example). In effect, contingent structures are mechanisms for carrying out policy.[72]

67. *ibid.*, p. 62.
68. Apter, *op. cit.*, p. 42.
69. *ibid.*, p. xiii.
70. Davies and Lewis, *op. cit.*, p. 64.
71. *ibid.*, p. 68.
72. *ibid.*, p. 69.

It may, therefore, be visualised that Apter's analysis, like any other structural-functionalist's, involves a search for the functional and structural requisites of the government.[73] However, the most representative contribution, in this direction, is that of Gabriel A. Almond who, though like Talcott Parsons and David Easton being in search of 'a functional theory of the polity', looks towards the problems of how political systems change from a traditional to a modern model and believes strongly that he has succeeded in elaborating such a theory whereby it "would ultimately make possible statistical and perhaps mathematical formulation."[74]

Almond proceeds ahead with certain considerations in his mind. First, he is for constructing a theory, or an approach, that may explain how political systems change from one type to another particularly from the traditional to the modern model. For this he subscribes, as well as contributes, to the theory of political development that hinges on the point of explaining transition from the predominantly agricultural to the predominantly industrial society that effects a simultaneous change in the political system. Second, he is for presenting a classification of political systems of what he calls 'an exercise in typology construction'. What informs Almond to present a classification of the political systems is the factor of *efficiency*. While one political system can efficiently perform its functions under a set of given conditions and another political system cannot, it is clear that one is more efficient than the other. To put it in concrete words, we can say that modern political systems can perform their functions well and so they are efficient, while the traditional systems are not inasmuch as they prove incapable in this regard. It is this line of distinction that provides ample material for making comparions in the field of comparative politics.

As one sets out to develop a science of comparative politics', Almond has certain assumptions. First, political change can be seen in terms of development alone. Thus, three degrees can be marked-traditional, transitional and modern. Second, since Almond is a structural-functionalist and since he is for studying the traditional political systems of the Third World in comparison with the modern political systems of the advanced and developed countries, he seeks "to identify the functions of the polity in modern Western systems, and then to pursue his analysis of political modernisation in non-Western areas by investigating how these functions, which are associated with distinctive political activities in Western systems, are performed elsewhere. The basis for this view is Almond's own belief that anyone who wishes to understand the process of modernisation in non-Western societies must first be capable of understanding the process of development and current behaviour of the societies which, he claims, can be called 'modern', that is Western societies."[75] Third, a political system is a set of interactions that take place as a result of the roles that the people play. Finally, political systems are like an 'open phenomenon' and, as such, they are engaged in communicating with entities and systems beyond their own boundaries, and they are affected by and react to what happens beyond these boundaries in their environment.[76]

It is obvious that Almond offers a systemic definition of the political system—within the framework of structural-functionalism—an analysis which looks at political systems as coherent wholes which influence and, in turn, are influenced by their environments. To Almond it is the presence of 'legitimate force' throughout the system – in the last analysis

73. *ibid.*, p. 68.
74. Almond in Almond and Coleman (eds.): *The Politics of the Developing Areas* (Princeton : Princeton University Press, 1960), p. 59.
75. Davies and Lewis, *op. cit.*, p. 33.
76. *ibid.*, p. 34.

holding it together—"that allows one to look at it 'in scientific terms; that is, as a whole."[77]

According to Almond, a political system has four characteristics that may be called 'legitimate patterns of interaction'. They are:[78]

(i) Every political system has its structures some of which may be more specialised performing more functions, while others may be less specialised performing less functions in it.

(ii) Whatever differences may be between the system and its structures, the same political functions are performed in all political systems.

(iii) Political structures perform a number of functions that may be termed 'multifunctional'.

(iv) All political systems being parts of the society as a whole have a culture of their own that is always a mixture of the traditional and the modern.

It is on the basis of this study of the 'legitimate patterns of interaction' that informs Almond to look towards those structures that perform different functions in different political systems for the sake of their stability and maintenance. It "attempts to shift the locus of analysis from the observable institutional political mechanisms to any areas where the actual performance of the functional requirements of the system are located. This approach is inclined to emphasise the search for processes that maintain the stability of the system."[79]

From a critical point of view, it may be said that, like Easton, "Almond is a victim of the search for the political 'Holy Grail', a theory of politics. At best, what he produces is a classification scheme, or perhaps a model, a very imperfect and loose model, that can be used to order political data and perhaps standardise observations of political phenomena. Whether or not, it should be employed for those purposes, depends upon empirical demonstration that the bundle of categories and that the model he suggests are, indeed, the crucial variables in politics...Almond is nothing, if not eclectic. He has in one ungrammatical sentence, combined Weber's definition of the state, Easton's conception of the authoritative allocation of the state and Parsons' view of the function of the political subsystem in society."[80]

Finally, we may refer to the contribution of Morton A. Kaplan who has rather written on the subject of international relations or world politics.[81] In systems engineering, a system is defined as a set of variables that can be considered as an entity against a given background. He makes use of this conception in his study. He defines a system as a set of variables so related in contradistinction to its environment that describable behavioural regularities characterise the internal relationships of the variables to each other and the external relationships of the set of individual variables to combinations of external variables. Systems are described in terms of 'states' and a state "is nothing more than a full specification of the values of the variables in the system. The behaviour of the system is stipulated in terms of changes in the variables which are called 'outputs'. Changes in the environment that influence the functioning of the system are called 'inputs'. Inputs that lead to radical changes in the system are called step-level functions. They alter the characteristic behaviour and even the structure of the system."[82]

77. Davies and Lewis, *op. cit.*, p. 34.
78. *ibid.*, p. 36.
79. *ibid.*, p. 37.
80. Meehan, *op. cit.*, pp. 175-76. This critic goes to the extent of saying that Almond is not clearly a political scientist without systematic training in functionalism." *ibid.*, p. 181.
81. See Kaplan's *System and Process in International Politics* (New York: Wiley & Sons, 1957).
82. Meehan, *op. cit.*, p. 182.

A scrutiny of the model of Kaplan at this stage shows that step-level functions are of prime significance in the study of the behaviour of systems. In his view, systems may be related or coupled, the output of one serving as an input for the other, coupling may be uni-directional or bi-directional. In the latter case, there is the feedback between the two systems. The two 'most important states of the system' are equilibrium and stability. "A system is equilibrium when the variables remain within specified limits for a given time; systems are stable when the variables remain within specified limits in spite of changes in output within a given range. Some systems are 'ultra-stable' meaning that they actively seek to adapt to the environment, either by making internal changes or by imposing changes in the environment."[83]

The principles governing the effects of equilibrium change in various kinds of systems may be stated in three broad terms:[84]

1. A system in equilibrium will remain so unless disturbed. If nothing in the environment is likely to change the state, the system is stable. If the environment contains disturbances but their effect depends on these strength, the system has local stability.
2. A system with local stability will change to a new equilibrium state or disappear entirely if disturbed with sufficient force. Systems capable of sustaining equilibrium change are ultra-stable.
3. If the disturbance appears and nothing else changes and the system fails to return to its earlier state, a system change has occurred.

No doubt, Kaplan's concept of the political system has its distinctive place in the study of international relations, it may be discussed in the field of comparative politics also, because he studies the whole pattern of political system in the context of 'sovereignty'. It is for this reason that, in his view, politics "is a contest to fill decision-making roles to choose alternative political objects, or to change the essential rules of the political system."[85]

Critical Appraisal

Despite the fact that structural-functional approach has occupied a very important place in the realm of comparative politics, it cannot be denied that it has some serious shortcomings that may be enumerated as under:

1. The structural-functional analysis "tends to focus on primarily static relationships rather than on dynamics. The approach is concerned, above all, with the problems of systemic survival, the requirements of the stable adaptation, and the operation of various functions and structures oriented towards systems maintenance."[86] Therefore, this approach is accused of being anti-change. The critics are not prepared to accept the interpretation of Merton who, while laying emphasis on the factor of dynamics, says that the concept of dysfunction, which implies the concept of strain, stress and tension on the structural level, "provides an analytic approach to the study of dynamics and change."[87] As such, this approach has the serious flaw of being 'concerned with the present' and having 'no perspective of the future'.[88] What this approach really aims at is to look at the existing political system as a subsystem within the social system as a whole and then to study its structures and their functions not for the purpose of suggesting radical changes in them but to devise ways and means to keep it like an ongoing concern. Thus, not change but stability is the sheet-anchor of the functionalists. It is for this reason that a critic like Gouldner

83. *ibid.*
84. *ibid.*, p. 183.
85. *ibid.*, p. 185.
86. Young, *op. cit.*, p. 32.
87. See Merton, *op. cit.*, pp. 25-37.
88. Bhambhri, *op. cit.*, p. 462.

accuses the functionalists of constituting the "sociological conservation corps of industrial society."[89]

2. The functionalists defeat the very purpose of their approach by misapplying their tools of empirical investigation while studying the political systems of the Third World. One may easily ask a question as to how the principles of empirical investigation devised in the sophisticated study rooms of the Chicago or Harvard universities can be rigorously applied to the study of poor and backward countries of the Afro-Asian world and that too for the sake of comprehending social and political reality. Edward Shils is quite forthright in his assessment when he says that the basic problem of the 'new states' is that they donot form a single civil society; they are scarcely able thus far to produce a polity that can supply the personnel necessary to run a modern society. They lack the affirmative attitude towards rules, persons, and actions that is necessary for consensus.[90] The problems of communalism, poverty, tribalism, linguistic chauvinism, sub-nationalism and the like, that are so much in force in various countries of the Third World, cannot be studied with the tools of empirical politics in a rigorous manner as hopefully devised by the sociologists and political scientists of the affluent countries of the Western world. As a critic says: "The masses in the Third World countries are struggling to resolve their basic social contradictions and Almond and other functionalists are suggesting'consensual model'for the study of such societies. The consensual model in politics emphasises fundamental agreements in societies, while the Third World countries are confronting fundamental disagreements between the entrenched and the emerging classes. The empirical reality, as it exists in these societies, cannot be analysed with the functional framework. Hence, the functional theorists in politics, with their consensual model and the view of the present which is devoid of any picture of future, fail to provide empirically validated answers to what is happening in the Third World."[91]

3. This approach suffers from, what is termed by Marion Levy, the 'fallacy of functional teleology'. That is, it suffers from the tendency "to explain the origins of a condition or pattern of action in terms of its being a functional necessity for the survival of the system."[92] The statement that a particular structural arrangement fulfils an important function is not an adequate explanation of its origin or existence. One may also find fault with the postulate of universal functionalism which suggests that all existing structures fulfil, wholly or partially, a particular function. It certainly overlooks the aspect of functional disintegration or breakdown. Likewise, one may hit at the fallacy of deductive functionalism that finds place in the tendency to develop deductively a list of functional requisites and then to make sure to find structural patterns which fulfil these requisites. All this "leads quite commonly to an unwarranted twisting and distorting of empirical realities in the interest of conceptual and theoretical neatness."[93]

4. A critical examination of the structural-functional approach from a strictly ideological point of view shows that it is all nothing else than an exercise to defend

---

89. See Gouldner, *op. cit.*, p. 332.

90. Edward Shils : "On the Comparative Study of the New States" in Clifford Geertz (ed.), Old Societies in the New States (New York, 1963) p. 22. A critic like John Rex holds that it "has yet to be shown that the functional requisites of even a simple society can be specified in empirical terms." *Key Problems of Sociological Theory* (London : Routledge and Kegan Paul, 1961), pp. 66-67.

91. Bhambhri, *op. cit.*, pp. 467-68.

92. Young, *op. cit.*, p. 35.

93. *ibid.*, p. 36.

Some Critical Observations on Structural-Functionalism

Functionalism blossomed in an era of consolidation and conservatism following the second World War.

— **Calv. Milly**
The Sociological Imagination (New York: Groove Press, 1959), pp. 25-49.

This theory is implicity designed to convert the reader to a belief in liberal democracy and liberal pluralism. It was also perceived as culture bound, establishmentarian, non-operational, formally inadequate. As a vehicle of research, it goes nowhere and as a language or discourse it leads to obfuscation. The pluralist neutralism of structural functionalism renders it useless as a theory.

— **Charles A. Powell**
"Structural Functionalism and the Study of Comparative Communist Systems: Some Caveats" in *Comparative Communism*, July-October, 1971, Vol. 4, p. 63

What Almond has to say could have been said without using this systems approach and it would have been said more clearly.

— **S.E. Finer**
"Almond's Concept of the Political System: A Textual Critique" in *Government and Opposition*, Vol. 5 (Winter, 1969-70), p. 4.

Ralf Dahrendorf castigated Parsons and claimed that his functionalism neither was relevant to facts nor reached a level of theory. Almond's work was ethnocentric in its emphasis on stability in the light of Anglo-American norms and political traditions.

— **R.H. Chilcote**
Theories of Comparative Politics : The Search for Paradigm Reconsidered (Boulder, Col.: The Westview Press, 1994), p. 138.

and justify the *status quo*. The real pursuit of the functionalists is to save a political system from changing towards socialism. A serious endeavour to maintain a system or its change, by all means, peaceful and gradual, in the direction of 'modernisation' aims at nothing else than an imitation or emulation of the *'western'* model that presents an anti-thesis of a communist system. The functionalists are, therefore, accused of being the 'defenders of the bourgeoisie at home and of imperialism abroad'.[94] A critic like W.G. Runciman has thus said that functionalism "can, indeed, be interpreted as a conscious alternative to Marxism. Some of its critics have even wanted to interpret it as a political ideology conditioned by the structure of American capitalism."[95] It is for this reason that the Marxists cannot appreciate this approach who are guided by this maxim that 'philosophers have so far interpreted the world, the problem is how to change it.'

5. It may be said further that while Easton and Parsons present an elaborate scheme of their 'system', Almond talks of functions without referring to a system in which functions have a meaning. That is, he is more concerned with his own sub-sets without first explaining and clarifying the premises of his main set. Moreover, whatever he says about his political system and its structural-functional mechanism is applicable to a western country. He has certainly failed to offer a workable formula whereby we may understand the social, economic and political reality of the poor and backward countries of the world. Likewise, his scheme of the classification of the political systems cannot be applied

94. Bhambhri, *op. cit.*, p. 469.
95. Runciman, *op. cit.*, p. 195.

to all countries of the world in a uniform or rigorous manner. Meehan has thus called it 'a very imperfect and loose model' that can be used to order political data and perhaps standardise observations of political phenomena. Again, he "has not produced a theory, of course, nor even a well-articulated classification scheme. The taxonomy is incomplete and ambiguous."[96]

6. Structural-functionalism in political science may also be criticised from the standpoint of conflict theory that has been accepted by the liberal as well as Marxist social theorists. The conflict theory contradicts the basic premises of structural-functionalism by assuming that (i) every society is at every point subject to the process of change, because social change is ubiquitous; (ii) every society displays at every point dissensus and conflict, because social conflict is also ubiquitous; and (iii) every society is based on the coercion of some of its members by others.[97] One may say that structural-functional theories also assume that conflict "can be rendered harmonious through the interaction and satisfaction of interests and claims by contending groups."[98] However, one may also say that conflict theorists from Karl Marx to George Simmel have taken divergent positions in this regard. While the latter takes a liberal view by holding that competition as well as compromise, coercion as well as conciliation, and contradiction as well as resolution are the motivational basis and foundation stones of a social life, the former view is that each stage of social development generates a level of contradictions which explode to instigate a new stage. Thus, the contradictions resolved in one stage generate new contradictions until the classless society is firmly established. If so, the Marxian view rejects the whole case of structural-functionalism that believes in the essential resolution of conflicts of social life even in a bourgeois system.[99]

7. Meehan's attack on the analysis of structural-functional analysis is worth quoting. He says: "It seems clear that the search for a general theory, functionalist or not, or for an all-encompassing model of politics is a false and misleading trail that leads to conceptual difficulties that are virtually insoluble. Pressed too strongly, the search can only lead to new metaphysics in which a great deal of time is wasted discussing the properties of metaphysical entities like the system, That problem can be avoided, in functionalism or elsewhere, by beginning with a set of concrete phenomenon and by employing concepts that are firmly rooted in empirical evidence. If we seek explanations of real phenomena, and not 'theories' with no reference, it is much easier to keep inquiry from straying into unproductive activity. The general rule is simple: No phenomenon, no explanation: no phenomenon, no suggestiveness; no phenomenon, nothing accomplished. Political scientists must be interested in and prepared to study carefully, some concrete steps of human behaviour... Functionalism is one conceptual behaviour that may be employed in the study of

96. Meehan, *op. cit.*, pp. 176 and 180.
97. See Ralf Dahrendorf : *Class and Class Conflict in Industrial Society* (London : Routledge and Kegan Paul, 1959), p. 162.
98. Apter : *Introduction to Political Analysis*, p. 409.
99. *ibid.* In defence of the same, Mao Tse-tung elaborates the idea of contradictions. He says : "Marxist philosophy holds that the law of the unity of opposites is a fundamental law of the universe. This law operates everywhere, in the natural world, in human society, and in man's thinking. Opposites in contradiction unite as well as struggle with each other, and thus impel all things to move and change. Contradictions exist everywhere, but as things differ in nature, so do contradictions. In any given phenomenon or thing, the unity of opposites is conditional, temporary and transitory, and hence relative; whereas struggle between opposites is absolute." *ibid.*

politics, and it seems quite promising, but it is by no means the only way of seeking explanations. Political scientists may choose to produce functional explanations of course, but the choice should depend on the nature of the phenomena and the kind of data that can be accumulated, not on some arbitrary criterion."[100]

Structural-functional approach has its advantages limited to the study of selected affluent western democratic countries where alone it may look quite attractive for a comparative analysis of the political systems. It may also be added in its favour that it deals for the most part with a manageable collection of variables; and it provides a set of standardised categories that can be applied successfully over widely disparate political systems.[101] The line of ideological criticism directed against it is not free from its own blame in view of the fact that Marxism has its own weaknesses. Both Marxism and systems analysis breakdown as full-fledged theories while dealing with the elements of social and political reality and its change in a strictly desired manner. We may not be oblivious to the fact that conflicts "are not as unilinear as Marx had tried to point out, nor harmony as integral a factor in social and political life as the system theorists would have us believe. Conflict and harmony, change and continuity, constitute the pattern of social life as it moves from one period of history to another."[102]

It is rightly said that there are two operational difficulties in particular-the difficulty of refining, operationalising and testing hypotheses. It is difficult to apply on a broad basis to include both historical and contemporary cases. The formulation also tends in effect to equate the modern political system with the modern Anglo-American democratic system. . . . its definitions employ too many dimensions and it neglects the problem of variation."[103]

---

100. Meehan, *op. cit.,* pp. 187-88.
101. Young, *op. cit.,* p. 33.
102. Varma, *op. cit.,* p. 191.
103. R.J. Holt and J.E. Turner: *The Political Basis of Economic Development, An Investigation in Comparative Politics* (Princeton: D. Van Nostrand, 1966), pp. 12-13.

6

Input-Output Analysis

> How do any and all political systems manage to persist in a world of both stability and change? Ultimately, the search for an answer will reveal what I have called the life process of political systems—those fundamental functions without which no system could endure—together with the typical modes of response through which systems manage to sustain them. The analysis of these processes, and of the nature and conditions of the responses, I posit as a central problem of political theory.
>
> **—David Easton[1]**

As pointed out in the preceding two chapters, systems analysis has its two important derivatives in the forms of structural-functional and input-output analyses. Whereas the former is a compound of two words, viz., 'structure' implying reference to any human organisation that can do things and have an effect on human beings and other human organisations and 'function' signifying relationship to the activity of the agency and its external effects,[2]- the latter "is simply a framework for organising, conceptualising, codifying and manipulating data."[3] However, one important thing common to both, and that has its source in their being the derivatives of the systems analysis, is that their analyses really aim at the maintenance and persistence of the political system giving just a semblance of emphasis on the processes of dynamism and change. In a conceptual and theoretical sense, both the approaches derive from the basic framework of systems theory that, for the very reason of being basically interested in seeing political system as an on-going concern, "is not likely to be popular with normativists and progressives."[4]

Input-Output Analysis: Implications and General Characteristics

If political system is a set of interactions having structures, each part of which performs its 'functions' in order to keep it like an on- going concern, it is also a set of processes routinely converting inputs into outputs; it is a complex cyclical operation that has a dynamic of its own and that is capable of being purposive and goal-directed. Going a step ahead of the structural-functional approach, the input-output analysis emphasises that "each segment of the operating cycle of a political system is susceptible to its own special types of stress and maintenance difficulties; but at the same time, there are typical regulatory processes that go with each segment of the cycle and that serve to counterbalance stress problems. The bulk of the input-output approach deals with the analysis of the workings of the political

1. Easton : *A Systems Analysis of Political Life* (New York : Wiley, 1965), p. 17.
2. James C. Charlesworth : "Introduction : Identifiable Approaches to the Study of Politics and Government" in his (ed.): *Contemporary Political Analysis* (New York : Free Press, 1971), p.6.
3. Oran R. Young : *Systems of Political Science* (Englewood Cliffs, New Jersey, Prentice Hall, 1968), p. 48.
4. Charlesworth, *op. cit.*, p. 7.

systems in terms of this second sequence of concepts followed by discussions of the common stress patterns and regulatory processes at each stage in the political cycle."[5] As input-output analysis presupposes political system as consisting of interacting roles, structures and subsystems and of the underlying psychological propensities which affect these interactions, it involves a process that may be viewed as "consisting of inputs from the environment or from within the political system itself, the conversion of these inputs within the system, and the production of outputs into the environment. Outputs may produce changes in the environment, which in turn may affect the political system (feedback)."[8]

The nature and implications of the input-output analysis may be made more clear, if we study some of its general characteristics:

1. Here the focus is again on the system as the basic unit of analysis and on the intra-system and inter-system behaviour of various systems as principal areas of research.[7]
2. The distinction between the concrete system and analytic system should be kept in mind. While the former refers to a collection of individuals and treats human beings as 'bask components', the latter relates to the abstractions with focus on selected elements of human behaviour. This approach refers to the analytic system existing and operating within an overall social system.[8]
3. It treats all political systems as both open and adaptive. Its most salient focus is on the nature of the exchanges and transactions that take place between a political system and its environment.[9]
4. Throughout the presentation, as so elaborately given by Easton and Almond, there is a very strong and underlying concern with questions relating to persistence of the system, the sources of stresses and modes of processes of regulating all tensions and threats that offer challenge to the stability and maintenance of the system.
5. It does not reject the issue of change; it cleverly interprets the process accommodating change that is invariably slow, peaceful and gradual but that by no means threatens the very stability and maintenance of the political system.

All these general characteristics of input-output analysis are well summed up by Young in these words: "Above all, the political system is seen as a conversion process performing work, producing outputs, and altering its environment, with a continuous exchange between a political system and its environment based on the steady operation of the dynamic processes. At the same time, the approach provides numerous concepts for dealing both with political dynamics in the form of systemic adaptation processes and even with purposive redirection in the form of goal-changing feedback. With this perspective it is possible to deal with changes in the system itself, although the approach focuses mainly on changes whose principal results are only to modify or streamline the system. It is, therefore, important to observe that the input-output approach does not dwell extensively on a third level of change and dynamics focusing on broader-scale and more far-reaching alterations. Revolutionary change is hardly mentioned and even the possibilities of evolution to new systemic forms

5. Young, *op. cit.*, p. 39.
6. G.A. Almond and G.B. Powell : *Comparative Politics : A Developmental Approach* (Boston : Little Brown, 1966), p. 25.
7. Young, *op. cit.*, p. 39.
8. *ibid.*, pp. 37-38.
9. *ibid.*, p. 38.

are not covered in detail. Though the adaptive consequences of phenomena like growth could certainly be treated under this approach, their broader aspects of qualitative change donot find much place therein."[10]

Input-Output Analysis in Comparative Politics: Interpretations of David Easton and Gabriel A. Almond

David Easton "is the first major political scientist who has developed a systematic framework on the basis of the systems analysis approach for the study of politics instead of merely adapting it from anthropology or sociology."[11] He has selected political system as the basic unit of analysis and concentrated on the intra-system behaviour of various systems as principal areas of social science research and investigation. He has defined political system as 'a set of interactions'and politics as 'making authoritative allocation of values'. "I have been exploring the utility of the system as the major unit, focusing on political life as a system of behaviour operating within and responding to its social environment as it makes binding allocation of values."[12]

The input-output analysis of Easton has three main variables in the forms of demands, supports and feedbacks.

1. ***Demand :*** Easton defines demand "as an expression of opinion that an authoritative allocation with regard to a particular subject matter should or should not be made by those responsible for doing so."[13] It means that the people as 'actors' make demands upon their political system that subserve their specific interests. Thus, the political system undergoes 'demand stress'. Sometimes, the weight of the stress is considerably enhanced either on account of quantitative excess what Easton calls 'volume stress' or due to the burden of qualitative elements what he terms 'content stress'. However, both situations create what he designates the 'overload'. The function of the structures of the political system thus becomes to convert these demands, correctly stated as 'inputs', into authoritative decisions, correctly stated as 'outputs'. Thus, there occurs the conversion process in which some demands are fulfilled, some are weeded out also. Since the political system has to operate in a way that its stability is maintained, it becomes essential that there should be four regulatory mechanisms. First, there should be 'structural mechanisms' to play the role of 'gatekeepers'. It means that certain structures of the political system should look towards the regulation of demands making their weight on the makers of the decisions. Second, there should be cultural mechanisms in the shape of firm beliefs and attitudes of the people in their political system in order to establish an influential criteria of appropriateness for the articulation of demands. Third, there should be 'communication mechanisms' in order to keep the 'actors' informed of the decisions of their 'rulers' and of the latter about the nature and intensity of the demands made by their people. Finally, there "should be the process of 'reduction mechanisms' having specific procedures for the collection and combination of compatible demands, intra-system gatekeeping procedures, and the requirement that general demands be converted into specific issues for purposes of political processing."[14]
2. ***Support :*** It is another variable dealing with the inputs. "Supports refer to the remaining input transactions between a system and

10. *ibid.,* pp. 44-45.
11. S.P. Varma : *Modern Political Theory* (Delhi : Vikas, 1975), p. 175.
12. Easton, *op. cit.,* p. 21.
13. *ibid.,* p. 38.
14. Young, *op. cit.,* pp. 40-41.

Some Important Statements about Input-Output Analysis

A political system will, therefore, be identified as a set of interactions, abstracted from the totality of social behaviour, through which values are authoritatively allocated for a society. Persons who are in the process of engaging in such interactions, that is who are acting in political roles, will be referred to as the members of the system.

– David Easton

The ideas of system, as an ordering concept, is a surrogate for these and comparable terms. Systems analysis is Easton's weapon against two ghosts he helped instal in the house of political science-we know them as the boundary and the units problem.

—Paul F. Kress

One of the most influential theories of revolution has been developed on the basis of the systems theory approach to politics. This approach implies that a political system will tend towards long-term stability as the 'outputs' of government are brought into line with the 'inputs' or presures placed upon it. In this light, revolutions can be understood as a form of 'disequilibrium' in the political system that is brought about by economic, social, cultural or international changes to which the system itself is incapable of responding.

—Andrew Heywood

its environment after demands have been subtracted."[15] Support may be either overt or covert. It is overt when an action is clearly and manifestly supportive, it is covert when it refers to the supportive attitudes. As one basically interested in the stability and maintenance of the system, Easton refers to 'support stress' that may be due to the output failure. If there is a decline or erosion of political support, resort must be taken to some devices. For instance, structural regulation should be revised by changing structural elements of the system. Changes in the system of representation or in the operation of the party system may be cited as clear examples in this regard. Another device is to engender diffuse support that refers to the use of various processes for developing the 'sense of community' among the people.

3. ***Feedback :*** Easton tells us that the outputs of a political system are the authoritative decisions and actions of the system's leaders that bear on the allocation of values for it. These outputs "not only help to influence events in the broader society of which the system is a part, but also in doing so, they help to determine each succeeding round of inputs that finds its way into the political system. There is a feedback loop, the identification of which helps us to explain the processes through which the system may cope with the stress. Through it, the system may take advantage of what has been happening by trying to adjust its future behaviour."[16]

The idea of feedback means that if the actions of the authorities are taken to satisfy demands or create conditions that will do so, information must be fed back, at least to those authorities, about the effects of each round of outputs. Without information feedback about what is happening in the system, the authorities would have to operate in the dark.[17] Easton, further, says that the feedback loop itself "has a number of parts worthy of detailed investigation. It consists of the production of outputs by the authorities, a response by the members of the

15. *ibid.,* p. 41.
16. Easton : "Systems Analysis : An Example on Functionalism" in Gould and Thursby (eds.): *Contemporary Political Thought* (New York : Holt, Rinehart and Winston, 1969), p. 208.
17. *ibid.*

society to these outputs, the communication of information about the response to the authorities and, finally, possible succeeding actions by the authorities. Thereby a new round of outputs, response, information-feedback, and reaction by the authorities is set in motion, forming a seamless web of activities. What happens in this feedback thus has a profound influence on the capacity of a system to cope with stress and persist."[18]

The input-output analysis of Easton shows that a political system is operated by the forces of environment that appear in the form of demands on it and the rulings of the men in power who take decisions in order to allocate binding values for them. That is, while the inputs refer to the role of 'demands' made on the political system, outputs are 'decisions' having an authoritative character for the purpose of allocation of values for it. Naturally, the outputs "are the results of the conversion process acting upon a great variety of demands and supports and can be conveniently divided into verbal statements and concrete performances."[19] The outputs may be either 'authoritative' in the form of specific decisions having a binding character, they may be 'associated' also in the form of decisions lacking the compulsory nature of the former. Moreover, the outputs may be oriented either in an intra-system or in an extra-system direction. They may, however, be different from the 'outcomes'. As Young says: "Outputs are the immediate or primary results of authoritative decisions, while the secondary and tertiary ramifications that occur over time are conceptualised as outcomes."[20]

The input-output analysis of Easton is an exercise in the sphere of having, what he calls, 'a flow model of the political system'. It is on account of his search for presenting a 'systems analysis of political life' that the formula of input-output has been devised. As he says: "Thus, a systems analysis of political life rests on the idea of a system embedded in an environment and subject to possible environmental influences that threaten to drive the essential variables of the system beyond their critical range. Such an analysis suggests that, to persist, the system must be capable of responding with measures that alleviate that stress. The actions of the authorities are particularly critical in this respect. But if they are able to respond, they must be in a position to obtain information about what is happening so that they may react in so far as they desire, or are compelled, to do so. With information they may be able to maintain a minimal level of support for the system."[21]

The method of systems analysis, as adopted by Almond is more representative than that of Easton for the simple reason that while the purpose of the latter is to make 'an enquiry into the state of political science', the field of the former is 'comparative politics'. Almond has used seven variables belonging to the input and output spheres showing that while the 'input functions' are performed by non-governmental subsystems, by the society, and by the general environment, the output functions are performed by government alone. What is peculiar about Almond's input-output analysis is that he has rather ignored the output aspect by referring to the functions of the legislature, executive and judiciary known in the new vocabulary of comparative politics as rule-making, rule-application and rule-adjudication departments respectively. In his systems analysis, it "is the input functions which are regarded as highly significant."[22]

18. *ibid.*, p. 209.
19. Young, *op. cit.*, p. 42.
20. *ibid.*
21. Easton, *op. cit.*, p. 210.
22. Varma, *op. cit.*, p. 171.

1. ***Input Variables :*** Almond discerns four input variables—political socialisation and recruitment, interest articulation, interest aggregation, and political communication. According to him, *political socialisation* is the process of induction into the political culture and leads to the development of a set of attitudes and beliefs among the members of the system towards their political system. Allied with this is the idea of political recruitment, or the initiation of members of the society into the politics of their country. Second, the variable of *interest articulation* refers to the existence and role of organised groups that play their part for the protection and promotion of their specific interests. These interest groups may be of different kinds—institutional or political, non-associational or ethnic and religious, anomic or spontaneous, and associational as trade unions and business organisations. The role of these groups may be, according to the stage of development, either specific or diffuse, general or particular, instrumental or affective. Third, the variable of *interest aggregation* refers to the existence and role of political parties that combine various interests and effect the recruitment of the personnel committed to a particular pattern of society. Almond presents a taxonomic illustration of the party systems and thus takes the bases of their organisation and style. On the basis of the former, he says that party systems may be authoritative, dominant, non-authoritative, competitive, two-party and multi-party; on the basis of the latter, they may be secular-pragmatic-bargaining, absolute-value-oriented or ideological, particularistic, or traditional. Last, the variable of *political communication* signifies the medium through which other functions in the political system are performed. The communication facilities are of the highest importance in determining the character of a political system inasmuch as they determine the flow of information about the society and its political system.

(2) ***Output Variables :*** Almond discerns three variables: rule-making, rule-application and rule-adjudication departments. The output functions, as Almond observes, "bear a strong resemblance to governmental activity as defined in traditional separation of powers theory. Here is a case in which new concepts are devised for traditionally recognised and otherwise named activities. The purpose of this is to shift the emphasis from description in terms of institutions which may be differently named in various countries and to substitute one set of functional concepts for describing the activities which these institutions perform, and which particular institutions may only perform momentarily."[23]

It is on the basis of these input-output variables that Almond calls his study of the political system as 'comprehensive'. It is comprehensive in the sense that it includes all interactions effected by the variables of inputs, that affect the use of physical coercion in all the structures, including undifferentiated structures, like kinship and lineage, and anomic phenomena like riots and street demonstrations, and not merely the interactions which take place within the structures associated with the state like parliament, executive and bureaucracies, and formally organised units like parties, interest groups and media of communications.[24] Almond's political system, like that of Easton, "belongs to a class of social system, with distinct characteristics of its own, but in the study of which concepts and principles of other disciplines in particular can be highly useful."[25]

---

23. Davies and Lewis, *op. cit.,* p. 39.
24. Varma, *op. cit.,* pp. 169.
25. *ibid.,* p, 167.

Key Concepts: Inputs, Outputs, Feedbacks and Capabilities

The input-output analysis is based on certain key concepts. Though we have made their meanings and implications clear at different stages, it shall be worthwhile to present their precise meaning here for the purpose of understanding the approach in a clear perspective. They are four in number:

1. ***Inputs*** : This term refers to the demands made by the people who play their 'role' in the political system. Since these demands come from the individuals belonging to different walks of life whether at the national or international level, it may be said, for the sake of convenience, that they come from the 'environment'. According to Almond, demands may be classified in many ways showing the degree of their range and variety that have their diverse impacts on the political system as:[26]

    (i) Demands for the allocation of goods and services such as demands for wages and hour laws, educational opportunities, recreational facilities, roads and transportation;

    (ii) Demands for the regulation of behaviour such as provisions for public safety, controls over markets and rules pertaining to marriage, health and sanitation;

    (iii) Demands for participation in the political system as right to vote, hold office, petition government bodies and officials and to organise political associations; and

    (iv) Demands for communication and information such as demands for the affirmation of norms, communication ot policy intent from policy elites, or the display of majesty and power of the political system in periods of threat or on ceremonial occasions.

According to this analysis, a political system may face demands in many forms, combinations and degrees of intensity. It should, however, be added that inputs necessarily come only from the society of which the political system is a part. It is typical of political systems that inputs are generated internally by political elites—kings, presidents, ministers, legislators, and judges. Similarly, inputs may come from the international system in the form of threats, invasions, controls, and assistance from foreign political systems. The inputs may come from any one of these three sources—the domestic society, political elites and the international environment.[27]

Inputs also include supports. As Easton says: "Inputs of demands are not enough to keep a political system operating. They are only raw materials out of which finished products called decisions are manufactured. Energy in the form of actions or orientations promoting or resisting a political system, the demands arising in it, and the decisions issuing from it must also be put into the system to keep it running."[28] Examples of support classifications are:[29]

(i) Material supports such as the payment of taxes or other levies and the provision of services such as labour on public works or military service;

(ii) Obedience to laws and regulations;

(iii) Participatory supports such as voting, political discussions and other forms of political activity;

(iv) Attention paid to governmental communication and the manifestation of deference or respect to public authority, symbols and ceremonials.

A proper balance should be maintained between the demands and supports for the smooth running of the political system. In case the stress of the demands is too great, the

26. Almond and Powell, *op. cit.,* pp. 25-26.
27. *ibid.,* p. 27.
28. Cited *ibid.,* p. 26.
29. *ibid.*

Almond's Model of Input-Output Analysis

Inputs	Conversion-Functions of a Political System	Outputs
(a) *Demands*		
1. Demands for goods and services such as wages and hour laws, educational opportunities, recreational facilities, roads and transportation;	1. Articulation of interests or demands;	1. Extractions which may take the form of tribute, booty, taxes or personal services;
2. Demands for regulation of behaviour such as provision of public safety, control over market and labour relations, rules pertaining to marriage and family;	2. Integration or combination of interests into policy proposals:	2. Regulation of behaviour which may take a variety of forms and affect some subset of the whole gamut of human behaviour and relations;
3. Demands for participation in the political system, for the right to vote, hold office, petition governmental bodies and officials, organise political associations and the like: and	3. Conversion of policy proposals into authoritative rules;	3. Allocation or distribution of goods and services, opportunities, honours, statuses and the like; and
4. Symbolic inputs such as demands for the display of the majesty and the power of the political system in periods of threats or on ceremonial occasions, or demands for the affirmation of norms or the communication of the policy intent from political elites.	4. Application of general rules to particular cases;	4. Symbolic outputs, including affirmation of values, displays and political symbols, statements of policy and intent.
(b) *Supports*		
1. Material supports such as the payment of taxes or other levies and the provision of services such as labour contributions or military services;	5. Adjudication of rules in individual cases; and	
2. Obedience to laws and regulations;	6. Transmission of information about these events within the political system from structure to structure and between the political system and its social and international environments.	
3. Participation such as voting, joining organisations and communicating about politics; and		
4. Manifestation of deference to public authority, symbols and ceremonials.		

conditions of the stability of the political system might be threatened and then it would become necessary to reduce the stress of demands or of the supports so that the political system survives and continues to run like an ongoing concern. As Almond says: "If the political system and the elites acting in its roles are to process demands effectively, supports must be received from other social systems and from individuals acting in the political system. Generally speaking, demands affect the policies or goals of the system, while supports such as goods and services, obedience and deference, provide the resources which enable a political system to extract, regulate and distribute—in other words, to carry out its goals."[30]

2. ***Outputs* :** The outputs of a political system "are the authoritative decisions and actions of the system's leaders that bear on the allocation of values for the system."[31]

The outputs are the results of the conversion process acting upon a great variety of demands and supports. In simple words, outputs are the transactions initiated by the departments of the political system that usually correspond too closely to the supports listed above, though they may or may not respond to demands depending on the kind of the political system obtaining there. In this regard, four processes may be pointed out:[32]

(i) Extractions which may take the form of tribute, booty, taxes, or personal services;

(ii) Regulations of behaviour which may take a variety of forms and affect the whole gamut of human behaviour and relations;

(iii) Allocation or distribution of goods and services, opportunities, honours, statuses and the like; and

(iv) Symbolic outputs, including affirmation of values, displays of political symbols, statement of policy and intents.

In brief, outputs are primarily means of generating specific support for a political system as they, according to Easton, "may help to maintain a minimum level of support for the various political objects."[33] Easton, further, says that it "is the aspect of the outputs that tends to be neglected in theoretical enquiry and which lies at the heart of this part of our analysis."[34]

3. ***Feedbacks* :** The flow of inputs and outputs includes transactions between the political system and the components of its domestic and foreign environments. But one thing that has its special role in the entire process is the feedback that "completes the cycle of political system and that makes it a dynamic and regenerative operation."[35] One may say that not one but many feedback processes go on within a political system, but the input-output approach "focuses primarily on the overall systemic feedback loop that links the consequences of outputs with the continuing flow of inputs."[36] Taking an analogy of the machine, Norbert Wiener says: "This control of a machine on the basis of its actual performance rather than its expected performance is known as feedback, and involves sensory members which are actuated by motor members and perform the function of tell-tales or monitors—that is, of elements which indicate a performance..."[37] However, social theorists and political scientists like Easton and Almond have used this term as "essentially a dynamic process through which information about the performance of a system is communicated in such a way as to affect the subsequent behaviour of the system."[38]

---

30. *ibid.*
31. Young, *op. cit.,* p, 42.
32. Almond and Powell, *op. cit.,* p. 27.
33. Easton : *A Framework for Political Analysis,* p. 347.
34. *ibid.*
35. Young, *op. cit.,* p. 43.
36. *ibid.*
37. Wiener : *The Human Uses of Human Beings* (Boston : Houghton, 1950), p. 12.
38. Young, *op. cit.,* p. 43.

The feedback has two aspects—negative and goal-changing. While the negative feedback deals with the regulation of an error, the goal-changing feedback deals with the problems of purposive redirection. Though the principle of feedback belongs to the subject of control engineering, its application in comparative politics, as suggested by Deutsch, has these main features:[39]

(i) The system must receive information concerning the position of the goal and concerning its own distance from it; and it must receive information concerning the changes in its distance from the goal brought about by its own performance.

(ii) The system must be able to respond to this information by further changes into its own position or behaviour.

(iii) The system should tend to move towards a state in which internal disequilibrium is reduced so that it can be reduced by bringing the whole system into some particular situation or relation *vis-a-vis* the outside world.

(iv) If these changes are effective and the system reaches the goal, some of the drive or inner tension usually will be lowered.

Thus, feedback "is essentially a regulative element in a political system, though it is subject to various pathologies itself as regards matters such as accuracy, responsiveness and time lags."[40]

4. ***Capabilities :*** Political scientists subscribing to systems analysis refer to the notion of 'capability' that relates to the extent to which the system can cope with inputs in a successful manner. The capabilities of political systems may be (i) extractive of resources, (ii) regulative of the behaviour of the individuals and groups, and (iii) distributive relating to the giving away of goods and prizes. Besides, the political system should also have the symbolic and the responsive capabilities in terms of national and international affairs. It means that a political system should be able to develop and maintain symbols that increase attraction or loyalty towards itself and respond adequately and with vigour to demands made upon it both from domestic and international environments.[41]

These four key concepts are used in the input-output approach to deal with the questions relating to the survival, stability and maintenance of the political system. It is in a study of the political system from this standpoint that its conceptual richness "goes substantially beyond the more useful and somewhat static analyses of stability and equilibrium and focuses on concepts such as disturbances, stress, regulation and purposive redirection, all of which lends a significant dynamism to the analysis of system-maintenance."[42] It may, however, be added that a system analyst is not unmindful of the change: what he really desires is that the change must be peaceful and gradual so that the maintenance of the system is not seriously threatened or reduced into disintegrative aspects. As Easton says "The idea of systems persistence extends far beyond that of systems maintenance; it is oriented towards exploring change as well as stability both of which may be interpreted as alternative avenues for coping with stress."[43]

Critical Appraisal

The input-output analysis on account of being a derivative of the systems analysis may be subjected to, more or less, those lines of criticism that we have discussed in the preceding two chapters. They may, however, be enumerated in the following manner:

39. Karl W. Deutsch : "Communication Models and Decision Systems," in Charlesworth (ed.) : *Contemporary Political Analysis,* p. 280.
40. Young, *op. cit.,* p. 43.
41. Varma, *op. cit.,* p. 173.
42. Young, *op. cit.,* p. 44.
43. Easton : *A Framework for Political Analysis,* p. 88.

1. This analysis is loaded with an obsession for borrowing and applying certain terms from other disciplines particularly those belonging to the categories of natural and exact sciences. It all happens at the expense of this fact that the concepts applied at one level of abstraction in one discipline and in a particular context are most likely to suffer from distortion if they are transplanted into another. It is on account of this that a sort of coagulation occurs. Whereas sociologists like Parsons look interested in the 'system', Almond talks of functions without referring to the system in which functions have a meaning. Easton lays so much emphasis on the input-output aspect that his widely adapted definition of the political system eventuates in a narrow and limited vision of political life. It is also found that various questions concerning patterns of control, power and influence donot play an important part in this approach. The result of all this is that this approach "does not emphasise various types of important and relevant questions that are simply not handled in detail by its conceptual apparatus and thus this approach lays focus on the operation of a system in fairly abstract terms rather than on the behaviour pattern of human beings."[44]
2. The input-output analysis suffers from several other deficiencies. For instance, it cannot be applied to the study of mass political phenomena such as voting, formation of political attitudes, street agitations and a host of other things in the form of demonstrations, strikes, *bandhs* and *gheraos*, etc. that take place mostly in the poor and backward countries of the world and that have been designated by Myron Weiner as the raw materials of the 'politics of scarcity'. It becomes more or less like an elitist approach inasmuch as care "is taken to restrict the application of concepts and hypotheses to the politically relevant members of the system. Although the notion of political relevancy is not precisely delimited, it is clear that it does not include mass phenomena".[45]
3. William Ross Ashby is of the view that the concept of feedback is nowhere important and that "so simple and natural in certain elementary cases, becomes artificial and of little use when the inter-connections between the parts become more complex. When there are only two parts joined so that each affects the other, the properties of the feedback give important and useful information about the properties of the whole. But when the parties rise to even as few as four, if everyone affects the other three, then twenty circuits can be traced through them: and knowing the properties of all twenty circuits does not give complete information about the system. Such complex systems cannot be treated as an interlaced set of more or less independent feedback circuits, but only as a whole."[46]
4. Finally, this analysis can be charged with harbouring a *status quo* bias. The central theme of this approach, like structural-functional approach, is to seek solution to the problems concerning persistence, adaptation and regulation of a political system. As Young says: "To continue, input-output analysis has little to say about the politics of decline, disruption and breakdown in political systems. The material on change that is included does not, for the most part, address itself to the more abrupt and pathological kinds of change under these headings. Easton himself admits that he is far more impressed with the self-maintaining capacities of political systems than with the phenomena of political decay and degeneration. And although some of the concepts in the approach could conceivably be turned

44. Young, *op. cit.,* p. 45.
45. *ibid.,* p. 46.
46. Ashby : *An Introduction to Cybernetics* (New York : John Wiley & Sons. 1963). p. 6.

towards analysis in this area, there is little scope for such analysis in the approach in its present form."[47] It is for this reason that this approach is accused of being conservative, for its fundamental theme is "to treat these institutions as given and unchallengeable in essentials..."[48] Obviously, this approach ignores the fact that the 'total system' "is never at rest, it is always being pushed, prodded and keel-hauled, it is always subject to strains and conflicts."[49]

It is for these important reasons that this analysis is charged with being conservative, anti-change and, above all, even inadequately empirical. Instead of looking at the realities of the 'politics of scarcity', it tries to fit the politics of the poor and backward countries of the world into a model that has been devised by the scholars of the 'bourgeois world'. The only point in defence of this approach can be said to lie in this affirmation that it has not been applied extensively so far in empirical political research. It may be expected that some of the points of its strengths and weaknesses will show up more dearly with the growth of its application. One may partly agree with Young that the input-output approach in the field of comparative politics "not only does present a nicely standardised set of concepts and categories that have the advantage of being logically inclusive, it is also pitched at a level that facilitates the piecing together of broad and comparable overviews of whole political systems, a characteristic that is highly desirable at present since the discipline is not yet very well prepared for detailed comparative work on many secondary and subsidiary questions. Moreover, the analysis is deliberately formulated at such a level of abstraction that it avoids the danger of becoming tied to any particular type of political system or to any specific variety of socio-cultural context."[50]

---

47. *ibid.*, pp. 45-46.
48. Gouldner : *The Coming Crisis of Western Sociology* (Delhi : Heinemann, 1971). p. 332.
49. See C.P. Bhambhri : "Functionalism in Politics" in *Indian Journal of Political Science*, Vol XXXIV, No. 4, October-December 1973, p. 459.
50. Young, *op. cit.*, p. 46.

7

Political Communication

> If you will imagine a communication system, you will realise that there is a great deal of variability about what comes out. The input and the output can, therefore, be described in terms of their variance (or their information). If it is a good communication system, however, there must be some systematic relation between what goes in and what comes out. That is to say, the output will depend upon the input, or will be correlated with the input. If we measure this correlation, then we can say how much of the output variance is attributable to the input and how much is due to random fluctuations of 'noise' introduced by the system during transmission. So we see that the measure of transmitted information is simply a measure of the input-output correlation.
>
> **—George A. Miller[1]**

The political communication approach, a relatively recent and fast-moving development in the field of scientific analysis, leans heavily on the fundamental orientations of cybernetics—the science of control and communication system.[2] It has received great impetus from the revolutionary developments "that occurred after the second World War in the spheres of engineering and technology. In keeping with the tradition of borrowing perspectives and frames of references extensively from other branches of knowledge, whether belonging to social or natural sciences, a good number of empirical political scientists like Karl W. Deutsch, in particular, have developed a new approach in the discipline of comparative politics whereby the analysis of political phenomenon is made on the basis of communication and control system. The main purpose of social theorists subscribing to this approach is that the developments in the new science of communications "have led to a diminution in importance of the differences for analytical purposes, between the behaviour of living things and that of social organisations. There has, consequently, he would also argue, been at least a lessening in the gulf between the methods used by natural scientists, on the one hand, and social scientists on the other. Concepts and methods drawn from analyse the behaviour of organisations, and Deutsch sees that the new sciences can now without fear of being misleading be used to state, as well as other types of political systems as, fundamentally, types of organisations."[3]

Political Communication: Nature and Meaning of the Approach: Clarification of Basic Concepts

The term 'communication' refers to a body of basic concepts underlying several contemporary approaches to human behaviour— including the interaction of nation-states.[4] This term may be used in both a narrow or *specific* and a wider

1. Miller cited in Karl Deutsch: "Communication Models and Decision System" in Charlesworth (ed.); *Contemporary Political Analysis* (New York : Free Press, Macmillan, 1967), p. 275
2. As understood in the disciplines of natural sciences, cybernetics is described as a science relating to controlof information and communication system.
3. Morton R. Davies and Vaughan A. Lewis : *Models of Political Systems* (Delhi : Vikas, 1971), p. 71.
4. Robert C. North : "The Analytical Prospects of Communication Theory" in Charlesworth (ed.), *op. cit.*, p. 300.

or *general* sense depending on its use or application by a student of natural or social sciences. As used by a mathematician like Weaver, it "includes all the procedures by which one mind may affect another."[5] Another writer belonging to the same discipline, while developing his theory of messages, used the word 'cybernetics' which he derived from the Greek word *kubernetes* meaning in English 'steersman', the same word from which 'governor' derives.[6] Used in a wider sense, the term 'communication' involves not only oral speech, but all human behaviour. In an even broader sense, it may be used with reference to the ways in which the physical environment excites signals in the central nervous system—together with the ways in which the human being operates upon the physical environment. In these terms the organism and the environment form a single system: the organism affects the environment and the environment affects the organism.[7]

It is for this reason, that the approach of political communication is also known by the name of 'political cybernetics.' As developed by Wiener and others, cybernetics is fundamentally "a body of theory and technique for the study of probabilities in different but analogous universes such as certain types of machines, animals, individual human beings, societies and nation-states—and the ways in which message transactions function to control such universes."[8] W. Ross Ashby, who is regarded as the pioneer of this approach, refers to cybernetics as the 'study of all possible machines', the word machine being construed to include men and animals as well as inanimate systems.[9] Thus, really speaking, cybernetics has its place in the natural sciences in view of the fact that it "is a theory of information self-regulating machines, computers, and the physiology of the nervous system. An important concept in the cybernetics is that of a machine which recognises stimuli, 'learns', adjusts itself automatically upon receiving feedback about its performance, and moves through a determined number of possible states."[10]

The term 'communication' has a different connotation when it is used in the context of 'political cybernetics'. Here it "consists of (i) a model drawn from the information theory and cybernetics, (ii) a theory of communication nets, and (iii) a set of propositions partially derived from other theoretical areas, such as democratic theory, organisation theory and decision theory, about the characteristics and effects of communications and their media on attitude change, public opinion formation, voting behaviour, maintenance and stability of a political system, consensus, coercion, political socialisation, political development, perception and ideology."[11] It should be cautioned at the very outset that ambiguity and confusion are compounded by the use of similar terminology with different definitions, but the best way to

---

5. Claude E. Shannon and Warren Weaver : *The Mathematical Theory of Communication* (Urbana : University of Illinois Press, 1959), p. 95.
6. North, *op. cit.*, p. 300. The term 'communications' has also come to include the concept of 'cybernetics' (steering) as developed by Norbert Wiener to signify the control of communication and the ability of a state to control is related to its ability to deal with information. Wiener, in fact, equates communication and control; every time we communicate, we control. Cybernetics, one might say, is concerned with a particular kind of system, namely one that is steered and that is conceived in terms of communication and information. See J.D. de Vree : *Political Integration : The Formation of Theory and Its Problems* (The Hague : Montana, 1972). But in strict cybernetic terms, the communication is political, if it involves the transmission of political messages, demands, supports and binding decisions. See R.L. Tooze : "Communications Theory" in Trevor Taylor (ed.) : *Approaches and Theory in International Relations* (London : Longman, 1978), pp. 205 and 215.
7. See W. Ross Ashby : *Design for a Brain* (New York : Wiley, 1960), p. 87.
8. Norbert Wiener : *The Human Uses of Human Beings* (Garden City : Doubleday, 1956), p. 15.
9. *ibid.*, p. 2.
10. Stephen L. Wasby : *Political Science: The Discipline and Its Dimensions: An Introduction* (Calcutta : Scientific Book Agency, 1970), p. 142.
11. *ibid.*

avoid such difficulties is to differentiate their centre of focus by describing them separately. It should be done in order to avoid the pitfalls of a least coherent theory like this.[12]

According to this approach, politics and government "appear in essence as processes of *steering* and *co-ordinating* human efforts towards the attainment of some set of goals."[13] In this framework we refer to the basic mechanism through which these processes manifest themselves in the *decision*. This approach, thus, may be taken as analogous to and also different from the decision-making approach, since it "devotes particular attention to the process of *making* decisions as contrasted with the actual *consequences* of decisions. It is a legacy of its background in cybernetics and *processes* rather than on the results of the decisions."[14] Such an interpretation leads to two orientations that this approach involves. First, it emphasises at all points problems of dynamics and of the various information flows attendant upon communications and decision-making. Therefore, the information flow constitutes the basic unit of analysis. The actual flow arises from the movement of the bits of information through the relevant system. Second, there are various structures that shape this flow of information with important consequences for the resultant decisions.[15]

It should also be borne in mind that the term 'political communication' as an important approach to the analytical study of modern political systems is different from the term 'communication' that relates to the media of dissemination of news. That is, communication and political communication are two different terms. We are not concerned here with the study of the means or channels of communications like press, radio and television, though they may" have their place within the wider study of political communication. Our purpose is to see communication as a dynamic movement of demands and decisions from one part of the political system to another as "no operation of the political system can take place unless parts of the system can communicate with each other. Communication links together the parts of the system and also the present with the past and the future, so that demands are followed by policies."[16]

The study of political communication approach is, therefore, integrally related to the study of political system. It is the communication that gives dynamics to the political system. As a result, we have to make a study of political communication in the same way as we study political system as a whole, *i.e.*, in terms of the inter-penetration and reciprocal influences between structures and behaviour. Such a study, therefore, raises three salient questions: First, what consequences follow from the general principle that the study of communication is truly the study of the dynamics of the political system? Second, what is the nature and what are the characteristics of these processes and structures of communication in various types of societies, and what is the relationship between these processes and structures? Third, what are the effects of these structures and processes on the communication levels of a given polity?[17]

The communications approach, as adopted by Karl Deutsch, may be said to have three main characteristics:[18]

1. It no longer seeks power as the key variable in the explanation of the political phenomena. Power is neither the centre nor the essence of politics. Instead the essence of politics becomes the dependable co-

---

12. *ibid.*
13. O.R.Young: *Systems of Political Science* (Englewood Cliffs, New Jersey : Prentice Hall, 1968), p. 50.
14. *ibid.*
15. *ibid.*
16. Jean Blondel: *An Introduction to Comparative Government* (London : Weidenfeld and Nicolson., 1969), p. 223.
17. *ibid.*, p. 224.
18. See R.L. Tooze in Taylor, *op. cit.*, p. 218.

ordination of human efforts and expectations for the attainment of the goals of the society.

2. There is a strong emphasis on the empirical nature of the concepts. The attempt is to 'operationalise' each concept through measurement and mapping. Quantitative data is not seen as a substitute for other types of analysis but as complementary in that it could do much to check, strengthen or confirm the judgment of the historian or political analyst.
3. It is not restricted to any one level of analysis. It is equally relevant to groups, peoples, organisations of any size, including the state, and relationships between the units.

Political communication, as a matter of fact, relates to the world of political engineering. As such, it has certain important concepts that should be understood before grasping the real meaning and nature of this approach. They are:

Concepts relating to operating structures : Every political system has some 'receptors' or 'reception systems' dealing with the intake of information from internal and external environments. It also covers several other functions beyond intake like scanning operations, selection of information and data processing. Within the decision-making apparatus, information is handled and acted upon by structures representing memory, value complexes and actual decision centres; while memory relates to the incoming information to the relevant past experiences concerning both processes and consequences, values perform the normative tasks relating to preferences. The structures of a political system operate to implement completed decisions and to feed information concerning performances back into the apparatus as a new unit.[19]

Concepts relating to flows and processes : Here we deal with channels, loads and load capacity. *Load capacity* is a function of the number and types of available channels, while *load* itself relates to the over-all intake of information at any given time. Load capacity is closely related to factors like responsiveness, fidelity, background, noise and distortion. *Responsiveness* refers to the facility of the apparatus in taking account of and handling incoming information: *fidelity* refers to the accuracy with which information is transmitted in the various processes of perception, selection and handling. The level of fidelity can be affected by several variables like *distortions* and *noise* that tend to obscure relevant information. Then comes the *recall* or the ability of the communication system to associate, locate and bring forth past experience that is relevant to the analysis of incoming information. All these process elements form the *combinatorial capacity* of the overall operation of a political system.[20] Thus, combinatorial capacity "is a measure of ability to deal with a wide range of information inputs in such a way as to make and implement actions with positive consequences for the attainment of the goals to the political system."[21]

Concepts relating to outcomes : Outputs in the form of decisions are the results of inputs. The question of outcomes raises several considerations as those of compliance, effectiveness and authority. Here figure in the concepts of *'feedback'* and *'feedback process'*. By feedback, according to Deutsch, is meant "a communication network that produces action in response to an input of information, and includes all the results of its own action in the new information by which it modifies its subsequent behaviour."[22] According to Snyder and others, it "refers to the messages about the actions or state of the system which are returned to the system. By means of a continuous flow of such messages it is possible for the decision-makers to have a more or less current picture of the success or failure of their actions and the

19. Young, *op. cit.,* p. 51.
20. *ibid.,* p. 52.
21. *ibid.*
22. Karl Deutsch : *The Nerves of Government* (New York : Free Press, 1968), p. 88.

relative adequacy of the system."[23] Feedback may be either positive or negative. Positive feedback occurs when the information fed into the system catalyses only actions that constitute an increment to or an augmentation of the original action. The result is not a regulatory process but an upward spiral of responses. It is for this reason that positive feedback processes are sometimes capable of inducting breakdown or radical change in the decision-making system. Different from this, negative feedback refers to the processes through which information about the consequences of taking decisions and implementing actions is put back into the system in such a way so as to alter the system's behaviour in directions that will lead closer to the attainment of relevant goals.

There are some more specific concepts that are central to an explanation of the operation of the negative feedback processes. They are: load, lag, gain and lead. *Load* refers to the extensiveness of the activities of a system relative to available feedback facilities and to the quantities of information involved in feedback processes relative to channel capacities. *Lag* is a measure of delay in reporting and acting on information about the consequences of decisions and actions, whereas *gain* represents the extensiveness of a system's responses to this information following its receipt. On the other hand, *lead* is the capacity to act in response to forecasts of future consequences as it is the case when one aims ahead of a moving object in order to hit it.[24]

The political communication approach lays stress on the point that all functions of a political system "are performed by means of communication."[25] It is communication that sustains and nourishes the body of a system. Hence, one "may liken the communication function to the circulation of the blood. It is not the blood but what it contains that nourishes the system. The blood is the neutral medium carrying claims, protests and demands through the veins of the heart; and from the heart through the arteries flow the outputs of rules, regulations and adjudications in response to the claims and demands."[26] Though this approach seeks to study the elements of change, it is more concerned with a change that may not bring about the destruction of the system. As such, it "is concerned with ways in which certain kinds of apparatus are maintained through 'feedbacks', that is to say, devices by which the entropy of a system is counteracted by returning some of its output into input."[27]

Functional Aspects of the Approach: Political Communication as a Variable for the Comparative Study of Political Systems

As pointed out above, all the functions in a political system are performed by means of communication. For instance, the heads of the family, school and college teachers and religious leaders perform the work of inculcating values in the people; leaders of the interest groups and political parties perform the function by communicating demands and policy recommendations; legislators make laws on the basis of information communicated to them by their fellow- parliamentarians and the ministers of the government; the administrators perform their functions on the basis of information communicated to them by the society and the organs of government. The judicial process is carried on by means of information communicated to the judges by the litigating parties and the decisions of the fellow judges sitting at higher echelons. Viewed thus, it might

23. Richard C. Synder, H.W. Bruck and B.M. Sapin : *Decision-Making as an Approach to the Study of International Politics* (Princeton, Princeton University Press, 1954), p. 88.
24. Young, *op. cit.,* p. 53.
25. G.A. Almond's 'Introduction' in his (with Coleman) (ed.) : *The Politics of the Developing Areas* (Princeton : Princeton Univ, Press, I960), p. 45.
26. *ibid.,* p. 47.
27. D. Emmet : *Function, Purpose and Powers,* p. 61.

appear that there is no political communication function as such, that communication is an aspect of all other political functions. Almond, however, cautions against this tendency and he suggests that a student of comparative politics should know that political communication function should be studied in a way different from other political functions of a political system inasmuch as failure to do so "would deprive us of an essential tool necessary for distinguishing among political systems and characterising their performance."[28]

In other words, it follows that the dissemination of information by the structure of a political system should not be likened with the principal function that it discharges such as interest articulation done by organised groups and interest aggregation performed by political parties. The process of decision-making should not be identified with the agencies that seek to influence it. Though a student of comparative politics is required to study the role of the input factors that have their definite impact upon the process of decision-making, he is also required to see as to how various subsystems of a political system operate at their own levels and how they make others operate by means of communicating information for the paramount purpose of keeping the system like an 'on-going concern'. For this it is necessary that there should be no violent change; if there is any change, let it be of a peaceful and gradual type so that the system is not pushed to the brink of breakdown. Keeping this in view, Young suggests four characteristics of the functional aspects of political communication approach:

1. It is certainly related to an emphasis on decision-making as a process rather than on the results or consequences of decisions. As a result, the approach tends to focus *onflows* of information and on the forms of various structures rather than on'the substance of either.[29]
2. It deals quite explicitly with various processes and dynamic movements so that it is quite well equipped to handle questions concerning change. Problems of 'modificatory' change are incorporated closely into the approach, since it is based on the notions of dynamic processes that accomplish objectives and, therefore, alter the situation of the decision-making operation.[30]
3. It is also attuned to the problems of evolutionary change, a fact which gives its real advantages in some areas of political analysis. Self-transformation, innovation and growth are given explicit treatment. Decision-making operations are likely to transform themselves completely over time in response to their own activities and to environmental changes, and this is an important perspective in the analysis of many political processes.[31]
4. It does consider certain externally imposed difficulties, such as overload, as well as internal problems like steering pathologies and amplifying feedback. Possibilities of revolutionary change are, therefore, not wholly neglected. Nevertheless, the approach focuses primarily on the problems of keeping systems going on and on the various processes of adaptation that can be utilised to meet destabilising forces.[32]

If so, the political communication approach can be utilised as a variable for making comparisons between different political systems. We may say that while a democratic system guarantees freedom for the flow of information in diverse channels with the result that political culture becomes fragmented and the role of various structures becomes

28. Almond, *op. cit.*, p. 46.
29. Young, *op. cit.*, p. 56.
30. *ibid.*, p. 58.
31. *ibid.*
32. *ibid.*

differentiated, it has a reverse form in a totalitarian system where the ruling party has its control over 'complete switchboard'. Coercion is the hallmark of a totalitarian order as a result of which there is the monopolistic control of the ruling party or its elite over the media of communications. Thus Almond adds: "Totalitarian communication directs the inflow of information to a single political culture, and limits the outflow of communication to the purpose of the communist elite. Thus only that elite has the necessary information on the basis of which it can calculate, devise strategies, control and eliminate anomic potentialities...A democratic system provides for a relatively free, multidirectional flow of information, thus making it possible for all the structures to calculate and to act effectively."[33]

Then, political communication can be used as a variable for comparing modern and primitive political systems. All structures of a political system—whether for mal like those of legislature, executive, judiciary, political parties and interest groups and informal like those of family, kinship, lineage groups, face-to-face groups, neighbourhoods, communities, village caste, status and class groups, ethnic and linguistic groups, etc. may be found involved in the performance of communication functions. As Almond says: "What distinguishes a modern political system from a traditional or primitive one is the fact that in the modern system the specialised communication structure is more elaborate, and that it penetrates the unspecialised or intermittent structures of political communication...Traditional or primitive political communication is performed intermittently by kinship, lineage, status, and village groups. Specialised media of communication are present only to a limited degree, if they are present at all."[34]

Finally, political systems may also be compared according to the ways in which they combine the 'styles' of communication such as 'manifest' or 'latent', 'specific' or 'diffuse', 'particularistic' or 'generalistic', 'affectively neutral' or 'affective'. Almond makes the implications of all these terms very clear by adding: "A manifest political communication is an explicit message; a latent one is a mood readable only from behavioural or expressive cues. A specific message is a statement of a political event which separates the political from the non-political and involves explicit cognitive discrimination. A specific political event is reported as having occurred, as occurring, or as likely to occur, with the estimate of probability, and sometimes with the consequences, spelled out. A particularistic message is one which by virtue of its language, or of its esoteric properties, cannot be easily transmitted at all beyond the limits of the esoteric audience. A general or universal message is one that is so couched as to be more or less transmissible throughout the entire communication network of the polity. An affectively neutral communication is an objective report of an event or events which may be combined with other reports and other data and be the ready object of analysis and inference. An affective communication creates difficulties in analysis and inference. It, cannot be as readily appraised or weighed, and fed into the stream of political inputs and outputs.[35]

Carrying his point further, Almond suggests four subvariables that should be taken into account while making a comparative study of different political systems. These are : homogeneity of political information, mobility of information, volume of information, and direction of the flow of information. It leads him to say that while in a developed and modernised political system we find homogeneity, mobility and multi-directional flow of voluminous information, we find heterogeneity and very little or almost no

33. Almond, *op. cit.,* pp. 47-48.
34. *ibid.,* pp. 48-49.
35. *ibid.,* p. 49.

mobility and restricted flow of information in traditional and transitional political systems. It is a study of the role of these subvariables that enables us to use the labels of 'open' and 'closed', 'modern' and 'primitive', 'developed' and 'developing' political systems. And it is on the basis of such an interpretation of the functional aspect of political communication approach that Almond comes to the point of suggesting how important is the communication function in the operations and cohesion of political systems.[36]

Quantification of Political Communication: Study of Social Cohesion and Change

Political communication approach "suggests the measurement of transactions of one state (or group) with other states (or groups) by 'metering' certain pertinent channels of the system. It also enables the investigator to locate an individual decision-maker within a number of nesting systems—the foreign minister within the cabinet and within the state, for example—and to relate data from each of these levels in an orderly fashion. One may, in effect, instal 'meter boxes' —anyone of a variety of measuring techniques—at four points in the state system; (1) just outside the input gate, so to speak, in order to measure objectively existent stimuli from the environment (especially the behaviour of other states); (2) 'inside' the foreign decision-making group, measuring the leadership's perceptions and attitudes towards the stimulus events taking place outside; (3) 'inside' the foreign decision-making group, measuring the leadership's perceptions of their own state's past, present and future attitudes, intents, purposes, and perferences towards other actors 'outside'; and (4) just 'outside' the output gate, in order to measure the overt behaviour that the decision-makers put in motion. Of course, it is also possible, wherever appropriate, to measure communications among component parts of a single nation-state system—between the Congress and the President, for example, or between pressure groups and an arm of the government, and so forth."[37]

This approach takes information as the basis of its expression. In general terms, information "can be defined as a patterned distribution or a patterned relationship between events."[38] A sequence of such processes forms a channel of communication and information is that aspect of the state description of each stage of the channel that has remained invariant from one stage to another.[39] It requires two conditions: first, at least some parts of the receiving system must be in a state of highly unstable equilibrium so that very small amount of energy carrying the signal is sufficient to start off a much larger process of change. Second, the receiver is required to use the standard of selectivity. It is owing to the application of this standard that there occurs a measurable distinction between the richness of information contained in different images. The upshoot of all this thus comes to be the emergence of information as a quantitative concept. Information "can be measured and contained, and the performance of communication channels in transmitting or distorting information can be evaluated in quantitative terms."[40]

If information can be measured, no matter in quite crude terms, we can also measure the cohesion or change of societies in terms of their ability to transmit information with smaller or larger losses or distortions in transmission. The smaller the losses or distortions, and the less the admixture of irrelevant informations (or noise) the more efficient is a given channel of communication or a given chain of command. Likewise, we can measure the speed and accuracy with which political information or

36. *ibid.*, p. 52.
37. See R.C. North, *op. cit.*, pp. 308-309.
38. See Karl Deutsch: "Communication Model and Decision Systems" in Charlesworth (ed.), *op. cit.*, p. 274.
39. *ibid.*
40. *ibid.*, p. 277.

commands are transmitted, and the extent to which the patterns contained in the command are still recognisable in the patterns of the action that are supposed to form its execution. For instance, we can measure that sympathies and antipathies of the people on a given issue of social, economic or political significance on the basis of information available with us and we may also make useful comparisons for the purpose of producing a well-tested and empirical analysis of social cohesion or change.[41]

Since information can be measured and results deduced therefrom, it should also be borne in mind in a study of informatics that society always remains in a state of flux. As there is change, proper information should be collected about the factors that bring about a change or retard its flow that may even lead to the emergence of conditions of violence and revolution. For this reason, political communication approach rejects the idea of equilibrium and seeks to offer an alternative to it. It is the idea of change that is contained in the notion of 'feedback'. As Deutsch warns: "If we think of a political system in terms of a classic mechanistic equilibrium, we are forced to think in terms of a system that is isolated from its environment and receives nothing important from the outside except disturbances. If these disturbances are small, the equilibrium will simply be restored through the automatic reaction of the system. If the disturbances are somewhat larger, we should expect them to elicit proportionately greater reactions tending to restore the *status quo*. If the disturbances are too great, we can only imagine that the system will somehow be overthrown or destroyed, but the equilibrium concept gives us little or no information as to just what will happen from then on, except vague indications of disaster. In short, the equilibrium concept is incapable of describing an important range of dynamic phenomena and it can indicate no time path for substantial change."[42]

It is with these standards that political communication approach strives to study problems relating to social (including political) cohesion and change. The collection of information and then its selection is taken as an instrument to understand the phenomena of stability versus change. The results may be put in quite quantified terms and the help of mathematical or statistical methods can be obtained for this purpose. It is the information that can conceivably be measured, though in an extremely crude way, in terms of the percentage of image points transmitted or lost on a line screen of given fineness, or in terms of the number of outstanding details lost in a slightly more refined way, information can be measured by the number of such details lost or transmitted in terms of their probability in the context of the possible alternative states of the communication channel; and their meaning could be estimated in the context of the probabilities of the set of details already stored in the receiver. Thus, Deutsch adds with a word of confidence: "The fact that the social scientists may have to use some of the cruder rather than the more refined methods for measuring the amounts of stored or transformed information, should not obscure the importance of being able to measure it at all."[43]

Exponents of the Communication Approach: Neuropolitics of Karl Deutsch

As already seen, cybernetics as developed by a mathematician like Norbert Wiener and a natural scientist like W. Ross Ashby "is fundamentally a body of theory and technique for the study of probabilities in different but analogous universes such as certain types of machines, animals, individual human beings, societies and nation-states—and the ways in

41. *ibid.*, p. 278.
42. *ibid.*, pp. 281-82.
43. *ibid.*, p. 277.

which message transactions function to control such universes."[44] Wiener was basically concerned with the characteristics and feedback systems—systems controlled on the basis of comparing an actual state with some pre-arranged norm or preferred state and then releasing energy to reduce.[45] As he says: "The process of receiving and of using information is the process of our adjusting to the contingencies of the outer environment, and of our living effectively with that environment."[46]

The concept of Wiener is thus summed up by Robert C. North : "On mechanical levels a controlled feedback system may be illustrated by thermostatic controls for maintaining desired temperatures within a house, by the self-aiming device of an anti-aircraft artillery piece, or the automatic pilot in a ship or aircraft. By force of analogy several of the basic functions of such servomechanisms can be compared with certain minimally necessary, if not sufficient, functions of living systems such as the individual human being, the work team, the corporation or the nation-state. Once these processes are identified, moreover, it should be possible to describe organisations on each level in terms of the probability that its components will perform their appropriate functions. In the long run it should also be possible with tolerance for insufficient information and random phenomena —to predict the system's behaviour and also the conflictual and cooperative or integrating transactions between or among systems."[47]

Political communication becomes political simulation at the hands of Kenneth Boulding who suggests the ways in which a human being operates according to analogous, complex, highly sophisticated, frequently illusive feedback or cybernetic principles. According to this theory of model-building, each one of us maintains an image of *what is* (the thermometer, so to speak) and an image of *what ought to be* (the preferred thermostat temperature setting). In highly over simplified terms, we behave in various ways in an effort to reduce the gap between the two parts of the image.' Viewed thus, he says that associations, organisations, societies and the nation-state itself" are built upon and held together by communications—by perceptions, by transactions, and by their willingness to validate a considerable portion of the expectations by appropriate reciprocal behaviours. Politics could not exist without communications, nor could wars be fought. In these terms, a modern nation-state may be viewed essentially as a decision and control system which relies on the exchange of messages in both its domestic affairs and its foreign relations."[49]

However, the most important name in this direction is that of Karl Deutsch whose general interest in the control of the political systems "has led him to broaden his perspectives to cover material concerning homeostatis and cybernetics."[50] If it should prove possible, as David Easton has suggested, "to devise a theory of the behaviour of political phenomena that can provide a complete explanation of the basic processes of those phenomena—whether they be found within the state or beyond its borders—then the work of Karl Deutsch *(The Nerves of Government)* will have constituted one of the major steps in this direction."[51] The aim of Deutsch "is to use the concepts and methods of the science of cybernetics to provide explanations for not simply the survival but the *growth* of political systems and to predict the consequences of changes that affect the structure of systems. His work can, in a sense,

44. R.C. North, *op. cit.*, p. 300.
45. *ibid., p. 301.*
46. *ibid.*
47. *ibid.*
48. Boulding : *The Image* (Ann Arbor : Univ. of Michigan Press, 1956), p. 11.
49. North, *op. cit.*, p. 301,
50. Young, *op. cit.*, p. 54,
51. See Davies and Lewis, *op. cit.*, p. 71.

be seen as an explanation of some of the assumptions underlying that of Easton, as well as an attempt to refine and further develop (if perhaps in a slightly different direction) the analysis of the 'life processes' of the political system that Easton has undertaken."[52]

The main features of Deutsch's neuropolitics may be thus summed up:

1. ***Society as a Machine :*** According to Deutsch, the social system with political system as its part survive and develop, because they contain mechanisms which allow or encourage habit forming and other activities that go with this : the acquiring of information; the selection and storage of this information (the facility of memory); the selection and development of norms relating to the use of information gained. Thus, he is able to conclude that the 'inner source of political power' (the relatively coherent and stable structures of memories, habits and values) depends on existing facilities for social communication both from the past to the present and between contemporaries and also to suggest that in a political system information precedes compulsion.[53]
2. ***New Definition of Politics :*** One of the important concerns of Deutsch is to reduce the importance of the notion *of power* as a component of continuing political activity. To him, politics is concerned with the attainment of social goals; it is the sphere in which the decisions are made with respect to the whole society—decisions which are enforceable. The 'core area' of politics is the 'area of enforceable decisions' and the 'essence of politics' for him is the 'dependable coordination of human efforts for the attainment of the goals of society'.[54]
3. ***New Notion of Government :*** The function of government is to control the direction of information into or away from particular channels of communication. Thus, its main task is to 'steer' information rather than to exercise 'power' over the individuals. Essentially speaking, control involves the transmission of messages and the understanding of control processes is a branch of communication engineering, not of power engineering. Government should be seen as involving this kind of steering rather than as involving, predominantly, the use of power. In a political system, the government is like the steering of a ship; it is a form of administration of communication channels.[55]
4. ***Miniature Communications System :*** The infrastructure of a political system is constituted by political parties and interest groups. They are interconnected and open, but they are also capable of steering themselves and with mechanisms (human and institutional) that allow them to adapt and modify their structures and behaviour. Conflicts between the political system and its subsystems should not be seen as 'contests of wills' but as the results of collusions caused because of the failure of steering facilities or of the signals of the systems.[56]
5. ***Homeostatis instead of Equilibrium :*** Deutsch desires to furnish a model that is not static but dynamic. That is, he is not for 'equilibrium' that indicates a stationary model of a political system. He calls the whole idea of equilibrium as being both mechanistic and excessively detached from the impact of environmental factors. Such an approach is not adequate to handle directional movement along a path through time. Politics is a changing phenomenon and thus he stands for a dynamic situation what he terms 'homeostatis'. Political

52. *ibid.*
53. *ibid.,* p. 73.
54. *ibid.,* p. 72.
55. *ibid.,* p. 74.
56. *ibid.*

system performs its functions and accomplishes its objectives in such a way as to change their basic position *vis-a-vis* their environments; it also has some ability to change itself in the course of steering towards various goals. Information should come from its past and present as well as from its external and internal environments to exercise its impact upon the operation of the political system. As information must be continuous, the system must remain open for change.[57]

6. ***Concept of Feedback or Servomechanism :*** Feedback is, indeed, the key concept in the neuropolitics of Deutsch. It means a network of communications that produces action in response to an input of information and includes the results of its own action in the information by which it modifies its subsequent behaviour. Feedback may be negative or positive. A negative feedback system is one which transmits back to itself information that is the result of decisions and actions taken by the system, and which leads the system to change its behaviour in pursuit of the goals which it has set itself. 'Load' indicates the total amount of information which a system may possess at a particular time. 'Lag' indicates the amount of delay that the system experiences between reporting the consequences of decisions and acting on the information that it has received. 'Gain' is an indication of the manner in which the system responds to the information that it has received. 'Lead' illustrates the extent to which a system has the capacity to react to predictions about the future consequences of decisions and actions.[58]

Deutsch's approach to the study of politics is quite novel. As he himself says elsewhere : "Politics, like all techniques of making and implementing decisions, is not an end in itself. Indeed, we have a range of generous visions, from early Christianity to H.G. Wells envisaging a state of social development where all social compulsions and with it all politics will become obsolete. Whatever one may think of these hopes, politics in the world of today is an essential instrument of social learning. It will

Deutsch's Model of Political Communication

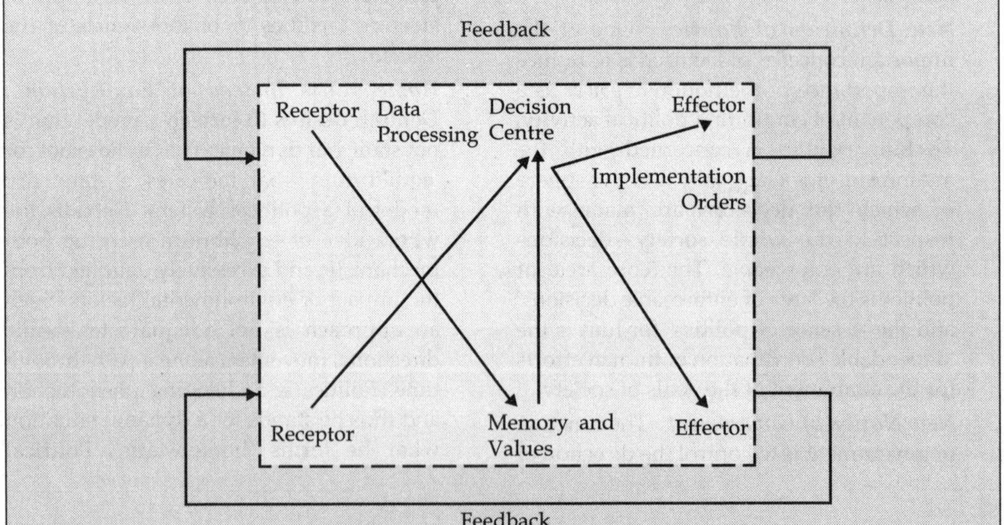

57. *ibid., p. 75.*
58. *ibid.,* pp. 76-77.

be more likely to function as an instrument of survival and growth, rather than destruction, if it is guided by the cognitive insights. All studies of politics, and all techniques and models suggested as instruments of political analysis, have this purpose : that men should be more able to act in politics with their eyes open."[59]

Critical Appraisal

The political communication approach, as discussed in the preceding sections, may be criticised on these grounds :

1. Political communication approach, though different from such an approach in other disciplines like neurophysiology, mathematics and electrical engineering, has been criticised for elaborating an essentially engineering and mechanistic orientation towards human behaviour. One may ask as to how the laws of a natural and fixed science like that of electrical engineering can be applied to the study of human behaviour that is never fixed and definite. Man is not a machine and thus society cannot be regarded as a mechanistic arrangement. Thus, it can be said that the exponents of this approach, particularly Karl Deutsch, exaggerate their conclusion in the direction of political simulation. The approach of political communication "offers a model that seems far more manipulable than most actual political operations; it often seems to discount irrational, fortuitous, or random behaviour, and above all, it does not deal adequately with the nuances of human thought processes, the psychological consequences of world views and value systems, the subsocieties of political leadership, and the nebulous quality of many political relations."[60]
2. It can also be said that the entire approach of political communication depends upon the extension of an analogy between a natural and a social system. What philosophers like Plato, John of Salisbury, Hobbes, Rousseau and Herbert Spencer did in order to understand and explain political phenomenon in their own ways, has now been done by others like Deutsch who have made use of the terms of natural sciences to describe and explain the same phenomenon. Such a shift from the language of natural sciences to that of a social science is bound to involve significant discontinuities and incongruities. Naturally, the model of Deutsch "ultimately becomes so complex that it tends to move away from being a working model and towards becoming a scheme. Though the core elements of the model are not unduly complex, great problems arise when Deutsch begins to expand the structure to deal with the nuances of political reality. What could remain a working model in the essentially operational field of communications becomes considerably more diffuse when applied to the more nebulous variables of political behaviour."[61]
3. There is not only the difficulty of applying models picked up from a natural to a social science, it is all the more difficult to make it useful for the purpose of social sciences. Some terms of electrical engineering may either remain unapplied, or they may be misapplied and for this reason it is likely that we get a confused picture of a political model. The theory thus "suffers from serious drawbacks both at the structural level and in substantive matters. It fails to demarcate the proper structures which are needed to deal with the information flows concerning political change, transformation and growth. It is, however, at the substantive level that the approach presents the largest

59. Karl Deutsch : "Communication Models and Decision Systems" in James C. Charlesworth (ed.), *op. cit.*, p. 299.
60. Young, *op. cit.*, p. 60.
61. *ibid.*, p. 61.

number of difficulties. It attaches far too great an importance to the qualities of formalism and excessive rationalism, whereas we know that the real decision-making procedures in political life are often incremental in nature rather than expressive of the rationality that Deutsch demands from them."[62]

4. It is true that social sciences are concerned with systems that are 'steered', it is also important to note that a cybernetic model is a very general, abstract one, and its principal concepts may acquire different meanings according to the particular system to which they are applied, be it a computer, an irrigation system, the human brain or society[63]. In a most abstract form, then, a cybernetic system is a set of communication processes through which certain impulses, information, which it receives from the environment, are processed into impulses which the system, in turn, releases into the environment.[64] In order to do this, certain structures within the system must receive and transmit information (detectors and effectors). However, a cybernetic system is steered towards a particular goal, and as the system exists in a changing environment, it needs structures to enable it to 'steer'. Deutsch characterises these as 'decision areas'. But the difficulty arises when we find that the key terms (like load, lead, lag, autonomy, perception etc.) cannot be reduced into a causal form in each and every situation and this all makes his theoretical import as 'skimpy.'[65] It is also remarked that, despite Deutsch's attempt to develop eventually a theory of politics, both national and international, his own formulations "were explicitly not theory but parts of an 'ongoing enterprise' to be developed into theory at some unspecified later stage."[66] Keeping it in view, a critic like Meehan has observed : "But the fact remains that Deutsch is still a very long way from making effective use of the formal structure embodied in cybernetics and in information theory."[67]

Though it is true that the cybernetic model loosely adopted by Karl Deutsch and others for analysing the stability and instability of political systems in the light of communications system is not rich enough to do all that they intend to do with it, we cannot ignore the fact that the work of an innovator is always subject to criticism.[68] Despite all points of weakness, as given above, it may be admitted that the approach looks promising too. "It would be premature, however, to settle upon any single model, paradigm, pre-theory, or particular set of tools. The most rewarding procedure seems to require, for the time being, at least, that encouragement of alternative methods and techniques with the hope that various investigations will serve to cross-check each other—and perhaps reveal important convergences. It is almost self-evident that communication approaches and decision-making approaches are complimentary. In the long run several competing measurement devices are likely to prove reciprocally reinforcing in somewhat analogous ways."[69]

---

62. S.P. Varma : *Modern Political Theory* (Delhi : Vikas, 1975), p. 329.
63. R.L. Tooze, *op. cit.*, pp. 215-17.
64. J.D. de Vree, *op. cit.*, p. 91.
65. M. Haas : *International Systems : A Behavioural Approach* (New York : Chandler, 1974), p. 365.
66. R.L. Tooze, *op. cit.*, p. 227.
67. Eugene J. Meehan : *Contemporary Political Thought : A Critical Study* (Homewood, Illinois : The Dorsey Press, 1967), p. 336.
68. Wasby, *op. cit.*, p. 44
69. Robert C. North, *op. cit.*, pp. 315-16.

8

Political Simulation

> Political Science has always resorted to metaphors, to the device of proceeding from the known to the unknown. Those who criticise the use of models need to understand that they too must use them. Accordingly, much of the conflict over the use of models is spurious. The choice is not between models and no models, but between critical consciousness of their use and an uncritical acceptance. An open and hygienic use of models may or may not aid us in developing empirically sound political theory, but it would enable us to run far less risk than we take with the hidden, implicit and rigidified metaphors that one frequently finds in the textbooks of Political Science.
>
> **—M. Landau[1]**

An interesting aspect of contemporary political theory finds place in the use of models as working intellectual constructs to represent social and physical situations. Though largely used in the disciplines of natural sciences, simulation is regarded as an attempt to reproduce the selected aspects of a system that may be real or hypothetical depending upon the findings and experiments of a researcher engaged in such an exercise in his laboratory or study room. Political simulation is, therefore, a study of the models and methods that are neither mutually exclusive, nor should they be invariably regarded by their exponents as complete substitutes for the traditional approaches in political science.[2] It should, however, be borne in mind that here an attempt is made to translate an imaginative situation into one in which human beings play their roles and try to react to a particular situation as if the real occupants would have acted. If so, simulation is a very old exercise in the sphere of this discipline. Thinkers like Plato, More and Hegel drew picture of an ideal state, while others like Aristotle, Montesquieu and Bryce gave us models of constitutions that would suit different societies at different stages of development. What is of paramount significance in this regard is that here we "treat the models as plain intellectual constructs, or frameworks of a rigid nature, which can help us in organising our main streams of thinking and in directing our research. A model may include various kinds of categories, assumptions, postulates and concepts, with the help of which we are able to sort out the data collected by us during our research, analyse the data so arranged and determine the relationships between one set of data and another. A model may be expressed in words, charts or graphs."[3]

Game Theory

Communication approach, game theory and decision-making analysis are the three main conceptual frameworks that should be studied as exercises in political simulation. While communication approach has already been

1. M. Landau : "On the Basis of Metaphor in Political Analysis" in *Social Research,* Vol. 28 (1961), p. 353.
2. P.K. Ghosh : *Studies in Contemporary Political Theory* (Calcutta : Minerva, 1972), p. 70.
3. S.P. Varma : *Modern Political Theory* (Delhi : Vikas, 1975), p. 311.

discussed in the previous chapter, here we shall take up only two theories relating to game of conflict and decision-making. Game theory is defined as a body of thought dealing with rational decision strategies in situations of conflict and competition, wherein each participant or player seeks to maximise his gains and minimise his losses.[4] This theory stands for the application of mathematical models to the study of a political phenomenon. As Shubik says: "Game theory is a mathematical method for the study of some aspects of conscious decision-making in situations involving the possibilities of conflict and, or, co-operation. It deals with the processes in which the individual decision-unit has only partial control over the strategic factors affecting its environment. The decision-unit may be an individual, a firm, a government or any formal or informal institution."[5]

Nature and Implications : As pointed out above, the game theory is an application of mathematical models to the study of political phenomenon. It operates on the assumption that the political process "is the confrontation like a chess game, or a contest between two merchants or brokers, or the manoeuvres of rival political candidates, or the counteractions of opposed diplomats. Needless to say, institutions and countries can be deployed as individuals."[6] As a matter of fact, this theory "owes its genesis to parlour games like chess, chicken, poker, or bridge with obvious elements of conflict decision-making and co-operation, played between two or more players, where the decisions of each player are contingent upon the decisions of others, and the central point, therefore, is the interdependence among the decisions of different players participating in the game. In a situation of this kind, where each player is interested in 'winning' the game and two or more individuals have to make choices and have preferences, regarding the outcomes of these choices, it is necessary that they have some knowledge of the choices available to, and made by, each other and of the preferences the other players have in their choices. The crux of the parlour games is that it is not possible for any one player to make a choice: whatever choice he makes depends inextricably on the choice or the choices made by the other players."[7]

Though game theory is a part of the decision-making analysis in the discipline of mathematics, in behavioural sciences it has been incorporated into the models and experiments of both conflict and decision-making in a conflict-ridden situation. As such, it can be named 'conflict theory' as well (see table given on next page) for the reason that conflict "has been conceptualised as an outcome of exchanges between individuals, as a spatial relationship, as dissensus or conflict of values, as competition or conflicts of interest, as incompatibility of role expectations and/or as a game."[8] We can find that in the exchange models constructed by some contemporary social theorists, conflict in a political system "takes the form of competition, which is conceptualised as the exchange by which reciprocal relationships between individuals and or groups are transformed into unilateral or superior-subordinate relationships."[9]

Leaving aside the case of some games incorporating mixed strategies, it is generally assumed that each participant's strategy is predicated on the strategy chosen by his opponent. It is the information about all possible

4. *ibid.*, p. 340.
5. Martin Shubik : "The Uses of Game Theory" in James C. Charlesworth (ed.) : *Contemporary Political Analysis* (New York : Free Press, 1967), p. 240.
6. Charlesworth: "Introduction", *ibid.*, p. 6.
7. Varma, *op. cit.*, p. 341.
8. Stephen L. Wasby : *Political Science : The Discipline and Its Dimensions : An Introduction* (Calcutta : Scientific Book Agency, 1970), p. 122.
9. *ibid.*

strategies, rules and pay-offs or their possibilities that enables each player to maximise benefits while minimising losses. These games "describe a process of interaction in which the players or decision-makers' ability to rank their preferences, estimate probabilities, and make impersonal comparisons is assumed. Predictions are made by the participants about the outcomes of future competitive and or co-operative interactions; the interaction, co-operative or competitive, is determined by this comparison."[10]

Type, Forms and Characteristics defining the Forms of Conflict[11] in Game Theory

Types of conflict	Forms of conflict	Characteristics defining the forms of conflict
Competitive (interest)	Games (zero sum)	Certainty or uncertainty Perception of mutually incompatible goal Objective : outwit and eliminate competition or compromise by saddle-point determination Use of threats and sanctions
	Games (non-zero sum)	Uncertainty Option of perceiving goals as mutually incompatible or temporarily mutually shared Perception of the alternative rules of games, but discrepant values leading to disagreement over selection of rules which shall be considered binding. Objective : if goals, mutually exclusive, outwit and eliminate competition; if goals, temporarily shared, incur a minimum level of risk and cost Use of threats and sanctions
Value	Fights	Uncertainty Mutually incompatible goals Discrepant values leading to disagreement over selection of rules which shall be considered binding Objective : eliminate competitor Use of threats and sanctions
Non-competitive	Debates	Uncertainty Mutually shared problems Discrepant cognitive processes in the beginning stage (s) Objective : change opponent's mind; do not eliminate him Absence of threats and sanctions

10. *ibid.,* p. 125.
11. *ibid.,* p. 124.

Concepts and Assumptions : It may be discerned from what we have said above that the theory of games has certain concepts and assumptions of its own. These are :

1. There are the *players* or the decision-makers; they may be individuals or institutions.
2. Each player is a *rational entity* with well defined objectives and he has at his disposal some set of resources with the help of which he tries to combat the forces against which he is playing his game.
3. There are the *rules of the game* that each player has to observe. It refers to the distribution of resources and the strategic possibilities open to each player in his employment.
4. There are certain situations that may be described as *outcomes* in a game. The players are supposed to be engaged in choosing alternatives for the sake of winning, or at least not losing, the game.
5. The full range of possible outcomes is called the *prospects.* The inventor of the game generally designs a very small range of prospects, limited in number and possible combinations.
6. The reward of the game is called *pay-off.* The best pay-off is victory, *draw* is the second best.
7. *Strategy* is the most important concept that informs the player to act in a way so that his purpose is served. The norm of rationality is, for this reason, sufficiently diluted. It leads to two supplementary concepts—minimax strategy—that means minimum of risk and maximum of pay-off for the player and saddle point in which the two parties end up with exactly the same pay-offs.

While applying the theory of games to the particular phenomenon of coalition formation, Gamson suggests these assumptions:[12]

1. The actors can be ranked by resources (votes), position or by some other characteristic.
2. The actors have the same information about the initial distribution of resources and the pay-off for any localition.
3. All coalition strategies are equally difficult or costly.
4. No actor can be eliminated from the group or added to the group, and no actor has veto power.
5. Each actor will expect the other actors to demand a share of the pay-off proportional to the amount of resources which each has contributed to the coalition.
6. The chooser will seek a minimal winning coalition which is characterised by maximum advantage or minimum disadvantage of strength relative to his coalition partner.
7. The chooser will seek a minimal winning coalition which is characterised by the fact that the defection of any member will make the coalition no longer winning.
8. The pay-off matrix is in the zero-sum form, i.e., no single alternative will maximise the pay-off to all participants and the decisions to be made involves more than two members attempting to maximise their pay-off.
9. The decision rule is a simple majority.

With the help of these concepts and assumptions, we can evolve a framework to show as to who will co-operate with whom to achieve a goal that cannot be attained in any other way. We can make even predictions that would provide the basis for linking conflict, coalition and integration theories. It may be said that co-operation itself is a type of competitive strategy, because after identifying the 'enemy', the actors form a coalition to outrank him and ultimately eliminate him from the competition. Seeing that he is about to be eliminated, the 'enemy' actor will tend to pursue a competitive expansion strategy to enlarge the size of the group to regain supremacy. This process may continue until

12. See W.A. Gamson : "A Theory of Coalition Formation" in *American Sociological Review,* Vol. XXVI, pp. 373-382 and 565-73.

one coalition can no longer recruit new supporters or until viable rules call an end to the competition.[13]

Types of Game Theory : Before we are in a position to judge the worth of this theory, it is necessary to point out that there are several types of this framework that may be put into two broad categories:

1. **Two-Persons Zero-Sum Games :** It is a game of pure opposition. It is strictly competitive. There is no need for communication, discussion or bargaining. There is no joint gain or savings to be had from reasoning or co-operation. It is completely meaningful to call the participants in such a struggle opponents. In such a situation, there are only two players with the result that the gains of one are always equal to the losses of another.
2. **Two-Persons Non-Constant-Sum Games :** It is conceivable that both sides gain by a settlement or by means of a *quid pro quid* arrangement in which other concessions or side payments are made between the two antagonists so that they can both benefit from following a co-operative solution to their differences.
3. **N-Person Non-Constant-Sum Games :** There may be two or more persons in contest and they may act on the basis of some coalition adjustment that will require that the pay-off is divisible on the basis of some principle of distribution. It may become possible for two or more players to co-operate against others by pooling their resources and making collective decisions during the play. The players may 'gang up' to form their 'protocoalitions' reducing the number of their adversaries.

A student of comparative politics may feel as to what is the relevance of all this study for his purpose. The answer is simple. This theory has two important dimensions. It has its application in the field of mathematics and statistics where its assumptions have an wholly abstract and symbolic character that have no relationship with the empirical world. In social sciences like economics, sociology and politics, the assumptions of this theory may, however, be applied to present a quantifiable and measurable analysis of the phenomenon. With the study of the concepts and assumptions of this theory we may describe several crucial areas of contest like elections, voting behaviour, process of negotiation, military movements, coalition formations etc. For this purpose, we should also look at the types of game theory where we are concerned with the number of players and interactions going on among them for the sake of having the best possible pay-off.

Application of Game Theory to Politics : The history of the application of mathematical apparatus to the study of politics dates back to the Greeks. Plato in his *Plutarch* said that 'God always geometrizes' and his student Aristotle wrote several complex treatises on mathematical logic. Thales and Pythagoras added abstractness, generality and intellectual respectability to Egyptian practical geometry. Right from the days of the Greeks to the present, there have been many eminent political thinkers like Thomas Hobbes and Bertrand Russell who sought to explain their ideas by the use of mathematical formulations. Hence, Howard Alker says that it "should not be a surprising discovery that mathematics has strongly influenced the development of Western political thought."[14]

The use of game theory developed in the 1920's as a result of the works of Emil Borel. However, it is John Von Neumann who made it very popular. His collaborator Oskar Morgenstern's contribution should also be lauded in this connection. Primarily it was made use of in the field of economics, but soon after its application was made to the study of political phenomenon in which the contributions of R. Duncan Luce, Howard Raiffa, Martin Shubik

13. Wasby, *op. cit.*, p. 128.
14. H.R. Alker, Jr. : *Mathematics and Politics* (New York: Macmillan, 1965), p. 1.

and Anatol Rapoport deserve special mention. Riker made its best use for the study of coalition behaviour, Schelling made its use for the study of conflict-ridden situations and Morton A. Kaplan showed how this theory could be utilised for the study of the systems and processes in the field of international politics.

Kaplan's *System and Process in International Relations* shows that, according to systems analysis, international system has among its subsystems a set of actors called international actors. The international actors are national actors and supra-national actors. The supra-national actors are the block actors and universal actors. The NATO and the COMINFORM are the examples of block actors. The United Nations is an example of universal actors. International action is taking place between international actors. International actors are treated separately as systems in such a case inputs from the international system would function as parameters. This holds also for the subsystems of nation-states. Again, the internal system of the international actors are considered as parameters for the international system and their outputs as the variables of the international system.[15]

The systems approach of Kaplan is full of weaknesses and one may not safely say whether his three chapters on 'strategy and statecraft' are meant as a guide for policy-makers, or they merely suggest the ways in which they may use their knowledge for some purpose. Schelling's *The Strategy of Conflict* has an importance of its own. Instead of applying the rules of the game theory to the study of politics at the national and international levels in an almost blind manner, he carefully looks towards the problems from a realistic standpoint. There is much difference between theory and practice; as such, the 'game' on a theoretical plane is different from the 'game' as it is played between and among the states and institutions. He has recognised the fact that most of the international relationships involve a certain degree of conflict and a certain amount of mutual dependence. For this reason, he has introduced the concept of 'bargaining games' or 'mixed motive games'. Accommodating psychological aspects of the situation, he has introduced certain new concepts also as 'making threats', 'giving promises', 'relinquishing the initiative', 'identifying friends and enemies', 'delegating authorities', 'accepting mediation', etc. The choice of strategy, according to him, "is defined by empirical considerations rather than by purely formal operations and involves, as an essential part of the study, an effort to understand the mixed motive game. Schelling, thus, has considerably enriched the game theory by the introduction of complex human experience into the procedures of decision-making."[16]

However, the most significant place is held by Riker's *The Theory of Political Coalitions* wherein his primary objective in applying the theory of games to the study of international politics is to find out some of the general principles that govern the formation of coalitions and associations whose decisions are controlled by the coalitions. He has applied three major principles—size principle, strategic principle, and disequilibrium principle. By 'size principle' he means that the players are concerned with the maintenance of the size of their coalition to a point that all will ensure winning. By 'strategic principle' he means that the players keep on changing their strategy for the purpose of having the best possible pay-off. They may form coalitions or protocoalitions in order to reduce the number of their adversaries and to divide the fruits of the pay-offs according to the principle of adjustments. Finally, by 'disequilibrium principle' he means that politics is always unstable. However, it is in the interest of the players to try to maintain a state of

15. D.C. Jha : "New Dimensions of International Relations" in *Indian Journal of Political Science,* Vol. XXXIV, No. 4, 1973, pp. 443-44.
16. Varma, *op. cit.,* p. 350.

equilibrium so that their strategy proves rewarding. He thus discusses the sources of disequilibrium and the means of maintaining equilibrium and examines exogenous and indogenous factors which influence them.[17]

Critical Estimate : It may be said that game theory has its own weaknesses. It is basically deductive and, for this reason, it cannot be successfully applied to an empirical investigation. It assumes that the decision-makers are perfectly rational creatures, or they are amoral in their calculations and they have perfect information available to them. This is never possible in practice. Even the best players may be having no information or wrong information about certain things and they may not act at all in a purely rational manner. Moreover, the theory is not concerned with ethics while man is an ethical being. It is concerned merely with 'situational ethics', as the player is concerned with the outcomes and not with the intermediate processes; he looks at the strategy of the partner he is likely to choose and not why he chooses that particular strategy. Motives and convictions are kept out of the room, since the player is concerned with the object of having the best possible pay-off. Thus, this theory "runs the same danger as any theory in being too abstract, even in the propensity of the theorists to forget, when they try to predict or to prescribe, that all their theory was based on some abstract premises whose relevance needs to be confirmed."[18]

Game theory, perhaps more than most of the tools of inquiry, can be criticised only within the context in which it appears; that is, unless the purpose of inquiry is stated very clearly, it is quite impossible to say, whether or not, game theory will prove useful.[19] Criticism, in general, usually avoids considering the relation between the purpose for which game theory is used and its accomplishments. It is one thing to recommend game theory on the basis for relational decision by governments and quite another matter to suggest that game theory can lead to a clarification of concepts or suggest ways in which particular phenomena like coalitions might be explained.[20] We may perhaps appreciate the view of Karl Deutsch that in the study of politics, use of game theory may not be very helpful.[21]

It is true that the game theory is not an empirical study of how people make decisions, it is a deductive theory about the conditions that their decisions would have to satisfy "in order to meet demands rationally or consistently."[22] It should also not be forgotten that in the context of politics it may be made use of for the study of several interesting issues like military generals engaged in the battles, diplomats involved in the processes of bargaining and negotiations, politicians attempting to influence the voters, legislators trying to put together the appropriate coalitions, etc. The only requirement is that this theory should be applied to the study of politics with abundant caution. As Shubik says: "Given a sufficient understanding of both political science and formal game theory, its uses are many though not necessarily all of spectacular import. At the level of political philosophy, formal game models help in the investigations of concepts such as power, freedom, and equity. In the study of bureaucratic process they help in

---

17. *ibid.,* p. 348.
18. T.C. Schelling : "What is Game Theory ?" in Charlesworth (ed.), *op. cit.,* p. 237.
19. See Eugene J. Meehan : *Contemporary Political Thought: A Critical Study* (Homewood, Illinois : The Dorsey Press, 1967), p. 311. For a very interesting study see Albert Wohlstetter's "Sin and Game in America" in Martin Shubik (ed.) : *Readings in Game Theory and Political Behaviour* (New York : 1954) and Anatol Rapoport and C. Orwant : "Experimental Games : A Review" in *Behavioural Sciences,* Vol. Ill, No. 1, 1962.
20. Meehan, *op. cit.,* p. 314.
21. Karl Deutsch : "Game Theory and Politics : Some Problems of Application" in Sidney Umer (ed.) : *Introductory Readings in Political Behaviour* (New York : Rand and McNally, 1961).
22. Varma, *op. cit.,* p. 352.

investigating communication, information and centralisation or decentralisation of the decision-making. In the study of the bargaining and negotiation they help to explore the meaning of concepts such as threat. They also raise questions concerning the meaning of social and political stability."[23]

Decision-Making Approach

Like game theory, decision-making approach is another exercise in the sphere of political simulation. Both theories "overlap in many of the units selected and the situations subsumed by each; they differ, however, in one of their major characteristics. While in the former, actor's behaviour is assumed to be at least partially determined by the behaviour of others, this relationship may be, but it is not necessarily assumed in decision theory. This difference becomes clearer when we consider the common conceptualising of decision-making."[24] It should also be noted here that while the theory of games has its particular place in the discipline of mathematics, the concept of decision-making is prominent in psychology, social psychology, economics, business administration, psychiatry and other disciplines in addition to political science and each discipline has its own particular emphasis. What is needed here is that a student of politics should keep himself confined exclusively to theorising about political decision-making and thus he should ignore the potential relevance of findings and formulations from non-political disciplines that, by analogy or adaptation, might usefully be applied to the study of decisions involving political issues and situations.[25]

Meaning and Characteristics : Decision-making is usually defined as a process or sequence of activities involving stages of problem recognition, search for information, definition of alternatives, and the selection by an actor (s) of one from two or more alternatives consistent with the ranked preferences identified in the first three stages that will maximise or 'satisfice' the actor's goal. In many instances, the last stage has been defined to include a relationship (additive or multiplicative) between possible alternatives, preferences or utilities attached to each of the alternatives, and the probabilities of alternatives becoming the outcomes. These probabilities may and may not include or depend upon the actions of others.[26] The conceptualisation of decision-making has prompted the decision theorist-researcher to attempt to deduce patterns and or to infer patterns from the data gathered to answer the following questions:[27]

1. Who made the decision?
2. What was the decision?
3. When was the decision made?
4. How was the decision made?
5. Where was the decision made?
6. What were the characteristics of the decision situation?
7. To what class or subclass of decisions does this decision belong?
8. Why was the decision made?

Keeping all these alternatives in view, Wasby thus says: "Decision-makers are variously defined as those individuals who have public or legal responsibility for certain classes of political decisions; these who actually participate or share in the decision-making; those who contribute information to individuals participating in decision-making; those who decide which decisions or alternatives will be considered; those who belong to the more powerful economic, political, military, and or social elites; those who participate in the most types of decision issues; those who are leaders

---

23. Shubik, *op. cit.,* p. 272.
24. See W.J. Gore and J.W. Dyson (ed.) : *The Making of Decisions* (New York, 1964), pp. 1-63.
25. James A. Robinson and R. Roger Majak : "The Theory of Decision Making" in Charlesworth (ed.), *op. cit.,* pp. 175-76.
26. Wasby, *op. cit.,* p. 131.
27. *ibid.,* pp. 131-32.

of interest groups; those who administer or carry out the decision; those who have veto power on a decision; and/or those who select the decision rules. The particular definition of decision-makers by a theorist-researcher appears to be at least partially determined by his perception of the issue area which he wishes to investigate."[28]

What creates a serious problem in the way of offering a precise definition of this term is how to distinguish between a political from non-political decision. Either we should be guided by the suggestion of Merriam that "only confusion will be created by trying to draw too sharp and exclusive a line between political and other forms of organisation" and that, on the contrary, "a clearer view is gained by frankly recognising the fundamental similarity between them and the parallel and frequent interchangeability of functions";[29] or we should accept the advice of Diesing that due distinction should be maintained between economic, legal, social, technical and political decisions on the basis of differences in rationality.[30] He defines political decisions as those that concern the 'preservation and improvement of decision structures'. As he says: "All decisions occur within a decision structure of some sort, but political decisions in addition have decision structures as their special subject-matter."[31] Same trend is visible in the works of Leoni who separates political decisions from the non-political ones on the basis that political decisions result 'in the emergence of power' or the modification of the previously existing power situation'.[32]

Decision Process Cluster : Let us see how decisions are made? The simple answer is that all decisions are made according to a process—the sum of the particular techniques, methods, procedures and strategies, whether conscious or unconscious, by which a given decision is made. The political process must be regarded as the intersection of numerous lesser processes or subprocesses, the final cumulative outcome of which is, what David Easton calls, the authoritative allocation of values. Though it is true that a distinction can be brought about between political and non-political decisions, the problem of the decision-making process is such that it involves several other dimensions such as psychological, social and mechanical. That is, apart from seeing as to how decisions are made, we are also required to see as to who decides, under what conditions or upon what occasion the decision is made, in what organisational context the decision is taken, or what might be the results of the decision and the like. Viewed thus, we must look at the processes of decision-making that may be of three kinds —psychological, social and quasi-mechanical.

First, we take up the case of the *psychological* process. According to classical economic theorists, men take that decision that offers them best alternative on the basis of known utilities. This may be termed 'rationalist' model that may be correct and also incorrect depending on the situations of the case. Different from this is the 'satisfying' model of Herbert Simon who says that decision-making process involves 'bounded rationality' whereby he means that a decision will be adopted when an alternative seems to meet minimal standards, or is good enough and that a decision is not dependent on the availability of all possible alternatives from which the best may be selected.[33] Other writers have laid emphasis on the role of psychological factors that play their part in the decision-making process. For

28. *ibid.*, pp. 134-35.
29. See Charles Merriam : *Political Power* (New York : McGraw Hill, 1934).
30. Paul Diesing : *Reason in Society : Five Types of Decisions and their Social Conditions* (Illinois, 1962), p. 198.
31. *ibid.*
32. Bruno Leoni : "The Meaning of 'Political' in Political Decisions" in *Political Studies* (Oxford: Clarendon Press, 1957), pp. 225-39.
33. Simon : *Models of Man : Social and Rational* (New York : Wiley, 1957).

instance, Harold Lasswell speaks of seven functional stages through which all decisions are processed:[34]

(a) information—problem identification and information search,
(b) recommendation—formulation of alternatives,
(c) prescription—sanctioned selection of alternatives,
(d) invocation—provisional enforcement,
(e) application—special implementation,
(f) appraisal—monitoring and review of the decision and its effects, and
(g) termination—renewal, revision or appeal.

In brief, the purpose of the writers on this subject is to suggest that certain psychological factors definitely play their part in the decision-making process.

Then, we come to see the *social* process that has its part in the sphere of making decisions. Here different writers have laid stress on different factors: Almond on interest aggregation, Riker on coalition formation, Bentley on group interaction and articulation, Boulding on the images made through feedback and communication process, Deutsch on cybernetics, Dahl on hierarchy and polyarchy, Lindblom on bargaining and price mechanism, etc. The purpose of social theorists, in this direction, is to show that the role of several social forces like those of manipulation, negotiation, bargaining, mutual adjustments, centralisation and decentralisation of leadership, etc. should also be taken into account while discussing how and why decisions are made.

`Finally, we take up the *quasi-mechanical* process that is characterised particularly by the unconscious role of the decision-makers. Writers like Snyder, Bruck, Sapin, Kuhn and Schubert have laid emphasis on the role of customs, habits, routines or established rules of law and justice in the process of making decisions. Referring to the case study of judicial decision, Schubert indicates that the process of decision-making is influenced by the attitudes of the individual judges, role of the interest groups operating in the social context and the judiciary in the formal legal institutions.[35]

The underlying point is that we find complementary interaction of psychological, social, economic and quasi-mechanical processes in the making of political decisions. The outcomes are definitely the results of interaction of various factors emphasised by different writers in different ways. It is, therefore, necessary that we disagree with the 'narrow' version of those social theorists who have sought to build up their theories on the basis of some particular factor and thus ignored the role of other factors in the decision-making process. It is well observed: "In the final analysis, decision-making cannot be understood adequately or decision outcomes predicted without taking into account all three process types. It is the interaction of these processes, and their cumulative effects, that best explains decision outcomes."[36]

`***Variable Clusters :*** Let us also examine decisions and decision-making approach in terms of major variable clusters each composed of an indeterminate number of similar, though not necessarily dependently related, specific variables. They are:[37]

1. ***Decision Situation :*** It is characterised by surprise or anticipation, response time and value implications. It has also been categorised by several different dimensions. Those interested in crisis or non-crisis conflict decision behaviour have specified these dimensions: structured and non-structured, threatening and non-threatening, hostile and friendly, short-term

34. Lasswell : *The Decision Process,* cited in' Robinson and Majak, *op. cit,* p. 180.
35. *ibid.,* p. 184.
36. Robinson and Majak, *op. cit.,* p. 184.
37. Wasby, *op. cit.,* p. 137.

and long-term, familiar and unfamiliar, planned and unplanned, zero-sum and non-zero-sum. Decision situations have also been categorised by location, community, committee and small group, national, legislative, executive, judicial, foreign, military, organisational and international. In other words, the environment and organisation in which decision-making takes place are hypothesised to be among the determinants of decision-making and decision outcomes.

2. ***Decision Participants :*** It is characterised by the personalities, social backgrounds and experiences and values or preferences of the actors. This unit may, however, not be defined in a precise way since the actor may be an individual, a group, a class, a community, a government, a nation, etc. The problem can be solved by the perception of the decision-maker that he has about the issue of his investigation.

3. ***Decision Organisation :*** It is characterised by the roles and units. The particular characteristics of the decision situation itself may partially determine the identity of the decision-makers. It may be safest in the beginning to define decision-makers by their formal position particularly in less economically developed and role differentiated political systems (including the international system) until one can infer from the data he has with him.

4. ***Decision Outcome :*** It is a policy outcome that has authoritative and legal sanctions. It may also refer to the consequences of having selected a particular alternative. These consequences may include (i) what happens to the decision when it is administered, (ii) what advantageous and disadvantageous effects it has on what groups in the political system, and (iii) how the decisions and its administration affect the ability of the political system to maintain itself, resolve conflict, integrate the system and/or allocate values.

The 'outcome cluster' is very important in this direction. It may, however, be distinguished from the 'outputs' and 'effects', though all these terms are used interchangeably to refer to the products of a process or a chain of processes. Decision-making "may be regarded as a total process composed of distinguishable subprocesses. It is sometimes convenient, therefore, to employ output to refer to the products of the various subprocesses in decision-making and to reserve the use of 'outcome' to designate the final product of the decision-making process as a whole....Thus the distinction between 'outputs' and 'outcomes' is twofold: (1) It is a difference between *intermediate* and *end* products, and (2) it is a difference in usage—'outputs' being used *within* the decision unit and to produce other 'outputs' and eventually 'outcomes'. 'Outcomes', in turn, are imposed upon the environment external to the decision unit. The 'implementation' or 'consequences' of 'decision outcomes' may be referred to as 'decision effects'.'[38]

Decision-Making Approach and Political Development : According to Wasby, research on national political development has revealed a number of findings of interest to the study of national decision-making processes. If one is willing to assume that progress is linear and that the stages of development through which the advanced countries have passed are relevant to most political systems, a number of countries can be said to exhibit similar characteristics at the same stage of political development irrespective of their democratic, authoritarian or totalitarian nature.[39] It is on this basis that he offers his threefold classification:

1. ***Traditional Political Systems :*** Decision-makers in such political systems occupy

38. Robinson and Majak, *op. cit.,* pp. 184-85.
39. Wasby, *op. cit.,* p. 139.

their position of significance on the basis of customs and traditions. Class, race, religion, ethnic group and family instead of skill are their qualifications for such position. They tend to perform many political and non-political roles, because specialisation is not yet developed.[40]

2. ***Transitional Political Systems :*** Decision-makers in such political systems depend primarily on loyalty and their charismatic relationships with their supporters for their positions. Aspiring decision-makers are perceived as revolutionaries. Age differences between the younger and the older decision-makers appear to be related to sharp differences in perception in general and political orientation in particular. There is no overlapping in decision-making between the political, economic and social systems. Because the general population is still not organised for making demands of the political decision-makers, decision-makers tend to have more latitude in determining policies. This lack of policy-making limitations is reinforced by the basis of their authority, i.e., their supporters are loyal to them personally, not because of positions taken on specific issues.[41]

3. ***Modern Political Systems :*** Decision-makers in such political systems take more defined positions on issues, for their positions depend upon their fulfilling a universal achievement criterion which has a rational legal basis. They exhibit skills, particularly managerial and bureaucratic skills to hold their positions. Citizens' group also tend to play a more important role in the formulation stage of policy by making their demands known to the decision-makers in non-crisis decision situations.[42]

As a matter of fact, the study of decision-making approach is of special significance in the case of modern political systems where the decision-makers "have to rely on technical experts or become knowledgeable themselves in systems analysis, information retrieval, and other uses of the computer. The need for expertise to understand and evaluate what is going on might discourage the participation of most laymen. One might even envision wars being fought on computers, but it is not necessary to go this far to be impressed by the potential effects of automation on decision-making at all levels."[43]

Application of Decision-Making Approach to Politics : The names of Herbert Simon, James G. March, H. Guetzkow, Richard C. Snyder, H.W. Bruck and B. Sapin are well known in this field. We shall, however, keep our concern confined to the contributions of two outstanding ones —Simon and Snyder. According to Simon, voting, legislating, adjudicating and administering have always been conceived of as decision-making processes. The tools of political analysis —legal, historical and behavioural—have always been adapted to the analysis of decisions. The use of a decision-making framework for political research is not novel, rather it represents continuing development along paths that stretch back to the beginning of political science. What is of special significance about Simon is that he seeks the criteria of, what he calls, 'correct decision-making'. According to him, when correctness is applied to factual propositions, it means objective and empirical truth. The process of validating a factual proposition is quite distinct from the process of validating a value judgment. The former is validated by its agreement with the facts, the latter by human fiat.

40. *ibid.*
41. *ibid.*
42. *ibid.*, p. 140.
43. *ibid.*

Simon offers a 'behaviour alternative model' in which a decision-maker does not begin with the ends, he begins by considering all alternative courses of action and their consequences and then decides which of the alternatives will maximise the achievements of his values. He argues that there may be limitations to the behaviour alternative model. The organisations limit the environment of decisions and thereby reduce the decision-making problems of their members to manageable proportions. He asserts that decision-making theory should be dynamic covering the whole spectrum of decision-making activity—attention directing, design and choice—and not just a theory of one segment.[44] "An adequate theory of political behaviour must be concerned with three aspects of decision-making process. It has to expound the rules that govern the shift and persistence of attention on particular political issues, it must state the principles that govern the invention or design of potential alternatives of political action; and it must set for the conditions that determine the actual choice of an alternative."[45] As Simon says: "In all three spheres of explanation, we may expect the laws to take the form of dynamic principles; expressing relations between the state of affairs at any particular moment in time, and the events that can be expected to follow shortly thereafter."[46]

However, the most outstanding contribution is that of Snyder who makes a refutation of the static analysis as adopted by the systems analysts and structural—functionalists. He is concerned with a *process analysis* that is capable of dealing with dynamic situations. To him a process analysis may be of two kinds dealing with *interaction* and *decision-making*. While the former can describe and measure the relationship between two situations without explaining why the situation evolved in a particular way, the latter by virtue of being a combination of time and change is concerned with the sequences of behavioural events involved in the study of change in relationships and conditions. He is thus critical of social theorists like David Easton and Talcott Parsons who tell us about the conditions under which changes take place without giving us the reasons that lead to such changes. Thus, Snyder "claims to go beyond Parsons and points out that the decision-making analysis needs a phenomenological approach rather than a Parsonian approach in the sense that it does not assume, like the Parsonian scheme, a rational model of action and does not try to impose the observer's criteria on the actor."[47] He "was so much carried off by his discovery that he later came out with a wider application of the approach and claimed that it could be applied not only to the international situation but to the study of political processes as a whole."[48]

Snyder begins with this simple notion that all political action is undertaken by concrete human beings and that if we want to comprehend the dynamics of this action, we should be prepared to view the world not from our point of view but from the perspective of the persons responsible for taking the decisions. His main concern is with two things—who made the key decisions that gave rise to a particular action, and how to assess the intellectual and interactive processes by following which the decision-makers reached their decision. Thus, he offers a model showing three main variables—internal setting, external setting and decision-making process that may be illustrated as given on the next page:[49]

---

44. Simon : *Administrative Behaviour : A Study of the Decision-Making Process in Administrative Organisations* (New York, 1957), p. 53.
45. P K. Ghosh : *Studies in Contemporary Political Theory* (Calcutta : Minerva, 1979), p. 74.
46. Simon, *op. cit.,* p. 21.
47. Varma, *op. cit.,* p. 333.
48. *ibid.*
49. J Synder and others : "Decision Making as an Approach to the Study of International Politics" in *Foreign Policy Decision Making* (New York : Free Press, 1962), p. 72.

Synder (with the collaboration of others like Bruck and Sapin) has suggested that foreign policy decision-making may differ from other types in the following manner:[50]

1. Wider range of possible objectives and projects subject to a wider range of possible interpretations.
2. Greater heterogeneity of 'clientele' and thus more potentially hostile or dissatisfied reactions and demands.
3. A greater number of perspectives have to be integrated before consensus is achieved.
4. The 'setting' and 'situation' of decisions are more complex, less certain; less stable,

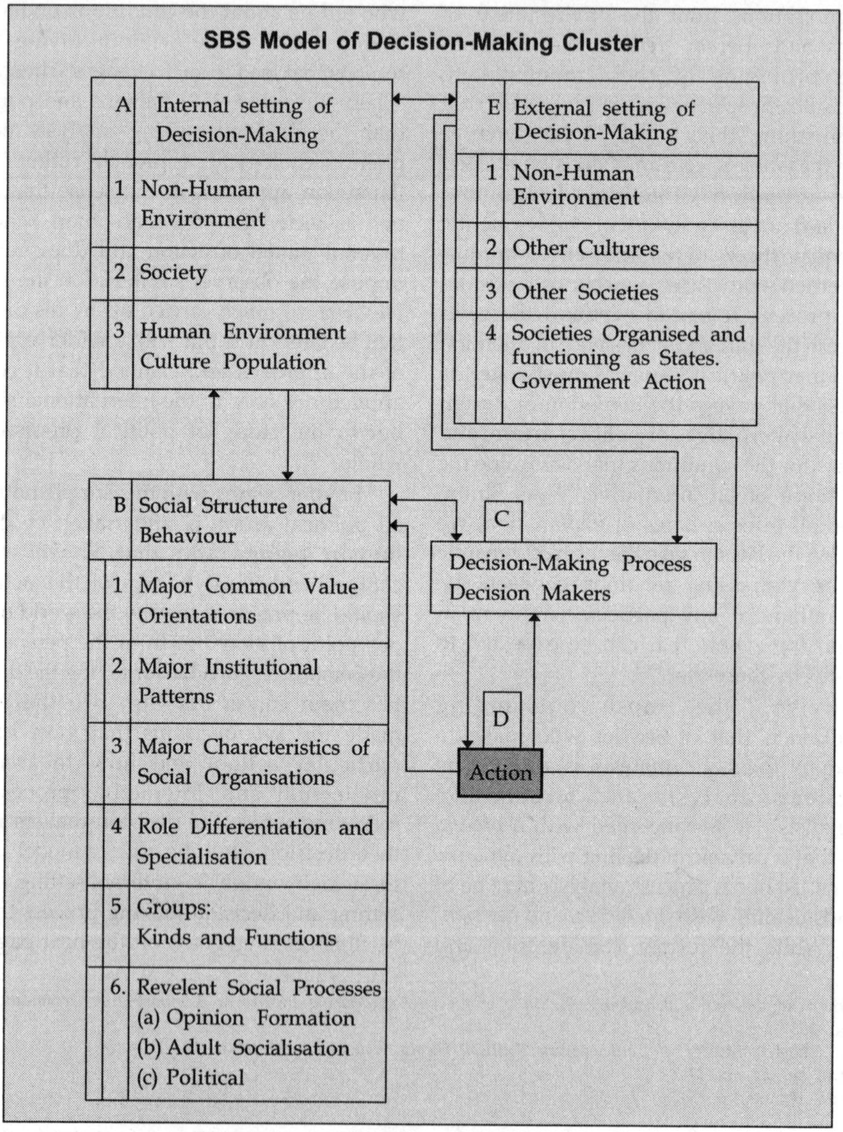

50. See Wasby, *op. cit.*, pp. 140-43.

the consequences of action are therefore harder to predict and control.

5. Sources of information are broader and less reliable and the necessity of 'classification' constitutes a special problem.
6. Relative lack of 'experimental opportunity' and infrequency of replicable situations.
7. Difficulty of measuring organisational effectiveness and policy results.
8. Necessity of discussing alternatives in terms which donot meet the simplest test of verifiability.
9. Time lag between the arising of problem situation and the unfolding of its full implications.
10. Greater possibility of fundamental conflicts and hence necessity for more extensive compromise.

In fine, the state is regarded by Snyder as a prime factor in international politics and its behaviour is always tried to be understood in the objective realities of its position in the world. Its goals and sources of behaviour are traced to geographical, historical, political and technological circumstances which are supposed to exercise a kind of compulsive influence on the behaviour of the state. The goals of a state and its national interests are generally identified by the objective circumstances in which it is situated at a particular time. The behaviour of the state is, in fact, the behaviour of the decision-makers and depends on how the decision-makers 'perceive' these factors. The state action is after all the action of its officials and the officials act according to what they regard as 'objective circumstances'.[51]

Critical Appraisal : Like the theory of games, decision-making approach may also be criticised for being too mechanistic and abstract, taking us far away from the world of empirical study. It requires a student of social science research to proceed as an amateur psycho-analyst in search of personality traits, private prejudices and uncontrolled drives that might underlie the behaviour of the officials. It certainly neglects the external setting and attaches too much importance to the internal setting. It informs us to assume that the decision-makers "act as if they were capable of rational calculation, *i.e.,* they can rank alternative preferences and consciously select the most efficient or feasible means consistent with their rank preference orderings of the alternatives for attaining explicitly stated goals. This assumption of rational behaviour, preferred most consistently by decision-theorists, obviously implies that a decision-maker's personal idiosyncracies donot determine the form of the process of selecting the alternatives."[52] Putting his reservations in a different way, Frankel says that we "seem to have allowed to grow up around us a decision-making process in which those who make key decisions are invisible and in their invisibility donot make themselves know that they are making such decisions. The result is a kind of organised irresponsibility built out of the decisions and actions of the countless disciplined and responsible men."[53]

It may also be added that decision-making approach may be applicable to the discipline of numbers where one is concerned with theoretical situations alone, it may not apply to the realities of human life where decisions are the consequences of political competitions or political participations in which the role of the undefined drives, traits, motivations or other attributes of human personality to provide a 'goad' or a 'spur' are neglected. "This is particularly characteristic of the decision-making theory in foreign policy area. It must be inferred that these drives and traits transform the static description of states into dynamic

51. Varma, *op. cit.,* pp. 335-36.
52. Wasby, *op. cit.,* p. 132.
53. Charles Frankel : *The Democratic Process* (New York : Harper and Row, 1962).

processes of decision-making. Part of the problem is the failure to make explicit whether the models depend for their dynamics on the decision-making process itself and/ or motivations of the individual participants. If the models depend on interaction for their dynamics, then there has clearly been a failure to define the dynamics of the process."[54]

As a last word, it may be said that neither the theory of games nor that of the decision-making may be treated as 'theories', they are just approaches or frameworks that can be made useful for the development of an empirical social or political theory in time to come. Decision-making theory, as it stands today, may be regarded as consisting of a set of categories that constitute an approach or a conceptual scheme consisting of a set of statements that specify relationship among different variables. Since the game and decision-making theories, as they are called, have been utilised to the study of various important political phenomena, it may be hoped that they will yield rewarding results. As Rosenau hopefully says: "Unencumbered by mystical concepts, unconcerned about refined abstractions, disinclined to search for objective reality, and willing to settle for replicable findings, practitioners are now free to devote themselves to the painstaking tasks of constructing and testing hypotheses about the behaviour of international actors. Now they can utilise the techniques of simulation and pursue the logic of game theory in meaningful and productive ways. Now they are free to enjoy the prime pleasure of empirical research: that endless sequence whereby new theoretical propositions exert pressure to gather new data which, in turn, initiate pressure for still newer theory. None of these opportunities or pleasures would have been available if an earlier generation had not cleared the way by calling attention to the centrality of decision-making phenomena."[55]

---

54. Wasby, *op. cit.,* p. 136.
55. James N. Rosenau : "Premises and Promises of Decision-Making Analysis" in Charlesworth (ed.), *op. cit.,* p. 211.

9

Political Development

> The idea that there should be such things as theories of development at all has helped a great deal to overcome the parochialism of individual studies of societies and has helped to relate our conceptual apparatus to the real world. Interest in theories of development was due simultaneously to policy requirements on the part of governments and international organisations, and to the interest taken by academics in the countries newly inducted, somewhat naked and bereft, into the international system. Moreover, the study of development has brought political scientists, sociologists and economists somewhat closer by differentiating between their respective autonomies and contributions.
>
> **—J.P. Nettl[1]**

The concept of political development that, in a quite large measure, was spoken about first by the statesmen and policy-makers and then by the scholars of economics and sociology has a very important place in the field of comparative politics in spite of the fact that there "is still considerable ambiguity and imprecision in the use of this term."[2] What prompted the modern political scientists, particularly those belonging to the United States, is the emergence of a large number of independent nation-states in the Afro-Asian and Latin-American regions which showed change from one position to another in a very rapid manner and thus informed them to refashion their tools of social investigation. The new generation of political scientists came to realise that the non-Western political processes, even though they were different from the Western political processes, could be successfully studied by them against the socio-economic and cultural background they themselves had inherited throughout the centuries in the West, and under the influence of which they had been operating now. The fact that these were different from the Western political processes, being rooted in, and drawing their sustenance from, different cultural backgrounds "induced them to widen their studies to the total context of the cultural and historical settings of the developing states."[3] The result was that the new approach in the study of comparative politics was so expanded as to include, besides the analysis of political institutions and structures, a wide range of ecological forces.[4]

Political Development: Meaning, Diversity of Definitions and Pye's 'Development Syndrome'

As pointed out above, the term 'political development' lacks a precise and standard definition the reason of which should be traced in the abundant studies made from the inter-disciplinary point of view all impinging on the subject of 'growth', 'modernisation' and 'development' of the new states of the Third

1. J.P. Nettl: "Strategies in the Study of Political Development" in Colin Leys (ed.) : *Politics and Change in Developing Countries* (London : Cambridge Univ Press, 1969), pp. 31-32.
2. Lucian W. Pye : *Aspects of Political Development* (Boston : Little Brown, 1966), p. 33.
3. S.P. Varma : *Modern Political Theory* (Delhi : Vikas, 1975), p. 270.
4. *ibid.*

World. The names of Lucian W. Pye, G.A. Almond. James S. Colemen, W. Howard Higgins, Leonard Binder, Herbert Feith, Myron Weiner, David Apter, Harold Lasswell, Karl Deutsch, Daniel Lerner, Talcott Parsons, Robert F. Boles, Edward A. Shils, N.J. Smelser, Joseph la Palombara, Robert E. Ward, Dankwart A. Rustow, Sidney Verba, W. W. Rostow, A.F.K. Organski, John H. Kautsky, C.E. Black, Claude E. Welch, Jr., F.W. Riggs, Robert A. Packenham, S.M. Lipset, S.N. Eisenstadt, Samuel P. Huntington, Robert T. Holt, John E. Turner, Alfred Diamant and a host of other social theorists may be referred to in this connection. They have made vast empirical studies of the nations of the Third World in particular from economic, social, psychological, anthropological and political standpoints in order to describe the process of change that has been taken over by the students of comparative politics. What is, however, especially noticeable about such a massive literature on the subject of political development is that it "illuminates a situation of semantic confusion"[5] and that behind this confusion there "does seem to be a certain more solid basis of agreement."[6]

Lucian Pye should be regarded as the leading light of the earlier batch of writers "to analyse the concept of development in depth, and has kept on evolving his ideas on the subject, and has left an abiding impression on the entire literature of political development."[7] Pye virtually set the pace in 1963 when he thought of political development in terms of cultural diffusion, and of adapting, fusing, and adjusting old patterns of life to new demands. He emphasised that the first step towards political development was the evolution of the nation-state system which he treated as a "basic concept supporting the gradual diffusion throughout all societies of what we might call a world culture."[8] At this stage, he told us that the signs of political development could be traced at three different levels – with respect to the population as a whole, with respect to the level of governmental and general systemic performance, and with respect to the organisation of the polity.[9]

Lucian Pye presents the case of political development in a quite elaborate form in his *Aspects of Political Development*. Before trying to furnish his own interpretation of the term 'political development', he discussesd diverse standpoints and goes ahead after accepting some and rejecting some other parts of each definition in the following manner :

1. ***Political Development as the Political Prerequisite of Economic Development :*** Political development should be taken as a result of the economic development. Economists like Paul A. Baran, Norman S. Buchanan, Howard S. Ellis, Benjamin Higgins, Albert O. Hirschman and Barbara Ward have laid stress on the point that political and social conditions can play a quite decisive role in impeding or facilitating the economic growth. Pye discovers four weaknesses in this concept of political development. First, it has a negative character in the sense that it is easier to be precise about the ways in which performance of a political system may impede or prevent economic development than about how it can facilitate economic growth. Second, such a concept of political development does not focus on a common set of theoretical considerations, for in some cases it would mean no more than whether or not a government is following intelligent and economically rational policies, while in other situations it would involve far more fundamental considerations about the basic organisation of the polity and the entire performance of the society. The

5. Lucian Pye, *op. cit.*, p. 33.
6. *ibid.*
7. Varma, *op. cit.*, p. 275.
8. Lucian W. Pye : *Communications and Political Development* (Princeton : Princeton Univ Press, 1963), p. 19.
9. *ibid.*

problems of political development would thus vary according to particular economic problems in each country. Third, it should also be taken into account that the prospects for rapid economic development have become exceedingly dim in most of the poor countries. Finally, in most of the under-developed countries people are clearly concerned with far more than just material advancement; they are anxious about political development quite independent of its effects on the rate of economic growth. Therefore, to link political development solely to economic events would be to ignore much that is of dramatic importance in the developing countries.[10]

2. ***Political Development as the Politics Typical of Industrial Socteties :*** Some social theorists like W.W. Rostow try to identify the process of political development with the pace of industrialisation. This point may be taken as an extension of the variable discussed above. Pye rejects it also on the ground that it ignores the role of several other factors like forces that threaten the hold of the vested interests, an appreciation of the values of orderly legal and administrative procedures, an acknowledgement that politics is rightfully a mechanism for solving problems and not an end in itself, a stress on welfare programmes and, finally, an acceptance of some form of mass participation.[11]

3. ***Political Development as Political Modernisation*** : A good number of social theorists like James S. Coleman, Karl Deutsch and S.M. Lipset have laid stress on the point that political development means a study of the developed western and modern countries and of their ways that the developing countries are trying to emulate. It means that the advanced western and modern countries are the pace-setters of political development. Pye feels that such a view has its own shortcomings inasmuch as it fails to distinguish between the 'western' and the 'modern' and that it ignores the fact that the backward or developing countries may have their own historical traditions that they may not like to give up for the sake of merely emulating everything that is western or modern.[12]

4. ***Political Development as the Operation of Nation-State :*** Some social theorists like K.H. Silvert, Edward A Shils and William McCord have pointed out that political development consists of the organisation of political life and the performance of political functions in accordance with the standards expected of a modern nation-state. Political development is thus identified with the politics of nationalism within the context of social and political institutions that a modern nation-state must possess. Rejecting this view, Pye says that nationalism is only a necessary but far from being a sufficient condition to ensure political development. Political development is identifiable with nation-building and not with merely a nation-state. "Development entails the translation of diffuse and unorganised sentiments of nationalism into a spirit of citizenship, and equally the creation of state institutions that can translate into policy and programmes the aspirations of nationalism and citizenship. In brief, political development is nation-building."[13]

5. ***Political Development as Administrative and Legal Development :*** Some social theorists like Max Weber, Talcott Parsons, A.M. Henderson and Joseph la Palombara have laid stress on the point that political development is intricately linked to the legal and administrative order of a community. Thus, the establishment of an effective bureaucracy is essential for the process of

---

10. Lucian Pye : *Aspects of Political Development,* pp. 33-34.
11. *ibid.,* pp. 34-35.
12. *ibid.,* pp. 35-36.
13. *ibid.,* pp. 37-38.

development. The administrative development is thus associated with the spread of rationality, the strengthening of secular and legal concepts and the elevation of technical and specialised knowledge in the direction of human affairs. Pye finds some weaknesses in this viewpoint also. It is quite possible that if administration is over-stressed, it can create imbalances in the polity that may impede political development. This view also entirely overlooks the problems of citizenship training and popular participation that are one of the essential features of political development.[14]

6. ***Political Development as Mobilisation and Participation :*** There are some social theorists like Clifford Geertz, Rupert Emerson, Bert F. Hoselitz and Eisenstadt who have stressed the point of the role of a politically awakened citizenry and the behaviour of the people in the direction of an expanded popular participation. Extension of franchise is taken as a mark of diffusion of the decision-making process through mass participation. Pye has taken into his consideration the disastrous effects of the politics of mass manipulation and thus pointed out that such a view of political development "is also fraught with the dangers of either sterile emotionalism or corrupting demogaguery, both of which can sap the strength of a society."[15]

7. ***Political Development as the Building of Democracy :*** Joseph la Palombara and J. Ronald Pennock are of the view that the case of political development is integrally connected with the building of democracy and inculcating 'values' of a democratic order in the minds of the people. Pye differs from this view and he points out that such a concept would exclude the cases of those countries where democracy is non-existent and that democracy is a 'value-laden' concept, while development is 'value-free'. "To use the building of democracy as the key to political development can thus be seen as an effort to push upon others American, or at least Western, values."[16]

8. ***Political Development as Stability or Orderly Change :*** Some social theorists like Karl Deutsch and F.W. Riggs have laid stress on the point that stability is legitimately linked to the concept of development in that any form of economic or social advancement does generally depend upon an environment in which uncertainty has been reduced and planning based on reasonably safe predictions is possible. Pye differs from this approach and says that it "leaves unanswered how much order is necessary or desirable and for what purpose change should be directed. There is also the question of whether the coupling of stability and change is not something that can occur only in the dreams of a middle class, or at least in societies that are far better than most of the currently underdeveloped ones. Finally, on the scale of priorities there is the feeling that the maintenance of order, however desirable and even essential, stands second to getting things done; and thus development calls for a somewhat more positive view of action."[17]

9. ***Political Development as Mobilisation and Power :*** Some social theorists like James S. Coleman, G.A. Almond and Talcott Parsons have taken the view that the concept of political development can be evaluated in terms of the level or degree of absolute power which the system is able to mobilise. According to this view, states naturally differ in proportion to their inherent resource base with the result that the measure of development is the degree to

---

14. *ibid.,* pp. 38-39.
15. *ibid.,* pp. 39-40.
16. *ibid.,* pp. 40-41.
17. *ibid.,* pp. 41-42.

which they are able to maximise and realise the full potential of their given resources. Pye is critical of this view also on the plea that such an explanation is applicable to the case of a democratic political system and thus it ignores the case of development in others where the mobilisation of power is deliberately kept limited.[18]

10. ***Political Development as one Aspect of a Multi-Dimensional Process of Social Change*:** Thus, some social theorists like Max F. Millikan, Donald L.M. Blackmer and Daniel Lerner have advanced the argument that it is unnecessary and inappropriate to try to isolate too completely political development from other forms of developments. Although, to a limited extent, the political sphere may be autonomous from the rest of the society, for sustained political development to take place it can only be within the context of a multi-dimensional process of social change in which no segment or dimension of the society can lag behind. Pye appreciates this view on the plea that here all forms of development are related, development is much the same as modernisation, and it takes place within a historical context in which influences from outside the society impinge on the process of social change just as changes in the different aspects of a society—the economy, the polity and the social order—all impinge on each other.[19]

11. ***Political Development as a Sense of National Respect in International Affairs*:** Finally, Pye refers to the problem of 'development syndrome' as pointed out by writers like James S. Coleman and Myron Weiner that takes into account the case of post-nationalism era where the sense of national self-respect and dignity in the international sphere shall inform and the nation-state will no longer be used as the basic unit of political life. Since Pye says nothing about the critical examination of this interpretation, it appears that he either accepts it or ignores it altogether and instead goes ahead to give his own explanation of political development that includes some element of all the diverse definitions and interpretations that he has discussed before coming to his own interpretation.[20]

The meaning of the concept of political development that Lucian Pye offers after scanning diverse definitions and viewpoints bears three characteristics :

i. ***Equality*:** The subject of political development does suggest mass participation and popular involvement in political activities. Participation may be either democratic or in a form of totalitarian mobilisation, but the key consideration is that subjects should become active citizens. At least, the semblance of a popular rule is necessary. It also means that laws "should be of a universalistic nature, applicable to all and more or less impersonal in their operation." Finally, it means that recruitment to political offices "should reflect achievement standards of performance and not the ascriptive considerations of a traditional social system."[21]

ii. ***Capacity* :** It refers to the capacity of a political system by which it can give 'outputs' and the extent to which it can affect the rest of the society and economy. It is also associated with governmental performance and the conditions that affect such performance. It entails the sheer magnitude, scope and the scale of political and governmental performance making it like a welfare agency. It also means effectiveness and efficiency in the execution of public policy. There is a trend towards professionalisation of government. Finally, it is related to rationality in administration and a secular orientation towards policy. The actions of the government are guided

18. *ibid.*, pp. 42-44.
19. *ibid.*, pp. 44-45.
20. *ibid.*, p. 45.
21. *ibid.*, pp. 45-46,

more by deliberations and justifications that seek to relate ends and means in a systematic manner.[22]

iii. ***Differentiation*** : It implies diffusion and specialisation of structures. The offices and agencies tend to have their distinct and limited functions and there is an equivalent of a division of labour within the realm of government. It also involves the integration of complex structures and processes. Thus, differentiation "is not fragmentation and the isolation of the different parts of the political system but specialisation based on an ultimate sense of integration."[23]

In addition to all this, Pye also makes two more points. First, all the three characteristic elements of political development may, and may not, fit together easily and thus there may, and may not, be tension between the demands for equality, the requirements for capacity and the process of greater differentiation. Thus, a pressure for greater equality "can challenge the capacity of the system, and differentiation can reduce equality by stressing the importance of quality and specialised knowledge."[24] Second, development is clearly not unilinear, nor is it governed by sharp and distinct stages, but rather by a range of problems that may arise separately or concurrently. A study of political development in the wider perspective of comparative politics also shows that while the characteristic of *equality* is concerned with *political culture,* the problems of *capacity* are related to the performance of the *authoritative structures of government,* and the questions of *differentiation* touch mainly on the performance of the *non-authoritative structures* and the general political processes in the society at large. "This suggests that in the last analysis the problems of political development revolve around the relationships between the political culture, the authoritative structures, and the general political process."[25]

Though much popularised by Pye, the concept of political development underwent a refinement in view of an agonising realisation about its deficient conceptual framework in respect of its application to the scenario of developing countries of the Third World. Hence, Leonard Binder came forward with his thesis of political development. It was appreciated by the Committee on Comparative Politics (USA) under whose auspices another important work appeared in which he attributed the following implications:[26]

1. Change of identity from religious to ethnic and from parochial to societal,
2. Change of legitimacy from transcendental to immanent sources,
3. Change in political participation from elite to mass and from family to group,
4. Change of distribution from status and, privilege to achievement, and
5. Change in the degree of administrative and legal penetration into the social structure and to remote regions of the country.

We may also refer to the views of Riggs at this stage who integrated the concept of political development with the forces of 'environment'. In his view, the term 'development' in the political context should be confined to connote 'an increasing ability to make and carry out collective decisions affecting the environment (not the context). It is obvious that the ecological dimension which the term 'environment' introduces in considerations of political decision making, requires that 'both the cultural and the human environment need to be added to the physical environment in order to form an adequate picture of the ecology of political administrative action.' Likewise, the term 'context' has a significance of its own that informs us to study state as a part of the international society. Thus, he defines: "My view of development, accordingly, is that it involves a growing understanding of both

22. *ibid.,* pp. 46-47.
23. *ibid.,* p. 47.
24. *ibid.*
25. *ibid.,* p. 48.
26. Binder : *Crises and Sequences in Political Development* (Princeton : Princeton University Press, 1971), p. 66.

constraints and resources of the environment. Moreover, and this is often the critical element in development, a society may choose to do things that change its environment so as to reduce the elements of constraint and increase the elements of resources, thereby expanding its own capacity to make decisions that will enlarge the scope of its own self-determination."[27]

It may also be added here that the concept of political development also covers the aspect of political decline or decay. That is, as a concept, it does not merely suggest that the movement is in a single direction, because institution grow and mature as well as decay and dissolve. The whole idea focuses attention between the ongoing social processes of modernisation on the one hand and the strength, stability or weakness of the political structures—traditional, transitional or modern—on the other. As Samuel P. Huntington says: "The level of institutionalisation of any political system can be defined by the adaptability, complexity, autonomy and coherence of its organisations and procedures. So also the level of institutionalisation of any particular organisation or procedure can be measured by its adaptability, complexity, autonomy and coherence. If these criteria can be identified and measured, political systems can be compared in terms of their levels of institutionalisation. Furthermore, it will be possible to measure increases and decreases in institutionalisation of particular organisations and procedures within a political system."[28]

In short, the concept of political development views the operation of a political system in terms of its increasing democratisation, while that of political decay does the same for its regression and disintegration leading to the advent of some form of totalitarianism. Moreover, as the concept has been developed by the American writers, it is naturally connected with what has happened in an advanced Western country like the United States. A look at the indices of political development, as pointed out by leading writers on the subject, shows that "the Anglo-American qualities most clearly approximate the model of the modern political system."[29] Moreover, as the advanced liberal democracies of the West have been able to solve their gigantic problems and face challenges in an effective manner, the idea of political development also involves the capacity of a political system "to control and co-ordinate various processes of change in society generated by the socio-demographic and structural changes."[30]

Concept of Political Development : Some Definitional Problems and Requirements of a New Theory

One thing is quite clear from all that we have seen in the preceding sections that the concept of political development cannot be precisely defined. As a matter of fact, this concept, as it has developed till now, carries a number of definitional problems that include:[31]

(a) A set of definitional priorities which constitute the meaning of development as a process and the notion of being developed or underdeveloped as a state;

(b) A set of values which make development desirable, if not mandatory;

---

27. Fred W. Riggs : "Further Considerations on Development" in *Administrative Change,* Vol IV, No. 1, (July-December, 1976), p. 2-8.
28. Huntington : "Political Development and Political Decay" in *World Politics,* Vol. XVII, No. 3, April 1965, pp. 393-94. Almond and Powell endorse : "It should also be pointed out that a decline in the magnitude or a significant change in the content of the flow of the inputs may result in development in the negative or regressive sense. The capabilities of the political system may decline or be over-loaded; roles and structures may atrophy; the culture may regress to a more traditional pattern of orientation." *op. cit.,* p. 34.
29. Almond and Coleman : *The Politics of the Developing Areas* (Princeton: Princeton University Press, 1960), p. 536.
30. S.N. Eisenstadt : *Modernisation : Protest and Change,* (New Delhi, 1969), pp. 1-19.
31. J P Nettl, *op. cit.,* p. 16.

(c) The inter-connection between the two categories of developed and underdeveloped societies, and

(d) The recognition of an implicit rank order of development— at least in the mind of the analysts, but possibly also in that of the participants.

Indices of Political Development and Decay

Positive Indices (Development)

1. State-building or territorial integration
2. Nation-building or national integration
3. Increasing franchise and free and fair elections with large voter turn out
4. Politicisation or participation of more and more people in the political process
5. Popular participation in decision-making bodies
6. Growing interest articulation by autonomous groups
7. Growing interest aggregation by stable political parties having democratic character
8. Freedom of the press and growth of mass media
9. Political and administrative decentralisation
10. Autonomy of the units of local/ self-government
11. Expansion of educational facilities
12. Effective role of legislative bodies and constituency service by the representative
13. Effective role of quasi-governmental agencies like public undertakings
14. Role of powerful organisations to oversee the working of public servants (like Ombudsman) and redressal of public grievances
15. Tolerance of dissent and control over anomic movements
16. Broadening of the social base of political elites
17. Openness in the working of government and accountability of the rulers to the ruled
18. Independence of judiciary and the existence of rule of law
19. Apolitical character of the armed forces,
20. Consensual politics implying use of constitutional methods.
21. Neutrality or anonymity of public services and
22. Secularisation of political culture.

Negative Indices (Decay)

1. Anti-national events
2. Communal and racial conflicts
3. Curtailment of the freedom of press and media
4. Electoral rigging and irregularities
5. Protest demonstrations by the use of violence
6. Anomic disturbances under-ground activities and armed attacks
7. Political defections for selfish gains
8. Fragmentation of political parties
9. Suppression of dissent
10. Idolisation of the rulers
11. Glorification of the official ideology
12. Political assassinations
13. Politicisation of the armed forces
14. Commitment of public services to the line of ruling party
15. Wide corruption and maladministration
16. Concentration of powers
17. Mass arrests and
18. Foreign interference in domestic matters.

Let us study all the four problematic situations, as pointed out by Nettl, in the following manner.

(a) ***Definitional Priorities*** : The concept of development originated in the discipline of economics and it came to have a wider perspective when social theorists took into their account the fact that several 'revolutionary' countries of the world after achieving independence generally opted for socio-political priorities, while the 'democratic' ones went for a more distinctly economic or economistic solution. Some social theorists like S.M. Lipset took into account the individual diversities and cultural constraints of different societies[32] and, as Rostow says, some people saw development as having to do with what was hopefully described as the attainment of specific and identifiable societal goals.[33] What further added to the confusion was that while some writers referred to the progress made by some advanced Western countries in all walks of life as the subject-matter of development and that should be taken by all developing societies as a model to emulate if not by specific institutional or quantitative replication but at least through functional equivalence. All this leaves an impression that in the concept of political development, there "is the hesitant and discordant division of development theories into socio-political and economic priorities, and also the see-saw battle between historical analogy and abstract models of utilitarian or rational emphasis."[34] Nettl thus feels that the basic contrast between a normative and a logical empirical ordering of categories remains in this as in almost every area of social science."[35]

(b) ***Set of Values*** : The subject of political development is made confused and perplexing when certain terms like 'traditionality' or 'modernity', 'free' or 'closed' societies, 'developed' and 'developing' social systems and the like acquire normative dimensions and thereby make the entire concept value-laden that should otherwise remain like a value-free subject on account of being a matter of empirical investigation. The result is that while some developing countries appreciate the Western model of development, some do not as they term it unattainable; not only this, some view "the Western model as 'destructive'; destructive in particular of stability, which had slowly become the unconscious but dominant preoccupation of the Western analysts. And the immutability of the Western world as a value in itself was also challenged from within Western society; far from the state of ultimate perfection which it appeared to be so long as it was a model for developing countries, it looked instead to be heavy with problems of its own. A new emphasis on societal goals on the part of leaders in developed countries was matched by academic preoccupations with the problems and values of so-called 'post-modernity."[36]

(c) ***Connection between the Developed and Less Developed World*** : A theory of political development must include within its range the entire world whether eastern or western, developed or developing, since there is inter-dependence between the two. As Nettl says: "What this amounts to is a rewriting of European, American and even Soviet history for developmental purposes. The modern world is no longer so much a goal or a process model but an historical abstraction of functional 'events' which, one way or another, must happen and be coped with by all countries aspiring to modernity."[37]

---

32. See S.M. Lipset : *Political Man* (New York, 1960), Ch 2.
33. See W.W. Rostow : *The Stages of Economic Growth* (Cambridge, 1960).
34. Nettl, *op. cit.*, p. 17.
35. *ibid*, p. 18.
36. *ibid.*, pp. 19-20.
37. *ibid.*, p. 21.

(d) ***Rank Order for Development*** : Though the subject of development originated from the discipline of economics and later became a fashionable tool at the hands of sociologists, it would be wrong to lay much emphasis on the predominance of any such discipline. Apart from throwing focus on the economic and sociological aspects, due emphasis should also be attached to the organisational criteria like capabilities of the political system to control or coerce, or on a wide sweep of economic, social, political and cybernetic indices which provide hard facts without any specific commitment to professed institutional or processual emphases. "If development is, indeed, a highly differential process according to particular societies and their goals, then rank ordering comparisons become meaningless."[38]

Having thus discussed the problems of presenting a precise definition of the term'political development', Nettl points out four 'requirements' that ought to be taken into account while explaining its meaning. They are :

(i) ***The Inter-Related World*** : The social theorists must understand this point that the world as a whole has inter-related countries and the study of development has an inter-disciplinary focus. Thus, undue emphasis should not be attached to any country or some countries or to any discipline or some disciplines like economics and sociology. No simple or direct relationship is discernible between the levels of economic growth and socio-political structures or processes and partly because at a conceptual level sociologists and political scientists "will not be tied in their work to *ex-ante* or *ex-post* economic priorities. Accordingly, future theories of development might increasingly discard the economic components of the Western experience and learn to live with the assumption that socio-political development in many countries in the world today might have to take place in a situation of industrial stagnation or even regression."[39]

(ii) ***Stability and Instability*** : Political development does not merely imply progress towards stability or growth; it also covers the case of drifting of things towards instability or disintegration where it becomes identifiable with, what S.P. Huntington calls, political decay. So far, social theorists have laid emphasis on factors like nation-building, integration, commitment to the universalism of a societal level instead of the parochialism of the village, achievement instead of ascription, mobilisation, institutionalisation and the like. Apart from this, a student of comparative politics must also look towards wars, inflation, insurrections, etc. no matter they bring about what is known as the breakdown of the political system. Though it "carries possible consequences for theories of development, we have not made it a basic part of any such theory, but relegated it to a special discipline concerned with conflict." [40]

(iii) ***Population*** : The social and political consequences of the demographic explosion need their special attention in a study of development. The population explosion creates several tedious problems that the nation-states have to tackle in a way that affords enormous material for the study of development. It contradicts the suggestion of some anthropologists that no relationship can be discovered between the density of population and political organisation. Connected with this are the often significant differences in age structure between elites and populations of developed and developing countries.[41]

---

38. *ibid.*, p. 22.
39. *ibid.*, *p.* 25.
40. *ibid.*, p. 28.
41. *ibid.*, p. 29.

(iv) ***Race*** : The theories of development eventually attempt to accommodate racial conflicts and racial differences. The Marxists have committed the mistake by reducing the nature of social conflicts to the denominator of class struggle; the anti-Marxists have committed the error by ignoring the factor of racial differentiation altogether. There "is an immediacy of primary identification and interpersonal conflict which is quite lacking in class formation and confrontation between classes; the very violence of personal conflict between black and white obviates the intervention of sociological collectivist notions as a means of creating identities and then hostility."[42]

What Nettl has tried to contribute is that political development is a very comprehensive and multi-faceted subject that cannot be defined precisely owing to certain technical difficulties and that certain factors should invariably be taken note of while a social theorist makes an attempt in this direction. He has nowhere made an attempt to underrate the contributions of social theorists; rather, he has reacted against the tendency of laying too much importance on the development of a country like the United States or on a particular discipline like economics. He has, however, recognised the importance of this subject and thus appreciated the fact that such a study "has contributed substantially to the infusion of a dynamic approach to the study of society" and that there "is no doubt that the salience of developmental problems has made social scientists more historically minded, and has helped to produce highly ingenious theories of how we ourselves became what we are."[43]

Political Development : A Synthesised Version of its Multi-Faceted Implications and Dimensions : The Issue of Problems and Crises

Though political development cannot be defined precisely, certainly its broad features can be outlined. David M. Wood makes an apt observation that, most commonly, political scientists studying the phenomenon of modernisation "have treated what they call political development as a dependent variable, using other facets of modernisation as independent variables."[44]

It should also be looked into as to what leads to the development of a political system. The answer is that the events which lead to political development "come from the international environment, from the domestic society, or from political elites within the political system itself."[45] It follows that events going on in the international sphere like wars or aggressions bring about conditions of change in the political system. Besides, events taking place within the system may also have the same effect. Development results when the existing structure and culture of the political system are unable "to cope with the problem or challenge which confronts it without further structural differentiation and cultural secularisation."[46] If so, let us look at the challenges that may lead to political development:

(i) ***Problem of State-Building :*** This problem arises when there is a serious threat coming from the side of a domestic or international environment so that the very question of the survival of the state comes into the forefront. A war or aggression occurring in the international sphere or a change in the political goals of the powerful elites may

---

42. *ibid.,* p. 31.
43. *ibid.,* p. 32.
44. See David M. Wood : "Comparative Government and Politics" in Stephen L. Wasby : *Political Science : The Discipline and Its Dimensions : An Introduction* (Calcutta : Scientific Book Agency, 1970), p. 504.
45. *ibid.*
46. G.A. Almond and G.B. Powell: *Comparative Politics: A Developmental Approach* (Boston : Little Brown, 1966), p. 34.

create serious threats to the very existence of the political system. "State-building occurs when the political elite creates new structures and organisations designed to 'penetrate' the society in order to regulate behaviour in it and draw a larger volume of resources from it. State-building is commonly associated with significant increases in the regulative and extractive capabilities of the political system, with the development of a centralised and penetrative bureaucracy related to the increase in these capabilities, and with the development of attitudes of obedience and compliance in the population which are associated with the emergence of such a bureaucracy."[47]

(ii) ***Problem of Nation-Building :*** It "refers to the process whereby people transfer their commitment and loyalty from smaller tribes, villages or petty principalities to the large central political system."[48] The problems of state-building and nation-building may be studied together, they may also be studied separately as it is not necessary that the two ever go together. There are several cases to show that while the problem of state-building has been solved, the problem of nation-building has still remained to create threatening postures for the very survival of the political system.

(iii) ***Problem of Participation :*** There are various interest groups in the society that strive to have a share in the decision-making process. Thus, political infra-structure comes into being in the form of political parties, groups, cliques, factions, etc. It leads to the expansion of 'demands' and also for participation in the process of decision-making so that 'outputs' are favourable to the interests of the claimants.

(iv) ***Problem of Distribution :*** Finally, there arises the problem as to how national income or wealth should be distributed or opportunities be given to all without any artificial discrimination on the grounds of religion, caste, creed, colour, etc. Talent should be recognised and that merit should be the deciding factor in the midst of 'equal opportunities' for all. It is also known by the name of the politics of welfare or general good.

Almond and Powell not only look towards the problems of political development from their structural-functional approach, they also hint at five major factors that must be considered in such an analysis. They are:

(i) ***Nature of the Problems Confronting a Political System :*** The stability or instability, or the development and decay, of a political system very much depends on the nature of the problems that a political system is confronted with. Different people demand different forms of participation, national integration, economic betterment, situations of law and order and the like. Since advanced countries have solved most of these problems over the years, the burden on their political system is not so heavy. Different from this is the case of backward and developing societies where such demands have come up suddenly and their effect is cumulative and reinforcing. Thus, it is generally recognised that a major problem in the new nations today "is the cumulative revolutions they must face."[49]

(ii) ***Resources of the System :*** A political system has to satisfy the 'demands' made upon it. It may be possible that the load of demands is too great that a political system may not bear or may do so at a heavy expense. For instance, the people of France had to terminate their Fourth Republic in 1958 and replace it with the Fifth under the leadership of Charles de Gaulle who had to make Algeria independent in 1962 despite the fact that he was inducted into the highest office for the very reason of saving the French colony.[50]

47. *ibid.,* pp. 35-36.
48. *ibid.,* p. 36.
49. *ibid.,* p. 39.
50. *ibid.*

(iii) ***Effect of Foreign Social Systems :*** When an economy develops new capabilities, new systems of production and distribution, the loading of the political system with demands for welfare may be significantly reduced and thereby affect political development. It is also possible that international institutions like the International Monetary Fund or World Bank may develop a regulative or distributive capability that reduces the pressures on the domestic political system. Thus, the existence or the development of capabilities in other social systems may affect the magnitude of the challenges confronting political systems, keep the flow "at an incremental and low-intensity level, and perhaps help avoid some of the disruptive consequences of cumulative pressures."[51]

(iv) ***Functioning Pattern of the System :*** The problem of political development or decay also depends upon the pattern of the political system. It means that a political system may, or may not, cope with the burden of 'inputs'. It may be resilient enough to bear the stress of 'loads' and thus keep itself going, it may also be weak enough to break down under the pressure of 'demands'. It is not necessary that all political systems may be geared for change and adaptation in an equal measure.[52]

(v) ***Response of the Political Elites :*** Finally, comes the problem of the role of the political elites. It is possible that powerful elites may change their goals in response to the pressure of demands and thereby save the political system from decay, or they may misjudge the seriousness and intensity of input fluctuations and thus either radically modify the system or fail to respond until it is too late with the result that there is the breakdown of the system itself.[53]

From the above, it is quite clear that the subject of political development is riven with certain crises that, according to Lucian W. Pye, may be enumerated as under:[54]

1. ***Identity Crisis :*** The people should identify themselves with their political system. That is, they must recognise their national territory as their homeland and they must feel that their own personal identities are in part defined by their identification with their territorially delimited country. It is found that there is a lot of contradiction between the traditional political culture having its roots in the loyalties of the individuals towards their community, tribe, religion, etc. and a modern political culture requiring that they should sacrifice their primordial loyalties at the altar of their national commitments.
2. ***Legitimacy Crisis :*** It refers to the problem of achieving agreement about the legitimate nature of authority and the proper responsibility of government. What should be the pattern of central or local authority? What should be the limits to the executive or bureaucratic authority? How much of the colonial structure of government should be maintained in the post-independence era? These are some of the problems that relate to the legitimacy crisis. This point has a more prominent place in backward societies ridden with theocratic values where people still cling to the idea that the political structure should conform to the precepts of their religion.
3. ***Penetration Crisis :*** It refers to the problem of the government in reaching down to the society and effecting basic policies. How much the government should do for the good of the people? What the government should not do? To carry out significant developmental policies, a government must be able to reach down to the village level

51. *ibid.,* p. 40.
52. *ibid.*
53. *ibid.*
54. Lucian W. Pye : *Aspects of Political Development,* pp. 62-67.

and touch the daily lives of the people. The problem arises when an endeavour of the government, in this direction, leads to the inculcation of 'demands explosion' that it feels hardly capable of solving.

(4) ***Participation Crisis :*** It occurs when there is uncertainty over the appropriate rate of expansion and when the influx of new participants creates serious strains on the existing institutions. A question arises as to whether freedom should be allowed for various political parties and groups to operate with a view to influence the decision-making process, or what restrictions should be imposed so that they are prevented from becoming anomic organisations. Such a question also covers the issue whether participation facilities should be given for a genuine democratic purpose or just for the sake of demonstrational politics.

(5) ***Integration Crisis :*** It deals with the extent to which the entire polity is organised as a system of interacting relationships, first among the officers and agencies of government and then among the various groups and interests seeking to make demands upon the system and finally in the relationships between officials and articulating citizens.

(6) ***Distribution Crisis :*** It refers to the questions about how governmental powers are to be used to influence the distribution of goods, services and values throughout the society. In some cases governments seek to meet the problem directly by intervening in the distribution of wealth; in other cases the approach is to strengthen the opportunities and potentialities of the disadvantaged groups.

Pye tries to show that the nature of these crises determines the sequence of political development in different countries of the world. It is, therefore, necessary that, ultimately, any useful theory of political development "must come to grips with the types of problems that may be subsumed under the category of crises."[55]

Political Development: Model of Stages and Search for an Approach

Broadly speaking, two types of schema "have been advanced for dealing with the tremendous wealth of political and extra-political phenomena which the study of political development conjures up."[56] Viewed thus, two conceptual models may be framed on the basis of which general theories of political development may be erected:

(i) ***Continuum Model :*** It "tends to view the developmental process in terms of a series of discrete variables each identified by a range of possible states that national entities may be in at various times with respect to some specific criterion."[57] This approach informs that the development of the nations of the world should be measured in quantifiable terms as gross national product and *per capita* income, percentage of the adult population, rate of literacy, number of the working people, participation in elections, growth of industrialisation, multiplication of political parties and groups, recruitment and promotion of government employees, etc. Such a model of development is subscribed to by social theorists who "posit a common movement along a broad array of fronts from less modern to more modern conditions, and who see a functional relationship between social, economic, psychological and political indicators of modernisation, find this type of conceptual model an economical and highly systematic way to portray the phenomena which interest them."[58]

---

55. *ibid.*, p. 67.
56. Wood in Wasby, *op. cit.*, p. 504.
57. *ibid.*, p. 505.
58. *ibid.*

(ii) ***Stages Model :*** Here the basis is transition from one stage of development to another. That is, it postulates three stages of development—*traditional stage* characterised by an overwhelmingly rural society and agrarian economy with appropriate political forms, *transitional stage* characterised by an economy embarking on the early stages of industrialisation and a political system which is accordingly undergoing transformation, and *modern stage* characterised by a largely urban society and a mature industrial economy with appropriate political forms. Viewed thus, Wood says: "In general sense, the political system moves from (1) the traditional focus upon local concentrations of power with little articulation between the centre and the periphery to (2) the transitional stage in which structures are .emerging to involve the increasingly available masses in the political system while improving upon the technical means of expanding the power of the centre into the periphery, and from there to (3) the modern state with its centrally engineered economy and its perfected institutional means of involving all members of society in the daily affairs of the individual; at the same time, the individual becomes involved in the national endeavour through whatever official means of participation that are available to him."[59]

It may be pointed out that both of these models have their own drawbacks. While the *continuum model* is inherent with the danger of the fragmentation of concerns, especially in the absence of any over-arching theory, the *stages model* lacks universal application in as much as it may be applied rigorously to a few but not to all countries of the world. Thus, while in the former we find a sort of tightly manipulated inter-connectedness of variables belonging to various social disciplines as economics, sociology and psychology, the latter represents a tendency to oversimplify the highly complex phenomenon and for forcing the experiences of particular countries into a mould that may not be applied to all parts of the world with the rigour of a methodology. One thing is, however, common to both that, in any event, they "are based upon an image of a largely dependent political realm and a largely independent extra-political realm, with movement in the economic, social, psychological and political realms highly interrelated."[60]

Political development approach is a result of the 'forward thrust' in the realm of comparative politics.[61] What really gave impetus to this trend was the focus on the study of political trends in the developing countries of the Third World. The trend was set by Roy C. Macridis in 1955 when he drew the attention of the political scientists towards the study of the political systems of the 'Third World' by forcefully arguing that the study of comparative politics had so far been 'parochial, insufficiently theoretical in orientation and formalistic'. It provoked a good number of leading figures like Gunnar Heckscher and G.A. Almond to make the study of comparative politics both fashionable and intellectually exciting by broadening the scope of their empirical investigations. The growing interest in the study of the political systems of the 'Third World' "branched off in two divergent though inter-related directions, reacting not only on the study of comparative government, but also on other sub-fields of political science. These trends involve first the use of quantitative and behavioural methods and second the strengthening of area studies and cross-disciplinary integration."[62]

Karl Deutsch deserves the credit for being the pioneer in promoting quantitative studies

59. *ibid.,* pp. 505-506.
60. *ibid.,* p. 506.
61. Fred W. Riggs: "The Theory of Political Development" in James C. Charlesworth (ed.); *Contemporary Political Analysis* (New York : Macmillan, Free Press, 1967), p. 318.
62. *ibid.,* p. 319.

to measure the forces of social mobilisation for cross-national comparisons in conjunction with other indices that could be related to political development. The Yale University became the centre of such studies. Banks' and Texor's *A Cross-Polity Survey* appeared as the leading contribution of the Yale Political Data Programme. Writers like Daniel Lerner and Fred Frey earned their names at the Centre for International Studies at the Massachusetts Institute of Technology. The Inter-University Consortium for Political Research established at the University of Michigan, the International Data Library and Reference Service set up at the University of California (Berkeley), Council for Social Science Data Archives with its headquarters at New York and a host of other such centres came into being in different American universities for the purpose of making cross-national studies by adopting the method of quantified analyses.

Side by side, developed the trend of area studies. It rested primarily on case studies of individual political systems of the developing world in the total context of their cultural and economic settings. Instead of paying attention to the measurableness of political data, writers taking to this trend tried to study the political systems of developing countries like Ghana, Burma, Sierra Leone and the like in a manner that the governmental system became an adjunct of the social system having economic, sociological, psychological and cultural dimensions. An inter-disciplinary focus became the tool in their hands with the result that it "tended to regard the governmental system as a dependent variable, an epiphenomenon based on social, psychological, cultural and economic determinants, or at best a mode of processing inputs generated by these forces and converting them into governmental outputs. The capacity to see politics itself as an essential, indeed a formative variable, in processes of social change was almost lost."[63]

Though both approaches—approach of quantitative methods and of area studies—became parts of an empirical theory, they differed from each other fundamentally. Whereas the former sought "to abstract from the rich complexity of real life a few measures or indices which are relatively amenable to quantification and therefore to comparison," the area approach directed attention to the unique variety of particular historic, geographic and cultural situations."[64] In other words, while the former should be called 'nomothetic', the latter as 'indeographic'. The political development approach should be regarded as the by-product of both these approaches or a bridge that joined the two within a broader framework. By the beginning of the sixties we came to hear about a good number of social theorists like Howard Riggins, G.A. Almond, Rostow, Philips Cutright, GB. Powell and Lucian Pye who started a new movement in this direction.[65]

It should, however, be pointed out that while political development approach became the most fashionable tool in the hands of new social theorists in the 1960s and 1970s, different writers took different lines that represented the growth of the approach towards its appreciation as well as a critique of the alternative approaches applicable to each other. It is that what Pye has called 'diverse definitions' and Nettl termed the problem of 'definitional priorities'. For instance, Rostow adopted the view of economic development[66] and, while following him and also differing from him,

63. *ibid.*, p. 325.
64. *ibid.*, p. 322.
65. The Princeton University Press brought out six volumes under the auspices of the Committee on Comparative Politics. They are Lucian W. Pye (ed.) : *Communications and Political Development*, Joseph la Palombara (ed.) : *Bureaucracy and Political Development;* Ward and Rustow (eds.) : *Political Modernisation in Japan and Turkey;* James S. Coleman (ed.) : *Education and Political Development;* Lucian Pye and Sidney Verba (eds.) : *Political Culture and Development;* Joseph la Palombara and Myron Weiner (eds.) : *Political Parties and Political Development.*
66. W.W. Rostow : *The Stage of Economic Growth* (London : Cambridge Univ. Press, I960).

Kenneth Organski suggested the process of political development through four stages – (i) political unification designed to achieve a centralisation of power in the hands of the state, (ii) industrialisation with a view to bring about economic development, (iii) national welfare where the result of the political and economic power gained by the state are available to the masses, and (iv) abundance where people begin to achieve high standards of material affluence.[67]

A sort of reaction, in this direction, started when certain keen observers came to realise that in a study of political development, there "had been too much dependence on sociology, especially on the structural-functional models as made familiar to political scientists by Gabriel A. Almond and his followers."[68] Thus, there occurred a shift in the focus and some new social theorists like Eisenstadt, Huntington, Diamant, Holt, Turner and Nye took to different lines that came to be known as 'will and capacity approach', 'problem solving capacity approach', 'institutionalisation approach', 'ability to sustain new goals approach', etc. Halpern talked_of the structural changes and demands let loose by the uncontrolled forces of transformation and will and capacity of political authority to cope with the changes and demands.[69] Eisenstadt defined political development as an institutional framework capable of continuous absorption of change.[70] The most important of all is the name of Huntington who not only freed this concept from the shackles of economics and sociology but also insisted on the aspect of 'decay' as an integral part of the study of political development.[71]

Pye and Almond write about political development. They ignore its reverse side, which is called political decay. S.P. Huntington removes this deficiency of the liberal theory of political development. In simple terms, it means that if the democratic system is developing more and more in a country of the Third World, it is development: if the things are moving in the opposite direction, it makes the case of political decay. For this purpose, he uses four variables and their antonyms to signify the marks of development and decay. These are.[72]

1. **Adaptability:** It means a long, regular and disciplined chain of leadership ready to welcome new changes and adapting the political, social and economic institutions accordingly. Its reverse aspect is *rigidity* which means that the leaders are fanatics who oppose change in the name of preserving their age-old institutions and patterns of life.
2. **Complexity:** It means that there is a network of institutions, each carrying its responsibility in a more or less free manner without interfering into the domain of others or without facing any interference from their side. Its reverse aspect is *simplicity* which means that the mode of operation is old and traditional in which there is no separation of functions.
3. **Autonomy:** It means that all institutions have their clearly defined sphere of activity and so one institution may not be a hindrance or a source of interference to others. Its reverse aspect is *subordination* which means that the institutions have no clearly defined area of activity of their own and so they remain under the control of some powerful institution of the state.
4. **Coherence:** It means a degree of consensus among different associations and institutions

67. A.F.K. Organski : *The Stages of Political Development* (New York : Alfred Knopf, 1965).
68. Varma, *op. cit.*, p. 278.
69. Malfred Halpern : "Towards Further Modernisation of the Study of New Nations" in *World Politics*, Vol XVII, October 1964, pp. 157-81.
70. See S.N. Eisenstadt : "Modernisation and Conditions of Sustained Growth" in *World Politics*, Vol. XVI, July, 1964.
71. Huntington, *op. cit.*
72. S. P. Huntington: " Political Development and Political Decay" in *World Politics*, Vol. XVII, No. 3, April, 1965, pp. 393-94.

Variables of Political Development and Decay	
Development	*Decay*
1. *Adaptability*	1. *Rigidity*
2. *Complexity*	2. *Simplicity*
3. *Autonomy*	3. *Subordination*
4. *Coherence or unity*	4. *Incoherence or disunity*

due to which unity prevails in the system. Forces of disruption are not there to disturb the operation of the political system. Its reverse aspect is *incoherence* or *disunity* that means the absence of consensus necessary for maintaining peace and unity in the state. The liberal writers lay emphasis on this key point that social and political change signifies evolution of society from incoherent homogeneity to coherent heterogeneity. The political development implies the growth of predictable patterns of behaviour in society, keeping pace with the growing mobility of the process of modernization. However, Huntington argues that the identification of political development with modernization is too vague and parochial, because it is wedded to one-way development and does not take into account the possibility of social regression.[73] Development and decay are the two polar points of a continuum and there are a series of countries at different points in it.[74] Eisentstadt identifies political development with the capacity of a political system to control and coordinate various processes of change in society generated by the socio-demographic and structural changes.[75]

Seeing all this, a critic may point out three weaknesses in this view of political development. First, there is a lot of disagreement among the writers on this subject about the implications and contours of political development. As a result of this, the concept, in all likelihood, is superficial and dysfunctional.[76] Second, it pertains to the bourgeois or market model of development and its real purpose is to justify the excellence of the Anglo-American model of development. It all makes the case of a distorted development as it may not be applicable to the poor and backward countries of the Third World. Almond and Coleman do not conceal their inhibitions when they observe that it "is clear from the list of attributes that the Anglo-American qualities most clearly approximate the model of the modern political system."[77] Last, no particular model of development may be prescribed for all countries of the world. China may adopt the Mao model, India may prefer the model of Nehru. "Just as different soils and climates produce different types of plants, similarly different social-economic factors require different strategies for their development."[78]

Marxian Model of Political Development

What we have said above relates to the model of political development as given by the American social theorists. It pertains to the 'democratic' model as evolved and now firmly established in advanced Western countries. It may be termed Anglo-American model of political development. Basically different from this is the communist model of political development. Here political development means movement from a discredited

73. *ibid.,* pp. 392-93.
74. *ibid.*
75. Eisenstadt: *Modernisation: Protest and Change,* pp. 1-19.
76. Rustow: "The Change to Change: Modernisation, Development and Politics" in *Comparative Politics,* 1971, p. 303.
77. G.A. Almond and J.C. Coleman: *The Politics of the Developing Areas,* p. 536.
78. V.R. Mehta: "The Concept of Political Development" in J.S. Bains and R.B. Jain (eds.): *Contemporary Political Theory,* p. 145.

bourgeois order to a fully socialist system in which the state is required during the transitional phase to accomplish the ideal of a classless society that would eventually culminate in a stateless condition of life. Obviously, the agent of political development is the bourgeois class in the first instance and the working class in the second. As Dodd says: "The crucial middle element in the pattern of development is the bourgeoisie."[79]

In other words, the Marxian view holds three assumptions: First, social class structure follows the distribution of economic forces. Second, socialism cannot emerge till the capitalist class exists. Third, consequently, socialism cannot be brought to the working class, but must emerge out of its conflict with the middle class. If applied to the study of the Third World countries, it signifies that a switch over from the so-called liberal democracy to the genuine people's democracy should be treated as the mark of political development.[80]

If so, for the Marxists, the ultimate aim of political development is something pre-determined—the coming of the communist system due to the inevitable application of the laws of historical materialism. Though one may discover some differences of emphasis at the hands of great Marxists like Lenin, Mao, Tito, Castro, etc., all are of one view so far as the crucial issue of the overthrow of the *status quo* and its substitution by a new social order under the 'dictatorship of the proletariat' is concerned. The most striking feature of this approach should, however, be traced in the fact that its protagonists "are much more concerned than most liberal democrats that history is on their side. Not only is the end of political development clear, the achievement of the end-state is to some degree beyond their control. Or at least, they must work within certain limits laid down by the Marxist interpretation of history".[81]

Though it is true that the concept of political development lacks a precise and universally acceptable definition, it is certain that the idea cannot be identified with a rigid or fixed pattern within which the over-all development of a country must take place. Just as different soils and climates produce different types of vegetation, similarly different socio-economic factors need different courses for their development. As a matter of fact, political development "is dependent upon the evolution of society from incoherent homogeneity to coherent heterogeneity."[82] Viewed in this context, we may frankly hit at the inherent shortcomings of both the liberal and the Marxian models. We may appreciate the view of Gunnar Myrdal who takes development as "a movement upward of a whole system of interdependent conditions as a complex process in which economic growth is only one of several categories of causally relevant conditions."[83]

Political Under-Development and Dependency Theory

A deeper study of the case of political development in the context of the colonial and semi-colonial countries at the hands of A.G. Frank, Paul A. Baran and F.H. Cardoso has led to the emergence of the idea of political under-development. It seeks to re-examine the situation obtaining in a semi-advanced country in the light of the 'exploitation' of the proletariat by the native bourgeois (and also feudal) elements in collaboration with foreign capitalists operating through 'multi-national organisations'. In other words, it may be taken as a study of 'neo-colonialism' that covers not only the poor and backward countries of the Third World but also a number of semi-advanced capitalist organisations of the world. In realistic terms, it implies a condition of

79. C.H. Dodd: *Political Development,* (London : Macmillan, 1972) p. 16.
80. *ibid.,* p. 19.
81. *ibid.,* pp. 11-12.
82. V.R. Mehta; *op. cit.,* p. 145.
83. Myrdal: *The Challenge of Poverty,* pp. 408-09. Prof. Daya Krishna holds that "the trouble with the concept of political development is that we donot quite know what is supposed to develop or whose development we are supposed to discern." *Political Development,* p. 10.

'double exploitation' of the people of these countries—exploitation of the native working class directly by the native capitalists and indirectly by the foreign capitalists through the network of multi-national corporations.

This theory of political under-development "derives from Marx who argued that in the long run it would have a detrimental effect on the industrial metropole as well as on the underdeveloped periphery."[84] In his thesis of 'imperialism as the final stage of capitalism', Lenin also stresses the point that the capitalist countries 'export' to their colonies not only innovation but their own internal crises as well. Therefore, capitalism creates gross social inequalities at home as well as in other areas under its control. As Paul A. Baran argues: "Far from serving as an engine of economic expansion of technological progress and of social change, the capitalist order in these countries has represented a framework for economic stagnation, for archaic technology, and for social backwardness. Thus, to the extent to which it depends on the volume of aggregate output and income, the economic surplus in backward capitalist countries has necessarily been small. Not that it has constituted a small proportion of total income. On the contrary,... the consumption of the productive population has been depressed to the lowest possible level, with 'lowest possible' corresponding in this case close to a subsistence minimum or to what in many underdeveloped countries falls notably below that benchmark. The economic surplus, therefore, while by comparison with the advanced countries small in absolute terms, has accounted for a large share of total output—as large as, if not larger than, in advanced capitalist countries."[85]

It follows that the case of under-development may be studied in the new role of native bourgeoisie working in alliance with multinational corporations. The capitalist class of a backward country aligns itself with the capitalist class of big and advanced countries and, as such, the consequent situation of 'double exploitation' places an independent country in the position of a semi-dependency. "Under-development goes hand-in-hand with economic dependency."[86] On this basis Fernando Henrique Cardoso presents the model of 'associated-development' that combines the idea of development with that of dependence. "Changes in international capitalist organisation have produced a new international division of labour, the key to which is the multi-national corporation. The interests of the foreign corporations become essential to the internal prosperity and growth of dependent countries. On the one hand, they help to produce growth of dependent countries. On the other hand, countries hosting multinational corporations are dependent for their development on their decisions and activities."[87] In the words of Cardoso": .... the consequence of imperialism with respect to dependent countries and nations (or colonies) was the integration of the latter into the international market. Inequalities among nations and economies resulted from imperialism's development to the extent that the input of raw materials and export of manufactured goods were the bases of the imperialist-colonial relationship. The reproduction and amplification of inequality between advanced economies developed as a by-product of the very process of capitalist growth."[88]

---

84. David Apter: *Introduction to Political Analysis,* p. 499.
85. Baran: *The Political Economy of Growth,* pp. 163-64.
86. Apter, *op. cit.,* p. 501.
87. See Cardoso: "Associated-Dependent Development: Theoretical and Practical Implications" in Alfred Stepan (ed): *Authoritarian Brazil.* pp. 142-76.
88. Cardoso: "Dependency and Development in Latin-America" in Hamza Alvi and Zendor Shanin (eds.): *An Introduction to the Sociology of Developing Societies.* As a matter of fact, under-development has emerged as the consequence of capitalist penetration and occupation of the developing countries. Within the latter in turn emerge national capitalism and national bourgeoisie which is unable to offer any way out of under-development. A.G. Frank says that under-development in a dependent region such as Latin-America cannot be understood as the product of a bourgeois policy formulated in response to class interests and structure, which are, in turn, determined by the dependence of the Latin-American satellite on the colonialist metropolis. *Lumpenbourgeoisie and Lumpenproletariat,* p. 1.

According to Andre Gunder Frank, the pioneer of the dependency theory, what is important for the purposes of development and under-development is not the sacrifice of the loser nation in terms of its actual loss of income or wealth or the absolute gain of the recipient country but the contribution of economic surplus accruing to the imperialist country from the colony. While the colonies and semi-colonies are denied the developmental possibilities of this capital, the metropolitan country can use it for its own economic development. The most unfortunate part of this phenomenon is that while the imperialist class may gain just a pound of flesh, the colonies or semi-colonies may lose a hundred times more in terms of their potential resources, their economic assets and their physical capacities. The reason behind it may be discovered in the control of the advanced capitalist countries over the sensitive and strategic areas of the colonial and semi-colonial countries. It may be seen in the case of the economies of the Third World countries like Guinea and Nigeria as well as in those of the so-called advanced states of Europe like Spain and Portugal. The difference of a big degree may, however, be marked out between the exploitation of the poor and backward countries of the Third World and of the semi-developed states of the Western World.

In this regard another great theorist is Immanuel Wallerstein whose 'world economic system' frankly asserts that "there are today no socialist systems in the world economy any more than there are feudal systems, because there is one world system."[89] It is world economy and it is by definition capitalist in form. This unified world economy system is three-tiered—the core, semi-periphery and periphery. (a) *Core economies* are the location for advanced economic activities such as manufacturing, banking and the processing of primary products. (b) *Semi-peripheral* areas trade with both core and periphery and occupy a kind of half-way position in terms of such features as profit margins and wage levels. (c) The activities of the *peripheral economies* are more or less restricted to the production of primary products. In this system of three circles, the semi-periphery plays a very important role in the operation of the world system as a whole.[90]

Frank and Wallerstein joined hands with other writers of the same view. Thus, they asserted in one of their important works:[91]

1. We believe that there is a social whole that may be called a capitalist world economy.
2. We believe that we cannot make an intelligent analysis of the various states taken seriously without placing their so called internal life in the context of the world division of labour, located in the world economy. Nor can we make a coherent analysis that segregates economic, political and social variables.
3. We believe that throughout the history of the capitalist world-economy, there has been increasing organisation of oppressed groups within the world system and increasing opposition to its continuance.
4. We believe that the hegemony of the US is declining owing to the 'increasing competitiveness' of West European and Japanese products, emergence of Washington-Tokyo-Beijing axis and wars among the states in the periphery.

Thus, the cases of political underdevelopment and the world economic system are interrelated. The whole analysis is constructed on the basis of centre-periphery relationship. "Centre and periphery are distinguished in terms of the market relations

89. See Wallerstein's *The Modern World System* (1971), *World Inequality* (1975), and *The Capitalist World Economy* (1979).
90. Roger Dale: "Nation-State and International System: The World System Perspective" in Gregor McLennan, David Held and Stuart Hall (eds.): *The Idea of the Modern State,* p. 192.
91. Samir Amin, Giovanni Aright, A.G. Frank and Immanuel Wallerstein: *Dynamics of Global Crisis* (New York, 1982), pp. 9-10.

that integrate them into the world capitalist system, whose expansion has brought about such differentiation. The centre develops on the basis of the expansion of its home market and in it the capitalist mode of production becomes the only mode of production. The capitalist mode of production is imposed on the periphery from outside, but in such a way that its penetration is incomplete."[92]

Dependency theory is jsut a corollary to the theory of under-development. It was through a discreet historical process, according to Celso Furtado, that development and under-development became parts of the same continuum. Dependency is a containing or a conditioning situation. So Santos says: "We can now define very clearly what is meant by dependence. In the first place, dependence is a conditioning situation in which the economies of one group of countries are conditioned by the development and expansion of others. The relationship of interdependency between such economies and the world trading system becomes a dependent relationship when some countries can expand through self-impulsion, while others being in a dependent position, can only expand as a reflection of the expansion of the dominant countries which may have positive or negative effects on their immediate development. In either case the basic situation of dependency causes these countries to be both backward and exploited."[93]

The dependency theorists or the 'dependistas' concede the point that some sort of capitalist industrialisation has taken place in the Third World and it has created the model of 'new dependency'. Since this sort of development is a dependent development, Faletto and Cardoso call it 'associated-dependent-development'. For them the structural dependency perspective focuses on the inter-relationship at three levels: the international economy, the nation-state and the alliance of social classes within the state. They are very clear that the state in Latin-America is in no sense a passive agency 'mechanically conditioned by external dominance.'[94] The state is a system of domination which relates dialectically to external factors and one of the tasks they set themselves is to develop concepts which will enable them to explain how internal and external processes of political domination relate one to the other.[95]

Wallerstein's Illustration

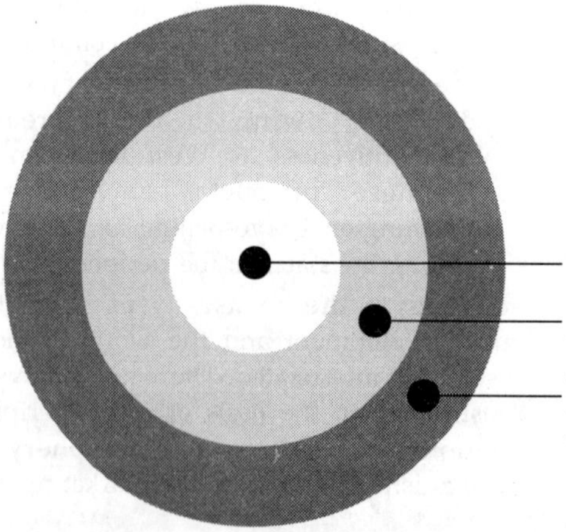

92. Roger Dale, *op. cit.,* p. 188.
93. T. D. Santos: "The Crisis of Development Theory and the Problem of Dependence in Latin-America" in Henry Bernstein (ed.): *Under-Development and Development: The Third World Today,* pp. 57-80.
94. Faletto and Cardoso: *Dependency and Development in Latin-America,* p. 173.
95. *ibid.,* p. xviii.

Essentially, the position of these two writers is that the process of economic expansion in the more developed countries of Latin-America (as Mexico, Brazil, Argentina and Chile) has posed the problem at the level of national politics of the incorporation of new social groups, the industrial and commercial bourgeoisie and elements of the popular sector. "The quest for the stake in the system on the part of such groups together with the need of the state to reconcile economic expansion with political stability, has led to the emergence of varying patterns of alliance. The variations from country to country depended upon their respective resource base before the period of ISI (import-substitution-industrialisation), the nature and degree of foreign involvement and the consequent balance of social forces."[96]

The chief cause of political under-development should be traced not only in the fact of 'satellite colonisation' of the poor and the backward countries of the world but also in the existence of feudal and bourgeois classes at whose hands the native proletariat suffers exploitation. It may be described as a case of 'double exploitation.' While the feudal aristocracy exploits the rural peasantry, the bourgeoisie exploits the urban working class. Thus, the feudal and bourgeois elements are combined and they acquire political power to perpetuate their hold. But contradictions develop within their ranks and, in order to remove them, the exploiters adopt tactics that leads to the vulgarisation and criminalisation of politics. It also happens that the disgruntled sections of the community take to the ways of violence as a result of which events of terrorism occur frequently to bring about structural changes in the social and economic system of the country.

Socialist development of a country may be described as a way out of this crucial difficulty. But we may take note of the fact that in most of the countries of the Third World, the clever leaders prefer to establish a kind of 'protosocialism'—a form of bureaucracy that elevates to power a new and essentially corrupt and repressive class. As a result of this, contradictions develop within the so-called socialist forces that create a more baffling situation. What more, a critical student of political economy may take note of the fact that the super-socialist powers like former USSR and China have their own vested interests in installing a kind of their satellite colonisation. Liberalisation trends in a satellite country like Hungary, Czechoslovakia and Poland were suppressed by force. It is also possible that an under-developed state like Chile or Guinea may become a 'proto-Stalinist' state in pursuit of its development through the course of socialism.

Such theories failed to have a long life. They became unfashionable in the 1980s for the main reason that their empirical base was very weak. It appeared that the socio-political consequences of under-development and dependency had been worked out without much precision and evidence.[97] Humza Alvi says that in post-colonial societies, the state is over-developed *vis-a-vis* the indigenous society and subservient to the metropolis.[98] The neoliberals question the efficacy of structuralist or nationalist economic strategies finding vindication in the increasing economic difficulties and ultimate collapse of the communist system in the countries of East Europe. Todaro comments: "Contrary to the claims of the dependency theorists, the neoclassical counter-revolutionaries argue that the Third World is under-developed not

96. Vicky Randall and Robin Theobald: *Political Change and Under-Development: A Critical Introduction* (London: Macmillan, 1998), pp. 147-48.
97. S.D. Muni: "Dependency Theory and Development Dilemmas" in Iqbal Narain (ed.): *Development, Politics and Social Theory* (New Delhi: Sterling Publishers, 1989), p. 89.
98. Humza Alvi: "The State in Post-Colonial Societies: Pakistan and Bangladesh" in *New Left Review*, Vol. 74, 1972, p. 36.

Critical Comments of Chilcote on Political Development and Under-Development

1. Mainstream perspectives have been found to be abstract and lacking in applicability to concrete situations, ethnocentric in the preference for the Anglo-American system, and favourable to capitalism.
2. Such writings have certain tendencies to look at conditions of exploited poverty and inequality; to stress exchange, circulation and trade rather than production and relations of production; to ignore relevant classical theories of political economy, including Marxism, to overlook issues around the role of state and class in the planned economy or market mechanism; to emphasise capitalist accumulation and its consequences; and to project idealistic and inevitable outcomes with concerete analysis.
3. Work on imperialism has been joined with developmental theory particularly by Bill Warren who stressed the progressive aspects of capitalism as releasing individual creativity and organised cooperation in production as well as serving as the basis for the advance to socialism as sensed by Brewer.
4. A further problem has been the miscasing of development as political or representative democracy with attention to Western style of governmental institutions and political parties, thereby diverting attention from capital accumulation and their impact (negative and positive) on the people.
5. Theories of development and under-development should serve further analysis as they have benefited past understanding dating to nineteenth century. Although these theories donot stand as polished or unified, they may help in understanding unequal development in an evolving consolidation of capital in the international order. They may stimulate awareness of problems associated with delayed capitalist development and lead to theoretical and practical thinking on ways for deprived people to relate to and resist oppressive manifestations of capitalism and to search for transition to democracy and socialism.

R.H. Chilocote: *Theories of Comparative Politics,* pp. 266-68. See Bill Warren: *Imperialism: Pioneer of Capitalism* (1980) and Anthony Brewer: *Marxist Theories of Imperialism: A Critical Survey* (1990).

because of the predatory activities of the First World and the international agencies that it controls but rather because of the heavy hands of the state and the coruption, inefficiency and lack of economic incentives that permeate the economies of developing nations."[99]

In fine, the story of under-development is an account of exploitation of the backward and semi-backward peoples at the hands of the highly advanced countries of the world. The native bourgeoisie plays its own part in the nefarious drama of political economy. It becomes the expoited force at the hands of multinational corporations in one respect and a partner with them in exploiting the 'proletariat' of of its own country for the sake of economic interests. It all occurs due to the existence of an imitated bourgeois state in the under-developed countries where the ruling party "as a mass movement is only a shell within which *compradors,* or local bourgeoisie, manipulate power, Inequality and unemployment flourish, with the result being agricultural stagnation, urban immigration, food shortages, inflation, balance of payments crises, further dependence on foreign finance, and a non-competitive domestic industrial sector."[100]

Critical Appraisal

The concept of political development, as discussed in the preceding sections, may be subjected to these lines of criticism :

1. This concept lacks a precise definition. Even after studying the enormous literature on this subject, one wonders as to what it

99. Cited in Randall and Theobald, *op. cit.,* p. 153.
100. Apter, *op. cit.,* p. 500.

really includes and what it really excludes. It becomes, like the very subject of comparative politics, 'either everything or nothing'. It entangles the case of political development into a labyrinth of all sorts of developments whether economic, or cultural, or sociological and the like with the result that anybody can keep anything within its fold. Thus Riggs rightly feels at the very outset of his study: "In fact, of course, there is as yet no such theory, although there are a host of speculations and even hypotheses. Nor is there any concensus on the meaning of the word 'development' in this context, or even, for that matter, of the word 'political'."[101] Even the large-scale publication programme brought under the six volumes published under the auspices of the Princeton University presents "a great deal of mature and sophisticated, as well as some immature and undigested, material before the reader."[102]

2. Studies of the subject of political development "suffer from the absence of any coherent political model of the developmental process and that the entire analysis is left at the point where extra-political factors have set the stage for political change."[103] That is, the entire study presents a very confusing picture and, in addition to that, it plunges the discipline of political science into the ocean of other social sciences like economics and sociology. Prof. S.P. Varma observes: "The relevance of social, economic, administrative, political and cultural variables in shaping political development could not have been denied, but it was difficult to determine what relative weight a particular factor carried. Many of those concepts could not be subjected to empirical tests. In most cases, the necessary data for testing them was not likely to be available. The greatest drawback of these studies, however, was that they treated political development as a dependent variable generated by something else, a world-wide wave of modernisation, nationalism or democracy and not as an independent, or intervening variable which, in its own turn, could shape things."[104]

3. The concept of political development does not offer a model that may be uniformly applicable to all countries of the world and, for this reason, be appreciated by social theorists belonging to any school, whether Liberal or Marxist. It cannot satisfy the communist scholars who look toward the building of a classless society, eventually moving towards a stateless one, as the only model of development. What is a peculiarly noticeable point at this stage is that, far from satisfying Marxist writers, it, has not been able to win the appreciation of the many anti-communist social theorists as well. Diverse analyses of political development given by the American writers are just like the critiques of one directed against another. It will, therefore, not be an error to say that the theorists of political development have certainly failed to understand the political reality of the countries of the Third World inasmuch as they have tried to look at the poor and backward peoples of the Afro-Asian region through the spectacles of the Chicago and Harvard Universities. It is due to this that whatever theories of political development have been developed so far they "lie in shambles today."[105]

4. Likewise, the Marxian approach to political development may be criticised for offering a deterministic course of social evolution. The Marxists look like faced with a

101. *ibid.*, p. 317.
102. Varma, *op. cit.*, p. 274.
103. David M. Wood, *op. cit.*, p. 506.
104. Varma, *op. cit.*, pp. 279-80.
105. *ibid.*, p. 290.

traditionality that confuses them and they find it very difficult to fit traditional societies into the rather rigid Marxian framework.[106] One may say how dictatorship of the proletariat may be treated as a sign of political development and not that of a decay or decline in view of the fact that here people have a closed society and a singularistic order under the iron hold of an elite of the Communist party. It may be commented that the dictatorship of the proletariat "would represent the actual interests of a minority which only by some metaphysical sleight of hand could be made out to represent not only the interests of the whole but of the future also."[107]

Despite these serious drawbacks, this approach has certainly broadened the scope of empirical political investigations by aligning the frontiers of comparative politics with those of other sister sciences and also by engaging the attention of a host of new social theorists towards the study of the political conditions of the new and developing societies of the Third World. Viewed thus, the study of political development has a relevance of its own and it "would be outright tragic if the fruits of development theory would present the Asian and African masses with a choice between continued frustration and chaos on the one hand and total submission on the other."[108] Almond and Powell also hopefully visualise: "The world of politics has never waited for the observer to finish his quiet contemplation. In the present century, political development seems to be proceeding at an ever-accelerating rate, overwhelming our comparative 'snapshots' by making them obsolete before we finish our books and articles. It is increasingly obvious that the study of politics must be a dynamic system-and-process analysis, and not a static and structural one."[109]

As a last word, it may be said that the concept of political development cannot be identified with a rigid or fixed pattern within which the overall development of a country must take place. Just as different soils and climates produce different types of vegetation, similarly different socio-economic factors need different courses for their growth. Viewed in this context, we may frankly hit at the inherent shortcomings of both the Liberal and Marxian approaches.

106. See T.P. Thornton (ed.) : *The Third World in Soviet Perspective* (Princeton : Princeton Univ. Press, 1964).
107. Daya Krishna : *Political Development : A Critical Perspective* (New Delhi : Oxford, 1979), p. 100.
108. Karl Von Vorys: "Use and Misuse of Development Theory" in Charlesworth (ed.), *op. cit.*, p. 363.
109. Almond and Powell, *op. cit.*, p. 41.

10

Political Modernisation

> Political systems and social change cross and meet at the processes of political entry. These processes are the reflectors oj social change: they can mirror changes in values, aspirations, perceptions of opportunities, as well as changes in actual structures and roles. At the same time, they exert their own influence in their distribution of status and prestige, their efficiency in selecting persons appropriate to the tasks to be carried out; by their flexibility they may contribute to system stability and development, by their rigidity they may create points of tension and breakdown.
>
> **—W.H. Morris-Jones[1]**

The political culture of a people involving their norms, attitudes, values and orientations and political institutions based on them change from one form to another either speedily by means of a revolution, or peacefully in a gradual and smooth manner, or by any means lying between the two extreme gradations. The essential point is that a study of change should be made in the context of many inter-related factors as industrialisation, urbanisation, technological development, education, commerce, cultural and sociological development and communications network. "The ultimate objective must be to construct a scheme that incorporates these factors in a comprehensive analysis of social change."[2]

Political Modernisation: Comprehensive Implications and Dimensions

Political modernisation, like political development, is a term that cannot be defined precisely though it can be understood, as Claude E. Welch, Jr. suggests, as "the process based upon the rational utilisation of resources and aimed at the establishment of a modern society", or as Benjamin Schwartz describes it as "the systematic, sustained and powerful application of human energies to the rational control of man's physical and social environment for various human purposes." This term stands for the transformation of the political culture in response to the changes in social and physical environments in view of this essential fact that political change "is intricately related to a wide spectrum of social and economic factors."[3] Huntington thus describes it as "a multi-faceted process involving change in all areas of human thought and activity."[4]

From the above, it is obvious that the subject of political modernisation is a comprehensive affair in as much as it includes much within the ambit of politics that is generally taken to cover the realms of economics, sociology, even psychology. It refers to the change in political culture and political institutions as a result of the process of modernisation—"that is

1. Morris-Jones : "Political Recruitment and Development" in Colin Leys (ed.) : *Politics and Change in Developing Countries* (London : Cambridge Univ. Press, 1969), p. 122.
2. Morton R. Davies and Vaughan A. Lewis : *Models of Political Systems* (Delhi: Vikas, 1971), p. 93.
3. *ibid.,* p. 98.
4. S P. Huntington cited in S.P. Varma : *Modern Political Theory* (Delhi : Vikas, 1975), p. 303.

everything like economic growth, increase of gross national product and *per capita* income, economic planning, greater industrialisation, accumulation of capital, increasing urbanisation and a reduction in the proportion of those engaged in agriculture, scientific advance, improved transport and a higher rate of literacy. The "take off' point for economic growth often occurs when agriculture claims less than forty five per cent of the working population. From the economic point of view, an implicit assumption is that economic and technological growth and increased consumption is inherently desirable."[5]

Modernisation is a multi-faceted process and, for this reason, political modernisation is a concept having several dimensions as:[6]

1. At the *psychological* level, it involves a change in the norms, values, attitudes and orientations of the people;
2. At the *intellectual* level, it involves a tremendous expansion of man's knowledge about his environment and the diffusion of this knowledge throughout society through increased literacy and mass communications,
3. At the *demographic* level, it implies improvement in the standards of living and progress towards the mobility of people and urbanisation,
4. At the *social* level, it has a tendency to replace the focus of individual's loyalty to family and other primary groups to voluntarily organised secondary associations, and
5. At the *economic* level, it involves the growth of market agriculture, improvement in commerce at the expense of agriculture, development of industrialisation and widening of the economic activity.

Thus, modernisation "is regarded as a comprehensive phenomenon which brings about radical changes in the field of economic development, mainly in the direction of industrialisation and material advancement, changes in the nature and content of the political systems and also changes in the social and psychological spheres of life."[7]

Certainly, the concept of political modernisation does not seem to be as vague as that of political development that we have studied in the preceding chapter. The reason for this should be discovered in the open-endedness of this concept. While the concept of political development may be described either as vague or as rigid pattern of social change, the idea of political modernisation is quite simple. It implies the existence of a traditional order that is to be changed for the better. That is, it is the effect of the new on the old, not the total eradication of the old and its substitution by the new one as is covered under the rubric of political development. "We feel more comfortable in asserting that a society is modernising than in claiming that it is developing... A modernised house is very different from a modern one—and often more comfortable to live in. Modernisation does not necessarily result in modernity."[8]

In other words, the concept of political modernisation refers to the case of political transformation as occurred in the European countries in particular in the modern period and then recurred in other countries of the world in recent times. In the political sphere, this transformation may be expressed as a syndrome of related characteristics of this term. Thus, as suggested by Pye, this syndrome may be said to include: (i) general attitude towards equality that allows equality of opportunity to participate in politics and compete for

5. Michael Curtis : *Comparative Government and Politics : An Introductory Essay in Political Science* (New York : Harper & Row, 1968), p. 65
6. Varma, *op. cit.*, pp. 302-303.
7. *ibid.*
8. C.H. Dodd : *Political Development* (London : Macmillan, 1972), p. 12.

government office; (ii) capacity of a political system to formulate policies and to have them carried out; (iii) differentiation and specialisation of political functions, though not at the expense of their overall integration; and (iv) secularisation of the political process—the separation of politics from religious and other influences.[9]

However, the concepts of political modernisation and of political development converge on a point when we deal with the capacity and capability of a political system to solve the problems arising out of the trend of renovation and change. The process of modernisation leads to the emergence of some crucial problems and challenges that a political system has to face and cope with so as to create the situation of 'development' or conversely speaking, so as to avoid the baleful situation of 'decay', 'decline', 'disintegration' or 'demise'. Viewed in this context, political development becomes identifiable "with a process which aims at a particular political condition, but one which creates an institutional framework for solving an ever-widening range of social problems."[10]

Stages of Political Modernisation: Apter's Paradigm of the Developing Countries

The subject of political modernisation has its special relevance in the case of the developing countries of the Third World which "are damned if they do, and damned if they don't."[11] Such is the dram before the Third World countries. The reason for this may be traced in their perennial quest for the way they should adopt to achieve the goal. The fact stands out that no country desires to relinquish the path of development or modernisation and, at the same time, most of the Third World countries fail to choose the option between liberal and socialist courses. Apter is of the view that while the liberal capitalist solution poses the problem of inequity, the Marxian socialist requires coercion. And yet the struggle for political modernisation persists because 'development embodies hope.'[12]

Like political development, political modernisation also takes place where it is most easily accepted or wanted. Thus, it signifies the 'transfer of roles from metropole to periphery.'[13] Moreover, it has its stages, each having its own predicaments. According to Apter, four stages may be earmarked in this regard:[14]

1. ***Stage of Contact and Control :*** It began with a few hardy and enterprising individuals with a particular strong sense of mission, or greed, or zeal, or desire for adventure. They paved way for innovation. Since it happened in the advanced countries of Europe in the seventeenth, eighteenth and nineteenth centuries, this stage found its start in the adventures of the British, French, German, Dutch, Portuguese and Italian colonialists.[15] Hence, the first stage of development represented a process by means of which the then new wealth of Europe and new technologies, by creating opportunities for trade, effected not only the settlement of trade centres but the acquisition of territory as well. It was accompanied by the belief that the condition of dependent peoples must be changed. A poet like Kipling shrewdly termed it 'white man's burden'. It was marked by the consolidation of the alien rule, erection of a stable system of authority and the beginning of urbanisation, health and schooling for an elite occurring at the end of this stage.

9. Lucian W. Pye : *Aspects of Political Development* (Boston : Little, Brown and Company, 1966), pp. 45-48.
10. Alfred Diament : "Political Development: Approaches to Theory and Strategy" in J.D. Montgomery and W.J. Suffin (eds.) : *Approaches to Development* (New York : McGraw Hill, 1966), p. 16.
11. David E. Apter : *Introduction to Political Analysis* (New Delhi : Prentice Hall of India 1978), p. 461.
12. *ibid.*
13. *ibid.*, p. 469.
14. *ibid.*, pp. 469-73.
15. See George Masselman : *The Cradle of Colonialism* (New Haven, Connecticut: Yale Univ Press, 1963).

2. ***Stage of Reaction and Counter-action :*** It showed the effects of Western colonialism. Innovative foreign elites of the bureaucrats, missionaries, traders and the like created new urban centres or renovated the old ones and the native persons drew closer to them. Rules and regulations required local authorities to assist in carrying out the dictates of the colonial regimes. What prospered even more were the cultural and racial notions of superiority used to justify alien domination. In this way, primitive countries were opened up to the benefits of civilisation, trade and commerce not always to their enhancement. At the same time, exploitation of the dependent peoples became more severe the most heinous type of which we find in the slave trade of the African people. The notable feature of this stage was that local and foreign elements interacted; new forms of association developed; and new interests arose. At the same time, nationalism led by an elite grew. The nationalist leaders demanded more and more participation in public affairs. The colonial masters played the strategy of winning over the nationalist elites to their side and repressing those who could not be tamed for their purpose.
3. ***Stage of Contradiction and Emancipation :*** With the growth of new elites, more complex associations in politics arose. The base of the nationalist movement widened. Elites developed in the rural and semi-urban areas and the nationalist leaders sharpened the pace of their struggle. Attacks on colonial authorities combined with the demand for sharing power and the events of revolution in the West like American War of Independence of 1776 and French Revolution of 1789 became the source of inspiration.[16] To face the challenge of the growing nationalism, the colonial powers devised the strategy of introducing their own democratic systems in degrees. Such responses, in turn, stimulated political organisations, mass movements, demands for greater independence, and other forerunners of the impending break with the colonising power. Intellectuals fomented rebellion, providing ideological arguments and alternatives. Charismatic or near-charismatic leaders promised a new unity with independence.[17]
4. ***Stage of Search for a New Generative Solution :*** It occurred after the advent of independence and, as such, it was marked by the inauguration of the second revolution in the social, economic and technological spheres. Thus, the main problem before the developing countries is to use political independence to produce more viable and effective communities without becoming ensnared in 'neo-colonialism'. This is partly a matter of prompting economic growth, partly an awakening to the predicaments or uneven change. To avoid such predicaments of modernisation, some 'political leaders opt for developmental socialist solutions.' Each proposed solution, however, and each type of political system soon generates its own problems and difficulties. Some rely on force at the expense of liberty. These spend large sums on police and army fire power. Others which emphasise liberty soon find themselves at the mercy of the rich or middle sectors of the population who claim access to politics (and supply a good many of the politicians) at the expense of the poor.[18] One striking point at this stage is that the nationalist leadership of the well-known nationalist figures loses its charismatic hold and the 'imported democratic system' is replaced by some authoritarian model provided by the only ruling party or military junta.[19]

16. See S.M. Lipset : *The First Nation* (New York : Basic Books, 1963).
17. Apter, *op cit.*, p. 474.
18. *ibid.*, p. 471.
19. See A.F.K. Organski : *The Stages of Political Development* (New York : Alfred A. Knopf, 1965).

We may take note of the fact that the analysis of Apter is based on the dichotomy of 'tradition' represented by the native forces and 'modernity'brought about by the alien masters.[20] The process of conflict between the two begins with the gradual establishment of the Western colonial system. At the same time, a sort of unique reconciliation develops with the passage of time. The processes of synthesisation and contradiction flow simultaneously with the result that the natives not only emulate and imitate the 'political culture' of their masters, they also cry for their emancipation. When national independence is achieved, they struggle for a suitable course so as to realise the aim of establishing social and economic democracy in the country.

Political Modernisation and Social Change

A study of political modernisation shows its inter-connection with social mobilisation—"a process by which major clusters of old social, economic and psychological commitments are eroded or broken down and the people become available for new patterns of socialisation and behaviour."[21] Viewed in this context, social systems of the world may be said to be of three varieties:

(i) ***Primitive and Backward Social Systems :*** This category includes highly backward social systems of the world where traditional responses, customs and rituals still carry the authority with them. Authority remains where it has been and no serious effort is made in the direction of political mobilisation, socialisation and recruitment. "The right to participate in deciding both in the institutions of government and in the limited number of voluntary associations is largely confined to members of particular kinship and lineage groups, or to those belonging to religious or caste communities. This hierarchical structure of authority results in either excessive submissiveness among the people at large, or adherence to extremist egalitarian ideals as a reaction against the established system."[22]

Several countries of the Third World like Nepal, Bhutan and Sierra Leone may be put in this category. Here primitive political norms and values are dominant. The high offices of the state are shared by the men of the same family or tribe or by the elites who enjoy a sort of charismatic hold over the destinies of their simple and innocent people. Urbanisation may have a start; the rate of literacy may increase slowly; industrialisation may be inching upward and mass media channels expanding; but many of the goals identified with political modernisation like democracy, stability, structural differentiation, achievement patterns and national integration seem to be, as Huntington says, beyond realisation as ever. What is peculiarly striking about the political modernisation of the countries belonging to this category is that in some of the cases, apart from a movement towards competitiveness and democracy, there have also occurred a shift in the reverse direction as is evident in the form of setting up an autocratic military rule or one-party powerful rule.[23] It is also found that national integration, instead of being within the possibility of achievement, is disrupted by ethnic conflicts and civil wars. "Even countries which had built up some kind of party systems or developed highly efficient

---

20. See S.N. Eisenstadt : *Tradition, Change and Modernity* (New York : Wiley 1973), pp. 98ff.
21. Karl W. Deutsch : "Social Mobilisation and Political Development" in *American Political Science Review*, Vol. LV, September 1961, p. 496.
22. Davies and Lewis, *op. cit.*, p. 97.
23. See Rupert Emerson : *From Empire to Nation* (Cambridge : Harvard Univ, Press 1960), Ch. V.

bureaucratic systems in the colonial days, saw them declining gradually."[24]

(ii) ***Developing Social Systems :*** The countries falling in this category show a dichotomy of tradition and modernity that may be visualised most clearly in those parts of the world where people have lived under the colonial hold of some European power. A cross-cultural phenomenon developed there as the masters imposed their political culture successfully over the social and political structures of the countries under their colonial domination. It is found that during the days of freedom struggles, these traditional attitudes and influences "'tended to be submerged in the unity maintained by the common goal of national independence. Once independence was achieved, the traditional pressures reasserted themselves usually becoming the basis for interest groups and political parties. The result is a complex mixture of the traditional and the modern, consisting of a series of modern institutions resting (often precariously) on a traditional base which is continually under the impact of increasing pressure of industrialisation and urbanisation."[25]

Two important points should be noted in this connection. First, though the pace of political modernisation becomes rapid, the element of tradition is not thoroughly eroded by the trend towards modernity. The case of Turkey is cited as the best example in this regard. We may see that Mustapha Kemal (Kemal Ataturk) sought to modernise Turkey through the process of political socialisation and his successors like Ismet Inonu did the same by laying stress on the new symbols of nationhood—national flag, national anthem, national history, national monuments, national education, etc.—the Turkish people could not be thoroughly westernised. Le Vine has, therefore, concluded that it is misleading to regard political values as something which "must be destroyed or replaced, they need to be combined with the new institutions and patterns of behaviour."[26]

Second, and it follows from the above, that no break with the past "can be complete, and even though far-reaching, and fundamental changes may be effected, an element of continuity remains.'[27] It is obvious, owing to this reason, that while the process of political modernisation, socialisation and recruitment is at work, the people cultivate blind faith in the social and political philosophy of their leaders with the result that they are deified and the state ideology is given the rank of a 'religion.'[28] The case of a country like India may be cited as a shining example in this regard where people not oniy followed Gandhi, they took Gandhism as the political religion of the country. Such a turn in the process of political socialisation creates a stumbling block. It then informs that a change in politics require first a change in State religion.[29]

(iii) ***Western or Developed Social Systems :*** This category includes those countries where the people are affluent and highly educated, the country is well urbanised and industrialised and institutional arrangements are such that the decision-makers "are either elected by the people at

24. See Varma, *op. cit.*, p. 304.'
25. Michael Rush and Philip Althoff : *An Introduction to Political Sociology* (London : Nelson, 1971), p. 64.
26. Robert L. Vine : "Political Socialisation and Culture Change" in Clifford Geertz (ed.) : *Old Societies in the New States* (New York, 1963), pp. 284-85.
27. Rush and Althoff, *op. cit.*, p. 68.
28. See David Apter : "Political Religion in New Nations" in Geertz, *op. cit.*, pp. 57-104.
29. See Rush and Althoff, *op. cit.*, p. 66.

large, or are legally answerable to, and act on behalf of, those who are representatives of the people. In this sense, the predominant characteristic of the authoritative decisions in these states is that they are democratically based."[30] It may be that there are some non-democratic institutionalised features that affect the decision-making process in these social systems as hierarchical nature of party organisations with much centralisation of power at the top, nevertheless the general degree of commitment to democratic form "is great and corresponding feelings of involvement in social and political spheres among the population make it unlikely that decisions will for very long go unchallenged."[31]

Countries like America Britain, and France can be placed in this category. Instances are there to show that an American President like Richard Nixon, though the real head of national administration, had to quit when he found the matters reaching the point of his impeachment. A great Prime Minister like Harold Wilson had to go to polls on the issue of Britain's joining the European Common Market. A strong President like Charles de Gaulle had to grant independence to Algeria, though he was inducted into the highest office of France for the cause of crushing the movement of the Algerian people for independence. It is clear that these social systems are well committed to the observance of democratic norms and, thus, they are far more advanced than those belonging to the second category which, as Shils says, "are a regime of civilian rule through representative institutions in the matrix of public liberties."[32]

Political Modernisation and Political Systems

If political modernisation can be used as a variable for classifying social systems, it may also be used for presenting a typological illustration of the political systems of the world. The name of Edward A. Shils is important in this direction who presents a classification of modern political systems into two varieties—democracy and oligarchy—and their further classification into political and tutelary democracies of the former and modernising, totalitarian and traditional oligarchies of the latter. Taking political modernisation as a plausible ground for the stratification of political systems, he begins with the case of primitive and backward societies where parochial loyalties make it difficult to achieve the norms of modern democratic life like rule of law and legitimate exercise of political authority and where availability of justice in administration and adjudication process is made difficult, even impossible, owing to the tendency of favour towards the kinsmen, castemen and co-believers.[33] In the middle, comes the case of developing societies where the inherited body of traditional beliefs, existing social structure, scarcity of the human material of politics, and normal and intellectual qualities of the elites themselves all affect the operation of the political system, revealing its true potentialities and thus affecting the nature of the ideal sought as well as the means of attaining it.[34] At the apex are the developed political systems of the world that have attained the goal of dynamism—concerned with the people, democratic and equalitarian, scientific, economically advanced, sovereign and influential.[35]

---

30. Davies and Lewis, *op. cit.*, p. 97.
31. *ibid.*
32. E.A. Shils : *Political Development in New States* (The Hague : Mounton & Co, 1962), p. 48.
33. Davies and Lewis, *op. cit.*, p. 95.
34. *ibid.*
35. Shils, *op. cit.*, p. 10.

Rustow and Ward on Characteristics of a Modern Polity*

1. A highly differentiated and functionally specific system of governmental organisation.
2. A high degree of integration within the governmental structure .
3. Prevalence of rational and secular procedures for the making of political decisions.
4. A widespread and effective sense of popular identification with the history, territory and national identity of the state.
5. Large volume, wide range and high efficiency of political and administrative decisions.
6. Widespread political interest and achievement in the political system though not necessarily in the decision-making aspects thereof
7. Allocation of political roles by achievements rather than ascription. and
8. Judicial and regulatory techniques based upon a predominantly secular and impersonal system of law.

* L.J. Cantori and A.H. Ziegler, Jr.: (ed.): *Comparative Politics in the Post-Behavioural Era* (Boulder, Colarodo: Lynne Rienner Pub., 1988), pp. 359-60.

Huntington on Characteristics of the Modernisation Process**

1. It is a *revolutionary* process. Change from tradition to modernity consequently involves a radical and total change in the pattern of human life.
2. It is a *complex* process. It cannot be easily reduced to a single factor or to a single dimension.
3. It is a *systematic* process. Changes in one factor are related to and effect changes in other factors.
4. It is a *global* process. Though originated in Europe, it has now become a worldwide phenomenon.
5. It is a *lengthy* process. The totality of the changes which modernisation involves, can only be worked out through times. Transition from tradition to modernity will be measured in generations.
6. It is a *phased* process. It is possible to distinguish different levels or phases of modernisation through which all societies will move.
7. It is a *homogenising* process. It produces tendencies towards convergence among societies.
8. It is an *irreversible* process. There may be temporary breakdowns and occasional reversals in the elements of modernising process as a whole, it is an essentially secular trend.
9. It is a *progressive* process. In the long run, it enhances human well-being, culturally and materially.

** S.P. Huntington: "The Change to Change", *ibid*, pp. 360-62.

The five-fold classification of the political systems, as furnished by Shils, includes the models of political democracy, tutelary democracy, modernising oligarchy, totalitarian oligarchy and traditional oligarchy. The essential characteristics of each model may be enumerated as under :

Political Democracy : It represents the best form of political system as one obtaining in a country like Britain or the United States.[36] It has these main characteristics :

(i) It has a legislature as the focal point of the political system organised on the basis of universal adult franchise and entrusted with the work of making legislation either on its own or on the initiative of the sovereign voters, or committees of the House. It exercises

36. *ibid.,* p. 95.

control on the government by censuring the conduct of the ministers, or by cutting the budget proposals, or by scrutinising the work of the administrators.

(ii) Political parties constitute an integral part of these systems and they form governments and carry out their policies and programmes on the basis of winning elections in order to fulfil their electoral commitments.

(iii) Power is held for a comparatively short and well-defined period under the conditions laid down in the organic law of the land.

(iv) Freedom of dissent or opposition is fully provided as an effective check on the abuse of power.

(v) Independence and impartiality of judiciary is maintained:

(vi) People exercise democratic self-control and thus use only constitutional means to correct or change their government.

(vii) People are expected to develop trust in their government;

(viii) There is a trained and organised civil service to carry out the decisions of the administrators chosen by the people.

(ix) Adequate police and armed forces are maintained to keep law and order.

(x) People are committed to the norms and values of a democratic order.

Tutelary Democracy : It constitutes the second best form of a political system as described by Shils. It refers to a political system that is committed to observe the norms and values of democracy and thus it tries to emulate the ways of countries known for having political democracy. It "is thus the result of pragmatic response by committed democrats to situations which seem to be inherently incapable of effectively operating democratic institutions."[37] It has these main characteristics:

(i) The executive is the real centre of power much more powerful than the legislature. Its authority is maintained by a strong personality or a group of very strong at the centre controlling both the party and the government.

(ii) Legislature operates under the strict control and supervision of the executive and thus has a considerably restricted role.

(iii) Channels of opposition are allowed, though the executive maintains its strong hold over the means of political communication.

(iv) There is a competent and loyal bureaucracy capable of providing dispassionate and informal criticism of projected policies.

(v) Sefeguards for rule of law and public liberties are scrupulously maintained.

Modernising Oligarchy : It refers to a system that is more than a traditional oligarchy, as discussed below, but less than a political democracy, as given above. Such a political system may either be in the hands of the civilians maintaining their control over the armed forces in order to prevent the subversion of their position, or in the hands of top military men keeping all power with them but also interested in gaining the cooperation of great civilian figures with a view to give a label of legitimacy to their authoritarian rule.[38] Its main characteristics may be enumerated thus :

(i) Parliament is like an acclamatory body meant for ratifying the decisions of the administrators. It is thoroughly deprived of any meaningful legislative authority.

(ii) Opposition is outlawed; free and fair elections are not held; political parties are banned; channels of mass communications are censured.

(iii) The position of bureaucracy is much strengthened as the administrators bank on its support and there are no

---

37. Davies and Lewis, *op. cit.,* p. 102.
38. *ibid.,* p. 104.

democratic channels to keep it under check or control.

(iv) An independent and impartial judiciary enforcing rule of law is non-existent.

Totalitarian Oligarchy : It means an all-powerful rule of a rightist variety as Fascism in Italy and Nazism in Germany or of a leftist variety as Communism in the former Soviet Union and China, the common point of both being distinct—commitment to a particular ideology.[39] It has these main characteristics :

(i) There is full concentration of authority in the hands of the ruling clique based on class, race or some other such feature.

(ii) It has a highly disciplined and well-organised elite bound together by its ideology through the institution of the party.

(iii) There is no place for rule of law, independent and impartial judiciary and a legally constituted opposition;

(iv) The entire paraphernalia of democracy like universal adult franchise, periodic elections, bi-cameral legislature, etc. is provided for propaganda purposes; and

(v) Attempt is made to create an intelligentsia supporting and justifying the official ideology and for creating an atmosphere of superficial consensus in the country.

Traditional Oligarchy : Finally, Shils takes up the case of traditional oligarchy that "is based on a strong dynastic constitution associated with traditional religious beliefs. Rulers emerge on the basis of kinship (or by a combination of kinship and selection of persons qualified by kinship to participate) in the selection process. The ruler's counsellors and immediate confidants form a palace retinue chosen by the ruler on the basis of kinship or personal choice.[40] It has these main characteristics :

(i) Since political authority is exercised by the ruler with the help of his chosen advisers, virtually no place is given to the legislative body even for propaganda purposes.

(ii) As the scope of state activity is highly limited, no need for having an efficient bureaucratic staff is felt.

(iii) The ruler keeps a small armed and police force to maintain his rule.

(iv) Feudalism prevails as a result of which small potentates belonging to the similar kinship or other such ties dominate at the local or regional levels.

(v) Opposition is non-existent; public opinion is not created and the ruler claims legitimacy of his rule on the ground of protecting the traditional culture of the community.

It may be commented that the taxonomic study of Shils fails to produce a quite plausible picture of the forms of modern political systems. One cannot place all prevailing political systems of the world in a neat and water-tight form in these five categories as suggested by him. What should, however, be taken note of is that Shils has only one element in his mind—the role of the political elites. Whether it is a full-fledged democracy or a 'political democracy' as called by him, or it is a democracy committed to similar values and moving in the direction of having a political democracy—a tutelary democracy as designated by him—it is the role of the elite that should be looked into. It is a different matter that the role of the elite is conspicuous in the case of oligarchy whether modernising, totalitarian or traditional and, for this reason, he keeps his attention on the elites of an oligarchical system. The case of transition from traditionality to modernity in all spheres of social life "depends to a great extent initially on the elite's ability to establish a working compromise with the claims of traditional beliefs,[41] and through time, on this ability to

39. *ibid.*, p. 106.
40. *ibid.*, pp. 109-110.
41. *ibid.*, p. 111.

Political Modernisation and Social and Political Systems

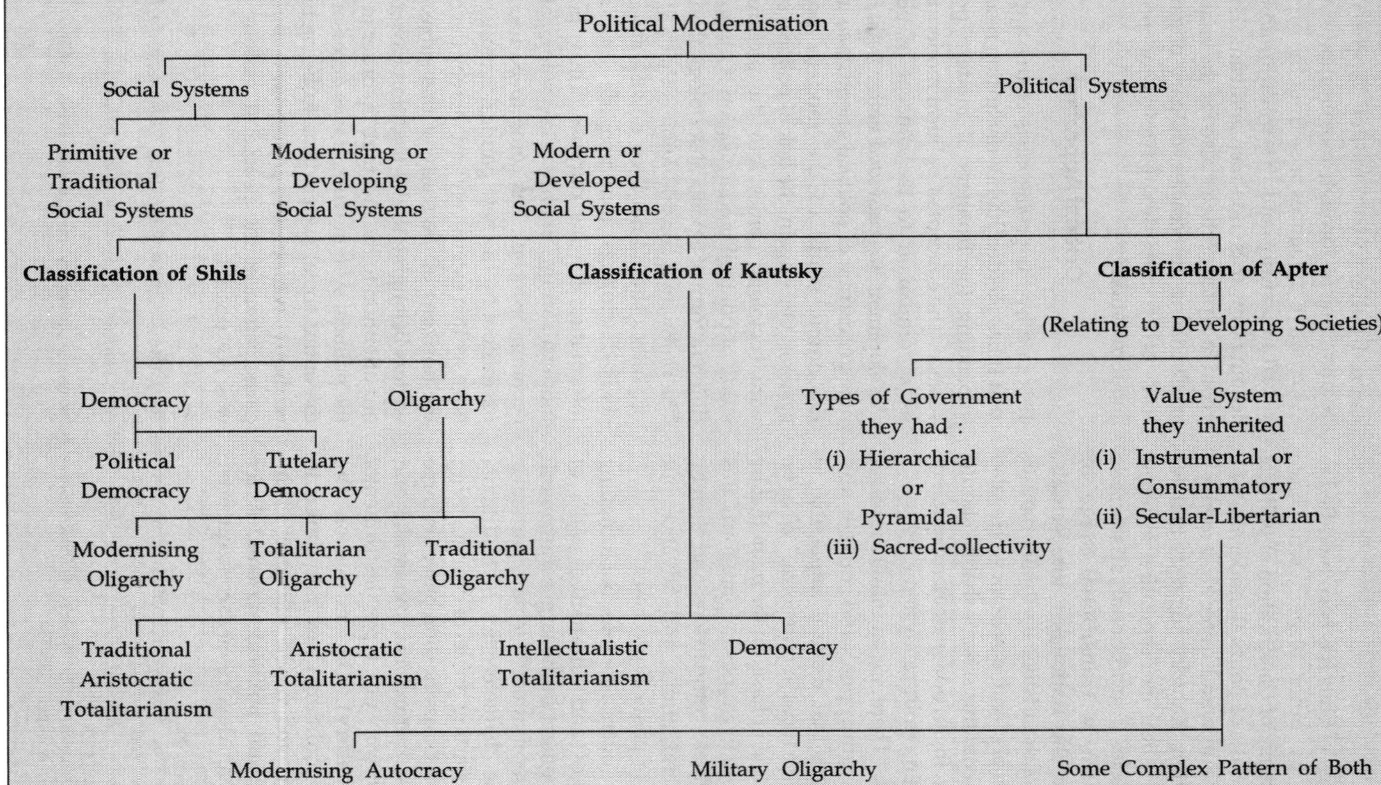

reinterpret traditional beliefs, adapt them to modern needs and translate them into the modern idiom."[42]

The typology of Shils has been modified in various ways by other writers who have adopted the scheme of classification of political systems on the basis of political modernisation. The names of Kautskyand Apter need mention in this connection. Kautsky suggests that we may analyse political modernisation in terms of five categories : traditional aristocratic authoritarianism, a transitional stage of domination by the nationalist intellectuals, totalitarianism of the aristocracy, totalitarianism of the intellectuals, and democracy. He also makes it clear about this scheme that it "should not be mistaken for an adequate description of any or all existing political systems."[43]

As he adds: "There are an infinite number of variations sub-types, and mixed and transitional forms that make it impossible to find any of the five types in pure form." What he has in mind is his emphasis on the point that by formulating these five types in 'pure form' it is possible to facilitate comparisons and thereby formulate generalisations and advance our understanding of political processes."[44]

David Apter offers a complex but intriguing theory of stages and alternative paths of political development in the larger framework of political modernisation.[45] He pays particular attention to the characteristics of traditional societies as the starting points of change, using a two-dimensional classification based on three authority types (hierarchical, pyramidal and segmental) and two value types (instrumental and consummatory). Depending on the character of the traditional base, and subject to the contradictory and varied influences of the Western social and political systems, Apter "discerns two main development consequences: a secular-libertarian model approaching democracy through mobilisation systems and a sacred-collectivity model approaching totalitarianism through mobilisation systems. Alternative sequences arise from the processes of ritualisation and 're-traditionalisation' leading towards non-mercantilism. There is room in Apter's scheme also for the analysis of modernising autocracies, military oligarchies, and other complex patterns of political modernisation."[46]

Critical Appraisal

It is said by the protagonists of this approach that it has yielded highly rewarding results by expanding the frontiers of modern political science. The concept of political modernisation as a companion to the concept of political development has provided better tools for the new generation of political scientists to make a taxonomic study of the modern political systems. Once again, the link of political science with sociology comes into the picture as a study of political modernisation is obviously a different form of a political-sociological analysis. The motivating consideration is that a student of politics should not keep himself aloof from sister-disciplines that provide him ample information for his purpose. Thus, political modernisation, mainly a sociological and economic concept, has come to be used as a useful tool by the new political scientists who have written extensively and thereby developed the horizons of the study of this subject. The writers belonging to this tradition have drawn our attention to the fact that "in order to make the political system work, it was necessary that the entire social system was to be mobilised, without which the necessary political participation of the people at various levels was not possible."[47]

42. Shils, *op. cit.*, p. 89.
43. F.W. Riggs : "The Theory of Political Development" in James C.Charlesworth (ed) : *Contemporary Political Analysis* (New York : Free Press, 1967), p. 333.
44. John H. Kautsky : *Political Change in the Under-Developed Countries : Nationalism and Communism* (New York : Wiley, 1962), p. 4.
45. See David E. Apter : *The Politics of Modernisation* (Chicago : University of Chicago Press, 1965).
46. See Riggs, *op. cit.*, pp. 333-334.
47. Varma, *op. cit.*, p. 279.

And yet the concept of political modernisation may be subjected to the same line of criticism that is levelled against the concept of political development. One may say that here we find an attempt to drown politics into the ocean of some other discipline like sociology or economics. Instead of keeping political science as an independent science, it is reduced to the status of a dependent variable. Under the impact of well-known sociologists like Talcott Parsons, Robert K. Merton and Marion Levy Jr., political scientists like David Easton, David Apter and Edward A. Shils look like developing a tendency to regard the governmental system as a dependent variable whose contours are determined by social, psychological, cultural and economic factors and whose main task consists of processing 'inputs,' generated by these forces and converting them into governmental outputs. Politics is thus treated as "a handmaid of social forces, a mere instrument which was fed by material from outside and which churned it out and returned it to the society— whether in a good, bad or indifferent form depending on the quality (or level of development) of the political system."[48] Sartori is thus right in saying that it "is an extraordinary paradox that the social sciences should be ever more prompted to explain politics by developing a fetishism for the invisible hand."[49]

---

48. *ibid.*, p. 278.
49. Giovanni Sartori : "Sociology of Politics and Politics of Sociology" in S.M. Lipset (ed.) : *Politics and the Social Sciences* (New York : Wiley, 1969), p. 94.

11

Political Socialisation

> Policy-makers and scholars have been equally troubled by how much importance they should place on the role of values and attitudes in the modernisation process. Among both groups there have been advocates of the view that the entire process of development depends on the final analysis upon certain changes occurring in the realm of the subjective.
>
> —Lucian W. Pye'

The concept of political development has two dimensions–sociological and psychological. Further studies in both the directions have led to the emergence of two more concepts that should be taken as the derivatives of the concept of political development. They are *political socialisation* in the psychological and *political acculturation* in the sociological spheres. If modernisation is a state of mind and to a student of empirical politics it seems that a political system can be operated effectively only by the people who share the lively and rational ingredients of the modern outlook, the task of political development thus boils down to the blunt need to change the attitudes and feelings of the people. According to this viewpoint, the argument about how best to facilitate development is again relatively simple : introduce the essential structure and performance changes—by persuasion if possible, arbitrarily if necessary— and the people will in course of time make the appropriate changes in attitudes. Evidence can be cited to show that "once people have been placed in a developed context, they can readily adapt their mind and spirit and thus there is little need to show excessive concern over such murky matters as the psychic state of affairs of transitional individuals."[2]

Political Socialisation: Nature and Essential Implications

H.H. Hyman, who coined the term 'political socialisation', laid emphasis on the perpetuation of political values across generations.[3] Picking up a thread from such an interpretation, Lasswell says that political socialisation "unquestionably meets the criterion of significance in as much as it is an important feature of every past, present and future body politic. Every community transmits with varying degrees of success the mature practices of its culture to the immature. Every stable sub-culture engages in a parallel process, since it also distinguishes between participation by the mature and the immature."[4]

Political socialisation "is the process by which political cultures are maintained and changed. Through the performance of this function individuals are inducted into the political culture, their orientations towards political objects are formed."[5] In other words, it

1. Lucian W. Pye : *Aspects of Political Development* (Boston : Little Brown, 1966), p. 89.
2. *ibid.*, pp. 89-90.
3. *Political Socialisation A Study in the Psychology of Political Behaviour* (New York : Free Press, 1959).
4. Refer to his paper captioned "Political Socialisation as a Policy Science" in S.A. Renshon (ed.) : *Handbook of Political Socialisation : Theory and Research* (New York : Free Press, 1977), p. 446.
5. Gabriel A. Almond and G.B. Powell, Jr : *Comparative Politics : A Developmental Approach* (Boston : Little Brown, 1966), p. 64.

refers to the learning process by which norms and behaviour acceptable to a well-running political system are transmitted from one generation to another. Thus, the aim of this concept is to train or develop the individuals in a way that they become well-functioning members of a political community. Obviously, it has a peculiarly psychological dimension in the sense that it "is the gradual learning of the norms, attitudes and behaviour acceptable to an on-going political system."[6]

The process of political socialisation generally acts in a causal or imperceptible manner. That is, it operates in a quiet or smooth manner without people's being aware of it. The people take the norms for granted without questioning their legitimacy. Thus, the subject-matter of this concept "is the process by which people acquire political values not simply during active political participation, but also in the period before they engage in an explicitly political activity."[7] Thus viewed, political socialisation would encompass all political learning whether formal or informal, or whether deliberate and unplanned, at every stage of the cycle of his life, including not only explicitly political learning which "affects political behaviour, such as the learning of politically irrelevant social attitudes and the acquisition of politically relevant personal characteristics."[8]

The principal emphasis of the concept of political socialisation is on the transmission of political values from one generation to another. The stability of a social or political system depends on the political socialisation of its members on account of the fact that a well-functioning citizen is one who accepts (internalises) society's political norms and who will then transmit them to future generations. For example, the members of a stable democratic system as operating in Britain are trained and made habitual of adopting constitutional means to affect changes rather than resorting to the techniques of taking the matters to the streets or creating conditions of a violent upheaval. Political socialisation thus covers the whole process by which an individual "born with behavioural potentialities of immense range, is led to develop actual behaviour which is confined with a much narrower range—the range of which is customary and acceptable for him according to the students of his groups."[9]

Simply stated, political socialisation desires to achieve the goal ol political stabilisation. It stands on the premise that a political system cannot function smoothly unless the process of the internalisation of political norms and values is at work simultaneously. As in the case of an individual organism so in the case of body politic, nothing but maintenance or survival is needed. And survival means nothing else than stabilisation. As Roberta Sigel says: "The goal of political socialisation is to so train or develop individuals so that they become well-functioning members of the political society... For without a body politic in harmony with the on-going political values and the political system would have trouble in functioning smoothly and perpetuating itself safely. And survival, after all, is a prime goal of the political organism just as it is of the individual organism."[10]

---

6. Roberta Sigel : "Assumptions about the Learning of Political Values" in *The Annals of the American Academy of Political and Social Sciences,* Philadelphia, Vol. 361, September 1965, p. 1. It shows that political socialisation refers to a gradual, continuous process of incremental change through childhood and adolescence during which the new generation acquires the norms prevailing within the adult population." D.C. Schwartz and S.K. Schwartz : *New Directions in Political Socialisation* (New York : Free Press, 1975), p. 5.
7. Stephen L. Wasby : *Political Science : The Discipline and its Dimensions:* (Calcutta : Scientific Book Agency, 1970, p. 333.
8. F.I. Greenstein: *"Political Socialisation" cited in Sigel, op.cit.,* p.2.
9. Irwin L. Child : "Socialisation" in G. Lindzey (ed.) : *Handbook of Social Psychology* (Camb, Mass, 1954), Vol. 2, p 655.
10. Sigel, *op. cit.,* p. 2.

Some Important Statements about Political Socialisation

Political socialisation is the process through which we learn about politics. It concerns the acquisition of emotions, identities and skills as well as information. The main dimensions of socialisation are what people learn (content) when they learn it (timing and sequence) and from whom (agents).

— **Hague, Harrop and Breslin**
Comparative Government and Politics : An Introduction, p. 63.

The impact of the so-called primary 'agents' of political socialisation, such as the family and the social class, has declined. Whereas once people acquired, in late childhood and adolescence in particular, a framework of political sympathies and leanings that adult experience tended to mollify or deepen, but seldom radically transformed, this has been weakened in modern society by greater social and geographical mobility and by the spread of individualist and consumerist values.

— **Andrew Heywood**
Politics. p. 203.

Political socialisation studies have been criticised as conservative, because they focus on continuities rather than discontinuities among agencies during different periods of individual's life. Important questions and issues are often overlooked.

—**R.H. Chilcote**
Theories of Comparative Politics., p. 184.

Political socialisation seeks to inculcate values, norms and orientations in the minds of the individuals so that they develop trust in their political system and thereby keep themselves like well-functioning citizens and also leave their indelible imprints on the minds of their successors. Political socialisation may thus be defined as the process by which an individual "becomes acquainted with the political system and which determines his reactions to political phenomena. It involves the examination of the social, economic or cultural environment of society upon the individual and upon his political attitudes and values. Political socialisation is the most important link between the social and political systems, but may vary considerably from one system to another. From a political point of view, political socialisation is extremely important as the process by which individuals become involved to varying degrees in the political system—in political participation."[11]

Development of Political Socialisation: Case of Open versus Closed Societies

Every society that wishes to maintain itself or to have its stability as a condition precedent to its survival has one of its essential functions in the socialisation of the young in order to enable them to carry on willingly the established values, orientations and norms of their collective life. A new-born child is not a socialised creature; he is socialised by means of a learning process. Moreover, such learning "is not limited to the acquisition of appropriate knowledge about a society's norms but requires that the individual so makes these norms his own — internalises them—that to him they appear to be right, just and moral. Having once internalised society's norms, it will presumably not be difficult for the individual to act in congruence with them."[12] Moreover, this process of norm-internalisation is not exhausted with

11. Michael Rush and Phillip Althoff: *An Introduction to Political Sociology* (London : Nelson, 1971), pp. 13-14. p. 63.
12. Sigel, *op. cit., p.* 2.

the age of adolescence; it also covers the young for the same reason which informs that a politically organised society has the same maintenance needs in which the young people have to play a quite responsible part. Let us, therefore, look at the norms– internalisation process at two stages–socialisation of the child and the adolescent and socialisation of the young people.

The process of political socialisation starts when the child becomes aware of a wide environment; he feels increasingly perceptive in response to particular situations and comes to have an outlook that becomes increasingly coherent and total where before it was fragmented and limited.[13] It is at this stage that the general attitude of the children towards authority, obedience, resistance, cooperation, aggression, etc. has its germination. What a child gets from the family has its furtherance in the school that cements his early convictions towards political values. Easton and Dennis posit four stages in the process of political socialisation at the childhood stage–(i) recognition of authority through particular individuals such as parents, policemen and the President of the country; (ii) distinction between public and private authority; (iii) recognition of impersonal political institutions like national legislature, judiciary and voting behaviour; and (iv) distinction between political institutions and persons engaged in the activities associated with those institutions so that idealised images of particular persons such as the President or the Congressmen are transferred from the Presidency and the Congress.[14]

If the factors of environment and experiential influences have their definite impact on the life of the individual in his childhood and adolescence, it is quite reasonable to assume that these influences have an importance of their own during the phase of adulthood. Thus, the process of socialisation continues even after the period of adolescence. The main outlines of future political behaviour "may well be determined in the earlier period, but this is more likely to create a situation in which there is interaction between early political socialisation and the environmental and experiential influences of later life than to preclude adult socialisation."[15] A study of the voting behaviour, for example, shows how the members of a legislature undergo a process of political socialisation during the war of votes and that their subsequent legislative behaviour is determined partly by their knowledge, values and attitudes as these existed prior to elections, and partly by their experiences within and reactions to their new environment in the legislature.[16] Electoral studies have demonstrated correlations between party preferences and characteristics of the voters which are related to environment and experience.

Though it is true that early socialisation lays the foundation of later socialisation, it does not imply that the pattern of later socialisation should strictly conform to the former. The effect of the later experiential influences "may bring about a change in the attitudes or orientations of men at an advanced stage of his life. "The knowledge, values and attitude acquired during the childhood and adolescence will be measured against the experience of adult life: to suggest otherwise is to suggest a static political behaviour. If the process of adult socialisation tends to reinforce those of childhood and adolescence, the degree of change may be limited to that of increasing conservatism with age, but where conflict occurs, radical changes in "political behaviour may result: such conflict may have its roots in early political socialisation, but it may also be

13. See Frank and Elizabeth Estava : *The Child's World* (New York, 1959), Chapters 3-8.
14. Easton and Dennis : *Children in Political Systems : Origins of Political Legitimacy* (New York, 1969), Part 3.
15. Rush and Althoff, *op. cit.*, p. 45.
16. *ibid.*

attributable to the experiences of later socialisation."[17]

It shows that the process of political socialisation covers the whole life of a man. Its foundations are laid in the early stages of a man's life, its superstructures may undergo change in the later stage on account of certain new experiences. What is strikingly noticeable at this stage is that the political socialisation of the young witnesses, what Almond and Verba call 'multi-directional flow of influences.'[18] The result is that what the individuals learn at their grown up stage, they strive to have it inculcated at the early stage of the life of their offsprings. While referring to the case of the United States, Almond and Verba point out that the people owing to the practice of political democracy in the country "subsequently demand the practice of democracy in school, shop and church. Since the demand is often met, school-children, workers and others acquire an articulation, debate and decision-making. These experiences, in turn, help them towards developing the skills with which to participate in political life and either to help bring about or to accept political change. Thus, the socialisation process contributes not only to a society's political stability but also to change and to the strain at ease with which changes take place."[19]

The process of political socialisation has two forms: (i) homogeneous or continuous signifying that the individuals cooperate with each other in an atmosphere of mutual trust towards their political system, and (ii) heterogeneous or discontinuous signifying that the individuals have an attitude of mutual suspicion and hatred towards each other that eventually leads them to have disaffection with their political system. Thus, while in the event of a homogeneous or continuous process of political socialisation, a political system can hope to receive a more or less dependable support from the individuals, but the entire political life "is likely to become restless, and turbulent leading to the frustration and demands for radical social change."[20] Obviously, "it is in the interest of the stability of a political system that it draws its sustenance from a homogeneous environment."[21]

It should be pointed out at this stage that though political socialisation desires, as a matter of fact, political stabilisation, it should not at all be construed as an anti-change concept. It may certainly be described as a conservative concept in the sense that it stands for a change that is neither radical nor rapid. It lays stress on this point that when change is the law of nature, it should be gradual and peaceful. Political socialisation, thus, emphasises that if the attitudes, orientations and values of the people change through time, a simultaneous change in the sphere of political culture must take place in order to avoid the risks of sudden changes that may bring about the decay or destruction of the political system. That is, the process of the shaping of political values and the process of change should run in conformity with each other. It requires that the rulers must

17. *ibid.*, p. 47. The process of political socialisation automatically involves the case of re-socialisation that takes place when individuals are inducted into new status for which no role models previously existed in the society. Most pre-industrial political systems undergoing rapid social change are faced with burdensome tasks of re-socialisation. The literature on totalitarian political systems (as Fascist Italy, Nazi Germany and Communist Russia) has also devoted considerable attention to this subject. Another form of resocialisation takes place when a group inducts an individual into a status for which he was not prepared by his earlier training. Social mobility would be a case in point. Only when the socialisation role of these secondary or intermediary institutions is understood, will we be able to explain with more confidence why the well-trained generation leads to revolution against the established order, or why, for example, "the radical Japanese adolescent becomes a conservative adult." K.P. Langton: *Political Socialisation* (New York : Oxford Univ. Press, 1969), pp. 19-20. Also see F.H. Houn : *To Change a Nation* (New York : Free Press, 1961).
18. See Sigel, *op. cit.*, p. 9.
19. G.A. Almond and Sidney Verba : *The Civic Culture* (Princeton: Princeton Univ. Press, 1963), Ch XI.
20. S.P. Varma : *Modern Political Theory* (Delhi : Vikas, 1975), p. 299.
21. *ibid*

remain very careful to prevent the occurrence of any major event like that of inflation or war that may lead to the inculcation of radical changes in the attitudes of the people. The men in power are thus duty-bound to see that the pressure of events does not reach a point that the loyalists are converted into the rebels, or the collaborationists become the aggressors, or the friends are transformed into the foes in view of the historical fact that if the process of socialisation "is slow, the waters of political culture will run smoothly, and a political system smoothly adjusted with the political culture of the country will be able to function effectively. Too rapid a process of political socialisation, on the other hand, is likely to throw everything out of gear."[22]

The nature of the process of political socialisation at work varies over tjme and according to the environment of which it is a part and to which it contributes. It is, therefore, related to the nature of the political system and the degree and nature of change. "The more stable the polity, the more specified the major agencies of political socialisation will be. Conversely, the greater the degree of change in a non-totalitarian polity, the more diffused the major agencies of political socialisation will be. The more basic the degree of revolution in a polity, the more specified the agencies of political socialisation will be."[23] The paramount fact may, however, not be lost sight of that though political socialisation may involve political orientations and behaviour patterns from the maintenance and replication of a given political system to its transformation or total destruction,[24] it, as a matter of fact, strives to emphasise the point that "the test for a stable political system is whether the socialising agencies are sufficiently flexible and inter-dependent to allow change without violent disruption."[25]

The process of political socialisation in the form of the acquisition of political orientations and patterns of behaviour is as applicable to non-democratic societies as it is to the democratic ones, though it cannot be denied that the emphasis placed on the role of the 'agents' or the system of mechanism may vary both in kind and in its effectiveness. An open society allowing room for dissent and opposition has a plural character wherein multifarious interests operate for the purpose of inculcating a multifaceted variety of political norms and values. Opposed to this is the case of a totalitarian society where the men in power impose their ideology or political values on the people as a whole with a view to de-educate the old and re-educate the young generations. The totalitarian societies "differ from modern democracies in the degree of control they exercise over the political socialisation of their members. All governments seek directly or indirectly to socialise members of society to varying degrees by the control of information, but in the totalitarian society, the control is all-pervasive."[26]

A totalitarian state is one that seeks to control all aspects of society and lays stress on the socialisation in general and political socialisation in particular. The ideology of the state "becomes the official basis of all the actions and pervades all activities. Political socialisation is not and cannot be left to find its own channels; nor to purview uncontrolled knowledge, values and attitudes which may contradict or undermine that ideology. The minds of men must be captured, guided and harnessed to the needs of the state through the vehicle of its ideology."[27] This is evident from

22. *ibid.*, p. 298.
23. See Yasamusa Kuroda cited in Rush and Althoff, *op. cit.*, p. 68.
24. Easton and Dennis, *op. cit.*, p. 66.
25. A.R. Ball : *Modern Politics and Government* (London : Macmillan, 1971), p. 73.
26. Rush and Althoff, *op. cit.*, p. 55.
27. *ibid.*, pp. 54-55.

the statements of great totalitarian leaders like Adolph Hitler: "We have set before ourselves the task of inoculating our youth with the spirit of this community of people at a very early age. And this new Reich will give its youth to no one but itself, take youth and give to youth its own education and its own upbringing."[28] Likewise, V.I. Lenin said: "Only by radically remoulding the teaching organisation and training of the young shall we be able to ensure that the results of the efforts of the younger generation will be the creation of a society that will be unlike the old society that is a communist society."[29]

A deeper examination in this regard, however, leads to this astonishing impression that the process of political socialisation is essentially a conservative concept, regardless of the case of democratic and totalitarian societies, in view of the fact that its real concern is with the survival or maintenance of a political system. Whether it is a free and open society like that of the United States or Britain, or it is the opposite of that as we find in China, the net over-all effect of political socialisation "is in the direction of supporting the *status quo,* or at least the major aspects of the existing political regime."[30] As Greenstein says: "Political socialisation in both stable and unstable societies is likely to maintain existing patterns."[31]

Major Agents of Political Socialisation

If political socialisation concerns itself with the orientation of the individuals towards political objects, let us look into the role of the 'agents' which play their part in the process of norm-internalisation. An inquiry in this regard covers the role of those factors that have their latent as well as patent influence on the mind of the individual and thereby make up his personality. Simply stated, it means that we should have a brief study of the factors that internalise political norms and values what men of earlier ages called lessons in civic education, training for citizenship, behaviour of men in authority and role of social and political institutions. Thus, the role of the family, school, church, peer groups, mass media and public relations, etc., should be looked into in order to find out the veracity of this statement: "Since the individual is continually being influenced in the shaping of his political attitudes, orientations and values, the process of socialisation goes throughout his life."[32] Or as Ball says: "Political socialisation is not a process confined to the impressionable years of childhood, but one that continues throughout adult life."[33]

First of all, comes the family that should be described as the 'child's first window on the world outside, it is the child's first contact with authority'.[34] The chief contribution of the family in forming the political personality of the individual derives from its role as the main source and locus for the satisfaction of all his basic and innate requirements. Thus, the child tends to identify with his parents and to adopt their outlook towards the political system. The father becomes the prototypical authority figure and thereby initiates the child's view of political authority. As Davies says: "The family provides the major means for transforming the mentally

---

28. *ibid.,* p. 54.
29. Lenin : *Selected Works,* Vol. II, (Moscow, 1947), p. 661.
30. Sigel, *op. cit.,* p. 9.
31. *ibid.*
32. Varma, *op. cit.,* p. 297.
33. Ball, *op. cit.,* p. 68. Thus David Apter is right in holding that political learning "is a consequence of the organisation of motivation around perceptions of appropriate values of affiliation and participation. It works by bringing children into a political culture and converting them into responsible adults capable of exercising the judgements and rights pertinent to that culture. The two go together in an open society, but this, in turn, requires an active politics. Participation is itself a socialising influence." *Introduction to Political Analysis* (New Delhi : Prentice Hall, 1978), p. 271.
34. *ibid.,* p. 69.

naked infant organism into adult, fully clothed in its own personality. And most of the individual's political personality—his tendencies to think and act politically in particular ways—has been determined at home, several years before he can take part in politics as an ordinary adult citizen and as a political prominent."[35] Robert Lane has suggested that there are three ways in which the foundations of political beliefs may be laid through the family—(i) by overt and covert indoctrination, (ii) by placing the child in a particular social context, and (iii) by moulding the child's personality.[36]

Then comes the school as a centre of primary education. Education has long been regarded as a very important variable in the explanation of political behaviour, and there is much evidence to suggest that it is a very important agent of political socialisation. Almond and Verba have pointed out that the more extensive an individual's education, the more likely he is to be aware of the impact of government, to follow politics, to have more political information, to possess a wider range of opinions on political matters, to engage in political discussions with a wider range of people, to feel a greater ability to influence political affairs, to be a member of and to be active in voluntary organisations, and express confidence in his social environment and exhibit feelings of trust.[37] It is for this reason that the selection of courses comes to have an importance of its own and the politically conscious people fight for the revision of the syllabi as pertaining to their interests. Thus, the leaders of the Muslim League in Kerala struggled for the expunction of certain portions from the school textbooks in which Jawaharlal Nehru had said about the communal and anti-national role of the League in the pre-independence days. To take another example, we may say that the American negroes have become more vocal in their criticism of the neglect of negro contributions in school text-books and have successfully demanded the inclusion of 'black studies' programme in many educational institutions.

What matters much in this direction is that the problem of political socialisation arises after the children emerge from the early influences of their family and primary schools into the world of higher classes—also known as the 'peer groups'—and thus "may become subject to other influences which may reinforce or conflict with early politicisation."[38] Martin Levin has found a tendency for individuals to adopt the majority group within the 'peer groups'.[39] The courses of study, debates, discussions and other extra-curricular activities have their own impact upon the attitudes of the grown up students. Thus, the centres of higher education play their part in proto-political context and thereby become effective sources of political enlightenment. In this way, pedagogy finds its integration with social sciences as the aim of both, as C. Wright Mills in his work *The Sociological Imagination* says, "is to help cultivate and sustain publics and individuals that are able to live with, and to act upon adequate definitions of personal and social relations."[40]

---

35. James C. Davies : "The Family's Role in Political Socialisation" in *The Annals of the American Academy of Political and Social Sciences,* Vol.361, September 1965, p. 11.
36. R.E. Lane : "Fathers and Sons : The Foundations of Political Beliefs" in *American Sociological Review,* Vol. XXIV, 1959, pp. 502-511.
37. Almond and Verba, *op. cit.,* pp. 315-24.
38. Rush and Althoff, *op. cit.,* p. 44.
39. See Martin L. Levin : "Social Climates and Political Socialisation" in *Public Opinion Quarterly,* Vol. XXV, 1961, pp. 596-606.
40. Edgar Litt : "Education and Political Enlightenment in America" in *The Annals of the American Academy of Political and Social Sciences,* Vol. 361, September 1965, p. 32.

Not merely the family and the educational institutions but social and political institutions as a whole play their part in the process of norm-internalisation. The role of religious institutions, for instance, need not be undermined. The effect of the church on political attitudes "is less apparent when it reinforces other socialising agencies, but the role of Roman Catholicism in many European countries, liberal-democratic and totalitarian, offers illustrations of its conflict with both state and education, and is possibly a vital factor in the political behaviour of women in some countries."[41] Youth movements do play an important part in the process of national integration particularly in the developing countries. Let us also have a look at the role of the political parties that are more diffuse because of their need to win wider support. The role of the government as a whole must be looked into, particularly in countries like Germany and Austria where financial support is given by the state to voluntary youth groups and organisations to encourage political education.[42]

Lasswell's Common Set of Categories

Factors	*Institutions*	*Effects*
Power	Government and Law	Giving and receiving of support in connection with important decisions (authoritative commitments enforceable if challenged by the use of severe deprivations against challengers)
Enlightenment	Mass Media and Scientific Publications	Giving or receiving of news or scientific information
Wealth	Industry, Money and Credit	Giving or receiving of services or resources
Well-being	Nutrition and Medicare	Giving or receiving of opportunity for safety, health and comfort
Skill	Occupation, Profession, Arts	Giving or receiving of opportunity to discover and perfect latent capabilities
Affection	Families, Larger Identities	Giving or receiving of opportunity for love and loyalty
Respect	Classes, Ranks, Castes	Giving or receiving of opportunity for recognition
Rectitude	Ecclesiastical, Ethical organisations	Giving or receiving of opportunities to facilitate and apply norms of responsible conduct.

41. Ball, *op. cit.*, p. 72.
42. *ibid.*

Wc should also examine the experiences that a man gathers during the course of his employment. One gains a great deal of insight into human nature by the way in which the employer behaves towards his employees. Brought up as a child in a family living on democratic lines and given to cooperation by nature, a person may develop a strong sense of resentment, even of violence, if he finds his employer behaving in a wrong manner. Herein figures the issue of the attitude of dominance towards the subordinates, attitude of deference of the subordinates towards their superiors, or a sort of sensitivity of power relationships. The job as well as the formal and informal organisations built around it, like unions and clubs, may constitute the channels for the explicit communication of political information and beliefs and any sort of participation in the process of collective bargaining or involvement with a strike can be a powerful socialising experience for workers and employers alike. The striking labourer not only learns that he can shape the authoritative decisions being made about his future, but he gains knowledge of specific action skills, such as demonstrating and picketing, which may be used in political participation.[43]

The channels of mass communication exercise their own impact upon the 'cognitive map' of the individual's personality. By reading newspaper reports, listening to radio talks and seeing television films, people develop taste as well as distaste for certain norms and values. Thus, while free mass media—press, radio and television—inculcate different sets of values in the minds of the individuals, a controlled system of mass communications may play a quite effective part in bringing about a lot of conformity in their views.

Besides, we may also refer to the role of 'symbols' as an important means of developing political orientations. Events such as May Day parades, general elections, street demonstrations, coronation, inauguration of Presidency, birth anniversaries of Marx, Lenin and Gandhi, observance of national rejoicing days, etc. lay stress on historical continuity as well on unity of the people. A young child not only sees such events, he also develops an affective and evaluative orientation towards the regime. Positive judgements of the incumbents of these roles precede actual knowledge among children, for instance, about party affiliations and actual authority of the American President and political neutrality as well as titular headship of the British monarch.[44]

Finally, we come to the influence of direct contacts with the political system. It will not be wrong to say that nothing can be as influential in shaping the attitudes and orientations of the individuals as their direct contacts with the institutions and processes of the political system under which they live and work. "No matter how positive the view of political system which has been included by family and school, when a citizen is ignored by his party, cheated by his police, starved in the bread line, and finally conscripted into the army, his views on the political realm are likely to be altered. Direct formal and informal relationships with specific elite in the political system are inevitably a powerful force in shaping orientations of individuals to the system."[45]

43. Almond and Powell, *op. cit.,* p. 69.
44. Dennis Kavangh : *Political Culture* (London : Macmillan, 1972), p. 33.
45. Almond and Powell, *op. cit.,* p. 69. R.D. Hess and J.V. Tordey postulate four models of political socialisation as : (i) Accumulation model : The more information of political system is fed to a child, the more knowledge he acquires, (ii) Interpersonal transfer model : By virtue of familial and other associations, the child develops diverse relationships to figures of authority; (iii) Identification model : The child develops his attitudes from significant older persons, (iv) Cognitive-development model : The thought processes of a child are based on a conceptual understanding of an order which will allow him to translate an understanding of the individual figure into an understanding of similar individuals and to their roles in a whole potential system. *The Development of Political Attitudes in Children* (Chicago : Aldine, 1967).

Critical Appraisal

The study of political socialisation "seems to be one of the most promising approaches to the understanding of political stability and development."[46] What has prompted the recent political scientists, political sociologists and political psychologists, particularly of the United States, is the desire for looking into the factors that have brought about transformations in the political systems and that have been playing their sinister part in this direction, particularly in the backward and developing countries of the world. As a matter of fact, what has motivated the scholars to render their contributions, in this regard, is their enthusiastic search for developing tools whereby existing political systems may be saved from their transformation into a form that is distinctly opposed to the domain of free and open societies. The result is that the concept of political socialisation may be accused of being conservative. As the entire concept of political development is an exercise for defending and preserving the *status quo,* the concept of political socialisation on account of the very fact of being a derivative of the same may be accused of in a similar vein.

As such, the concept of political socialisation may not serve the purpose of those who subscribe to the school of Marxism-Leninism, nor can it fully satisfy those who are in search of a real alternative to the school of scientific socialism. The Marxists openly declare that the philosophers have so far interpreted the world, the problem is how to change it. For this reason, they reject any concept of an 'open' society like that of political socialisation as another ingenuous gift of the bourgeois mind. What is peculiarly noticeable is that the entire approach of the political psychologists has failed to satisfy the scholars of the free world, though they have never rejected it like their counterparts subscribing to the school of Marxism-Leninism. The new generation of American political scientists has found many faults with the pattern variables and their empirical specifications not only in regard to their application to the developing countries of the Third World but to their own countries so terribly caught up in the problems like those of inflation, unemployment and war all assuming threatening postures to the survival of their own political systems.

A study of the political development of countries belonging to the Third World reveals that the model of political socialisation, as given by many distinguished American writers, may hardly apply to them in the midst of "too many armies, too much bureaucratic parasitism, too much unequal distribution and not enough production, too much concentration on display of projects and neglect of infrastructure, too much articulation of conflicts. between communities, in short, too much politics for the elites and not enough authentic participation for the masses. For anything but in the very long run, the Western model began to be regarded as unattainable, especially given the absolute character of the values and goals of many Third World leaders."[47] As the two American critics comment: "The investigators rarely ask hard political questions about who benefits, who controls, and who attempts to control the processes they study. That children have a benevolent image of the political world is vastly a myth. But it is dead certain that the political socialisation theorists do."[48]

---

46. Almond and Powell, *op. cit.,* p. 65.
47. J.P. Nettl: "Strategies in the Study of Political Development" in Colin Leys (ed.): *Politics and Change in Developing Countries* (London : Cambridge Univ, Press, 1969), p. 19.
48. R.W. Connell and Murray Goot: "Science and Ideology in American Political Socialisation Research" in *Berkeley Journal of Sociology,* Vol. 17.

12

Political Culture

> Instead of casting all our old prejudices, we cherish them to a very considerable degree, and to take more shame to ourselves, we cherish them because they are prejudices; and longer they have lasted, and the more generally they have prevailed, the more we cherish them. We are afraid to put man to live and trade on his own private stock of reason; because we suspect that this stock in each man is small, and that the individuals would do better to avail themselves of the general bank and capital of nations and of ages.
>
> **—Edmund Burke[1]**

The study of the concept of political culture constitutes an examination of the sociological aspect of the subject of political development. Ever since this term was popularised by some leading American writers like Ulam, Beer and Almond, it has come to stand as a very important variable for a morphological study of the political systems. It has influenced the system-theorists to assert that one political system is distinguished from another not only in terms of its structure but also in respect of the political culture in which it lays embedded. It is on account of this very fact that while a parliamentary system of government could develop and work well in a country like Britain, it failed to have a similar success in many backward countries of the Third World. The realisation has, therefore, now come to stay that the attitudes, sentiments and cognitions that inform and govern political behaviour in any society "are not just random congeries but represent coherent patterns which fit together and are mutually reinforcing, that in any particular community there is a limited and distinct political culture which gives meaning, predictability and form to the political process, that each individual must, in his own historical context, learn and incorporate into his own personality the knowledge and feelings about the politics of his people and his community."[2]

Political Culture : Meaning and Components : Concept of Secularisation

A political culture "is composed of the attitudes, beliefs, emotions and values of society that relates to the political system and to apolitical issues."[3] It is defined as "the pattern of individual attitudes and orientations towards politics among the members of a political system."[4] The people of a society share a common human nature like emotional drives, intellectual capacities and moral perspectives. The common human nature expresses itself in the form of certain values, beliefs and emotional attitudes which are transmitted from one generation to another, though with greater or lesser modifications, and thus constitute the

1. Bonn (ed.) : *Works of Edmund Burke,* Vol II, p. 359.
2. Lucian W. Pye : "Introduction : Political Culture and Political Development" in Pye and Sydney Verba (eds.) : *Political Culture and Political Development* (Princeton : Princeton Univ. Press, 1965), p 7.
3. A.R. Ball : *Modern Politics and Government* (London : Macmillan, 1971), p. 56.
4. G.A. Almond and G.B. Powell : *Comparative Politics : A Developmental Approach* (Boston : Little Brown, 1966), p. 50.

Some Important Statements about Political Culture

Political culture refers to a people's psychological orientation. It implies a pattern of orientations to political objects such as parties, governments and constitution expressed in beliefs, symbols and values.

—Andrew Heywood
Politics, p. 200.

Political culture refers specifically to the basic norms for political activity in a society. It is a determining factor in what ideologies will dominate a country's political regime; it is unique to a given country or group of people.

— Patrick O'Neil
Essentials of Comparative Politics, pp. 78-79.

To say that a group of people share a particular political culture does not mean that they agree on all of the important issues of politics and governance. Rather it means that they are likely to share a common perspective about their public surroundings, including their political leaders, governmental structure and the enduring symbols and values of public life. It includes citizens' general feelings towards government, including their desire (or lack thereof) to participate in political issues. It also captures a sense of people's understanding of the decision-making process, including attitudes about its merits.

—December Green and Laura Leuhrmann
Comparative Politics of the Third World, p. 198.

general culture of that society. "Certain aspects of the general culture of a society are especially concerned with how government ought to be conducted and what it shall try to do. This sector of culture we call political culture."[5] It "is the set of attitudes, beliefs and sentiments that give order and meaning to a political process and that provides the underlying assumptions and rules that govern behaviour in the political system."[6]

The political culture, then, may be seen "as the over-all distribution of citizens' orientations to political objects."[7] R.C. Macridis writes of it as "the commonly shared goals and commonly accepted rules."[8] Robert A. Dahl has singled out political culture as a factor explaining different patterns of political opposition whose salient elements are :[9]

1. Orientations to problem-solving; are they pragmatic or rationalistic?
2. Orientations to collective action; are they cooperative or non-cooperative?
3. Orientations to the political system; are they allegiant or alienated?
4. Orientations to other people; are they trustful or mistrustful?

However, Lucian W. Pye has studied the meaning of political culture in the context of his concept of political development relating to the case of new states of the Third World and, for this reason, he has included three factors in its study :[10]

1. Scope of politics; how ends and means in politics are related ?
2. Standards for the evaluation of political action; and

5. Beer and Ulam : *Patterns of Government* (New York : Random House, 1962), 8th Ptg, p. 32.
6. Lucian W. Pye : *Aspects of Political Development* (Boston : Little Brown, 1966), p. 104.
7. Dennis Kavangh : *Political Culture* (London : Macmillan, 1972), p. 11.
8. Macridis : "Interest Groups in Comparative Politics" in *Journal of Politics*, Vol. XXIII, 1961, p. 40.
9. Dahl : *Political Opposition in Western Democracies* (New Haven: Yale Univ. Press, 1966), pp. 352-53.
10. Pye : *Politics, Personality and Nation-Building* (New Haven, Yale Univ. Press, 1962), pp. 122-23.

3. Values that are salient for political action.

Thus, political culture may be described as "a short-hand expression to denote the emotional and attitudinal environment within which the political system operates."[11] Borrowing from Talcott Parsons, we "can be a little more precise at this point and say that we are concerned with *orientations* towards *political objects*. Orientations are pre-dispositions to political action and are determined by such factors as traditions, historical memories, motives, norms, emotions and symbols.'[12]

It is obvious that the concept of political culture finds place in the subjective realm. According to Almond and Powell, "such individual orientations involve three components—(i) *cognitive orientations* implying knowledge, accurate or otherwise, of the political system, (ii) *affective orientations* implying feelings of attachment, involvement, rejection, and the like about political objects, and (iii) *evaluative orientations* implying judgments and opinions about the political objects, which usually involve applying value standards to political objects and events."[13]

From the above, one may infer that political culture has certain components having their place in the world of sociology. They are: values, beliefs and emotional attitudes of the people towards their political system. We may observe that the people have, in general, certain political values as elections should be held periodically and also in a free and fair manner; that the ministers should resign if they forfeit the confidence of the people or their chosen deputies, that no person should be made to suffer in body or in goods unless a verdict is given by a competent court of law following a procedure established by the organic law of the country, etc. Closely linked with political values is the component of political beliefs about the actual behaviour of men and countries. It includes certain norms such as that adult population of a country has the right to take part in the political discussions. The significant cause of the beliefs should also be traced in this fact that ideas that "donot appear at first glance to have relevance to politics may be intimately connected with it through the belief system of the political culture."[14] Finally, we come to the component of emotional attitudes, the tone and temper of the people. While attitudes inherited from a past full of struggles for a constitutional democracy, as in Britain, may inform that the speakers must behave courteously, the tone of discourse must be conversational and the whole style of behaviour and speech must conform not only to the rules of procedure of the Parliament but also to a complex and largely unspoken set of conventions[15], attitudes inherited from a long authoritarian past may impede the operation of a democratic system, even though most of its members sincerely accept the democratic ideal.[16]

A political culture hinging on the fact of people's attitudes and beliefs towards the political system, whether homogeneous or heterogeneous, is a product of several inter-related factors—historical, geographical and socio-economic. Moreover, it is not static, it is dynamic and thus responds to the needs generated within the political system or imparted or imposed from outside. A pragmatic orientation, in this direction, is known by the name of 'secularisation' of the political culture. Let us first examine the three factors that constitute the foundations of the political culture.

A study of history offers ample authentic evidence to prove the continuity or discontinuity of a political system behind which the foundations of a political culture can well be

11. Kavangh, *op. cit.*, p. 10.
12. *ibid.*, pp. 10-11. Also see Parsons and Shils : *Towards a General Theory of Action* (New York, 1962), pp. 55ff.
13. Almond and Powell, *op. cit.*, p. 50.
14. Beer and Ulam, *op. cit.*, p. 41.
15. *ibid.*, p. 43.
16. *ibid.*, p. 45.

found out. The importance of political continuity in a country like Britain, for example, lies in the fact that there older values "have been allowed to merge with modern attitudes undisturbed by violent internal strife or domination by foreign power."[17] France offers a sharp contrast in the chain of historical development. While the revolution of 1789 violently overthrew the existing structures and subsequent events showed the highly emotional attitudes of the French people, the English leaders expressed their shock at the events of 1789 and a leading parliamentarian like Edmund Burke could successfully draw the attention of his countrymen towards the horrors of such a violent upheaval. Such a political culture had its impact upon the fate of the colonies as well. Thus, while the Indians learnt from their British masters the values of parliamentary democracy and efficacy of the constitutional means, the people of Algeria and Vietnam learnt from their French masters the lessons of an insurrectionary struggle. Burke rightly understood the role of historical development in the formulation of political culture when he repudiated the logic of French revolution and thereby laid down his doctrine of the 'prescriptive constitution.' For instance, while criticising rabidly the logic of the French revolution, he said: "Our constitution is a prescriptive constitution. It is a constitution whose sole authority is that it has existed time out of mind."[18]

Geography has its own part in laying the foundations of a political culture. The insular character of the British Isles protected the country from foreign invasion and also from the massive influx of foreign races that could have created the problem of ethnic differences. Different from this, the limitless frontiers of a country like India opened the ways for the foreigners to invade and even stay here with the result that we developed the values of independent egalitarianism in the midst of sharp ethnic differences. Instances can be gathered to show that in case the ethnic differences are allowed to develop in the direction of hostile political cultures, national integration suffers heavily and different people in the name of their different nationalities struggle for their separate sovereign states. Thus, the Government of Kenya, for instance, has to wage a relentless fight against its Somali tribesmen demanding their union with Somaliland. The factor of political geography engages our attention when we find that the rebellious tribesmen very much thrive on the support of the alien enemy nations as the Nagas of India, or the people of a country like West Germany were forced to accept the existing political structures of a neighbouring state like that of East Germany—virtually an integral part of their own—because of the geographical compulsions and also because of the competing international alliances then led by the United States and the Soviet Union.

Lastly, we take up the determinant of socio-economic development. "A predominantly urban industrialised society is a more complex society, putting a premium on rapid communications. Educational standards are higher, groups proliferate, and participation in the decision-making process is, by necessity, wider. Rural societies are not geared to change and innovation, and states with a predominantly peasant population are more conservative.[19] Developments in the field of science and technology have their impact on the growth of agriculture and industry; they also have their impact on the process of transportation and communications, migrations and immigrations, imports and exports, revolutions and warfares.

It all leads to changes in political values and beliefs of the people. Thus, the labour classes become 'embourgeoisiefied' in rich countries of the Western world. It contradicts the Marxian law of increasing misery, degradation and pauperisation of the

17. Ball, *op. cit.*, p. 58.
18. Bonn (ed.) : *Works of Edmund Burke,* Vol. IV, p. 146.
19. Ball, *op. cit.*, p. 61.

proletariat in the industrially advanced countries of the world. The Americans, for instance, abandoned their foreign policy of splendid isolationism at the time of the first Great War and they adopted the policy of effective intervention after the Second world War for containing the growth of communism. It is also possible that an industrially developed nation may outstretch its imperialistic arms to subjugate another country and cause a transformation of the political culture of the subjugated people before it withdraws its control as happened in Japan where the promulgation of the Peace Constitution in 1946 at the hands of the Americans led to the superimposition of liberal-democratic values over the feudal political culture providing sanction to the norms of military behaviour.[20]

Allied with this is the subject of secularisation of the political culture. It has two attributes—(i) pragmatic and empirical orientations and (ii) movement from diffuseness to specificity of cultural orientations. Times change and so change the beliefs and values of the people. This change should, however, be in a pragmatic and empirical direction and that too in a way from diffuseness to specificity. That is, the political beliefs and values of the people must change from a parochial to a mundane variety, the people must learn more and more the meaning of political participation and political recruitment and their knowledge of political involvement should grow so that they may grasp the implications of the idea of political legitimacy. Thus, the process of the secularisation of political culture means increasing political awareness of the people enabling them to have a growing information about their political system and their role as a political actor in it. "It is through the secularisation of political culture that these rigid, ascribed and diffuse customs of social interaction come to be over-ridden by a set of codified, specifically political, and universalistic rules. By the same token, it is in the secularisation process that bargaining and accommodative political actions become a common feature of the society, and that the development of special structures such as interest groups and parties become meaningful."[21]

Political Culture and the Issue of Political Stability and Change

A study of different political systems of the world, whether western and advanced or eastern and developing, from this standpoint leaves this impression that political culture plays a very important role in the sphere of political stability and change. We may put the same thing in a different way by adding that if political culture "is the pattern or patterns of knowledge, evaluation and communications relating to political authority,"[22] it informs us to treat political orientations of the people towards 'authority' as a very important determinant or "an explanatory variable in accounting for the stability, effectiveness and representativeness of a democratic political system."[23] Thus, a line of difference may be drawn between the cases of Britain and France. While a large part of the political stability of the former may be explained by the deferential norms which dominate political as well as social relationships,[24] the conventional view of the French political culture may be seen in the appreciation of absolute conception of authority. "The rivalry between the two sub-cultures of the political right committed to principles of order and hierarchy and of the political left committed to principles of change and equality, means that the values of autonomous leadership and popular control of the government are not blended within individuals."[25]

20. Sec A.W. Burks : *The Government of Japan* (London, 1966), II Ed., p. 267.
21. Almond and Powell, *op. eit.*, p. 60.
22. Peter Nettl : *Political Mobilisation* (London, 1967), p. 57.
23. E.A. Nordlinger : *The Working Class Tories* (London, 1967), p. 49.
24. Kavangh, *op. cit.*, p. 18.
25. *ibid.*, p. 17.

It follows that the system of parliamentary democracy cannot be imposed on people having their faith m the tenets of authoritarianism. More than hundred fifty years ago, John Stuart Mill was right when he held that despotism was the best form of government for the barbarians, while representative government for the civilised ones. Examining the case of the Weimer Republic of Germany established after the First World War, Eckstein, for this reason, concludes that the reason of its instability should be related to the wide gap between the democratic rules of the conduct of government and the authoritarianism found in the military, the bureaucracy, the political parties and the family.'[26] Likewise, while referring to the case of Japan, Frank Langdon has observed that the strength of the support attached to the *status quo* and to traditional norms is a source of hindrance to the tasks of social and political modernisation.[27]

The dichotomy between tradition and modernity on the cultural front thus creates the problem of political bi-culturalism. The makers of the new states are, therefore, confronted with this dilemma and it depends upon their sagacity and magnanimity as how to take their country to the path of political modernisation. Evidence shows that a sudden or total change amounts to the breakdown of the new political system, because the tradition-bound people donot appreciate change that stands in total contradiction to the values of their conventional culture. On the other hand, the leaders who strive for a gradual change get ample success in their endeavours. In this way, the "very stability and integration of the political culture depend on promoting orderly changes and achieving a political consensus depends on the politician's ability to strike a balance between the old and the new."[28]

If so, the case of political development has both conservating and innovating aspects. The former aspect may be seen in vehement opposition to any move towards total change, the latter may be traced in the endeavours of the leaders like Kemal Ataturk of Turkey, Nasser of Egypt and Nehru of India to infuse political modernisation in degrees. The latter course proves eminently successful, because the process of incremental change finds its simultaneous assimilation with the traditional culture and that effects its legitimisation in an imperceptible way.[29] What strikes us here is that the leaders of such countries appreciate the existence of diverse cultures in the midst of which a sort of astonishing homogeneity prevails. Nehru calls it by the name of 'unity in diversity'. The burden of their argument is that "if all people spoke the same language, or had the same religion, or belonged to the same race, all the diversity and cultural richness that these differences represent would be lost."[30]

It is true that the stability of Anglo-American political systems may be described as a result of the factor of cultural homogeneity, but it would be a mistake to agree with the view of Parsons and Sutton that societies may be divided into two categories—industrial and agricultural—and that a uniform value system

26. *ibid.*, p. 18. Also see H.H. Eckstein : *Division and Cohesion in Democracy* (Princeton : Princeton Univ. Press, 1966).
27. Langdon : *Politics in Japan* (Boston : Little Brown, 1967), pp. 74-75.
28. Kavangh, *op. cit.*, p. 39.
29. Rajni Kothari : "Tradition and Modernity Revisited" in *Government and Opposition*, Vol. Ill, No. 3, 1968.
30. D.E. Apter : *Introduction to Political Analysis* (New Delhi : Prentice Hall, 1978), p. 250. "This factor has a special relevance in the study of the developing countries of the Third World. Keeping it in view, David E. Apter has suggested several general uses of political religion in the new states: reinforcing the values of hard work and sacrifice; developing a 'collective orientation', making citizens aware of their shared ties : developing a political structure; endowing the new order with moral principles; and legitimising the incumbent elite's continual monopoly of office. He develops the analogy further by adding that political religion may come to serve as a universal church. Its agents are the missionaries. Opposition to it appears as a new form of imperialism." *The Politics of Modernisation* (Chicago: Chicago Univ. Press, 1965), p. 366.

may be found in industrial societies. As a matter of fact, values "are mixed within individuals and within nations."[31] Myers is, for this reason, justified in holding that any simple distinction between societies involves a loss of discrimination about differences without the industrialised societies and an empirical examination "strengthens the argument that the logic of industralisation is to create different value orientations among different social classes."[32]

However, the reconstruction of political culture is a fascinating affair in the case of developing societies of the the Third World. Four reasons may be assigned for this. First, if culture change is to be effected speedily, it will have to be directed by the state—usually by means of secondary and formal agencies. Second, the scope of politics is large in such states; society becomes identified with the state, the good man or citizen is the good party man. Third, given the recent discontinuities in the histories of many new states, the creation of new attitudes is important in weakening the pre-revolutionary or pre-independence outlooks. New orientations are necessary to support new institutions and new forms of activity. Last, the internalisation of regime-approved norms and values is important in strengthening the regime's legitimacy and in encouraging voluntary compliance with its commands.[33]

Ideology and Political Culture : Phenomenon of a Well Defined Admixture of Political Values

The role of ideology must also be understood in the formation and change of people's commitments towards certain political values. The reason for this may be traced in the fact that cognitive aspect of ideology connects fundamental beliefs to 'deep structures' or the internalised values that make up the mental attitude of the people. Ideology is, therefore, a pre-disposition or a long-term orientation of thought.[34] If so, it "stands on the intersection between philosophical principles or ends, individual preferences and beliefs, and general and particular values. Values, interests and preferences obviously overlap. Ideologies are combinations of these attributes —sometimes coherent and sometimes not. Preferences can be converted to interests and interests to values, or they may be elevated to the status of values in order to achieve interests."[35]

A study of ideology and political culture, in this context, enables us to distinguish between its rigid and flexible dimensions. In the former, as taken by the Marxists and the Fascists, it becomes like a dogma or a sort of 'religious belief' and thereby desires a pattern of uniformity in respect of convictions and commitments of the people. Dissent is not at all allowed. The new rulers use force to replace the old beliefs of the people by a set of new 'socialist values'. Such a movement is lauded as 'cultural revolution'. The entire community of the dissenters is tortured and a great leader like Stalin or Mao proudly demands that the people must change their mental orientations so as to run the new social, economic and political system. "At the very core of such an ideology is the notion of class conflict; indeed, this is the mechanism through which the promised perfect society is to be gained."[36]

---

31. Kavangh, *op. cit.,* p. 38.
32. See Frank Myers : "Social Classes and Political Change in Western Industrial Systems" in *Comparative Politics,* Vol. II, No. 3, 1970.
33. See Kavangh, *op. cit.,* p. 40.
34. See H.C. McClosky, P.J. Hoffman and R. O'Hara : "Issue Conflict and Consensus Among Party Leaders and Followers" in *American Political Science Review,* Vol. 54, June 1960, pp. 406-27.
35. Apter: *Introduction to Political Analysis,* p. 242.
36. Daniel Bell : *The End of Ideology: On the Exhaustion of Political Ideas in the Fifties* (New York : Colliers, 1961), pp. 431-32.

Different from this is the case of flexible dimension of ideology where, according to the interpretation of Freud, it is like a way of rationalisation so as to cope with the pressures, threats, tensions and conflicts to which the human organism is subject. Viewed thus, liberalism becomes an ideology in its own way. It emphasises that all people "have, besides the opinions they hold on particular issues, fundamental commitments by means of which their views on any particular issue are likely to be slanted. No one participates in supporting or opposing the issue of socialised medicine, or a more expanded range of welfare benefits, or taxation to pay for those things, without fitting these beliefs into some previously defined system of notions or prerequisite preferences (like the value of the individual over the state, self-reliance over socialism, freedom over bureaucracy, or some other advocacy). Ideologies may not always be consistent, but they are interrelated. Political parties sometimes clearly and strongly, sometimes more vaguely, stand for the primacy of some of these sets of interests over others."[37]

It is, therefore, obvious that the ideology of liberalism does not plead for the case of a single political culture. The room for interpretations is not closed, though unanimity in respect of fundamental convictions cannot be ruled out. Faith in the principles of liberty, equality, rule of law, justice and the like remains unshaken, though different people have their divergent views on questions relating to the nature and scope of each political value. "Independence is prized; men say they would rather be known for their capacity to get along in a discussion; they value leaders who give the impression of independence."[38]

Whether it is the rigid dimension of ideology or the flexible one, this much is certain that ideology has its objective manifestation in the form of action. This is corroborated by the fact that people prefer to die for the sake of their principles rather than to live like cowards and their names have a conspicuous place in the annals of history. Thus, ideology may be seen in the form of motivation or the 'conversion of ideas into social levers', as said by Bell. For the ideologue truth arises in action, and meaning is given to experience by the 'transforming moment.' One might say, "in fact, that the most important latent function of ideology is to tap emotion."[39]

A study of ideology and political culture, as a matter of fact, becomes organically inter-related in view of the fact that here we are concerned with the subjective and objective aspects of the same phenomenon.[40] Civic culture is nothing else than an objective manifestation of what each society teaches its members by way of a certain religious conviction. For this reason, the role of political culture has an importance of its own in the modern political analysis, for it alone "maintains the balance between power and responsibility."[41] As Apter says: "High congruity in the political culture equals great stability in the political system. The ingredients, and the style, of various political cultures are thus of critical importance. Comparative analysis of different systems can be useful in analysing the validity, or the durability, of various political cultures."[42]

Political Culture and Political Systems : Morphological Analyses of Almond and Finer

The political culture approach is markedly different from the legal-institutional approach

37. Apter, *op. cit.*, p. 248.
38. R.E. Lane : *Political Ideology* (New York : Free Press of Glencoe, 1962), pp. 19-20.
39. Bell, *op. cit.*, p. 371.
40. R.D. Putnam : *The Beliefs of Politicians* (New Haven : Yale Univ Press 1973).
41. Almond and Verba, *op. cit.*, p. 249.
42. Apter, *op. cit.*, p. 250.

in the sense that while the latter lays stress on the legal structure of political institutions and decision-making process according to the framework of the fundamental law of the land, the former goes a step ahead by emphasising that in addition to the formal institutions of the political organisation, the student of politics, as Almond suggests, "must take into account the parts played by family ties, mobs, electorates, causal and persistent groupings, and all foci of power and influence in the political process if his analysis is to be directly relevant to political system as they are."[43] It is obvious that the concept of political culture involves a study of non-political contexts to a quite considerable extent. Starting with this premise that the legal-institutional approach does not result in any meaningful comparisons of actual systems, Almond makes an attempt to construct a scheme for the methodological comparisons of political systems by adopting concepts borrowed from the disciplines of sociology and anthropology and thus comes to lay down that major political systems which "exist in the world of today can be classified according to a common set of categories."[44] The starting point of this American political scientist is that a political system "is a system of action about which there is no difficulty in gaining information, that is political activity is empirically observable behaviour."[45]

Political culture may be classified according to the active or passive part that the members of a society take in the political process. That is, whether they play a part with an ardent expectation of tangible benefits from the governmental activity, or whether they have very little, or almost no, knowledge of the decision-making process, and thus have no hopes for a share in the power. Almond begins with this assumption that political culture and political structure are interrelated as one is affected by the other. In order to elucidate the relationship between the two, he introduces the concepts of *roles* and *orientations to political action*. He regards the political system as a set of interactive roles, or a structure of roles in which each individual or group is taken as a political actor. Not only this, each actor plays a multi-dimensional role: for instance, as a minister in one capacity, as a legislator in another, and as a party leader in still another.

The second assumption of Almond is that a political system operates within a framework of set of meanings—attitudes of the people towards political activity. Thus, there appears a thing like the pattern of orientations to political action that may be described as another name for political culture. It requires the study of a political actor's knowledge and information about, involvement with and judgment on four counts: (i) system as a whole including its historical development, size, location and power and constitutional characteristics; (ii) input process, i.e., forces that affect the decision-making process like political parties, pressure groups and mass media agencies; (iii) output process, *i.e.*, the work of the rule-making, rule-implementing and rule-interpreting departments; and (iv) self, i.e., his own assessment about the part he plays in the political sphere. In this way, political culture is determined by the frequency of different kinds of cognitive, affective and evaluative orientations towards the political system in general, its input and output aspects, and the self as a political actor.[46]

---

43. Morton R. Davies and Vaughan A. Lewis : *Models of Political Systems* (Delhi : Vikas, 1971), p. 112.
44. *ibid.*
45. *ibid.*
46. G.A. Almond and Sidney Verba : *The Civic Culture* (Princeton : Princeton Univ. Press, 1963), p. 17.

Almond's Morphological Illustration of Political Culture and Political System

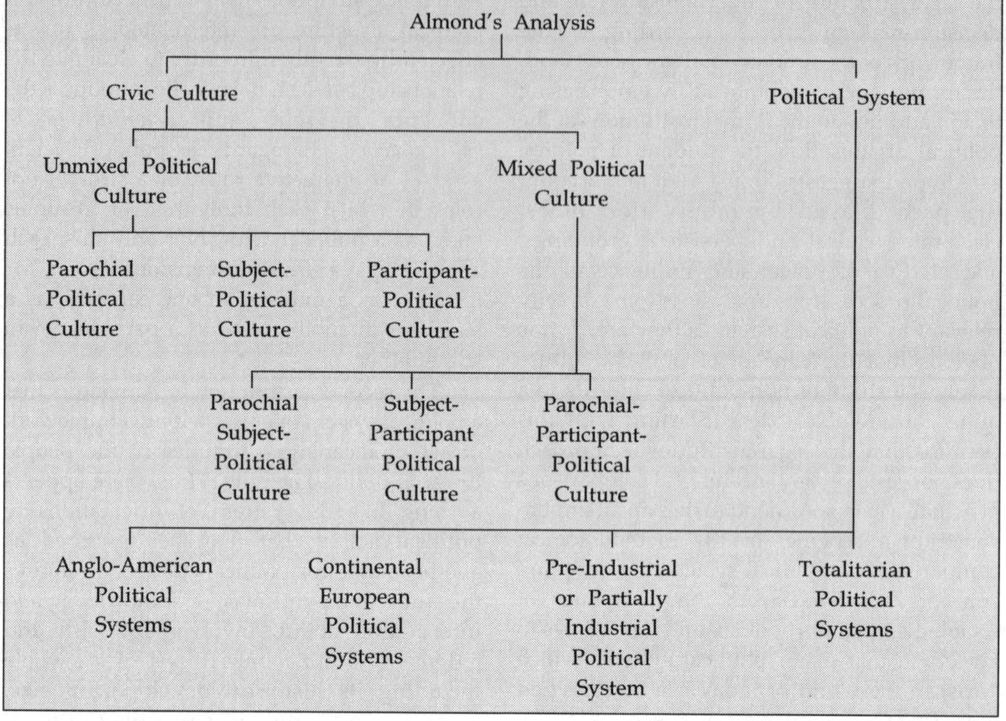

Almond presents a classification of political cultures on subjects-participants basis and his classification of the political systems on the basis of different political cultures. In the classification of political cultures the basic factor is his emphasis on the roles of the subjects and the participants. Persons aware of the political system may be either subjects (those individuals who are oriented to the political system and the impact which it outputs, such as welfare benefits, laws, etc. may have upon their lives, but who are not oriented to participation in the input structures) and participants (those individuals who are oriented to the input structures and processes, and engaged in or view themselves as potentially engaging in the articulation of demands and the making of decisions).[47] Almond further says that orientations to politics include the notions of the individual about himself as a political actor.[48]

With these standpoints, Almond presents a tripartite division of political culture that may be briefly discussed as under:

1. ***Parochial Political Culture :*** It exists in simple traditional societies in which there is very little specialisation and where actors fulfil a combination of political, economic and religious roles simultaneously.[49] Here we find a pattern of undifferentiated role structure as a chieftain performing the role of the arch-administrator, arch-priest, arch-economist, etc., and the subjects living under him donot show any awareness of their political system as such, though they have much awareness of their community as a

47. Almond and Powell, *op. cit., p. 53.*
48. *ibid.,* p. 54.
49. Davies and Lewis, *pp. cit.,* p. 115.

whole. It may be that on account of development, some of the individuals may become aware of the existence of central political authority, but their feelings for and evaluation of the system as a whole "have not crystallised sufficiently for them to establish for themselves norms and standards to regulate their relations with the system."[50]

2. ***Subject Political Culture :*** It exists where there is a high frequency of orientations to the system as a whole and to its specifically output aspects. It occurs in dependent colonies where the people either feel pride or cultivate hostility towards their political system. That is, they either accept the decisions of their rulers as legitimate, or struggle against them in the name of their right for self-determination. It is a different thing that Almond lays too much emphasis on the part of the people's blind acceptance of the political system as legitimate and he ignores the latter part of their hostility that results in the form of movements repudiating the authority of the decision-makers by calling their laws as 'black' and demanding nothing short of complete independence.

3. ***Participant Political Culture :*** It exists in highly developed societies where people take active part in the political sphere by considering themselves as active members of the polity. They are well conscious of their rights and duties. "Evaluation and criticism of the system exist at all levels, and it is generally accepted as discernible that political activity should be under the close scrutiny of individuals and groups within society."[51] Almond, however, makes it clear that as political cultures are more politically homogeneous, individuals should not be taken as uniformly oriented to political actions.

In addition to this, Almond points out two more variables that should be taken into account. First, apart from all these varieties of the political culture of an unmixed type, he also refers to the political culture of a systematically mixed variety. Here he deals with situations where there are significant proportions of more than one pattern of orientations. Thus, he lays down three varieties: (i) parochial subject-political culture, (ii) subject-participant political culture, (iii) parochial-participant political culture, and (iv) civic culture.

Second, political cultures and political structures are never stationary and the process of congruence versus incongruence operates over a period of time owing to rapid scientific and technological changes. There "is no inevitable tendency for a movement towards or away from congruence to complete itself. It is possible for cultural patterns to stabilise at a point short of congruence, that is, where individuals have accurate knowledge of the political system which they are prepared to tolerate but with which they have no sense of involvement or about which they have no positive, favourable opinions. Alternatively, a pattern of development may be "established in which slow cultural changes are accompanied by slow structural changes, thus maintaining a balance between the two which closely approximates, but never actually achieves congruence. This pattern of development is particularly likely to appear in those societies in which individuals are positively oriented to the input process, that is, in situations in which popular volition can make itself felt, or at least where popular opinions are politically influential when called into being by a rival set of leaders."[52]

Then, Almond presents a typological illustration of the political systems that may briefly be discussed as under.[53]

---

50. *ibid.,* p. 116.
51. *ibid.,* p. 117.
52. *ibid.,* p. 119.
53. See G.A. Almond : "Comparative Political Systems" in *Journal of Politics,* Vol. XVIII of 1956.

Anglo-American Systems : This is the first variety operating in advanced Western democratic countries like Britain and America whose salient characteristics may be enumerated thus :

(i) Such systems are characterised by multi-valued political cultures that are homogeneous and continuous in the sense that there is general agreement about political ends and means to their realisation;

(ii) Politics becomes like a game in which several players, though rivals, play their part but they never take their differences to the extent of converting the atmosphere of the game into that of a battlefield;

(iii) Politics also looks like a market-place where decision-makers offer their outputs as exchanges for winning votes or people' support. Thus, bargaining process takes place between the rulers and the ruled, the elected and the electors, between leaders and their followers;

(iv) Society has a plural character in which different parties and interest groups operate in order to influence the decision-making process in response to their respective interests;

(v) There is the diffusion of power and influence. Thus, there is a full and well-functioning arrangement of checks and balances. Legal institutions are checked by the channels of mass communication and mass education so that the prospects of authoritarian rule are mitigated, even eliminated; and

(vi) Finally, there is the stability of differentiated roles. Different institutions perform their respective functions; they may also perform the functions of others with the result that the administrators become legislators in one and the adjudicators in another respect; or the bureaucrats become legislators in one and the adjudicators in another respect and the like.

Continental European Political Systems : This is the second variety operating in less developed Western democratic countries of Europe like France, Italy, Sweden, Norway, etc. whose salient features may be thus enumerated:

(i) The political culture is fragmented where different sections of society establish different patterns of cultural development, while some are more developed than others. For this reason. the political culture has with it a train of political sub-cultures that may be effected either by virtue of scientific and technological innovations or on account of their importation from the advanced ruling country. Such a particular culture has much of its past coming from the days of feudalism and also tries to emulate the higher values of countries belonging to the above category;

(ii) Each political sub-culture develops a separate sub-system of roles with the result that various cultures become the focal points of the whole system. Thus, one has to look at the infrastructure also after he makes a study of the legal-institutional framework; and

(iii) The process of political bargaining is virtually non-existent that creates a situation in which politics becomes like a game. The result is that various sub-cultures are at war against each other and one poses itself as superior to other or the others and thus tries to impose its norms on the rest.. Thus, instead of bargain, there is warfare among groups competing for power.

Pre-Industrialised or Partially Industrialised Political Systems : This category includes a large number of countries which have emerged from the days of long colonial domination. In such a political system the political culture of the rulers is imposed over the political culture of the subjects. It has these main characteristics:

(i) The political culture of the masters is super-imposed over the political culture of the subjects. The result is the erosion of the political culture of the subjects and the super-imposition of the political culture of the rulers that is deemed as superior in all respects;

(ii) The leaders may try to establish a synthesis between the old and the new and thereby develop characteristics providing a new source of legitimacy to the system. It is, however, possible that there occur violent outbreaks that may make the whole system unstable if the charismatic leadership is exposed or replaced by another leadership of the same variety; and

(iii) Here two or more political cultures may be at work within a single structure of roles. For instance, a particular family or a caste may remain in power in reference to particular traditions and also emulating the ways of western democracy.

Totalitarian Political Systems : Finally, Almond takes up the case of a totalitarian country like the former Soviet Union and China. It may be said to have these characteristics:

(i) The quality of the acceptability of the legitimacy is artificially created. The characteristic orientation to authority tends to be some combination of conformity or apathy produced by the central control or the means of communication and of the agencies of violence;

(ii) Coercion becomes the hallmark of the exercise of authority. All organisations are surrounded by an atmosphere of coercion exercised by an all-powerful state; and

(iii) There is all-concentration of power that negatives the principle of diffusion of authority. The men in power count heavily on the support of bureaucracy, police and army.

Political culture "includes not only the attitudes to politics, political values, ideologies, national character and cultural ethos, but also the style, manner and substantive form of politics."[54] It is due to this that the varieties of political culture can be discovered. While paying special attention to the role of military in the political life of a country, Professor S.E. Finer suggests three variables of political culture:[55]

(i) ***Mature Political Culture :*** As obtaining in Britain, America, Australia and the Netherlands, it shows that the political consensus and its degree of organisation are very high; the need of the government for counting on the support of the armed forces is at a minimum; and long habituation to this situation has brought not only the public but even the armed services to an almost unquestioning belief in the principle of civil supremacy.

(ii) ***Developed Political Culture :*** It refers to a society where the public is highly organised, though, from time to time, it becomes sharply polarised on either the legitimacy of its institutions and procedures or on the incumbents who hold office as a consequence of these. We may find that the civilian governments are often threatened, even subverted, by military pressures and the people, in general, are either silenced by the force of arms, or they feel solace in getting politically alienated. Countries like Egypt, Algeria and Cuba can be placed in this category.

(iii) ***Low Political Culture :*** It is found in countries with narrow and weakly organised publics, often self-divided on the legitimacy of the regime or the incumbents in office. In such countries, public opinion is too feeble or self-divided or both to offer any sustained resistance to authoritarian rules. Countries like Vietnam, Iraq, Syria, Bhutan, and Indonesia may be placed in this category.

54. S.P. Varma : *Modern Political Theory* (Delhi : Vikas, 1975), p. 292.
55. Finer : *Comparative Government* (London : Allen Lane, 1970), pp. 537-40.

Critical Appraisal

According to the protagonists of political culture approach, it has made a highly significant contribution to the development of modern political theory. It is said that it "may provide us with a valuable conceptual tool by means of which we can bridge the micro-macro gap in political theory."[56] Professor S.P. Varma points out five main contributions of this approach :

1. It has made Political Science a more complete social science through its insistence on a combined micro-macro approach.
2. It has focused our attention on the study of the political community or society, as a dynamic collective entity as distinct from the individual and thus on the total political system.
3. It has encouraged political scientists to take up the study of social and cultural factors which are responsible for giving the political culture of a country its broad shape.
4. It has helped us in combining the study of the rational factors which shape the actions of the individuals to a large extent with the more latent, the irrational, determinants of behaviour that may be subjected to empirical research to a quite considerable extent.
5. It is the political culture approach which "helped us to understand why different political societies, inevitably moved in different directions of political development, or may be, find themselves suffering from severe constraints, socio-economic as well as political, which force them to move towards political decay."[57]

However, the political culture approach has some weaknesses that may be pointed out as under :

1. Being a derivative of the political development approach, it suffers from the stigma of conservatism and reaction. It is not progressive but reactionary in character. Even Almond and Powell have realised that this approach cannot be taken as a correct barometer of individual behaviour. They affirm that a careful analysis of political culture "still provides no sure guide, perhaps at best a probabilistic one, for the prediction of individual behaviour in a given case. Individual actions can at times have great impact on the performance of the political system, but it is unlikely that any analysis of the political culture of the United States could have predicted the behaviour of a Lee Harvey Oswald. Nor can a consideration of the political culture of Ghana fully explain the actions of Nkrumah."[58]
2. The political culture approach cannot be described as a very precise variable for presenting a morphological study of modern political systems. The terms coined by the protagonists of this approach are neither very clear nor very precise as a result of which a student of comparative politics is often confronted with a confusing situation. Thus, it has been pointed out that the concept of political culture "is an attempt to find one rubric to include what, in the past, have been variously described as attitudes to politics, political values, ideologies, national character, and cultural ethos, etc. None of these terms are sufficiently broad to provide a basis for classifying political systems, though each

---

56. Almond and Powell, *op. cit.*, p. 51. So Harry H. Eckstein says that it is the social structure, such as the family and the school, and the potential structure such as parties and pressure groups which are 'adjacent' to the government, which prepare individuals for governmental roles. Consequences between governmental and other structures redress strains and bring about appropriate expectations for future roles. *Division and Cohesion in Democracy* (Princeton : Princeton Univ. Press, 1966).
57. Varma, *op. cit.*, pp. 296-97.
58. Almond and Powell, *op. cit.*, p. 51.

one of them separately is relevant to the study of comparative politics, but each one is vague and ambiguous and, as such, serves only as a source of confusion for those attempting to compare political systems methodically."[59]

3. If political culture is nothing else than a set-of beliefs and sentiments about politics as embodied in the verbal and non-verbal behaviour of the people and depending upon the specific content of the notion of 'political development', it is bound to be conducive or antagonistic to it. The problem arises when there is a measure of difference between the political culture of the rulers and that of the ruled. In such a situation, the question would arise "as to which of these different cultures may be considered more relevant to political development."[60] Lucian Pye has taken note of this fact that in no society there is is a fundamental distinction between the culture of the rulers or power holders and that of the masses.[61] If so, then it "is obvious that the relation of political culture to political development, howsoever conceived, would have to be conceived in a far more complex and differentiated manner."[62] Not only this, diversity of political culture may be seen even in the community of the ruling class. One party may come into power after replacing another with its own set of political notions, beliefs and commitments. If so, it would have its own effect on the pace of political development and political modernisation of the country. The problem, in fact, compounded as political culture itself is a sub-system of the culture in general. Or, if it be objected that there "is no such thing as culture in general but rather cultures as differentiated with respect to particular domains, the problem may be.reformulated and articulated in terms of the homogeneity or heterogeneity of the culture obtained in the political domain with those obtained in other domains."[63] Keeping it in view, Prof. Daya Krishna says: "Seen either as a lubricating oil for the creaking joints of the social machine or as a compensatory dream which makes the oppressive repression of social reality bearable or as a beautiful mask which hides hideous reality, it is always treated in relation to something other than itself and as an instrument thereof. The talk of 'political culture' is no different, and it is primarily seen in terms of political development"[64]

It may, however, be admitted that the concept of political culture "is an attempt to gain the rigour and comprehensiveness which these other concepts lack."[65] Keeping this all in view, Kavangh has pointed out that describing subjective attitudes about the political system "is not tantamount to a realistic description of the system itself in view of the fact that there may be sharp differences of opinions about the very meaning of old and modern attitudes of the people. In this way, the "fatal attractiveness of the political culture approach is that it may be made to explain too much. It has been used to cover so many disparate phenomena that it is easily used as a residual factor."[66] He goes on to add: "Values and attitudes are undoubtedly relevant to an explanation of the performance of political systems, but eventually we have to go back and explain how the political culture came to be formed and expressed the

59. Davies and Lewis, *op. cit.,* p. 114.
60. Daya Krishna : *Political Development: A Critical Perspective* (New Delhi: Oxford Univ. Press, !979), p. 151.
61. Pye, *op. cit.,* p. 13.
62. Daya Krishna, *op. cit.,* p. 151.
63. *ibid,* p. 152.
64. *ibid.,* pp. 149-50.
65. Davies and Lewis, *op. cit.,* p. 114.
66. Kavangh, *op. cit.,* p. 55.

way that it is."[67] More specific is the charge that the study of norms., sentiments and beliefs, which are often taken for granted, is not amenable to survey methods.[68] It informs him to add further that, in reality, the political culture "is almost certainly differentially determined by the individuals according to their political weight and the intensity behind their particular orientations. Aggregation is only legitimate where the units to be aggregated are similar. In most cases, it is the political elites, the leaders, activists and writers, who play the major role in creating and interpreting the 'political formula' of a group or nation, and their responses should be given greater weight by the researcher. Moreover, the emphasis on the individual's orientations to and participation in politics is very much a 'culture-bound' approach."[69]

67. *ibid.*, p.59.
68. *ibid.*, p. 61.
69. *ibid.*, pp. 61-62.

13

Political Ideology

> Political ideas are part of the political environment, they are a result of that environment. They change with the pressure of events and they provide a mould for political change. They may be badly articulated preferences with little relevance to other political values held by the individual or the group such as the 'them and us' variety, or they may be linked to a whole host of other attitudes, such as one finds in nationalist movements. These ideas may find their sources of inspiration in all sorts of different fields such as religion, etc., but it is their nature and their function in the political process that are of most importance.
>
> **—Alan R. Ball[1]**

A study of political values within the framework of a 'science of ideas' or ideology, as generally understood, has a significance of its own in the field of comparative politics in view of the fact that "in every type of political system, policies are formulated and decisions made within a value-framework."[2] It is the comparative study of different value and belief systems that involves an attempt to explain why the substantive contents of ideologies such as conservatism in Great Britain, liberalism in the United States, fascism in Italy and Spain, nazism in Germany, socialism (or communism) in the former Soviet Union and China etc. vary from one extreme to another. Allied with this is the issue that a comparative study of ideologies should explain why the same social groups in certain countries of the world develop different ideologies pertaining to the promotion of their specific interests. These differences and similarities "can only be accounted for in terms of such factors as the effectiveness of political parties, the existence of habits of compromise, the tradition of political leadership, the productivity of the economy, and so on. The study of ideological trends among key groups like those of the army and the intellectuals is especially important during periods of rapid political change. The nature and intensity of ideological conflict provides valuable clues to the degree of stability and instability in a given system. Thus, virtually every aspect of a political system can be illuminated by examination of the relationship between groups and ideologies."[3]

Political Ideology: Meaning, Nature and Characteristics

Political ideology or doctrine "is a type of political theory which upholds a certain political system (broadest sense) and the values and ideals that sustain it, as the final proximation of the human mind to an ideal arrangement, and, therefore, claiming this finality seeks to realise it."[4] The test of a political ideology "lies in its 'application'."[5] Thus,

1. A.R. Ball : *Modern Politics and Government* (London : Macmillan, 1971). p. 250.
2. *ibid.,* p. 247.
3. B.E. Brown : *New Directions in Comparative Politics* (Bombay : Asia Publishing House, 1962), pp. 18-19.
4. Frank Thakurdas : "The Expanding Frontiers of Political Science" in *Indian Journal of Political Science,* Vol. XXXIV, No. 4, 1973, p. 415.
5. *ibid.,* p. 416.

Preston King says that an ideology "will either involve the actual application of a coherent system of political ideas to a political system in such a way as to direct its activities, or it involves the serious distinction of making this application."[6] In other words, ideology refers to an 'action-related system' of political ideas in the sense that they are sets of ideas concerning change or defence of existing political structures and relationships.[7] Ideology involves 'commitment and action' as a part of the political process.[8] It "may or may not possess a logical or philosophical character at all; but it must possess a political character, *i.e.*, a content without which it cannot be described an ideology—a guide to direct political action."[9]

If so, the real meaning of ideology differs from that of certain other terms that are mistakenly regarded as interchangeable with it. For instance, ideology and mentality cannot be taken as analogous terms. While an ideology "is a system of thought which has been intellectually worked out and organised usually in written form by scholars and intellectuals or with their help, mentality denotes a way of thinking and feeling which is more emotional than rationalised -something like a 'cast of mind."[10] Ideology also differs from philosophy and, for this reason, political ideology and political philosophy cannot be regarded as synonymous terms. Political philosophy "evokes reflection and understanding, while ideology is more likely to imply commitment and action."[11]

Keeping in view the essential fact that a political scientist cannot base his entire analysis on empirical knowledge alone and that he has to choose and approach his particular field of specialisation equipped with the values and attitudes of his own political culture that will affect his political analysis, we may pinpoint certain general characteristics of the term 'political ideology' as under:

1. Ideologies are not the same as values and attitudes of the political culture. They are programmes for action and instruments of evaluation. They are a response to and a means of defending or changing existing political systems; they provide a language to conduct an examination of the political process.[12]
2. It is not the content of the ideologies alone that distinguishes one from another, it is the function of the ideology within the political system that creates differentiation. Ideological emphasis is a significant characteristic of the totalitarian states, but in liberal democracies the role of the underlying ideologies is often less obtrusive but no less important in different respects.[13]
3. Ideologies do change, but this is not necessarily due to their being 'corrupted' or to the 'death' of their role in the political process; nor are the changes simply the result of the political opportunism. An ideology is impossible to translate directly into practice; there has to be accommodation to political realities, a translation which may result in ideological splits between former ideological colleagues and a distortion of reality to fit the ideological interpretation. It may be that ideologies need 'enemies' to establish their credibility.[14]
4. Ideologies may be classified according to their role in relation to the political system as rightist or leftist, reactionary or

6. *ibid.*
7. See Carl J. Friedrich and Z.K. Brzezinski : *Totalitarian Dictatorship and Autocracy* (New York, 1965), p. 88.
8. Preston King cited in Frank Thakurdas, *op. cit.*, p. 416.
9. *ibid.*
10. S.E. Finer : *Comparative Government* (London : Allen Lane, The Penguin Press, 1970), p. 43.
11. See Preston King and B. Parekh (eds) : *Politics and Experience* (Cambridge, 1969), p. 351.
12. Ball, *op. cit.*, p. 256.
13. *ibid.*, p 255.
14. *ibid.*, p. 254.

progressive, conservative or revolutionary, reformist or radical and the like. No political system is, however, absolutely free from the 'bond of ideology'. It is a different thing that the adherents to the ideology of liberalism may claim and cry for the 'end of ideology'.

5. It is the ideology that constitutes the keystone of the arch of a political party or a group. It may be asserted that a scuffle between two leaders (as Stalin versus Trotsky) in Russia, or between two groups (as between Maoists and Liuists in China), or between two countries (as former Soviet Union and China) is conducted 'within the framework of ideological arguments'.[15]

A study of the term 'political ideology', after keeping in view its general characteristics and diverse ramifications, shows that ideological politics "is doctrinaire, didactic, dogmatic, transitory, prescriptive, polemical and propagandist, partisan, combative and destructive; whose appeal is in the nature of a religious belief, which would not suffer either doubt or criticism. It is the creedal character that makes it thoroughly impervious to scepticism or to a critical scrutiny. To doubt is to destroy; and all of them save Communism are far from clear and coherent."[16] It should also be kept in mind that the qualities as of truth and knowledge "are not its criteria; hence demand a total commitment and a total allegiance (e.g., Mao Tse-tung's 'Red Book' provides us with the latest, nay classic example)— as guides to action."[17]

Political Ideology and Political Power: Varieties and Functional Aspect of the Action-Related Values in Politics

What we have said above leads to this impression that ideologies "attempt to be a description of political reality and a blueprint for action."[18] The function of the ideology, in this way, becomes either to bring about a change or to justify an existing political system. A student of comparative politics is thus concerned with the subject of political power in respect of its distribution between the people and their rulers. The result is that, according to a writer on comparative politics, ideologies "are as much a factor in stability and political unity as a source of challenge to existing political structures. They can be used to support the dominant political elites and to disarm their political rivals, and they can be useful in diverting attention from difficult internal problems. Above all, they are a means of legitimising the government and the policies of that government."[19]

Viewed thus, a 'system of action-related values' in politics has two important dimensions—one relating to the study of the existing political system with special reference to the issue of 'distribution of power' and the other relating to its role in being an instrument of change. The two aspects may be thus designated—politics as an art of having a legitimate government and politics as a struggle for power for making a change in the existing political system with special reference to the

---

15. *ibid.*
16. Frank Thakurdas, *op. cit.*, p. 416.
17. *ibid.* The term 'ideology' has been defined and interpreted by many writers in their own ways. For instance, Fredrick Watkins suggests that ideology comes almost entirely from the political extremes. It is always opposed to the status quo. It proposes an abrupt change in an existing order. *The Age of Ideology* (Englewood Cliffs, New Jersey : Prentice-Hall, 1964). David Ingersoll says in a little different way that each ideology includes an assessment of the status quo and a view of the future. The future is always represented as something, better than the present or the past. Each ideology contains a definite plan of action by which the better future can be attained. See L.P. Baradat : *Political Ideologies : Their Origins and Impact* (Englewood Cliffs, New Jersey : Prentice-Hall, 1979). p. 33. Quite different is the view of L.T. Sergent who says that ideology is based on the value systems of various societies. It "provides the believer with a picture of the world both as it is and as it should be, and in so doing, . . . organises the tremendous complexity of the world into something fairly simple and understandable." *Contemporary Political Ideologies* (Homewood, Illinois : Dorsey Press, 1972), Rev. Ed., p. 1.
18. Ball, *op. cit.*, p. 256.
19. *ibid.*

distribution of power so that the political order has a legitimate character. Let us first study the aspect of ideology desiring change in the political system for the sake of bringing about 'a truly legitimate political system' that may be termed as the 'ideology of scientific socialism' as given by Karl Marx and then look at the ideology of the *'status quo'* that is basically antithetical to the ideology of Marxism and that has its diverse manifestations in the forms of liberalism and fascism.

Ideology of Marxism : According to Marxism, all fundamental historical changes are determined by the means of production or economic forces. A change in the means of production brings about a corresponding change in the relations of production. If the hand-mill creates a society with the feudal lord, the steam mill creates a society with the industrial capitalist. It creates the two classes in the society—the 'haves' and the 'have-nots'; while the former are the rulers, the exploiters and the oppressors, the latter are the ruled, the exploited and the oppressed. The function of Marxian ideology is, therefore, to explain the nature of social relationships and to suggest ways so that the present 'bourgeois' society is substituted by a new 'socialist' order. The rule of the bourgeoisie is thus to be replaced by the rule of the masses—the workers, artisans, peasants and all those who toil. For this reason, Marx exposed the liberal myths that surrounded the political institutions of modern societies and he accused all social theorists, who analysed social relationships in terms of power, as 'victims of the illusions of the epoch'. He criticised them for 'accepting as truth what was, in fact, part of the ideological support of the ruling class.'[20]

Marx lived and wrote in the nineteenth century that was the age of capitalism; it was his orthodox disciple Lenin who saw the development of capitalism into the final phase of imperialism and thus he made Marxism up-to-date by adding his interpretations. While Marx predicted in his *Communist Manifesto* of 1848 that the law of dialectical materialism would automatically operate to bring about the doom of capitalism, Lenin gave a peculiar twist to this prophesy by adding that in the changed conditions of the twentieth century, revolution would have to be created and the party of the workers and peasants would play the role of a vanguard in the bloody revolution whose object would be to bring about a socialist society. The ideology of Marxism-Leninism, therefore, takes the society as a theatre of struggle going on between the two rival classes of the exploiters and the exploited and desires its substitution by a new order that has a classless character during the transitional phase culminating into a condition of statelessness in the final phase of socialism. The function of ideology is thus to understand political reality in terms of the 'doctrine of class war' according to which the class conflict between the 'haves' and the 'have-nots' "would inevitably end in the victory of the larger classes, the proletariat, and this triumph would usher in the classless society."[21]

The essence of the ideology of Marxism-Leninism may be seen in the statement of Finer. He says that it has three variants: "firstly, that society is monistic and therefore minority or sectional rights must be eliminated. It is denied that the government ought to recognise and accept the existence of various sections of society and undertake to conciliate the claims of one as against another; on the contrary, only one section of society—the proletariat and its allies—is worthy, and the government has the duty of suppressing all other sections and governing in the interests of this worthy section alone. Secondly, a government so functioning is supposed to be doing it in the name of some transcendent end—of something which has been described as 'a consummatory value': one

20. See Geraint Parry : *Political Elites* (London : George Allen and Unwin. 1969), p. 27.
21. See Ball, *op. cit.*, p. 257.

to which all individuals and groups in society, and present generation as against future generations, must be subordinated. In the communist case, this consummatory value is the realisation of an ideal social system, called communism, on an international scale. And, in pursuing this ideal, Marxist philosophy suggests that the government of the state is simply 'giving history a push'. Since the laws of society, as discovered by Marx and Lenin, indicate that the transition to communism is an ineluctable trend in society. Thirdly, these 'laws' of society are held to be scientifically demonstrable, and so, instead of judgements on society and morals being regarded as matters of individual choice or conscience, they are held to be matters of scientific certainty."[22]

Ideology of Fascism **:** Opposed to Marxism are the ideologies of Fascism (also Nazism) having a totalitarian character and liberalism pertaining to a democratic model. Both may be treated as 'rightist' in the sense that they are opposed to the substitution of the present order by a new one and that too by means of a bloody revolution. The common point between the ideologies of Marxism-Leninism and Fascism, however, finds place in the fact that both subscribe to the system of totalitarianism and, in this respect, both are basically different from the ideology of liberalism that attaches sanctity to the principles and norms of a democratic order. A student of comparative politics is, therefore, concerned with the role of three ideologies having points of resemblance and difference between one another without agreeing with this observation of some critics that liberalism cannot be given the place of an ideology.

The ideology of Fascism, as it developed in Italy, desired, what the founder-father of this doctrine Bennito Mussolini said, a 'Corporate State'. Laying emphasis on the essential characteristics of this state, Mussolini said: "Three conditions are necessary for the full, complete, integral and revolutionary fulfilment of the Corporate State: a single party by means of which there shall be effectuated political control as well as an economic control and which shall be above the competing interests a bond which unites all in a common faith. Nor is that enough. We must have, as well as, the single party, the totalitarian state, *i.e.*, the state which absorbs in itself, to transform and make them effective, all the energy, all the interests and all the hopes of the people. The third . . . is to live in a period of the highest ideal tension."[23] While Mussolini pinpointed the word 'Corporate State', Hitler did the same for 'Idea' that signified the exclusive and unassailable leadership of the supreme figure. As, in a mood of resentment, Hitler said that every member of the party "has to do what the leader orders. The Leader incorporates the Idea and alone knows its ultimate goal.."[24]

The ideology of Fascism has two essential characteristics—totalitarianism and anti-Marxism. Its totalitarian characteristic is contained in these words of Mussolini: "Fascist conception is for the State, and it is for the individual in so far as he coincides with the State, and it is for the individual in so far the universal conscience and will of man in his historical existence."[25] Similarly, Hitler, leader of the Nazi party in Germany, said that the "individual is transitory, the *Volk* is permanent. The position of this single echo is exclusively determined by the interest of the *Volk* as a whole."[26] The whole ideology of Fascism "is dominated by the dogmas of sovereign state and irresistible government. All particularistic interests of individuals must be suppressed by an omnipotent, hierarchical organisation of the nation. A citizen's political obligations are more important than his rights. This is the Fascist

22. See Finer, *op. eit.,* p. 77.
23. *ibid.,* p. 88.
24. *ibid.,* p. 89.
25. *ibid.,* p. 82.
26. *ibid.,* pp. 82-83.

'totalitarianism', which recognises no sphere of individual life as immune from political authority."[27] The true Fascist, says Gentile, "is Fascist in his home, school and workshop as well as in his politics."[28] The keynote of Fascism is contained in these words of Mussolini: "Nothing against the State, nothing over it, nothing beyond it."

Fascism pertains to the category of rightist totalitarianism in view of the fact that it stands for the protection and promotion of the interests of the 'bourgeois' class and also patronises religion that, as the Communists say, goes to the exclusive advantage of the same class. Both Mussolini and Hitler made serious plans to destroy the Soviet Union. Thus, it is said that Fascism "is anti-Marxism which seeks to destroy the enemy by evolvement of a radically opposed and yet related ideology and by the use of almost identical and yet typically modified methods, always, however, within the unyielding framework of national self-assertion and autonomy'"[29] It is on account of the rightist character of Fascism that it "is seen as conservative in that it is counter-revolutionary,"[30]

As already pointed out, one important point common to both ideologies is that they stand for totalitarianism—a form of political order that crushes individual liberty, tolerates no opposition, desires complete state centralisation, glorifies the nation and emphasises the idea of state as a power system, exalts conditions of world war and denounces conditions of peace and tranquillity and has no faith in the ideals of liberalism and humanism. In other words, both ideologies stand for a non-democratic system about which Bernard E. Brown thus observes : "All non-democratic regimes, whether autocratic or totalitarian, reject democratic assumptions concerning the value of criticism and the uses of representative institutions."[31] In contrast to traditional autocracies, a modern totalitarian state secures the participation of the *masses* (not just the palace circles) in some great endeavour. Totalitarian states are always in movement, since inaction permits the opposition to rally. Coercion and terror are used against opponents, but the legitimacy of the regime in the long run depends upon popular identification with the goals of the leadership.

Ideology of Liberalism : Opposed to the ideology of totalitarianism, whether 'rightist' 'or leftist' is the ideology or philosophy of liberalism that stands for the values of freedom, democracy and humanism. Its assumptions may be said to lie in the paraphernalia of a democratic order having representative government, responsible executive, socio-economic and political checks and balances, independence of judiciary and rule of law. It has three fundamental assumptions—limited government, pluralistic society, and abundant scope for human choices. The government operates in a world of autonomous, spontaneously self-creating, voluntary associations *i.e.* at a margin of social activity. The society has a pluralistic character. It implies that it "is made up of a host of autonomous sections and associations, but to believe that each enshrines values or interests dear to its members."[32] Finally, the scope for choices implies that truth "is a matter of individual conscience where all consciences are held by an act of faith, to be equal either in the sight of God or in the sight of man. Two working conclusions follow from this, namely, toleration and the qualification of majority rule."[33]

---

27. F.W. Coker : *Recent Political Thought* (New York : D. Appleton Century, 1934), pp. 482-483.
28. *ibid.*
29. E. Nolte : *Three Faces of Fascism* (London, 1965), pp. 20-21.
30. Ball, *op. cit.,* p. 250.
31. Brown, *op. cit.,* pp. 77-78.
32. Finer, *op. cit.,* p. 64.
33. *ibid.,* p. 65.

The really difficult problem about the ideology or trend of liberalism finds place in its essentially flexible character that takes it to the pole of being thoroughly democratic on the one hand to that of being authoritarian on the other, despite the fact that the three assumptions of liberalism cannot be found in all countries of the world on account of varying political cultures. Democracy involves more than the existence of a particular political structure. Historical evidences are there to confirm that the American and the British systems of government "could easily evolve into dictatorship of the executive in the absence of an organised opposition, free elections, a free press, and deeply rooted traditions of individual rights. Democracy can work only when the values associated with it (particularly those relating to speech and opposition) are fully understood and accepted by all the people. This in turn is dependent upon a whole cluster of social conditions"[34]

It is on account of the recognition of this fact that liberalism stands for justifying government control over the liberties of the people in varying degrees according to the exigencies of social interest. Realising this essential fact, a great liberal thinker like John Stuart Mill endorsed : "A people may be unwilling or unable to fulfil the duties which a particular form of government requires of them. A rude people, though in some degree alive to the benefits of civilised government, to be really advantageous to them, will require to be in a considerable degree despotic; to be one over which they donot themselves exercise control, and which imposes a great amount of forcible restraint upon their actions."[35]

It is, however, as a result of either misunderstanding or deliberately distorting the real state of affairs that some writers like Daniel Bell have spoken of the 'end of ideology' in liberal-democratic societies. The issue of economic development has come to stay in the forefront and the state of political stability has almost become a well settled phenomenon. The people have developed firm faith in the institutions of their political culture and, as such, they have nothing to fear in that regard. However, the issue of economic development has come to be the main goal that they want to achieve by living within the broad framework of a well-established democratic system. It is for this important reason that there is hardly any difference of opinion between the leaders of the Democratic and Republican parties in the United States and not so basically hostile relationship between the Conservative and Labour parties of Great Britain. In spite of all this, it would be a mistake to say that the ideology which "was once a road to action, has come to a dead end."[36]

In this important direction, the fact is that the shackles of ideology have become a bit loose with the result that while the liberals have taken to diverse stands that often makes them look like ideologically neutral, the socialists and the communists have, likewise, shown their proneness towards a gradual acceptance of the liberal-democratic values. All this should be interpreted not as an end or decline of ideology but as a change from one position to another. It indicates that, like the world itself, the ideology is also in a state of constant flux that may be discerned even in the changing behaviour of the socialist and communist parties of various major countries like France, Italy, Germany and the Russian Federation. As Ball says : "The actual ideological standing of various parties may be the subject for a more detailed debate and may demand terminological variations, but the important point is that this sort of movement does not necessarily imply the end of ideological adherence, and that the supporters of the 'end of ideology" arguments have, in fact, made this

34. Brown, *op. cit.,* p. 80.
35. Mill : *Considerations on Representative Government* (1861), Ch 1.
36. D. Bell: *The End of Ideology* (New York, 1960), pp. 369-70.

Some Important Statements about Ideology

Marxism: While it deprecates ideology as 'false consciousness of social reality', it presents an ideology of its own. It is more or less a coherent set of ideas which purport to explain and justify social position of the two rival classes. In political terms, it seeks to change the status quo by overthrowing the rule of the dominant class of the exploiters and the oppressors. Revolution alone can usher in the socialist society. The state known as the 'dictatorship of the proletariat' is an all-powerful institution to protect the interest of the class of the workers and the toilers that would wither away in the final stage of social development. Socialism would replace capitalism and eventuate into communism. Marxism-Leninism may be described as totalitarianism of the left.

Fascism: It seeks to maintain the status quo so as to protect the interests of the affluent and privileged sections of the society. The state is omnipotent, nothing against it and nothing above it. It may be described as totalitarianism of the right.

Liberalism: It stands for the values of liberty, democracy and humanism. It has a flexible character by virtue of which it cannot be taken as a ideology. And yet its stern commitment to the norms of freedom and tolerance makes it so. "Give me liberty or give me death", says Thomas Jefferson.

mistake because of their narrow definition of ideology as a concept interchangeable with revolutionary utopianism."[37]

Ideologies and the Nature of Political Power : Elitism Versus Marxism

Let us now look at the conception of power (or authority) that "provides a framework of decision-making" and that "defines within broad limits what power various participants shall have and how they shall proceed in making decisions'"[38] Here we are concerned with two approaches that are basically opposed to one another While the approach of elitism stands invariably for the rule of the 'minority' over the majority, the approach of Marxism does the same for the substitution of the 'rule of the class' by the rule of a classless society. The essential point of difference lies in the nature of the ruling authority. Thus, while elitism adheres to, what Michels calls, the 'iron law of oligarchy', Marxism stands for, what Parry terms the 'concept of the mass'. The approaches are, however, interconnected in the sense that one.cannot be understood without knowing the other, for both are essentially concerned with the distribution of political power.

Elitism, that was described by its ardent protagonists like Pareto, Mosca, Burnham and C. Wright Mills as a 'formula', asserts that political power is unevenly distributed in society. It resides in the hands of a very small minority or a group of chosen few that is known as the elite. The ruling class is always an elite and whenever there is a change in the ruling class, it means the replacement of one elite by another. The sources of power of the political elites are many like military, economic and religious, though the factor of organisational skill may be said to have its own importance. Though there are points of difference among leading elitist writers in this direction, there "is agreement that forms of representative government are merely disguises to cover minority. There are problems of who actually constitute the political elite and whether it is defined narrowly or widely; also there are differences on the means of recruitment, but there is unanimity on the inevitability of the minority rule."[39]

37. Ball, *op. cit.*, p. 253.
38. Beer and U!am : *Patterns of Government* (New York : Random House, 1968) 8thPtg.,p. 49.
39. Ball, *op. cit.*, p. 253.

The principle of elitism thus rejects the findings of earlier political scientists who had concerned themselves with the assumption of government as a rule of the people, whether few or many. Mosca says that past political thinkers "were less concerned with determining constant trends in human societies than with the arts by which an individual, or a class of individuals, might succeed in achieving supreme power in a given society and in thwarting the efforts of other individuals or groups to supplant them."[40] In the name of his 'historical method', Mosca asserted that previous generations lacked the accurate knowledge of history, since they ignored this "incontrovertible truth' that political power was always held by the 'very few' people.[41] Following the same trend, Michels said that the 'law of oligarchy', which he formulated on the basis of the 'facts of experience', was 'inevitable' and 'an essential characteristic of all human aggregates' and 'historical evolution, mocks all the prophylactic measures that have been adopted for the prevention of oligarchy."[42]

In brief, the doctrine of elitism rejects the proposition that political power is held by the people or even by a class of people. The idea of the sovereignty of the people, as held by a thinker like Rousseau, or that democracy being the rule of the people as eulogised by Lincoln are misleading. Following the tradition of Aristotle that inequality is ordained by nature and yet disagreeing with him on the issue as to 'who really rules', a leading elitist like Pareto expressed his ideas in his usual castic tone : "It is paradoxically, precisely the inequality of men which prompts them to proclaim their equality."[43] Summing up the ideology of elitism, Parry observes: "Government in a democracy was certainly *of* the people, it might even be *for* the people, but it was never *by* the people but only by the ruling class. The supposed 'law' which required refutation was that asserted by socialists according to which a classless, egalitarian society would be the inevitable outcome of the class conflict which had characterised all previous history. The law was a mere pious hope which deceived the lower classes in society, but at the same time significantly bolstered their confidence."[44]

Fundamentally opposed to this is the Marxian view of political power. Here the emphasis is on the word 'class'. The forces of history find their tangible embodiment in the contending social classes. Hence, the history of all hitherto existing societies is the history of class struggle. The dominant class does not capitulate once its economic basis becomes important and its political role obsolete. As freemen and slaves in the slave society and lords and serfs in the feudal age, were contending for the seizure of power so the capitalist and the working classes are at war against each other in the present bourgeois system. The socialist society would emerge out of the present one and then this class war would come to an end with the establishment of a classless society. Thus, the need for a revolution in which the working class would seize the reins of the state remains for the Marxists 'an article of faith.'[45]

The ideology of Marxism, therefore, contends that political power is always in the hands of the socially dominant class. Once it was with the freemen, then with the feudal lords, now it is with the capitalists. The 'religion' of the workers is to struggle for the seizure of power so that the bourgeois class rule is replaced by the rule of the proletariat. In this way, Marxian ideology offers to the working class a hope; it also presents what appears to be, and what is claimed to be, a science of

40. Mosca : *The Ruling Class* (edited by A. Livingstone) (New York : McGraw Hill, 1939), p. 1.
41. *ibid.*, p. 3.
42. Robert Michels : *Political Parties* (New York : Free Press of Glencoe, 1915), p. vii.
43. Cited in Parry, *op. cit.*, p. 25.
44. *ibid.*
45. Beer and Ulam, *op. cit.*, pp. 599-600.

End of Ideology—Ideologisation Versus De-ideologisation

Theories of De-Ideologisation

When capital was the key to economic success, social conflict was between the rich and the poor. In recent times, education has become the difference that divides. Politics also reflects the new division. In the United States, suspicion and resentment is no longer directed to the capitalists or the merely rich. It is the intellectuals who are eyed with misgiving and alarm.

– J.K. Galbraith

The intellectual historian of the future will be challenged by a strange phenomenon of the later half of the 20th century - the second coming of Karl Marx. In the second coming he appears not as the dusty frock coat of an economist, as the author of 'Capital', nor as a revolutionary sans-caulotts the inspired pamphleteer of the *Communist Manifesto.* He comes robed as a philosopher and moral prophet with glad tidings about human freedom valid beyond the narrow circles of class, party or faction. In his train flock not the industrial workers of the world but the literary intellectuals.... not the proletariat but elements of the professoriat, not the socially disinherited but the psychologically alienated, and a varied assortment of writers and artists.

– Sidney Hook

The social function of management becomes decisive for the organisation of production. The industrial society is characterised by a technical approach to nature and human activity.

– Daniel Bell

No End of Ideology

(Operation of modern revisionism in socialist clothing)

The only choice is either bourgeois or socialist ideology. There is no middle course, for mankind has not created a third ideology, and moreover, in a society torn by class antagonisms, there can never be non-class or an above class ideology.

– V.I. Lenin

The struggle of today's revisionism against Leninism is more than an ideological debate. It is a blow to the international workers' movement with the aim of depriving it of the revolutionary theoretical gains of the last sixty years. It is an attempt to throw back international workers' movement to the level of the period preceding the Great October Socialist Revolution.

– Alfred Kosing

However, despite the fact that the theory of de-ideologisation is obviously groundless and tendentious, it, like other theories connected with it, has become rather widespread in the West. The reason for its relative popularity is that in the conditions of the profound crisis of bourgeois social thought as a whole, it conforms to the social practice and interests of certain social groups and political trends in contemporary bourgeois society.

– V. Kortunov

society that explains the nature of class relationships within the existing and all hitherto existing societies and predicts the eventual inevitable dominance of the working class to be followed in turn by the replacement of the rule of a class by the rule of a society without the classes of the exploiters and the exploited, the oppressors and the oppressed. Such an assurance must have seemed all the more urgent, since the working class is already armed with an ideology masked as a science of social revolution. It is said in a tone of its appreciation:

"The comprehensive character of Marx's social analysis was unrivalled. The status of politics and political leadership, the role of the middle class and of representative institutions, the character of ideology, the situation of the masses— all were within the compass of 'scientific socialism."[46]

Ideologies and Party System : Transformation in Social Structure and Decline of Ideological Controversy

Political parties are said to be the 'most important ideological carrier and interpreter.'[47] It is the factor of ideology that provides comprehensive theories of politics and that makes it unnecessary to deal with individual issues on their individual merits. As Beer and Ulam observe : "Ideologies are like theoretical sausage machines; one feeds in problematic meat at one end and out comes a string of policy sausages at the other, beautifully integrated and consistent. And because they obviate real thought on individual issues they can become terribly necessary under certain conditions, particularly when the political system presents an unusually large number of unsolved issues, or, putting the same point another way, when an unusually large area of behaviour is subject to political decision-making."[48]

Broadly speaking, political parties, from the standpoint of their ideological foundations, may be put into two kinds—rightist and leftist. While the rightist parties are those that stand for the maintenance of the *status quo* or desire very slow and peaceful changes, the leftist parties stand for breaking the *status quo* and advocate rapid and violent changes. There are a number of intermediate varieties between these two poles. For instance, the rightists or conservatives may be either traditional or authoritarian and the leftists or radicals may be either liberal or authoritarian all assuming diverse nomenclatures as socialist, democratic socialist, liberal democratic etc. It is also possible that there may be a party having no ideology but organised and working on 'populist' lines. The Congress Party of India offers a unique example in this regard. What is peculiarly noticeable in this regard is that even some communist parties have loosened the bond of ideology to the extent that they have been accused by their critics of being sold to bourgeois elements. The name of the Communist Party of France may be cited here about which a critic has said: "Not at any moment did the Communist Party and the C.G.T. further an uprising. Not at any moment did they wish to torpedo the Gaullist government whose foreign policy corresponds to their fondest wishes and which permits their progressive integration into French society. Obviously they would have taken care of the state if it had been handed to them. But their constant objective was not 'to make a revolution' but not let themselves be outflanked on their left by the students, by the Maoists, by the young workers..."[49]

As pointed out above, Indian National Congress affords the peculiar case of a party without ideological moorings. It has a distinctly amorphous character keeping which in view it is described as a 'platform' and not a party by its critics. Once it was essentially a freedom movement. Being in politics in the pre-independence days "almost meant being in Congress...for reasons of high idealism, prestige and spirit of service in the cause of the country."[50] The same trend has continued even after the advent of independence, no matter it adopted the ideal of socialistic pattern of society in 1955. The triumph of this party under the stewardship of Nehru and its resurgence under

46. Parry, *op. cit.*, pp. 26-27.
47. Ball, *op. cit.*, p. 260.
48. Beer and Ulam, *op. cit.*, p. 99.
49. Raymond Aron cited in H.W. Ehrmann : *Politics in France* (Boston : Little Brown, 1968), p. 329.
50. S.C. Kashyap : *The Politics of Power* (Delhi : National, 1974), p. 63.

the leadership of Indira Gandhi has been owing to this important reason that it has been like "an Aristotelian party, a party, of the middle way, if it was to survive and succeed. And the Congress political leaders became moulded as a man of the centre, normally permitting himself the luxury of only a shade of emphasis on one side or the other."[51]

If the role of ideology in comparative party systems is made from a sociological standpoint, it may be found that the stiffness of ideological bond has declined owing to transformation in social and economic spheres. Prof. Otto Kirchheimer has referred to this as the emergence of the 'unified middle class society,'[52] which includes the working class, civil servants, white collar workers, and professionals. Agreeing with the view, Brown says: "On the one hand, the old independent artisan and shopkeeper is disappearing. The new middle classes tend to gain their livelihood in some kind of bureaucratic enterprise (whether public or private), within which they have a degree of autonomy. They have lost the independence, or illusion of independence, which in the past gave them a consciousness of superiority over workers. On the other hand, percentage of national wealth allotted to the working class has vastly increased. Members of the working and middle classes have thus come to experience the same kind of social discipline and to share the same aspirations, values, tastes, dress and the leisure-time habits. They seek a larger portion of the national income in order to better enjoy a common way of life. Politics thus becomes a matter of slicing up the cake, not debating whether to bake something else."[53]

Though the issue of 'the end of ideology' became very prominent in the 1960s, it may be found that leading social and political theorists of the West have interpreted the situation in different ways. A look at the writings of sociologists like S.M. Lipset, B. Moore, H. Marcuse, H.S. Hughes, H. Kenniston, Anthony Giddens and J. Meynaud shows that the 'end' of ideology has been identified with several related and unrelated situations like 'de-radicalisation', de-ideologisation' and 'de-motivationalisation' of politics. Lipset has paid too much importance to the fact of 'pragmatism' in this regard commitment to which has blurred the distinction between the right and the left. He has confined his attention to the doctrine of Marxism in his study of the term 'ideology' and thus come to hold that the end of ideology and the decline of Marxian revolutionary ideas amount to the same thing. Others like Meynaud have confused the whole debate by coining the phrase of 'ideological pluralism' in advanced countries resulting in the situation of 'ideological appeasement.' In the view of C. Wright Mills, ideology is like a 'mood' and, for this reason, "any political reflection that is of possible public significance is ideological." Haber contends that the alleviation of mass discontent by government action has brought about the 'end of a revolutionary alternate.'[54]

A forceful assertion of the same may be seen in the writings of Anthony Giddens. In his view, "the world we live in today is not one subject to tight human mastery, the stuff of the ambitions of the left, and, one could say, the nightmares of the right. Almost, to the contrary, it is one of dislocations and uncertainty, a run-away world."[55] It is the age of 'generative politics' which seeks to allow individuals and groups to make things happen rather than have things happen to them in the context of over-all social concerns and goals. "Democratisation of democracy is needed. It pursues development of personal relationships

51. W.H. Morris-Jones : *The Government and Politics of India* (London : Hutchison Univ Library and B.I. Pub of Bombay, 1971), III Ed. p. 172.
52. See Brown, *op. cit.*, pp. 33-34.
53. *ibid.*, p. 34.
54. See Martin Seliger : *Ideology and Politics* (London : George Allen and Unwin, 1976), pp. 42-47.
55. Antony Giddens: *Beyond Left and Rigth* (London : Polity Press, 1994), p. 3.

in which active trust is mobilised and sustained through discussion and the interchange of views rather than by arbitrary power of some sort or another."[56] With a sense of certainty, he asserts: "The spectre which disturbed the slumbers of bourgeois Europe, and which for more than seventy years took on solid flesh has been returned to its nether world. The hopes of radicals for a society in which, as Marx said, human beings could be truly free, seem to have turned out to be empty reveries."[57]

The critics of the 'end of ideology' theory deprecate the efforts of the bourgeois writers of the West in the name of offering a new ideology to preserve and justify the discredited capitalist system. In particular, the Marxists call it a 'new ideology' in the age of welfare state allowing political pluralism, decentralisation of power, mixed economy and parliamentary democracy. Such contentions draw inspiration from the philosophy of *status quoism* and pragmatism and thus, instead of exposing the hollowness of the intellectual systems of the bourgeois world, endeavour to distract the attention of the progressive social and political theorists from the real state of affairs. In fact, the end of ideology theory "is an ideology of an end to maintain the base intact by slight modifications in the superstructures."[58]

Critical Appraisal

Though it is true that there may be cases where the element of ideology is either absent or very weak as the basis of political parties and groups that struggle for giving stability or strength to a political system or to bring about a change in it, it cannot be overlooked that political ideas and values that constitute the moorings of an ideology have a significance and a relevance of their own. One may disagree with Dante Germino's thesis of 'ideological reductionism,'[59] or may find fault with the 'positivism' of August Comte who said that men have walked out of the 'theological' and 'metaphysical' stages when they were under the influence of supernatural ideas. Among recent writers, one may also refer to Easton and Cobban who have spoken of the 'decline of ideology' and moved ahead more and more in the direction of 'factualism' and 'hyperfactualism'. Thanks to the contributions of writers like Michael Oakeshott, Hannah Arendt, Bertrand de Jouvenel, Leo Strauss and Eric Vogelin that the place of ideology in political theory has been re-recognised.[60]

The significance of ideology in the study of comparative politics is thus well borne out in the observation of Prof. Ball: "Thus, to claim that political values are irrelevant to the functioning of the political system is like Canute ordering the water to recede. Political ideas bring together discoordinate demands into a more coherent pattern producing order and arrangement. Most of all they provide a criterion of relevance, a yardstick by which to judge political aspirations and actions. This is not to deny that they also provide a camouflage to hide materialistic aims within a mass of value-loaded generalisations; most political actors claim a wider relevance for their demands than mere self-interest, yet even this is a significant aspect of the political process. Political ideas allow the expression of preferences; the basis and source of these ideas may be relatively unimportant for an analysis of the system. The truth or falsity of the ideas themselves is a matter for theologians and political philosophers; we are concerned with their political significance."[61]

---

56. *ibid.,*
57. *idid.,* p. 1.
58. K. Seshadri : *Studies in Marxism and Political Science* (New Delhi : People's Pub., 1977), pp. 190-91.
59. See Dante Germino : *Beyond Ideology : The Revival of Political Theory* (New York : Harper and Row, 1967).
60. See S.P. Varma : *Modern Political Theory* (Delhi : Vikas, 1975), p. 127.
61. Ball, *op. cit.,* pp. 247-48.

14

Constitutionalism

> In conclusion, then, we may fairly say that if national democratic constitutionalism is to be preserved, we must be ready to admit that democracy can take many shapes and that it may be necessary to experiment greatly in order to discover the ideal form of it, that nationalism has both good and bad aspects, and that it should become possible to sacrifice some of its badness in order to achieve permanent international peace without in the least diminishing its power to benefit mankind through the instrumentality of the limited nation-state.
>
> **—C.F. Strong[1]**

The study of political constitutionalism occupies a significant place in the sphere of comparative politics in view of the fact that it is the constitution that, as Dicey says 'directly or indirectly affects the exercise of the sovereign power of the state.'[2] A political scientist is concerned with the origin and development of the state, with its nature and organisation, with its purpose and functions, and with the theory of the state and its possible forms. If so, he is naturally concerned with all these facts of the subject in a certain manner. Since the study of the political constitutions is 'a branch of political science or the science of the state', a student of this subject "is interested chiefly in the institutions which the state builds up for its peace and progress without which the state could not maintain itself, any more than a society could maintain itself without the state."[3]

Meaning of Constitutionalism : Concepts of 'Constitution' and 'Constitutional Government'

Constitutionalism is a modern concept that desires a political order governed by laws and regulations. It stands for the supremacy of law and not of the individuals; it imbibes the principles of nationalism, democracy and limited government. It may be identified with the system of 'divided power.'[4] As Friedrich says: "Constitutionalism by dividing power provides a system of effective restraints upon governmental action. In studying it, one has to explore the methods and techniques by which such restraints are established and maintained. It is a body of rules ensuring fairplay, thus rendering the government 'responsible.'"[5] Constitutionalism, .thus, stands for the existence of a constitution in a state, since it is the

1. Strong: *Modern Political Constitutions* (London : Sidgwick and Jackson, 1966), ELBS Ed., p. 364.
2. A.V. Dicey : *An Introduction to the Study of the Law of the Constitution* (London : George Allen and Unwin, 1948), p. 23.
3. Strong, *op. cit., p. 4.*
4. Carl J. Friedrich : *Constitutional Government and Democracy* (Calcutta : Oxford and IBH, 1964), 9th Ptg, p. 25.
5. *ibid.,* p. 26.

Some Important Statements about Constitutionalism

In its broad sense, the rule of law is a core liberal-democratic principle, embodying ideas such as constitutionalism and limited government to which most modern states aspire. In particular, the rule of law imposes significant constraints upon how law is made and how it is adjudicated.

– Andrew Heywood
Political Theory: An Introduction, p. 155.

The concept of constitutionalism is that of a polity governed by or under a constitution that ordains essentially limited government and rule of law as opposed to arbitrary or authoritarian rule. Constitutional government, therefore, should necessarily be democratic government.

– Dr. S.C. Kashyap
Our Constitution, p. 2.

A constitution is a set of laws and rules setting up the machinery of the Government of a State and which defines and determines the relations between the different institutions and areas of Government, the Executive, the Legislature and the Judiciary, the Central, the Regional and the Local Governments. In fact, a constitution is the source of the jurisprudential fountain-head from which other laws must flow, succinctly and harmoniously.

– Prof. M. V. Pylee
Select Constitutions of the World, p. 8.

instrument of government, or the fundamental law of the land, whose objects "are to limit the arbitrary action of the government, to guarantee the rights of the governed, and to define the operation of the sovereign power."[6]

In order to have a proper understanding of the term 'constitutionalism,' we must first understand the meaning of terms like 'constitution' and 'constitutional government'. A constitution "may be said to be a collection of principles according to which the powers of the government, the rights of the governed, and the relations between the two are adjusted."[7] In other words, it may be described as "a frame of political society organised through and by law, in which law has established permanent institutions with recognised functions and definite rights..."[8] According to Wheare: "The word 'constitution' is commonly used in at least two senses in an ordinary discussion of political affairs. First of all, it is used to describe the whole system of a government of a country, the collection of rules which establish and regulate or govern the government. These rules are partly legal, in the sense, that the courts of law will recognise and apply them, and partly non-legal or extra-legal, taking the form of usages, understandings, customs, or conventions which courts donot recognise as law but which are not less effective in regulating the government than the rules of law strictly called. In most countries of the world the system of government is composed of this mixture of legal and non-legal rules and it is possible to speak of this collection of rules as the 'Constitution.'[9]

The constitution of a state may be a deliberate creation on paper effected by some assembly or convention at a particular time; it may be found in the shape of a document that has altered in response to the requirements of the time and age; it may also be a bundle of separate laws assuming special sanctity of being the fundamental law of the land; or again, it

6. Strong, *op. cit.,* p. 12.
7. *ibid.,* p. 11.
8. *ibid.,* p. 15.
9. K.C. Wheare : *Modern Constitutions* (London : Oxford, University Press, 1956), p. 1.

may be that the bases of a constitution are fixed in one or few fundamental laws of the land, while the rest of it depends for its authority upon the force of the custom. A look at the constitutions of the countries of the world shows that for most of them the constitution "is a selection of the legal rules which govern the government of that country and which have been embodied in a document."[10] However, Britain affords the peculiar case where the constitution is not in the form of a document; it is a growth and not a make. Bolingbroke thus said about the English constitution : "By constitution, we mean, whenever we speak with propriety and exactness, that assemblage of laws, institutions and customs, derived from certain fixed principles of reason ... that compose the general system, according to which the community hath agreed to be governed."[11]

Whereas the constitution refers to a frame of political society organised through and by means of law and in which law has established permanent institutions with recognised functions and definite rights, a constitutional state "is one in which the powers of the government, the rights of the governed and the relations between the two are, adjusted."[12] According to Wheare, constitutional government "means something more than a government according to the terms of a Constitution. It means government according to rule as opposed to arbitrary government; it means government limited by the terms of a Constitution, not government limited only by the desires and capacities of those who exercise power."[13]

From the above, it may be inferred that a constitutional government is one that operates within a universe of positive restraints. It is, however, a different matter that the degree of restraint may vary from one political system to another. That is, while one state may be constitutional by virtue of being set in a universe of more restraints, the other may be of the same category by virtue of being set in a universe of few restraints. The charge of being 'unconstitutional' can be levelled against a state only if it has'no restraints'as specified by Friedrich in his paradigm :[14]

It is, therefore, clear that, like all true functional concepts, the notion of constitutional government is essentially descriptive of two poles : very strong restraint and very weak restraint. Between these two poles, all actual governments can be ranged. Carl Friedrich, however, makes it very clear that the case of an unconstitutional state can be conceived in mere theoretical terms as every state of the world has a constitution of its own that places restraints to some degree at least. As he shows in his paradigm and says : "The unreal limits are 'complete restraint' and 'no restraint'."[15] "Moreover, constitutionalism" as Blondel says, "is clearly a dimension : it is an oversimplification to classify regimes as 'constitutional' or 'non-constitutional', as it is an over-simplification to classify them as 'liberal' or 'authoritarian'. Dichotomies may be useful in practice, but a general theory of constitutionalism must take into account the fact that the regimes stretch along a continuum ranging from complete authoritarianism to full

Friedrich's Paradigm

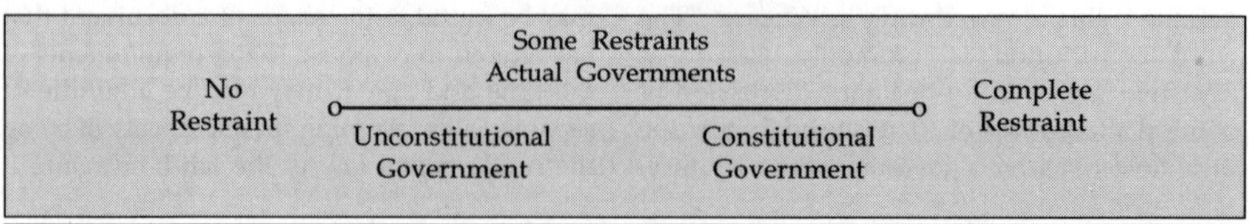

10. *ibid.*, p. 2.
11. *ibid.*
12. Strong, *op. cit.*, p. 15.
13. Wheare, *op. cit.*, p. 137.
14. Friedrich, *op. cit.*, p. 125.
15. *ibid.*

liberalism and that a replica of this continuum is provided by an axis stretching from 'full constitutional government' to 'pure non-constitutional rule'."[16]

Constitutionalism, in this way, desires a political order in which the powers of the government are limited. It is another name for the concept of a limited, and for this reason, a 'civilised' government. The real justification of the constitution finds place in having a "limited government" and of requiring those who govern "to conform to laws and rules."[17] We are required to see how the constitution of a state works in actual practice and whether usages and conventions operate to strengthen or weaken the machinery of the constitutional arrangement. We may find that, apart from those limitations that have their place in the provisions of the constitution, there are well-established customs and norms that have their own effect for the same purpose. Keeping such empirical facts in mind, one may say that there exists no government in the world that may not be called constitutional, though he may also say that such a government hardly exists in a country under a totalitarian rule where the constitution is seen with 'contempt'. For this reason, it is only in a democratic country that constitutional government can be said to exist.[18]

Development of Constitutionalism: An Historical Process of the Rise of Constitutional State

The rise of a constitutional state is essentially an historical process whose chief material is contained in the history of political institutions coupled with the history of western political ideas right from ancient to modern times. The history of the development of constitutionalism is thus a history of the growth of political institutions that had their first important manifestation in the soils of ancient Greece and Rome and thereafter they witnessed their rise and growth in the middle and modern ages. Side by side, reference should be made to the ideas of great political thinkers who either drew stimulus from the development of political institutions, or who thought in terms of having a particular form of polity under the ideal or obtainable conditions. The movement is still going on with a view to seek the improvement of political institutions in the direction of having a legitimate constitutional order. We may study the history of the development of constitutionalism under these heads:

Greek Constitutionalism : The Greeks occupy the first place in this direction who had 'political separatism' as a marked characteristic of their life. They had city-state system in which the benefits of citizenship were open to the freemen only. Most of the city-states had a direct democratic system, though Sparta was under the rule of military junta. The Greeks, however, had a peculiar notion about the state and the role of the people (citizens) therein. As Strong says: "A Greek citizen was actually and in person a soldier, a judge and a member of the governing assembly...The state to the Greek was his whole scheme of association, a city wherein all his_needs, material and spiritual, were satisfied..."[19] The Greek philosophers like Plato and Aristotle, however, studied the case of political institutions from an ethical point of view with the result that the political constitutionalism became a handmaid of normative and moral notions. The ideal state of

16. Jean Blondel : *An Introduction to Comparative Government* (London : Weidenfeld and Nicolson, 1969), p. 249.
17. Wheare, *op. cit.,* p. 137.
18. *ibid.,* p. 4. C.H. Mcllwain is right in observing that, in whatever sense, the broad and perhaps somewhat vague concept of constitutionalism is being used, it always presents an essential feature : 'limitation on government by law'. *Constitutionalism : Ancient and Modern* (Ithaca, New York : Cornell, 1947), Ch 1. Likewise, a Dutch writer says : "A form of government can only be classified as constitutional when the rulers are subject to a body of rules and principles, which limit the exercise of their power. Constitutional government is the anti-thesis of arbitrary rule." S.P. Ybema : *Constitutionalism and Civil Liberties* (Leiden: Leiden Univ. Press, 1973), p. 1
19. Strong, *op. cit.,* pp. 16-17.

Plato under the all-powerful rule of a non-corrupt and incorruptible philosopher-king looked like a 'utopia', while the best practicable state of Aristotle having 'polity' signified a type of middle-class rule "striking a balance between the unrealisable, or at least transitory, best and the intolerable worst."[20] It is true that while Plato thought in terms of the ideal state of a superman and Aristotle in terms of a best practicable state under the super-science of law, both failed to look beyond the horizon of a city-state with the result that Greek constitutionalism failed to move with the pace of the changing conditions of history. As Barker says: "Neither the enlightened monarchy which Plato had suggested, nor the mediating middle class on which Aristotle set his hopes could avail to set the city-state; and to be rescued from itself it had to lose its cherished independence."[21]

***Roman Constitutionalism* :** A great change occurred after the eclipse of the city-state system and the establishment of a great empire under the Romans. The intellectual life became more diffuse and driven into different channels. Men retreated with themselves; ethics became independent of politics; society and state ceased to be equivalent terms and the individual, apart from the state, became the chief object of contemplation. C.H. Mcllwain, thus, observes that there "was gradually emerging an individual who was something more than a citizen, a society that was wider than any possible political unit and a humanity more extended than any single race; individualism and cosmopolitanism are the most marked of the newer aspects of political philosophy."[22] The imperial rulers of Rome evolved their constitution as a determinate instrument of government—"a mass of precedents, carried in men's memories or recorded in writing, of dicta of lawyers or statesmen, of customs, of usages, understandings and beliefs, upon the methods of government, together with a number of statutes." With the termination of monarchy about 500 B.C., there emerged the Republic that had a 'mixed,' constitution. The offices of the Consuls (of whom two were elected annually each with a right to veto another) represented the monarchical element of the terminated system; the Senate (a small body with vast legislative powers) represented the aristocratic element; the democratic element existed in the meetings of the people in three sorts of conventions according to the division of land or people (curies, centuries or tribes). It is a different thing that, in course of time, the era of irresponsible autocracy came to prevail in Rome when the office of the Emperor was revived. Despite this, Roman constitutionalism made certain important contributions to the development of this concept. They codified their law and laid down the principle of representative government that came to be the most celebrated principles of constitutionalism. The two-pronged conception of the legal sovereignty of the Emperor—that his pleasure had the force of law and that his powers were ultimately derived from the people—persisted for many centuries and influenced throughout the medieval period the views on the relations between the rulers and the ruled.

***Medieval Constitutionalism* :** A great change took place after disintegration of the Roman Empire in the fifth century A.D. and its substitution by the establishment of a number of feudal states. The Teutons brought with them certain new ideas as the personality of law based on the force of folk customs that bound the authority of the king. The invasions of the barbarians caused the emergence of a haphazard political and economic set up in which the old nomadic relationship informed the formation and character of the society and political institutions. The state of incessant warfare finally gave way to innumerable scattered political and economic 'sovereignties'

20. *ibid.*, p. 17.
21. E. Barker : *The Political Thought of Plato and Aristotle*, p. 497.
22. Mcllwain : *The Growth of Political Thought in the West*, p. 98.

not on a national and territorial but on local levels due to which Europe "became a dismal swamp of individual feudal allegiances."[23] The era of feudalism represented a phase of transition, decentralisation, and disintegration. From the political point of view, it exhibited an age of 'statelessness' since every lord could conduct warfares or regulate commerce, or coin currency, or discharge judicial responsibilities. From an economic point of view, it "meant a state of society in which all or a great part of public rights and duties are inextricably interwoven with the tenure of land, in which the whole governmental system—financial, military, judicial—is part of the law of private property."[24]

Curiously, universalism came to be the keynote of this era of transition, decentralisation and disintegration as a result of the spread of the religion of Christianity. With the conversion of more and more people to the new religion, 'Christendom' came into being and Biblical law took the place of Roman law. A happy synthesis occurred between the Roman and Teutonic ideas and practices. For instance, the Roman conception that the people were the ultimate source of the royal authority and the practice of the barbarian tribes that the king was under the law of the folk happily coincided. The coronation ceremony in the presence of the chiefs and nobles coupled with the swearing in ceremony of the king became a clear indication of the fact that the monarch was the holder of temporal powers in the name of the ultimate authority of his people. These events led to the growth of democratic constitutionalism.

However, what retarded the pace was the domination of the church. Political thinkers followed the trend set by St. Augustine and St. Thomas in making secular authority subservient to the authority of the church that signified the rule of the bishop over the authority of the monarch and of the Pope over all secular and religious heads of the Christian world. This baleful state of affairs could not be remedied until, after a period of about 800 years, the national monarchs raised their heads to overthrow the discredited hold of the Papacy. The trend of nationalism reared its head particularly in France, England and Spain that witnessed the emergence of the 'actual germs of the modern constitutional state', for in these countries, practical politics "outstrode the legal theories and the ghost of the Holy Roman Empire was irrevocably laid."[25]

Constitutionalism during Renaissance Period : The medieval world came to an end 'with the pestilence of the Black Death of the Fourteenth century.'[26] The renaissance marked the re-emergence of a humanistic and scientific outlook. It indicated that the European people had developed a new consciousness of life and a new sense of liberty. Achievements in the fields of arts, literature and science threw off medieval forms and looked for new values. Inspiration was derived from the models of the classical world. Along with the renaissance, another movement that brought the Middle Ages to an end was the Reformation that destroyed the medieval concept of universalism and scholasticism and supplemented the work of each other by creating modern secular and sovereign national states. The general effect "was at once one of atomisation and one of integration: it atomised the medieval world but integrated individual states."[27] However, one thing that still retarded the pace of a constitutional state was the emergence of absolute monarchy. The unassailable position of a single Pope was taken over by a number of despotic rulers that forced the people to take the matter to the revolution for a final settlement.

23. C.C. Maxey : *Political Philosophies,* p. 107.
24. F.W. Maitland : *Constitutional History of England,* p. 23.
25. Strong, *op. cit.,* p. 27.
26. R.H.Murray: *The History of Political Science from Plato to the Present,* p. 104.
27. Strong, *op. cit.,* p. 27.

Machiavell's *Prince* and Bodin's *Six Books on the Republic* became the chief sources of attraction. The result was that after the decline of the Papacy, absolute monarchical rules were established in England, France, Italy, Spain and Prussia. For this reason, it is commented that the Renaissance state "was not truly a constitutional, much less a democratic, State."[28]

Constitutionalism in England : Britain occupies the most significant place in the development of constitutionalism. The age of Tudor Despotism ended with the 'golden age' of Queen Elizabeth. The Stuart monarchs had to face the opposition of the people. The civil war of 1640-48 was conducted on the issue as to who was supreme—the law *(lex)* or the king *(rex)*. The defeat of the king and the victory of the people confirmed the sovereignty of the people. What remained undone in the civil war was accomplished in the Glorious Revolution of 1688 that laid the foundations of the sovereignty of the Parliament. The movement for the democratisation of the system continued with the result that the great Reform Acts were passed in 1832, 1867 and 1884 that enfranchised more and more people. The Parliament Act of 1911 crippled the House of Lords and its amendment of 1949 further reduced the area of authority of the House in matters of passing a non-money bill. The rise of two political parties had its own contribution to the development of constitutionalism in this country. It made the functioning of the parliamentary government a possibility.

As a result of all these developments, the sovereign stands removed from the area of political authority; the power is exercised by the ministers accountable to the Parliament; and that all citizens of the country, irrespective of their social and political position, enjoy the boons of liberty and equality, what Dicey calls the 'rule of law'. What is of special importance in this regard is that English constitutionalism has supplied a "continuity of life to liberal institutions through many .centuries when elsewhere they were dead or had never lived, permitted the growth of its own institutions among those communities in all parts of the world of which England herself was the mother and supplied the pattern of a constitution when the moment came for any newly-liberated community to found one."[29]

Constitutionalism in France : France could not remain immune from the influence of modern constitutionalism. The voice of Rousseau's *Social Contract* that 'man is born free, he is everywhere in chains' had its clear echo in the Declaration of the Rights of Man and Citizen adopted by the National Assembly in 1789 that said : "Men are born free and equal in rights...The aim of every political association is the preservation of the practical and imprescriptible rights of man." The Constitution of 1791 based on the ideals enshrined in the Declaration could not last as the legislative assembly that was created under this instrument of government failed to arrest the state of anarchy in which the country was caught up.

Moreover, what acted as a great impediment in the way of a well-established constitutional government was the emergence of Napoleonic dictatorship. The monarchy that was terminated in 1789 had its revival in 1799 that continued till the 'total' defeat of the Emperor in 1815. The country witnessed the rise and fall of several unstable monarchs until the Third Republic was created in 1875. It had a parliamentary government, a constitutional President and a responsible ministry. It continued till it was shattered by the Second World War in 1940. The Fourth Republic came into being in 1946 with the parliamentary system of government, a constitutional President and a responsible executive. Since the government of France failed to check the rise and growth of revolutionary conditions in its colony of Algeria, a new Constitution came

28. *ibid.,* p. 27.
29. *ibid.,* p. 54.

into force in 1958 that marked the establishment of the Fifth Republic under Charles de Gaulle. The new arrangement provides for a strong President and a weak Prime Minister with a weaker Parliament. It may be termed quasi-presidential or quasi-parliamentary. However, keeping in view the very strong position of the President, it has also been called a 'monarchist constitution'. The contribution of France in this regard should be discovered in the fact that here we find the first example of a constitution frankly based on the ideals of 'liberty, equality and fraternity.'

Constitutionalism in America : The spirit of the *Social Contract* of Rousseau had its echo in the United States also where the Declaration of Independence of 1776 categorically stated that "all men are created equal: that they are endowed by their Creator with certain unalienable rights- that to secure these rights, governments are instituted among men, deriving their just powers from the consent of the governed; that, whenever any form or government becomes destructive of these ends, it is the right of the people to alter or abolish it, and to institute a new government, laying its foundations on such principles, and organising its powers in such form, as to them shall seem most likely to affect their safety and happiness."

Guided by these ideals, the Founding Fathers of the American republic established a form of federal government based on the principles of separation of powers as so elaborately presented by a French thinker (Montesquieu) and supplemented it with the principle of checks and balances as evolved by them. The result was that America came to have a government with executive, legislative and judicial powers vested respectively in the President, the Congress and the Supreme Court.

The three organs of American government are separated from each other and, at the same time, they check each other so that the balance may be maintained. Thus, all appointments and foreign treaties made by the President must be ratified by the Senate; the Congress may remove the President by the process of impeachment; and the Courts can invalidate any order or decree issued by the President in case it goes beyond the constitution or is against the due process of law. Likewise, the Congress cannot make a law that violates the letter and spirit of the Constitution. A bill passed by the Congress requires the assent of the President and the Courts may invalidate it if they find that the impugned law is against the constitution or the due process of law. Finally, the Courts are checked by the authority of the President and the Congress. The Congress may pass a law to enhance the jurisdiction of the Courts, or the number of the judges and their emoluments and may also remove a judge by the process of impeachment. The judges of the Supreme Court and other federal courts are nominated by the President and the Chief Justice acts under an oath of office that is administered to him by the President.

In this way, the American constitution has materialised the maxim that 'power cuts power' or that 'power checks power'. The result of all these constitutional arrangements has come to be that democracy in America "rests upon the expectation that lawful conduct is the standard to which both governments and men will conform."[30] The most outstanding feature of the development of constitutionalism is that herein we find the "true beginning of modern documentary constitutionalism."[31]

Constitutionalism after the First World War: The period following the first Great War came as an era of great surprise since, instead of bringing about a rich harvest of constitutionalism after the termination of hostilities in a world that could be made 'safe for democracy', it witnessed serious authoritarian reactions against the process of

30. J.H. Ferguson and D.E. McHenry : *The American Federal Government* (New York : McGraw Hill, 1969), X Ed., p. 31.
31. Strong, *op. cit.*, p. 37.

constitutionalism hitherto set in the direction of representative and responsible government. The emergence of communism in Russia, Fascism in Italy and Nazism in Germany can be cited as the concrete instances in this regard. The new constitutional devices adopted in these countries contained two elements that distinguished them from a constitutional state hitherto known—political dictatorship through the dominance of a single party to the exclusion of all others and a totalitarian system that used the political machine to control and direct every aspect of economic, social and even religious life. However, one remarkable aspect of the post-First War period was the establishment of the first international organisation called the League of Nations that aimed, by constitutional means, at preventing or peacefully settling conflicts between the sovereign states. It marked a new and unprecedented stage in the development of constitutionalism. Constitutionalism, thus, came to have one more attribute called internationalism.

Constitutionalism after the Second World War: While the dictatorships of Italy, Germany and Japan were destroyed in the second Great War, the model of the Soviet Union survived that now witnessed its proliferation in other countries of the world. As a result, a new model of constitutionalism came to have its place that may be found in all the communist countries of the world. A good number of countries became free that sought to adopt the English or American models or a peculiar combination of the two. For instance, while India adopted the Westminster model in 1950, Pakistan switched over to the American-model in 1958 and then got back to the English model in 1972 subverted in 1977. The poor and backward countries of the Third World, called the developing countries, made several interesting experiments with constitution-making in order to have a constitutional state. The establishment of the United Nations at the debris of the League of Nations cemented the fact that constitutionalism not only stands for nationalism and democracy, it also includes the attribute of internationalism. So we take note of the fact that in the Japanese Constitution of 1946, renunciation of war has been specifically incorporated so as to confirm its character as a document of 'peace'. The Constitution of India includes a directive principle in its Part IV (Art. 51) saying that the State shall strive for a peaceful and secure international order, promote international law and justice and seek pacific settlement of international disputes.

A study of the theme of the development of constitutionalism, as contained above, leaves certain important impressions.

1. Constitutionalism signifies 'addiction to constitutions or the fundamental law'.[32] That is, it desires that every state should be governed by means of a constitution that may be taken as a clear proof of the fact that the rule of law and not that of man is the prime necessity of a civilised political order.
2. Constitutionalism, in course of time, has come to have three essential attributes—nationalism, democracy and self-government. We have neither city-states of the ancient model nor an empire of the medieval form but sovereign nation-states. Then, every state is committed to the ideal of a democratic form. Thus, constitutionalism desires that power should be with the people and that all changes should be effected in a peaceful and lawful manner.
3. Internationalism requires that every state must subscribe to the principle of a super-world federation in which each state is a member and it has to keep faith in the principles of the charter of this international organisation.
4. Since modern state is a social welfare state, it is also needed that the constitution of a state must be such that the idea of social and economic welfare of the people be realised so as to ensure an equitable social, economic and political order.
5. In a country with diverse religions, cultures, languages and ways of life, constitu-

32. Ferguson and McHenry, *op. cit.*, p. 30.

tionalism enjoins the adoption of a federal system in consonance with the urges and aspirations of the people and exigencies of the prevailing conditons.

6. Serions attention should be paid to incorporate provisions touching new themes like protection of human rights, preservation of a healthy environment, and observance of the norms of international law and morality.
7. Existing provisions of the constitution should be suitably amended, or new ones should be incorporated, so as to meet the requirements of the new trends of globalisation and liberalisation.

One thing is, however, certain that the idea of constitutionalism is still in an experimental stage and that it is under the stress of a severe challenge coming from the side of the communist model. Since modern state is a social welfare state, it is also needed that the constitution of a country must be such that the ideal of the socio-economic welfare of the people should be realised along with the realisation of the purpose of securing a stable political order. The ideal of national democratic constitutionalism, ancient though its origins may be, "is still in an experimental stage and that if it is to survive in competition with more revolutionary types of governments, we must be prepared constantly to adapt it to the ever-changing conditions of modern society. The basic purpose of a political constitution is, after all, the same wherever it appears: to secure social peace and progress, safeguard individual rights and promote national well-being."[33]

Varying Concepts of Constitutionalism: 'Liberal' Versus 'Socialist' Interpretations: Case of 'Developing' Countries

Constitutionalism, as already stated, stands for a system having division of powers and an arrangement of checks and balances so that the government remains responsible; it also desires that the system be provided with adequate techniques and procedures that can bring about a systematic and orderly change. It does not stand for a particular form of government, though it may be described as essential for a democratic polity in view of the fact that it limits the powers of the government and seeks to check the 'abuse of power'. One may hardly agree with this interpretation that constitutionalism is against any form of centralisation of powers wherein there is no harmony between the authority of the state and the liberty of the individuals. Such an interpretation refutes the case of constitutionalism in a country having a fascist or communist model of government. A look at the views of eminent writers on this subject shows that there are two varying concepts given by the 'liberal' scholars on the one hand and by the 'socialist' writers on the other, though we may also refer to the case of the concept of constitutionalism in the 'developing' countries of the world.

Liberal Concept of Constitutionalism : Western writers like Thomas Paine, Alexis de Tocqueville, James Bryce, Harold J. Laski, Herman Finer, Charles H. Mcllwain, C.F. Strong, Carl J. Friedrich and a host of others have taken the view that constitutionalism is both an end and a means; it is both value-free and value-laden; it has both normative and empirical dimensions. The provisions of the constitution not only provide for the composition of various organs of the government and the powers entrusted to them, they also attach sanctity to the norms of liberty, equality, justice, rights, etc. For instance, the Constitution of India in its Preamble enshrines the ideals of Justice, Liberty, Equality and Fraternity. According to this view, the constitution is not only an end that ought to be respected by all, it is also a means to an end, the end being the achievement of security and the protection of liberty of the people.

33. Strong, *op. cit.*, p. 55.

The western concept of constitutionalism stands for a constitution that is either in the form of a document, or it is like an assemblage of numerous laws, institutions and customs. The 'rigid' view of some scholars like Thomas Paine and A. de Tocqueville that there 'exists no constitution in England' is hardly convincing in view of the fact that a constitution may not necessarily be in the form of a specific 'document' made at a particular time of history. The rules may either be written, or they may exist in the form of conventions of the constitution and both of them may have the same force of application. What makes a constitution, therefore, is the actual observance of recognised principles relating to the government of a country. James Bryce has rightly added that such principles do exist in England in the form of a host of conventions, usages, judicial decisions, etc. that have acquired general acceptance together with a number of formal charters and statutes. It is for this reason that we find uniqueness in the character of the English constitution. As Neumann says: "What makes the English constitution so unique is the uncommonly large number of its rules which are based solely on conventions and the fact that no act has a higher degree of authority than a simple act of Parliament."[34]

Whether the constitution is in the form of a document made at a particular time of history as the American constitution was made by the Philadelphia Convention in 1787, or it is in the form of numerous laws, institutions, and conventions as in the case of the English constitution, the western concept of constitutionalism lays emphasis on this point that the basic laws of the land should be such that difference between the government of the people and the constitution of the state is discernible. The constitution is more important than the government. It makes adequate arrangement for the establishment and maintenance of restraints so that the areas of a civilised government are well preserved. These restraints may be embodied in the legal framework, they may also be in the form of informal arrangements. What is really needed is that the restraints must be effective so that the government remains limited and also committed to realise the ideals of the constitution. The problem of effectiveness "involves a factual situation and an evaluation and existential judgment of that situation. If no one has 'absolute' power, if in actual fact there exists no sovereign who holds unrestrained power in a given community, then the restraints may be said to be effective."[35]

The western or liberal concept of constitutionalism desires a 'constitutional state' that has a well-acknowledged body of laws and conventions for the operation of a limited government. It has a legislature, an executive, and a judiciary all required to work within the prescribed framework by following the defined procedure. If there is a change, it should be peaceful and orderly so that the political system is not subjected to violent stresses and strains. There is the rule of law ensuring liberty and equality to all; there is the freedom of the press to act as the 'fourth estate'; there is a plural society having freedom for all interests to seek the 'corridors of power'; there is a system that strives to promote international peace, security and justice. Thus viewed, constitutionalism becomes 'an addiction' to the existence and operation *of* a democratic political system that is fundamentally different from those systems where constitution "is treated with neglect or contempt."[36]

Socialist Concept of Constitutionalism : Different from this is the case of the Marxist concept of constitutionalism. In a'socialist' country, the constitution is not an end in itself, it is just a means to implement the ideology of 'scientific socialism'. It is a tool in the hands of

34. R.G. Neumann : *European and Comparative Government,* p. 24.
35. Friedrich, *op. cit.,* p. 123.
36. Wheare, *op. cit.,* p. 4.

the 'dictatorship of the proletariat' that seeks to establish a classless society that would eventually turn into a stateless condition of life. The purpose of having the constitution is not to limit the powers of the government but to make them so vast and comprehensive that the ideal of "workers' state" is realised and 'a new type of state' comes into being.[37] The real aim of the constitution in such a country is not to ensure liberty and equality, rights and justice for all but to see that the enemies of socialism are destroyed and the new system is firmly consolidated. In this way, the real aim of the constitution is "to firmly anchor the new socialist discipline among the working people."[38]

The socialist concept of constitutionalism is based on the principles of the particular ideology of Marxism-Leninism according to which the state is viewed as a class institution whose *raison d'etre* is to act as an instrument of exploitation and oppression by one class over another. If the bourgeois class makes use of this instrument to perpetuate its rule of exploitation and oppression over the working class, the proletariat will make use of the same instrument for the purpose of liquidating the enemies of socialism and all counter-revolutionary forces. Thus, not the constitution of the state but the policy of the Communist Party is supreme. Without concealing his mind, Stalin once frankly asserted: "No important political or organisational problem is ever decided by our Soviets and other mass organisations without directives from the Party."[39] The Communist Party is the 'vanguard of the working class' and it is the party that has to see that the gains of the revolution are firmly consolidated. Hence, after the victory of socialism, there "can be no juxtaposition of public and private rights and interests in the Soviet society. The interests of the state, society and personality are synthesised in a new unity. Hence, all branches of law are part and parcel of the same uniform law—Soviet law."[40]

As in the former Soviet Union so in the People's Republic of China, the constitution is a sort of mainfesto, a confession of faith, a statement of ideals that, as Wheare says, makes 'excursions into political theory'.[41] Though a brief document, it lays down in detail the political, economic and social objectives of the regime. It deals not only with the present 'that which actually exists'; it also deals with the future and 'that which has yet to be achieved'. The constitution clearly states the determination of the country "to ensure the gradual abolition of systems of exploitation and the building of a socialist society." It is, therefore, clear that like the *Common Programme,* the Mao Constitution (1954) "is an important political manifesto announcing the basic principles of state power, military organisation, economic, cultural and educational policy, and foreign policy."[42]

It may well be discerned as to how different is the concept of constitutionalism when we examine the case of a communist country. The Marxist writers not only eulogise their concept of constitutionalism, they also denigrate the western concept as basically misleading. To them parliamentary democracy is a sham as it is another name for the oppressive and exploitative model of the bourgeois order. The model of 'western government' suits the interests of the class of the exploiters and the oppressors. As Lenin writes: "At each step in the most democratic bourgeois state, the oppressed masses encounter a lamentable contradiction between the formal equality

37. A.Y. Vyshinsky : *The Teachings of Lenin and Stalin on Proletarian Revolution and the State,* p. 76
38. A.Y. Vyshinsky : *The Law of the Soviet State,* p. 500.
39. J.V. Stalin : *Leninism,* Vol. I, p. 33.
40. Julian Towster : *The Political Power in the USSR,* p. 16.
41. Wheare, *op. cit.,* p. 46.
42. Paul H. Clyde : *The Far East,* p. 739. The Constitution of 1982 has inserted many new features making China free from Marxist—Leninist—Maoist trappings.

proclaimed by capitalist democracy and the thousands of factual limitations and complications making hired slaves of the proletarians." Fundamentally different from this, the Soviets were the councils of the workers endowed with the aim to draw the whole of the poor into the practical work of administration. It was a power that was open to all, that did everything in the sight of the masses, that was accessible to the masses, that sprang directly from the masses. The Marxist concept of constitutionalism, thus, stood for the system of the Soviets wherein "is realised the universal participation of the working people, one and all, in the management of the state."[43]

Concept of Constitutionalism in Developing Countries : It is very difficult to suggest the precise features of the concept of constitutionalism in poor and backward countries of the Afro-Asian world that have recently emerged as sovereign nation-states and are struggling hard for achieving the ideal of a social welfare state. It appears that they are torn between the poles of imitating the system of some European country under which they remained for a sufficiently long period of colonial domination on the one hand and going for a better and more workable system having much of the indigenous elements coupled with something of the 'socialist' systems of the world on the other. It is also found that several developing countries are experimenting with the imported constitutional arrangements and trying to establish a synthesis between the ideals of the liberal-democratic constitutional state on the one side and the demands and aspirations of the local people on the other. It is for this reason that countries like Pakistan and Bangladesh can be seen involved in alternating from parliamentary to presidential systems and *vice versa.* It can also be found that the failure of the constitutional state has led to the collapse of the popular system and its replacement by a system of military rule that should be regarded as the breakdown of constitutionalism in most of the countries of the Third World like Egypt, Iraq, Iran, Turkey, Sudan, Afghanistan, Pakistan, Myanmar, Bangladesh, Indonesia and Thailand.

The case of constitutionalism in developing countries may, however, be said to have some broad features: First, some countries like India and Sri Lanka have been able to incorporate the values of a western constitutional state, though the ideals like those of liberty, equality and justice have been suitably tempered with the requirements of a social and economic welfare of the society. Second, some countries like Ghana, Tanzania, Uganda, Pakistan, etc. have not yet been able to choose the correct options and they still feel that the western concept of constitutionalism may not serve their real purpose, though they have not yet reached the stage of losing their faith altogether in this concept so far. Third, a definite shift towards imbibing the values of a socialist concept are definitely visible to solve the pressing problems of a nascent social welfare state. It is for this reason that essential liberties of the people have been suitably curbed in countries like South Africa and Afghanistan. As a matter of fact, many developing countries are faced with a grim challenge, something that was felt by President Lincoln when he said: "Must a government, of necessity, be too strong for the liberties of its own people, or too weak to maintain its own existence."[44]

Problems and Prospects of Constitutionalism

Mention, at this stage, must be made of the forces that work against the operation of a constitutional government and whose results shake our faith in the concept of constitutionalism as an addiction to the establishment of a democratic political order. Three factors may be discussed in this regard—

43. Vyshinsky : *The Law of the Soviet State,* p. 84.
44. See Wheare, *op. cit.,* p. 142.

war, emergency and socio-economic degeneration. It is in the war time when the government claims absolute power and in the name of defending the realm from foreign aggression goes to the final extent of crushing the essential liberties of the people. The government undertakes several measures like compulsory conscription, military training, nationalisation of major industries, censorship of the press, etc. for the sake of defending the country. It appears that the framework of a constitutional government is subverted during war times. Such a statement may and may not be correct depending upon the nature of the case. Thus, whereas a constitutional government had its total doom in countries like Italy, Germany and Japan during the days of the Second World War, it could not have the same fate in other countries like France and Britain. A return to the normal constitutional government occurred after the termination of hostilities.

A constitution may incorporate a particular clause saying that the powers of the government shall be unlimited during the days of war or armed rebellion as we may see in the case of the Irish constitution. It, however, depends upon the nature of the case whether such a categorical provision goes against the very spirit of constitutionalism or not. It is said that the emergency powers of the President, as given in the Indian constitution, look like a replica of the Weimer constitution wherein the seeds of future totalitarianism were embedded. One may well disagree with such a rash judgment and endorse the sane observation of Wheare: "The extent to which constitutional government has been suspended in time of war varies a great deal. It need not be assumed that war means the destruction of constitutional government in every case. Yet it is certain to put a strain upon it and it usually suspends it in some degree."[45]

Allied with this is the second factor of emergency. The suspension of the constitutional government is justified if there are the conditions of national emergency. It was under these conditions that President Lincoln went to the unprecedented extent of using troops to crush the revolt of the southern States of the American Union that had raised their heads in opposition to his mission of banishing slavery. The British government took several important measures to meet the conditions of emergency during the days of the first and second world wars. American President Roosevelt went to the length of having 'New Deal' legislation in the 1930's to face the conditions of great depression. The Government of India had made several important arrangements after the proclamation of national emergency in 1975 that were dubbed by its critics as the 'murder of democracy'. What we have said above applies here also. It depends upon the nature of the case whether conditions of emergency entail the doom of the constitutional government or not. Thus, while countries like the United States and Britain returned to the era of a limited government after the termination of the conditions of emergency, others like Italy, Germany and Japan took the matter to a point that their 'constitutional governments' had a quite inglorious end.

Finally, there is the factor of the social and economic distress. Eradication of the conditions of starvation, famine, illiteracy, disease, poverty, squalor, prestilence, etc. requires discretionary action of the state. The government is called for to take immediate and drastic action to alleviate the sufferings of the people. What the Government of India has been doing since the inauguration of the five year plans can be cited as a clear instance in this direction. We may once again reiterate the same point that the outstretched authority of the government to alleviate the conditions of social and economic distress may, and may not, entail the destruction of the constitutional government. It depends upon the sagacity and wisdom of the men in power that by extending the area of their discretionary authority they may save the

45. *ibid.*, p. 138.

country from the challenge of social and economic disintegration, or they may push it to the most disastrous consequences. Wheare rightly suggests that conditions of national emergency or socio-economic distress "lead to the suspension of the ordinary limitations upon government in order to permit swift and effective action. Crisis or emergency government can seldom be constitutional government : peace and prosperity are in truth strong allies of constitutional government. Their prospects are its prospects."[46]

Latest Perspective

A pertinent question arises as to how these serious problems should be dealt with. Or, what should be the outlook for constitutionalism in the present age of globalisation, liberalisation and demoeratisation.

The attribute of nationalism occupies the first place in view of the fact that the modern constitutional state is necessarily a nationalist organisation. The constitutionalism should recognise the principle of national self-determination. We may quote several instances to show that the edifice of a constitutional state was shattered by the forces of nationalism that raised their heads and ultimately caused the disintegration of the constitutional state. The emergence of the republic of Bangladesh may be cited as an instance of the same fact. The Soviet constitution had given the right to every nationality to secede from the Union that had made the federation analogous to a confederation. It may be feared that certain minorities may take undue advantage of claiming autonomy as we find in the case of the French community in the province of Quebec in Canada or of rebel Nagas and Mizos in the north eastern region of India. Such movements may create serious problems for the government. However, the solution to all such difficulties and problems lies in the successful realisation of the ideal of national integration.

The new trend must be taken note of that the concept of nation-state with the attribute of sovereignty has been steadily in the process of erosion for the last many years. Nationalism is being imperceptibly supreseded by trans-nationalism the example of which may be seen in the successful working of the European Union. The member-states of this trans-national organisation have made necessary adjustments so as to harmonise their political institutions with the constitutional set up of the European Union. The British Parliament is no longer a sovereign body as taken by A.V. Dicey in 1885. A member-state of such a trans-national organisation is no longer the exclusive locus of power within its own territorial boundaries. Its powers are limited, and so the powers of the Union are limited in relation to the individual member-states. It is specifically given in the Maastricht Treaty of 1992 that every person holding the nationality of a member-state shall be a citizen of the European Union. The case of the Association of South-East Asian Nations may also be counted in this regard. The operation of such supra-regional organisations is certainly adding a new dimension to the case of constitutionalism.

Though constitutionalism does not strictly stand for a representative and responsible government as conceived by the liberals, it nevertheless attaches prime significance to a rule that is opposed to a totalitarian government. "If constitutional government is limited government, it follows that one of its enemies is absolutism of any kind. Any body of opinion and any organised movement which aims at establishing omnipotent government is clearly a force opposed to constitutional government."[47] The provisions of the constitution must, for this reason, pertain to a democratic model, though the degree of democratisation may vary from one country to another as per obtaining social, economic and political conditions.

46. *ibid.*
47. *ibid.*

It should also be kept in view that the idea of constitutionalism that had an aristocratic nature at the outset has now come to assume a democratic character. Achievements made during the days of the Jacksonian presidency in the United States, the democratisation of franchise in England and civil war in France—all covering the middle portion of the nineteenth century—have brought about a basic change in the concept of constitutionalism. The result is that if nationalism is one essential attribute of constitutionalism, democracy is another. The fears of totalitarianism should be dispelled by the provisions of more and more democracy. The constitution must provide room for essential freedoms of the people, safeguards for the rights of the minorities, protection of the legitimate social and economic rights of the people, guarantee of freedom for the channels of mass communication and the like. We should understand the significance of this motto that the best way to defend freedom is to have it and to struggle for it.

A new definition of the term constitutionalism should be thus furnished that it "embodies the simple proposition that the government is a set of activities organised by and operated on behalf of the people, but subject to a series of restraints which attempt to ensure that the power which is needed for such governance is not abused by those who are called upon to do the governing. There is no apparent reason why a greater or lesser amount of such governmental activities should be incompatible with effective restraints provided the concentration of power in one group or man is guarded against."[48]

A very ticklish problem has been created by the philosophy and practice of socialism that has contributed to the modification of the meaning of constitutionalism. We may agree with the observations of 'western' writers that the ideology of scientific socialism as contained in the works of Marx, Lenin, Stalin, Mao and others refutes the very essence of constitutionalism, since it combines an advocacy of force and violence during the revolutionary and post-revolutionary periods and "a ready acceptance of the dictatorship of the working class with a vague and anarchical type of democracy after all classes except the labour class have been destroyed."[49] Opposed to this is the interpretation of democratic socialism that takes the state as a 'welfare agency' whereby it (state) is treated as a great balancer of different interests and classes of society.

This is the age of nationalism, democracy and socialism. Hence, the concept of constitutionalism must imbibe the ideals of all the three. If English constitutionalism can accommodate the philosophy and practice of Fabianism, or if the constitution of China can accommodate the thought of Socialism with Chinese characteristics, or if the Indian Constitution can be successfully run by those irrevocably wedded to realise the ideal of a socialist pattern of society or to establish a socialist cooperative commonwealth, it can be easily suggested that constitutionalism "is combinable with a considerable variety of economic patterns. Constitutionalism rests upon a balance of classes in society. But this balance is not a hard and fast one, it is an equipoise of mechanical weights, but rather a moving equilibrium of a kaleidoscopic combination of interests. The government, through the parties, operates as a balancer of these combinations."[50]

The outlook for constitutionalism must recognise the significance of the concept of federalism as well that desires a new interpretation of the idea of sovereignty in the national and international spheres. It is the device of federalism that can realise the ideal of 'unity in diversity'. It is this device alone that

48. Friedrich, *op. at.*, p. 35.
49. *ibid.*, p. 33.
50. *ibid.*, p. 35.

can bring about a happy reconciliation between local and regional, or regional and national interests in a way so as to strengthen the very framework of the constitutional state. Examples should be cited of the United States, Switzerland, Canada and South Africa to show how the problems of a multi-national constitutional state have been solved by adopting the device of federalism. Even a unitary state adopts the policy of 'devolution' of powers to have a well-ordered constitutional system as we find in the cases of Britain and France. What has happened to the astonishment of all, in this direction, is that a modern federal state, though based on the principle of division of powers, has struck a good balance between the principle of the distribution of powers and their concentration in the hands of the national government. May has, therefore, observed that a federal system "falls somewhere between a unitary government and a loose association of sovereign states."[51]

Not a mere territorial division of powers but a functional division also can make the device of federalism more meaningful. A federal plan should be devised so that the society, apart from being a federation of territorial units is also a federation of all kinds of associations in which all people "do in practice express themselves far more freely than they do through the normal political organisation. It implies the establishment of semi-sovereign bodies with definite rights within the sphere of their action corresponding to such rights at present enjoyed by the federating units in such federations as the United States and the Commonwealth of Australia, the difference being that they would have no political but economic, religious or social functions. The state would, of course, remain, as it is bound to remain, to coordinate these new parts and maintain order among them. But in this case the state becomes an association of interests which every citizen can appreciate. "Sovereignty then begins to assume a new guise; it becomes instead a fixed legal idea, a pliant tool for man's welfare. And once this is felt of it, there is hardly any limit to the possibilities of constitutional development, whether national or international."[52]

Then, we may take up the factor of internationalism. Modern constitutionalism is confronted with the issue of how to reconcile the framework and operation of a constitutional state with the requirements of a new international order. The constitution of a state should be such that recognises the ideals of international law and justice, renunciation of the policies and programmes of war or irrational protectionism, observance of the decisions of the international organisation and the like. As already pointed out, the constitution of Japan has done a great thing by incorporating a specific clause (Art. 9) speaking of the renunciation of war as an instrument of national policy. The Indian constitution goes a step ahead by incorporating a directive principle in its Part IV (Art. 51) that says that the state shall strive to promote international peace and security, foster respect for international law and treaty obligations and encourage settlement of international disputes by peaceful means.

No right-thinking person can deny that some kind of world authority is the only alternative to international anarchy that has produced two devastating wars and must, if not checked, end in such, rather a far bigger, holocaust entailing total destruction of the human race. It requires that the constitution of a state should be so devised that it does not act as an impediment to the growth of a better international order. A constitution desiring 'export of revolution' or propagation of an ideology of totalitarianism, or subscribing to the eulogy of wars and the like should be deemed as the very enemy of the idea of

51. Ronald J. May : "Decision-Making and Stability in Federal Systems" in *Canadian Journal of Political Science*, Vol. III, No. 1 (March, 1970), pp. 74-75.
52. Strong, *op. cit.*, p. 362.

constitutionalism. We may once again invoke the device of federalism that can . serve our purpose in this regard very well. A constitutional state must subscribe to this idea that the ultimate objective is the 'establishment not of an international but of a supra-national authority to which the nations would sacrifice their external authority."[53]

In addition, three more features may be enumerated which have come into limelight in the age of globalisation and liberalisation. These are related to the protection of human rights, prevention of environmental pollution, and observance of the principles of international law and morality. It is for this reason that the new constitutions of some countries like China, Russian Federation and South Africa have some provisions in this regard. Though a communist country, the Chinese constitution of 1982 has a set of general principles one of which says that the state 'shall give permission to foreign enterprises, whether individual or collective, to invest their money in this country and to enter into economic cooperation with Chinese entrepreneurs'. The constitution of the Russian Federation of 1993 has provisions for the protection of a healthy environment. It recognises the norms of sustainable development. The constitution of South Africa of 1996 honours the principles of international law. Hence, the state is enjoined to observe its international treaties and commitments.

Two important points arise to engage our attention at the end of this study from what we have discussed so far. First, an analysis of constitutionalism would be incomplete if it does not attempt to assess efforts made to combat the forces of totalitarianism that is its biggest enemy. Any movement in the direction of weakening the civil rights of the people in the name of the'reason of the state'is a challenge to the concept of constitutionalism that should be faced to revise the meaning of constitutionalism in the light of new and still newer conditions. We should look at the forces that have an essentially totalitarian character and yet they have a potential attraction for the people. Conditions should be generated in which the models of social and economic democracy are strengthened. Such a model of democracy "is not a miracle which comes to life at a particular moment and then continues to function automatically, but it is rather a political task upon which it is necessary to work continually."[54]

Second, change is the law of nature that should be welcomed as it is inevitable. It calls for the revision of the old values and systems in the light of new hopes and aspirations of the people. We have seen that it is on account of this change that the content of constitutionalism took a turn from an aristocratic to a democratic side after the events of the middle phase of the last century and that socialism came to be added as one more attribute to it after those of nationalism and democracy. In other words, it signifies that the meaning of constitutionalism should not be given a rigid or fixed form; it should be treated as a dynamic affair that changes with the emergence of new conditions, new challenges, new problems and new issues. And change "is not something to be feared and avoided, as Aristotle thought, but it is of the very warp and weft of modern constitutionalism."[55]

---

53. *ibid.*, p. 364.
54. Arthur Rosenberg: *Democracy and Socialism*, p. 216.
55. Friedrich, *op. clt.*, p. 35.

15

Federalism

> Traditional federal theory for, the most part, simplified this picture into two major aspects. First, it paid little regard to the inter-dependence of the Centre and the various units, because it effectively ignored the direct influence of government's policy output on the policy outputs of other governments through persuasion, influence and bargaining, and implicitly assumed that the demands made by each electorate on its respective government were separate and independent as between governments. Second, while recognising differences between units, it assumed implicitly that the policy outputs of the various units are, in general, sufficiently similar that the units may be regarded as a collectivity.
>
> **—Ronald J. May[1]**

Political systems may be classified in terms of the methods by which the powers of administration are distributed between the government of the whole country on the one hand and regional or provincial governments that exercise authority over the parts of a country on the other. On this basis, they may be designated as 'federal' and 'unitary' models, though the possibilities of a political system having a queer blending of both may not be ruled out. In a federal system, the powers of the government "are divided between a government for the whole country and governments for parts of the country in such a way that each government is legally independent within its own sphere. The government for the whole country has its own area of powers and it exercises its authority without any control from the governments of the constituent parts of the country, and these latter in their turn exercise their powers without being controlled by the central government. In particular, the legislature of the whole country has limited powers, and the legislatures of the states or provinces have limited powers. Neither is subordinate to the other; both are coordinate."[2] In a unitary system, on the other hand, the legislature of the whole country "is the supreme law-making body in the country. It may permit other legislatures to exist and exercise their powers, but it has the right, in law, to overrule them; they are subordinate to it."[3] As pointed out above, there may be a political system in which the elements of both are blended in a strange way that the position of the Central government is far stronger than that of the regional governments. Such a system may be designated as 'quasi-federal'.

1. May : "Decision-Making and Stability in Federal Systems" *in Canadian Journal of Political Science.* Vol. Ill, No. 1. 1970, pp. 74-75.
2. K.C. Wheare: *Modern Constitutions* (London : Oxford Univ. Press, 1966), p. 19.
3. *ibid.* J.W. Garner says : "Federal Government, as contradistinguished from a unitary government, is a system in which the totality of governmental power is divided and distributed by the national constitution or the organic act of parliament creating it, between a central government and the governments of the individual states or other territorial sub-divisions of which the federation is composed. These latter governments are not the creations of the central government of the union : in most federal systems the reverse is the case, that is, the central government has been created by the constituent members through the act of federation; they are something more than parts, or agents of the central organisation; their sphere of autonomy is determined not by the Central government but by the general constitution of the federation or, as in the British dominions, by an act of the imperial parliament which serves the purpose of a constitution. Consequently, they donot exist by the sufferance of the Central government, nor may their competence be restricted by it." *Political Science and Government* (Calcutta : World Press, 1952), p. 348.

Federal System: Meaning and Dynamic Implications

Political systems of the world are either federal or unitary or a queer mixture of both. While countries like the United States, Switzerland, Australia, South Africa, Canada and India should be placed in the category of 'federal states', others like Britain, France, Sri Lanka and China are the examples of 'unitary states'. Different from both, some countries having a system based on the principle of the division of powers along with very high level of concentration of powers in the hands of the Central government are treated as 'quasi-federal'. The case of Canada falls in this category. It is a different matter that a great writer like Wheare places India too in this category. It is, however, certain that the elements of centralisation of powers are unmistakably present in every federal system of the world and, for this reason, no political system can now be described as the model of an idea! federation.

Federal system, according to Daniel J. Elazara, provides a mechanism which 'unites separate polities within an over-arching political system so as to allow each to maintain its fundamental political integrity."[4] This mechanism is constituted by the distribution of powers between two governments, general and constituent, in a way designed to protect the existence and area of authority of both which, according to traditional norms, are considered to be 'coordinate governments'.[5] Obviously, the basic aspect of federalism is pluralistic inasmuch as its fundamental tendency, as Max Hildebert Boehm points out, "is harmonisation and its regulative principle is solidarity."[6] If federalism signifies the existence and operation of a double set of government, it naturally requires that basic policies be made and implemented through understanding and negotiations in some form so as to ensure participation of the central and provincial governments in the decision-making and decision-executing processes. Federalism thus provides a convenient and workable arrangement to unite 'political' forces with certain 'unpolitical' forces—ideological, sociological, psychological etc. which, if carried to extremes in certain situations of dissatisfaction and desperation, may become highly anarchical demanding solution of the issues, in question, without much loss of time. It is evident that a federal system in the face of a tendency to establish 'complete unitarianism' becomes a principle of opposition.[7]

A penetrating study of the principle of federalism reveals its flexible and cooperative character in such a way that neither level of government "is wholly dependent on the other, nor wholly independent of the other."[8] However, a degree of difference does appear in the traditional and modern interpretations of this term. True that a total policy output in a federal system comes as a product of complex process of interaction between central and provincial governments which share decision-making and decision-executing process, the traditional interpretation of federalism, for the most part, implies an obsolete situation of inter-relationship which is hardly in tune with the latest orientation of constitutional systems.

Modern federal system "falls somewhere between a unitary government and a loose association of sovereign states."[9] It has developed a difference of kind with a confederal model, it has brought about a difference of

4. David I. Sils (ed.): *International Encyclopaedia of Social Sciences,* (New York : Macmillan, 1968), Volumes 5-6, p. 358.
5. An eminent writer on the 'federal principle', K..C. Wheare, defines it as 'the method of dividing powers so that the general and regional governments are each within a sphere coordinate and independent'. *Federal Government* (London: Oxford University Press, 1963), 4th Ed., p. 10.
6. Seligman (ed.) : *Encyclopaedia of the Social Sciences* (New York : Macmillan, 1964), 4th Ptg., Vol. 5, p. 169.
7. *ibid.*
8. M.C.J. Vile : *The Structure of American Federalism* (London, 1961), p. 197.
9. May, *op. cit.,* p. 76.

degree with a unitarian system.[10] The national and regional governments may be 'coordinate' according to traditional statement constituting 'independent political systems'at the general and constituent levels; according to modern interpretation, both constitute a single system 'containing within it several overlapping sub-systems'.[11] As a result of this, decision-making and decision-executing processes are influenced and determined not only by means of mutual participation of national and regional governments but also by means of the bargaining power and skill in the midst of 'supreme' position of the centre by virtue of an unmistakable tendency of centralisation of powers and 'superior' capacity of the units *inter se* by virtue of their respective position—demographic, strategic, political, economic etc.[12]

It is further inferrable from the study of the latest trends that if the Centre dominates the units, the units themselves dominate one another, including the Centre, in a particular situation through the mechanism of cooperative federalism by virtue of their bargaining skill and capacity in addition to their geographical size, population, natural resources, strategic situation, etc. Ronald J. May aptly suggests that unit inequalities "are reflected in the Central government's decision-making functions in two ways. First, because of superior number and perhaps, wealth, that part of the central government's electorate which resides in the large units is likely to exercise stronger influence over the Central government's policy output than that which resides in the small unit; second, to the extent that relative size and wealth affect the bargaining capabilities of unit governments, the government of the large unit is likely to have more influence over the Central government's policy output than the government of the small unit. The policy output of the Central government is, therefore, more likely to correspond to the interests of the large unit than to those of the small unit."[13] True, both central and provincial governments exercise their powers in a way enabling them to neutralise or turn to their advantage those conditions which they find uncongenial for their purposes, but "to what extent they are able to do so will always depend upon their legal power, political influence and resources."[14]

Furthermore, the traditional theory of federalism should be restated in the light of new materials ranging from studies and interpretations of constitutional arrangements to the facts and figures covering the areas of centre-state relationship in their diverse ramifications. In other words, the study of federalism should be re-interpreted as "a constantly changing process resulting from the inter-action of mass political parties, widespread bureaucracies, a large number and variety of interest groups, and elected governments with expanded functions rather than as a static model or formula for political organisation (as 'ism')."[15]

---

10. See R. Davis : "The Federal Principle Reconsidered" in *Australian Journal of Politics and History*, Brisbane, 1955-56, Vol. I, Nos. 1-2.
11. *ibid*, p. 78. While dealing with the case of a revised approach to the study of cooperative federalism in a counrry like India, Prof Amal Ray thus furnishes a plausible point: "Reorientation of federalism is primarily based upon cooperation between two sets of authority in the task of attaining national objectives. Increasing discussions between the centre and the units would provide basis as in India for agreement on broad policies and programmes. The units cannot claim absolute autonomy within their jurisdiction, because in the closely integrated contemporary societies, the central and state spheres defy exact demarcation, and often they overlap." *Inter-Governmental Relations in India: A Study of Indian Federalism*, (Bombay : Asia Publishing House, 1966), pp. 6-7.
12. See Max Beloff: "The Federal Solution in its Application to Europe and Africa" in *Political Studies*, Oxford, 1953, Vol. I, No. 2, pp. 127-28.
13. May, *op. cit.*, p. 79.
14. A. Chatterji : *The Central Financing of State Plans in the Indian Federation* (Calcutta : F.K.L. Mukhopadhyay, 1971), p. 6.
15. See Marcus F. Franda: "Federalising India : Attitudes, Capacities, and Constraints" in *South Asian Review*, Vol. III, No. 3 (April, 1970), pp. 199-215.

Essential Conditions for the Successful Organisation of Federal Government

Contradistinguished from a unitary state, a federal state is one in which a number of co-ordinate states unite for certain common purposes. As such, federal system "partakes of a character of a treaty. It is an arrangement made between certain bodies politik which wish to retain certain rights. Thus the constitution will state either the rights that are to be retained by the federating units or the rights that the federal authority takes over."[16] Since federal state has the character of a 'composite' state, its successful organisation requires the existence of some important conditions that may be enumerated as under:

1. *Geographical Contiguity :* A federal state must have a geographically contiguous area. The size of the state may be very large or very small. What is needed is that the entire area of the state must be geographically contiguous. If the parts of a state are cut off from one another by a big distance, federal system cannot be successfully worked out there. For instance, a country like Indonesia cannot have a successful federal system as she is an archipelago and her worst enemy is her geography. Such a system operates successfully in a vast country like the United States, Canada and India for the obvious reason that these countries have the advantage of geographical contiguity. It is on account of this that a federal state expects its unit to take part not only in its own affairs but also in the affairs of the national government.
2. *Community of Interests :* What provides cementing force to a federal system is the community of interests in the sphere or spheres of language, religion, culture and the like. A federal system desires, as Dicey said, a 'union' and not a 'unity'. It stands on the principle of 'unity in diversity'. It aims at forging a union and creating a 'united nations'. The cases of the United States, Switzerland, Canada and India illustrate that in each one of them there are prevailing diversities that are sought to be preserved. Though the people have diverse religious, ethnic or cultural patterns of life, they have also developed a sense of common identity that they donot desire to lose. This is not to deny that, in spite of these social or cultural differences, there must be an overriding sense of unity to bind the diverse people together.
3. ***Similarity of Social and Political Institutions:*** It is required that the pattern of governmental systems should be the same both at the national and regional levels. That is, the Centre and the States must have the same form of government. We find in federal countries like Canada and India that the parliamentary form of government prevails at the Centre and also in the Provinces or States. Likewise, in the United States, presidential form of government prevails at the Centre and also in the States. When we see the case of Switzerland, we find that the 'republican' form of government prevails at the national as well as cantonal levels. In the Russian Federation, the republican system prevails at the central as well as at the regional levels. Whether the constitution specifies the powers of the central government and assigns residuary powers to the states (as in the United States), or it enumerates the powers of the Provinces and assigns residuary powers to the Centre (as in Canada), or it clearly mentions the powers of both (as in Australia and India), it is required that the same form of government prevails at both the levels. It is, for this reason, provided in the constitution that the Centre may veto or invalidate any action of the regional government in case it violates the basic features of the national constitution.

---

16. C.F. Strong : *Modern Political Constitutions* (London : Sidgwick and Jackson, 1966), p. 64.

4. ***Absence of Marked Inequality :*** As far as practicable, the units of a federal state should enjoy equality of status in respect of their powers though not in respects of their territorial and demographic compositions. It is not possible that all units of a federal state are of equal size, or they have equal density of population. It is, however, essential that there should be no inequality in matters relating to the distribution of powers, as far as possible. For instance, all the units of the .United States send equal number of representatives (2 each) to the upper house of the national legislature. Different from this is the case of India where the number of deputies sent by the State governments to the Rajya Sabha varies from 1 to 31. The factor of inequality creates dissatisfaction that has its harmful effects on the political behaviour of the provincial governments. Care should also be taken to remove regional economic imbalances. If one area of the state is very rich and economically advanced and the other very poor and backward, it will lead to agitations as we find in the movements for the construction of a steel plant in Andhra Pradesh or for the creation of a separate state of Telangana.
5. ***Socio-Economic Development :*** A federal system cannot work successfully unless there is social and economic development of the country. It is required that the people are educated and modernised so that they can keep themselves away from the influences of parochial tendencies. Economic development is also equally necessary. As federal system is a very expensive arrangement, it needs ample economic resources to run the double set of governments. Moreover, it is also essential that social and economic development covers the entire country. There should be no imbalance in this regard. In case the people of one part of the country are well-developed, socially and economically, others will resent it and then come out with their demands for speedy social and economic development that may culminate in their movement for seceding from the union.
6. ***Political Ability :*** The political ability of the people has its own significant part to play. It refers to a developed political culture. Unless the people have their own ideas, beliefs and commitments to the values of their political system, no political system can work successfully. More so, in a federal state, it is required so that the people understand the meaning of their allegiance towards a double set of governments. National leadership must be in the hands of those who have national image and who can infuse the sentiments of national integration in the minds of the people.
7. ***Political and National Integration :*** The people of a federal country should be integrated politically as well as nationally. The political map of the country should be drawn or redrawn in a way that the local urges and aspirations of the people for having a separate state of their own are reconciled with the over-all requirements of national integration. Then, people should learn that the interests of the nation as a whole over-ride their primordial loyalties. If so, then divisive movements would be arrested and the people saved from the disastrous effects of those forces that balkanise a country.
8. ***Centre-State Coordination :*** There should be a happy coordination between the central and regional governments. Though the areas of their respective jurisdictions are specifically earmarked, it is also required that some inter-linking arrangements be devised so that the two governments remain connected with each other. Federalism should have a cooperative and not a competitive, a persuasive and not a coercive, a flexible and not a rigid and, above all, a positive and not a negative character. The annual conferences of the heads of central and regional governments may be suggested as a positive step in this direction.

9. ***Reasonable Trend Towards Centralisation :*** As already pointed out, centralisation of powers has become an unmistakable trend in every federal system of the world. No federal state can live in its 'true' or classical form under modern political conditions. The regional governments must appreciate this dynamic political truth and thus, instead of resenting, they should accept the reasonable moves of the central government, no matter they go to attenuate the scope of their authority to some extent. At the same time, it is required that the central government should not take to the course of finishing the autonomy of the states. The move of the central government must be 'reasonable', that is, it should be supported by, some plausible justification. For instance, the President of India may convert the federal system into a unitary one during times of emergency (vide Art. 352). Such a drastic step amounting to the extinction of the autonomy of State governments can be taken only when the country is faced with the conditions of war, external aggression or armed revolt.

If these conditions are existent, a federal system can work successfully. We may cite the leading instances of some countries like the United States, Switzerland, Australia and India. The case of a communist country, like the former Soviet Union, was basically different where the network of the Communist Party played its own part in making the federal system run successfully. The USSR afforded the singular instance where the units had been given the power to secede from the Union. It, however, never occurred, nor could it ever occur, as the 'leading and guiding role' of the Communist Party was always there to put its heavy hand on such a move if it ever arose.

Unitarian Federalism

In view of the fact that federalism as an organisational device cannot be divorced from the requirements of the age, its classical model has been changing so as to be more and more in tune with a new pattern that is neither purely federal nor unitary. It may conveniently be designated as unitarian federalism. It is for this reason that every constitution taking a federal premise too seriously, can hardly escape becoming anachronistic.[17] A historical study of the growth of federal systems brings home the political truth that what has happened during the last decades is that the central governments have developed their powers more and more intensively at the expense of the areas originally allotted to the regional governments. It is due to this that the national governments "have grown in importance in comparison with the regional governments, because they began from nothing and because they were endowed with control over most of the important matters with which regional governments have to deal."[18]

The main forces that have contributed to the growing strength of the central government at the expense of regional governments seem to have been fivefold—war politics, depression politics, welfare politics, technopolitics, grants-in-aid politics and party politics. The horrible conditions of war and economic depression demand unitary control for the effective protection of national interests. They impose heavy financial burdens which the national government alone can bear. The conditions of war and economic depression, though temporary, are detrimental to the growth and stability of a federal system. Similarly, the ideal of social welfare state has enjoined upon the national government to increase its scope of activity more and more to eradicate gigantic evils of poverty, unemployment, disease, starvation, ignorance, squalor, etc. One may say that the ideal of

---

17. K. Loewenstein : "The 'Living' Constitution" in J. Blonde! (ed.) : *Comparative Government* (London : Macmillan, 1969), p. 152.
18. Wheare, *Federal Government*, p. 238.

Heywood's Analysis of Federal System

Features common to federal systems of the world

1. *Two relatively autonomous levels of government :* Both the central (federal or national) government and the provincial (regional or state) governments possess a range of powers that the other cannot encroach upon.
2. *Written constitution:* The responsibilities and powers of each level of government are defined in a codified constitution. Therefore, the relationship between the centre and the periphery is conducted within a legal framework.
3. *Constitutional arbiter :* The formal provisions of the constitution are interpreted by a supreme court, which thereby arbitrates in the case of disputes between federal and state levels of government.
4. *Linking institutions :* In order to foster cooperation and understanding between federal and state levels of government, the regions and provinces must be given a voice in the process of central policy-making. So the upper chamber of the national legislature has representatives of the units.

Case for Centralisation

1. *National Unity :* Central government alone articulates the interests of the whole rather than the various parts. That is, the interest of the nation rather than those of national, ethnic, or regional groups. A strong centre ensures that the government addresses the common interests of the entire community; a weak centre leads to rivalry and disharmony.
2. *Uniformity :* Central government alone can establish uniform laws and public services that help people to move easily from one part of the country to another.
3. *Equality :* Decentralisation has the disadvantage that it forces peripheral institutions to rely on the resources available in their locality or region. Only central government can rectify inequalities that arise from that fact that the areas with the greatest social needs are invariably those with the least potential for raising revenues.
4. *Prosperity :* Economic development and centralisation invariably go hand in hand. Only central government can ensure sustainable growth.

Case for Decentralisation

1. *Participation :* Local government is certainly more effective than the central government in providing opportunities for citizens to participate in the political life of their community. The benefits of widening the scope of political participation include the fact that it helps to create a better educated and more informed citizenry.
2. *Responsiveness :* Peripheral institutions are usually 'closer' to the people and more sensitive to their needs. This both strengthens democratic accountability and ensures that government responds not merely to the overall interests of society, but also to specific needs of particular communities.
3. *Legitimacy :* Physical distance from government affects the accountability or rightness of its decisions. Decisions made at a local level are more likely to be seen as intelligible and therefore legitimate. In contrast, central government may appear remote, both geographically and politically.
4. *Liberty :* As power tends to corrupt, centralisation threatens to turn government into a tyranny against the individual. Decentralisation protects liberty by dispersing government power, thereby creating a network of checks and balances. Peripheral bodies check central government as well as each other.

Andrew Heywood: *Politics,* pp. 158-62

welfare state is not inimical to the growth and stability of a federal system as social service activities are shared by the national and provincial governments. However, experience being the better guide shows that regional governments have not been able to realise the commitments enshrined in the constitution and political resolutions due to lack of economic resources and largely corrupt and inefficient public services. As a result, the national government has increased the area of its activity despite its telling effect upon the functional, if not structural, aspects of a federal system.

Technopolitics means the study of political institutions in the light of scientific and technological developments having their impact upon the working of governmental machinery. As every government is run by the experts—persons well-trained in the art of public administration—bureaucracy occupies a very significant position so much so that what people take as their representative government virtually becomes a new leviathan devouring their fundamental liberties and privileges. It may be discovered that not the leaders chosen by the people but the experts and the technicians stress goals of development and lay down policies and programmes. As these specialised services are mostly provided by the national government, the regional governments have to carry out the plans, programmes and instructions prepared by the technocrats working behind the rulers of the central administration. Such a role of technical experts is bound to have a reprehensible form when the public servants are recruited and controlled by the agencies of central government while they serve and draw their salaries and emoluments from provincial governments.

The factors of war and economic depression belong to a temporary phase of national or financial emergencies and the factor of technopolitics has an invisible, though not so reprehensible, role. However what smacks of the highly attenuated autonomy of the component units of a federal state is the politics of grants-in-aid. The regional governments live in a perpetual condition of financial difficulties. They have meagre resources; more than that, they are forced to collect money that they cannot spend. They are also forced to spend it in a particular way, the money that they do not collect. In many cases, the provincial governments have to stand like 'beggars' at the door of the Centre. Politics having its own part in this regard is discoverable in the policies of the shrewd leaders of the central government who either liberalise or tighten the rules and norms of financial grants to oblige, appease or punish certain regional governments.

Finally, we come to the point of party politics. A political party plays the role of an extra-constitutional agency in the running of a federal system. Though a formal federal system in all respects, the very system is reduced to a unitarian model when political parties run the machinery of general and regional governments without federalising their own character. The case of Congress or BJP in India affords a shining case in this regard. The High Command of this party (consisting of top leaders running the central government) is the final authority in matters like composition of the Union and State ministries, selection of the Prime Minister and Chief Ministers, imposition or revocation of emergency in a State under Art. 356, etc. The result is that both the Union and State Governments in India are virtually controlled by the all-powerful party. On account of this fact, our federal pattern has become a matter of form, while its spirit has become unitary under the rule of the party in power.

The relationship between federalism and party structure manifests that the organisational structures of political parties tend to correspond to the governmental patterns under constitutional democracy. This "is very natural, since it is one of the purposes of the parties to gain control of the government; therefore, if the government is federally structured, parties must adapt themselves to such a structure."[19] However, as seen above,

19. Carl J. Friedrich : *Trends of Federalism in Theory and Practice* (London : Pall Mall, 1968), p. 47.

this point lacks universal applicability. The case of India under Congress rule at the Centre and in most of the States defies the case of a comparative analysis of party systems vis-a-vis federal models. Likewise the case of a communist country stands out with the only difference that while in a democratic country, like India, the dominance of one party is a matter of accident, in a communist country it is a matter of normal constitutional sanction. It is because of the centralisation of powers that some systems of the world have been designated as 'quantitative', 'quasi', or 'super' federalisms. The Soviet Union was regarded as a quasi-federal state where formal division of powers between the central and regional governments was interpreted as a method of social integration through the mechanism of the Communist Party rather than of perpetual diversification pertaining to the development of a pluralist society. In such a political system, though federal in form, the basic stress is on cultural autonomy rather than on political self-government. Likewise, Indian federalism has been described, by a critic like Prof. Wheare, as a unitary system with certain subsidiary features of a federal model rather than a federal model with certain subsidiary features of a unitary state.

A word of caution may, however, be added at this stage against the wrong notion of regarding federalism as obsolescent. To say that the rights of the regional governments are 'dead', or that nobody cares for the 'finished' autonomy of the states is to misread the fact of Centre's standing like a colossus. It is a misargued statement that a federal system is out of date in view of the fact that it preserves hard and fast regional divisions in a world where social and economic life is becoming more and more a single whole. The fact is that federalism offers plurality to the singularity of life in a way that diverse factors are harmoniously reconciled. As political institutions must change according to the needs of the age, federalism is no exception and a term like unitarian federalism has been coined to represent not a unitarian model tampered with a federal process but a federal model revised in the light of new conditions of the age and requirements of the people. Federal government "is still desired by some regions in all the federations. There is no conclusive evidence that federal government is to be no more than a stage in the process towards unitary government."[20]

Cooperative Federalism

A federal system not only stands for the distribution of powers between central and regional governments, both autonomous (in the traditional sense) in their respective spheres, it also desires sincere cooperation between the two sets of political organisations in order to ensure that the ideal of coordination and complete administration of the divided spheres is attained as effectively as possible. It is needed for the obvious reason that there is the area of inter-regional relationships disallowing any component unit to keep itself completely cut off from others in the interest of administrative efficiency and nationalist sentiments. Wheare rightly visualises that if each regional government "keeps completely to itself, many matters will suffer from diversity of regulation, and government itself will be less efficient because the experience of other states will have been neglected."[21]

Hence, some agencies of inter-governmental cooperation have been devised in various federal systems of the world. Taking the case of the Australian federal system, we find Inter-Provincial Conference and Premiers Conference, the latter being very influential by virtue of its annual meeting in the month of May when State Premiers and Commonwealth Prime Minister meet and discuss matters of general and particular interest, ranging from financial

20. Wheare, *op. cit.*, p. 242.
21. *ibid.*, p.227.

resources and relations to constitutional reforms. The Loan Council may be cited as another important agency in this regard with the only difference that while Premiers' Conference has its roots and record of evolution in usages and conventions, it has a statutory status. The Governors' Conference in the United States and Dominion-Provincial Conference in Canada are the cases of similar institutions in the two other federal states of the world.

The study of Indian federalism reveals that while such a headline has nowhere been mentioned specifically in the text of the Constitution, it is well understood that our constitutional system has envisaged 'a series of federal institutions' that would be 'appropriate to the political environment'.[22] The language of Art. 1 of the Constitution is quite specific to illustrate India as 'a Union of States'. Moreover, our constitutional system, apart from pertaining to the formal federal framework, necessitates 'a process of bargaining' between Central and State Governments in which experiment, cooperation and persuasion are requisitioned both to testify generally accepted norms and the usual procedural patterns of interaction between national and state governments.[23] That is, our constitutional system stands on the foundation of cooperative federalism presuming interdependence of national and regional governments of a federal union instead of granting them absolute independence in the allotted sphere pertaining to a classical federal model. In the midst of a strong Central Government, our Founding Fathers sought to ensure that it "would not necessarily result in weak provincial governments that are large administrative agencies for Central policies."[24]

The fact that Indian constitutional system stands on the foundation of 'cooperative federalism,'[25] what Morris-Jones calls 'bargaining federalism',[26] is traceable in the existence, formal as well as tacit, and operation of various institutional agencies whether provided in the text of the Constitution or set up to implement its ideals as enshrined in the Preamble and Directive Principles of State Policy as Planning Commission and National Development Council (NDC), Finance Commission, Inter-State Council, Zonal Councils and a host of statutory bodies for the adjudication of disputes with respect to the use, distribution and control of inter-state river, water etc. That is, the Constitution envisages the appointment of a number of high-level commissions, both permanent and *ad hoc,* for the specific purpose of reconciling diverse and conflicting interests with the cooperation of Union and State Governments. In other words, our Constitution allows experimentation with a variety of federal arrangements and devices in which inter-dependent Central and State Governments are involved. That is to say, our Constitution allows experimentation with a variety of federal arrangements and devices in which inter-dependent Central and State Governments are necessarily brought together just to make the envisaged system a successful affair or, in negative terms, to avoid the situation of failure of a great system which has already become 'a source of enlightenment' in many Asian and African countries of the world.[27]

22. Marcus F. Franda : *West Bengal and the Federalizing Process in India* (Princeton : Princeton University Press, 1968), p. 179.
23. See W.H. Morris-Jones : *Government and Politics of India* (London : Hutchinson, 1971), second edition, p. 150.
24. Granville Austin: *The Indian Constitution: Cornerstone of a Nation* (New York : Oxford University Press, 1966), p. 186.
25. Austin, *op. cit.,* pp. 186-87. It ought to be made clear that Indian cooperative federalism covers much more than the financial sphere. Thus, the case of Indian federalism is quite distinguishable from the study of American, Canadian and Australian federal systems as presented by A.H. Birch in his *Federalism, Finance and Social Legislation* (London : Oxford University Press, 1955), p. 305.
26. Morris-Jones, *op. cit.,* p. 150.
27. Ronald J. May, *op. cit.,* p. 73. Also see T.M. Franck (ed.) : *Why Federations Fall* (New York, 1968).

In the end, it ought to be kept in view that, despite formal division of powers, a federal system, what Lees says about the American pattern and is equally applicable to others also, "has never been a neat system of distinct governmental activities and functions."[28] There has been no standard way of measuring the degree of centralisation of a particular federal polity and on that basis presenting a taxonomic representation of federal systems of the world. The net result of all is that every viable federal system has the characteristics of being creative and cooperative as well as quasi and quantitative, though in varying degrees.

Inter-Governmentalism and International Federalism

A Study of federalism aoross national boundaries enables us to look at the new themes of inter-governmentalism and international federalism. Inter-governmentalism looks like confederalism in view of the fact that it implies a union or alliance of several nation-states in which each member-state preserves its independence and sovereignty and thereby retains its distinct political entity. As such, it has the option to remain in the union or to leave it if its interest is not properly defended or served. The case of the General Agreement on Trade and Tariffs (GATT) formed in 1948 and its substitution by World Trade Organisation (WTO) in 1995 may be referred to here. So the cases of the North Atlantic Treaty Organisation (NATO) formed in 1949 and the East European Defence Treaty (Warsaw Pact) formed in 1955 (expired in 1990) may be cited at this stage. Such inter-govermental organisations are confederal in character. As Heywood says: "Such treaties and alliances are highly specific: they involve agreement on a particular area of policy-making, whether economic or military, and rarely address general or broader issues. Moreover, in signing such treaties, states donot formally surrender national sovereignty. Treaties are signed and alliances are made in pursuit of national interests. States are, therefore, only likely to fulfil their obligations if they perceive that the treaty continues to reflect these interests, there being no institutional means of treaty enforcement."[29]

However, the case of international federalism is different in terms of its conceptualisation and operation. In the present age of globalisation, states are drawing closer to each other. The forces of political, economic, social and cultural integration are at work the examples of which may be seen in the formation and working of the European Union. Here an irresistible move from inter-governmentalism to international federalism may be noticed having its clear manifestation in the gradual erosion of the sovereignty of the nation-state. The Treaty of Rome (1957) established the European Economic Community. The Luxemburg Compromise of 1966 enshrined the sovereignty of the member-states. It accepted the general practice of unanimous voting in the Council of Ministers and granted each member-state an outright veto on matters threatening vital national intetests. However, things have taken a turn towards emerging international federalarchy. As a result of the Single European Act (1986) and the Maastricht Treaty of European Union (1993), the practice of qualified majority voting which allows even the largest state to be outvoted was applied to a range of policy areas, thereby narrowing the scope of national veto. The European Commission has established its supremacy over the ministries and the European Court of Justice has established its jurisdiction over the judiciaries of the member-states. The result is that now the European Union "has both inter-governmental and federal features."[30]

---

28. John D. Lees: *The Political System of the United States* (London: Faber and Faber, 1969), p. 49.
29. Andrew Heywood: *Political Theory: An Introduction*, p, 111.
30. *ibid.*, p. 114.

Some Important Statements about Federalism

Federalism in the West has always been associated with liberalism. It has been gradually assumed that the two orders of government (national and regional) that comprise the federation must enjoy the freedom that is associated with liberal principles.

– Doughlas V. Verney

International society exists when a group of states, conscious of certain common interests and common values, form a society in the sense that they conceive themselves to be bound by a common set of rules in their relations with another and share in the working of common institutions.

– Hedley Bull

Global governance is multi-layered and pluralistic, embracing a significant range of actors. International society as a form of world order may be understood as a situation in which states do more than simply coexist in an international system.

–Stephanie Lawson

Federalism has been in existence at the regional and national levels. Now in the age of globalisation, it has carved out its place at trans-national, continental or international levels. The member-states of an organisation (as the EU) may boast of their willing association with it which they may quit as per their will. But the facts speak otherwise. National interest demands its harmonisation with international interest and so a member-state would hardly like to quit such an organisation in the face of its political and economic compulsions. More and more nation-states of Europe are in the race to join it, none has so far talked about renouncing its membership. Progress leads to more progress, it cannot be pushed in the reverse direction. Once city-state, then feudal state, then nation-state and now a trans-national state. Further move in the same direction would lead to a bigger state based on the principles of federalism. It may be hoped that the obstructions and the contradictions would be surmounted by the human genius. It is well observed: "Inevitably, nationalism, regionalism and globalism would be dialectically inter-related with contradictions and complimentarities."[31]

Critical Appraisal

Finally, we may look into the merits and demerits of a federal system. Since it is opposed to the unitary or centralised system of government, the merits of one are the demerits of another and *vice versa*. First, we discuss the case for federalism :

1. Under a federal system, small states may unite themselves into a more powerful commonwealth and thereby obtain certain manifest advantages, both internal and external, which flow from the union without at the same time wholly surrendering their separate existences and sacrificing their right to govern themselves in respect to matters which concern them alone. It, thus, combines the advantages of national unity with those of local autonomy and the right of self-government. In return for this advantage, the people are reconciled to the loss of power which they attain through the delegation to the central government of the authority to regulate certain affairs of general interest to all the states composing the union. It furnishes

31. M.P. Singh: "The Impact of Global and Regional Integration" In B.D. Dua and M.P. Singh (eds.): *Indian Federalism in the New Millennium* (Delhi: Manohar, 2003), p. 381.

the means of maintaining an equilibrium between the centrifugal and centripetal forces in a state of widely different tendencies.[32]

2. It is the only political system which makes it possible to have uniformity of legislation, administration and adjudication throughout the country in respect to those matters concerning which uniformity is desirable and, at the same time, makes possible diversity where it is desirable by reason of the varying conditions and standards which prevail in different parts of the country. It is, therefore, adapted to states of vast area and diversity of conditions and also to those small ones whose people are separated by racial, geographical and other barriers and who can be reconciled to live under a common regime only when they are permitted a certain degree of autonomy.[33]
3. By permitting the inhabitants of each component state a large measure of self-government, their interest in public affairs is stimulated; they are better qualified for determining their own policies and regulating their own local affairs than uninformed, over-burdened, distantly removed bureaucrats are; and in consequence of the division of competence, the central authorities—legislative and administrative—are relieved of the burdens and congestion which oppress them where the unitary system prevails.[34]
4. The component units may experiment with new legislative and administrative approaches to the constantly changing problems presented by a technological age, and often such laboratory experiments by a single state serve as a guide for federal legislation.[35]
5. A federal system provides a model for world government. If the dreams of those who are contemplating a design for one world, one state, one government, one citizenship and the like are to be realised, the pattern of international administration would be possible on the federal lines.[36]

A federal system has its own weaknesses, inherent as well as circumstantial, which may be enumerated as under :

1. It is a weak government on account of the division of powers between the centre and the units. Thus, in times of national crisis it faces numerous difficulties. The central government is not powerful enough to deal with all fissiparous tendencies that entail from the distribution of authority between two coordinate governments.
2. A federal system creates a twilight zone that becomes a source of unnecessary complexity and confusion. There is duplicity of legislation, administration, taxation, adjudication and the like. It entails heavy expenditure at the cost of the tax-payer. There arise so many situations when the federal government "may lack constitutional authority to act, yet where action by individual states may be futile without concerted action by all of them. Such uniform state action is difficult, if not impossible, to achieve, particularly where individual states see a short-run advantage in nonconformity."[37]
3. It is said that many problems of a federal system may be solved by making necessary changes in the constitution of the state. But this cannot be done so easily, because the process of constitutional amendment is deliberately made rigid and cumbersome. Where the amending process is difficult

32. See J.W. Garner, *op. cit.,* pp. 417-18.
33. *ibid.,* p. 418.
34. *ibid.*
35. C.C. Rodee, T.J. Anderson and C.Q. Christol : *Introduction to Political Science* (New York : McGraw Hill. 1957), pp. 42-43.
36. See M.M. Ball and H.B. Killough : *International Relations* (New York : The Ronald Press, 1956), p. 586.
37. Rodee and others, *op. cit.,* p. 44.

and slow, as in the United States and Switzerland, much time may elapse before urgent problems are met—if, indeed, the proposed amendment is ever ratified.

4. A federal government is a weak government and, for this reason, the fear of disintegration always remains. Any unit may challenge the authority of the Centre and thereby take to the path of secession. Only a strong centre can meet the challenge of the rebels as was done by the government of President Lincoln in America in the 1860s. Congo had a different fate in 1960 and Pakistan in 1971.
5. A federal state cannot pursue a vigorous foreign policy because of its likely repercussions on the attitudes of the governments of the units. For instance, the American states by virtue of their reserved powers over the rights of person and property, may create difficulties for the central government by making laws affecting the aliens.

It is true that a federal system has its own points of strength and weakness, a plausible conclusion would be that, in spite of several inherent difficulties, it alone is suited for the countries having a vast area and/or diversity in respect of racial, religious, linguistic and cultural factors. It is for this salient reason that several countries of the world have adopted it. In such a country, only a federal system provides solution to the major problems of the people and they feel 'less danger from the rise of a despotic centralised government, usurping their rights'.[38]

38. See James Bryce : *The American Commonwealth,* Vol. I, Chapters 29-30.

PART II

POLITICAL INSTITUTIONS AND STRUCTURES

A people may be unwilling or unable to fulfil the duties which a particular form of government requires of them. A rude people, though in some degree alive to the benefits of civilised society, may be unable to practise the forbearance which it demands ... In such a case, a civilised government, to be really advantageous to them, will require to be in considerable degree despotic; to be one over which they donot themselves exercise control, and which imposes a great amount of forcible restraint upon their action.

—John Stuart Mill[1]

The subject of politics, like the subject of justice, is inherently a diffuse, multi-faceted human concern. Those who aspire to excessive rigor of definition within it risk irrelevance, It is precisely because of this ambiguity of political terminology that we need to supplement our knowledge of the input *side of politics of how the system* works*—ostensibly—with evidence of what it actually* does. *The latter is, in part, an empirical verification of the former.*

—Alexander J. Groth[2]

Democracy, in effect, shields the inner life of the community from the necessarily brusque actions of government . The state is a tool of the greater society: the ultimate meaning of democracy is that (in Henry Thoreau's phrase) men should not become the 'tools of their tools'.

—Bernard E. Brown[3]

1. Mill : *Considerations on Representative Government* (London : Parker Son and Bourne, 1861, reprinted by Chicago : Regners, 1962), Ch 1.
2. Groth : *Comparative Politics : A Distributive Approach* (New York : Macmillan, 1971), p. 9.
3. Brown : *New Directions in Comparative Politics* (Bombay : Asia Pub, 1962), p. 77.

16

Party Politics

> The study and analysis of political parties constitutes a new branch of science. It occupies an intermediate field between the social, the philosophico-psychological, and the historical disciplines, and may be termed a branch of applied sociology. In view of the present development of political parties, the historical aspect of this new branch of science has received considerable attention. Works have been written upon the history of almost every political party in the Western world. But when we come to consider the analysis of the nature of party, we find that the field has hardly been touched.
>
> **—Robert Michcls[1]**

The discussion of political parties and pressure groups forms part of a wider study of the subject of politics for the reason that it takes one beyond the traditional range of political theory and practice in its past and present forms. Much is included here what. in contravention of the traditional political theory, comes within the disciplines of psychology and sociology. In recent years this study has become so important and interesting that a new title of 'stasiology' has come into prominence.[2] Traditional analyses and statements of writers on the subject of party politics have mostly outlived their significance in view of the fact that much has come to be studied within this discipline that forms part of sister disciplines known by the names of political sociology or sociological politics and political psychology or psychological politics. It reveals an uncompromising unwillingness on the part of modern political scientists to ignore what was formerly regarded as 'beyond the scope of constitutional framework'; it instead demands adoption of new approaches and techniques, though extensively and indiscriminately borrowed from other disciplines like sociology and psychology, to understand and evaluate those socio-economic forces which influence the mechanism of modern government and the underlying significance of their operation that naturally makes the study of formal political structures an affair of secondary importance. It is owing to such realisation that in 1958 a great English writer like Sir Ivor Jennings regretted his inability (in the preface to the second edition of his celebrated work on Parliament) to write just a sketchy chapter on the momentous subject of party politics in his country, since it required a comprehensive treatment of the complex phenomenon of 'political emotions'.

Party Politics : Momentous Importance of the Subject in Recent Times

Political parties have become like a common feature of our daily life. However, the puzzling,

1. Michels : *Political Parties : A Sociological Study of the Oligarchical Tendencies of Modern Democracy,* Translated from German into English language by Eden & Cedar Paul, (New York : Dover Pub, 1959), pp. viii-ix.
2. It is a term meaning scientific study of party politics. It originates from a Greek word *stasis* which means a faction interested in 'sedition' or 'destruction'. Stasiology implies a scientific study of party politics with special emphasis on the role of factions and groups operating within political parties so as to have a thoroughly empirical study of the subject.

as well as interesting, point in this direction is that they "are both taken for granted and constantly criticised, continuously discussed and unsystematically assessed. Events lead us to pass judgment on the life of the parties, both at home and abroad, but always or nearly always from a Lilliputian viewpoint. If a local party takes a decision which we donot like, we are apt to generalise about 'lack of democracy'. If a Third World party is created or maintained by a strong charismatic leader, we are quick to make the point that it is merely the mouthpiece of this leader. When parties are swept away by the army, we notice that they are the means by which corrupt politicians can organise patronage. If some event demonstrates the extent of restrictions on freedom in an Eastern country, we conclude that Communist parties are but the instruments of ruthless dictatorship."[3]

It may be asked at this stage as to what factors have played their part in enhancing the importance of the study of political parties in recent times. For this, certain factors may be highlighted that have not only laid focus on the importance of this subject but also informed the students of political science and political sociology to lay down certain empirical theories on this subject. These are:[4]

1. At the very outset, reference should be made to the movement of behaviouralism in the United States in the post-Second World War phase emphasising insistence on data and theory, use of new scientific methods and techniques and the degree of faith in the possibility of establishing more general laws or explanations regarding political phenomena. Moreover, despite some initial rigidity and excessive evangelical zeal, there has appeared ample room for a large variety of approaches, themes and methods.
2. The fact of internationalisation of the study of political parties may be described as another important factor in this connection. Prior to the Second World War, the study of this subject was 'culture bound'. The lion's share of attention was devoted to the political parties of the advanced European and American countries. An important change took place after the Second World War when the students of this subject took an increasing interest in the party politics of undeveloped and developing countries of the Third World. An interesting development, in this direction, should be studied in the role of one-party system that in the beginning looked like a contradiction in terms to the political scientists of the Western countries. Naturally, it broadened the vistas of study and these events, in the context of stricter scientific perspectives and aspirations, became both meaningful and directive.
3. The subject of party politics came to be examined in the perspectives of the rise and fall of parties. It led to the emergence of 'developmental approach' in this important direction. It informed more and more students to study the subject of party politics in the light of its integrative and disintegrative aspects. It also enthused them to study this subject in the context of increasing saliency of issues, declining hold of the parties on the legislative bodies and instead enhancing position of the executive departments.

Obviously, these factors or trends "began to combine in ways that were unanticipated and to produce both concrete events and scholarly findings that shattered key articles of the conventional wisdom and left professional observers doubtful as to how to interpret the present or forecast the future."[5]

As pointed out above, the most attractive feature of the study of political parties now is

3. Jean Blondel : *Political Parties : A Genuine Case for Discontent* (London : Wildwood House, 1978), p. vii.
4. Louis Maisel and Joseph Cooper : *Political Parties : Development and Decay* (London : Sage Publications, 1978), Vol. 4, pp. 8-9.
5. *ibid.*, p. 9.

the use of new theories, some of which may be referred to as under:[6]

1. ***Developmental Theory*** : Also known by the name of modernisation theory, it is particularly concerned with the dynamics of party politics. Here a student is concerned with the case of systemic crises (covering the themes of nation-building, industrialisation, mass mobilisation, etc.) or with the notion of broad systemic needs and functions (as integration, legitimisation, conflict management, etc.) and, finally, with the idea of systemic loads or their burdens imposed by the order in which the system operates. However, one difficulty in the comprehension of this theory is that leading writers have taken a.highly normative view of the idea of 'development', conversely that of 'decay', that creates confusion to a new student of this subject. For instance, Chambers views development in terms of system characteristics, adaptive capacity, other capabilities, structural differentiation, maintenance of integration etc., Myron Weiner and Joseph la Palombara take development in terms of solving crises and meeting needs of the system. But S.P. Huntington views modernisation in terms of systemic characteristics such as rationalisation of authority, differentiated structures and mass participation.
2. ***Cleavage Theory*** : As developed by eminent writers like Upset, Rokkan and Allardt, it seeks to study party politics in terms of economic, religious, regional, urban-rural, ethnic and tribal conceptions of a legitimate authority. In other words, a student of this subject is advised to study various factors that cause cleavage in the social life of the people and have their definite impact on the operation of the party politics.
3. ***Realignment Theory*** : As contributed by eminent writers like Sandquist and Burnham, it lays emphasis on change in the levels of political participation, intensity and divisiveness of partisan feelings, distribution of political and economic power among the elites in the character of key political institutions.
4. ***Spatial Theory*** : Mainly contributed by Giovanni Sartori, it throws focus on issue divisions, approaching them in terms of economic assumptions and techniques of analysis.
5. ***Permeation Theory*** : It examines the role of various cliques, factions, elites, etc. that operate within a political party. Maurice Duverger and Daalder have tried to highlight the role of such agencies that, in fact, permeate the institutional structures of a political system as well as the results that follow from varying degrees of success.

No doubt, the utilisation of these theories has done a lot to enrich the discipline of 'stasiology', we may also refer to some more theories on this subject contributed by the Marxist writers in particular that will add to the stock of knowledge in this regard.

Broad Functional Dimension of Party Politics : The Concept of Linkage

A political party is not an isolated institution. It operates in an 'environment'. As such, a study of party politics requires its study in the context of all those forces, institutions and agencies that interact with each other. In other words, an empirical study of party politics requires that we must look into the interactions in which political parties are very much involved and, as a result of that, not only political but other dimensions of our collective life as well—say economic, social and cultural—are naturally affected. The reason for this can be traced in the fact that a political party can be put to almost any political or governmental purpose. It can articulate and aggregate demands and interests, recruit and remove leaders, make or unmake government policy,

6. *ibid.,* pp. 19-21.

carry out or obstruct the implementation of a policy decision, effect adjustment or protraction of disputes, and even go to the extent of educating or coercing the people.

One may point out that not only political parties but other non-political institutions (like religious bodies, social groups, labour unions, cultural organisations, professional entities and the like), whether public or private, also perform linkage functions. However, what distinguishes political parties from all others "is their emphasis on linkage. Parties are seen both by the members and by others as agencies for forging links between citizens and policy-makers. Their *raison d'etre* is to create a substantive connection between the rulers and the ruled."[7] The reason for this should be easily traced in the fact that the existence and operation of parties "by no means eliminates selfish and unscrupulous motives. The power-seeking drives of politicians remains constant."[8] Even if the party politician is motivated by a crude self-interest, his behaviour must depart—if the constraints of the system are operative—from the motivation-... Parties are instrumental to collective benefits of the contestants. Parties link people to government."[9]

Simply stated, the idea of linkage implies a series of connections or a chain of relationships like alignments between parties and the voters, recruitment of party leaders and legislators with the support or approval of the people or partymen and the like. It signifies a connotation of interaction. It is found that the elements linked thus behave differently from which four dimensions may be earmarked:[10]

1. **Units being linked :** The concept of linkage, as a matter of fact, has been employed to study inter-connections among all levels of government. As J.N. Rosenau says : "It leads itself to all forms of 'across system' study or to efforts to specify how and under what conditions political behaviour at one level of aggregation affects political behaviour at another level."[11] The analyst of linkage who is always ready to ignore long standing conceptual boundaries and think anew about interaction across different levels of aggregation is not content to presume that the parties that are lawful at the level of aggregation that interests him can be adequately explained by holding other levels constant. Thus, he is impelled to expand his explanatory net beyond the dynamics operative at the level of his dependent variables. Rosenau makes it clear that for him the term 'system' can be applied to any level of political life—local, national or inter-national —and he specifically sanctions the widest possible interpretation. Slightly different is the view of Prof. V.O. Key, Jr. to whom linkage refers to the interaction between mass opinion and public decisions—his units of analysis are thus individual citizens (aggregated in polls and election results or operating independently via written or personal contact with officialdom), intermediate collectives (parties and pressure groups) and government.[12]
2. **Units that instigate linkages :** Linkage may be described as a metaphor for democracy and also as a synonym for representation. As such, it includes the case of wider political participation by the people. It refers to citizen activity in constitutive processes

---

7. K. Lawson : *Political Parties and Linkage : A Comparative Perspective* (New Haven, Connecticut : Yale Univ. Press, 1980), p. 3.
8. G. Sartori : *Parties and Party Systems : A Framework for Analysis* (London : Cambridge Univ. Press, 1976), p. 25.
9. *ibid.*
10. Lawson, *op. cit.*, pp. 5-11.
11. Rosenau: "Theorising Across Systems: Linkage Politics Revisited" in Jonathan Widenfeld (ed.) : *Conflict Behaviour and Linkage Politics* (New York : David McKay, 1973), p. 25.
12. V.O. Key, Jr. : *Public Opinion and American Democracy* (New York : Alfred A. Knopf, 1964), pp. 409ff.

(like leadership recruitment, campaigning and elections) as well as in petitioning processes by organised groups. In simple terms the idea of linkage covers all units that constitute the stuff of people's role in the political process of the country.[13]

3. **Processes by which linkages are established:** Finally, we may refer to the processes by which the establishment of linkages becomes a fact. Rosenau refers to two processes in this regard that occur by means *of penetration and reaction.* The process of penetration involves two situations : (i) Governments locate their agents openly or covertly in citizen organisations. (ii) Citizens place some of their members in government via electoral processes or acts of revolution thus establishing a new government altogether. Then, it also occurs by means of *reaction* that involves three situations: (i) governments engage in acts of representative response to citizens' views on policy, (ii) governments engage in acts of coercion to which citizens must perforce respond, and (iii) governments and citizens exchange rewards for votes.[14]

However, an easier illustration of the same is offered by Prof. A.H. Somjee. It covers three important directions:[15]

1. **Interest Linkage :** It refers to various structures in a society that interact and articulate their respective interests. Party organisations, in order to have the support of different social structures formulate programmes balancing the demands of such organisations. Parties also become the supplier of information and bring together unacquainted individuals who share political beliefs, interests and aspirations.
2. **Normative Linkage :** Shared normative perspectives provide necessary links between as well as within different systems. At the level of the political system itself, the ideals of commonwealth are provided by the ruling elite, by the media and by the exponents of party programme. These leaders of public opinion evaluate the quality of public life, identify critical issues facing the society as a whole, and inculcate new directions to take place. They also engage in mutual criticism and evaluate competing policy proposals in terms of what would lead to an improved common welfare.
3. **Operational Linkage :** Those who direct their energies to the task of building and sustaining a structure of support for their party organisations is what sustains in the last analysis a system of party linkages. Most of these hard-working activists are motivated by the hope of personal benefits. They seek their reward in the form of power, status, or material benefits and without such a pay off. The linkmen involved in the operational linkage activity are the office-holders, the party activists, and the marginals.

Obviously, the whole idea of linkage refers to the study of party politics in a democratic environment where competition is open and both the individuals and their groups play a free role in the political process of the country. We may, therefore, appreciate the view that the essence of democratic and dictatorial rule "is embodied in the daily life of the parties."[16]

---

13. Heinz Eulau and Kenneth Prewitt treat linkage as a synonymn for participatory politics. See *Labyrinths of Democracy : Adaptations, Linkages, Representation and Policies in Urban Politics* (New York : Bobbs and Merril, 1973).
14. See Lawson, *op. cit.,* pp. 205-7.
15. Somjee : "Party Linkages and Strife Accommodation in Democratic India". *ibid.,* pp. 205-7.
16. Sigmund Neumann : "Towards a Comparative Study of Political Parties" in his (ed.) : *Modern Political Parties : Approaches to Comparative Politics* (Chicago : Univ. of Chicago Press, 1956), p. 403.

Some Definitional Statements about a Political Party

A political party is a group of people organised for the purpose of winning government power, and usually displays some measure of ideological cohesion.

—**Andrew Heywood**

A political party is an association organised in support of some principles or policy which by constitutional means endeavours to make the determinant of government.

—**R.M. MacIver**

A Political party consists of a group of citizens, more or less organised, who act as a political unit and who by the use of their voting power, aim to control the government and carry out their general policies.

—**R.G. Gettell**

A political party is a more or less organised group of citizens who act together as a political unit. They share or profess to share the same opinion on public questions and by exercising their voting power towards a common end, seek to obtain control of the government.

—**Stephen Leacock**

In politics shared hatreds are almost always the basis of friendship.

—**Alexis de Tocqueville**

Meaning and Nature of a Political Party: Liberal Versus Marxist Interpretations

The institution of a political party has now assumed an honourable place after having a notorious past. The reason for this lies in the fact that now a political party is considered fundamentally different from a destructive body like a clique or a faction. The views of a critic like George Washington of the United States and Voltaire of France no longer hold good who deprecated political parties in the name of 'violence of the faction' and forces 'swallowing up the republic'. A well known authority on this subject like Giovanni Sartori, therefore, holds that now the term 'party' may be interchangeable with a 'faction', if it is not 'seditious'[17]. He goes on to say that the difference between the two is that the 'faction' applies to a *concrete group*, whereas 'party' is far more an *analytic partition*, a mental construct, than a concrete entity.[18] We may, however, distinguish between Liberal and Marxist views :

Liberal View : Though it is true that the institution of a political party has assumed a respectable place now, its meaning, nature and role are still a matter of serious debate. While the liberal view appreciates the existence and role of political parties as the agencies of organised public opinion with the help of which a political system operates, the Marxian view examines it within the framework of class antagonism. Not only this, divergence of opinion may be discovered even within the camp of the liberals. It is evident from the fact that while the English, French and Italian writers lay emphasis on the factor of'principles' on which a political party is organised and functions, the typical American view is to treat a political party just like a machine or a platform for taking part in the struggle for power on democratic lines.

17. Sartori, *op. cit.*, p. 3.
18. *ibid.*, p. 5. The classic statement of Madison in this regard is quoted by this writer who once said : "By a faction I understand a number of citizens, whether amounting to a majority or minority of the whole, who are united and activated by some common impulse of passion, or of interest, adverse to the rights of other citizens, or to the permanent and aggregate interests of the community." *ibid.*, pp. 11-12.

The typical English view as contained in the classic affirmation of Edmund Burke signifies that a political party "is a body of men united for promoting the national interest on some particular principles in which they are all agreed."[19] Reiterating the same idea, Disraeli described political party as 'a group of men banded together to pursue certain principles.'[20] Likewise, Benjamin Constant says that a party "is a group of men professing the same political doctrine."[21] This view is not shared by a majority of the leading American writers who deliberately avoid reference to the sanctity of 'principles' and treat political party as an 'instrument'for taking part in the struggle for power. For instance, a leading writer like Schattschneider ridicules the English notion as symbolised by Burke. He uses a new phraseology by observing that a political party "is first of all an organised attempt to get power, but it is equally just to say that parties are held together by the cohesive power of public plunder."[22]

When we refer to the American notion of a political party, we find that a political party is regarded as a vote-catching machine or an agency to mobilise people's support for a candidate at the polls, or an instrument for the aggregation of interests that demand their vociferous articulation. Thus, Sigmund Neumann suggests : "We define a political party generally as the articulate organisation of society's active political agents, those who are concerned with the control of governmental power and who compete for popular support with another group or groups holding divergent views. As such, it is the great intermediary which links social forces and ideologies to official governmental institutions and relates them to political action within the larger political community."[23]

Such a notion of a political party makes it hardly distinguishable from a pressure or interest group. A 'specific' interest may constitute the foundation of a political party. Thus, differences between or among political parties may be sought on the basis of different specific interests. For this reason, Dean and Schuman observe that political parties have become essentially political institutions "to implement the objectives of interest groups."[24] A similar vein may be discovered in the interpretation of Crotty who says : "A political party is a formally organised group that performs the functions of educating the public-.that recruits and promotes individuals for public office, and that provides a comprehensive linkage function between the public and governmental decision-makers. It is distinguished from other groups by its dedication to influencing policy-making on a broad scale, preferably by controlling government and by its acceptance of institutionalised rules of electoral conduct more specifically capturing public office through peaceful means."[25]

Since political parties play a very crucial role in the working of a democratic system, a workable definition of the term finds its succinct manifestation in its part in the struggle for power through the battle of the ballot box. Thus, Epstein treats political party as "any group seeking votes under a recognised label."[26] Harold Lasswell in his *The World Revolution of*

19. Burke : *Thoughts on the Causes of the Present Discontent,* p. 16.
20. See J. Jupp : *Political Parties* (London: Routledge and Kegan Paul, 1968), p. 2.
21. See Maurice Duverger : *Political Parties : Their Organisation and Activity in the Modern State,* Translated from French into English language by Barbara and Robert North (London : Methuen, 1964), p. xiv.
22. E.E. Schattschneider : *Party Government* (New York : Holt, Rinehart and Winston, 1942), pp. 35-37.
23. Neumann, *op. cit.,* p. 396.
24. Cited in David E. Apter : "Political Parties" in Eckstein and Apter (eds.) : *Comparative Politics : A Reader* (New York : Free Press of Glencoe, 1963), p. 328.
25. William J. Crotty : "Political Parties Research" in Michael Hass and Henry S. Kariel (eds.) : *Approaches to the Study of Political Science* (New York : Chandler, 1970), p. 294.
26. L.B. Epstein : *Political Parties in Western Democracies* (New York : Praeger, 1967), p. 9.

our Time says : "For many purposes, it is enough to define a political party as an organisation specialised with regard to presenting candidates and issues under its own name in elections."[27] Likewise, in another book *A Framework for Political Enquiry* (written in collaboration with Kaplan), he says that a political party "is a group formulating comprehensive issues and submitting candidates in elections."[28] Riggs also takes a structural view of the role of a political party and then identifies it with "any organisation which nominates candidates for elections to an elected assembly."[29]

In brief, the whole notion of a political party, as conceived and developed mainly by the American political theorists is based on the classic affirmation of Schumpeter that a party is not a group of men who intend to promote.public welfare upon some principles on which they are all agreed (as said by Burke), rather it "is a group whose members propose to act in concert in the competitive struggle for political power."[30] A simplified version of the same is available in the interpretation of Myron Weiner and Joseph la Palombara who hold that by the term 'political party', "we do not mean a loosely-knit group of notables with limited and intermittent relationships to local counterparts. Our definition requires instead, (1) continuity in organisation, that is organisation whose life-span is not dependent upon the life-span of current leaders; (2) manifest and presumably permanent organisation at the local level with regularised communications and other relationships between local and national units; (3) self-conscious determination of leaders at both national and local levels to capture and to hold decision-making power alone or in coalition with others, not simply to influence the exercise of power, and (4) the concern on the part of the organisation for seeking followers at the polls or in some manner striving for popular support."[31]

From what we have said above, following essential features of a political party may be earmarked so as to offer a comprehensive meaning of this term :

1. A political party is not a loosely-knit organisation of some persons. It is required that the members of a political party must be organised on some specific principles or interests in a tight manner so that the party may be distinguished from any oligarchical entity.
2. There must be close and intimate relationship among all the members of a party. An intermittent relationship between the 'lords' and the 'vassals' does not constitute a party in this sense.
3. There must be a clear line of distinction between 'principles' and 'personalities'. Despite the weighty influence of the personalities of a few leaders, the life of the party must not depend upon the life of its members.
4. The leaders of a party must endeavour and struggle for maximising their base of popular support and legitimising the circle of the decision-makers.
5. In the end, a party must adopt constitutional means for the seizure of power so as to implement its policies and programmes, or to protect and promote some specific interests.

Keeping all these features in view, Jean Blondel observes that political parties "are groupings but groupings of a particular kind.

27. See Jupp, *op. cit., p. 3.*
28. See Sartori, *op. cit.,* p. 62.
29. F.W. Riggs : *Administrative Reforms and Political Responsiveness : A Theory of Dyndmic Balancing* (London : Sage Pub., 1970), p. 580.
30. Schumpeter : *Capitalism, Socialism and Democracy* (New York : Harper, 1942), p. 283.
31. Joseph la Palombara and Myron Weiner (eds.) : *Political Parties and Political Development* (Princeton : Princeton Univ. Press, 1966), p. 3.

Clearly it is not sufficient to say that they are 'political', while other groups are not: politics being a procedure, a body is political only to the extent that it participates in the procedure of solution of conflicts."[32] He further says: "It is because aims are general and membership open that the parties want to take power and are highly politicised. They donot confine themselves to a limited number of issues; they are interested in all national decisions. They cannot, therefore, be confined to intermittent influence, but are concerned with overall influence."[33]

Marxist View : The Marxist view of a political party and its role is quite different from one we have seen above. Here the liberal emphasis on party as a 'doctrine' has been replaced by the idea of a party as a 'class' that will fight for inaugurating a new era culminating in the phase of 'communism'. Developing the idea of Marx in the name of making it uptodate, Lenin says that the proletariat "has no weapon in the struggle for power except organisation....Constantly pushed down to the depths of complete poverty, the proletariat can and will inevitably become an unconquerable force only as a result of this: that its ideological union by means of the principles of Marxism is strengthened by the material union of an organisation, holding together millions of toilers in the army of the working class."[34]

Thus, Lenin made his own contribution to the development of Marxism in the twentieth century. If Marx said that the fact of exploitation at the hands of bourgeoisie would force the working class to develop the necessary 'consciousness' that would act as the force to take them to the path of a revolution, Lenin modified the idea by adding that an organisation of the proletariat would play a crucial part in arousing class consciousness and thereby creating a revolution. In this way, as Sabine says, the communist party "becomes a staff organisation in the struggle of the proletarian class for power, and Marxism is the creed that holds it together, the guide of its action, and the subject-matter by which it extends the circle of class-consciousness. Ideal union through the principles of Marxism and material union through rigid organisation and discipline were the two foundation stones on which, from the beginning of his career, Lenin proposed to build a revolutionary movement."[35]

Lenin described the communist party as the 'vanguard of the revolution' for the working class. It is evident from the text of a resolution adopted at the Congress of Communist International in 1920 that *inter alia* said : The communist party is a part of the working class: its most progressive, most class-conscious and, therefore, most revolutionary part. "The communist party is created by means of the selection of the best, most class-conscious, most self-sacrificing and far-sighted workers.. The communist party is the lever of political organisation, with the help of which the more progressive part of the working class directs on the right path the whole mass of the proletariat and the semi-proletariat along the right road."[36]

It is clear that a political party is an instrument whereby the working class develops class consciousness so as to overthrow the bourgeois order. Lenin's theory of party, in addition to this, has a more formidable characteristic. The party is not only the 'vanguard' of the working class, it alone is the custodian of all power and any opposition to

32. J. Blondel : *An Introduction to Comparative Government* (London : Weidenfeld and Nicolson, 1969), p. 100.
33. *ibid.*, p. 102. A well-known American writer like J.S. Coleman says : "Political Parties are associations formally organised with the explicit and declared purpose of acquiring and/or maintaining legal control, either singly or in coalition or electoral competition with other similar associations, over the personnel and the policy of the government of an actual or prospective sovereign state." J.S. Coleman and C.G. Rosberg : *Political Parties and National Integration in Tropical Africa* (Berkeley : University of California Press', 1964), p. 2.
34. Lenin's *One Step Forward, Two Steps Backward* (1904) cited in G.H. Sabine *A History of Political Theory*, p. 724.
35. *ibid.*
36. Jane Degras (ed.) : *The Communist International, 1919-43, Selected Documents* (London. 1956), Vol I, p. 28.

it is, for this reason, visited with severe punishment. The communist party stands on the principle of 'democratic centralism'. It means two things. First, the party is a hierarchy in which members of the higher ranks are elected by those of the lower ranks. Moreover, all units have intra-party democracy whereby the members may discuss and debate matters at their organisational level and also elect and remove their office bearers. Second, the lower organs are bound to follow the decrees given by the higher unit with the result that power is centred at the top. A very small band of the arch-leader and his most trusted followers constitute a clique that holds unlimited and absolute power. A critic may, therefore, point out that "the communist-type organisation is, in fact, a structure or *vertical centralism.* Its secret is to sever horizontal communication lines, and especially descending ones. No democratic party has been able, or shown as yet the desire, to go that far."[37]

It may also be taken note of that, in the view of Lenin, the emphasis is not only on the leader or his most trusted followers, it also covers the position of the 'militants'. Thus, an 'inner circle' becomes everything what we can identify with the elite of communist party. On this point, Maurice Duverger well observes: "The ideas of Lenin seem to concern not only the leaders but also the militants. In practice, in so far as the latter are maintained by the party, they are naturally given positions of control, because they alone dispose of sufficient leisure to fill these positions effectively. To create a 'class of professional revolutionaries' is equivalent to creating a 'class of professional leaders of revolutionary parties', an inner circle which stirs up the masses and which is founded upon the official duties performed within the party; it is equivalent to (creating a bureaucracy, that is to say an oligarchy. If the posts for party's permanent officials were strictly elective, bureaucracy could coincide with democracy. But this is not so and cannot be so: the militants who are capable of filling a permanent position and willing to do so are not very numerous; the leaders of the party are anxious to keep close control of them so as to be certain of their technical ability and of their political trustworthiness: the leadership is largely made up of permanent officials already in office. Thus, there is born an authentic oligarchy which exercises power, retains it, and transmits it by means of co-option."[38]

We may, or may not, agree with the Marxian view of a political party, its nature and structure, its *raison d' etre* and the issue of militant leadership and the like, it is certain that this view is basically different from its liberal counterpart. It has ample material for research on the subject of party politics as prevailing in different countries of the world. It has its own significance in a perspective of comparative politics. Even a critic like Duverger has admitted that the Marxist schema "is true in one respect: the 'bourgeoisie' and the 'proletariat' donot perhaps constitute two classes, defined in strictly economic terms, but they characterise two states of mind, two social attitudes and two ways of life, the distinction between which throws light on certain problems concerned with the structure of parties."[39]

---

37. Giovanni Sartori, *op. cit.,* p. 96.
38. Duverger, *op. cit.,* p. 155.
39. *ibid.,* p. xv. The Marxian view of a political party is not appreciated by the liberal writers who refuse to find out the basis of a political party and its role in the fact of class antagonism. They contend that most of the parties are not based on 'classes' except in the rather tenuous sense that a majority of social class may vote for one party in preference to another. It is said that the Leninists "have tried to solve the dilemma by arguing that non-Marxist working class parties are objectively serving" the interests of the bourgeoisie. This definition juggling is hardly tenable. It is particularly difficult to sustain for the very large number of parties in the under-developed world which are clearly based on religions, tribes or language groups. All that it leads to is a scientifically spurious application of labels like 'national bourgeoisie' which are changed to 'progressive forces' when Soviet foreign policy demands it." Jupp. *op. cit.,* p. 3.

Horizontal and Vertical Elements of a Political Party : Duverger's Thesis on its Organisation and Membership: Case of Interior and Exterior Parties

A study of the organisation and membership of a political party may be made on certain scientific lines without delving deep into essential differences between Liberal and Marxian interpretations of the meaning and nature of a party. The contribution of Maurice Duverger has an importance of its own in this regard who has taken the view that a political party "is not a community but a collection of communities, a union of small groups, dispersed throughout the country (branches, caucuses, local associations etc.) and linked by co-ordinate institutions."[40] In other words, he takes a very comprehensive view of the horizontal and vertical elements of a political party. He includes every organisation operating through a party by terming it an 'indirect party' the examples of which can be found in numerous groups, associations, unions, corporations, professional bodies, etc. In this way, while for example, the Labour Party of England is a 'direct party' in a superficial sense, it is made up of numerous labour unions that, in themselves, bear the stamp of an 'indirect party'. Not only this, an empirical examination of the organisation and working of a political party shows the role of several 'inner circles' that may be termed caucuses, cells, branches, militia, etc. Moreover, it is their meaningful role that enables us to distinguish between democratic, fascist and communist variants of a political party.

Keeping this in view, Duverger says about the following elements of a party's organisation:[41]

1. **Caucus :** Identifiable with a small unit like clique, core committee, coterie and the like, it is a very small entity having a 'limited nature'. Its size is deliberately kept as small as possible. Its strength does not depend upon the number of its key members but upon the quality they possess. It is, indeed, a group of notabilities chosen because of their influence. It plays a very important part in the decision-making process, though it reaches its peak on the eve of elections. Thus, it may be likened with an institutional elite. Caucuses may be of 'direct' and 'indirect types.' They belong to the first category (as in the case of French Radical Socialists) where they are composed of 'notabilities' chosen for their individual qualities and personal influence; they belong to the second one where (as in the case of Republican and Democratic parties of the United States) they are composed of the 'experts' in the art of fighting elections.
2. **Branch :** It designates a basic element which is less centralised than a caucus. While the latter deliberately seeks to live away from the masses, the former appeals to them and also appreciates its growing proximity with them. It is by and large an invention of the Socialist parties which desire to maintain their intimate touch with the people at large. It is found that the leaders of the Socialist parties come to the branch members and talk about their problems and then a free exchange of ideas takes place. An attempt is also made to recruit more and more members with the help of branch organisations and to disseminate political education among the people. The result is that the branches of a political party become very important in the day-to-day functioning of the party. Besides, its impact upon the people in general is so abiding that they see in politics a means of bettering their position. In this way, branch system corresponds to the working class mentality.
3. **Cell :** It is an invention of the Fascist and Communist parties where the 'occupational' units of the ruling party are scattered in every nook and corner of the

40. Duverger, *op. cit.,* p. 17.
41. *ibid.,* pp. 17ff.

country and every cell has a much greater hold on its members than the caucus or a branch. The members of a cell carry much importance than the members of a party. The secretary of a cell can control the activity of his unit by virtue of his strong influence. The party solidarity is also very strong, because cell is a unit of about a dozen members or so who know each other intimately. Above all, the cells have an ideological orientation and they are a source of every clandestine action. The entire network of the cells is controlled by the highest unit of the party composed of the 'real decision-makers at the top'.

4. **Militia :** The Fascist party of Mussolini in Italy and the Nazi party of Hitler in Germany (and so Communist Party of China under Mao) made another experiment by taking militia as the basis of their party's organisation. Mention may be made of Hitler's Storm Troopers, Mussolini's Shock Troops and Mao's Red Guards. The members of these organisations remain civilians, though they are given military training, wear prescribed uniforms, hold party flags and act at the behest of the party leaders working under the supreme command of the chief of the organisation. It is a kind of private army of the party in power sufficient to combat and finish the enemies inside the country.

The whole idea of Duverger is contained in his affirmation: "The branch allows only a slack, superficial, intermittent discipline; the cell, on the contrary, because of its size and its permanence, ensures a regular, tight and sound discipline. It is certain that the work of the cells deters many from becoming its members. They prefer the branch debates. But these are precisely the less good, the less sincere, the less dependable members. The others, on the contrary, find in the cells, a means of immediate, precise, serious action as well as a means of education. The cell system certainly constitutes one element in the strength of the Communist parties. But it will be seen that because of it the centre of gravity of political action is changed. The caucus is essentially an electoral and parliamentary organisation, an instrument suited for winning over electors and bringing pressure to bear on those elected; it makes it possible to organise an election and to put citizens in touch with their representative."[42]

Besides, the concept of 'membership' has its own relevance in a study of political party. It is true that every party has a very large number of its own members, but the nature of the membership varies from one system to another. For instance, the membership of a democratic party is quite different in nature when it is compared with a totalitarian party, whether of the right or of the left. Keeping it in view, Duverger says about two types of parties:

1. **Cadre Party :** It is a grouping of notabilities who constitute the structure of a political party. It believes in the principle of 'selection'. The notable figures take a very important part in the formulation of its policies and programmes, nomination of candidates for elections, prosecution of electoral campaigns, collection of funds for the party and the like. Here quality is the most important factor. Prestige of a person, his expertness in the techniques of fighting elections and his power of gathering financial sinews for the organisation count very much. Not only this, such people prepare a sort of cadre for the party whose support for it at the time of elections is a foregone conclusion. Reference, in this direction, may be made to the Communist parties that have a cadre of their own in the influential figures of labour and peasant organisations.

2. **Mass Party :** The growth of franchise is responsible for converting cadre parties into mass parties to a very great extent. Different from a cadre party, a mass party is one that believes in the principle of 'election' so as

42. *ibid.*, p. 35.

to win the title of popular legitimacy. It tries to enrol more and more members and act with their confidence and consultation. The membership is an open affair that is available to every one who subscribes to its basic policy. Regular subscription is the source of its finances and the vast size of its membership is the stuff of its activity. In this way, mass party technique replaces the capitalist financing of electioneering by democratic financing.

Studied from a critical angle, while we may appreciate the overall framework of Duverger, we may find some fault with it also. The Marxists may refute his interpretation whereby a communist party belongs to the category of a cadre party on the ground that it is a people's party and its ultimate purpose is to replace the bourgeois democracy with the 'people's democracy'. It may also be said that, in modern times, electioneering has become a very costly affair. The subscription paid by the members is very meagre and no mass party can function without the help of 'political funding' from big industrialists or business magnates of the country. The difference between a cadre and a mass party, as pointed out by Duverger, for this reason, becomes irrelevant and we are ultimately forced to endorse the view of Lenin that every political party, except that of the Communists, is a bourgeois and petty bourgeois organisation.'[43]

Duverger makes a division of party system into its 'interior' and 'exterior' forms keeping in view the emergence and development of political parties in various countries of the world. The case of the interior party system represents its emergence and development in response to the growth of the trends of democratisation in the countries of the western world in particular. The extension of franchise and progressive institutionalization of parliamentary democracy enthused many conscious citizens to create small associations like Bretton Club in France. Likewise, groups inside the legislative chambers came into being to protect and promote respective interests. Owing to the enhancement of egalitarian feelings among the newly enfranchised people leading to a desire to oust traditional social elites, there came into being electoral committees to capture power of the votes even by means of their sale and purchase. As the process of democratisation in the shape of the extension of franchise went on unchecked, these groups improved their ways of organisation and working in the form of maintaining records of written rules, subscription of members, minutes of meetings and list of office-bearers, etc. Moreover, their expansion to cover other areas of the country meant their conversion into a national organisation with central, provincial, regional and local hierarchical units. Political parties thus came out of the crises.

However, externally created political parties are those which came into being and made their development to realise some revolutionary objective, or safeguard some interest—religious, communal, economic—or to fight for the achievement of national liberation. In many countries the birth of communist parties was associated with the activities of revolutionary groups and secret organisations which either succeeded in capturing power (as in Russia), or they were allowed to operate under the strict surveillance of the government, if not totally outlawed, and thereby forced to live underground. In many countries, religious and communal organisations came into being to fight for their 'interests' as Anti-Revolutionary Party of the Calvinists in Netherlands and Muslim League in India. Protection and promotion of certain economic and industrial interests led to the establishment of many organisations as Canadian Conservative Party of the Bankers of Montreal in Canada and Forum of Free Enterprise in Bombay. Lastly, people under the alien or despotic rule organised parties to win political freedom or establish a constitutional government.

43. See Bernard E. Brown : *New Directions in Comparative Politics* (Bombay : Asia Pub, 1962), pp. 81-83.

It is, therefore, obvious that while an internally created political party is one which emerges gradually from the activities of the legislators themselves, an externally created party is one that emerges outside the legislature and invariably involves some challenges to the group in power together with a strong representation. La Palombara and Weiner thus define the two terms of division : "Where the local organisation and the local parliamentary connection is established as the result of initiative exercised by those who are already in the legislature or who hold national public office, we can speak of political parties as having been created internally...Externally created parties are those that emerge outside the legislature and invariably involve some challenge to the ruling group and a demand for representation. Such parties are more recent phenomena; they are invariably associated with an expanded suffrage, strongly articulated secular or religious ideologies, and, in most of the developing areas, nationalistic and anti-colonial movements."[44]

Duverger finds three lines of distinction between 'internally' and 'externally' created parties. First, while the former develop from 'in' to 'out', the latter show the reverse tendency.[45] In the case of the former, local units widen themselves to become a national organisation; in the latter case, wider units move towards the trend of centralisation. That is, while in the former case, the local committees which are in existence first create a central organisation to co-ordinate their activity and consequently limit their powers, the extent to which the extra-parliamentary institutions creating the party is decentralised obviously has an influence on the degree of decentralisation of the latter. Second, for similar reasons, parties arising outside the cycle are generally more coherent and more disciplined than parties of electoral and parliamentary origin. The former have at their disposal an organisation already in existence which binds together all the cells at their base; the latter have all these bonds to create with no starting point than the co-existence of a few representatives within the one parliament.[46]

Last, again for some analogous reasons, the influence exercised by parliamentary groups over party organisation and policy is very different in the two types of parties. It is obviously much more in the case of interior parties than in that of the exterior ones. The attitude of the two differs radically towards their parliamentary organisations and their working. For the interior parties the winning of seats in legislative assemblies is like the supreme purpose of life; while for the exterior parties, although the electoral and parliamentary struggle remains important, it is only one of the elements in the general activity that they use to realise their political ends. For instance, for a communist party, the electoral campaigns are only one element and that too of a secondary character in an all-embracing strategy aiming at the complete seizure of power and the exercising of it in a totalitarian form.[47]

Leadership and Its Autocratic Tendency : Michels' Iron Law of Oligarchy

The issue of leadership has a relevance of its own in a study of the organisation and structure of a political party. Every party works under the stewardship of a person who "can enthuse, influence, inspire and control other persons, in such a manner that he can guide or direct the thoughts, feelings and actions of the persons he leads."[48] If power is the essential touchstone of politics and every political party takes part in the struggle for power, naturally "power

44. Joseph la Palombara and Weiner, *op. cit.*, pp. 9-10.
45. Duverger, *op. cit.*, p. xxxiv.
46. *ibid.*
47. *ibid.*, p. xxxv.
48. Suma Chitnis : "The Nature of Leadership : A Sociological Point of View" in J.W. Airan (ed.) : *The Nature of Leadership : A Practical Approach* (Bombay : Lalwani, 1968, p. 3.

and leadership become part of a system of social causation."[49] The concept of leadership now engages our attention so as to study the "relationship between an individual and a group built around some common interest and behaving in a manner directed or determined by him."[50]

"The character of leadership is 'transactional' in most of the cases, it is also of a 'transformational' type. It pertains to the former category when we find that the leader and his followers are bound to each other by the simple logic of give and take. The followers desire to follow a person who can give them expected rewards in return of the services they render by following his directives. This type of leadership is a universal phenomenon. But the higher and noble variety of the same may be discovered in the transformational aspect where the leader renders immortal service in "elevating, mobilising, inspiring, exalting, uplifting, preaching, exhorting, evangelising."'[51] The most outstanding name in this regard is that of Mahatma Gandhi who transformed the character of the Indian National Congress.

The character of political parties may be distinguished on the ground of leadership.[52] It is democratic when leaders are elected by the followers in a free and frank manner; policies are formulated by discussion and decisions are taken out of the alternatives offered by the leaders; members have freedom to choose options by means of compromise and conciliation; above all, criticism of the leaders is appreciated. Basically opposed to it is the case of totalitarian leadership where it is adulated; dissent is forbidden; leader's voice is the final voice; leader lives aloof from the rank and file; above all, leadership is personalised. On this ground we may say that, for instance, while Conservative, Liberal and Labour parties of England, Democratic and Republican parties of the United States, Indian National Congress, Janata and Bharatiya Janata parties of India may be designated as 'democratic', the Communist parties of Cuba and China, Golkar party of Indonesia and Baath party of Iraq may be put in the opposite category.

Whether it is the case of democratic or totalitarian leadership, Robert Michels has sought to prove that it is always an oligarchical affair. It always resides in the few for the simple reason that it cannot be shared by the multitude. As he says : "Leadership is a necessary phenomenon in every form of social life. Consequently it is not the task of science to inquire whether this phenomenon is good or evil, or predominantly one or the other. But there is a great scientific value in the demonstration that every system of leadership is incompatible with the most essential postulates of democracy...Now, if we leave out of consideration the gratitude of the led towards the leaders, and the general immobility and passivity of the masses, we are led to conclude that the principal cause of oligarchy in the democratic parties is to be found in the technical indispensability of leadership. The process which has begun in consequence of the differentiation of functions in the party is completed by a complex of qualities which the leaders acquire through their detachment from the mass. At the outset, leaders arise spontaneously; their functions are accessory and gratuitous. Soon, however, they become professional leaders, and in this second stage of development, they are stable and irremovable."[53]

---

49. J.M. Burns : *Leadership* (New York : Harper and Row, 1978), p. 13.
50. Richard Schmidt : "Leadership" in E.A.R. Seligman (ed.) : *Encyclopaedia of the Social Sciences* (New York : Macmillan, 1967), Vol. IX, p. 282.
51. Burns, *op. cit.*, p. 20.
52. Sigmund Neumann makes a convincing point by holding : "Just as leaders and lieutenants carry different meanings in democracies and dictatorships, so do parties also." *op. cit.*, p. 395.
53. Michels, *op. cit.*, pp. 400-01.

What Michels said in the period preceding the First World War is supported by another leading writer on this subject like Duverger in the period following the Second World War. Leadership is integrally connected with the autocracy, whether it is 'open' and thus an exception, or 'disguised' and thus a rule. By all means, the leader is a superman. It is a different matter that he may be just like a titular head when some other forces are in the background that may be described as 'second power'. Here the fact of leadership may be traced in the hands of, what the Americans call, 'bosses'. Laying special focus on the party politics of the United States, Duverger says that real leadership resides not in the hands of the party stalwarts like Wilson or Truman, it is with the bosses of the pressure groups who wield economic power. "Leadership may also fall into the hands of a 'technocratic oligarchy' in a totalitarian country (like Italy and Germany in the pre-Second World War period) where "courses are set up for leaders inside the party which one must attend before being given the post of a leader."[54]

Though Duverger has followed the line of Michels, it cannot be denied that he has also made an improvement upon it by laying down the doctrine of 'inner circle.' Distinction between democratic and non-democratic party systems can be drawn if we scrutinise the fact of "inner circle leadership" that undergoes frequent changes in the former but not in the latter categories. The non-democratic parties are highly centralised with the result that their leadership remains strongly entrenched and those who occupy the inner ring cannot be replaced unless there is some violent revolt or a coup. The supreme leader goes either with his death, or when there is a major shake-up in the ranks of the inner circle. Different from this, democratic parties stand on the principle of decentralisation as a result of which inner circle remains in a state of frequent renewal.

The most sinister dimension of leadership may, however, be seen in its 'personalised' variety. Not only in a totalitarian system but also in a system committed to a democratic model, the fact of personalised leadership may be said to have its indelible impression in most of the cases. It is all the more striking in the politics of the Third World countries where a single person identifies himself with the party or, in other words, the party is condensed in him. His voice is the voice of the party; his 'aye is the aye and naye the naye of all'. The names of Col. Nasser in Egypt, Nkrumah in Ghana, Soekarno in Indonesia, Kenyatta in Kenya, Patrice Lumumba in Congo, Abdul Rahman in Malaysia, Sihanouk in Cambodia, Ben Gurion in Israel and, to some extent, Indira in India immediately engage our attention.[55]

Three factors may be said to play an important part in this connection. First, a leader risen from the people develops a sort of autocratic tendency, because he seeks to capitalise on the myth of 'hero-worship' that supplies sustaining force in a backward country. Second, the element of efficiency also enthuses a leader to tread the path of authoritarianism. The leader renders certain useful services . to the people and thereby obliges them to obey his dictates meekly. Last, the element of 'charisma' has its own role in the countries of the Third World where the people are swayed by the exceptional qualities of a leader by which he "is set apart from ordinary men and treated as endowed with super-natural, super-human, at least superficial exceptional powers."[56]

Critical Appraisal

Following important impressions may be gathered from what we have discussed in the preceding sections :

54. Duverger, *op. cit.,* p. 155.
55. See W.A. Hannah : *Eight Nation-Makers: Southeast Asia's Charismatic Statesmen* (American Universities Field Staff, 1964).
56. See Gerth and Mills : *From Max Weber: Essays in Sociology* (New York : Oxford Univ Press. 1946), p. 328.

1. Political parties are one of the important inventions of our age. They are now an essential part of our political life. The people of an undeveloped, or of a developing, country may not know in detail as to what their parties really stand for, they at least have a general image of their policies and past records. They can choose the parties they prefer. It may also be added now that party politics cannot be finished. If a dictator outlaws party system, he has to restore the same in a different form. The examples of Egypt, Indonesia, Pakistan, Bangladesh, Myanmar etc. sustain the fact that parties re-emerge from their own ashes. "The best that the authoritarian leaders can do is to domesticate them by controlling their number, their personnel, their programme."[57]
2. The progress that has been made in the study of political parties has been attained despite continued inability to resolve a number of key conceptual problems. Most prominent among these are—how to define a party, how to classify or categorise parties and party systems, how to conceptualise the environment or context within which a party functions including the operation and impact of a party and the interaction between it and its environment. The surprising development in this regard is that, despite all these difficulties, students are engaged in making an empirical study of party politics with the aim of refining the discipline of stasiology.[58]
3. Political parties have widened their area of concern so much so that they are no longer a mere political organisation. A sociological study of a political party reveals that its ramifications cover other aspects also like social, economic and cultural. By aggregating diverse specific interests represented by pressure groups and in that way by integrating its activity with them, a political party has taken upon itself the ardous task of politicising the social and economic life. Such a role of the political parties may well be studied in the spheres of political acculturation, political modernisation and political development. It shows that, particularly in modern mass democracies, a political party "has taken on an ever-increasing area of commitments and responsibilities assuring an individual's share in society and in incorporating him into the community".[59]

Despite the fact that party politics is characterised by the hold of oligarchical and autocratic tendencies releasing a saga of undistinguished battles through which some individuals strive and hope to dislodge others and they also care little for putting into practice what they so loudly profess and proclaim, it is certain that they are the principal means by which a system of representative democracy can be introduced and maintained in modern times. They are the "main means by which demands from below and leadership from above can uneasily blend into one complex and unchanging world."[60] We may end our study with the fine observation of Jean Blondel that parties "deserve neither the praise nor the criticism which they periodically receive. It may be unrealistic to expect parties to unite a divided country, genuinely represent the population, and provide the basis for social and economic development. The oscillation between cynical criticism and exaggerated hopes may simply reflect the failure of observers to recognise that a human institution can only achieve limited results in a short period of time."[61]

---

57. Jean Blondel: *Political Parties,* p. 3.
58. Louis Masel and Joseph Cooper, *op. cit.,* p. 10.
59. Sigmund Neumann, *op. cit.,* p. 405.
60. Blondel, *op. cit.,* p. vii.
61. *ibid.,* p. 11.

17

Party System

> Instead of attending to the structure of government, many are focussing their interest upon popular participation, or what is sometimes termed the 'political process'. There is concern for political dynamics for the ways in which leaders, political parties and social groups achieve power, and a quest for the mainsprings of action unrepealed by a study of more publicised formal structures of government.
>
> **—Doughlas V. Verney[1]**

Modern representative democracy has brought about party system as an indispensable factor in every political society. It may be laid down that political party in one form or another "is omnipresent.*"[2] This fact lays stress on the maximisation of political participation by enjoining upon the members of a political elite to take the people at large in confidence either for the sake of observing the myth that 'voice of the people is the voice of God', or to justify the very legitimacy of their popular leadership and authority. It also indicates political modernisation in the sense that it calls for the involvement of more and more people into the process of, what Easton calls, the 'authoritative allocation of values'. Whether it is the rule of a single person (monarch or dictator), or of the few (assembly or elite), or even of the many, the norms of party system demand sanctity to this maxim that the masses must participate in the political affairs of the country as much as possible.

Nature and Essential Implications

Undeniable is the fact that party politics has become a universal phenomenon. Leaving aside the case of some tradition-ridden states like Saudi Arabia and Maldives, every state of the world has a party system of its own whether it pertains to a one-party model, or to a bi-party model, or to a multi-party model, or to a peculiar admixture of them. Thus, in a study of party system we have to study the network of political and para-political parties and, in addition to that, all those organisations that, in the words of Maurice Duverger, play the role of 'indirect parties'. If so, the scope of study is widened so as to include every political party whether big or small, operating at the national, regional or local level, with ideological commitment or neutrality, and the like. Giovanni Sartori has, therefore, advised us to include the following kinds of parties in a study' of the party system :[3]

1. Verney: *An Analysis of Political Systems* (London: Routledge and Kegan Paul, 1959), p. 1.
2. Joseph la Palombara and Myron Weiner : *Political Parties and Political Development* (Princeton : Princeton Univ. Press, 1966), p. 3.
3. Sartori: *Parties and Party Systems : A Framework for Analysis* (London : Cambridge Univ. Press, 1976), Vol. I, p. 327.

1. witness parties, those uninterested in maximising votes,
2. ideological parties, those interested in votes primarily via indoctrination.
3. responsible parties, which donot submit policies to maximising votes,
4. responsive parties, for which winning elections or maximising votes take priority, and
5. purely demogogic, irresponsible parties, which are only vote maximisers.

Obviously, such a view is broad enough to embrace every political party that has some place in the stasiological configuration of a country.[4]

A study of party system is, however, beset with one difficulty : a political party "is notoriously difficult to define accurately."[5] It "is not always easy to differentiate it from a faction, an interest group, or a parliamentary group which may have a life of its own independent of electoral opinion as in France, or from a political movement which may temporarily transcend a number of parties or groups as did the RPF in France, the Rassemblement Democratique Africaine, the National Union of Popular Forces in Morocco, the National Front in a number of systems"[6] As a matter of fact, the meaning of political party is so flexible that it may mean any group or organisation from one having a smaller number of members and committed to the protection and promotion of a specific interest to that having a wider base and, as Frank Sorauf in his work *Political Parties in the American System* says, organised on the basis of any incentive like patronage, obtaining special treatment by the government, career opportunists, economic benefit, personal rewards, ability to wield influence, or ideological gratification.[7] Keeping all such essential points in view, Curtis goes to the extent of saying : "Essentially, party signifies a group of people who hold certain political beliefs in common or who are prepared to support the party candidates, work together for electoral victory, attain and maintian political power."[8]

One thing is clear from what we have said above. We should not be led away by just what Burke said about two hundred years ago ; we should also take into consideration that political parties are "specialised associations whose purpose is to secure power within a corporate group for their leaders in order to attain ideal or material advantages. They may spring up within trade unions, corporations, universities, parliaments or the state itself—in which latter case they are political parties. Parties are thus specialised associations and become more complex, organised and bureaucratic as a society approaches the modern type."[9] The central object of a political organisation is to capture power either singly; or in collaboration with others. It is this goal of attaining political power that distinguishes political parties from other groups in the political system, although the distinction "is

4. On this basis, Sartori refutes the theory of Anthony Downs who assumes that "citizens in a democracy primarily act to maximise their self-interest and their utility income, that parties formulate in order to win elections, rather than win elections in order to formulate policies." If so, the primary object of politicians is to 'be elected.' *An Economic Theory of Democracy* (New York : Harper & Row, 1957), pp. 28-30. The mistake of Downs is that he assumes parties to be 'teams' and indeed coherent and unified teams rather than largely disconnected and multi-faceted coalitions. Sartori, *op. cit.*, p. 327.
5. Michael Curtis : *Comparative Government and Politics* (New York : Harper and Row, 1968), p. 136.
6. *ibid.*
7. *ibid.*, p. 37.
8. *ibid.*
9. Bernard E. Brown : *New Directions in Comparative Politics* (Bombay : Asia Pub. House, 1962), p. 21. Keeping this difficulty in view, Louis Masel and Joseph Cooper point out : "Equally important, the distinctions ultimately established between parties and other political groups—*e.g.* factions and interest groups—are highly relative with the result that the universe of groups remains exceedingly kaleidoscopic in character." *Political Parties : Development and Decay* (London : Sage Publications, 1978), Vol. 4, p. 11.

rather blurred at times, especially in regard to pressure groups."[10]

It is, therefore, a hard job to differentiate between a political party and a pressure group in all cases. There are certain borderline situations where we find the two being analogous to each other. For example, the Irish Nationalists in the House of Commons before 1918, or the poorly represented Welsh Plaid Cymru and Scottish Nationalist groups today display many of the characteristics of both a political party and a pressure group. The weaknesses of the party systems in most of the undeveloped countries of the world add to our difficulty in this regard. One may say that the Shiva Sena in Maharashtra is not a political party but a pressure group, or one may call it a political party in view of its 'open' political commitments and activities.

The difference between a political party and a pressure group may, however, be made on a conceptual plane. It may be said that a political party is an organisation of numerous people who are openly committed on broad matters of public policy and they want to assume direct responsibility for their policies by seeking to monopolise or share with other parties in a position of political power. Contrary to this, a pressure group does the work of interest articulation and strives to protect and promote its specific interest through governmental agencies without being ready to assume direct responsibility for the same. It plays the game of hide and seek in politics. The difference between the two is thus borne out by Neumann : "Fundamentally, pressure groups are the representation of homogeneous interests seeking influence. The interest group is strong and effective when it has a direct specific purpose. Political parties, on the other hand, seeking office and directed towards policy decisions, combine heterogeneous groups. In fact, it is one of their major themes to reconcile the diverse forces within political society. Theirs is an integrative function which is not the domain of the interest groups".[11]

Determinants and Functions of a Political Party

Manifold are the determinants of the party structure. They vary from religious and social to economic and political. Certain political parties are associated with a religious faith like the MRP in France, Christian Democrats in Italy and Germany, Christian People's Party in Norway, Protestant and Catholic Parties in Holland, Muslim League and Hindu Maha Sabha in India and Komei-to (political wing of the Soka Gakkai) in Japan. There are some parties depending on ethnic or racial connection such as Tamil Federal Party in Sri Lanka, People's Progressive Party of the East Indians and People's National Congress largely composed of the Negroes in Guyana. Some political parties may be based on sub-nationalism as Flemmish Nationalists in Belgium, or on the factor of linguistic chauvinism as Radical Party in France. In some cases, caste may play the role of a determinant as we find in the case of DMK and A-IADMK in India. It is also found that some political parties are held together by a clique led by an attractive leader, or by patronage as Maurice Duplessis and the United National in the province of Quebec in Canada : some look largely as a receptacle for those disenchanted with other major parties such as Social Credit Party of Canada. There may also be parties like a confederation of various socio-economic groups or various regional organisations like the Mapai of Israel and the Liberal Party of Australia.

Though the determinants of party structure may be different, they may be reduced to three main factors—historical, socio-economic and

10. A.R. Ball : *Modern Politics and Government* (London : Macmillan, 1978), II Ed.,-p. 102.
11. *ibid.*, pp. 102-3.

ideological. In the first place, historical factors are of great importance in the determination of party structures. Parties are the conditions of modern political processes and their emergence presupposes a necessary degree of urbanisation and development of mass communications. It is the extension of franchise that leads to the creation of political parties. As the process of suffrage grows, the organisation of political parties has a wider and still wider base. The National Union of England, for example came into being as a result of the conditions after the implementation of the First Reform Act of 1832. Thus, political parties "arise when historical changes occur and these are not subject to scientific laws. Therefore, the development of parties is more haphazard and uneven than general classifications make apparent. Certainly particular changes are necessary such as the need for the dominant political elites to seek wider political support, and for a significant change in the political attitudes."[12]

Second, the socio-economic factor has a significance of its own. The level of economic development influences the nature of party competition. We may find that there is a different response to urban and rural societies and to those in which class conflict is a significant aspect of the political process. In a liberal-democratic state parties with a totalitarian structure may hardly find a congenial place to live in and operate, since there is open electoral competition that allays possibilities of all such developments. Nationalism and religious divisions may be more important than those of class in forming the basis of political parties. Of course, the attitudes and values prevalent in society and political culture may be of vital significance in determining the types of political parties that emerge in any society.[13]

Last, there is the factor of ideology. It has its application in some special cases. Socialist and Communist parties are organised on the basis of a particular ideology. These parties are called 'leftist', because they struggle to change the *status quo* what they call 'the era of injustice' perpetrated by the class of 'bourgeois' exploiters and oppressors over the 'proletarian' class of the workers and toilers. There may be parties based on the 'rightist' ideology as Fascists in Italy, Nazis in Germany and Bharatiya Janata in India. Such parties stand for the maintenance of the *status quo* that goes to the advantage of the existing rulers hailing from the affluent class of the society. It is not necessary that every political party is committed to some ideology. The political parties of the United States have nothing like ideological commitment for which reason the Democrats and the Republicans have been described by Lord James Bryce 'as two bottles of wine, liquor being the same but different labels'. Hence, it is said that American political parties "are primarly electoral machines, decentralised, laying little emphasis on ideological differences, exercising little disciplinary control over their members, and recruiting many of their presidential and congressional representatives from outside the party structure."[14]

Political Parties perform several important functions in modern political systems which may be enumerated as under :

1. The parties unite, simplify and stabilise the political process. They bring together sectional interests, overcome geographical distances and provide coherence to sometimes divisive government structures. The American Democratic Party provides a bridge to bring together the southern conservatives and northern liberals; the German Democratic Party bridges the gulf between the Protestants and the Catholics in Germany. In federal systems all political parties emphasise the uniting of different

12. *ibid.,* p. 85.
13. *ibid.*
14. *ibid.,* p. 86.

government structures, the extreme case being that of the former USSR. In this way, political parties tend to provide the highest common denominator.

2. The parties struggle for capturing power; they strive to form order out of chaos. They seek to widen the interests they represent and harmonise these interests with each other. Though interest articulation function is performed by the pressure groups, the work of interest aggregation is done by the parties. For instance, the Conservative Party of Britain, in spite of the nature of its internal organisation and distribution of power, depends upon the support of diverse economic, social and geographical sections in English politics. It may be said that all parties strive to extend the area of their support whether it is a bi-party system or a multi-party system of competitive electoral politics, or it is a single-dominant party system where political process operates under the dominance of a single party and, in doing so, other parties not only reflect division in society but also tend to mitigate them.

3. The parties provide a link between the government and its people. They seek to educate, instruct and activate the electorate. That is, they perform the job of political mobilisation, secularisation and recruitment. In a liberal-democratic system, the parties use means of mass media to give political education to the people. The parties may organise and control some unions or organisations for the purpose of, what S. Hening and J. Pindar call, 'occupational and social implantation'. The Communist Party of France may be said to be its best example. In a totalitarian system, the party in power works for the mobilisation of support by activating the people by means of rallies, uniforms, flags and other displays of unity to emphasise the identification of the individuals with the political party in power.

4. While increasing the scope of political activity and widening popular participation, political parties perform the important function of recruiting political leaders. Men in authority are recruited by some channel. In political systems having weak and ill-organised political parties, power remains in the hands of the elites that are recruited from the traditional groups like hereditary ruling families or military organisations. In totalitarian countries where only one party is in absolute power, political recruitment is made from the ranks of the same party. It is only in countries having a liberal-democratic order that competitive party system prevails and political recruitment is made from different political parties.

5. The parties present issues; they set value goals for the society. All parties have philosophical bases, no matter how blurred and no matter how divorced from the actual political behaviour of the party they are. Though American political parties have, what Robert Dahl says, 'ideological similarity and issue conflict', they have no disagreement on the fundamental goals of the society. The two parties of Ireland (Fianna Fail and Fine Gael) are prototypes of the two parties of the United States in respect of 'ideological similarity and issue conflict' nature. Single political parties in totalitarian systems set more rigid ideological goals for society. For instance, the Communist parties proclaim socio-economic equality of all after establishing the dictatorship of the proletariat.

6. The parties serve as the broker of ideas by selecting a number of issues and focusing attention on them. In a democratic system revolutionary parties (or those hostile to the established order as such) act not as conciliatory elements in aggregating the largest number of common interests but as focal points of discontent and organised opposition. The compromise needed in democratic political behaviour is never

acceptable to them. These parties may adhere to the political left, as the Communist parties do, or to the right as done by the Fascist and Nazi parties (respectively in Italy and Germany) or the Poujadists as in France, or to revolutionary nationalism as with the Aprista in Peru, the Revolutionary Nationalist Movement in Bolivia, or the Accion Democratica in Venezuela. In a non-democratic system, revolutionary parties may not simply be the mechanism through which the political system operates, they may be real core of the system itself with power being exercised by party leaders rather than by governmental officials.

7. In the newer and developing nations of the world where political habits and traditions are yet to grow up, political party does or parties do the job of political modernisation. That is, they strive to give a particular shape to the government, provide the main link between different social and economic groups, constitute the chief agency for political education and socialisation, break down traditional barriers and act as the binding force in communities divided by groups based on tribal affiliation, religious denomination or national origin. The role of the Congress party in India may be said to be the best example of this type where its great leaders played a monumental part in the framing of the constitution and running.the government on the lines of parliamentary democracy.
8. Political parties also perform social welfare functions that may be termed their 'non-political activities'. The parties work for the alleviation of the sufferings of the people during days of famine, drought, epidemic, wars, etc. They also work for the eradication of social evils like illiteracy, untouchability, ignorance, disease, etc. In Australia citizens may lead their lives from cradle to grave within the frame of organisations linked to a party which include not only trade unions and welfare groups but also stamp collecting societies pigeon clubs and weight-lifting associations. The Indian National Congress and Bharatiya Janata Party often engage themselves in massive activities of social welfare and public service.

While dealing with the functional aspect of the political parties, their 'dysfunctional' dimension cannot be ignored. One should also look at the distorting features of the functions of political parties. They "may polarise opinions in ways dangerous to the stability of the political system."[15] The French Fourth Republic reached a stage of near collapse in 1957 owing to the upper hand of the Communists and the Gaullists, for both were hostile to the constitutional framework of the country. The doom of Italy and Germany during the Second World War should be attributed to the 'dysfunctional' role of the Fascist and Nazi parties respectively.

A Typological Illustration: Recent Paradigm of Sartori

A typological illustration of the party systems as obtaining in different political systems, whether developed or developing, even undeveloped, of the world is governed by several factors like the nature ot social composition, economic divisions, religious and ethnic affiliations, cultural diversities, and political differences over matters of internal and external policy of the state. Maurice Duverger's too simplistic classification is now out-moded. He had formulated a simple classification of one, two and multi-party systems and thereby sought to place all the party systems of the world in one of the three relevant categories. As a matter of fact, significant developments have taken place in the realm of comparative politics keeping which in view it may be emphasised that a typological illustration needs restatement in order to be as scientific as possible.

15. *ibid.*, p. 80.

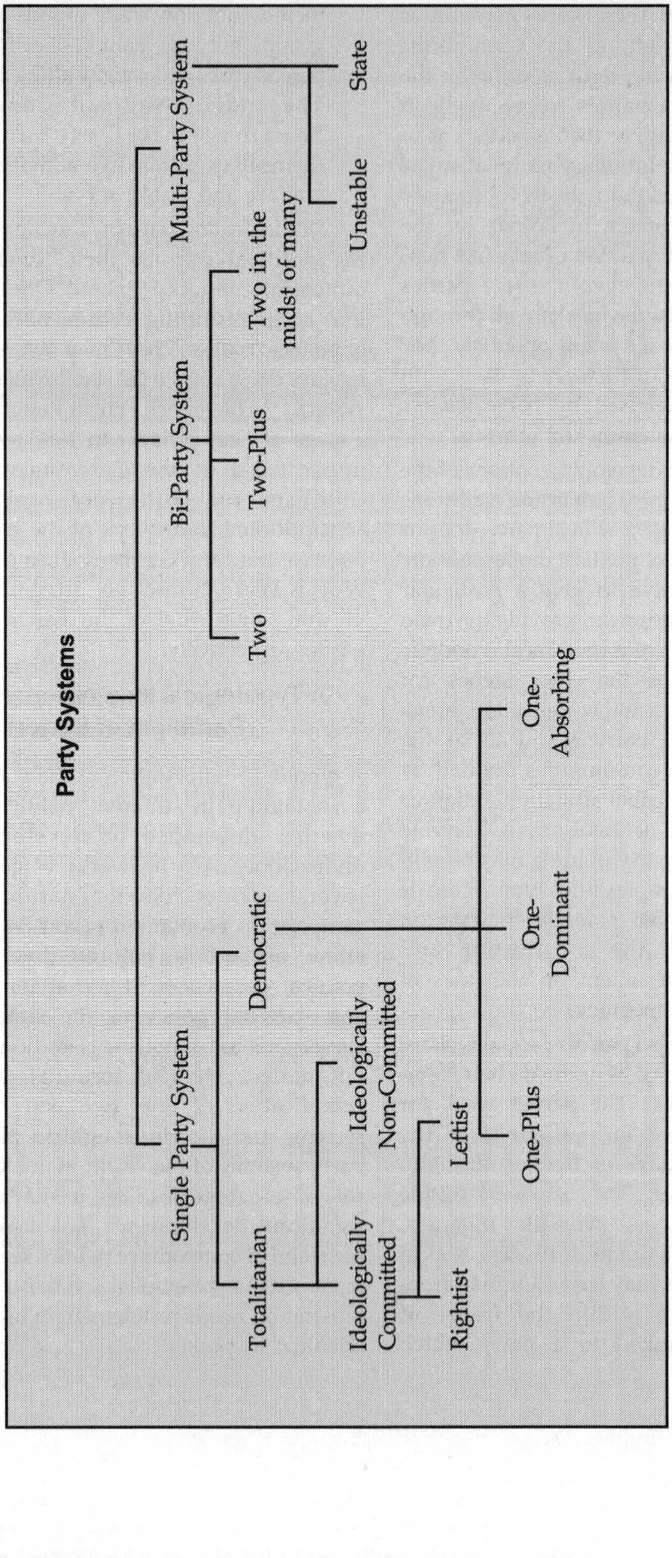
Party Systems
Single Party System
Bi-Party System
Multi-Party System
Totalitarian
Democratic
Two
Two-Plus
Two in the midst of many
Unstable
State
Ideologically Committed
Ideologically Non-Committed
One-Dominant
One-Absorbing
Rightist
Leftist
One-Plus

Viewed thus, we may discover the fact that the three categories of single, bi- and multi-party systems have their own sub-categories that may be explained in the following manner:

Single Party System : This category "is characterised by the party in power either dominating all other groups, trying to absorb the political opposition, or in the extreme case suppressing all opposition groups which are regarded as counter-revolutionary or subversive of the regime as forces dividing the national will.[16] This principal category has two sub-categories—totalitarian and democratic. The case of a single party system of the totalitarian model obtains if the party in power allows no other party or group to live or act in opposition to its authority; it is democratic in case the ruling party tolerates the existence of other parties in opposition, or it may sometimes take the help of another party or parties for living in power, or there may be several parties that, even when put together, may not be in a position to wrest power from the dominant party, or there is one party absorbing all other parties within its fold. The outstanding feature is that the party in power allows other parties and groups to exist and operate. In this situation, the party in power enjoys a dominant position. To carry the point of categorisation further, we may say that even the totalitarian model of a single party system may be said to have two more subcategories—ideologically committed and ideologically neutral. That is, the party in power may, and may not, be committed to a particular ideology. Moreover, even this ideological commitment may be of two types—rightist and leftist. While the ideology of the right stands for the maintenance of the *status quo,* the ideology of the left aims at the liquidation of the present system and its substitution by a new one that is more equitable and just for the interests of the weaker, oppressed and exploited sections of the community.

In order to support our categorisation with the help of factual cases, we may say that while the Fascist and Nazi party systems constituted the case of a totalitarian party system committed to the ideology of the right, the communist party systems belong to the latter category where a single party system is committed to the ideology of the left. While we may put Spain and Portugal in the first category, we may place China, Cuba and North Korea in the second one. When referring to the category of a single party system under an ideologically non-committed party, we may cite the names of some countries like Indonesia under the Indonesian National Party before 1965, Bangladesh under the Awami Muslim League before 1975, Egypt under Arab Socialist Union, Burma under the Lanzin party and Iraq under Baath Party before 2003.

The democratic category of a single party system has three subcategories, namely, 'one-plus' party system where the dominant party seldom takes the help of some other party as we could see in the case of Liberal Democratic Party of Japan until 2009; 'one-dominant' party system where one party enjoys a position of far more influence than all other parties put together as in the case of Indian National Congress before 1967; finally, 'one-absorbing' party system where one party absorbs all other major and minor political organisations within its fold as in the cases of Institutional Revolutionary Party (PRI) of Mexico, Kenya African Naiional Union (KANU) of Kenya and National Renovating Alliance of Brazil.

Bi-Party System : A two-party system may be said to exist where there are only two parties sufficiently strong to take part in the struggle for power. There may be other parties, but the alternation of power remains between the two major ones. A two-party system may be said to have three sub-categories, namely, two-party system where alternation of power takes place between two major parties; 'two-plus' party

---

16. Curtis, *op. cit.,* p. 165.

system where some other party or parties may seldom have a chance to share power with either of the two major parties; and 'two-party system in the midst of many' where parties other than the two .major ones have chances, now and then, to share power.

In order to carry our point of typological illustration further, we may say that the two-party system has its two sub-categories—distinct and indistinct. The case of a distinct two-party system occurs where two major parties have their policies and programmes, clearly different from each other on the basis of which they take part in the struggle for power. The Conservative and Labour parties of England find their place in this category. The case of indistinct bi-party system finds its example in the United States where the Democrats and the Republicans have no 'ideological differences' or, as Dahl says, they have 'ideological similarity and issue conflict'.[17] In a 'two-plus party system', there are two major parties that sometimes take the co-operation of some other party or parties to run their coalition governments. The cases of Germany and Canada may be put in this category. It may also be possible that the two major parties, off and on, take the help of other minor parties that makes it 'a two-party system in the midst of many'. The cases of Belgium, Luxemburg and Ireland may be referred to here.

Multi-Party System : It is a system in which no party is able to obtain clear majority in the legislature entitling it to form government. Coalition governments are formed that may, and also may not, have a stable existence depending upon the political culture and circumstances of the country. As prevailing in many countries of the world, it is of two types—stable and unstable. It is stable where many parties struggle for power and they run the government without going to the extent of making the political system unstable. The case of Switzerland is very conspicuous in this regard where Social Democrats, Radical Democrats, Liberal Democrats and Communists struggle for power without creating conditions of political uneasiness with the result that the political system is not pushed towards its decay. Different from this is the case of France. The Socialists, Communists, Gaullists, Liberals and Republicans take matters to such an extent that the very existence of the political system becomes a matter of serious concern. Yet another example is afforded by Italy where the Communists, Socialists and Democratic Socialists follow more or less the lines of their French counterparts,

It may be pointed out at this stage that bi-party and multi-party systems are a result of certain important factors. In this direction, we may appreciate the view of Sigmund Neumann who says: "Historical precedents may suggest the following favourable circumstances for a two-party development: social homogenity, political continuity, an early sanction of responsible political parties striving for political control, and their orientation at one elective office (the U.S. presidency, the British premiership) as the desired prize. Whenever fundamental cleavages in social structure evolve and continue to exist because of differences in nationalities, regions, religions or classes which are often fostered by outside influences like *irredenta* movements and revolutionary internationals; whenever political revolutions coincide with great social transformations, as in France, Central and Eastern Europe and the Near and Far East, whenever a controlling elite, through the divide and rule device, prevents parties from fulfilling their genuinely political functions of presenting clear-cut policy alternatives, as in Bismarck's strategies, for example, whenever the political machinery of state diffuses the electorate's division by numerous choices—whenever any or all of those complicating factors enter the national

17. Robert A. Dahl : *Pluralist Democracy in the United States* (Chicago, 1967), p. 222.

political scene, a multi-party system finds its *raison d' etre.*"[18]

A more neat taxonomic illustration of party systems has been given by Giovanni Sartori in his latest study on this subject.[19] The notable feature of his classificatory illustration is that he has discovered several sub-varieties within the one party system and then differentiated the two-party and multi-party systems on the basis of 'pluralism' and 'atomism'. The basic touchstone of his classification is the fact of real participation in power what he terms 'competition'. If so, only two broad categories can be earmarked with the designation of'competitive'and 'non-competitive' models. While the case of one-party system falls into the former category, the cases of two-and multi-party systems belong to the latter category.

In the view of Sartori, the single-party system is one where political competition between different political parties is either non-existent, or is not very effective. The single party model may be said to have three main varieties. It *is monopolistic* when political power is wielded by one party alone and no other party is permitted to exist at all. A deeper study of such a party system shows that it has three sub-varieties. It is *totalitarian* and has the rubric of 'dictatorship' where the degree of coercion is very high; policies adopted by it are highly destructive to the opponents; only official ideology is sacrosanct; no autonomy to other groups is sanctioned and the element of arbitrariness is unbounded and unpredictable. Then, it is *authoritarian* when the criteria of ideology is weak and non-totalistic; degree of coercion is medium; some autonomy is available to different groups; and the element of arbitrariness is within predictable limits; Last, it is *pragmatic* when the hold of ideology is very feeble, even irrelevant; degree of coercion is quite low; sub-group independence is also allowed; and the element of arbitrariness is limited. In other words, while the totalitarian and authoritarian parties are assumed to reflect different ideological intensities, the one parte pragmatic represents that end of the continuum at which an ideological mentality gives way to a pragmatic mentality. One can equally say that totalitarianism and authoritarianism appear as different points of an ideological scale whose lowest point is called pragmatism.[20]

Another variety of the single party system is its hegemonic position. Here we find that while the existence of other parties is allowed, only one party counts more than all. The other parties live like its 'satellites' or subordinate entities without posing any challenge to its hold. The hegemonic party "neither allows for a formal nor a *de facto* competition for power. Other parties are permitted to exist, but as second class, licensed parties; for they are not permitted to compete with the hegemonic party in antagonistic terms and on an equal basis. Not only does alternation not occur in fact; it *cannot* occur, since the possibility of a rotation in power is not even envisaged. The implication is that the hegemonic party will remain in power whether it is liked or not."[21] The case of a hegemonic party has two sub-varieties—ideological and pragmatic. It pertains to the former category if the ruling party is committed to a particular ideology like the Communist Party of Russia, or it is pragmatic when the ruling party has no such commitment the type

18. Neumann : "Towards a Comparative Study of Political Parties" in his (ed.) : *Modern Political Parties : Approaches to Comparative Politics* (Chicago : University of Chicago Press, 1956), pp. 401-2.
19. See Sartori, *op. cit.,* Chapters 5, 6 and 7.
20. *ibid.,* p. 223.
21. *ibid.,* p. 230.

of which we find in the case of PRI (Institutional Revolutionary Party) of Mexico.[22]

Finally, we may refer to the case of predominant party system as another variety of the single party system. Here we find a power configuration in which one party governs alone without being subjected to alternation as long as it continues to win absolute majority in the elections. In this model, one party outdistances all others, for it is significantly stronger than all of them even put together. The cases of India, Japan, Turkey and Uruguay fall in this category. A degree of difference between the hegemonic and predominant party models can be traced in the fact that while the latter remains submissive to the conditions that make for a responsible government, no real sanction commits the former to responsiveness. Whatever its policy, its domination cannot be challenged.

In the scheme of Sartori, two- and multi-party systems embody the common characteristic of 'polarised pluralism' that has the following important features :[23]

1. Different parties exist and operate including those relevant anti-system ones that may go to the extent of undermining the legitimacy of the regime. However, the anti-system character of a party or parties should not be confused with a 'revolutionary' character.
2. The existence of bilateral and multilateral oppositions and counter-oppositions is a fact with the result that interaction may be biangular, triangular, quadrangular and the like.
3. The metrical centre of the system is occupied by one party, that faces opposition at both ends—right and left. The system is multipolar in that its competitive mechanism hinges on a centre that must face both a left and a right. In this way, a centre party that attempts to outdo the parties located at its right and left will contribute, more than to anything else, to a crescendo of escalation and extremisation.
4. The degrees of ideological distance may be discovered between different parties. Cleavages are likely to be very deep, consensus is surely low, and that the legitimacy of the political system is widely questioned.
5. Centrifugal drives prevail over the centripetal ones. There is the enfeeblement of the centre, because the centrifugal strains appear to counteract successfully any decisive reversal of the trend.
6. Ideological patterning may also be visualised here. Polities contain parties which disagree not only on policies but also, and more importantly, on principles and fundamentals.
7. We may also find the existence of irresponsible opposition in this model. The frustrated parties may go to any extreme. Moreover, governmental instability and shifting or quarrelsome coalitions obscure the very perception of who is responsible for what.

---

22. The PRI of Mexico affords a peculiar example. It includes within its fold a rightist organisation like PAN (National Action Party) and a leftist one like PPS (Socialist People's Party) and also a centrist one like PARM (Authentic Party of the Mexican Revolution). To a foreign student, it may.all appear very puzzling and he may desire to know its reason. First, according to the law of 1963, it has been laid down that each minority party must win at least 20 seats in the Congress. This ceiling has been raised to 25 in 1973, on the basis of given percentages. Second, Mexico is under a dictatorial presidency as a result of which the legislature does not have any meaningful say in the administration of the country. The people are happy to see that they "avoid personal dictatorship by retiring their dictators every six years." Brandenburg : *The Making of Modern Mexico* (Englewood Cliffs, New Jersey : Prentice-Hall, 1964). Below the president is a seven-member central committee of PRI that takes all important decisions. Since it is not a democratic country like the United States, it is a foregone conclusion that the PRI must win. It is a routine affair that in case there is any danger to the victory of the PRI, ballot boxes are stuffed or replaced. See Barry Ames: "Basis of Support for Mexico's Dominant Party" in *American Political Science Review*. March, 1970. The PRI lost its hold in the presidential election of 2000.
23. Sartori, *op. cit.,* pp. 132-40.

8. Last, we find the politics of outbidding or over-promising. The ruling party or other ones may cause inflationary dis-equilibrium by making tall promises to the voters.

Despite the fact that 'polarised pluralism' is the common feature of hi-party and multi-party systems, a line of distinction between the two may be drawn. A bi-party system is one where the existence of third parties does not prevent the two major parties from governing alone and, therefore, coalitions are unnecessary. It involves these important conditions: (i) two parties are in a position to compete for the absolute majority of seats, (ii) one of the two parties actually succeeds in winning a sufficient parliamentary majority, and (iii) this party is willing to govern alone, and (iv) alternation or rotation in power remains a credible expectation.[24]

What is quite astonishing at this stage is that Sartori has included the case of countries having stable coalition systems (like Germany, Belgium, Ireland, Switzerland, Denmark, Netherlands, Iceland and Norway) in this category. That is, this model is not only available in a country like the United Kingdom, it is equally applicable to one where one coalition is opposed by another coalition and the political system remains in smooth operation. Curiously, he has excluded the case of the United States from this model on the plea that this applies to a country having a cabinet government, not a presidential government where presidency and the legislature may, or may not, be captured by the same party. When it does not synchronise, presidential government becomes basically different from a parliamentary form of government in a study of the party systems.[25]

Finally, we come to the point of extreme polarism that is the hall-mark of an 'atomised' party system. A multi-party system having a highly fragmented character leads to the existence of highly fluid party politics. Here we find that no party is in a position to cast a noticeable effect on the other. All those parties must be excluded which have almost no place in the bargaining process and thereby represent their structured consolidation. An atomised party is fragmented leader by leader, with very small groups revolving around each leader. As such, it "has no significant fractional articulation beyond the face value of all that characterises a political party."[26]

One important point may, however, be mentioned in the end. A very precise, neat and water-tight classification of the party systems cannot be presented that may be of universal and eternal acceptance for the obvious reason that the subject itself is of a very complicated nature and that political developments take place so quickly as to disturb the conclusions of a serious study. One may also say that a particular country should, or should not, be placed in a particular category in case one is able to discover some other variable(s) in a study of the stasiological configuration. For instance, one may say that India has a multi-party system, since several parties have had a chance to be in power as the Akali Dal in Punjab and DMK and A-IDMK in Tamilnadu and Janata, Lok Dal and Congress(S) at the Centre. One may also say that Britain does not afford the case of a two-party system, it is a case of the two-plus party system in view of the fact that the Labour Prime Minister Wilson had to run his minority government with the help of Liberal Party for some time in 1974 and now the emergence of Social Democratic Party looks like a curious development. In 2010 the Conservative Party formed its government in alliance with Liberal Democratic Party. What is, however, required on the part of a student in this direction is that he should fulfil the prime

24. *ibid.,* p. 188.
25. *ibid.,* p. 211 n 88.
26. *ibid.,* p. 75.

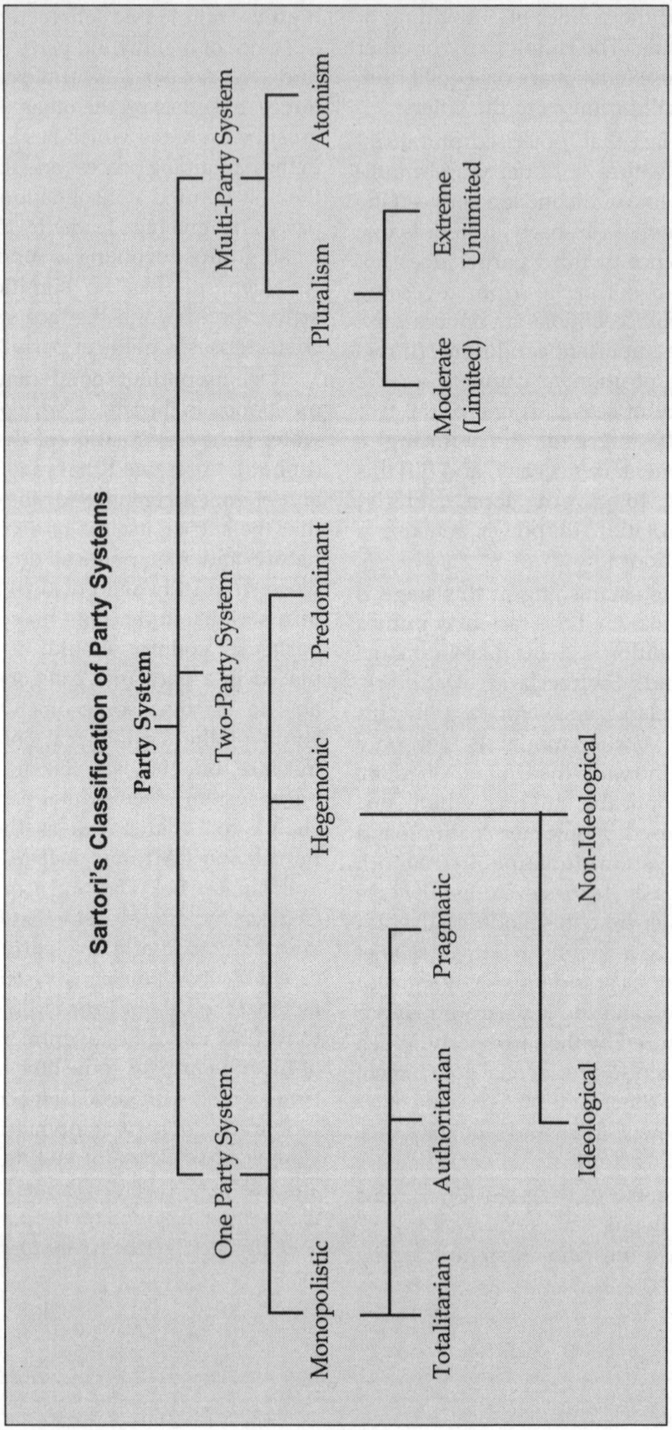

Sartori's Classification of Party Systems

Lijphart on three kinds of Party Systems

1. *Consensual Party System:* The political parties commanding most of the legislative seats are not too far apart on policies and have a reasonable amount of trust in each other and in the political system. Bargaining may be intense and politics may be exciting in these systems which seldom threatens the system itself.
2. *Conflictual Party Systems:* The legislature is dominated by the political parties which are highly antagonistic towards each other on issues.
3. *Accommodative Party System:* It exhibits a mixture of the above two systems. The parties have an accommodative attitude on some issues or occasions, and they are antagonistic to each other on some other issues or occasions.

Arendt Lijphart : *Democracy in Plural Societies* (New Haven: Yale University Press, 1977).

qualification[27]—whether the one model used, in spite of inevitable anomalies, allows general conclusions to be drawn which are true and informative.

Party Systems: Western and Non-Western Paradigms

If party system is an omnipresent affair, it has varieties of its own depending upon the political culture of the people and the political system of the country. Confining attention to the major parts of the western world, two broad varieties of party systems have been earmarked to call them 'democratic' and 'totalitarian', it is pointed out that the 'democratic model' allows elements of 'opposition' leading to the existence of a big or multi-party system, while the 'totalitarian model' signifies the existence and leading role of a single political party. In the former, opposition is allowed and parties operate within the constitutional framework so that parties and government become different institutions; in the latter case, opposition is tabooed with the result that party and government are not only identified, the latter becomes a shadow of the former. This is why, it is sometimes argued that party system of a totalitarian model is a negation of what we find in a democratic country and also what is often accepted within the compass of the meaning of a political party. As Verney remarks: "Political parties, as the term is commonly understood, can, therefore, flourish only in liberal societies where there is general agreement on fundamentals, the acceptance of the integrity and good faith of one's opponents."[28]

While distinguishing between the democratic and totalitarian models, Apter observes : "In Western practice a political party is a function of a larger system in which it operates; that is, it is a servant of the constitutional framework. Totalitarian parties are different; and to understand their role, it is necessary to examine totalitarian societies and governments. In other words the totalitarian party is coterminus with the state itself."[29] Again : "In the democratic tradition political parties assume a constitutional framework of government and operate within its rules. In the totalitarian tradition, parties change the rules to serve their own purposes and the state is thus subordinated to the party. In the new nations the legitimacy of the state and the effective discipline of the party often vary independently of one another, thus causing political parties to have special responsibilities

27. See Gabriel A. Almond : "Introduction : A Functional Approach to Comparative Politics" in Almond and Coleman (eds.) : *The Politics of the Developing Areas* (Princeton : Princeton University Press, 1960), pp. 40-45. Almond distinguishes four major categories with some sub-divisions. These are: authoritarian (with a separate sub-category of totalitarian); dominant 'non-authoritarian'; competitive two-party; and 'competitive non-party; working and *immobilistic.*
28. Verney, *op. cit.*, p. 125.
29. Apter, *op. cit.*, p. 328.

Apter on Party-State Relationships and Characteristics

Social Units	*Democratic Parties*	*Totalitarian Parties*
Party	*Pluralistic* : Competitive with other parties.	*Monopolistic* : Seeks to eliminate other parties.
Community	*Representative* : Seeks to incorporate divergent view in order to win widest following.	*Directive* : Seeks to amalgamate grievances to overthrow existing order, or if in power to bend the community towards goals laid down by the party.
Government	*Constitutional* : party action is limited by constitution, convention and electoral rules.	*Extra-constitutional* : Accepts legal order only in so far as it is forced to, when in control the party bends the government and the constitution to its own ends. Party makes the state sub-servient to itself.

for the establishment of a constitutional framework."[30]

However, this major division of party system into two models is further divisible into its allied varieties. True to say that democratic countries like Britain, France and the United States fall within the 'democratic model', but they have their different systems. Both Britain and the United States are the models of a bi-party system, yet they are different in the sense that while the American political parties lack rigid organisational discipline and clear-cut ideological commitments, the English party system represents cohesion, effective organisation and specific ideological commitments. As Apter argues : "American political parties are not centres of passion. Today they are part-time organisations, kept alive between special election of minor ones, state and local, by patronage and by some spoils."[31] In contrast to this, "disciplined parties, effective parliamentary organisation, a high standard of ethics, all these now characterise the British political party system in spite of occasional lapses from political virtue and internal cohesion."[32]

Moreover, while the British and the American party systems are the models of bi-partyism, many other countries of the western world (like France, Italy. Switzerland, Germany, and Canada) have multi-party systems. In such a model, political parties, more than two in number, operate to fight for power and the machinery of government is run either by a single party provided it gets the mandate of the people to make its majority, or by a coalition of parties that make up their strength for the required purpose. However, this phenomenon of multi-partyism may be limited and orderly (as in Holland and Switzerland), or it may be anarchic and disorderly (as in Italy and in pre-1958 France), or it may take an intermediate situation (as in Germany and in post-1962 France). However, by and large, the situation of multi-partyism is not appreciated for the reasons of its tendency to bring instability, disorder and anarchic trends of pre-modernisation period which sometimes establishes a line of similarity between multi-partyism and non-partyism. As Duverger points out: "Multi-partyism is often confused with absence of parties. A country in which opinion is divided amongst several groups that are unstable, fluid,

30. *ibid.,* 329.
31. *ibid.,* p. 327.
32. *ibid.,* p. 328.

and shortlived does not provide an example of multi-partyism in the proper sense of the term: it is still in the pre-historic era of parties; it is to be situated in that phase of general development at which the distinction between bi-partyism and multi-partyism is not yet applicable because there are not yet true parties."[33]

The study of party system reveals more astonishing features when attention is paid to the cases of under-developed or developing countries of the African and Asian regions. Party system in such countries is a product of historical circumstances. While European political parties emerged as 'internally created' phenomenon in response to the growth of democratic trends like extension of franchise and parliamentary system, the political parties in a subject country came into being and developed as 'externally created' institutions. That is, parties came into existence not for the sake of running the government but for the purpose of fighting for national liberation. They had an anti-foreign character. They not only laid stress on the significance of indigenous factors but. in many cases, refused to cooperate with the ruling foreign power in its proposed system of parl:amentary democracy. Sometimes, the anti-foreign tirade mounted so high that the colonial power outlawed a nationalist organisation and thereby forced it to operate in a clandestine or underground form.

The emergence of party system in a colonial country witnessed the coming up of some anti-nationalist organisations as well to counteract the growing force of a nationalist party. This happened either due to the policy of 'divide and rule' pursued by the colonial power or due to the resentment of certain ambitious leaders against the 'entrenched leadership' of the elite of the nationalist organisation. The case of Muslim League in India affords a leading instance in this regard that came into being as a pampered child of the British colonial genius and that came under the leadership of Jinnah who had already developed a very critical attitude towards the leadership of Mahatma Gandhi. As a result of this unfortunate trend of events, the force of nationalist movement became weak and the country had to suffer from the disasters of territorial disintegration. As Joseph la Palombara and Weiner observe: "The expansion of the League into a mass movement was clearly associated with an integrationist crisis that ultimately resulted in the partition of the subcontinent. Elsewhere in Asia, religious, linguistic and tribal minorities have often organised political parties in opposition to the nationalist movement and advocated special protections within the framework of an accepted colonial rule, or else favoured the creation of several nation-states where there had previously been none."[34]

One more characteristic feature of the party system in a subject country of Asia and Africa is that a nationalist party came mto being as a small body of men determined to oppose their colonial masters or serve them in a way of their own choosing as far as possible. Here developed a situation of mutual adjustment and also of mutual tug-of-war. In case the nationalist party agreed with the co stit tional gifts of the colonial power and sho ed its readiness o embrace parliament y democracy, the nationalist party could no develop as a mass movement and it remain d hardly anything else than a small elite of the nationalist organisation.[35] However, where this elite felt dissatisfied with the achievements of its influence upon the colonial administrat , it strove for th expansion of its memb hip more and more to have a mass base a to struggle for the availability of more and opportunities to wrest power in its own hands.

33. Maurice Duverger : *Political Parties* (London : Methuen, 1964), p. 228.
34. La Palombara and Weiner, *op. cit.,* p. 16.
35. For a better study see Howard Wriggins : *Ceylon : Dilemma of a New Nation* (Princeton : Princeton University Press, 1960).

It is due to this tug-of-war between the nationalist organisation and foreign power that the nationalist leaders remained divided between moderate and extremist sections, while ultra-extremists often resorted to violent activities to overthrow the alien regime.[36]

The historical factor exercised its impact upon the party system of the developing countries even after the advent of independence. The biggest nalionalist organisation held power after the exit of the foreign colonial rule and established 'quasi-democracy'—democracy under one party's dominance. In a country like India, it set up its all-powerful rule without formally outlawing opposition and the specific interest groups of the country sought to operate within the framework of this nationalist organisation.[37] However, in a country like Pakistan the enjoyment of power in the absence of healthy opposition made this organisation more and more corrupt and the gradual loss of legitimacy entailed the decline and doom of the very organisation which ultimately meant the replacement of even that truncated democracy by the rule of the military elite.

Political developments of many countries (like Egypt, Pakistan. Burma, Indonesia and Bangladesh) confirm this trend. The exceptional case of India where the Congress party found its rejuvenation under the leadership of Indira Gandhi after the great split of 1969, repeated in 1978, affords the instance where the biggest nationalist party having a glorious record of its role in the freedom movement could re-emerge through the democratic process of parliamentary elections. Different is the case of several Asian and African countries where nationalist parties "often found it relatively easy to establish one-party system and place extraordinary restrictions on civil liberties precisely because no organised group in the society with any measure of popular support was committed to the maintenance of a competitive framework."[38]

Operational Dimensions of Party System : Peculiar Case of the Communist Party

Party system provides normal means of fighting political battles and its existence is universal, although some exceptions are found relating to very 'primitive' societies, or where the powerful elite employs institutionalised techniques to ruthlessly suppress structures of a party system.[39] However, the cases of both 'primitive' societies and ultra-totalitarian polities are not very realistic, because there is hardly any 'primitive society' worth considering within the framework of comparative politics and that there can hardly be a regime that holds the capability of running the machinery of government without the mechanism of the party system. Even military regimes, after the consolidation of their dictatorial rule, form their own party (as Arab Socialist Union in Egypt and Golkar Party in Indonesia) and gradually seek to legitimise their hold in the name of this organisation designed to establish national integration and better administration on democratic lines as far as possible. So many factors relating to the processes of social modernisation and political acculturation have their definite impact upon the operation of party system in every country, whether democratic or totalitarian, developed or developing. It "is this ubiquitous tendency for parties to emerge in one form or other that leads us to think that there do exist conditions of technology, communication, and organisation that make the political party itself a strong probability in the contemporary world."[40]

36. See La Palombara and Weiner, *op. cit.,* p. 16.
37. For a better and illuminating study of Congress in India, see Rajni Koihari: *Politics in India* (Boston : Little Brown & Co., 1970), Ch. VIII.
38. La Palombara and Weiner, *op. cit.,* p. 11.
39. Blondel, *op. cit.,* p. 99.
40. La Palombara and Weiner, *op. cit.,* p. 23.

What strikes us at this stage is that even a dictatorial system may not uproot the structures of a party system in entirety. The party system exists even under the iron-law of dictatorship: opposition parties either live underground to work for the overthrow of the established regime, or cleverly operate like organised interest groups within the framework of the party in power. No amount of repression can terminate the existence of opposition elements. Totally outlawed parties assume a clandestine form to hatch and prosecute conspiratorial activities (as F.L.N, in Algeria) adversely affecting the long-range political development of the country. Moreover, any deliberate endeavour to suppress the party system totally leads to political instability and compels the powerful elite to convert itself into a party of its own so that other elements may be accommodated. Resultantly, a mono-party system emerges to force all dissident elements either to change their strategy by manipulating to sit inside the sleeve of the official organisation or drag the situation towards the mutilation of the men in power in a revolutionary upheaval. The 'vanguardhood' of a party is just a shrewd device to hoodwink the people in general, or to coerce them into forced submission, or to sacrifice their opponents at the altar of 'socialism'.

However, any attempt in the direction of the 'simplification of a complex party system' cannot be identified with ths case of ruthless suppression of all opposition parties. In the former case, the official party (as P.N.I, in Indonesia before 1965) tries to arrest the 'disease' of multi-partyism, though in the interest of its own power it still leaves some room for other 'dissident' elements to coalesce with others so as to manipulate their configuration and thereby operate to have their programme. In the latter case, a deliberate effort is made to efface the existence of every shade of opposition. The change in the electoral method of the President of the Republic in France in 1962 is clearly an example of the former type where the new arrangement (amounting to amendment in the Constitution without the utilisation of proper procedure) forced many small parties and splinter groups to come together and thereby reduce the gross multi-partyism of the country.[41]

Development of the systems of communications and technology has its own impact upon the rise and growth of party system. Better services of transport and communications enable people of a country to have wider contacts. This process facilitates the task of making bigger organisations. Nettl rightly contends that knowledge evaluations, being the main criteria of cultural level, are meaningless except in the context of communication structure.[42] It is owing to this that the Indian National Congress gathered more and more popularity and widened its base by including within its fold leading nationalists from all parts of the country. However, it ought to be made clear that the process of communications has a political significance of its own. While the free process of communications is the hallmark of a democratic system, its controlled flow is seen in a totalitarian country. Free press, radio and television communicate news to the people to enable them to form their views according to their standard of judgement, while a totalitarian order keeps monopoly over the media of communications. As a result, totalitarian communication "directs the inflow of information to a single political structure and limits the outflow of communication to the purposes of the communist elite.'"[43]

Factors leading to the emergence and operation of party system are governed by the process of modernisation. Historical and political crises materialise and respond to the

41. See Samuel E. Finer : *Comparative Government* (London : Allen Lane, The Penguin Press, 1970), pp. 307-08.
42. J.N. Nettl : *Political Mobilisation* (London : Faber and Faber, 1967), p. 58.
43. Almond and Coleman, *op. cit.*, p. 47.

situations which operate in this regard to mould the configuration of party system. Since party system has an extra-constitutional character, not written rules formulated by a constitutional convention or a legislative assembly as such, as evolution of healthy traditions is required to substantiate the phenomenon of political modernisation. In the absence of healthy conventions, party system remains vitiated by the evils of defections, counter-defections and growth of splinter groups all making the party system a baleful phenomenon of representative democracy. It would thus appear that it "is the occurrence of political crises of systematic magnitude at a point in time when sufficient modernisation has taken place to provide conditions for party development that causes parties to emerge."[44]

However, the elite in power, in the form of a junta or a clique identifying itself with the state, may not be likened with a political party for the reason of its being monolithic in orientation and hostile to any shade of opposition. It endeavours to hinge on the central point of 'total integration' and its 'arsenal of instrument for political control includes everything from mild pressure to organised terror.'[45] Whether the constitution specifically prohibits the formation of another political party (as in the former Soviet Union) or it keeps silent on this issue though with the same intent (as in China), in such political systems, the state itself "is an instrument of a monolithic party which has ideological goal—the total use of power for the restructuring of the society's social and economic system."[46]

The apologists of such a system claim that it serves a double purpose—single party is both an elite and a bond. Its aim is to replace the traditional elites with new elites—to create a new ruling class, to unite and to shape the political leaders capable of organising the country, for the masses cannot govern themselves. Through its youth organisations, their hierarchy, and the channels which take their members into the party itself, or by its organisation of controlled methods of entry into party after a waiting period, sponsorships and tests, the party "forms a sieve which retains the elite in its meshes. It instructs them: at the same time, it makes them capable of fulfilling their tasks: it also organises them in a permanent fashion; it gives them a structure and a hierarchy, the elite thus chosen and prepared can fulfil its role of leadership having seats everywhere, from the Council of Ministers to the smallest local or special committees; from the Civil Service to the Trade Unions, Co-operatives, Cultural Associations, etc"[47]

Critical Appraisal

The party system has its own points of strength and weakness. First, we take up the case of its merits. It is said that parties are in accord with human nature. Since people differ in respect of their ideas, beliefs and commitments, they have different political parties. The successful prosecution of democracy demands a successful party system. Far from being in conflict with the theory of democratic government, party system is the mechanism which renders the latter feasible. "A modern democratic State without this somewhat artificial and yet essential unanimity would become a brawling chaos of individual opinions."[48] Party system avoids the risks of direct legislation. If parties "always distort public opinion in some degree, they also prevent the still larger distortion caused by sudden waves of excitement, -party organisations are inclined to check political vagaries....[49] It is on account of the party system that elections are made easy and possible and

44. La Palombara and Weiner, *op. cit.*, pp. 21-22.
45. *ibid.*, p. 40.
46. *ibid.*
47. Duverger, *op.cit.*, pp. 257-59.
48. Stephen Leacock : *The Elements of Political Science*, p. 313.
49. A.L. Lowell : *Public Opinion and Popular Government*, pp. 96-97.

Functions of Political Parties

1. Selection or nomination of official personnel
2. Formation of public policies
3. Conducting and criticism of government
4. Political eduction
5. Intermediation between individuals and governments.
6. Development and maintenance of a sense of national unity.
7. Coordination of the branches of government particularly in a government such as the United States where the separation of powers would encourage deadlocks without the integrating force of the party system.
8. Minimising the clash of economic forces by establishing a basis of compromise under a common party platform, and
9. Making it possible for the electorate to function in a organised and effective manner.

Source: F.G. Wilson: *The Elements of Modern Politics*, p. 332.

1. Framing of political issues for the people
2. Selection of candidates
3. Establishment of a collective and continuing political responsibility, and
4. Serving its agencies of civic eduction or keeping the interests of the people alive.

Source: W.B. Munro: *The Government of the United States*, pp. 133-36.

1. Parties develop and maintain a sense of national unity.
2. They coordinate the branches of government wherever there is separation of powers.
3. They minimise the clash of economic interests, for the demands of various economic groups find expression in party platform.
4. They permit the electorate to function.
5. They formulate policies.
6. They seek to control the government.

Source: Patterson: *American Government*, pp. 175-76.

legislative excellence is promoted. The tendency of Caesarism is checked. "The existence of a party of opposition, with a programme fairly within the limits of a possible public opinion, is a bulwark against the tyranny, not only of a despot but also of a practical political majority."[50] Bryce thus sums up the value of party system: "The parties keep a nation's mind alive as the rise and fall of the sweeping tide freshens the water of long ocean inlets...so few people think seriously and steadily upon any subject outside the range of their own business interests that public opinion might be vague and ineffective if the party searchlight were not constantly turned on."[51]

The party system has its demerits too. It is described as an unnatural political phenomenon. Members belonging to different parties, as Leacock says, remain in a state of 'wilful inconvincibility with individual judgment frozen tight in the shape of the party mould."[52] It creates factionalism as it "tends to make the political life of a country machine-like or artificial. The party in opposition, as it is

50. *ibid.*, pp. 97-98.
51. James Bryce : *Modern Democracies*, Vol. 1, pp. 134-35.
52. Leacock, *op. cit.*, p. 312.

Merits of Party System*

1. The parties harmonise the organs of government. They give coherence to the very complicated mechanism of government established under the federal and state constitutions. To some extent they mitigate the disadvantages of the federal system, by harmonising the policy of the state and nation in those cases where political action, to be effective, must take place simultaneously in both quarters. But far more important is their service in neutralising the effort of the checks and balances system which as, Woodrow Wilson said, was intended by the framers of the constitution to keep government in a sort of mechanical equipoise by means of a standing amicable contest among its several organic parts and particularly to prevent the will of the people as a whole from having at any moment an unobstructed sweep and ascendancy.
2. The national party organisations alone make it possible for the enormous electorate to function at all effectively. Without them our national politics would take the form of a conflict between innumerable competing groups, a conflict so confused, so obscure, and so unintelligible that public opinion could not be ascertained at all.
3. The parties have been instrumental in developing and maintaining a sense of national unity. Parties check religious intolerance. They tend to assimilate foreign elements and they soften the clash of economic interests.

* E.M. Sait: *Political Institutions,* pp. 159-64.

Demerits of Party System**

1. Parties cause a bias and every voter is more or less attracted or repelled to such an extent that he is unable to form an entirely unbiased judgment either on questions of policy or on the merits of the candidates.
2. Parties produce unnatural divisions and thus falsify public opinion. Men are naturally separated from hard and fast lines into two or more compact groups, but pursue every kind of combination of opinion. Further, to maintain an outward unity, internal differences among members are not integrated, they are only not allowed to result in rupture and active dimension.
3. Two parties especially involve only 'yes' or 'no' to only one proposition. It means that the differences are not integrated. Every vote is given not for the whole, but for a *partial* cause.
4. It is the extreme element that always leads the party; the moderate elements are mere hangers on. They merely follow; they donot break away from the party, because they can do no other. This means public opinion remains falsified.
5. Sometimes, the extreme element fires the heads of the leaders to do and say things which the latter donot desire. In that case too, the real opinion remains unrepresented.

** A.L. Lowell: *Public Opinion and Popular Government,* pp. 86-95.

sometimes called the outs, is always antagonistic to the party in power or the ins."[53] The talent of the people is ignored on account of party politics and the interest of party is given precedence over the interests of the nation. Hollowness and insincerity get encouragement. The vision of the party members is narrowed and their individuality crushed with the result that the evils of favouritism, nepotism and spoils system are multiplied. The system of

53. R.N. Gilchrist : *Principles of Political Science,* p. 361.

administration is de-stabilised on account of rapid changes in the position of the parties. There is wastage of money, explosion of opportunity to self-seekers and excessive pandering to the masses. Marriott rightly fears that party allegiance, if carried to excess, "may easily obscure the claims of patriotism. Concentration upon the business of vote-catching may tempt party leaders and party managers to ignore or to postpone the higher call of the country."[54]

Though the subject of party system may be concluded with a brief enumeration of its merits and demerits, two more points should be emphasised at this stage. First, the idea of 'parlyless democracy' is purely utopian. It has nothing more than academic significance. Such a theory having its roots in the political philosophy of the American Federalists like George Washington and James Madison and finding its reasoned argumentation in the works and utterances of recent Indian thinkers like Mahatma Gandhi, M.N. Roy, Acharya Vinoba Bhave and Jayaprakash Narayan is far from the world of political reality. As Brown says: "Demands for a 'parlyless democracy' are utopian. Parties are the main institutions through which responsibility of the rulers is enforced. If parties are unable to perform this function, then other institutions whose purposes are similar will likewise fail."[55] Second, though abundant literature has appeared on the subjects of elections and modern representative government, a standard theory of political parties 'is still lacking.'[56] As a well-known authority on this subject says: "It is at the present time impossible to give a valid description of the comparative functioning of political parties: yet it is essential to do so. We find ourselves in a vicious circle: general theory of parties will eventually be constructed upon the preliminary work of many profound studies; but these studies cannot be truly profound so long as there exists no general theory of parties. For nature answers only when questioned and we donot yet know what questions this subject demands."[57]

54. Marriott : *Mechanism of Modern Slate,* Vol. II, p. 431.
55. B.E. Brown, *op. cit.,* p. 24.
56. David Apter, *op. cit.,* p. 328.
57. Maurice Duverger, *op. cit.,* p. xiii.

18

Pressure Group Politics

> How different are the problems of public policy-making in a society where there are no effective mechanisms for the articulation of public demands, from one in which there is an elaborate set of structures for the formulation of demands. and the transmission of these demands into the party and governmental systems'? The kind of interest groups which are present in a society, the specificity or diffuseness of their demands, their conceptions of the political arena and of the rules of the game, the ethos which they bring with them into the political process—these are the raw materials of policies— which some set of mechanisms must transform into political personnel and public policy.
>
> —**Gabriel** A. **Almond**[1]

The study of pressure groups (also known as the interest, organised and catalytic groups) within a conceptual framework constitutes an interesting as well as an important subject of comparative politics that has been designated by eminent writers in various phrases.[2] It highlights those underlying forces and processes through which political power is marshalled and applied in organised societies, perferably in democracies. It, however, does not imply their total non-existence in a society having an authoritarian system for the simple reason that even in a totalitarian order such groups exist though they are highly circumscribed and thereby "serve merely as instruments of the state for securing ends which are state-determined, or they may become part of the facade of government for legitimising decisions."[3] A line of demarcation possibly subsists in the degree of involvement. A pluralistic society, with a democratic order, recognises their existence and ensures widest possible participation to the extent of making them the principal avenues of activity out of the 'official administration'. A totalitarian order, on the other hand, encourages and permits them to work in a particular direction congenial to its own interest. However, the paramount fact remains that in every society, whether democratic or totalitarian, interest groups seek to influence public policy in a desired direction without being ready to accept the responsibility of public office as well as by declining to hold direct responsibility for ruling the country.[4]

Pressure Group Politics : Significance of a New Area of Study

This study has recently gained much importance in the realm of comparative politics because, over the last few years, political science has lost much of its connection with history and ethics; it has moved closer to the disciplines of psychology and sociology. A new meaning of 'politics' has come into use whereby it is

---

1. Gabriel A. Almond : "A Comparative Study of the Interest Groups' Political Process" in *The American Political Science Review,* March 1958, pp. 270-82.
2. Prof. S.E. Finer calls it 'anonymous empire'; D.D. McKean names it 'invisible government' and Thorstein Sellin and Richard D. Lambert designate it as 'unofficial government'.
3. Abraham Holtzman : *Interest Groups and Lobbying* (London: Macmillan, 1966), p. 1.
4. See Graham Wotton : *Interest Groups* (Englewood Cliffs : New Jersey, Prentice Hall, 1970), p. I.

regarded as a process by which social values are authentically allocated. Such a study regards politics not merely as a science of state and government in the traditional sense of the term, it implies the process of decision-making. Since these decisions are often made as a result of group conflict, it stretches its scope of study to all such groups which are involved in the process of decision-making. This new approach amounts to the formulation of a 'descriptive', if not 'explanatory' theory, and belongs to what is sometimes called 'informal' politics. Naturally, it has added material to the stock of literature on comparative politics, and, though the approach is not appreciated by many 'frontier-minded' writers, the whole study, more appropriately called a study of 'political sociology', "will continue to play a very important role in comparative politics research."[5]

In other words, this study revolves around the pivot of a new man, called the Political Man, distinguished from the Economic Man or the Moral Man. It considers man not as an 'isolated atom' but as 'a creature of groups'. The problem is thus not 'man *versus* the state' as designated by Herbert Spencer in the vein of an extremely individualistic philosophy; it is 'groups *versus* the state' as suggested by Ernest Barker in the line of modern interpretation of liberalistic individualism. When men united into groups have their interests and use 'pressure' for the sake of their protection and promotion, as Hagan points out, the life in society, in all its phases, can be stated in'groups of active men'.[6] The allocation of social values is done by means of decisions which are taken by diverse activities, each not being quite separate from the other, though the mass of activity, having common tendencies, in regard to such decisions is manifest in the form of groups. Thus, what determines the making of decisions is nothing but a constant struggle between different groups and interests. Viewed in this context, a new definition of politics is furnished by the exponents of this theory. For instance, Eckstein says: "If we say that politics involves the making of decisions, the decisions are made as a result of group conflict, that groups are the same thing as interests, that both groups and interests are mass of activity, then we say merely that politics is activity."[7] As such, a study of group politics is like a newer wave in the direction of modernisation of this subject, and though much more useful theories are yet to come, it is certain that the ice "has most decidedly broken."[8]

However, a study of pressure groups is beset with the task of precise nomenclature and other problems of a procedural and substantive character. All groups are not the same, though they are distinguished as such. For instance, some represent vested interests or interests of a particular social or economic group having some sort of objective characteristics common to each other; others represent and safeguard the interests of a particular point, regardless of their objective characteristics. Then, these groups are of different types—self-seeking and altruistic from the viewpoint of purpose; ephemeral and long-term keeping in view the point of tenure; and with formal or informal bureaucratic organisation taking in view the fact of power position. Likewise, these groups are different from each other as regards their concentration of efforts either on the legislative bodies or on the voters as a whole. Differences are also visible when we examine the functional impact of pressure politics upon a particular policy and, that is why, some groups frequently achieve their goals while others fail to do so. On the whole, pressure groups have a very

5. See Harry Eckstein : "Group Theory and the Comparative Study of Pressure Groups" in Eckstein and Apter (eds.) : *Comparative Politics: A Reader* (New York : Free Press of Glencoe, 1963), p. 389.
6. Hagan : *Approaches to the Study of Politics,* Cf. *ibid.,* p. 390.
7. *ibid.,* p. 392.
8. Eckstein, *op. cit.,* p. 389.

important role in a modern political system where the state is irrevocably wedded to the ideals of representative democracy and social welfare.

One thing needs to be pointed out here. Organised interest groups are active in every political community, more so in a representative government committed to the realisation of the ideal of a social service state. But a degree of difference exists in that they are more varied and active in a rich and prosperous society, as distinguished from a poor and backward country. But in spite of this degree of differentiation, it is certain that in the political process of western democracy their significance is enhanced by the factor of modernisation which acts as a lubricant in the machine of functional differentiation. The multiversal character of society in the shape of division of labour and functional specialisation fragments it into a very large number of interests, thus making possible a social organisation made up of groups. More so, when the state is committed to the ideal of a welfare state, it assigns to social groups a greater stake in politics and thereby mobilises them to a much greater extent. At the same time, when the state adopts a policy of positive role in the sphere of planning and social service, it makes itself increasingly dependent upon the aid and advice of such groups.

This, however, does not imply that these groups are thoroughly non-existent in a totalitarian country. They seem to be relatively great in a highly pluralistic structure of society with a democratic form of government recognising the principle of decentralisation of authority and small in a highly monolithic system where the dictator at the top, in the language of King Louis XIV of France, identifies himself with the state. Hence, the role of interest groups is evident even where centralism and regimentation of justice inform all institutions of social and political control with the result that diverse groups are not allowed to germinate and progress freely to establish special relationships with politicians, statesmen and other leaders of the country. On the whole, the point of difference is that whereas in a democratic system dominant direction of flow is from the groups to the government, in a totalitarian system it is just the other **way** round.

From the above, it follows that a democratic state, with a pluralistic society, offers far greater opportunities of access to the process and activity of decision-making and effective participation of the organised interest groups in it. Such a condition of life encourages even weaker interests to participate in politics alongwith other interests. It thus politicises the character of every grouping to some extent, big or small. The result is the politicisation of the entire group structure of society. As Roman Kolkowicz says : "In pluralistic systems we have come to accept the idea and reality of interest groups as central to the political and social processes. They are presumed to be a vital faction in the political process and social transaction in which the political leaders manipulate or accommodate various interest groups' demands. In a totalitarian or authoritarian political system, however, when a single party claims hegemony in respect to political and social authority, the concept of interest group needs some clarification, since the single party denies the very existence of such particularistic entities and views the possibilities of their emergence as anathema."[9]

Political Parties and Pressure Groups : Inter-Action and Inter-Penetration

One peculiar development of modern political systems finds place in the inter-penetration of political parties and interest groups whether it is a two-party system characteristic of the peculiarly English and American models or a

9. Roman Kolkowicz : "Interest Groups in Soviet Politics", in *Comparative Politics*, New York, Vol. 2, No. 2 (April, 1970), p. 445.

multi-party system indicative of their French and Italian counterparts.[10] This inter-action and inter-penetration is existent even in a communist society where trade unions and other cultural organisations work in unison with the only dominant political party. What counts in politics is power. For the sake of having power both the parties and the organised groups have to depend upon the help and cooperation of each other.[11] Hence, either some groups combine together to form or support a particular party as a political counterpart of their organisation or coalition, or a political party controls some group or groups and thereby imparts a politico-ideological content to their activity. The result is not only a process of interaction but interpenetration: when the party controls groups, it inhibits the capacity of groups to formulate pragmatic specific demands, but when the groups control a party, they inhibit the capacity of a party to combine specific interests into programmes with wider appeal.[12]

It follows that in a political system organised interest groups not only constitute necessary elements, they also play a very important part in the political process as a whole. The process of interaction and interpenetration between the two is so strong that to account for the directions and control of public policy, both must be taken into the scope of study. However, this inter-action and inter-penetration may take place in three degrees :

1. A group may pursue its objective in dealing with governmental agencies almost independently of a political party. That is. by virtue of its privileged position and favourable circumstances, it may have a mechanism of communications with the governmental functionaries autonomous of party control.
2. A group may seek to realise its goal by means of active collaboration with a single political party.
3. A group may neither be so powerful as to work independently of party control nor so conservative as to live invariably under the hold of a single political party. Thus without having a formal mask of partisan orientation it may have affiliations with any party or parties as per its own interest.

It is due to this reason that on the national scene certain major pressure groups "cluster around each party. The policy orientation of the parties plough a furrow through the group system, and most of the major groups—and some of the lesser groups—find one party far more congenial to their tastes than the other."[13]

A political party is pledged to have a partisan orientation and this factor contributes to the inelastic character of a party organisation. But with pressure groups the case is entirely different. Even if a group moves from its advocacy of a particular narrow interest to the

10. Many eminent American writers have a peculiar notion about the meaning of a political party. To them a political party is a 'vote mobiliser' made of 'alliance of interests'. See Pendelton Herring : *The Politics of Democracy* (New York : Rinehart & Co., 1940), p. 55. A. more authentic version is given by Truman : "The meanings to be attached to the term 'political party' are thus extremely varied. What activities are implied by the designation depends upon the time and place, the level of government, and the section of the country involved. Viewed from the national level the so-called party system gives an impression of disorganisation, if not of unrelieved chaos. Such an impression is not strictly accurate, but it is apparent that the national party at any given time is fluid and unstable consisting more of temporary personal alliances than of continuing institutionalised relationships. It follows that relations between political parties and other political interest groups will be similarly protean. The appropriateness of the political party as a means of group access to government proper will depend, therefore, not only upon the claimant groups involved but also upon the characteristics of the party at the particular time, place, and level of government under discussion. Generalisation in the area is hazardous." *The Government Proces* (New York: Alfred A.Knopf, 1951), p. 282.
11. It conforms with the view of Max Weber that politics "means striving to share power or striving to influence the distribution of power either among states, or among groups within a state." See his "Politics as Vocation" in Garth and Mills : *From Max Weber : Essays in Sociology* (New York : Oxford Univ. Press, 1946), p. 78.
12. See Gabriel A. Almond : "A Comparative Study of the Interest Groups and Political Process" in *The American Political Science Review*, Vol 52, No. 1 (March, 1958), pp. 270-82.
13. V.O. Key, Jr. : *Politics, Parties and Pressure Groups* (New York : T.Y. Crowell Co., 1964), p. 156.

Interest Group Systems and Their Characteristic Features

Pluralist Interest Group Systems

1. Multiple groups may represent a single societal interest.
2. Group membership is voluntary and limited.
3. Groups often have a loose or decentralised organisational structure.
4. There is a clear separation between interest groups and the government.

Democratic Corporatist Interest Group System

1. A single peak association normally represents each societal interest.
2. Membership in the peak association is often compulsory and nearly universal.
3. Peak associations are centrally organised and direct the actions of other members.
4. Groups are often systematically involved in making and implementing policy.

Controlled Interest Group System

1. There is a single group of each social sector.
2. Membership is often compulsory.
3. Each group is normally hierarchically organised.
4. Groups are controlled by the government or its agents in order to mobilise support for government policy.

whole range of public questions, it endeavours to stick, as far as possible, to the facade of non-partisanism and thus its alliances of opinions and attitudes are supplemented by relations of mutual defence and offence. Sometimes, a group may adhere to a particular line of thinking or action and thereby create a point of sharp difference with a similar group and come very close to a particular political party. Such a situation creates a degree of collaboration between the party and the group where the latter has to wind itself up generally on one side of the fence. The result is, as Key suggests, "not necessarily party adoption of the group programme, it may be modified in the light of the broader objectives of the party as a whole."[14]

Political parties and pressure groups resemble each other in a way that both seek to realise their objectives by influencing the decision-making agencies in their favour.[15] However, a striking difference between the two finds place in that while a party is a full-fledged political organisation and plays politics by profession, a group becomes a political association for a particular purpose only to play politics for the sake of expediency. A group is formed just for the sake of some interest to exercise influence upon the decision-making body to the extent its range of interest is involved. Very often a pressure group lives and acts in a most disguised manner and strives for its political promotion according to the ethos of its existence That is, a group keeps or unkeeps its political complexion just for the sake of expediency. It is thus very rightly pointed out by Harry Eckstein that pressure group politics "represents something less than the full politicalisation of groups and something more than utter depoliticalisation; it constitutes an intermediate level of activity between the political and the apolitical."[16]

14. *ibid.*, p. 156.
15. Key, Jr. remarks that both political parties and pressure groups "are informal and extra-constitutional agencies that provide a good deal of population for the formal constitutional system." *ibid.*, p. 154.
16. See Harry Eckstein : *Pressure Group Politics* (Stanford : Stanford Univ. Press, 1960), pp. 15-39. Also see G.A. Almond, G.B. Powell, Jr., Kaare Stron and R.J. Dalton: *Comparative Politics Today: A World View* (Singapore: Pearson Education, 2001), pp. 69-71)

Pressure Groups and Electoral Process : Recruitment of Legislators

The role of organised groups in the political process of a country covers certain areas—elections, legislature, executive, bureaucracy, judiciary and public opinion. To interest groups, elections are an object of primary concern, for they afford them an opportunity of pushing their 'favoured' men into the main agency of administrative mechanism. They have a stake in the matters of public appointments for the obvious reason that men occupying high positions in the governmental set-up make policies and take decisions which ultimately affect their interests in varying degrees. fit requires that men of their choice be inducted and as elections constitute the open channels of filling highest offices, interest groups make use of them for the desired purpose. Group politics, thus, comes to have its part at various levels of an electoral process—nominations, canvassing campaigns and post-electoral results. It is a different thing, however, that groups follow a policy of eating and keeping their cake too; they do take part in the politics of elections and, at the same time, profess to be absolutely non-political.[17]

Organised groups play a special kind of politics in the elections. Almost all groups have their stake in the polls in some measure and their profession of keeping out of politics implies nothing else than a secret and shifting identification with some political party. Instead of implying complete aloofness from involvement in open and continuous connection with a political party, it involves a game behind the curtain. Its basic reason emanates from the fact that politics is a risky game and, in general, groups lack both courage and capability to face the hazards of contingency. Why should an interest group live in open and continuous commitment to one particular party when it is likely to cost more and pay less by such an affiliation ? It is very likely that open and well committed support to a particular person or a party may drag a group to 'extreme peril of isolation' if the electoral results are not in its favour.[18] Much weight lies in the statement of Key, Jr. that public identification of a candidate with a particular group "may be of negative value, group endorsement may drive away more votes than it attracts. A group leadership sensitive to the proprieties consults a candidate before the announcement of its support."[19]

The process of electoral contests begins from nominations. Various groups struggle to conscript names of their favoured candidates and tickets are distributed among them through the process of elimination in which rival factions manoeuvre to negotiate either with one another or with a dominant one to have their purpose served to the best possible extent. Grounds of popularity, social and economic status, caste and religion, etc. are implored to show the prospects of success or defeat of a particular person supported by a particular group before the controversy of his candidature is finally settled. However, the form taken by group politics at the time of nominations is a matter of tricks and tactics. First, a group may promote the fortunes of an aspirant through some party by securing its useful organisational support. Second, a group may contribute to much of the financial sinews of a political party and thereby secure party labels for its favoured candidates. Third, it is possible that a group may agree to the names of those candidates who are widely acceptable and on that occasion utilise an opportunity of obliging them by withdrawing the names of their hostile aspirants. Fourth, a group may justifiably

17. Key, Jr. is right in holding the view that groups 'tend to develop behind the non-partisan facade to perform the functions of recruiting and backing candidates." He further points out that if there are some non-partisan political groups, they "create a politics of low temperature." *op. cit.*, p. 385.
18. Schattschneider : *Party Government*, p. 86.
19. Key, Jr. *op. cit.*, p. 160. It is evident from the warning of David Dubinsky, Head of the International Ladies Garment Workers' Union, that labour "must be in social politics but not in party politics." Cf. in Mills (ed): *The New Men of Power*, p. 163.

convince others of a sizable cohesive bloc of voters in its pocket and thereby secure some names on the basis of adjustments. Finally, some groups may increase their strength by joining hands with others and, in this way, force a political party to choose candidates in a way that goes to their best possible satisfaction. In such a situation nomination becomes an affair of the coalition of interest groups and the party becomes, more or less, an abstraction.

But it is certain that status counts for the participation of groups in the war of nominations. The story of nomination is incomplete until one's personality, social and economic status and other relevant points are taken into consideration. It is owing to this that some persons of outstanding eminence enjoy the rare privilege of automatic access. Groups choose their names as they are massive vote-getters and their success at the polls is taken for granted. Naturally, when the effectiveness of a nominee's claim is based on his personal standing, group control over him becomes limited and the person enjoys a lot of autonomy even after his triumphant election. However, the list of such influential persons is very limited and, thus, a host of other names are chosen on the basis of group adjustments. Individual standing of a candidate requires the support of collective standing of a group. Thus, the status of a group comes into question. Leading members of a very important group figure prominently in the list of nominees; whereas other groups resort to the alternative channels of promises and threats and thereby manage to gain some of the favoured names to the exclusion of others.

Obviously, pressure group politics plays its part at the time of nominations. Tickets are, in many cases, distributed on the basis of status of the nominees and their groups. A man of unparalleled status or repute finds a very easy, rather automatic, access and almost every group may prefer to propose his name with one voice. However, as such cases are rare, leadership has become diffused like a collective entity and thus at the time of the distribution of tickets not the personality of a person as such as the status of his group counts more. The personality of a man is subordinated by the personality of his group. However, in both the cases, the outstanding consideration is that of securing access by many alternative means which "depends upon the group's internal politics, its position in the constituency, the character of the party organisation, patterns of influence in the constituency, and the nature of the formal legal procedures governing nominations and elections."[20]

War of nominations is a manipulated affair; electoral campaigns take place in the open market. As such, pressure group politics is not so visible in the conducting of electoral campaigns as may be discovered in the nomination controversy by a careful investigator. Leaving aside the case of some weak groups which refrain from taking part in elections, whether open or concealed, for some strategic reasons, i.e., fear of losing the privilege of patronage in the event of defeat of their supported leaders, many groups take part, actively though not openly, either by contributing to the funds for election campaigns or by publicising the merits of the candidates, or both. Lest the labours should go unrewarded with a kiss of political death, every group taking part in the electoral process seeks to thrive on two factors—monetary assistance and personality of the candidate.

Election is, indeed, a very costly affair. It is seldom that a candidate can meet all the expenses out of his own pocket. It opens floodgates for the inflow of money and the interest groups seek to make their hay when the sun shines. Any party, or candidate having

20. Truman, *op. cit.*, p. 295. This writer cites the case of a representative from Georgia elected to the Association of Life Insurance Presidents who in very candid terms thus wrote to one of his superiors : "—the method is to interest ourselves in key men before they are elected; help them to be elected, and then they owe us something instead of our owing them. That is the whole secret." *ibid.*, p. 291.

better prospects of success at the polls has the luck to bank upon the financial support of the groups intending to utilise the recipient of aid as their 'agent' in the government. Donations and contributions at the time of elections are thus given by many groups and taken by the parties and candidates just for the sake of securing access to power in their own ways and seeds of corruption, favouritism and spoils etc. lay embedded in such huge monetary investments whose real figures are never given to the public, although it may be required by many statutory measures of the state. Obviously, money spent on election as such, whether in the form of donations or contributions, to a party or a candidate is like a 'bribe' given by the donor to the donee to have access to the power of government through him—a necessary and basic condition of escape from the iron hands of law for doing anti-social activities.[21]

Money makes the mare go; yet it should not be treated as the single decisive factor. The personality of a candidate carries its own weight. In some rare cases, it appears that money loses where personality wins. Voters are influenced by the great services that a man renders to his community. Supporters of such a candidate invoke his great sacrifices and the voters come to form an indelible impression of his great personality. In such a situation groups seek to take advantage of a candidate's personality. They rally their support behind a great leader of charismatic personality whose victory at the polls is a forgone conclusion, or whose voice in the party acts as a determinant of policy matters. The assumption of crude theory of politics that each voter behaves like an atomistic individual does not lay down a decisive conclusion and, as such, a voter may be influenced by the charms of money as well as by the sentiments of religion and caste, etc. He may not act so irrationally as not to pay his electoral homage at all to the personality of the great leader of his land.

We have seen that two factors count most in elections—money and personality.[22] But available evidence authentically demonstrates that, out of the two, the former plays a more important role. Men of 'personality' are very rare; men of 'money' are many. The result is that men elected on the basis of monetary investments have their 'legs into the coffers' and as the keys of coffers are with wealthy groups, they have the key of the movements of the legisators in their hands. It is like mortgaging the head and heart of an elected leader to his supporters. One term as a legislator is not enough; lust for power yearns for another. So, how can a man elected on the support of a group dare to break his connection with his roots? It is, therefore, obvious that even after victory at the polls, the elected leader lives and acts like an agent of his trustees. Distinguished members of legislative bodies are thus controlled by invisible reins—greater the group, stronger the strings.

Pressure Groups and Rule-Making Department : Influencing the Process of Legislation

Target structures of interest groups involve the entire paraphernalia of a modern legislative organisation beginning from electoral struggles to the point of policy formulation. Their role may be discovered in the writing of party manifestos, distribution of election tickets and the formulation of legislative policy. Hence, the role of pressure groups, in this regard, may be discovered at three tiers— elections, party and parliament. In the first place, these groups concentrate their efforts on the electoral system by helping agencies that may work to their advantage at the time of polls. It is accomplished by creating a strong and favourable public opinion for a certain political party and its nominees. Second, they resort to the help of a party by contributing to its electoral funds and

21. See Lasswell : "Bribery" in Seligman (ed.): *Encyclopaedia of the Social Sciences,* Vols 1-2.
22. For a standard work in this connection see Alexander Heard : *The Costs of Democracy* (Chapel Hill : Univ. of North Carolina Press, 1960).

thereby winning tickets for their favourite parliamentary nominees. In such a situation they are successful in infiltrating their 'agents' into the legislative chamber for a more effective participation in the decision-making process of the highest representative body.[23] But the outspoken role of these groups is manifest in the legislative organisation where debates on important aspects of public interest take place and decisions are made in that respect.[24]

However, the nature of the role of pressure groups varies from one state to another owing to either different constitutional systems or national temperament. In a parliamentary form of government with a stable two-party system and in a land of conservatism as the hallmark of national temperament like Britain, these groups work in a more disciplined manner. Even in the event of grave dissatisfaction they donot shirk faith in the ethics and usefulness of peaceful and constitutional channels. When the groups maintain their association with one particular political party, they have a good chance of controlling legislative machinery in the event of that party's winning at the polls by a comfortable majority. However, in the event of strict party control through whips, they are not in a position to act haphazardly by pulling in contrary directions. But in America the case is different. Here federalism and separation of powers have decentralised the whole political system to such an extent that, despite a stable bi-party system, pressure groups work freely for the sake of their instrumental objectives and, in the absence of strict control exercised by the party whips, resort to the practice of 'pork-barrel' and 'log-rolling' for the realisation of their objectives. More outspoken is the manifestation of interest politics in the Senate where the device of filibustering is used to obstruct the proceedings for no other reason than the realisation of some specific interest. Likewise, the device of gerrymandering is a shrewd way of redrawing electoral districts on the eve of elections for increasing the prospects of the victory of the favoured nominees at the expense of the n minees of the opposition. However, in both Britain and the United States, pressure groups entertain moderate, secular and constitutional objectives in the legislative process. France, Italy and India present a different example. In these countries the groups are more expressive in extra-legislative spheres. In an attempt to influence legislative policy, here groups resort to many extra-constitutional, even undemocratic, devices.

If the legislative process of a representative body be examined, it appears that the role of legislators occupying very important capacities in the committees strengthens the position of organised groups in the legislative sphere. This point is very important in the context of American legislative politics where Congress in the committee rooms "is said to be Congress at work."[25] As Holtzman analyses : "Probably the most important focal point in the legislative process for interest groups is the committee. What it recommends is generally adopted by the legislature. In the Congress, what is opposed in the legislative committees, almost invariably dies there, and that which is moved on for consideration by the entire chamber may

---

23. What Prof. D.M. Berman writes about the American national legislature is applicable in varying degrees to other legislative bodies of the world also : "Members of Congress, especially those in the House of Representatives, often find themselves virtually in the pockets of pressure groups compelled to do their biddings with far greater strength than the Congressmen feel themselves obliged to do at the biddings of the Party. How and why it happens is rather very simple. The Congressman more than anything else wants to help maximise the possibilities of his election. And the election campaign needs money. So, the member is always on the lookout for money, Money is not available with the party. Thus he goes to the pressure groups for that money and gets it. But he must pay the price for the money that he obtains." See his paper "The Legislative Process in the US Congress" in *Journal of Constitutional and Parliamentary Studies* (New Delhi), Vol 2, No. 1, p. 41.
24. *ibid.*
25. Woodrow Wilson : *Congressional Government,* p. 79.

be radically altered in the committee."[26] The withdrawal of the official bill (dealing with the drastic reform proposals of the House of Lords) by Labour Prime Minister Wilson in April, 1969 after its heated debate in the Committee illustrates the fact that the influence of pressure groups has penetrated even into the institutions of British Parliament despite strong party discipline exercised by the leader of the party in power through his whips.[27]

It is obvious that pressure groups desire to keep control over the legislative organ and for this the question of means, methods and techniques engages their attention. Again, the question of techniques is closely related to the system of political administration as well as the socio-economic conditions of the people. For instance, in a very prosperous and advanced country like the United States, more stress is laid on propaganda and investment of money (amounting to bribery and distribution of offices, also called the spoils system) so that the legislative policy is controlled by them in consonance with their particular interests. But the same situation does not exist in a country having a system of proportional representation in as much as the formation of hotch-potch ministries puts a very heavy premium on the working of stable coalitions. The people of a culturally and also politically fragmented society choose their legislators in proportion that leads to the protection of local, instead of national, interests with the result that standing committees of the legislative assembly are colonised by powerful specific interests in many respects.[28]

Pressure Groups and Rule - Implementation Department : Influencing the Political Executive

Pressure groups strive to approach and influence the rule-implementing department for the reason that public policy is formulated by it whereby national administration is carrried on. Support rendered to the American President in his electoral contest affords a big handle in the hands of organised groups to advise him to lay down or give up a particular policy, send messages to the Congress, or veto a bill passed by the national legislature. Budget-making is a job of the executive and the interest groups, on the basis of their built-in strength, may go to the extent of influencing the government to incorporate into or delete some provision from the income-expenditure account of the government. Since the President makes appointments, subject to Senatorial confirmation by simple majority, pressure groups may force the Chief Executive to make or unmake some appointments on the threat of engaging filibusters in the upper chamber of the American national legislature. American experiences demonstrate that (in some States) the Governors appoint legislative councils to act as their liaison agents with the State legislatures and also to deal with certain interest groups.

However, in a parliamentary government, pressure groups seek to influence the executive through legislature. Questions, adjournment and call-attention motions, and votes of censure are the various devices through which the legislators induce, threaten or force the ministers to implement or stay a particular policy-decision in the light of the interest of their pressure groups. Ministers are, after all, elected by the people and electoral fight needs money as well as cadre-support. Naturally a minister elected with the help of a group is hardly in a safe position to frustrate the hopes of his makers. Legislative support is required to pass a resolution, adopt a bill and carry through a budget inasmuch as defeat of an official motion (in a cabinet government) amounts to a vote of censure. It is obvious that the ministers have to count upon the support of the dominant groups of the legislature in order to avert their defeat. As Holtzman says : "A hostile or indifferent legislature may cut the agency's appropriations,

26. Holtzman, *op. cit.*, p. 93.
27. See J.C. Johari: "Proposals for Reform of the House of Lords" in *The Indian Journal of Political Science*, Vol. XXXI, No. 2, April-June 1970, pp. 153-66.
28. See Henry W. Ehrmann : *Organised Business in France* (Princeton : Princeton Univ. Press, 1957)., Ch V.

alter or even eliminate progress, dictate administrative policy and procedures, and harass its personnel. Within the legislature, moreover, parts of the executive may find support for challenging other agencies and for resisting the political leadership in the executive."[29]

The establishment of several committees and sub-committees for advice and consultation by the departments affords a very convenient channel for organised groups to protect and promote their interests. Now every democratic state relies on the view that these agencies "form, in brief, a deposit of expertise upon the different aspects of policy which, effectively used, create an atomosphere of responsibility about governmental acts. If the minister acts upon their opinion, he is at least building upon a foundation of experience; if he rejects them, the creation of an opposition and, as a consequence, of the discusion that is the life-blood of democratic governance, is adequately assured."[30]

Here a situation of give and take develops in that while the department receives useful advice, the 'group representative' seeks to safeguard his interest. Holtzman says : "An executive unit that services or regulates part of the general public needs the cooperation of those who are the recipients of its activities. As active organised units representing such recipients, interest groups have much to offer to an administrative or political executive. They can provide an alternative pipeline of information and ideas to that of the administrative bureaucracy. They may furnish special staff services for which the agency has neither the appropriations nor the skills, or that it considers too sensitive politically to undertake. They can feed back to the administrator the feelings and discontent of those most affected by his agency. Within his administrative frame of reference, therefore, they are valuable adjuncts of his leadership and useful allies for his agency."[31]

It is notable that administrative boards entrusted with the task of determination of policy are generally staffed with an eye on group interests and any possibility of change in this behaviour is inevitably connected with the infiltration of new members and also to some extent with the adoption of a new policy by the old ones under forced circumstances. Anyway, the men in power protect and promote the interests of some group or groups and others feel compelled to sit willynilly in the position of petitioners rather than claimants. Identification of a group interest with an administrative unit makes the established line of access rigid against which preparations, open and underground, are made by the sufferers to change the existing order.

A situation of inter-penetration of group and administrative activity can be seen in three ways—advice, administration and propaganda. In the name of technical and complicated matters faced by a department, various consultative and advisory bodies are formed either in pursuance of a legislative measure or of an executive decision whose basic purpose is nothing else than to facilitate acceptance of the agency's action by the groups represented on such bodies. However, the device of working through the committees is more a handicap than a positive advantage for the simple reason that the terms of reference are very limited and the recommendations given after any serious deliberation are purely of an advisory character. The members of an advisory committee also

29. Holtzman, *op. cil.*, p. 118.
30. Laski : *A Grammar of Politics*, pp. 80-81. In other words, the general testimony is that departmental advisory committee is rendering valuable service not only by bringing to the departments information and advice based on first-hand knowledge but "by inspiring greater public confidence in administrative authorities as being guided by such information and advice rather by sheer theory of bureaucratic presupposition." See F.A. Ogg: *European Governments and Politics*, p. 111. For a study of committees in India, see Shriram Maheshwari : "Committees in the Central Government" in Supplement to the *Indian Journal of Public Administration* (New Delhi), Vol. IX, No. 3, pp. 186-200.
31. Holtzman, *op. cit.*, p. 116.

feel short of total support from their group. Even if a group is well-cohesive and its advices are given with a sense of unified conviction, the department may not be able to accept it in entirety or without hesitation for the fear of opposition by other groups whose interests are adversely affected. More useful for group interest is the device of administration. A situation characteristic of the occupational licensing boards and similar independent agencies comes to take place when one homogeneous interest group is directly or indirectly charged with the administration of a function. Then we have a more or less complete control of administrative action through the delegation of governmental power, especially rule-making power, to the organised interest group. Quite different is the situation where two or more conflicting groups share responsibility for decisions.

Finally, we come to the device of administrative propaganda employed as a means of protecting the access of one set of interests and restricting that of others by altering their relative strength.[32] An administrative agency charged with a highly ambiguous mandate by the 'labourers of demagogic leadership' is almost used to force propaganda in order to control access to its decisions. It is likely that the battle of propaganda may take the shape of a 'guerilla warfare' compelling the government to check its sinister development.

This is owing to the fact that now executive organ has emerged as the most important department of every political organisation. Neither legislature nor judiciary but executive "is the aggregate or totality of all the functionaries or agencies which are concerned with the execution of the will of the state as that will has been formulated and expressed in terms of law."[33] It naturally calls for the infiltration of political executive with 'men of choice' for inducting favourable personnel in the departments, formulating a policy congenial to their interests, giving priorities to certain items in the national budget, supporting or obstructing legislative measures etc. Only an effective executive can hold up pressure and counter-pressure against forces intruding upon it in a certain direction, since he is "active in organisations outside of government in order to mobilise their support when he needs it."[34]

Pressure Groups and Bureaucracy : Influencing the Permanent Civil Servants

The protection and promotion of specific interests through bureaucracy is a matter of dexterous mechanism of modern government. Taking of a decision by the legislative body and its eventual implementation by the department is just a superficial matter if the nature of modern public administration is carefully examined with the new tools of research. Legislative declarations are either very sketchy or controversial and it is the business of the administrators to convert them into a routine affair. For want of time as well as of necessary capabilities, the legislative bodies leave a lot to be accomplished by the departments supposed to function under their control. The administrators then inherit a resolution of adjustment among conflicting interests with the mandate of implementing it within an area of operation. New grants of power are made by the legislative bodies to expand the stock of administrative activity. And again, when the legislature is confronted with an insurmountable difficulty of ample time and necessary expertise, the authority of the department automatically multiplies. Consequently, in terms of distribution of both formal governmental power and informal

32. See J.L. MacCanny : *Government Publicity : Its Practice in Federal Administration* (Chicago : Chicago Univ. Press, 1939) and H.M. Stoke : "Executive Leadership and the Growth of Propaganda" in *American Political Science Review,* Vol. XXXV, No. 3, pp. 490-500.
33. Herman Finer : *The Theory and Practice of Modern Government,* p. 575.
34. See M.H. Bernstein : *The Job of the Federal Executive* (Washington, D C.: The Brookings Inst., 1958), p. 133.

political influence, the administrative services have become the principal inheritors of the declining representative bodies.[35]

As a matter of principle, bureaucracy should remain uncolonised by political complexions. However, when in the complex of public administration every organ of government is affected by the activities of interest groups, bureaucracy can be no exception. The penetration of influence into the sphere of public services, however, does not occur at the immediate level as we find in the cases of the legislature and the executive. That is, in terms of target, bureaucracy occupies a secondary place. The first target is the'open'organs of government (legislature and executive) and the groups strive to exercise their influence on them as a matter of policy. However, their penetration affects bureaucracy when both the legislature and the executive fail to protect their interests to the extent they desire. In such a case, the activities of interest groups touch non-political branches of national administration and civil services happen to constitute a dominant area of their concern. Obviously, in such a situation, bureaucracy tends to be multi-functional by protecting and promoting diverse interests. As such neutral and independent character of the bureaucracy is seriously affected.

However, the nature of the interlinking of interest groups with bureaucratic agencies is not common throughout the world. In countries like France and Italy, where party system in not very strong and healthy conventions are also non-existent, civil services are colonised by powerful groups struggling for the protection and promotion of their specific interests. This situation is quite different from that of Britain where legislature (Parliament) and executive (Cabinet) exercise effective control over the civil services. The result is that neutral character of civil services is not seriously tampered with owing to strong parliamentary control over the political executive.

The relationship between interest groups and bureaucracy in a non-Western country has its own salient aspect. Contradistinguished from the West, the penetration of influence in the civil services finds place at the primary or immediate level. Bureaucracy in the countries of Asia and Africa lives like a congeries of diverse interests pertaining to some religion, caste, raco, language, economic status, etc., and the groups donot look to it as a secondary target. Instead of using legislature and executive as their first or immediate target, the groups place more reliance on public services and, for this reason, bureaucracy becomes the dominant area of their concern. The tendency is more outspoken in a country ruled by a single dominant political party or a military junta where a single 'hero' having a charismatic personality is supported by a 'powerful elite'.

Bureaucracy is quite susceptible to the penetration of influence of the interest groups. But this penetration depends upon the techniques which they want to employ and the objectives they seek to realise through a political system operating in the midst of socio-economic conditions of the people. The means may range from their peaceful form (like negotiations and consultations) to violent form (like militant demonstrations and gheraos including other bad ones like bribery and nepotism). Likewise, the aims and objectives may vary from traditionalism and conservatism to modernism and progressivism. Finally, the nature of penetration is either favoured or forced—'favoured' when the tendency of leadership is towards modernisation and 'forced' when it is towards both authoritarianism and conservatism.

Interest groups take part in electoral politics to induct men of their choice into the seats of political executive, but their concern with

35. That now the civil servants play a vital role in national administration may be evident from the oft-quoted observation of Joseph Chamberlain : "I have a shrewd suspicion that you can do with out us (ministers). But I have an absolute conviction that we could not do without you." Refer to C.W Boyd (ed.) : *Speeches*, Vol. II, p. 7.

bureaucracy is no less important. Administrative departments have an army of officers who are 'experts' and who control their 'lay masters'. It is these experts who influence their respective heads at the time of policy-making and decision-taking. As such, it is they on whom interest groups count for an effective realisation of their purpose. Political prudence informs that it is always judicious and profitable to look to the real masters placed in comfortable chairs than to those whose tenure is subject to shifty elections and whose wisdom, knowledge and experience are controlled by their subordinates. The field of appointed posts is always prone to expansiveness; the field of elected ones is narrowed by the war of nominations and the results of elections.[36]

A logical relationship between the authority vested in the office of a bureaucrat and the sphere of interest of a group can be established. The head of a department is an ordinary human being like a legislator or a minister or a judge and, as such, has his principles, educational accomplishments and areas of interest. While in office, he may be confronted with a struggle between the tradition of the department and the philosophy of his life. Though an incumbent is selected on the basis of some written examination, oral interview, medical check-up, etc., he has to see that his loyalties are in conformity with the tradition of the department. The protection and promotion of the interests of various groups is closely associated with the nature and philosophy of those who are selected for filling so many public offices. Thus, the notion of an administrator as a neutral public servant without conflicting motivations is misleading inasmuch as he "is not a blank-sheet of paper on which the organisation can write what it wills."[37]

In a certain respect, even administrative agencies are like pressure groups; they not only administer what is given to them by legislative mandates but also act as "originators of proposals for legislation and often exert an influence in the making of new policy."[38] The civil servants have a tradition of their own and to budge from it is not an easy affair. It is wrong to say that they are just 'clay' in the hands of their masters (that is, ministers responsible to the people as their elected deputies), since they often initiate movements leading to the formulation of a new policy which may sometimes run even counter to the inclinations of the party in power. It is found that at times they act as representatives of group interests and thereby exert their weight in matters of management of programmes of procurements and expenditure that significantly contribute to the fortunes of great economic concerns. Facts may be furnished to prove that vast aggregations of public servants animated by traditions, aims and interests have a major role in the political process of a democratic country. A degree of relationship between the pressure groups and administrative agencies can be established to prove that they "are elements in the pattern of politics that may be jarred or re-aligned by the result of an election but are seldom completely thrown from power."[39]

It follows that bureaucracy acts like an attorney of some interest groups and strives for the protection, maintenance and furtherance of their interests. Administrative agencies usually exert their strength to defend themselves from criticism in the legislative chambers. They also tend to have a vested interest in the making and enforcement of a legislative measure and when they are indirectly attacked by some men

36. Truman thus comments : "It is far less risky to wager on the outcome of a race between two contestants than to try to pick up the winner from a field of three or four or twenty. To have backed the winner before he was nominated is likely to pay high dividends in access, but to have backed one of his unsuccessful opponents is even more likely to result in isolation." *op. cit.,* p. 295.
37. Simon and Thompson : *Public Administration,* p. 78.
38. Key, Jr. *op. cit.,* p. 691.
39. *ibid.,* p. 692. Also see J.L. Freeman : "The Bureaucracy in Pressure Politics" in *Annals* (September, 1958), pp. 10-19.

of organised groups in the legislative body, they resort to the assistance of their legislative friends. They thrive on the support of their political heads who, well aware of their own weaknesses, have to rely upon their permanent staff. Group interests are thus safeguarded and promoted by skilful administrative politicians and, as a result of this, departmental policy tends to ripen and harden into a tradition that resists change. It all happens over a fairly long period when a line of tradition giving to the department a personality of its own "comes to permeate the organisation; and if new recruits donot have the departmental attitude, they acquire it in time."[40]

From the above, it may be inferred that legislative declarations are routinised by the executive departments. However, two things strike us at this stage—the nature of administrative determination and the relative position of contact between the administration and the groups. Literal enforcement of a resolution adopted by a legislature and a decision consequently taken by the department may be made or vitiated by the subordinate officials either by means of an ingenious interpretation of its clauses, or by securing a judicial pronouncement over the controversy so arisen. The second factor of relative position has got its own significance. Any change in the sphere of environment, technology and social and economic structures may affect the situation of relative strength.[41]

The penetration of pressure group politics into the domain of public services has its own ground of justification. Men conducting administrative services are not merely an inert mechanism to translate the will of a legislative body into action. They are living human beings like others engaged in various other fields of official and non-official activities. Thus, being a very powerful force in the political process, they play a very important role in the determination of what is to be done in the name of the state. Politics and administration are no longer separate things; they have become a unified discipline under the complex life of a modern state and, as such, pressure groups cannot tolerate a life of complete aloofness from administrative agencies. Conflicting interests, therefore, not only contend for the penetration of their influence, they also prevent the possibilities of bureaucratic parochialism of the pettiest type.[42]

Indisputably, such a struggle combats the stock of forces that militate against the time-honoured and conservative tradition of a particular department. The defect, no doubt, is equally serious. Pressure groups play politics of a low variety and the apolitical character of public services is seriously undermined with its penetration. One suggestion that may be offered for the eradication of this malady is that the leadership of both legislative and executive wings should be in the hands of able, competent and conscientious persons. Key, Jr. adroitly concludes that the problem of bureaucracy "is, in fact, not a problem of bureaucracy at all;" it is rather a question of attracting into party service an adequate supply of men competent to manage and control the bureaucracy from their posts as the transient but responsible heads of departments and agencies."[43]

Pressure Groups and Judiciary : Influencing the Adjudicators

The penetration of the politics of interest groups in a judicial system is, however, indirect. Different from the legislative and executive organs of the government, judges "are insulated from outside political pressures."[44] The purpose must be served somehow. What the organised

40. Key, Jr. *op. cit.,* p. 695.
41. See R.C.S. Sarkar : "Role of Government Department in the Legislative Process" in *Journal of Constitutional and Parliamentary Studies,* New Delhi. Vol. II, No. 1, pp. 1-12.
42. Charles Merriam : "Public Administration and Political Theory" in *Journal of Social Philosophy,* Vol. 5 (1940), pp. 305-6.
43. Key, Jr. *op. cit.*
44. Holtzman, *op. cil.,* p. 133.

groups fail to get through the legislature and the executive, they desire it to be done through the judicial process keeping in view that judiciary is the ultimate guardian of the rights of the people and the protector of the constitution. Hence, the penetration of the politics of interest groups into the judicial system is inescapable despite every possible arrangement of maintaining the independence of judges. The reason is that the judges are "selected without regard to their political affiliations, that once selected they shall hold office for a long term—for life, or during good behaviour, that they shall not he subjected to dismissal by the executive or may be removed only for misconduct as established by a formal process of impeachment or address on the part of both houses of the legislature, and that their compensation shall not be withheld or diminished during their term of office."[45]

This penetration may take place in many ways. First, the method of the appointment of judges engages our attention. In the case of America, political considerations intrude at the time of the selection and nomination of judges. Senatorial debates exhibit that at times interest groups do intervene either to veto the nomination of a candidate (whom they regard as holding views contrary to their own interest), or to ensure that only that nomination is confirmed that is acceptable to them. The withdrawal of the nomination of Fostera for the post of Chief Justice of the Supreme Court by President Johnson in 1968 in the face of filibustering is an instance in this regard. The result of all this has been that the Chief Executive "has only half the appointing power, the Senate has the rest."[46] The selection of K. Subba Rao (Chief Justice of the Supreme Court who had earned name in the opposition circles after his decision in the Golak Nath Case in 1967) as an Opposition nominee for the Presidency against the official Congress nominee (Dr Zakir Hussain) informed the Government of India "to discriminate between candidates for judicial appointments on the basis of their social philosophy."[47] The second device is the use of an organised bar. Any canvassing by the bar associations strengthens or weakens the case of a candidate to be selected by the President or his proposal to be ratified by the Senate afterwards. In 1930, the Senate rejected the nomination of Parker for the American Supreme Court (made by President Hoover) when some bar associations highlighted his patently anti-negro sentiments as contained in one of his earlier affirmations that participation of negroes in the American politics was a 'source of evil and danger to both the races'. An Indian example may be furnished here to demonstrate the growing significance of bar associations in a move that was initiated to frustrate a contemplated step of some 'leftist' MPs for impeaching the two Supreme Court judges who had given their verdict against the Government in the Bank Nationalisation Case of 1969.[48]

The pressure groups may also use the technique of *amicus curiae*. That is, they may seek access to the courts when issues pertain to their interest. In such a situation they may secure permission to file briefs and present arguments before a court even if they are no direct party to the case in conflict. It may obviously afford them an opportunity to be in temporary alliances with others in order to influence the minds of the judges. Sometimes it does happen that by providing the court with

45. W.W. Willoughby : *The Government of the Modern State,* p. 434.
46. W.B. Munro : *The Government of the United States,* p. 192.
47. Z.M. Quraishi : "The Presidential Election in India" in *Indian Political Science Review,* Delhi, Vol. II, Nos. 1 & 2, p. 37.
48. J.C. Johari : "Lobbying in India: Independence of National Judiciary and Supreme Court Bar Association" in *Indian Journal of Politics,* Aligarh, Vol. VI, No. 1, Jan-June 1972, pp 39-55. In 2010 Chief Justice K.G. Balakrishnan withdrew his recommendation relating to the appointment of P.D. Dinakaran as a judge of the Supreme Court in view of its stern opposition by the bars of Karnataka and Tamilnadu.

well-developed and other alternative legal approaches to the issue in conflict, the groups' interests "coincide with courts' interests in arriving at a just decision."[49] However, the worst situation obtains in the people's court of a communist country where much of the sanctity of justice is destroyed not by political appointments of the judges but by mass participation in trial proceedings. It is found that a number of persons indoctrinated in the ideology of official Marxism throng the court hall and even during the course of prosecution raise slogans demanding drastic punishment to the accused persons.[50]

An effective onslaught of public opinion is a very clever tactic in the hands of interest groups to influence the judicial process from a distance. The bombardment of personal or anonymous letters, despatch of telegrams, picketing or *gherao* of judges, etc., are neither desirable nor permissible. But the creation of a strong public opinion becomes a democratic way of influencing the judges. Collection of thousands of signatures in favour of acquitting an accused and wide publicity through the press can be cited here. Likewise, publication of articles and reviews in papers and magazines or display of public resentment in television serials may go to the extent of shaping the mind of the judges. It is said that Chief Justice Warren of the American Supreme Court "publicly expressed the opinion that the leading law review articles were making available to the judges some of the best legal thinking in the country."[51]

Pressure Groups and Public Opinion : Influencing the Mass Media

The role of interest groups in the formation of public opinion is an important affair in the study of a modern political system irrespective of the fact that it is a British system with its moderate interest groups functioning effectively in a two-party system, or it is a French system with groups making activities of a radical nature in a multi-party system, or it is the American system in which organised associations openly engage themselves in public informational activities on a large scale. The ways in which these groups appeal to their audience and represent their interests through the mediums of mass communication (like press, radio and television) throws ample light on the functioning of the political system as a whole. Whatever be the form of political process, the pressure groups "play an important role in the formation of public opinion. Some exert pressure very infrequently, others almost continuously. Of primary importance are the large, powerful groups that do so much to mould and shape mass opinion and public policy."[52]

Three strategies of the pressure groups may be mentioned in this regard as suggested by Childs. First, pressure groups use the strategy of argument to appeal to the minds as per the reasoning capabilities of their audience. They publish annual and special reports, books, pamphlets, etc., and display pictures to argue their case. Religious, scientific and other empirical evidences are employed, speeches delivered, press conferences engineered, panel discussions held and a host of other similar arrangements made for this purpose. Then, they utilise the strategy of persuasion to arouse hate, fear, love or any other emotion that transforms intellectual conviction and acceptance into votes, attendance, purchases and loans. It is noticeable that everywhere groups are prompt in appropriating and applying whatever psychological, sociological or other findings about human nature may serve their purpose. Finally, they employ the tactic of publicity to call attention to their appeals. This device "is concerned with the most effective use of

49. Holtzman, *op. cit.*, p. 135.
50. Quigley : *China's Politics in Perspective*, p. 111.
51. Holtzman, *op. cit.*, p. 138.
52. Childs : *Public Opinion* (Princeton, D. Von Nostrand, 1965), p. 237.

communication media, not only of mass media, but of personal contact, small groups, local papers, bill boards, radio and television stations."[53]

Organised groups in a society compete with one another and find that the most successful method to build up influence in the realm of public policy, under a democratic government, is through propaganda or special pleading with the electorate. These groups are the principal makers of a political propaganda. In the midst of special pleadings with these interest groups, it "is vital that the most important generalised power structure in society (government) explains its activities for the benefit of all the people. When partisan petitions, have been heard, weighed and evaluated, and decisions made, based upon compromise among the whole spate of special pleadings of all interest groups, it is the responsibility of the government to publicise the decision and the reasons which support it."[54]

Determinants of Pressure Group Politics

Finally, we turn to the determinants of pressure group politics which may be thus illustrated :[55]

Pressure groups seek favourable policy decisions and administrative dispositions. They tend to adjust the form of their activities not so much to the formal constitutional structure of governments as to the distribution of effective power within a governmental apparatus. Thus, the form of group politics is determined by the interplay of governmental structures, activities and attitudes *vis-a-vis* the scope or intensity of their interest. In other words, the form and nature of group polices is conditioned by the structure and administrative agencies, activities of the political organisation and attitudes of governmental agencies towards them.

As regards governmental structure, it may be pointed out that one should look to the type of a political system. For instance, a pressure group may assume a very important, powerful and well-organised position even at the national level if the work of policy-making and its implementation is assigned to the central branch of administration. Obviously, in a country with a unitary system of government, groups have their highest units in the national capital. But in a country with a federal system of government (where authority is decentralised and localised), many groups have their units at the local and regional levels too. Secondly, the

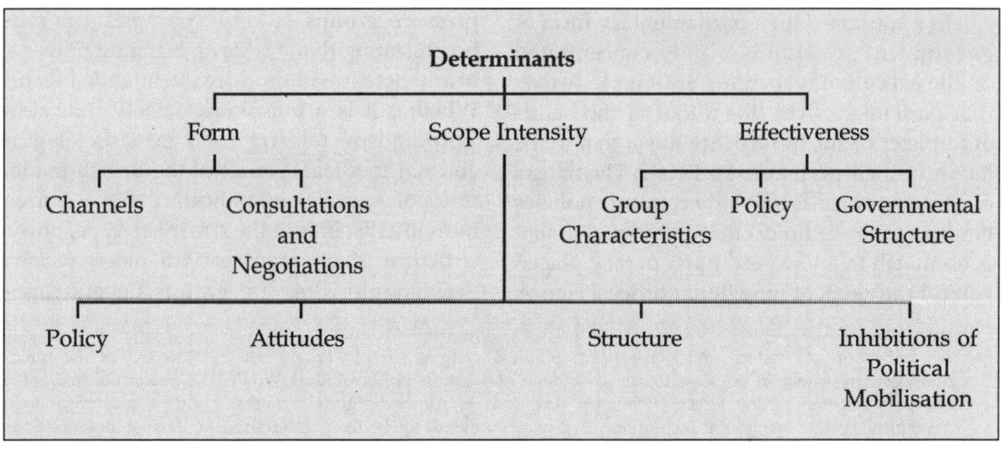

53. *ibid.*, p. 245.
54. Rodee, Anderson and Christol: *Introduction to Political Science* (New York : McGraw-Hill, 1957), p. 433.
55. See Eckstein and Apter (eds.) *op. cit.*, pp. 408-18.

politics of pressure groups is conditioned by the channels of governmental activity. One should look to the place where decisions are actually taken. It is owing to this that groups concentrate their attention on legislature and executive. Serious efforts are made to form public opinion and huge amounts of money are spent to secure victory for 'favoured' candidates at the polls. However, when the agencies of parliament and cabinet transmit their authority to bureaucracy and other minor branches of administration, pressure groups tend to penetrate their influence to the extent that even the neutral character of civil services is seriously affected.[56]

Lastly, the attitudes of administrative agencies towards pressure groups also play an important part. That is, if popular ministers and elected representatives occupying legislative seats are very responsive to the demands of these groups, they feel a sense of favoured access to the government. Conversely, when the leadership is of an authoritarian or of a traditional or conservative type working to the disadvantage of a particular clique in a single dominant political party or a military junta, the groups have a feeling of dissatisfaction and start operating through more inconspicuous channels.

In a country with a parliamentary form of government pressure is mainly concentrated on the executive branch for the simple reason that parliament lives like a tool in the hands of ministers who, in turn, are like a tool in the hands of their permanent officials. The nature of contemporary social and economic policies has become so technical that a 'lay' parliament is no match to an 'expert' bureaucracy placed behind the cloak of ministerial offices. Hence, the proper place where decisions are actually taken is not the 'open parliament' but the 'closed department' and, as such, pressure groups concentrate their attention on the 'closed' branch of administration. It, however, does not preclude the possibility of exercising influence upon policy-making through members of legislature who can use their political influence by means of asking questions, putting adjournment motions, making private representations and also utilising the source of their prestigious contacts. Moreover, many groups maintain clandestine connection with a political party either by paying donations or rendering other kinds of assistance at the time of electoral contests. They just pose a form of political neutrality in order to save themselves from the dangers of oscillation of power from one political party to another. In this way, interest groups strive to have their prosecutors first in the party and through it in the parliament and, as the powers of a parliament have been usurped by the executive in every form of government, they seek to exercise their influence upon the ministers and civil servants for the sake of having a share in the effective power of policy-making.[57]

If one asks about the ultimate aim of pressure groups, a very appropriate answer lies in stating that it rests on bringing power to bear where it will produce the intended result. Whether it is a uni-centric society indicating 'corporatism' (a term used in a sociological and not in a legal sense) of the British model, or a poly-centric one indicating with a perfect individualist bias of the American type, power structure of government is a more decisive desideratum. Pressure groups depend upon

56. A comparison of western and non-western political systems sharply brings out the 'latency' of the typical non-western system in contrast to the overtones of western politics. See L.W. Pye : *Guerilla Communism in Malaya* (Princeton : New Jersey, 1956), pp. 334 ff. G.A. Almond rightly remarks : "Any characterisation of a political system would be incomplete if it was confined solely to a description of current organisational patterns and processes. Latent interests may not only result in future changes in organisation and process, it establishes an atmosphere which effects the contemporary operations of the political process." See Eckstein and Apter, *op. cit.*, p. 400.
57. For the case of Britain see S.H. Beer : "Pressure Groups and Parties in Britain" in *American Political Science Review* (March 1956), pp. 5-6.

having negotiations with necessary administrative channels for the realisation of their purpose. However, the factor of necessity calls for the pressure groups to have a small body of 'pet' representatives capable of having consultations and negotiations with principal administrative channels with a sense of discretion vested in them and on the basis of which they may conveniently make some concessions and commitments. It should be taken for granted in advance that not their body as a whole but only their small organ of a bureaucratic type can have successful negotiations with the decision-making bureaucratic organ of the government. For this only an informal and unostentatious contact is the *sine qua non.*

However, when groups are of a very small and weak type and their influence on the decision-making body of the government is very little, perhaps nothing, then not the formal structure of government but the power-base of the groups plays a more important role in determining pressure group behaviour. In the case of extremely segregated pressure groups, negotiations take place first among the groups themselves to win reciprocal cooperation for the sake of making an effective voice. As unity lies in strength, very weak and little groups combine to make a strong impact before resorting to establish contacts with official agencies. And if, in spite of this, they fail to have access to formal official agencies, the ways of their behaviour become erratic, even unconstitutional and undemocratic involving intrigues and violence, which may better be described as 'cessation of politics' rather than of a particular form of it.[58]

The scope and intensity of pressure groups politics are determined by many factors like policy, attitudes, structures and inhibitions on political mobilisation. The policy pursued by a government has a natural relationship with the creation and working of pressure groups. The tendency of a group towards taking a more active interest in politics is accentuated when it finds something to gain or to lose pertaining to its interest from governmental decisions. In some cases, we find interaction going on among various groups to obtain favourable legislation for the sake of regulating intra-group relationship or impending rival groups competing for cutting one another's throat. In such a situation, group politics casts a very important impact upon governmental policy. The result is a two-way traffic and Eckstein very carefully makes Bentley stand on his head by arguing that if interaction among politically active groups produces policy, policy in turn creates politically active groups.[59]

Then, the factor of attitudes has its own place. Every pressure group requires a legitimate existence in order to take part in politics and, for this reason, the attitude of its members and also the attitude of others (non-members) comes into question. For example, a group may not hold the position of taking part in politics if the attitude of its doing too revolutionary and rebellious is not approved by others. Labour unions are permitted to work only when they pose no danger to national security and today in all democratic countries they are not dubbed as 'instrumentalities of class treason' or 'agencies of the conspirators'. However, when a union of workers resorts to frequent strikes and other forms of violent activities amounting to the disruption of essential services, the imposition of a ban on its existence becomes a matter of necessity. The nature and temperament of the members lays down a code of internal ethics and, as such, a group may prefer 'active politicisation' either for the sake of expediency or faith.

58. Harry H. Eckstein : "The Determinants of Pressure Group Politics", see Eckstein and Apter, *op. cit.*, p. 412.
59. *ibid.*, p. 413. Eckstein further says: "We may regard political systems as amalgams of potential and actual pressure groups : groups which form a political standpoint are merely categoric groups which have actually been drawn into politics chiefly through the impact of public policies, either policies actually adopted or policies which are threatened."

Furthermore, we should look at the structure of government. In a single party state, pressure groups cannot enjoy freedom of organisation and activity for the simple reason that opposition is tabooed under a totalitarian regime. Hence, in a political system manifesting an anti-thesis of democracy, group politics revolves around the centre of power. As a result, only those groups are permitted to live and work which consistently champion the interests of the men or party in power.[60] The case with multi-party democracies is different. In a bi-party state groups live and operate freely. They either thrive under the camouflaged support of a leading political party or maintain intimate relationship with the party in power by posing a state of political neutrality. But in a multi-party state, the degree of difference between a political party and pressure group is lessened and leaving aside the case of a very few important parties, the rest are fully politicised groups. The fundamental point in this direction is the expectation of success and, as such, in a democracy pressure groups either have their necessary 'immutable' connection with a single big political party or a 'mutable' link with the party in power. A group may even exist and operate like a 'minor' political party.

Finally, there is the factor of inhibiting political mobilisation. The ways in which pressure groups define their aims and evaluate their prospects of success and the extent to which they may ably exert their influence on decision-making agencies of the government constitute a relevant aspect of study. Two things emerge out of it social set-up and political organisation. If the society is 'modern' and 'non-primitive', its high degree of social differentiation certainly contributes to the intensification of group politics. Such a society has many interests for whose protection and promotion numerous interest groups come up with their own goals. Likewise, in such a political system intense political activity is the order of the day that finds its manifestation in the role of numerous groups engaged in exerting influence upon the decision-makers or affecting public opinion to capture power.

The effectiveness of a pressure group is determined by various factors—economic, social and political. As money plays a very significant role in modern political life, a group may more effectively influence the arena of decision-makers if it can lavishly contribute to party donations or purchase eminent leaders, writers, statesmen and publicists. Not only this, by spending huge amounts of money it may recruit a very competent staff on whose expertise governmental agencies have to count before taking any final decision. Social status of a group also contributes to its ability to achieve the desired purpose. The size of membership and the list of dignified members assign to the group a sort of prestige value that not only contributes to the creation of a favourable public opinion, it also leaves a quantitative weight upon those who occupy government chairs to make all vital decisions.

The political factor should also be taken into account. Since a popular government is made and unmade by elections, electoral process plays a significant part. As such, while in a system of proportional representation groups concentrate and depend upon their proportion, they have to diffuse and widen their area of influence for the sake of securing quantitative strength of numbers otherwise. Then, in a government run by a powerful cabinet controlling parliament by the use of whips, such groups have to confine their manipulative activities mainly in the area of executive as distinct from one where executive and legislature live in separation from one another.

What is implied here is that interest groups look not so much to the agencies of government but to the instrumentalities of political organisation enjoying distribution of effective

60. Refer to Almond's article "A Comparative Study of the Interest Groups and the Political Process" in *The American Political Science Review* (March 1958), pp. 270-82.

power within a governmental system.[61] The pressure which they exercise is either indirect (that is through the parties) or direct (that is in the shape of a minor political party or a legitimate union) for the protection and promotion of interest with or without posing a state of political neutrality. This process of interaction and inter-penetration has its definite impact upon the character and financing of a legislative organ. When the party controls interest groups, there are better prospects for the penetration of influence inasmuch as a party having a sizable strength in the legislature and functioning with the help of its whips acts with responsibility and its voice inside the legislative chamber is heard with respect.

Conversely, when the groups control a political party, the character and functioning of a legislative body are vitiated. A legislature penetrated by relatively narrow interests and uncompromising ideological tendencies, off and on, witnesses instability, even want of parliamentary decorum, and is used as a place of contention for particular interests. In the absence of a well-organised party system and in the absence of one party majority government controlled by the whips, these groups stage a very pernicious drama of criss-crossing and fail to signify an effective and timely formulation and support of large policy decisions. Naturally, legislature becomes a place where diffused, revolutionary and uncompromising tendencies struggle for the sake of protecting and promoting their interests as a result of which there is neither a stable government nor a coherent opposition. In such a situation, resort to extra-parliamentary, even extra-constitutional means takes place and the power-hungry groups feeling dissatisfied with the achievements of a legislature look to other areas of government. In order to have their 'raw' and 'unaggregated' demands of specific interests, they donot hesitate to violate the sanctity of bureaucratic and judicial organs and with their penetration into such spheres of administration, integrity and neutrality of the public services (including judiciary) are seriously affected. In particular, in a non-western and economically backward country, ridden with parochial loyalties, organised groups may be visualised to have faith less in the means of negotiation and bargaining than in methods of an extremely militant kind, as violent demonstrations, total strikes, riots, arson, etc.

Critical Appraisal

As a last word, it may be commented that interest groups have opened a very wide channel of study and thereby broadened the scope of Political Science to include rather every association or group committed to the protection and promotion of its interest through governmental activity. Prof. J.W.M. Mackenzie takes a very cautious view to define pressure groups and yet restrict the scope of study by observing a formula of the "field of organised groups possessing both formal structure and real common interest in so far as they influence the decisions of public bodies."[62] But Stewart prefers to amend the latter part of observation to read in so far as they "seek to influence the process of government."[63]

However, the combination of persons bound together by shared goals and attitudes in order to obtain decisions favourable to their preferred values by all means at their disposal, especially by gaining access to the governmental process, has got its own points of strength and weakness. Quite convincing is the view of Tom Driberg that there "are only two things to do with a pressure group. If you agree with it, remember it, embrace it and welcome its support; if you disagree with it, ignore it..."[64]

61. Lasswell and Kaplan : *Power and Society* (London: Routledge and Kegan Paul, 1950), pp. 126ff.
62. Mackenzie : "Pressure Groups in British Government" in *British Journal of Sociology* (June, 1955), p. 137.
63. J.D. Stewart: *British Pressure Groups* (Oxford, Clarendon Press, 1958), p. 1. However, he makes it plain that the title 'pressure groups' "may not be entirely unfortunate, but it has established itself too firmly in the language of political science to be worth trying to dislodge it." *ibid.*
64. Driberg, *op. cit.*, p. 271.

19

Pressure Groups

> Groups are naturally the first type of structure which we encounter in the analysis of political systems. But the study of groups raises very serious practical and theoretical problems. This is because groups are not as such part of the study of politics: we are interested in groups to the extent that they enter the political process, but not in the groups themselves. Some of them may be involved so often in politics that they cannot easily be separated from political life : but even these are not wholly in politics. Conversely, however, any group, or almost any group, is involved from time to time in the political process. Thus, we become concerned with practically all the groups which exist in society.
>
> **—Jean Blondel[1]**

Recent studies of the role of pressure groups in the sphere ol modern empirical political theory have appeared as a refined version of the philosophical and deductive theories of pluralism. Here the atomistic liberalism of Locke and the idealistic collectivism of Green that had their clear manifestation in the works of great pluralists like Figgis, Maitland, Cole and Laski have been replaced by, what may be called, analytical pluralism of David Truman, V.O. Key, Jr. and Earl Latham who have taken inspiration from Bentley's *The Process oj Government* published in 1908. The group theorists, as they are called, take it for granted that society is a mosaic of numerous groups living in interaction with each other. Curiously, the groups make claims on the government and the government, in turn, acts as the adjuster or the balancer of the interests of the social groups. The result is that each of the major social groups "tends to associate itself with a distinctive interpretation of politics or ideology."[2] The emphasis on the dynamics as well as the processes in group theory "is essentially a criticism of the formalism and static quality of the institutional approach to political analysis that was prevalent in the early phase of the twentieth century. In addition, the tenacious insistence of group theorists on the central position of the group was a reaction not only to the atomistic individualism of the so-called classical liberals but also to a kind of simple psychologism that purported to deal with social events in terms of human ideas and ideals without a very adequate theory of perception."[3]

Group Theory: Meaning, Nature and Functional Dimension

This theory shows a great deal of interest in the internal organisation and processes of various groups and discusses questions relating to their boundaries, size, territoriality and other forms of integration. Matters dealing with the degrees of organisation, patterns of control and fluidity of membership are also taken into consideration.

1. Jean Blondel: *An Introduction to Comparative Government* (London : Weidenfeld and Nicolson, 1969), p. 59.
2. Bernard E. Brown : *New Directions in Comparative Politics* (Bombay : Asia Pub., 1962), p. 18.
3. Oran R. Young : *Systems of Political Science* (Englewood Cliffs, New Jersey: Prentice-Hall, Inc, 1968), p. 80.

Society is taken as a mosaic of groups living in interaction with each other and the government is described as a form within which the group struggle can proceed in the presence of certain over-arching boundaries and limits. According to group theorists, the government can be distinguished from other groups in terms of the mechanics and processes of adjustment they provide for the purpose of handling the ongoing struggle for political interest groups. The government, thus, "comprises of groups representing within its framework broader social processes, as well as interests and claims, thus making available to outside groups a number of points of access, at which it is open to influence."[4]

At this stage, a pertinent question arises as to what a group implies. In simple words, a group means a collection of individuals. However, in terms of group theory, it has a different connotation. According to Bentley—the author of this theory—a group "means a certain portion of the men of a society, taken, however, not as a physical mass cut off from other masses of men, but as a mass (of) activity, which does not preclude the men who participate in it from participating likewise in many other group activities."[5] Truman says that a group is a collection of individuals which "on the basis of one or more shared attitudes, makes certain claims upon other groups in the society for the establishment, maintenance, or enhancement of forms of behaviour that are implied in the shared attitudes The shared attitudes constitute the interests."[6] Though one may discover certain points of difference between the views of Bentley and Truman, it may be pointed out that, according to both, group "is a mass of activity directed by interest, and the social system, which consists of a large number of groups, marks the arena for the interaction of group activity."[7]

A group, for the reason given above, has an interest of its own and it also represents a pattern of process rather than a static form. As such, a group can emerge only when the interactions among its individual members are both relatively frequent and sufficiently patterned to produce directional activity. It should be noted that groups are also different from each other as regular and coincidental or 'categoric' and the fact that the same individuals may belong to various groups, and they also do so, makes it amply clear that the activity particular to the group is more important than its structural composition. What binds the individuals of a group is the *interest*— a shared attitude concerning a claim or claims to be made by one group upon certain other groups in a social system. Bentley has laid great emphasis on the element of interest, because it leads to the 'organisation of groups'. It is because of this very element that one can imagine a large number of interests that have not found expression in any group and, for this reason, they remain unrepresented until they find such expression. Keeping this in view, we may talk of the 'potential' groups and those that are in the stage of 'becoming' so.[8]

The group theory, thus, leads logically to a particular concept of the social system and of political behaviour and it is through the social system that the various groups seek to realise or maximise their interests. The society "is a single universe of groups which combine, break, federate, and form coalitions and constellations of power in a flux of restless alterations and is kept going by the push and resistance between groups."[9] Like other behaviouralists, the exponents of this theory "are interested in the

4. S.P. Varma : *Modern Political Theory* (Delhi : Vikas, 1975), p. 251.
5. Arthur F. Bentley : *The Process of Government : A Study of the Social Pressures* (Chicago : Chicago Univ. Press, 1952), p. 211.
6. David B. Truman : *The Governmental Process* (New York : Knopf, 1964), op. 33-34.
7. Varma, *op. cit.,* p. 248.
8. *ibid.*
9. Earl Latham : *The Group Basis of Politics : A Study in Basing-Point Legislation* (Ithaca, New York: Cornel Univ. Press, 1952), p. 49.

fact that the society keeps going and, in order to explain how it can keep going in spite of the perpetual conflict among groups in which each is frantically pursuing its own narrow self-interest, the theory of a kind of automatic balance of power is brought in, the theory of the balance of the group pressures as Bentley has described it."[10]

From what we have said above, some salient features, as so elaborately marked by Young, may be thus pinpointed:[11]

1. A group is seen as a mass of activity and not as a mere collection of individuals and also as a patterned process rather than a static form.
2. A group lives and acts in the midst of group interactions that are relatively frequent and sufficiently patterned to produce directional activity.
3. A group has an interest of its own that should be studied positivistically. The interest of a group is taken to be the sum of its policy oriented and directional activities.
4. A genuine group should be distinguished from a coincidental collection or a 'categoric' group and that the individuals hold simultaneous memberships in a number of groups with varying degrees of intensity.
5. The real core of the group approach is found in the analysis of the interaction process of the very large number of groups that make up a social system.
6. The state of society at any given time is constituted by the balance of the group pressures.
7. The strength of a group varies from others on account of several factors like number of the members, intensity of concern and forms of organisation.
8. All group activity cannot be taken as 'political'; it is non-political as well. Politics is involved only when the groups make their claims through or upon the institutions of the government.
9. The government is concerned with the establishment of regularised adjustment process for handling the struggle among political interest groups.
10. In addition to functioning as an adjuster of the over-all group struggle in society, government tends to harbour a variety of groups that are themselves often in conflict with each other.

According to this theory, society is made up of groups and the government is represented by them as playing the role of a mediator in the struggle among groups and the source of rules and restraints. The government "functions to establish and maintain a measure of order in the relationships among groups."[12] Action, according to Bentley, is always and invariably a group process—never found in one man himself, it cannot be stated by adding men to men. It must be taken as it comes in many men together by men in groups. Society, nation, government—legislation, politics, administration-all are comprised of groups of men, each group cutting across many others. Moreover, these groups are in a state of perpetual interaction with each other, and politics "consists in the shunting by some men of other men's conduct along changed lines, the getting of forces to overcome resistance to such alterations, or the dispersal by one grouping or forces by another grouping."[13]

The group theorists find a great stabilising force in the operation of several social groups. The competing groups that make up society are seen as participating in an unconscious balancing process. The vast mosaic of groups involved in the process of interaction and competition and the existence of the divergent lines of conflict guarantee that all individual

10. Varma, *op. cit.,* p. 249.
11. Young, *op. cit.,* pp. 81-86.
12. Truman, *op. cit.,* p. 32.
13. Cited in Varma, *op. cit.,* pp. 247-48.

groups are kept in check by the simultaneous activities of other groups. Another stabilising force also stems from the phenomenon of overlapping or cross-cutting memberships. The individuals belong to various groups and they are not prepared to give their undivided support to one particular group at the expense of their association with other groups. Above all, the balance within a society is powerfully supported by what the group theorists call the rules of the game, or, what Bentley calls, 'habit background'. The rules of the game "are seen as unorganised though widely accepted interests that set up certain criteria of acceptability for the conduct of inter-group conflict and that are capable of active organisation in the event that these criteria are seriously violated. In formal terms, therefore, these rules are potential groups of a very powerful sort."[14]

The study of the existence and operation of pressure groups in every political system, whether democratic or totalitarian, developed or developing, has over the last few years emerged as a subject of much interest. The writers have taken pains to highlight an 'anonymous empire' or a new dimension of relationship between the individuals organised in groups and the state. The group theorists have repudiated the contentions of political philosophers of state absolutism like Hobbes and Rousseau who idealised state authority at the expense of the role of social groups by denigrating them respectively as 'worms in the body politic' and 'forces of obstruction between the individual and the general will'. Indeed, this form of study has raised interesting issues for the twentieth century political organisation and enthused a number of empirical political scientists to discover hitherto obscure material in order to ex-examine the nature of politics from the standpoint of the theory of interest articulation. Finer observes: "Today, so strong and persistent are these interest groups in pressing claims for laws and administration that political scientists have almost lost sight of the millions of individuals who are not members of them."[15]

The group theory of politics may be subjected to these lines of criticism :

1. It is said that group theorists have used certain important terms like 'group', 'access', 'interest', 'equilibrium' etc. without giving a precise definition of all of them. It is also found that there is no unanimity among the group theorists on the standard meaning of these terms. For instance, Truman does not agree with the interpretation of Bentley that group means a 'relation' between men or a process of adding man to man. It is not made clear whether a particular interest leads to the creation of the group or the group itself may have a creation of some specific interest. Though we may understand that every group tries to have access to the decision-makers, it is not clear whether the role is played by the groups outside the government as well.[16] How the group theorists would explain a situation in which President Nixon, for example, took a decision on the advice of his Secretary of State Henry Kissinger: whether Kissinger is a man or a group who influenced the actual decision-maker of the United States.
2. The group theory may be taken as half-correct and half-incorrect if we closely examine the actual functioning of a government. All decisions of a government are not taken under the pressure of groups. While some decisions are definitely made on account of the pressures exercised by the interest groups, others are not. The role of other factors like consideration for the

14. Young, *op. cit.*, pp. 86-87.
15. Herman Finer: *The Major Governments of Modern Europe* (London: Methuen, 1962), p. 10.
16. Peter Odegard : "A Group Basis of Politics : A New Name for an Ancient Myth" in *Western Political Quarterly*, Vol. XI, No. 3, September 1958.

good of the people, or feelings and ideas of the people, or character and temperament of the nation may not be entirely lost sight of. It is clear that group theorists "have tried to banish reason, knowledge and intelligence from the governmental process, which, according to them, is governed only by force, tension and pressure. While one may agree with the group theorists in holding that a great deal of politics is made up of pressure, force, intimidation and self-interest, it would be difficult to believe that reason and logic are complete strangers to the decision-making process."[17]

3. The group theory lacks the quality of goal orientation. It simply tries to study things as they are without telling us as to what should be the goals of our social life. It also fails to tell us as to how changes take place in the social and political system. According to this theory, man is reduced to the level of a creature of material interests whose mission in life is nothing more than to struggle for the protection and promotion of certain mundane interests. Group theory, like other empirical theories, may be criticised for, what is called, 'implied reductionism'. Even its empirical character can be challenged in view of the fact that it has nothing to tell us about how changes take place in the political life. Hence, it is pointed out: "A theory lacking in the very definition of goals certainly is much less capable of explaining social change. It is surprising that while group theorists are all the time talking of 'masses of activity' and 'dynamic processes', which implies that change is one of the fundamental facts of the group theory, there seems to be no attempt to use the theory for the understanding, explanation, or direction of any fundamental systemic changes.. Changes envisaged by the theory are primarily within the limits of stability-oriented system and refer, at their maximum, to the shifting balance among individual groups within the system."[18]

4. Last, the group theory is excessively'culture bound'in the sense that it is, indeed, an outgrowth of the American political process. Truman had no reservation when he defined the very term 'group' as "a part of the American politics so intimately related to the daily functions of those constitutionalised groups—legislature, chief executive, administrative agencies, and even, courts—that make up the institution of government and that the latter cannot be described adequately if these relationships are not recognised as the weft of the fabric."[19] Young thus points out : "This problem seems to be a natural outgrowth of the over-riding interests of many of the leading group theorists in American political processes. In short, the principal conceptions of group theory seem to be peculiarly relevant to a highly differentiated, economically modernised, and largely capitalistic social system such as the United States."[20]

Pressure Groups: Meaning and Nature

The politics of pressure groups hinges on the psychological foundation of self-interest. It is the cardinal factor of self-interest that forces men to be in unison with other 'like-minded' ones in order to enhance their position and power to the point of gaining recognition, legitimisation and realisation of their specific interest. That is, it depends upon the fact that "a man's skin sits closer to him than his shirt. And so men think more carefully, as a rule, about their immediate concern than about their general welfare; they are more likely to perceive their own interests in

17. Varma, *op. cit.*, p. 255.
18. *ibid.*, p. 258.
19. Truman, *op. cit.*, p. 46.
20. Young, *op. cit.*, p. 92.

politics than the larger framework."[21] However, the interests of a man are many and multifold. He lives not in a 'universe' but in a 'multiverse' of interests, unless he is a recluse or a man living away from the life of his community. Keeping this in view, it is noted that the study of pressure group politics must be made within the general framework of man's diverse interests and issues coming out of their interaction, inter-relation and interpenetration. As J.D.B. Miller says: "The individual is then a universe of interests; their orbits intersect, their influences upon him vary with time and circumstances. It is the exceptional man (in a developed society) who serves only a single interest all the time."[22]

It follows that the individuals live in a 'multiverse' of interests. They have many interests and struggle for their protection, furtherance and realisation. A social whole is a 'vast complex of gathered union'[23] some of which are clearly organised bodies, while others are amorphous collections of individuals having ephemeral existence or appearing only at certain times. As a member or supporter of a political party, an individual may agree to reduce his independence to the position of a cog in the machinery of a political organisation, yet he may keep himself free to move in and join other'para-political' organisations called pressure or interest groups for the protection and promotion of his interests. These basic divisions are inevitable and permanent, but the social system manages to accommodate them and keep them in some sort of balance, though uneasy, as the situation of balance changes its pattern from time to time. Through the interpenetration and interplay of various conflicting interests, people, in the main, "learn to live with one another, through a sense of interdependence, through a sense of what is possible, and through the intervention of the forces of law and order."[24]

It may now be possible to frame a simple definition of the term 'pressure group'. It is employed "to describe any collection of persons with common objectives who seek their realisation through political action to influence public policy. Still more simply, an interest group is any that wants something from the government."[25] Prof. Maclver says: "When a number of men united for the defence, maintenance or enhancement of any more or less enduring position or advantage which they possess alike in common, the term 'interest' is applied both to the group so united and to the cause which unites them. In the sense, the term is most frequently used in the plural, implying either that various similar groups or advantages combine to form a coherent complex, as in the term vested interests or that the uniting interest is maintained against an opposing one, as in the expressions conflict of interest or balance of interests. Interests so understood usually have an economic-political character."[26]

A pressure group has been defined as "an organised aggregate which seeks to influence the context of governmental decisions without attempting to place its members in formal governmental capacities."[27] Thus, the important aspects of the pressure group activity "are that pressure groups are firmly part of the political process and that they attempt to reinforce or change the direction of government policy, but donot wish, as pressure groups, to become the government. They range from powerful employer organisations and trade unions operating at the national level to small and relatively weak local civic groups trying to improve local amenities."[28] A peculiarly

21. D.G. Hitchner and W.H. Harbold : *Modern Government : A Survey of Political Science* (New York : Dodd, Mead & Co, 1965), p. 233.
22. Miller : *The Nature of Politics* (London : Gerald Duckworth & Co, 1962), p. 44.
23. J.N. Figgis : *Churches in the Modern State* (London, 1913), p. 70.
24. Miller, *op. cit.*, p. 44.
25. Hitchner and Harbold, *op. cit.*, p. 235.
26. See R.M. Maclver : "Interest" in Seligman (ed.): *Encyclopaedia of the Social Sciences,* Vols 7-8, p. 144.
27. H. Zeigler : *Interest Groups in American Society* (Englewood Cliffs, New Jersey : Prentice-Hall, 1964), p. 30.
28. A.R. Ball : *Modern Politics and Government* (London : Macmillan, 1971), p. 103.

American interpretation of the term 'pressure groups' has been given by Henry A. Turner who says: "By definition, pressure groups are non-partisan organisations which attempt to influence some phase of public policy. They do not themselves draft party programmes or nominate candidates for public office. Pressure associations do, however, appear before the resolutions committees of the political parties to urge the endorsement of their programme as planks in the parties' platforms. They often attempt to secure the endorsement of both major parties and thus remove their programme from the arena of partisan controversy. Many groups are also active in the nomination and election of party members to public offices."[29]

Pressure groups play their part in every political society. It would be worthwhile to enumerate their characteristic features to highlight their different dimensions and areas of operation in order to understand the working of a modern political system from a micro-angle of vision. An enquiry in this regard starts with the presupposition that practical or applied politics is a matter of continual tension, of unstable equilibrium between various conflicting interests of the people. Any attempt in the direction of considering as to how these interests take their shape to emerge in the form of political forces having their definite impact upon the nature and working of a political system naturally becomes a matter of great significance. Keeping in mind the picture of organised groups operating in a political system, the characteristic features of pressure groups may be enumerated thus:

1. A specific interest is the root of the formation of a pressure group. It follows that there can be no group unless there is a specific interest forcing the individuals to actively resort to political means in order to improve or defend their positions, one against another. As birds of the same feather flock together, individuals having a common interest come together to fight for the protection and promotion of their interests. As this fight requires active participation for the sake of potential articulation, it becomes essential that the members of a group have a serious and stable base. That is, there is no group at all where a body of people take things non-seriously, or they disperse after signing a resolution or witnessing a football match. In the true sense, a particular organised group "claims to represent, not only those who are actually members of it, but also all those who are potentially members of it, by virtue of some common characteristic which they share with the groups."[30]
2. Pressure groups play the role of hide-and-seek in politics. That is, they feel afraid of coming into politics to play their part openly and try to hide their political character by the pretence of their being non-political entities. It sometimes creates the problem of their political character and it becomes a matter of dispute to say whether a particular group is a political entity or not as it seems to confine its interest to the domain of economics or sociology. The part played by them for the sake of expediency leads to the problem of their role identification. It may, nevertheless, be pointed out that the role of pressure groups dwindles between the poles of full politicisation like that of political parties and non-politicisation like that of social or cultural organisations. Eckstein is very right in his assessment that pressure group politics "represents something less than the full politicisation of groups and something more than utter depoliticisation: it constitutes an intermediate level of activity between the political and the apolitical."[31]

29. Turner : "How Pressure Groups Operate" in *The Annals of the American Academy of Political and Social Sciences*, Philadelphia, Vol.319, September 1958, p. 65.
30. Miller, *op. cit.*, p. 41.
31. Harry Eckstein : *Pressure Group Politics* (Stanford : Stanford University Press, I960), pp. 15-39.

Almond's Classification of Pressure Groups

Associational Groups : Groups which are formally organised in the form of registered bodies having their constitution or rules, finances, records, addresses of the office-bearers and the like. The existence of such groups is known to all and so they can be easily identified as groups of the businessmen, workers, farmers, professionals and the like.

Non-Associational Groups : Traditional groups based on religious or caste or racial loyalties having no formal organisation. Their existence is not known to the public, though they show their identity in a critical situation. Such groups have an intermittent existence. They appear when their interest is at stake and then disappear. The names of their office-bearers or their mailing addresses cannot be easily located. Groups of the tribals or of indigenous people may be referred to in this regard.

Institutional Groups : These are groups of public servants who operate the system of governance. Surprisingly, they have their existence inside the government. They manage to influence the decision-makers and thereby protect and promote their interests without making a powerful protest. Such groups may be seen in the ranks of the bureaucrcy, the judiciary and the defence services.

Anomic Groups : Groups which often take to militant means and whose behaviour is unpredictable. Like an angry child, the members of such groups may indulge in violence at any turn of moment. The groups of the students and ultra-leftists may be put in this category.

3. The above point leads to the issue of differentiation between a pressure group and a political party. While the latter is a bigger organisation committed to certain principles and programmes and plays an open role in the politics of the country, the former has a limited clientele and strives to play the role of either a splinter group within a political party or shifting its loyalty and support from one party to another and, at the same time, pretending its aloofness from politics. However, both have a political complexion. While a political party plays politics by virtue of its profession, a pressure group does likewise for the sake of expediency. They, for this reason, resemble each other in being "informal and extra-constitutional agencies that provide a good deal of propulsion for the formal constitutional system."[32]
4. Keeping in view the degree of political involvement, pressure groups may be termed either 'sectional' or 'cause' groups.[33] They may also be called political and semi-political groups. They are political or sectional groups when they have a long-range interest and strive to have a part in the political process for the common needs of their members which are not of a transient kind. In contrast, cause groups are formed for a very short occasion to protect or propagate a certain belief, as religious or humanitarian, and all of their activities are by no means related to the process of governmental activity. While the former "represent a section of the community" and their concern is confined to looking after the interest of their members (as farmers or labourers or businessmen), the latter represent some belief or principle (as abolition of capital punishment) and "seek to act in the interest of that cause."[34]

Viewed in a wider perspective, pressure groups may be classified into four parts- 'institutional' groups (like government departments) which exist to perform functions and keep the governmental process in operation, 'non-associational' groups based on

32. V.O. Key, Jr : *Politics, Parties and Pressure Groups* (New York : T.Y. Crowell Co, 1964), p. 154.
33. See A.M. Potter : "British Pressure Groups" in *Parliamentary Affairs,* (London : Autumn, 1956), pp. 418-26.
34. J W. Stewart : *British Pressure Groups : Their Role in Relation to the House of Commons* (Oxford : Clarendon Press, 1958), p. 25.

class, kinship, religion or other traditional characteristic bases of communication being informal, or intermittent, 'anomic' groups appearing in the form of spontaneous uprisings like demonstrations, processions, marches, riots, etc. and 'associational groups formally organised to represent the interests of particular persons also to enjoy the advantages that such association provides in dealing with other political structures.[35]

Existence and Articulation of Pressure Group Politics

If politics means the reconciliation of interests by the role of group pressures, it becomes all the more essential to examine the forces which have their impact upon the governmental process by means of their potential articulation. Believing that many pressure groups, unlike political parties, are not solely political organisations and that they donot possess the tendency to prefer politics at every turn of time, it is yet to be admitted that they provide a significant channel of popular representation. They are, in short, second or auxiliary circuit of representation.[36] A study of pressure groups after the study of party system makes a sister-analysis in view of the fact that while the party system provides political representation, the network of pressure groups and their operation constitutes the functional part. It is irrespective of the fact that by no means do all such groups, or even a majority of them, "normally have the slightest concern in what the government is up to; but at any point of time, they might be so concerned and might wish to try to influence its policy."[37]

In order to examine the existence and articulation of pressure groups in various countries of the world, we may classify world political systems into four categories—presidential, parliamentary, presidential-cum-parliamentary and totalitarian. First, we take up the case of a country having presidential system of government like the United States where the legislature and the executive are separated from **each** other and, for this reason, the pressure groups have to exercise their influence upon two organs of the government separately. They have their eyes fixed mostly on the President who is the virtual ruler of the country and when they fear some frustration, they apply their potential articulation through the legislative bodies with the result that there is pressure and cross-pressure to bear upon the government. Lobbying assumes a very serious proportion to act as a counterblast to the authority of the President and thus we often notice the cases of deadlock between the President and the Congress.

Even if the legislature and executive are found to have a similar outlook going to the detriment of the interest groups, they have a resort to judicial intervention to make that executive order or legislative enactment null and void. Moreover, in the absence of a strong and well-organised party system the legislators and the President as well as his ministers donot work according to the 'official' party line which not only affords them ample freedom of action but brings about a marked line of difference between an individual's political behaviour and group action. Thus, there "is the paradoxical situation that the most popular theory is one of individualism as the correct basis of political action, whereas actual political practice depends very much upon group intervention."[38]

---

35. See Almond : "introduction" in Almond and Coleman (eds.): *The Politics. of the Developing Areas* (Princeton: Princeton University Press, 1960), pp. 33-34.
36. Samuel H. Finer in Macridis and Ward (eds.) : *Modern Political Systems: Europe* (Englewood Cliffs, New Jersey: Prentice-Hall, Inc., 1968), p. 58.
37. *ibid.*
38. Doughlas V. Verney : *An Analysis of Political Systems* (London: Routledge & Kegan Paul Ltd, 1959), pp. 135-36.

The same degree of freedom of action for the interplay of pressure groups is not allowed in a parliamentary system of the British model where political parties on the basis of their numerical strength form either the Government or the Opposition and run their organisation on the basis of strict discipline. Besides, the party commanding majority in the popular chamber forms the government and thereby implements its policy and programme as given in the party manifesto or announced at the platform. And yet it does not imply that there are no pressure groups in Britain. Sir Winston Churchill once frankly admitted: "We are not supposed to be an assembly of gentlemen who have no interests of any kind. That is ridiculous. That might happen in Heaven, but not happily here."[39]

The main point of difference between the American and British patterns of government is that in Britain, unlike the United States, the "pork-barrel is kept locked up in 10, Downing Street."[40] The machinery of legislative process at the Westminster is propelled not by the force of pressure groups emerging in the shape of open or clandestine lobbying but by the decision-making agency of the executive (cabinet) which formulates the policy of national administration and makes the Parliament and the entire administration run accordingly. It is a different thing that the party in power accommodates the interests of a particular group in its programme and thereby frustrates the advantages of others, as instead of legislation "depending upon pressure groups, it depends upon whether the Government (and the civil servants) want to introduce it, and however much the Government finds it convenient to consult with interests affected, it insists that the policy shall be determined by itself alone."[41]

In the British political system the functions of the interest groups and political parties "are sharply differentiated. Interest groups articulate political demands in the society, seek support for these demands among other groups by advocacy and bargaining, and attempt to transform these demands into authoritative public policy by influencing the choice of political personnel, and the various processes of public policy-making and enforcement. Political parties tend to be free of ideological rigidity, and are aggregative, *i.e.*, seek to form the largest possible interest group coalitions by offering acceptable choices of political personnel and public policy. Both interest group systems and the party systems are differentiated, bureaucratised and autonomous. Each unit in the party and interest group system comes into the 'market', so to speak, with an adjusting bargaining ethos. Furthermore, the party system stands between the interest group system and the authoritative policy-making agencies and screens them from the particularistic and disintegrative impact of special interests. The party system aggregates interests and transforms them into a relatively small number of alternative general policies. Thus, this set of relationships between the party system and the interest group system enables choice among general policies to take place in the cabinet and parliament, and assures that the bureaucracy will tend to function as a neutral instrument of the political agencies."[42]

Pressure groups play a very powerful, and also a very irresponsible role in France not because her political system is quasi-parliamentary but because French people have a different temperament and their sectional interests "tend to take precedence over the national interest."[43] It is, in other words, owing to the fact that this country has never accepted

39. See Beer : 'Pressure Groups and Political Parties in Britain" in *American Political Science Review*, March 1956, p. 6.
40. See Ivor Jennings : *Parliament* (London, 1957), p. 200.
41. Verney, *op. cit.*, p. 137.
42. See G.A. Almond : "A Comparative Study of Interest Groups and the Political Process" in *American Political Science Review*, Vol. LII No. 1, March, 1958, p. 275.
43. Bernard E. Brown : "Pressure Groups in France" in *Journal of Politics*, cited in Verney, *op. cit.*, pp. 137-38.

the full "mplications of parliamentarism like the people of Britain but retained a peculiar situation of the predominant position of the National Assembly before the de Gaulle Constitution of 1958 and of the President after the termination of the Fourth Republic. However, the existence and articulation of pressure groups in France has a very striking feature in that while they are 'solidly organised', they "are also divided that they often fail to generate a common strategy and action."[44]

The multi-party system of France with traditions of violent revolutions is responsible for making the position of institutional and anomic groups more important than that obtaining in Britain. The Communist Party has its groups in the trade union organisations and certain institutional groups (like the Catholic Church) have their colonies in the political parties (like CFTC) with the result that the parties and pressure groups interpenetrate each other. In fact, the significance of institutional and anomic interest groups "is directly related to the uneven effectiveness of associational interest groups, the absence of an effectively aggregative party system, and its fragmented or isolative political culture. Parties and interest groups in France donot constitute differentiated, autonomous political subsystems. They interpenetrate one another."[45]

This type of articulation of interest groups has resulted in blurring the borderline between social and political systems and accentuating the tendency of high incidence of anomic interest articulation, what the French people call 'poujadism'. Though a country of Europe having much of a parliamentary system of government even under the Fifth Republic, the lobbies of France "are quite similar in their methods of action to American lobbies. They give financial support to candidates; they place their spokesmen in the legislature and in the Civil Service; they have their own journals and hand out news releases in an attempt to sway public opinion to their point of view; they often exact pledges from the candidates they support and sponsor study committees in the legislatures to promote their own interests."[46]

Almond in his paper on a comparative study of interest groups and the political process further puts: "When parties control interest groups they may, and in France do, inhibit the capacity of interest groups to formulate pragmatic specific demands; they impart a political-ideological content to interest group activity. When interest groups control parties, they inhibit the capacity of the party to combine specific interests into programmes with wider appeal. What reaches the legislative process from the interest groups and through the political parties are, therefore, the 'raw' unaggregated demands of specific interests, or the diffuse, uncompromising, or revolutionary and reactionary tendencies of the Church and the movements of the right or left. Since no interest group is large enough to have a majority, and the party system cannot aggregate different interests into a stable majority and a coherent opposition, the electoral and legislative processes fail to provide alternative effective choices. The result is a legislature penetrated by relatively narrow interests and uncompromising ideological tendencies, a legislature which can be used as an arena for propaganda, or for the protection of special interests; by veto or otherwise, but not for the effective and timely formulation and support of large policy decisions. And without a strong legislature, special interests and ideological tendencies penetrate the bureaucracy, and undermine its neutral, instrumental character."[47]

44. Macridis : "Social and Economic Foundations : The Mainsprings of Change in France" in Macridis and Ward (eds.), *op. cit.*, p. 193.
45. G.A. Almond, *op. cit.*, pp. 37-38.
46. Macridis, *op. cit.*, p. 193.
47. Almond, *op. cit., p. 276.*

A comparison of British and American pressure groups creates the impression that they "only have overweening power in parliamentary systems when the element of parliamentarism is not strong enough to withstand them."[48] Now we take up the case of a country having totalitarian form of government. It is wrong to assume that pressure groups have their operation only in a free and democratic country. These groups do exist and operate even under a totalitarian system with the difference that they "tend not to be independent: the embodiment of the goals of the system by associations requires the creation of new associations which donot have any internal legitimacy and thus rely on the political system to grow and to be maintained."[49] Jn contrast to the situation of a democratic country, pressure groups in an authoritarian system are allowed a very circumscribed role and serve merely "as instruments of the state for securing ends which are state-determined, or they may become part of the facade of government for legitimising decisions."[50]

As a corollary to the above case, we may refer to a system of one party's monolithic position in the midst of weak and disarrayed opposition. Such a political system is quite different from the totalitarian model for the obvious reason that here opposition is not forbidden. Such type of 'dominant non-authoritarian party systems' are usually to be found where nationalist movements "have been instrumental in attaining emancipation."[51] The line of difference between a totalitarian system and a political system run by a single powerful political party lies in the fact that while pressure groups operate in the former by means of intrigues, denunciation, passing the buck and other such oblique methods, they operate in the latter without facing the onslaughts of purge and suppression and discover their place within the structure of the party in power.[52]

Finally, a reference should be made to the developing societies where pressure groups do exist though in a rudimentary and poorly organised form. The techniques they often adopt are of a very crude type. When a serious crisis comes, the military supervenes to finish the obtaining order and establish its dictatorship by virtue of its coherent organisation, similarity of outlook and the capacity to organise the coup. In such a society other interests "may be powerless to move because of their lack of organisation and discipline; they will have to come to terms with the colonels, but will retain some strength, since the colonels cannot run the state without at least some cooperation from them."[53]

Whether it is a free or a totalitarian, a developing or a developed country, the existence and articulation of interest groups cannot be ignored, though it may be manifest or latent, specific or diffuse, general or particular, instrumental or affective in style. It is *manifest* when it is an explicit formulation of a claim or a demand; it is *latent* when it takes the form of behavioural or mood cues which may be read and transmitted into the political system; it is *specific* when it takes the form of a request for a particular legislative measure and a subsidy; it is *diffuse* when it takes the form of a general note of dissatisfaction or resentment; it is *general* when the demands are couched in general class or professional terms and it is *particular* when they are put in individual or family terms; it is *instrumental* when it takes the form of a bargain with consequences realistically spelled out; finally, it is *affective* when it takes the form of simple expression of anger or gratitude etc.[54]

48. Verney, *op. cit.,* p. 138.
49. Blondel, *op. cit.,* p. 69.
50. Abraham Holtzman : *Interest Groups and Lobbying* (London : Macmillian 1966), p. 1.
51. Almond, *op. cit.,* p. 41.
52. Miller, *op. cit.,* p. 77.
53. *ibid.,* p. 78.
54. Almond, *op. cit.,* pp. 34-35.

Heywood's Analysis of Pressure Groups and their Merits and Demerits

Distinction between Political Parties and Pressure Groups

1. Parties aim to exercise government power by winning political offices (small parties may nevertheless use elections more to gain a platform than to win power).
2. Parties are organised bodies with a formal 'card carrying' membership. This distinguishes them from broader and more diffuse social movements.
3. Parties typically adopt a broad issue focus addressing each of the major areas of government policy (small parties, however, may have a single issue focus, thus resembling interest groups).
4. To varying degrees, parties are united by shared political preferences and a general ideological identity.

Merits of Interest Groups

1. They strengthen representation by articulating interests and advancing views that are ignored by political parties, and by providing a means of influencing government between elections.
2. They promote debate and discussion, thus creating a better informed and more educated electorate, and improving the quality of public policy.
3. They broaden the scope of political participation, both by providing an alternative to conventional party politics and by offering opportunities for grass-roots activism.
4. They check government power and, in the process, defend liberty by ensuring that the state is balanced against a vigorous and healthy civil society.
5. They help to maintain political stability by providing a channel of communication between government and the people, bringing outputs into withinputs.

Demerits of Interest Groups

1. They entrench political inequality by strengthening the voice of the wealthy and privileged, those who have access to financial, educational, organisational or other resources.
2. They are socially and politically divisive, in that they are concerned with the particular, not the general, and advance minority interests against those of society as a whole.
3. They exercise non-legitimate power, in that their leaders, unlike politicians, are not publicly accountable and their influence bypasses the representative process.
4. They tend to make the policy process closed and more secretive by exerting influence through negotiations and deals that are in no ways subject to public scrutiny.
5. They make societies ungovernable, in that they create an array of vested interests that are able to block government initiatives and make policy unworkable.

Andrew Heywood : *Politics*, pp. 248 and 277.

Critical Appraisal

The existence and articulation of organised interest groups in every political system has been dubbed as a sinister development, an exercise in partial as opposed to total representation and the interplay of unprincipled and corrupt forces undermining the existence of what Rousseau called 'general will'. In the politics of pressure groups it is the shrewd and corrupt leadership which enjoys a position of special advantage. Then, the behaviour of these groups is hardly democratic either towards other groups operating in the country or even towards those which come to render their support on some occasions. The organisation of leadership and other hierarchical units operates in the hands of unscrupulous persons indulging in quite selfish and irresponsible ways. Their game of hide-and-seek in politics brings about a situation of their difference with political parties with the result that they cannot be held to account for their policies, their leaders cannot be turned out of public office and punished at the polls. Finally, it appears that though selfish and narrow interests effectively organise, important and socially significant ones go unrepresented. "The battle between producers and consumers, for example, is notably uneven."[55]

Various pressure groups operating in a political society are viewed with moral indignation and alarm owing to their sinister penetration in the mechanism of modern representative system. It is further charged that the technique of lobbying, as practised by these groups, constitutes a whole congeries of abuses, corruption and fraud manifestly weakening people's faith in the system of popular government. While referring to the sinister interplay of pressure groups behind the legislative process in the American Congress, Woodrow Wilson discovered that the wishes of the Congress were really the wishes of the interest groups. It is also contended that any degree of appreciation of the role of pressure groups in a modern political system becomes reminiscent of the Fascist corporate state. Hence, it "may be said that the genuine representative significance of all organisations arising in connection with men's activities within the total context of modern industrial life has become sufficiently apparent to make it necessary to reckon them as pretenders to the throne of government. Where the interests are sharply divided, certain of these groups have proceeded to take over the government and to revolutionise it in such a way as to suit their particular needs and conceptions. Such efforts accompanied by dictatorial methods relapse into crude techniques of government which violate the fundamental premises of constitutional limitation."[56]

Despite these objectionable points, the utility of pressure groups in the working of a modern constitutional system cannot be dismissed. Exponents of the group theory of politics and others subscribing to the school of modern pluralism emphasise the fact that there is an organic relationship between the individual and the groups owing to which the individuals "are the heirs of the head, while the groups are limbs on which the body depends."[57] If political parties are inevitable for the working of a modern democratic system, pressure groups have their own significance in the political process. Any fear of contradiction between individual and group political participation can be avoided by looking upon politics as a process rather than as a simple relationship between formal structures of a political system. It is unwise to purge or finish conflicting interests, rather the task "remains of distilling the general public interest out of the often-conflicting special interests which constitute part of the whole."[58]

It leads to the satisfying conclusion that there is every need for keeping control over the interest groups in order to regulate their existence and working to the best possible extent. It is necessary to assure that, while making their contribution to the political process of a country, the groups are not allowed to lose their touch with their own members or other groups of the society, or doing anything against public interest or general good. The case of public recognition of group participation carries with it the understanding that interest groups conform to the same standard of political behaviour which is expected from the individual electors. True that the unorganised individuals at the ballot box have often become powerless to achieve anything in contrast to the highly organised lobbies with their direct access to the centre of power, but there remains nothing

55. Hitchner and Harbold, *op. cit.*, p. 252.
56. Carl J. Friedrich : *Constitutional Government and Democracy* (Oxford and IBH, Indian Ed., 1966), p. 484.
57. Verney, *op. cit.*, p. 144.
58. Friedrich, *op. cit.*, p. 484.

to prevent the state from reforming and regulating the pressure groups which exist and enjoy power without responsibility.

The real significance of pressure groups in a political society must be examined in the light of two main considerations. First, they are of numerous advantages to political parties and thereby contribute to the sustenance of the modern representative system. Power corrupts man and power alone checks power. The pressure groups thus act as a powerful check upon the arbitrary exercise of power and as they themselves are prone to abuse their share of power, it is essential that various interest groups be allowed to act as a check upon one another in order to establish and sustain the system of 'checks and balances.' It also implies that when the groups act as a check upon the government, the latter must see to it that the activity of group politics is saved from deterioration to the extent of vitiating or destroying the political system itself. As Verney holds : "The use of the term 'pressure groups' suggests that outside interests are obtaining special favours at the expense of the public, but it is also true that groups help to prevent Governments from imposing unfair burdens on the unorganised masses. Moreover, where party programmes tend, of necessity, to be general, group policies and proposals can be usefully specified."[59] Second, the utility of pressure groups must be examined in the light of new approach to the meaning of politics. Politics is a struggle for power creating conflicts and tensions and then discovering and offering their solutions and adjustments. As Miller says : "Politics rests ultimately upon the conflict and accommodation of interests, brought into being by the manifold inequalities of a society; broadly speaking, political decision will follow the course along which it is led by the relative strength of interests."[60]

59. Verney, *op. cit.*, p. 143.
60. Miller, *op. cit.*, p. 101.

20

Techniques of Pressure Politics

> Individual interest groups generally function in a pragmatic and opportunistic fashion, using any method or technique which they believe will serve their purpose effectively. Undoubtedly, dictating most pressure groups' activity is the criterion : what action will produce the maximum desired result with the minimum expenditure of time and resources. The techniques and tactics which any particular group employs will be determined largely by such factors as size and geographic distribution of the membership, cohesion of membership, financial resource, prestige, position of the organisation, quality of leadership and staff, and relations with the political parties and other organised groups.
>
> **—Henry A. Turner[1]**

Coercion or exercise of pressure by means of force is the ultimate weapon used by the individuals and their groups to secure compliance of their wishes and the acceptance of their demands. It is in the nature of a reserve which is to be used when other techniques of politics of persuasion fail to serve the desired purpose. In order to see that specific interests are protected and promoted, as far as possible, pressure groups emerge "to promote, defend, threaten, inform, educate, destroy and so on."[2] Hence, we may now study various techniques that are employed by the pressure groups in this regard. They are many, depending upon the temperament of the nation, limits of the constitutional provisions, availability of legal sanctions and socio-economic conditions of the people. In this chapter, we shall, therefore, deal with four techniques—lobbying, strike, *bandh* and *gherao*, the last two being peculiarly Indian and that have had their manifestation over the last few years.

Lobbying

Lobbying is a favourite technique of the pressure groups operating in every political system, whether it pertains to liberal democracy or totalitarianism for the simple reason that politics is the struggle for power in which they play their part. That is, any group that makes claims upon other groups or upon the society as a whole finds it well-nigh impossible to stay out of politics. As in a strictly *laissez faire* system of the nineteenth century, the government had to provide the legal framework within which social action takes place, so in a modern industrial society (where regulation extends in some degree to almost all human activities and relationships), the decisions of public officials are of crucial importance. They "are and must be subject to the close and continuous attention of the groups they affect. Even the most authoritarian rulers must take into account the army, the priesthood or some other politically influential elements."[3]

1. Turner: "How Pressure Groups Operate" in *The Annals of the American Academy of Political and Social Sciences*, Vol. 319, September, 1968, p. 64.
2. Childs : *Public Opinion* (Princeton : D. Van Nostrand, 1965), p. 237.
3. *Encyclopaedia Britannica*, Vol. 14, p. 175.

The term 'lobbying' is used both in a narrower and a wider sense. In the narrower sense, it refers to approaches made to the members on a large scale by outside organisations inasmuch as it is not restricted merely to activities occurring within the precincts of the parliament. In the wider sense, it means an attempt on the part of organised groups to influence any organ or agency of governmental departments to seek maintenance, protection, furtherance and realisation of their specific interests. That is, lobbying is a political technique and its sole *raison d'etre* "is that of influencing the government."[4] An authoritative definition of lobbying in this regard is thus furnished : "In its original meaning lobbying is referred to the efforts of the individuals to influence the votes of legislators, generally in the lobby outside the legislative chamber. In its broadest modern sense, it means any attempt by individuals or groups to influence the decisions of government. It is most commonly associated with the activities of private interest groups, often called pressure groups, although even public officials may be said to lobby when they attempt to influence the making of public policy by other officials."[5]

The existence of pressure groups and the use of the technique of lobbying is conspicuous in a free or open society where the obligation of the government to consult the governed is recognised and institutionalised through guarantees of freedom of speech, press and assembly alongwith the right of the people to petition the government for the redressal of their grievances. Thus, lobbying "occupies a preferred position in the constitutional system because it is necessary to the preservation of self-government."[6] It, however, does not imply that the existence of pressure groups and the operation of the technique of lobbying are confined to the countries having representative form of government; even countries with a totalitarian system are no exception in the strict sense of the term. It is an historical fact that even a Caliph like Harun-ul-Rashid visited his people in disguise to know their feelings and thereby redress their grievances just to legitimise his autocratic rule. Recent examples show that anomic (spontaneous) groups may come up to challenge the authority of the despots in a country like Afghanistan, Pakistan, Bangladesh and Myanmar. Though they are repressed, they provide an indication of the only means available to the people groaning under the iron hold of a totalitarian regime tied to the apron strings of a powerful leader. It shows that even under a despotic government, the ruler "must find some means to act from time to time as a politician with his ear to the ground."[7]

The operation of lobbying occurs mainly in the area of legislative activity in a free and democratic society. Hence, we first refer to the employment of this technique in relation to the organisation and working of a legislative body. Here it signifies a very effective weapon in the hands of pressure groups to bear their influence upon the legislators. Its most sensational form is mass lobby. The object of this technique "is to persuade the Member of Parliament of the degree of feelings in his constituency on an issue and incidentally to put some arguments to him."[8] In a leading case (*US* v. *Rumely*, 345 US 41), the American Supreme Court interpreted that lobbying "should be construed in its commonly accepted sense a representation made directly to the Congress, its members or its committees."[9] Likewise, while upholding the constitutional validity of a lobbying law,

4. D.V. Verney : *An Analysis of Political Systems* (London : Routledge and Kegan Paul Ltd, 1959), p. 132.
5. *Encyclopaedia Britannica,* Vol. 14, p. 175.
6. *ibid.*
7. D.G. Hitchner and W.A. Harbold : *Modern Government : A Survey of Political Science* (New York : Dodd Mead & Co, 1965), p. 233.
8. J.D. Stewart : *British Pressure Groups : Their Role in Relation to the House of Commons* (Oxford : Clarendon Press, 1958), p. 207.
9. *Encyclopaedia Britannica,* Vol 14, p. 176.

the Supreme Court (*US* v. *Harris*, 347 US 612), reinforced its re-interpretation of the narrow scope of the law.'[10]

As lobbying is a technique of influencing the body of legislators, it may take any form such as personal meetings, delegations and deputations to representatives of the legislative bodies, writing of letters and making telephone calls, sending cables and telegrams, making demonstrations, and so on. In addition, support rendered to the candidates at the time of electoral battles with men and money and threats of withdrawal of such support at the time of the ensuing elections belong to this category. It is the constituency which provides the group with a sure way of catching the attention of the members of parliament, no matter an open display of such weapons amounts to the breach of parliamentary privileges in some respects. While withdrawal of support or its threat is no contempt of the House,[11] the issuance of threat may amount to the same although the offer of monetary assistance in any form is certainly a breach of parliamentary privileges.'[12] It is, however, a different thing that clever groups exercise the weapon of veiled threat to avoid the risk of parliamentary criticism, or an astute leader like Churchill may epitomise the situation by arguing that threats and political abuses are parts of the life of a member of parliament.[13]

A member of a legislative body is elected by the votes of his people who have certain demands on and expectations from him. It is only at the open risk of losing next chance that the chosen delegate may, like Edmund Burke, reveal his heart by acting according to his judgment on the frank admission that the elected person is not at all a slave or a loudspeaker of his constituents. True to say that a representative chosen by the people, several thousands in number, cannot reduce himself just to the status of their mouthpiece at every turn of moment, he is certainly expected to exercise his judgement, as far as possible, in a way plausible to them in case he has to maintain his goodwill in his constituency. As Stewart says : "Members of Parliament exist in a distinctive atmosphere. In it, certain ideas and principles are taken for granted. One of them is that a member has his duty to the constituents. The MP is there to represent his constituents and though this does not mean accepting their views on all issues, it does mean paying attention to them."[14]

Lobbying in the form of electoral support to the contesting candidates is governed by the consideration of inducting 'agents' into the legislative chamber. Support rendered during electoral fights in the shape of 'open' manpower or 'disguised' monetary assistance keeps the elected representatives "virtually in the pocket of pressure groups"[15] However, the nature of the operation of this technique differs from one state to another owing to different constitutional systems and socio-economic

---

10. *ibid.* While referring to the special case of the United States, it is reported that there are, moreover, not 1 but 51 governments, each exercising powers guaranteed to it by hard-to-amend the Constitution. In this framework, the national parties are merely federations of state and local parties, incapable of carrying out a promised programme of action. Power is further dispersed in Congress among Standing Committees, and localism is strengthened by the individual member's dependence on his constituency. With political power so fragmented, the group struggle is bound to be public. This makes it easy for the participants to denounce the lobbying of the other side; as Sen Jim Reed once said, 'a lobbyist is any one who opposes legislation 1 want." *ibid.*
11. See Erskine May : *Parliamentary Treatise,* 15 Ed., p. 123.
12. It is highly improper to bribe a member as the offer of money or other advantage to any member of Parliament for promoting any matter whatsoever, depending or to be transacted in the legislature, "is a high crime and mis-demeanour and tends to be subversive of the English Constitution." *ibid.*
13. Stewart, *op. cit.,* p. 222.
14. *ibid.,* p. 218.
15. D.M. Berman : "The Legislative Process in the U.S. Congress" in *Journal of Constitutional and Parliamentary Studies* (New Delhi), Vol 2, No. 2, p. 41.

conditions of the people. For instance, in a rich country with a presidential system working on a loose party organisation, like the United States, lobbying plays a very outspoken and legally recognised part by the professional organisations. Different from this, in a prosperous country with a cabinet system of government based on rigid organisational discipline of two political parties and standing on the conservative temperament of the people, like Britain, lobbying is allowed to play a very limited and 'concealed' role by the exigencies of the conventions and not by the provisions of a parliamentary statute.

It is further noticeable that while in a country with a hotchpotch of parliamentary and presidential systems vitiated by multi-party system and radical temperament of the nation in the midst of elegant conditions of life, like France, lobbying seems to play a more significant part around the office of the real executive (President) not accountable to the legislature than that of his nominee (Prime Minister) responsible to the National Assembly.[16] Finally, in a backward country having remnants of a feudal economy and torn by a multiparty system, like India, lobbying takes the shape of violent manifestations as strikes, *bandhs, gheraos* etc. Moreover, as every legislative body works with the help of committees where detailed considerations take place over bills and other measures of proposed legislation, lobbyists fix their mind on these legislative committees where they strive to have their 'colonised' agents.

Lobbying, in a wider sense, covers all organs of a government, and, as such, its penetration is discoverable even in the spheres of administration and adjudication. Executive has become the most important organ of the government by virtue of its policy-making and policy-implementing powers and, as such, lobbyists have their eyes on the real executive whether he is the President as in the United States or France, or he is the Prime Minister as in Great Britain and other countries following the model of cabinet system of government. The establishment of many committees for the purpose of advice and consultation affords a very convenient channel. Bureaucracy is the essential part of the executive and hence the lobbyists endeavour to influence the appointing authorities to colonise administration with their own men so that they have, in addition to their chosen legislators, an alternative pipeline of supporters in the sphere of administration. It follows that in every system of government obtaining today, the lobbyists have their eyes fixed on agencies concerned with national administration for the obvious reason that it calls for the infiltration of the administration with the man of their .'choice' "for inducting favourable personnel in the departments, formulating a policy congenial to their interests, giving priorities to certain items in the national budget, supporting or obstructing legislative measures etc. Only an effective executive can uphold pressure and counter-pressure against forces intruding upon it in a certain direction, since he is active in organisations outside of government in order to mobilise their support when he needs it."[17]

The penetration of the tactic of lobbying in a judicial system is, however, of an indirect type as, unlike the members of a legislature and an executive, the members of a judiciary are insulated from outside political pressures. The basic factor is that the purpose must be served and in case lobbying fails to achieve it through the instrumentalities of a legislative body or its committee or that of an executive and bureaucracy working under it, the act of judicial intervention must be taken under consideration to win the game. Hence, the matter of the appointment of judges comes up. To colonise the judiciary with 'agents' is desired. When the matter is before the court, judges must be influenced from a distant source. As forces deemed proper for influencing the

16. See Henry W. Ehrman : *Organised Business in France* (Princeton : Princeton University Press, 1957), Ch V.
17. See H.M. Bernstein : *The Job of the Federal Executive* (Washington D.C. : The Brookings Institute. 1958), p. 133.

legislators and administrators are not allowed in the case of influencing the judges, the most effective channel finds place in the creation of a strong public opinion to have some definite impact upon the minds of those who occupy the seats of justice.[18]

It is obvious that lobbying is a favourite technique in the hands of pressure groups to play a bigger but unofficial role in a governmental process. It has become a remunerative profession in the hands of very shrewd persons. So important has become the practice of this technique, particularly in the opulent societies of the West, that the necessity of legislative safeguards has been emphasised to control its evil aspect, much less to derecognise it. It is generally accepted that as it is based on the foundation of self-interest, it cannot be conducted on ideal principles. Nothing useful has come out in the United States by the Federal Regulation of Lobbying Act of 1946. Neither can its flow be outlawed in a democratic system, nor can it be circumscribed by the exigencies of a law, though the usefulness of legislative measures cannot be absolutely ruled out. Owing to this situation, many social scientists hesitate in accepting the view that lobbying "is not inherently bad and have, indeed, recognised that this form of group representation may be useful provided the public interest is protected."[19]

A proper sanction to the practice of lobbying must be discovered within the framework of democratic government which recognises every man's right to struggle freely for the protection and promotion of his interest and which also demands the sacrifice of private interest for the sake of national good. As in every society some men are more assertive to make their rights meaningful than others, this has meant, in practical terms, that those interests with much to spend for protection have proclaimed 'lobbying for all men' as an almost sacred article of faith.[20] Viewing various aspects of this complex issue, Stewart suggests that it would be unwise to call any lobbying tricks improper as it is a matter for the group to decide. These weapons "provide the group with its means of appeal. Without them it would be more dependent on the government than seems desirable. It may be that many of these methods donot seem very elegant and that they would have no place in an ideal political system. But in the present system they provide many groups with the means of campaign which safeguard their position. They are part of the communication of our society and as such valuable and important, even though at times distasteful."[21]

Strike

Strike is the commonest pressure tactic in the hands of one party to coerce the other so as to concede its demands. In very simple terms, it means 'the stoppage of work'. An eminent American writer, Florence Peterson, says : "A strike is a temporary stoppage of work for specific reasons entered into with the expectation that work will be resumed when a settlement of the grievances is effected. So far as the intentions and the attitudes of the strikers are concerned, they look upon themselves as continuing to retain the status of the employees and of the company against which they are striking, with vested interests in their individual jobs and with the right to return to their jobs when they have reached a mutual agreement over the matters in dispute, or if unsuccessful, when they are willing to return to work on the terms offered by the employer."[22]

18. Abraham Holtzman : *Interest Groups and Lobbying* (London : Macmillan, 1966), p. 138.
19. See E.P. Herring : "Lobbying" in E.A.R. Seligman (ed.) : *Encyclopaedia of the Social Sciences* (New York : Macmillan, 1933), pp. 565-68.
20. Roche and Levy : *Parties and Pressure Groups* (New York : Harcourt Brace and World, 1964), p. 192.
21. Stewart, *op. cit.*, p. 237.
22. Peterson : *American Labour Unions* (New York : Harper & Row, 1963), p. 153.

However, as the stoppage of work cannot be done by a single person, it involves plurality of men with the same intent of compelling the other party to meet their demand (s) or grant a redressal of their grievances. Moreover, a refusal to carry on the work requires concerted action for the realisation of their objective. A statutory definition of the term' strike' is thus given in Sec. 2(q) of the Indian Industrial Disputes Act: "Strike means cessation of work by a body of persons employed in an industry acting in combination, or a concerted refusal under common understanding or of any number of persons who are or have been so employed to continue to work or to accept employment."

It is evident that the two definitions given above concern industrial aspects only. But the ingredient of both—'cessation of work' by a body of persons for the realisation of some objective through concerted action—is applicable to every strike whether it is in a commercial or industrial undertaking or in an office, workshop, school, college, university etc. Hence, with a view to give another definition of the term strike applicable to every place of work, it may be added that it means a combined action of a body of men amounting to the quitting of work with a specific purpose mainly related to their interest. Undoubtedly, strike is a typical case of this straightforward application of pressure. "The strike is commonly used," writes Bondurant, "to effect economic pressure, and is intended to hurt business, or to strain relationship so that normal functions are brought to a halt, or at least inhibited. Normal functioning cannot be resumed until policy changes are instituted. The process of strikes or passive resistance in its most common forms amounts to the intensification of pressure or the shifting of the points of attack until a settlement is reached through capitulation or through compromise."

Such an interpretation of the term 'strike' leads to the study of its nature and intent. As regards the nature of strike, it may be said to include three ingredients, namely, the number of men involved, effect resulting in the stoppage of work, and their combined endeavour to achieve their purpose. The tactic of strike cannot be employed by a single person inasmuch as it needs a concerted action of a group of men. The practical manifestation of a strike reveals stoppage of work in which the consideration of periodicity is immaterial. As such, a strike may continue for minutes, hours, days, weeks or months. But the purpose of the strike cannot be achieved without concerted action appearing in the shape of mass 'leave' on some fake and flimsy ground, or the exercise of persuasion and force upon others to do likewise. However, a person on leave or absent on some other ground may be said to have been on strike if there is a convincing evidence to demonstrate an element of common understanding between him and other strikers.

Next, the element of 'intent' constitutes a difficult situation. Stoppage of work can be effected when the persons involved in it quit their work for any purpose and with any motive whatsoever whether having any connection with the nature of their employment or not. Even legal opinion in this regard is divergent and it cannot be said with certainty whether stoppage of work by a group of men on account of their mass movement to witness a football match or to join a funeral procession, for example, constitutes a strike or not. The general view is not to regard any concerted action of a group of men as strike when the employers are not at all confronted with the situation of conceding the demands of their employees. However, it may be just a lame excuse to avoid a difficult situation. Any action of a group of persons amounting to the cessation of work and defiance of authority is, nonetheless, a strike whether the intent or motive of the strikers is political, economic, humanitarian and the like. In this regard, an Indian lawyer's point of view is quite convincing when he observes that it "is implicit in the definition of the word 'strike' that the cessation of work should be in defiance of the authority of the employer. Where the cessation of work is not in defiance of the employer's authority, it does not amount to a strike, though the act of cessation might be concerted."[23]

However, refusal to or quitting of work amounting to the defiance of authority for any sake does not constitute a strike when the employer wants to engage his employees in some additional work going beyond the terms of contract of employment. However, a situation of strike may arise even in a case of overtime work when a group of persons induce, persuade or force others not to do additional work. Again, there is a strike when the persons involved therein refuse to carry on their work not wholly but partially. Duty and parts of a duty go together and if the persons quit not their duty as a whole but its part or parts, it is certainly a strike though, for the sake of a more befitting appellation, it may be termed 'partial' strike.

Such a study of the term strike leads us to look into its varieties having, as well as not having, any connection with the nature of employer-employee relationship. As such, a strike may take place where the persons involved are in direct clash with their employers; it may also occur in a way where the employer's interests are effected incidentally or remotely; it may also happen when the interests of the employers are not at all affected. Besides, strike may also be visualised as an instrument of pressure politics either affecting a particular industry, office, institution, place of work or paralysing the whole country or its major parts. Viewed thus, strike may be said to have various types and forms as mentioned below :

First, there is a case of 'sympathetic' strike if the persons involved in it resort to the cessation of work in sympathy with their fellow-workers with or without having any specific demand or grievance of their own pertaining to their economic relationship with their employers. Sometimes, the workers feeling reluctant to go on a strike because of the 'fears' of hardships or consequences, resort to a 'token strike' which means stoppage of work for a very short duration though it may issue a warning signal about the shape of things to come.[24] When the persons involved commit an act of strike with the object of forcing their government to adopt or scrap a particular policy, to pass or abrogate a particular form of legislative measure, appoint a commission of enquiry or dismiss a minister etc., it becomes a political strike.

Again, in some cases, when the area of striking activity covers the whole country or its major part and thereby affects 'key' administration as a whole, it is called 'general' strike. What we call 'bandh' is an instance of this type. Such a strike is generally undertaken by the workmen against all masters. A French socialist leader Blanqui defines the term 'general strike' as not necessarily a strike of all workers. On the contrary, it is not to be expected that an adequate number of workers will be animated by a sufficiently vigorous class conscious spirit to strike simply and solely for the purpose of terminating the capitalist system. "What is wanted is a strike on the part of a sufficient proportion of the workers in key industries to secure the paralysis of capitalism."[25]

Labour legislation has many provisions for the adjudication of labour disputes and normally the workers are not required to resort to strike as per their pleasure or satisfaction. But the right to strike is recognised by certain statutory provisions in a particular situation in

23. V.P. Arya : *Strikes, Lock-outs and Gheraos* (Calcutta : Oxford & IBH, 1969), p. 12.
24. According to Prof. F.W. Coker, there is a sympathetic strike in which various groups of workers that "have no particular quarrel with their employers quit their jobs in order to force attention to the demands of some other group engaged in an unsuccessful strike. It is different also from the ordinary political strike which is used as a means of upsetting an oppressive political regime or of intimidating a government into granting particular concessions" *Recent Political Thought* (New York : Appleton Cent., 1934), p. 237.
25. See C.E.M. Joad : *Modern Political Theory,* pp. 69-70.

order to have a 'justified' character. Strike cannot be undertaken on a false pretext or without exhausting all avenues of peaceful settlement of disputes. A proper notice is necessary. If it takes place without any proper notice given in advance especially in case of a 'public utility service', it is called 'lightning' strike. It pertains to the technique of the quick unheralded stoppage of work amounting to irritation, annoyance and harassment of the employees. It is also called 'quickie' in the United States. As there is no limit to human ingenuity, the workers of a particular public utility or essential service may stage a new kind of strike variously called as 'regulation strike' or 'go-slow strike' or 'work-to-rule strike'. It means workers being in place but adhering to rules and regulations in a very meticulous way really going against all canons of normal working behaviour.

It creates a peculiar situation where we have a strike in the midst of no strike. However, such a strike is different from its another variety called 'stay-in strike', 'pen-down strike', 'chalk-down strike', 'tool-down strike', etc. In the latter case, the workers remain on duty without doing any work; they also refuse to vacate the premises of their work on the plea of 'being on duty' in a peaceful and non-violent manner. The salient feature of a sit-down strike in addition to refusal to work, "is taking over the possession of the property of such business with a view to refuse access to others desiring to work. It is more a blockade of plant and machinery than of the owners. The strikers neither do work, nor leave their places, nor allow any of the persons to work."[26] Such a strike is likely to take the shape of a violent activity as destruction of furniture, papers, machinery, etc. amounting to criminal trespass and hence punishable under the criminal law of the land. The employer is justified in using even police force to get his premises vacated.

An element of trespass is definitely involved in the sit-down strike in view of the fact that a group of employees and others interested in realising a certain objective in a particular business forcibly take over possession of the property of such business. Teller goes to the extent of calling such a strike as trespass by all means, since the men involved in it not only establish themselves inside the premises, they also stop production, refuse to do what is their duty and do many other things causing damage to the business.[27] A different view has been taken by the Indian Supreme Court in the *Punjab National Bank Case* wherein their lordships held that such a situation would not be 'unjustified' or 'illegal' if the workers on duty remained throughout non-violent and peaceful. In such a case, the Court found that no amount of civil or criminal trespass was involved and the workers exercised their right of entering the premises of their office no matter for going on a strike. As such, stay-in-strike is not *per se* anything different from strike.'[28]

However, the most reprehensible form of strike is fasting or 'hunger strike' where a person stages 'satyagraha' without taking any food or drink. Fasting is a religious ritual and, as such, it is considered a sacred way of self-purification. Under the law, fasting is a crime if undertaken to the point of starvation and death. But fasting in public in the name of 'satyagraha' has got a political significance. Curiously, a fasting satyagrahi may be found living on Ganga water, or holy louse, or ending his life by sheer starvation for a great cause. Though the declared nature of fasting is often non-violent, it may tend to degenerate into an ugly situation of violence. The most pernicious aspect of hunger strike finds place in the declaration of a 'satyagrahi' that after such period he would perform 'self-immolation' publicly in case his demands are not met in a satisfactory way.

26. A.P. Aggarwal : *Gherao and Industrial Relations* (Bombay : N,M. Tripathi, 1968), pp. 14-15.
27. Ludwig Teller : *Labour Disputes and Collective Bargaining,* Vol I, Sec. 109, p. 321.
28. See Arya, *op. cit.,* pp. 19-20.

Take any form of strike, it is different from boycott and picketing, no matter both may often be seen in co-existence with it. Boycott consists in dissuading public from having any affinity for or connection with an offending employer in order to put him in a situation of serious loss. For instance, during Swadeshi Movement, Indian Congressmen appealed for the boycott of foreign goods.[29] Available information shows that labour in India has not made much use of this tactic. But strike and picketing, in spite of their co-relationship, have a degree of difference. Picketing means posting of men involved in a strike near the place of work so that they may persuade, win over, or stop, even forcefully check, the non-strikers from resuming work or maintaining any connection with the offending employer.[30] For this sake, dissemination of information by means of propaganda is needed to arouse favourable sentiments. It is described as "marching to and fro before the premises of an establishment involved in a dispute generally accompanied by carrying and display of a sign, placard or banner by the picketers bearing statements in connection with the dispute."[31]

If one looks at the practical manifestation of a strike, picketing is a necessary accompaniment in most of the cases. The men on strike raise slogans such as 'shame shame' and use many violent remarks with the object of dissuading the non-strikers ('blacklegs') from going to resume their work. Not picketing but strike is 'legal' and justified under certain circumstances. Even peaceful and non-violent picketing is punishable under the law of Indian Penal Code for the simple reason that a picketing of 'innocent' type hardly ever, rather never, exists in actual practice and it always involves some degree of force and violence. In a leading case, the Bombay High Court has observed that even a peaceful picketing "may engender a feeling of fear or fright and thus deter a person from entering or approaching any place of business" and that it "has to be remembered that peaceful picketing by its nature should, in all probability, not result in any violence. But we have seen frequent instances where peaceful picketing has degenerated into violence."

The technique of strike has certain dangers. Strike as a Gandhian technique has its own justification in view of its being based on the forces of truth and non-violence, otherwise it is always a method of violence in the hands of the employees to coerce their employers. The work by means of effecting a concerted and organised stoppage of work in essential industries shows that it is the only sure means in their hands for compelling the dominant social groups to take action for the redressal of their political and economic grievances. Sometimes, the workers take the situation to the final extent of paralysing the administration of the country that compels the government to take repressive measures. Undoubtedly, the technique of strike assumes a very serious form at the hands of the Syndicalists (or those influenced by them) who describe it as "primarily a demonstration of the latent social power of wage earners; by simultaneously quitting work in essential industries, they can paralyse the whole economic and social life of

---

29. According to Coker, boycott is "refusal to take employment with or purchase article made by a firm". *op. cit.*, p. 240.
30. Teller, *op. cit.*, p. 321. Picketing means simply the stationing of men for observation, or for the purpose of attempting to induce the workers to quit their employment or intending workers not to seek employment, or for the purpose of apprising the public of the dispute with the employer and influencing them to withdraw their patronage. Florence Peterson says : "Picketing is the presence of one or more persons at the approach to a work place during a labour dispute for the purpose of (i) informing the public and employees that a strike exists or that the employer is on the union's 'unfair' list. (2) persuading the workers to join or to continue the strike or boycott, (3) preventing persons from entering or going to work." *op. cit.*, p. 121.
31. See Arya, *op. cit.*, *pp.* 27. A leading jurist of India, G.C. Kothari, is of a different view. He puts : "Mere persuasion without coercion or intimidation is not picketing. Peaceful picketing is legal." *Labour Law and Practice in India* (Bombay : N.M. Tripathi, 1964), p. 178.

the community and thus force the privileged group to yield to their demands. Particular strikes, however extensive, should therefore be regarded chiefly as means of preparation and training for a final and mighty general strike by which the workers are to make themselves the masters of society."[32]

The strike is a favourite technique in the hands of the leftist forces which attach importance to it as means of evoking and strengthening the sentiments for a wage earners' war against the capitalists and their state. It is strike that brings all groups of workers into a co-ordinated and co-operating class, intensifies their class consciousness, and cultivates a militant feeling among them. An economic strike becomes more intense, becomes less the separate act of a special group of workers and more the act of a class fighting for the ultimate triumph of its formidable revolutionary aims. In this way, "strike becomes a direct action for a general economic and social revolution; a weapon for forcing a general capitulation of employers and governors to workers."[33]

Bandh

Literally, *bandh* or *bundh* means 'closure' that, for the sake of convenience, may be likened with a general or total strike of all whether offices, shops, markets, transport and the like. It is more sinister than a strike, whether partial or total, since it is a destructive technique of organised violence for any political purpose concerned with anything like toppling or formation of a government, weakening or strengthening of an alliance, humiliating and harassing the leaders in power or in opposition and the like. The instances of *bandh* illustrate that it is a mischievous device of enacting a managed riot involving mob-violence and mob manipulation. It is even identifiable with a civil war in some very extreme cases inasmuch as, despite all claims made by the users of its being a legitimate and peaceful and democratic affair, it is the manifestation of a blind rebellion staged by political parties, pressure groups, students and others to obstruct, weaken, or overthrow the established order against which this pernicious technique is employed.

It is found that for people having a vested interest in creating conditions of a mass upheaval to capture power by means other than those of the ballot box, the use of such a revolutionary method well represents the first step in the direction of their ultimate goal. It is obvious that for such people having faith in extra-democratic methods, *bandh* is the latest addition in a series of militant tactics conveniently placed at their disposal by the very nature of democracy which they seek to destroy. Viewed thus, the argument that, in essence, this technique is in no way different from a legitimate form of democratic protest like a general strike is ridiculous through and through.

Bandhs, as they have occurred in the form of violent disturbances in major towns of the country and as they have usually been staged by the communists, para-communists, fascists and their sympathisers, may conveniently be labelled as 'rehearsals of a bloody insurrection'. That is, they have been wrongly construed as people's resentment against the failures of the government on different fronts—whether language policy, food problem, rising prices, increasing unemployment and the like. The entire manifestation of this pernicious technique fits well in the strategy of the fascists and ultra-progressive elements who strive to create a violent revolution through various stages as :[34]

1. Infiltrate agents into strategic organisations and mass media, mobilise crowds, slip operations into newspapers, radio, stations, trade unions, civic associations, university departments, student organisations, even military and police units.

---

32. Coker, *op. cit.,* p. 239.
33. *ibid.*
34. See Eugene Methvin : "How the Reds Make a Riot ?" in *Reader's Digest,* February, 1965.

2. Soften up the populace with symbols and slogans like bread, civil liberties, imperialism, etc.
3. Draw together mob nucleus by using the standard bally-hoo methods of newspaper publicity, leaflets, radio announcements and offer of free transport.
4. Agitate the crowds to rise up in revolt against the police and military authorities even at the expense of their life.
5. Manufacture martyrs by taking out funeral processions and thereby commemorate the death of 'comrade hero' to enliven the fanatical struggle atmosphere.

It is, unfortunately, found that most people ignorant of the real state of political affairs are hired and engaged by the shrewd politicians and made to become an object of violent demonstrations. Curiously, the ultra-leftist elements somehow manage to requisition the support of other political parties and groups, including their hard-line opponents, by injecting the pretext of people's cause in their activities of subversion. Thus, revolutionary leaders successfully instigate the people to do simple things like making slogans at the top of their voice, while the 'shrewd brains' stand behind the facade of popular uprising and do disastrous activities like cutting telephone and electricity wires, arsoning transports, dismantling buildings, removing fish plates of railway tracks and doing a number of other mischiefs of sabotage and disruption. From all available circumstantial evidence it is inferrable that the leaders engaged in a *bandh* "seem to follow closely the above methods while staging a demonstration, as it is so well organised and controlled that it has compelled even their opponents to praise their efficiency in organising demonstrations or gaining their pre-planned object through them."[35]

It should, thus, be borne in mind that *bandh* is certainly a very dangerous weapon devised in recent years by the leftist forces, in particular. It is not at all a further extension of the Gandhian technique of strike based on the forces of *satyagraha* and non-violence. In its practical manifestation all the tricks from the communist literature may be conceived to have been employed and the frustration that most opposition parties must experience has added to its viciousness. It all revolves around the conviction of Lenin : "When we have companies of specially trained workers-revolutionaries who have passed through a longer course of schooling, no police will be able to cope with them". Thus a critic says : "The communists, after taking the leftist political parties and students into confidence, are organising *bandh* in one state after another which are nothing but a prelude to their revolution. Before the date of *bandh* in any state, they shout at the top of their voice that it would remain peaceful and is simply a legitimate form of peaceful protest which a democracy must permit, but they make secretly all preparations for violence and plan for cutting of telephone lines, sabotaging railway tracks, setting fire to railways, Government buses, bridges, factories, Government offices, including post offices, and court buildings etc., blowing up vital installations, attacking police, capturing Government arms stores, etc. and they, in fact, actuate their violent programmes."[36]

Gherao

Like *bandh, gherao* is another Indian term that has become a household word owing to its applicability in every walk of our collective life whether social, economic, political or educational. In simple words, it implies 'encirclement' or 'confinement' of the employers by the employees for coercing them to meet their demands as per their satisfaction.[37] The main ingredient of this peculiar tactic lies in the confinement of the other party for any length

35. V.B. Sinha : *Red Rebel in India* (New Delhi : Associated Pub, 1968), p. 199.
36. *ibid.*, p. 200.
37. See Arya, *op. cit.*, p. 61.

of time. That is, it is a form of lock-in of management, employers, managers; the officers are sometimes 'besieged' in their offices by their employees or subordinates for hours and days until their demands are met.[38] It may mean encirclement in the sense of 'blockade' or a complete and partial encirclement with the object of preventing egress to or ingress from a particular place whether it is some office, workshop, factory, even a place of abode, in which situation the point of trespass may arise.[39] As Dr. S.C. Kashyap says : "When employers and factory managers, etc. are encircled in their offices or elsewhere by the labourers and are prevented from freely moving about or out for hours or days together until their demands are conceded, the action is called *gherao.*"[40]

Instances of this coercive technique witnessed their most terrible frequency in the State of West Bengal, in particular after the installation of a non-Congress ministry headed by Ajoy Mukherji of the Bangla Congress. As a result, the matter was taken to the courts. In the leading case of Jay Engineering Works, the Chief Justice of Calcutta High Court in a lengthy judgment dated Sept. 29, 1967, observed : "*Gherao* is a physical blockade of a target either by encirclement or by forcible occupation. The target may be a place or persons usually the managerial or supervisory staff of an industrial establishment. The blockade may be complete or partial and is 'invariably accompanied by wrongful restraint and/or wrongful confinement and occasionally accompanied by assault, criminal trespass, mischief to persons' property, unlawful assembly and various other criminal offences. Some of the offences complained of are cruel and inhuman, like confinement in a small space without lights and fans, and for long periods without food or communication with the outside world. The persons confined are beaten, humiliated and abused and not allowed even to answer calls of nature and subjected to various other forms of tortures, and are completely at the mercy of their besiegers. The object is to compel those who control industry to submit to the demands of the workers, without recourse to the machinery provided by law and in wanton disregard of it. In short, to achieve their object not by peaceful means but by violence."[41]

However, the tactic of *gherau* is different from the Gandhian technique of *satyagraha.* The latter is based on truth and soul-force, while the former involves violence on account of having no care for the plight of the other party and no regard to the sanctity of means. Similarly, '*gherao*' is different from a demonstration. The latter is a democratic right whereby any number of persons may hold a public exhibition of their grievances or demands without resorting to violence, while the former is a disorderly demonstration where the party resorting to it forces its will upon the party under confinement. Then, *gherao* is different from a stay-in strike. The latter means refusal to work by the workers and also their control over the industry with a view to refuse access to others desiring to be on duty, the former is related to mere confinement of the management staff with or without the situation of the stoppage of work and may occur even at the hands of those who may be regarded as 'unconcerned elements'. Finally, *gherao* is different from picketing. The former is a basic tool that may take place even without the prior existence of a strike, since its essential ingredient is the confinement of the opposite

38. See J.C. Johari : "Gherao : A Pernicious Technique of Agitational Politics in India" in *Journal of Constitutional and Parliamentary Studies,* New Delhi, Vol. IV, No. 2 (1970), pp. 231-40.
39. G.L. Banerjee : *Gherao* (Calcutta : Firma K.L. Mukhopadhyaya, 1969) p. 50.
40. S.C. Kashyap : *The Politics of Defection* (Delhi : National, 1969), p. 344.
41. *The Statesman* (Calcutta), September 30, 1967.
42. Teller, *op. cit.,* p. 321.

party, while the latter is the marching to and fro of the persons in order to boost up the morale of the strikers.'[42]

Undoubtedly, *gherao* is the most reprehensible technique of agitational politics and its occurrence cannot be justified even by the canon of expediency. Nothing but the storehouse of ruination—moral, mental, political, economic, social, cultural and psychological—is the net result. *Gherao* is not merely one crime, it is a bundle of crimes involving criminal trespass, wrongful restraint and confinement and a host of other wrongs punishable under the penal law of the country. Its net result "is the proliferation of indiscipline all around."[43] Persons involved in this pressure tactic are liable to be arrested without warrant and punishment with imprisonment and fine. By any standard of justification, *gherao* cannot be appreciated as a form of collective action to shake up the administration, unmask black marketeers and hoarders and deal with the profession of social culprits. To talk of a peaceful and non-violent *gherao* is an exercise in self-contradiction inasmuch as no instance of *gherao* could ever achieve a good objective.[44]

43. B.S. Sharma and M.M. Sankdher : "Gandhi and Agitational Politics in India" in *The Indian Political Science Review*, Delhi, Vol. IV, No. 1, 1970, p. 87.
44. Aggarwal, *op. cit.*

21

Typology of States

> The apparent differences between states and the diversity of points of view from which they may he considered have led to numerous attempts to classify them. The literature dealing with the subject is very large, but on the whole it is unsatisfactory because the classifications which have been attempted too often rest upon no scientific principle by which states can be distinguished from one another in their fundamental characteristics... The things which differentiate one state from another are not differences of constituent elements but rather external phenomena or characteristics. The most important of these latter are the forms and character of their governmental organisations.
>
> **- J. W. Garner[1]**

Viewed from the morphological standpoint, modern nation-states may be classified into two broad forms—liberal-democratic and totalitarian. While the former stands on the foundation of democracy signifying residence of power in the hands of the people and its utilisation by their chosen representatives; the latter is an antithesis of the former where political power lies in the hands of a group of power-hungry politicians or a junta of military oligarchs who strive to secure legitimacy of their rule by means of 'force and fraud'. The totalitarian form of state has been justified by its protagonists on the grounds of political stability and socialistic achievements and thereby claimed to be more democratic than the model of a liberal-democratic state. Curiously, in between the two, the model of an authoritarian (autocratic) state may be inserted. Another variety popularly known by the name of 'welfare state' has emerged as a harmonious blending of the two having cardinal virtues of both—liberty of the former and welfare of the latter—and discarding the cardinal weaknesses of both—*laissez faire* of the former and regimentation of justice of the latter. The concept of welfare state has been devised to meet the challenge of the totalitarian state. It has brought about a reinterpretation of the case of liberal-democratic state so much so that the line of distinction between a liberal-democratic state on the one hand and a welfare state on the other has almost blurred, while the boundary line between a liberal democratic state on the one side and a totalitarian state on the other has become sharp and clear-cut.

Liberal-Democratic State

As its name suggests, the model of a liberal-democratic state signifies a political system in which democracy or 'the rule of the people' prevails to make the regime 'legitimate' in the real sense of the term. The machinery of government is run by the chosen representatives of the people who are accountable to them for their policies and actions. Freedom of speech, discussion and expression of views, universal adult franchise and free and fair periodic elections, etc. all entail a continuous test of the legitimacy of this government. Whether it is a direct democracy of the Athenian model, or a representative government of the Anglo-

1. Garner : *Political Science and Government* (Calcutta : World Press, 1952), II Impression, p. 240.

American model, or even a mixture of the two (as in Switzerland where, despite the system of elected representatives, three agencies of direct democracy like initiative, referendum and *landsgemeinde* or town parliament operate), the fact remains that power lies with the people and it is the will of the people that plays a decisive part in the organisation and working of the government.

Assumptions : If the liberal-democratic system stands on the foundation of democracy, it also implies the recognition of certain assumptions. In the first place, such a system recognises the existence of democracy in a qualified sense. The government is not an end in itself but a means for the realisation of the greatest good of the greatest number. The authority of government is not absolute but limited by the laws and conventions which constitute the fundamental law of the land. Hence, the government cannot take upon itself the task of totally covering the life of man; it, as Maclver says, can deal with only those things 'which are Caesar's'. State is one of the associations of social organism which "cannot legislate the whole of myself."[2] It revolves around the idea that the state "is confronted not merely by unassociated individuals but also by other associations evolving independently, eliciting individual's loyalties, better adapted than the state because of their select membership, the special forms of organisation and action for serving various social needs."[3]

This interpretation informs us to make a passing reference to modern pluralism that undertakes to transform the 'discredited state' (Barker), or "criticises it, discredits it, and seeks to reduce it from its place of honour to a place of servitude."[4] That is, the case of a liberal-democratic model rejects the mystic notion of the divinity of state as propounded and emphasised by the thinkers of the idealist tradition like Plato, Rousseau and Hegel and also by the champions of the imperative school like Hobbes, Bentham and Austin. However, the tinge of pluralism does not over-shadow the liberal-democratic system: it simply contributes an incidental element where the notion of absolute authority of state is dismissed to keep the state within the area of its own concern. As Laski says: "Political group refuses the swaddling clothes of finality and becomes a shifting conception. It cannot be Hegelianised into a permanent compromise. It asks the validation of men and actions in terms of historical experience."[5]

In a way, the model of a liberal-democratic state desires a pluralistic society—a view inherent with the assumption that the government "sets out to rule, not in the interest of any one group or alliance of groups, but in the common interest of all."[6] Such a system discards the notion of state infallibility as emphasised by the Hegelianised tradition of idealism. State, being a superior but not the supreme institution, can regulate the ordering of social affairs and thereby circumscribe the life of other associations and groups on some valid justification. Its *raison d'etre* is the maintenance of a social order of peace and prosperity which by no means entails either to neglect the minorities or suppress the dissidents. This itself "implies that such government is rather tender-minded towards the minorities and gives them a long run for their money. It

2. H.J. Laski : *A Grammar of Politics* (London : George Allen & Unwin 1938), p. 270.
3. F.W. Coker : *Recent Political Thought* (New York : Appleton Century, 1934) p. 508.
4. K.C. Hsiao : *Political Pluralism,* p. I.
5. Laski : *Authority in the Modern State,* p. 166. While explaining this statement of Laski, Prof. H.A. Deane comments : "In the pluralistic and pragmatic philosophies of James and Dewey, he found a point of view that was extremely congenial to his own position to idealism and monism and to his conviction, which makes him an heir to the utilitarian tradition of Bentham and Mills; that the state is to be judged in the light of its actual contributions to the well-being of its citizens." *The Political Ideas of Laski,* p. 21.
6. S.E. Finer : *Comparative Government* (London : Allen Lane, Penguin Press, 1970), p. 65.

also carries the implications, however, that judgment is fallible, and that there are many points of view and all of these have to be considered and, if possible, reconciled by the government."[7]

Finally, the case of a liberal-democratic model lays emphasis on secularism implying freedom of conscience and morality. The state has no official religion or ideology of its own to impose it upon the people by means of force and fraud. The very requirement of modern statehood assumes a political organisation to stand on the principle of secularism in order to keep those religious and communal forces in check that have the potentialities of undermining its modern and democratic foundations. It should never be forgotten that modern nation-state having the attribute of sovereignty is the product of historical circumstances which forced the church to lose its medieval prestige and authority and become 'either a voluntary association or a partner of nation government.'[8]

Characteristic Features : Apart from these assumptions, the case of liberal-democratic states has certain essential features. In the first place, it implies a government of the people through their chosen representatives. Different from the case of classical or direct democracy or the system of representative government, a term popularised by J.S. Mill, it signifies that delegates freely chosen by the people "act on their behalf as watchdogs over the Government."[9] As direct democracy of the Athenian model is an impossibility in modern times, it requires a representative system in which free and fair elections take place periodically to enable the people to exercise their franchise through secret ballot. Such a system guarantees freedom of thinking, speaking, writing, fighting elections, etc. to influence the working of the government. The people have the right to express their views and grievances so as to mould public opinion which the government need not and cannot falsify. Sometimes, the agencies of initiative, referendum and recall are introduced to check any possible abuse of power by the government and to confirm that it is the view of the people and not the voice of the man or group in power that would count. Also there is an independent and impartial judiciary to act as a check on the arbitrary exercise or power either by the legislators or by the administrators.

Second, the existence of a free legislative body to make laws according to the will of the people is not enough, it is also needed that the executive organ of the government must act according to the established norms of a liberal-democratic order. As the executive has a 'forward looking' function of the government, it includes both the lay politicians and the expert civil servants who jointly run the machinery of administration and thereby become the most important part of the political organisation. It is quite possible that the executors, being the most powerful organ of the government by virtue of their vast administrative authority, may transgress their frontiers and degenerate democracy into executive despotism, or the civil servants may go to the final length of keeping their political chiefs under their control to further degenerate executive despotism into bureaucratic tyranny. It is, therefore, required that while the political executive must behave democratically, the civil

7. *ibid.*
8. G.H. Sabine: *A History of Political Theory,* p. 334. For practical purposes, the liberal-democratic state stands on the assumption that majority's will should be taken as the will of all; it further assumes that conditions ought to be created where minority may improve itself to be the majority on some other occasions and then have the advantage of being in the position of majority. Establishment of necessary safeguards is needed for this purpose to justify that the minorities "must be given a chance to become ,a majority; and that means therefore that they must be given a chance, status and a means to convert the majority." See Finer, *op. cit.,* p. 66.
9. D.V. Verney : *Art Analysis of Political Systems,* p. 115.

service must remain politically neutral and a harmonious cooperation between the two must go on to keep the machinery of representative government well in operation. Neither an uncontrolled bureaucracy of a 'rickety' democracy nor a corrupt regime of the 'bureaucratic politicians' of an authoritarian system but a different order is called for where political and civil executives operate in harmony and cooperation to make the operation of constitutional government a successful and workable ideal for others to emulate.[10]

Third, the edifice of a liberal-democratic state stands on the principle of limited government. The powers of the three organs of government are not concentrated but separated and also inter-connected by the institutionalisation of the system of checks and balances. Whether it is the presidential system having legislature and executive apart, or it is the parliamentary model having executive joined with legislature, the system of a liberal-democratic state stands on the principle that liberty requires 'power cut into pieces.' It informs that the government has three organs, independent of each other, with their respective areas of jurisdiction.[11] Apart from following the classical doctrine of separation of powers, it further demands inner checks to keep the three organs of government in a situation of 'democratic balance'. Hence, the legislature is divided into chambers to check the conservatism of the upper and rash progressivism of the lower ones. A federalised pattern of administration is also desired to bifurcate the area of authority so that national and provincial governments exercise their respective powers in a way that both union and unity remain preserved. The essential point behind these devices "is to bring friction, delay and the necessity for consultation and compromise into the operation of government. All of them demand that, if government is to go forward, consultation must take place and some form of consensus between the contending bodies must be arrived at."[12]

Finally, there is the arrangement of socio-economic checks and balances. As various groups are formed to protect and promote specific interests, they are allowed to live and operate to make up the pattern of polyarchical democracy. Society is not a universe but a multiverse of interests because of which various groups—religious, communal, economic, social or cultural—come up to compete for power to protect and promote their specific interests. It is not the purpose of political authority to suppress them or dismiss their real significance. A liberal-democratic order lays emphasis on according proper recognition to the personality of various groups and professional associations. The business of the government is to reinforce harmony and co-ordination among these groups and bodies and not to coerce them into forced submission. It, however, does not mean equalisation of all such associations by the iron law of a despotic system; yet it does mean that any serious effort undertaken by the state in the direction of increasing curbs on the life and autonomy of a professional association must have a valid justification to sustain the sanctity of its legitimacy. It is owing to the fact that the bulk of the economic decisions in liberal-democratic societies "is not taken by the government, but by a multitude of private firms and their

10. As Carl J. Friedrich points out : "The popular anti-thesis between bureaucracy and democracy is an oratorical slogan which endangers the future of democracy. For a constitutional system which cannot function effectively, which cannot act with dispatch and strength cannot live." *Constitutional Government and Democracy*, p. 57.

11. Finer very ably suggests by means of an example thus: "The principle is similar to that of a three-legged race : running on his own, a child can moderate or accelerate his pace as he wishes; if he is tied to another, then he must adjust his pace to that of his fellow. If he stops and the other child does not, one or the other will fall down flat. Not unnaturally this slows down the speed of the race to that of the slower runner." *op. cit.*, p. 72.

12. *ibid.*, p. 73.

associations through the play of the market mechanism."[13]

Above all, a liberal-democratic state stands for political modernisation and political acculturation. It desires maximisation of people's participation in political affairs and thereby encourages bi-and multiparty systems to forge close and strong links between the masses and their chosen masters. Naturally, party system, though an extra-constitutional framework, develops more and more so as to recruit new participants, integrate individuals and groups into societies, transform social and political values from one generation to another, harmonise conflicts, contain diverse interests and provide channels of communication within a socio-political order all amounting to the development of a democratic nation-state. Obviously, in such a comprehensive system based on the norms of democracy, the role of the political parties becomes much more than mere involvement in the decision-making process. As Berger notes : "In addition to representational, aggregative, articulative, and decisional roles in government itself, parties have a role, along with other organisations, in a variety of functions."[14]

According to Ball, liberal-democratic system has the following characteristics :[15]

1. There is more than one political party; the parties are able to compete freely with each other for political power.
2. The competition for power is open, not secretive, and based on established and accepted forms of procedure.
3. Entry and recruitment to positions of political power is relatively open.
4. There are periodic elections based on a wide franchise.
5. Pressure groups are able to operate to influence government decisions. Associations such as trade unions and other voluntary societies are not subject to close governmental control.
6. Civil liberties such as freedom of speech and religion and freedom from arbitrary arrest, are recognised and protected by the government.
7. There is an independent judiciary.
8. The mass media, that, is, television, radio, newspapers, are not monopolised by the government and have, within certain limits freedom to criticise the government.

All this brings us to the point that a liberal-democratic state, whether it falls into the list of 'successful' countries of the West like Britain and the United States or comes into the category of 'experimental' countries of the East like India and Japan, is one which stands for the preservation of the entire paraphernalia of a representative government. Realising it well that democracy has become the battle cry of the day and every system assiduously claims to be democratic despite having a rank authoritarian character, the sanctity of the case of a liberal-democratic state remains unvitiated by the spectre of a totalitarian order. The fact stands out that while power is divided and diffused in a liberal democratic system, it is freezed and concentrated in the opposite model known by the name of totalitarianism. It may, however, be added that concentration of power in a totalitarian system "does not mean that many others donot participate in the exercise of power, but it does mean that their participation takes place at the pleasure of the ultimate, absolute controller, that is, only as long as the despot pleases."[16]

Totalitarian State

Contradistinguished from the model of a liberal-democratic state, a totalitarian state is one where the authority of government is total and absolute claiming jurisdiction over the whole

13. *ibid.*, p. 70.
14. A.S. Burger : *Opposition in a Dominant Party System* (Bombay : Oxford University Press, 1969), p. 3.
15. A.R. Ball : *Modern Politics and Government* (London : Macmillan, 1971), pp. 46-47.
16. Friedrich, *op. cit.*, p. 5.

Liberal Democracy	Totalitarianism	Authoritarianism
1. Based on formal, usually legal rules 2. Guarantee of civil liberties and individual rights 3. Institutionalised frgmentation and a system of checks and balances 4. Regular elections that respect the principle of 'one person, one vote' and 'one vote, one value' 5. Party competition and political pluralism 6. Independence of organised groups and interests from government 7. Private enterprise economy organised along market lines	1. An official ideology 2. A one-party state usually led by an all-powerful leader 3. A system of terroristic policing 4. A monopoly of the means of mass communication 5. A monopoly of the means of armed combat 6. State control over all aspects of economic life	1. A small group of individuals exercises power over the state. 2. Government is not constitutionally responsible to the public. 3. Public has little or no role in selecting leaders. 4. Individual freedom is restricted. 5. Authoritarian regimes may be institutionalised and legitimate.
Andrew Heywood: *Politics,* (2005)	C.J. Friedrich and Zbigniew Brzezinski : *Totalitarian Dictatorship and Autocracy (1963)*	Patrick O'Neil: *Essentials of Comparative Politics* (2004). p, 120.

of a man's life. That is, no part of a man's life is outside the detailed supervision and control of the state. It implies that state becomes absolute, permanent and a super-naturally sanctioned institution, or as Hegel says, it 'is the march of God on earth' and his disciple Trietschke commands that 'man should fall down and worship the state". The Foreign Policy Association of America defined it as: "For the pluralism of the modern democractic state, where the government is only one of several groups which have the individual's allegiance, fascism has substituted the totalitarian state which embraces all the activities of individuals and subordinates them to national ends." That is, in a totalitarian state, political authority is monopolised in the hands of a single person or his group (party). Among recent writers, Finer defines it as : "It is therefore the veritable contradictory of the liberal-democratic type of government. The scope and authority of government not limited, but just the reverse, is total."[17]

Meaning : Known by any name, whether Bonapartism in France, Fascism in Italy, Nazism in Germany and Communism in Russia, totalitarianism "is solidly opposed to any institutional division of power."[18] It stands for the monopolistic and hierarchical organisation of a single party, group or junta having both *de facto* and *de jure* authority to control and run the machinery of administration according to the official creed, partly through its monopoly of the mass media and partly through the use of brute force to establish its reign of terror. That is the reason to identify this type of government with one having extra-legal authority."[19] As Mussolini said : "All within the state, none outside the state, none against the state."[20]

17. S.E. Finer, *op. cit.,* p. 75.
18. Friedrich, *op. cit.,* p. 173.
19. Ford : *Dictatorship in the Modern World,* p. 27.
20. See Herman Finer : *Mussolini's Italy* (New York : Grosset & Dunlop, 1965), p. 198.

The case of a totalitarian state finds justification in philosophical interpretations as well as political practices of its exponents. The tradition of state absolutism coming from the writings of Plato makes a bold endeavour to justify the concept that state is an ideal institution requiring man's unquestioned obedience if he desires his moral development. The all-wise philosopher-king of Plato is a masterless man having 'unlimited and untrammelled discretion' in the ordering of state's affairs.[21] That is why, Plato has been dubbed as the first 'Fascist philosopher'. Likewise, the sovereign of Hobbes is a monarch with absolute authority and the "judge of the means necessary for the defence of the state; has the right to decide what doctrine shall be taught among the subjects, the law-making power, the judicial power, the right to carry war, the right to appoint officers, the rewarding and punishing power."[22] However, an idealistic defence of state absolutism appears in the writings of Rousseau whose concept of General Will, in practical terms, signifies justification of majority tyranny. Most pernicious aspect of this tradition appears in the philosophical contribution of the arch-German idealist, Hegel, in whose view the state "becomes a greater being, a spirit, a super-personal entity, in which individuals with their private consciences or claims of rights, their happiness or their misery, are merely subordinate elements."[23]

Apart from these philosophical justifications, the tradition of state absolutism finds its reiteration in political practices as well if we examine the cases of Italian Fascism, German Nazism and Russian Communism. The Fascist leader (Mussolini) asserted : "We must have, the single party as well as the totalitarian state, i.e., the state which absorbs in itself, to transform and make them effective, all the energy, all the interests and all the hopes of a people."[24] Likewise, Nazi leader Hitler impatiently broke out : "The National Socialist State is the pure political State, controlled by the Party, the incarnation of what is political : the embodiment of a *volkisch* community-will-for-self-preservation regardless of all other controversial issues within that community."[25] Justification of state absolutism in the name of 'dictatorship of the proletariat' is the same thing at the hands of the communists sworn to follow every line of Marxism-Leninism. That is why, Russian communist state was described as totalitarian regardless of the assertions of its leading jurist that it "is democratic in social essence, because it is directed to the defence of the interests of the maiority of the toilers against the exploited minority."[26]

Characteristic Features : The model of a totalitarian state has its peculiar features. First, it is dictatorial in nature and, as such, it is opposed to the norms of liberalism and parliamentary democracy. Whether it is a single leader or a group or a political party, the ruling power controls administrative apparatus at all levels permitting the members of this apparatus no latitude or discretion. As the Fascist leader says : "All is the State and nothing human or spiritual exists, much less has any value, outside the State. In this sense Fascism is totalitarian and the Fascist State, the synthesis and unity of all values, interprets, develops and gives power to every aspect of the life of the people..."[27] It becomes perfectly obvious that totalitarianism means total politicisation of the society and the reduction of that to one point : "All conscious and arbitrary movement or organisation is *totally* controlled by the State; the State is totally expressed in the actual

21. W.A. Dunning : *A History of Political Theories,* Vol. I, p. 46.
22. C.E. Merriam : *History of the Theory of Sovereignty Since Rousseau,* p. 26.
23. L.T. Hobhouse : *Metaphysical Theory of State,* p. 27.
24. Cited in Herman Finer, *op. cit.,* p. 231.
25. See Aurel Kolnai : *The War Against the West,* p. 159.
26. A.Y. Vyshinsky : *The Law of the Soviet State* (New York : Macmillan, 1938), p. 162.
27. See Herman Finer, *op. cit.,* p. 201.

governing authority and coincides *totally* with the ruling body."[28]

Second, totalitarianism imposes its official ideology or myth on its people by the iron law of despotism. All means of communications are in the hands of the state that are used for propaganda purposes. Secret police and intelligence forces are organised for the manhunt of the dissidents and their eventual persecution to establish a reign of terror. Official glorification of the leader, his party and the race also takes place. The regime uses both persuasion and force of deterrence to inculcate the official myth and secure its general acceptance. Several arrangements like grant of universal adult franchise and holding of periodic elections by means of secret ballot are made to hoodwink the people or to make them behave as the regime chooses. That is, the purpose must be served and in case persuasion falls short, coercion, even terror, is resorted to. One might even go to the extent of arguing that the crucial control in the totalitarian political system "is not coercion—although it is essential—but the monopoly of the media of communication."[29]

Third, totalitarianism of a political party means identification of the party with its government as a result of which secret party mechanism becomes more important than the formal constitutional framework. The constitutional law of the land outlaws opposition; it also imposes a ban on the existence of any other political party. As Finer holds: "The government is to the party what the glove is to the hand. The central institution of such totalitarian states is the party. It is the party which wields all these powers: the powers of persuasion, of deference, of the licensing and control of expressed opinion, of the control of elections."[30]

Fourth, totalitarianism stands for the monistic character of society. Nothing but state becomes everything with the result that other social associations are either disallowed or made to starve. Complete statification of man's life entails his total allegiance to the state. Man's independence is forfeited and he becomes a mere cog in the machinery of the state. Reading of party literature, writing for party papers, propagation of official ideology and activities of the party bosses, expression of views in the light of official standpoint, etc. all regulate the life of a member as desired by his party. The result is that all his life "is brought within the party framework, dominated by the party and devoted to the service of the party."[31]

Last, it is surprising that, despite so many rigorous limitations, totalitarianism generates mass movements. The leaders manage to win support of the masses by creating an hysterical environment. Promises of plenty to eat and drink, eradication of poverty and unemployment, annihilation of national enemies, etc. enthuse the people in general to support the regime with all means at their disposal. Popular frenzy mounts so high that people register their approval of official policies and thereby accord legitimacy to what their astute leaders want. In most of the cases they look like oblivious to the fact that appeal of the regime "is made not to reason but to the baser passions of man, with the result that the masses obey the behests of the State in a blind and mechanical manner. They are drilled and disciplined so thoroughly that they rush to the battlefield and the conquest of other people's territory like a swarm of locusts which are driven to action by some kind of blind and unreasoning instinct."[32]

According to Ball, a totalitarian system has the following characteristics.[33]

---

28. See Kolnai. *op. cit.*, pp. 160-61.
29. Almond and Coleman : *The Politics of the Developing Areas* (Princeton : Princeton University Press, 1960), p. 47.
30. S.E. Finer, *op. cit.*, p. 92.
31. Maurice Duverger : *Political Parties* (London : Methuen, 1964), p. 117.
32. E. Asirvatham: *Political Theory* (Lucknow: Upper India Pub, 1944), pp. 613-14.
33. Ball, *op. cit.*, p. 48.

1. All aspects of individual and social activity are theoretically the political concern of the government.
2. One party is politically and legally dominant. All political activity is channelled through this party, and the party provides the only institutionalised basis for competition, recruitment and opposition.
3. There is an elaborate ideology, which, in theory, regulates all political activity within the system.
4. The judiciary and the mass media are rigidly controlled by the government and the civil liberties, as defined in liberal democracies, are seriously curtailed.
5. Totalitarian regimes emphasise constant mobilisation of the population to win mass support for the regime, to provide it with a democratic base. The regime is legitimised by the consent and participation of the people.

All these characteristic features make it clear that the case of a totalitarian state presents an anti-thesis of a liberal-democratic model. While the process of decision-making is dispersed in a liberal-democratic model, it is concentrated in a totalitarian state; while the former strives for the maximisation of political participation in a sincere way to secure legitimacy, the latter wants minimisation of the same for the sake of consolidating its foundations by all possible means. So, while the former stands for a pluralistic society having various autonomous social associations with their recognised personalities, the latter either starves them or forces them to live like its own emanations or colonies. As Finer says: "Nothing throughout the society escapes the party except through accidental or administrative incapacity."[34]

Autocratic State

This type of political system, though quite close to the totalitarian model, is such that "gives rise to even more problems of clarification and exact definition than the other two."[35] Ball mentions gives these characteristics of an autocratic state."[36]

1. Important limitations are imposed on open political competition, *i.e.*, political parties and elections.
2. There is the absence of a dominating political ideology such as communism or fascism, although racialism and nationalism often provide some basis for attempted political uniformity.
3. The definition of what is 'political' is more restricted in totalitarian systems, although this may be the result of a lack of modern administrative and technological methods to impose a wider definition.
4. The political rulers often place greater emphasis on force and coercion to obtain political uniformity and obedience.
5. In contrast to liberal democracies, civil liberties are weakly supported and the mass media and the judiciary are more directly controlled by the government.
6. The basis for rule is found either in a traditional political elite or in a new modernising elite, often the army, which has seized power by a coup or as the result of a colonial war of independence.
7. It is usually one group that monopolises political control in contrast to the pluralism of liberal democracies.

An autocratic or authoritarian system resembles with as well as differs from dictatorship. Ordinarily, it need not, strictly speaking, "be a dictatorship and may well not be totalitarian. The essential element is that it is one in which stern and forceful control is

34. S.E. Finer, *op. cit.*, p. 94.
35. Ball, *op. cit.*, pp. 49-50.
36. *ibid.*, p. 50.

exercised over the population with no particular concern for their preferences or for public opinion. The justification for the rule may come from anyone as a matter of ideologies, but it will not be democratic ideology, and ideas of natural rights or civil liberties will be rejected in favour of government's right to rule by a command, backed by all the force it needs. It is very much tied to the idea of a command and obedience, of inflexible rule, and a denial of the legitimacy of opposition, or even counter argument."[37]

Such a system may have the under-pinning of an ideology that takes it very close to fascism and communism. However, the essential point is that in such a system politics is driven entirely by the whims of those in power. Naked and unabashed use of violence is used to suppress dissidence of any kind. The sanctity of rules and norms is mercilessly discarded so much so that the supreme leader himself becomes the regime. All decisions flow from the ruler, unfettered by political institutions of any sort.[38] Cases of Kim Jong Il of North Korea, Castro of Cuba and Gaddafi of Libya may be referred to in this regard. The fact stands out that "a small group of individuals exercises power over the state without being constitutionally responsible to the people. The public does not play a significant role in selecting or removing leaders from office and so they have much greater leeway to develop policies that they 'dictate' to the people."[39]

Corporatist and Neo-Corporatist State

The idea of a 'corporatist state' was the brain-child of the Italian fascist dictator (Mussolini) who in the late 1920s established a network of corporations throughout the country under the supreme control and direction of the national fascist corporation. Each corporation was a band of chosen people who had the right to speak for various sectors of society. The dictatorial state patronised and funded the groups of selected labour unions, agricultural associations, student groups, neighbourhood communities and the like who would settle the disputes of the employers and the employees and thereby maintain cohesion between the capital and labour as desired by the fascist leader in power. In other words, it "emerged as a method by which an authoritarian system attempted to solidify its control over the public by creating or sanctioning a limited number of organisations to represent the interests of the public, and restricting those not set up or approved by the state."[40]

This type of corporatism is undemocratic, for it allows no room for competition among and the overlapping memberships of unions and associations that is the hallmark of a pluralist society. It seeks to arrange society in an hierarchical manner, with each organisation empowered by the state to have a monopoly of representation over a given isue or a segment of society. Hence, the system of Mussolini was widely criticised for being a shrewd attempt to legitimise his dictatorial hold by the association of the hand-picked leaders of the associations and groups working as the instruments of his fascist system. But in the period after the Second World War, corporatism emerged in a new form in many democratic states and pluralist societies. It has been given the name of neo-corporatism. Under it state, society and market "are viewed as a single organic body with each element cooperating and performing its own specific and limited role."[41]

However, the democratic nature of the corporatist state cannot be denied. "It refers to the widespread tendency across the advanced capitalist countries for industrial relations between employers and trade union organisations to be resolved and institutionalised

37. David Robertson: *A Dictionary of Modern Politics* (London: Europa Publications, 2002), III ed., p. 3.
38. Patrick O'Neil: *Essentials of Comparative Politics* (New York: W.W. Norton and Company, 2004), p. 121.
39. *ibid.*, p. 120.
40. *ibid.*, p. 132.
41. *ibid.*

at the level of the state itself."[42] The state permits the role of non-state agencies to take part in the political process of the country. The representatives of the employers and the employees negotiate with each other in the presence of the officers of the state and then manage to settle their matters. Various interest groups bargain not only among themselves but also with the state officials and thereby affect the decision-making process of the government. One may say that functional representation, as once conceived by G.D.H. Cole, has replaced parliament as a means of policy—formation and of securing general state legitimacy. The unofficial unions or organisations receive some kind of state sponsorship in formulating national plans and in managing the public sector.

It may be said that neo-corporatism has changed the nature of state activity and, to a considerable extent, blurred the distinction between social and political spheres. The classical pluralists attacked the concept of sovereignty and warned that the state should not encroach upon the domain of social groups. But the neo-corporatist state goes ahead in the same direction. It invites the participation of non-state bodies in the decision-making process as a result of which some interest groups have immensely increased their strength and significance. As Bob Jessop says: "Societies are being increasingly corporatist. Rather than there being a relatively open process of group-state interaction, some groups are developing increasingly integrated relationship with the state. In particular, economic policy decisions are made through the process of bargaining between state actors and peak economic actors."[43]

Neo-corporatism has its natural confluence with neo-pluralism, since it "reflects the transgression of the division between state and society as previously assumed in the pluralist and liberal-democratic traditions."[44] Laski, as a pluralist, desired that 'if society is federal, the authority should also be federal'. He never meant that the two should draw closer and closer as has happened now. So Schmitter finds that increasing centralisation of organised interest groups as those of capital and labour has replaced the picture of many power centres based upon voluntary groups as conceived by the pluralists of the past. In advanced countries the role of the state is tripartite. The state is neither invisible nor neutral, it may be seen as a broker for independently vying social constituencies. In a communist country the state is everything and the economy run by it has the notorious appellation of 'command economy'. But in a democratic country the market is open, the role of the organised groups is active and the state plays the role of a fair or even-handed umpire.

Obviously, the model of a corporatist state is the creation of a fascist system, the model of a uni-partite state is the creation of the communist system. If so, the case of a neo-corporatist state cannot win the appreciation of those who in some form or the other desire to set up a closed system in which there is no room for social groups and organisations to compete with each other and to take part in the decision-making process either as a result of their effective pressure on the government or as a shift or change in the operation of the political system leaning more and more towards neo-corporatism. The pluralists may call it transgression of the social sphere by the state, but the Marxists call it' straightforwardly a form of class collaboration. "The unions are duped into a false sense of social recognition and are 'incorporated' into the logic of capitalist economic restraint. Corporatism is thus a state strategy operating directly on behalf of the capitalist class."[45]

42. Gregor McLellan: "Capitalist State or Democratic Polity?" in McLellan, David Held and Stuart Hall (eds): *The Idea of the Modern State,* p. 100.
43. Jessop: *The Capitalist State.*
44. McLellan, *op. cit.,* p. 101.
45. *ibid.,* p. 102.

Corporatism and Neo-Corporatism

Corporatism, in its broadest sense, is a means of incorporating organised interests into the processes of government. It has two forms:

Fascist or Authoritarian Corporatism : It is an ideology or economic form closely associated with Italian Fascism. It was characterised by the political intimidation of industry and the destruction of independent trade unions.

Liberal or Societal or Neo-Corporatism : It refers to the tendency found in mature liberal democracy (as Germany) for organised interests to be granted privileged and institutional access to policy formulation. The mechanisms through which it is achieved vary considerably, as does the degree of groups integration in contrast with its authoritarian variant. Liberal corporatism strengthens groups in relation to government, not the other way round.

Andrew Heywood *Politics,* p. 275.

Features of Corporatism

1. By it an authoritarian system attempts to solidify its control over the public by creating or sanctioning a limited number of organisations to represent the interest of the public, and restricting those not set up or approved by the state. These organisations are meant to replace independent organisations with a handful that alone have the right to speak for various sectors of society.
2. As opposed to the overlapping memberships, competition and ever-changing nature of organisations and political parties in a pluralist society, corporatism arranges society in a hierarchical manner, with each organisation empowered by the state to have a monopoly of representation over a given issue or segment of society implying that no other organisation may act in that area or speak on that issue.
3. State, society and the market under corporatism are viewed as a single organic body with each element cooperating and performing its own specific and limited role.

Features of Neo-Corporatism

1. It is a system of policy-making involving state, labour and business groups. Economic decisions are made through the competitive interaction of business and labour. Workers demand better or higher wages or better safety conditions, striking or quitting their jobs whenever necessary and the employers hire, fire, negotiate with workers as they find fit.
2. In some cases this relationship can be quite antagonistic, leading to conflict that can hurt business and result in violence. Thus even in liberal societies a certain level of business and labour regulation exists to protect both workers and business from each other. Such a conflict is seen as a necessary and positive part of human economic relations.
3. It rejects limited role of state. Instead, it uses policy in order to build consensus over competition by creating a limited number of associations that represent a large segment of business and labour. Many decisions are left to the state alone, or result from the interaction of business and labour in a cooperative and organised fashion.

Patrick O'Neil: *Essentials of Comparative Politics,* pp. 132-33 and 101-02.

State in the Third World Countries

The meaning of 'state' applicable to an advanced industrialised country is different from one that is applied to a backward and developing country of the world. It is true that the Third World countries have their states or political systems, but they range from a established democracy as in India to a semi-democracy as in Mexico and thereon to a party-state as in China. Theocracy prevails in the states of Saudi Arabia, Iran, Israel, Syria, Pakistan and Bangladesh, secularism is the ideal of countries like India and South Africa. Analysing the differences among these varied types of political systems is one of the most important and interesting tasks in the study of comparative politics. But it is also important to note some of the political characteristics shared by the Third World countries which distinguish them politically from the industrialised nations. In this regard, these points may be enumerated:

1. In all the countries, politics and government are shaped by the basic facts of scarce economic resources, extensive poverty and inequality, and a relatively weak position in the international system. The political leaders have fewer options available in resolving problems or in responding to demands from various groups for a bigger piece of the national economic pie. Thus, economic conflicts are more likely to arise as the agitations of the farmers and the workers and the rulers are often found involved in the cases of rampant corruption and maladministration.[46]
2. In these countries, the political legitimacy is very weak. It is true that the people obey the laws and cast their votes in the elections, but they donot see the government as being very relevant to their lives or as being able to do anything about their most serious concerns. They may even regard the government as having a negative impact on their lives, and their citizenship in the state may be negligible as a source of their political identity.[47]
3. The effective power of government in most of such countries is also very limited. The state may have little real ability to exert its authority much beyond the capital city and a few large urban centres. In the rural and backward areas patron-client relationship may be visualised. That is the wealthy and the powerful people exploit the poor and weak people and also help them in some respect that is in some cases neither legal nor moral. Thus, the formal aspects of government such as laws, parties and elections are less important than the informal politics of patron-client relationships.[48]
4. In most of the countries the state exists without its specific identity. The people identify their state with their society, their government, their party in power and even with the personality of their supreme leader. The leadership of the state is in the hands of those who may be labelled as a denationalised and demoralised lot and who, in the words of Callaghy, know how to convert the state into a 'lame leviathan'.
5. The general experience of the Third World indicates increasing dependency on the countries organs like police, paramilitary and military forces. The increasing role of the coercive apparatus and marginalisation of the developmental wings suggests that the state is getting back to its primitive role. For it is gradually abandoning the functions that it acquired during the course of civilisational development. The use of force without a developmental ideology in poverty-ridden societies is bound to create legitimacy crisis. It "creates a situation where different sections of the society would resort to aggressive protests and rebellious behaviour. The rebellious movements can destroy the existing structures but would not be able to offer an alternative."[49]

---

46. W.A. Joseph, Mark Kesselman and J.Krieger: *Third World Politics at the Croosroads* (Lexington: D.C. Heath & Co. 1996), pp. 11-12.
47. *ibid.*
48. *ibid.*
49. C. Hargopal and C. Chandrasekhar: "The State Appartus in the Third World" in Neera Chandhoke (ed.): *Understanding the Colonial World* (New Delhi: Sterling, 1994), p. 183.

Such a version of state in the countries of the Third World cuts across the Marxian view that classes create the state. The facts speak otherwise. The state creates classes. The state is like a complex reality that may be understood in terms of its operational apparatus. Ethnic, tribal and religious and communal forces have their powerful sway. The legislative wing exists of course without its brilliance as it is occupied by the incompetent and inefficient persons, but the executive wing dominates in a way that it looks not only as concrete instrument of state power, it enjoys considerable political space. The army of the experts having its seat in the bureaucratic organisation becomes an integral part of the power structure.

In the Third World countries the concept of state, in most of the cases, has emerged out of a popular revolution or mass uprising proclaiming goals of democratic government, social justice and nationalism. In the chaotic years just after the successful revolution, the state effectively created conditions for political integration, social tranquillity and economic development. The relationship between state and society has been shaped by a strong belief that capitalism, unless carefully monitored by the government, creates economic injustice, because the private sector's pursuit of profit causes it to exploit workers and disregard the good of the community for its own advantage. The factors that encourage the development of a strong state also increase its power in relation to civil society. Liberalism has its blending with the tenets of socialism in varying degrees as a result of which the model of welfare state becomes the common choice. Since that model has failed under the weight of its own contradictions, most of the countries are now in a quandary as to how the goal of social and economic justice be realised. The state is caught up in "a peculiar mix of fore and right that constrains and shapes the lives of generations."[50]

This category of the political system is, indeed, of a very heterogeneous type, since it differs from the liberal-democratic model in kind and from a totalitarian model in degree only. It may be that such a model is converted into a liberal-democratic system with the growth of political modernisation and development. It may also be admitted that autocracies are transitory regimes, lacking industrial and economic development to blossom forth into either liberal democracies or totalitarian systems. However, given these criticisms, we may include in this category states with traditional ruling groups such as Saudi Arabia and Ethiopia and modernising states with either military governments as Nigeria and Indonesia or with civilian governments as Algeria and Egypt.

Welfare State

The concept of welfare state (also known by the names of positive state or social service state) represents a happy blending of the two varieties of states—liberal-democratic on the one hand and communist-totalitarian on the other. It rejects the thesis of an individualist state (earlier form of liberal-democratic state) that the business of the state is to protect but not to promote; so it discards the policy of a totalitarian (communist) state that the welfare of the people, being the paramount concern of the state, can be accomplished only at the expense of fundamental liberties of the people. While the concept of welfare state discards the cardinal evils of both types of state, it also accepts the cardinal virtues of both. It borrows the element of freedom from a. liberal-democratic state and mixes it with the emphasis on public welfare of a totalitarian state and, in this way, presents the model of a new state that embraces the virtuous aspects of both democracy and socialism.

Meaning and Nature : The concept of a welfare state finds its theoretical or philosophical expression in various doctrines relating to the functions and ends of a political organisation. Theories in this regard have ranged from various directions—from those

50. David Held : "Central Perspectives on the Modern State" in Mclellan and others, *op. cit.,* p. 73.

who deny the necessity and utility of the state and consider it as an instrument of exploitation and oppression on the one hand to those who laud it as the mightiest creation of human mind, the noblest expression of human purpose, and an essential institution by which all kinds of progress can be achieved on the other. At one extreme, there are the Anarchists who emphasise the violent and coercive character of authority and insist on its abolition root and branch. At the other extreme, there are the Collectivists who regard the state as a welfare agency and thus contend for the maximisation of its activity. Between these two opposite poles, there are the Individualists who characterise the state as a 'necessary evil' and lay stress on the point that the sphere of state activity "should be restricted to the narrowest possible limits, consistent with the maintenance of peace, order and security."[51] In addition, there are the Marxists who denounce the state as a class institution and declare that, during the period of transition, it would forcibly suppress the opponents of the proletariat in order to consolidate the gains of the revolution.

It follows that such a system borrows the idea of liberty from the school of Individualism and of welfare from that of Communism and blends the two in such a way that it looks like a half-way house. While, on the one hand, it guarantees essential liberties (as of thought, expression, faith, profession, property, etc.) to its people; on the other, it adopts a policy of abolishing gigantic evils that make the life of the people miserable. Hobman, thus, defines it as "a compromise between the two extremes of Communism on the one hand and unbridled Individualism on the other, and, as such, in spite of its all imperfections, it sets a pattern of any human and progressive society. It guarantees a minimum standard of subsistence without removing incentives to personal enterprise. It also brings about a limited redistribution of income by means of graduated high taxation, yet it does not pretend to establish economic equality among its citizens. All are assured of adequate help in case of need, whether the need is due to illness, old age, unemployment, or any other cause."[52]

As pointed out above, it is clear that the concept of welfare state has two main ideals. Firstly, it guarantees essential liberties to the people and respects them with a sincere intent. In this respect, it adheres, to a great extent, to the spirit of *laissez faire* and keeps faith in the dictum of Mill that 'over himself, his own body and mind the individual is sovereign'. The liberty of a man can be restricted only when he becomes a nuisance to the liberty of another person. It, however, does not mean that such a state permits freedom of the woods, rather it refrains from imposing those limitations which definitely destroy the fabric of social freedom and reduce the individual to the status of a mere cog in the wheel of governmental machinery. It undertakes to maintain those conditions which help man to raise himself to the full stature of his personality. Its legal, adminstrative and judicial set-up helps the establishment and continuous existence of those conditions under which the individual can develop his faculties and plan his life as he deems fit and proper. Obviously, this type of state, as Dewey said, fully recognises that the freedom unrestrained by responsibility becomes a mere license and responsibility unchecked by freedom becomes a mere arbitrary power.

The welfare state necessarily performs certain police functions. For the sake of its own existence, it maintains military and police departments. In order to secure life, liberty and property of the people as well as to defend the territorial integrity of the country from foreign aggressions, it maintains sufficient defence

51. Garner, *op. cit.*, p. 451.
52. D.L. Hobman : *The Welfare State*, p. 1. E. Strauss defines it as "organised public interference with the functioning of the private enterprise system and the rights of property and as systematic redistribution of the national income through taxation and social benefits for certain unpriviledged groups." *The Ruling Servants*, p. 104.

force. It keeps police force to make the life of the people safe and peaceful. However, the characteristic mark of a welfare state lies in the use of its power in a way that the fundamental liberties of the people are not deliberately crushed. It is but for the sake of public welfare that the essential liberties of the people can be circumscribed. The essential requirement is that welfare programmes should not be carried out at the cost of individual liberty. However, if in a particular case, individual liberty has to be circumscribed, the state may do so in the name of public good. In other words, it implies that the state should not follow a policy unnecessarily jealous of individual liberty, particularly one motivated by the ideology of class war.[53]

The second important characteristic of a welfare state lies in the discharge of socially useful services. Dr Abraham thus characterises it as a community where state power "is used deliberately to modify the normal play of economic forces." Similarly, Dr. N.R. Sirkar observes that the determining factor of this state "lies in the assumption of certain basic responsibilities by the State." T.W. Kent regards it as a state that "provides to its citizens a wide range of social services. The primary purpose is to give to the citizens a security. The state undertakes to help him, if the ordinary member loses his source of income." MacIver says : "But the order so understood is a larger task. Order within the community is justified only as it serves the needs of the community. It is not order for the sake of order but for the sake of protection, and conservation, and development."[54]

Prof. MacIver devotes much attention to the question relating to the nature of modern welfare state. He very resolutely maintains that if the state is designed to maintain order, it is also enjoined upon it to render welfare services. In order to give a clear and thorough representation to his succinct thesis, he presents an exhaustive tabular representation showing area and nature of state activity in the internal sphere. It covers three heads—Order, Protection, Conservation and Development. In the first category, he puts establishment of the areas and frontiers of political authority and control of the forms of transport and communication, setting up of the units of measurement and computation of value, specification of general rights and obligations of citizenship and territorial residence, determination of the rights and obligations of various associations, regulation of marriage, contracts, currency, occupational status relating to population and trades, etc. In the second category, he includes the responsibility of the state to secure the person and goods of its citizens, justice, liberty, rights, decent living, wage rates, employment, upbringing of children, prevention of destitution and social wreckage. Finally, in the third category he puts promotion and regulation of the physical conditions by maintaining centres of health, recreation and profession, utilisation of natural resources, planning, rural and urban development, education and scientific research, centres of cultural and historical study, museums, promotion of industrial, agricultural and financial development for general good, and provisions for the means of enquiry into social problems of general significance.[55]

Obviously, the social welfare state discards the individualistic notion of the least possible interference. It repudiates the thesis of the 'struggle for existence' and 'survival of the fittest' and substitutes it with the new doctrine that it is the duty of the state to protect the weak against the strong. For this, its policies are so determined and laws so formulated that equal

53. The welfare state should not mitigate the chances of popular participation. Prof Appleby thus suggests ; "Action through democratic government is, in an important and valid sense, self-help, since the government has no means with which to be helpful except those which are produced by the people." *Public Administration in a Welfare State,* p. 9.

54. R.M. MacIver : *The Modern State,* p. 185.

55. *ibid.*

opportunities are provided to all to grow and expand and no one is denied, as far as possible, the basic amenities of health and living except the accidents of birth and misfortune which are beyond human control. So the state makes suitable arrangements for ensuring freedom from want and fear. It provides to its citizens several amenities like minimum wage, public assistance and effective guarantees in cases of risks, hazards, or contingencies of life. In the words of Maclver : "This expansion has done much to change the very conception of the state, so that from being, in the eyes of those subject to it, mainly an instrument of power it has become, so far as its internal activities are concerned, in large measure an agency of service."[56]

From this, it may be inferred that the welfare state does not kill the prospects of private incentive. Although it does much for the public welfare, it still leaves room for private enterprise. It realises that all-round development of its members constitutes its primary end, its interference is justified in relation to that primary end alone. That is, it should prove that the limitation of the freedom of citizens "helps ultimately to secure for them more freedom than abstention would guarantee."[57] In economic terms, it implies the existence of a pattern of mixed economy where state power competes with private initiative but does not aim at its complete liquidation. Undoubtedly, the powers of the government in a welfare state "are great enough for it to be able to secure for itself the means of securing maximum social welfare."[58]

In brief, the welfare state is a social service state and, as such, instead of confining its role to the office of a policeman, it also renders the services of a physician, an engineer, a teacher and the like. For the sake of the welfare of its people, it adopts schemes of public health, maintenance of hospitals and dispensaries. By preventive and curative measures it fights against epidemics and other fatal diseases which take a heavy toll of human life. It guarantees schemes of social insurance and for this takes upon itself the responsibility of compensating the individual as well as his family in the event of an unfortunate accident. As leisure and recreation are also necessary with work, it regulates working hours, service conditions, wage and bonus systems, old age pensions and holidays during the year. For the sake of proper and healthy dissemination of knowledge, it fights against ignorance and opens schools, colleges and other institutions so as to enable the citizens to acquire capacity of creative self-expression. Above all, it fights against the monstrous evils of mass poverty and unemployment. By pursuing the goal of social justice, it seeks to remould the pattern of national economy so that the vast disparities of wealth are diminished to a fair and an equitable extent.[59]

Distinct Identity : As a matter of fact, the welfare state has been devised to meet the challenge of a communist state established in the Soviet Union. The communist writers deprecated every other system as a 'bourgeois order' and defended their own system in the name of democracy and socialism. From this point of view, the political order of the Soviet Union had been lauded by its protagonists as a 'welfare state', smce it guaranteed fundamental rights, universal adult suffrage, bicameral legislature, secret ballot, recall, judicial process, etc. It was further claimed that national economic life was determined and directed by the state national economic plan, with the aim of increasing the public wealth, of steadily

---

56. *ibid.*
57. R.H. Soltau : *An Introduction to Politics,* p. 253.
58. Piet Thoenes : *The Elite in the Welfare State* (Eng. Trans, by J.E. Brigham), p. 133.
59. W.A. Robson is of the view that the idea of welfare state has two aspects-negative and positive. The determination of negative aspect is an easy affair, since it stands for the provisions of social welfare, but the positive side is a controversial affair and it cannot be easily said as how that welfare is to be achieved. See *The Welfare State,* pp. 15-17.

raising the material and cultural standards of the working people, of consolidating the independence of the country and strengthening its defensive capacity. The Russian system was based on the dictum of Lenin that economic freedom preceded political freedom and that Soviet democracy was a million times more democratic than any other bourgeois democracy in the world. Defending this system, Stalin once said : "Only where exploitation is annihilated, where there is no oppression of some by others, no unemployment, no beggary, and no trembling for fear that a man may on the morrow lose his job, his habitation. his bread—only there is true freedom found."

Undoubtedly, the model of welfare state has been devised to meet the challenge of the communist order. A communist regime endeavours for public welfare by the regimentation of justice. The welfare state naturally commits suicide when the state assumes a totalitarian character—a factor that is the hallmark of a communist system. In a communist system this form of political order finds its natural extinction in the presence of several stern reservations and safeguards. Hence, the sanctity of the respect for essential liberties is replaced by the fact of state absolutism and whatever welfare services are rendered, they are done for the sake of consolidating the roots of the party that has captured power. Obviously, a communist order cannot be regarded as the model of a welfare state inasmuch as the regimentation of justice leaves no room for the essential liberties of the people.

Similarly, the case of welfare state is different from a paternalistic system. Apparently, a paternalistic state represents an anti-thesis of the individualistic order and moves very close to the idea of a positive government by adopting measures for the welfare of its people. The functioning scope of a paternalistic government is not confined merely to restrain wrong-doing and protecting private rights, it goes much further and undertakes to promote, by various means, the social well-being of its citizens. For this it may establish and operate various industries, provide old-age pensions, grant financial assistance to the destitutes and the incapables and safeguard the social interests of the people in so many ways. In fine, the paternalistic order "undertakes to perform for society many services which might be performed as easily through private initiative on the ground that they can be more efficiently and economically done by the government than by public individuals."[60]

However, in a paternalistic system the tendency of camouflaged coercion persists and this creates a point of its difference from the positive state. By calling its people as 'children' and thus by taking upon itself the responsibilities of a'pater', paternalistic system may even assume the role of 'forcing the individuals to be free'. It may even imbue the sentiments of its infallibility in its people by teaching them the lesson of Hegel that the state can never act unrepresentatively. The welfare state has its distinct identity. It pays respect for essential liberties, undertakes programmes of public service and yet refrains from playing the role assigned to it by Hegel and his followers. Instead of preaching the lessons of its infallibility or passive obedience, it draws attention towards the consolidation of democracy in the political, economic and social spheres. Obviously, a paternalistic regime may, and may not, subscribe to the order of a welfare state and, as such, it should not be wholly identified with it.

Although the concept of welfare state is a modern affair, every political system may not necessarily be of this kind. Now every state is 'modern' in the sense that it possesses the attributes of sovereignty and nationalism. Among others, it also claims to contain within itself the characteristics of secularism, democracy and socialism. However, its

60. Garner, *op. cit.,* p. 361.

fundamental mark is national sovereignty that was distinctly absent in the ancient and medieval ages. Laski defines the modern state as "a territorial society, divided into governments and subjects, whether individuals or associations of individuals, whose relationships are determined by the exercise of this supreme coercive power."[61] But every modern state cannot be a welfare state, unless it fulfils the essential requirements as already pointed out. In other words, while a welfare state represents a curious mixture of the tenets of liberalistic democracy and collectivistic socialism, a non-welfare state, though a modern state, may assume the shape of a totalitarian or an autocratic system. In this connection, it may also be pointed out that while the modern state has a life of about four hundred years and is now a phenomenon complete in itself, the welfare state is entirely a new experiment having a life of some four decades and what more, its concept is still in the process of making.[62]

While analysing the nature and distinct character of a welfare state, Piet Thoenes lays emphasis on four cardinal characteristics. First, it is a society though it has the word 'state' and thus it is commensurate with every type of society endeavouring for public welfare whether ancient, feudal, medieval or modern. Second, it adheres to the material welfare of its people and thus takes effective measures to put. into practice the ideals that it preaches. Third, it offers a guarantee of collective security; makes concerted efforts for the social care of its citizens and thus reaches quite close to a socialist society though quite away from a liberal society. Last, it retains the capitalist type of production with certain modifications and restraints. Keeping all these features in his view, Thoenes defines it as "a form of society characterised by a system of democratic government sponsored welfare on a new footing and offering a guarantee of collective social care to its citizens concurrently with the maintenance of a capitalist system of production."[63]

Welfare State in Practice : Though welfare services have been rendered by the state even in the past, Britain has been credited with being the birth-place of modern welfare state. Historical evidence shows that even during the Middle Ages, charities were dispensed through the guilds and ecclesiastical institutions. When epidemics and conditions of starvation assumed formidable proportions, an act was passed in the days of King Henry VIII for the regular collection and distribution of alms. As these measures proved quite inadequate, the Poor Act was enforced during the reign of Queen Elizabeth I. It established once for all the responsibility of the state for those who were destitute. It also provided that all able-bodied poor persons be forced to work, but those who were in want through no fault of their own. the aged, the sick, and the children, were to be looked after and provided for out of a compulsory tax which was to be levied and realised by the parish overseers.

In the eighteenth century, attempts were made to impose the Workhouse Test which wanted the poor to apply for assistance by entering some workhouse. A policy which enabled the employees to keep down wages at the expense of the rate payers was widely adopted and it remained in force until the Poor Law Amendment Act was made in 1834. It abolished outdoor relief, in theory if not in practice, and forced those families to go into the workhouses if they were incapable of supporting themselves. Hence, the economic historian Lipson in his work *The Growth of the English Society* says: "In one sphere of national life—the relief of the poor—state intervention has had a continuous history extending over many hundreds of years ...The virtual right of the indigent to receive succour in case of need

61. Laski : *The State in Theory and Practice,* p. 21.
62. Piet Thoenes puts his impression that a remarkable feature of the Welfare State "is that nobody has the courage to propagate it properly and completely." *op. cit.,* p. 133.
63. *ibid.,* p. 125.

is implicit in the whole series of poor law enactments stretching back to the middle ages. It constituted a degree of recognition on the part of society that it had a duty, however imperfectly fulfilled towards its impoverished members."[64]

In spite of the fact that during the nineteenth century some voluntary organisations did much to alleviate the common distress and to show the way for reforms in many directions, the amount of charity was inevitably spasmodic and insufficient to meet the general need, nor was it given to every deserving person as a matter of right. Hence, writers like Dickens, Hood and Kingsley emphasised that the destitutes might have a legal right to be kept alive. Among the statesmen, it was Disraeli who really made the startling announcement that his people consisted of two nations – the extreme rich and the extreme poor. Then, General Booth in his book *In Darkest English and the Way Out* compared the deplorable conditions of his poor people with the residents of Dark Africa. He laid stress on the formidable evils of squalor, ill-health, drinking and sexual adulteration and held the English state guilty of sheer negligence. Similarly, Charles touched the public conscience in his work *Life and Labour of People in London* and helped to secure provisions for old age pensions.

A philosophical justification of welfare state was given by the Oxford Idealist T.H. Green. As a philosopher by thought, he insisted on the negative character of state activity and as a reformer by action, he desired that three gigantic evils of pauperism, ignorance and intemperance be eradicated by the compulsory action of the state. Contrary to the implications of Bentham and Mill, he defined liberty as a postive power of doing or enjoying something worth doing or enjoying in common with others. He held that the proper action of the state seemed necessarily to be confined to the removal of obstacles or to maintain conditions of life in which morality would be possible; and morality consisted in the disinterested performance of self-imposed duties. In this context he strongly urged that the removal of these evils by the state could not be stopped by any plea either of natural rights, or vested interests, or any other rights, or again by doctrine, however honestly propounded of the need of leaving scope for free will to ride triumphant of itself over illiteracy, intemperance and indigence.

However, the growth of relief by this time was gradual and piecemeal and poverty was by no means conquered, until a committee was set up under the chairmanship of Lord William Beveridge to make a comprehensive survey of social insurance. As a result, the Beveridge Report on Social Insurance and Allied Services was issued in 1944. It highlighted five gigantic evils, namely, want, disease, ignorance, squalor, and idleness. It suggested that social insurance should be regarded as part of a policy of national minimum; It very strongly demanded that the state should offer security for service and contribution. At the same time, it urged full scope for private initiative. In Part I. Sec. 9, the Report stated : "The State in organising security should not stifle incentive, opportunity, responsibility; in establishing a national minimum, it should leave room and encouragement for voluntary action by each individual to provide more than the minimum for himself and his family."[65]

The Beveridge Report was accepted by the Coalition Government with certain exceptions. All the three political parties of Britain agreed to the idea of making this great experiment in an effort to overcome poverty and create the welfare state. The British Parliament passed the Butler Act which, among other things, provided for secondary education. In 1946 Family Allowances Act was passed. The adoption of these measures became characteristic of social legislation and entitled

64. Cf. Hobman, *op. cit.,* p. 2.
65. Cf. ibid., *op. cit.,* p. 12.

the British Government to become the pioneer of welfare state. Hobman thus admires : "It is an error to imagine that the welfare state dropped like a manna from heaven into the open mouths of the expectant people; it is rather the fruits of the British political genius, budding and slowly ripening on a tree which was planted four and a half centuries ago."[66]

Like Britain, India has accepted the goal of welfare state and is committed to its realisation in full. The Constitution is an authentic case in this regard. The Preamble lays stress on Justice—social, economic and political; Liberty of thought, expression, faith, belief and worship; Equality of status and of opportunity; Fraternity assuring the dignityof the individual and unity and integrity of the nation. For the proper fulfilment of the requirements of the welfare state, two parts have been incorporated. Part III contains a comprehensive list of Fundamental Rights whereby rights relating to equality, freedom, non-exploitation, religion, education and culture and constitutional remedies have been guaranteed. Part IV of the Constitution embodies a comprehensive list of the Directive Principles of State Policy and declares that although they are not enforceable by the courts, nevertheless they shall be treated as fundamental in the governance of the country. Article 38 very specifically lays down that the state "shall strive to promote the welfare of the people by securing and protecting as effectively as it may a social order in which justice—social, economic and political—shall inform all the institutions of national life."

As the welfare state is not a mere theoretical creed but also a working ideal, India has done a good number of things in this regard. By now much work has been accomplished through Five Year Plans. The Union and State Governments have done much in the field of social welfare. The community development projects and the national extension services have been implemented. The result is that striking improvement has taken place in the directions of agriculture, irrigation, education, public health and social welfare. It is indisputable that the purpose of all such schemes is to create a new India—happy, prosperous and great. In this way, it may be appreciated that the state in India has been making strenuous efforts to justify the case of a positive state and thereby reject the Hegelian theory that state "is a metaphysical entity, independent of and overshadowing the individual, whose only end is to secure its own existence."

Criticism : Although the concept of welfare state has gained worldwide significance, it has been debunked as 'nefarious', 'deceptive' and 'unsatisfactory'. Two points may be thrashed out in this regard. First, from a theoretical point of view, it is alleged that the model of welfare state cannot satisfy those who frankly hold an anti-authoritarian approach. That is, those who denounce the state as an instrument of oppression, tyranny and exploitation, can never feel satisfied with it inasmuch as the violent character of state survives while rendering social welfare services. The followers of the Marxist-Leninist school would not like to abandon their hope for a day when the state 'will wither away' and classless society would eventuate into a stateless condition of life. Since in the name of rendering welfare services the area of state activity widens, the Pluralists also disfavour this tendency from another standpoint—curtailment of the role of other groups which also meet the requirements of a man's life.

However, a very scathing line of criticism comes from the side of the Marxists who denounce every other state as a bourgeois 'organisation.' The concept of welfare state, according to them, is nothing but another form of a capitalist state to exploit and oppress the class of workers. Since the state is a temporary institution which is to be made use of in the revolution, as Engels said, it is absurd to talk of a free and popular institution. The welfare

66. *ibid.,* p. 1.

state is a re-interpretation of the capitalist state. Naturally, it is anything but a compromise with the unjust capitalist system.

The significance of the social welfare state, however, is not diminished by such allegations. Ever since the days of Aristotle, state has been regarded as an instrument of welfare, moral and material. Whatever be the shortcomings, it is indisputable that state is the first condition of a civilised life, a guarantee against 'return to the state of nature' as once conceived by Hobbes. The concept of welfare state is a powerful response to the challenge of the Anarchist and Marxist tendencies. It is not merely a theoretical creed emphasising certain requirements of a political system, it has practical dimension too whereby it demands specific commitments and accomplishment by the state for the welfare of its people. The welfare state has thus assumed universal significance by accepting obligations "to meet certain dependent needs of the individual and the family."[67]

67. Titmuss : *Essays en the Welfare State*, p. 54.

22

Rule-Making Department

> But almost all political analysts are aware that the golden age of parliaments is over. To be effective they must be provided with more information on the formulation and execution of policies. This necessitates specialist committees which are acknowledgeable enough to prepare legislation and to examine the ministers on their policies. But even the most enlightened of regimes are not always ready to accept this development, and parliamentary assemblies find it difficult to compete with the executive power.
>
> **—Michael Curtis[1]**

The study of legislature (technically known as the rule-making department in the field of comparative politics) in a modern political system presents an interesting as well as an astonishing spectacle that ranges from its reverential aspect of being 'a grand inquest of the nation', as said by John Stuart Mill, to a modern interpretation of its being in a state of 'decline', nay 'demise', as bemoaned by Lord James Bryce. The study of legislature thus swings between the pole of normativism on the one side to that of empiricism on the other. The normative interpretations describing legislature as a 'mirror of the nation', 'embodiment of the general will of the community', 'a committee of grievances', 'a congress of opinions' and the like have been overshadowed by the empirical statements hitting at its real significance as a 'talking shop', 'an institution of class exploitation and oppression', a 'demised body,' and the like. What has really contributed to the declined, if not to the wholly demised, position of the legislature is the increasing authority and influence of the executive (rule-application) department. Modern political scientists in agreement with the fact of executive ascendancy have come to feel that legislatures, in general, "have been reduced to mere sound boards or mere rubber-stamps endorsing policies already framed by the executive."[2]

Legislature : Meaning and Functions

Legislature, most commonly known by the name of 'parliament', forms the first important organ of a political organisation. The word parliament that originally meant 'a talk', is derived from the French word *parler* (to speak or parley) and the Latin *Parliamentum.* In the latter form, it is applied to the after-dinner conversations held by the monks in their cloisters, talks which the monistic state of the 13th century condemned as unedifying. The term was also used to describe conferences such as that held between Louis XI of France and Pope Innocent IV in 1245 and the diplomatic parleys between Alexander II of Scotland and Richard Earl of Corwell a year earlier. Matthew Paris of St. Albans was the first to apply the word parliament to a great council of prelates, earls and barons in 1239 and again in 1246.[3]

1. Curtis : *Comparative Government and Politics* (New York : Harper and Row, 1968), p. 201.
2. R.B. Jain : "Legislative Role Differentiation in Contemporary Societies" in *Journal of Parliamentary Information,* New Delhi, Vol. XXI, No. 3, 1975, p. 360.
3. Norman Wilding and Philip Laundy : *An Encyclopaedia of Parliament* (London : Cassel, 1968), p. 509.

It is said that modern parliaments arose through a fusion of the legislative and judicial functions and the voting on taxation or supply. In medieval times, a parliament was usually a meeting of the king-in-council to which the judges were summoned for the consideration of pleas and petitions (or bills) to the king to redress grievances. On the other hand, the word 'parliament' might be applied to what was more usually described as a colloquium, a meeting of the clergy, or any or all of them. Such a colloquium might be summoned, for instance, to discuss measures for dealing with raids by the Scots over the border, or the sending of any army to the Gascony. More often the purpose was to obtain assent for the levying of an aid or customs duties.[4] In fine, parliament signifies a body of persons assembled for discussion.

The place and significance of the rule-making bodies, from a functional point of view, varies from the 'sovereign' English Parliament to the non-sovereign National People's Congress of China or from' the 'powerful' American Congress to the 'powerless' Cortes of Spain' —a body 'supinely acquiescing in the will of the ruler'[5]. While taking a synthesised view of the functions of legislative bodies, Curtis enumerates them in the following manner :[6]

1. Legislatures choose the head of the state; they may also remove him by the process of impeachment, or they can change the law of his succession or election. For instance, the British Parliament can change the law of primogeniture or the method of abdication. The parliaments of Israel (Knesset) and India (Samsad) elect the President of the Republic; the House of Representatives of the United States has the right to elect the President in case no candidate gets absolute majority in the Presidential polls. The legislatures of the United States and India can also remove their Presidents by the process of impeachment. It is also possible that the legislatures may approve the choice of the head of the government (real or working) as the nomination of the Chancellor in Germany is approved by the Bundestag. The parliaments of Canada, New Zealand and Australia recommend three names to the English sovereign and one of them is nominated by him/her to act as the Governor-General of the country.
2. The legislatures also approve the choice of the Prime Minister and his ministers in some countries. All ministerial nominations made by the President in the United States are ratified by the Senate. The list of entire cabinet is approved by the Knesset in Israel. The Parliament of Switzerland elects seven presidents (ministers) of the Federal Council. The nomination of the Prime Minister made by the King must be approved by the Diet in Japan. The Prime Minister nominated by the President in France has to seek vote of confidence in the Parliament in order to have the constitutional validation of his appointment. In countries having cabinet form of government like Britain and India, the ministers (including the Prime Minister) can remain in office so long as they enjoy the pleasure of the legislature.
3. Legislatures may influence or control government behaviour, or seek to make the executives accountable to them. Votes of no-confidence, censure motions, interpellation procedures, debates on budgets and major policies of the government, process of impeachment, etc. are the various devices in the hands of the legislators to exercise their control over the government. We know that the American Congress took up impeachment proceedings against President Andrew Johnson in 1868 who could survive by a single vote; the process was initiated against President Nixon in

4. *Encyclopaedia Britannica,* Vol. 17, pp. 376-77.
5. Curtis, *op. cit.,* p. 183.
6. *ibid.,* pp. 183-88.

1974 who could save himself by tendering his resignation. In 1999 impeachment proceedings were initiated against Bill Clinton, but he was acquitted. The exit of English Prime Ministers like Attlee in 1949, Eden in 1956 and Macmillan in 1963 confirm the fact of the controlling authority of the Parliament. Likewise, the exit of Chancellor Erhard of West Germany in 1966 shows that the Bundestag has its control over the government. It is a different matter that some restrictions are laid down in the constitution to make the process of censuring the government a tedious affair. For instance, it is given in the French Constitution that a censure motion must be signed by at least 1/10 members of the National Assembly, who cannot sign such other motion in the same session; to be carried, the motion must be voted by an absolute majority of the House after a minimum interval of 48 hours. Likewise it is required in Italy that a motion of no-confidence in the government be signed by at least by 1/10 members and that there be a three-day interval before it is put to debate.

4. Legislatures choose their office bearers and they can also remove them. Moreover, they can also disqualify their members on the charge of proved 'misbehaviour' or committing an act of corruption or treason. The American Senate disqualified its two members William S. Vare and Frank Smith on the charge that they had spent huge amounts of money in their elections. The Chairman (Speaker) and the Deputy Chairman (Deputy Speaker) are elected by the rule-making bodies and they may remove them by a vote of no-confidence. Assemblies may also take up the case of the breach of their privileges and for this they can either authorise their presiding officers or keep the power with them for the admonition, reprimand and imprisonment of the persons involved in the breach of their special rights or privileges. Wilkes Case has its own importance in England in this connection.

5. However, the most important function of the legislatures is to make laws or rules. Hence, it is called the rule-making department. The bills are moved, debated and then passed with or without any amendments, or they are adopted after some other procedure is followed. In most of the countries having 'democratic' form of legislative behaviour, it is a common affair that bills are given three readings and references to the committees are made invariably to discuss the whole proposal threadbare. Basically different from this, however, is the case of a Communist country where not the legislature as such but its small committee (as Standing Committee in China) adopt a bill (called decree) at the invisible behest of the party in power that is adopted by the legislature afterwards to have the form of a proper legislative measure. We also find that in India the ordinance issued by the Head of the State (an executive instrument having the force of law) is ratified by the legislature within a period of six weeks from the date of the commencement of the session.

What we have seen above constitutes, for most of the part, a superficial study of the legislative behaviour. It may also be called a traditional interpretation of the functions of the rule-making bodies. It is with this approach that John Stuart Mill said about a century and a half back that "the function of the assemblies is to serve as an organ in which popular demands could be articulated and wants made known as forums for the discussion of all opinions on public matters, and as mechanisms for watching and controlling the operation of government." Finding some element of truth in this normative interpretation of Mill, Curtis says that "probably the most significant contemporary function of assemblies is the supervision over and inquiry into the performance and behaviour of governments"[7] It was this possibility of control over government that led Cavour to say that the worst of chambers is always better than the best of antechambers. Traditionally speaking, the role of a well-organised assembly "is to analyse, criticise, and pass or reject the policies and proposals of the government; to voice the desires and anxieties of the mass of the citizens; to protect their liberties against any abuse of power by the Government; to educate public opinion through its debates; and finally—as the term legislature implies—to participate in the process of law-making to the extent this is still possible in an area that relies increasingly on the expert and the administrator."[8]

'Emergency Role' of Legislatures: A Modern Interpretation

Apart from making a traditional study of the functions and role of the rule-making bodies, let us also look into their 'emergency roles'. Richard Sisson and Leo Snowiss have suggested three different dimensions in this regard:[9]

1. ***Legislatures as Law-Affecting Bodies*** **:** The involvement of legislatures in the making of law must be considered their central and most fundamental function. In this regard the power with which legislative assemblies have to influence the direction and contours of public policy-making is decisive. So fundamental is this process that we find it difficult to imagine legislatures performing any other function effectively without somehow participating in the formulation of law.
2. ***Legislature and the Control of Executive Power*** **:** The capacity to control the potential excesses of executive initiative and power has always been considered a task of legislatures in modern theories of representative government. It is intrinsic to the idea of cabinet responsibility in a parliamentary system of government and to Congressional overview in the presidential system. It may be said that only when popular assemblies participate in the moulding of law, the necessary power for controlling the executive can be built up and expanded.
3. ***Legislature and the Mobilisation of Consent:*** The advocates of strong executive-centred government for modern or modernising societies assume that legislative institutions ought to serve as auxiliaries in the mobilisation of public support for policies advocated by the executive. As Bernard Crick has observed in his work *The Reform of Parliament* that we "have never had government by Parliament . . . but always government through Parliament."

The'emergency role' of the rule-making bodies cannot be performed unless there are some essential conditions. As R.B. Jain says : "The effective mobilisation of consent through legislative institutions must be accomplished through a complex infrastructure of political support which is ultimately grounded in the capacity of the legislature to affect law-making. It is the ultimate effect which legislatures have upon public policy which transforms election into vigorous systems which mobilise consent by encouraging the articulation of interests and the organisation of groups to pursue those interests in the larger political system."[10]

The functions of the legislatures should be studied in the context of political modernisation and development also if we want to make our study in tune with the norms of comparative politics. As already seen in the chapters on political modernisation and political development, it may be pointed out that

7. Curtis, *op. cit.*, p. 188.
8. Jain, *op. cit.*, p. 362.
9. Sisson and Snowiss : "Legislatures in the Context of Modernisation", a paper presented at the Second International Conference on Legislative Development, State University of New York, Albany, January 20-24, 1975, referred to in Jain, *op. cit.*, pp. 364-66.
10. *ibid.*, p. 366.

parliament, originally a consultative body for the kings, then a body making law and registering grievances of the people, "has increasingly faced competition from more specialised consultative, law-making and adjudicative agencies." It has happened on account of political development that brings a multiplication of political structures, each more specialised than the multifunctional institutions, of the old regime. In this context, the term 'political development' "must be defined as the will and capacity of the system to cope with, and to generate, continuing transformation toward whatever value seems appropriate in a particular context—among them three values: economic development, personal freedom and socio-economic justice would usually rank higher than the Western type democracy or strong legislatures."[11]

Confining attention to the legislatures of the 'developing' countries of the Afro-Asian and Latin American world, Robert Packenham has outlined three important roles of the assemblies:[12]

1. ***Legitimation Function :*** It means fostering acquiescence in, or support for, the moral right to rule the government among the population at large as well as political elites, either by simply meeting regularly and uninterruptedly, or by overt, conscious, legislative stamp of approval on executive initiative the legislature produces, among the relevant populace and elite, a wider and deeper sense of the moral right of the government to rule than would otherwise have been obtained.
2. ***Safety Valve Function :*** The legislatures reduce 'tensions,' provide reassurance and generally enhance satisfaction with or acquiesence in the policies and programmes of the government. They also provide scope for the articulation of interests. They perform 'exit functions' meaning that when the political system seems to have reached an impasse and the normal decision-making process seems incapable of providing a way out of the situation,, the elites sometimes turn to the legislatures for either the substance or the form, or both, of a decision which will take the system out of the impasse.
3. ***Administrative Overview, Patronage, Recruitment, Socialisation and Training :*** The legislatures exercise their control over the ministers and the civil servants working under them; they exercise patronage by ratifying the actions of the executive; they recruit leaders and provide them opportunities to go higher. By serving as training ground for the future leadership of the country, they strengthen 'consensual institutional continuity and they often constitute the only means of administrative overview available in the country.

It is in the context of these important directions that the rule-making bodies of the developing countries may play their significant roles. However, what pricks Packenham is the 'obstructionist role' of the legislatures. They "tend to represent all over the world more conservative and parochial interests than executives, even in democratic polities. This seems specially to be the case in presidential, as contrasted with parliamentary, political systems. In societies that need and want change, and where political modernisation may be defined as the will and capacity to cope with and generate continuing transformation, it may not make much sense to strengthen the decision-making power of an institution that is likely to resist change."[13]

Modern Legislatures : A Typological Illustration

Legislatures may be classified into two kinds—unicameral and bi-cameral. A unicameral legislature is one that has only one house as

11. *ibid.,* p. 367.
12. *ibid.,* pp. 368-69.
13. *ibid.,* p. 369.

the National People's Congress of China. A bicameral legislature is one that has two houses as the English Parliament having the House of Lords and the House of Commons. Since bicameralism has become a matter of constitutional fashion now, most of the legislatures of the world have two chambers known as the first (lower or popular) and the second (upper) chambers, though the Marxist writers donot agree with the practice of using such marks of distinction. A different form of typological illustration can be provided in case we use 'functional dimension' as the the basis of our study. We may refer to Blondel who constructs four types of legislatures in the modern world :[14]

1. *'Nascent' or 'Inchoate' Legislatures :* These are the lowest types of legislatures (as in former East Germany and the Soviet Union) whose ostensible activities are very small and almost non-existent and whose effectiveness or influence is hardly of any value. Such assemblies are nearer to 'limited surgeries' or 'low-grade ombudsmen'.
2. *'Truncated' Legislatures :* These are some legislatures (as in Singapore, Jordan and a number of African countries) that have a degree of influence within the context of their declared activities. They have a very limited influence.. They are not allowed to be concerned with very important matters, though they are given to discuss such matters to the extent the executives deem proper or relevant. We may say that legislatures have the opportunity to discuss the bill and policy matters but to the extent desired by the real rulers of the land.
3. *More 'Inhibited' than 'Truncated' Legislatures :* In this category we can include legislatures that have a better position than that discussed above, though not as good as discussed in the following category. However, it shows a higher degree so far as participation in power is concerned. The assemblies discuss all bills and policy matters and they seem to be appreciably involved in general questions of great importance, but they lack the position of influencing the executive to an extent that their will prevails over the will of the executive. The legislatures of France, Switzerland and India can be placed in this category.
4. *'True' Legislatures :* This is the best category that includes the legislature of very advanced democratic countries of the world like Britain and the United States. These legislatures are said to fulfil in a generally adequate way the functions of channelling demands and articulating interests of various sections of the people. They pass bills and budgets and discuss policy matters so much so that they can force the government to change a decision in a particular direction. Not only that, the legislatures can censure the conduct of the government and force the executive to resign after passing a vote of no-confidence or adopting the resolution of impeachment.

One may, or may not, agree with the four-fold classification of Blondel, or say that such a country can, or cannot, be placed in such a category. The reason for this should be discovered in the view one takes of the functional dimension of a modern legislature that is drastically changed owing to the emergence of new political conditions. For intance, there occurred a momentous change in the character of the Indian Parliament in 1975-76 under the weight of serious political developments with the result that the view of Blondel in placing it in thc third category gathered more weight. A study of political development in other developing countries of the world like Pakistan and Bangladesh may lead to similar impressions. To a student of comparative politics in agreement with the fact

14. Jean Blondel : *An Introduction to Comparative Government* (London: Weidenfeld and Nicolson, 1969), pp. 136-41.

Functions and Role of a Legislator : Price's Paradigm of a Senator

1. Instigation and publicising	: . . . the public or private advocacy of an issue as one worthy of attention and ameliorative action. Typical instigators include the staff man or lower-level bureaucrat who calls a problem to his superior's attention, the congressmen who highlights an issue through investigative hearings, or the author who documents and dramatises a social need.
2. Formulation	: . . . devising and advocating a specific legislative remedy for a supposed need. The formulator draws boundaries around and establishes a focal point for its further consideration.
3. Information gathering	: . . . collecting data on the nature of hazards and abuses; the alternative schemes for solving problems and their costs, benefits, and inherent difficulties; the likely political impact of each scheme; and the feasibility of various compromises. Information-gathering is crucial to each of the other functions—to devising a workable proposal well as to plotting its political course and building a sense of need and legitimacy.
4. Interest aggregation	: . . . responding to the needs and wishes of individuals or groups affected by a given proposal. In one instance, it might mean the championing of one group over or against others, in the stimulating of latent group sentiments. Such activities may both resolve and exacerbate conflict; that may, on the one hand, contribute to the instigation and mobilisation effort, or on the other, give rise to attempts at modification or obstruction.
5. Mobilisation	: . . . the exertion of pressure, persuasion, or control on behalf of a measure by one who is able, often by virture of his institutional position, to take effective and relatively direct action to secure enactment. Whether an issue goes beyond the publicising and formulating stages usually depends on the support it receives from individuals, groups, or governmental units that possess authority and legitimacy in the policy area and on the extent of 'intra-elite organising' by key leaders. Mobilisers may become involved in other functions as part of these efforts, but they may benefit from—or be stimulated by—those who were active at the 'earlier' stages as well.
6. Modification	: . . . the marginal alteration of a proposal, sometimes 'strengthening' it sometimes granting certain concessions to its opponents in order to facilitate final passage. Modification may, or may not, complement actions taken at earlier points, but in any case the modifier shares responsibility for a bill's final form.

See David Price: *Who Makes the Laws*? (Combridge, Massachusetts : Schenkman, 1972), pp. 82-84. Also see David E. Apter: *Introduction to Political Analysis* (New Delhi: Prentice Hall of India, 1978), pp. 350-51.

of 'decline of legislatures', it may deem proper that the development of assemblies has been more in the reverse direction. That is, legislatures are being demoted to the lower category on account of the increasing authority of the executive. The trend is towards the truncation of the powers and position of the rule-making departments and not towards, what Blondel calls, the 'true legislatures'. However, we may safely appreciate the view of Prof. R.B. Jain that such a typology of legislatures, as presented by Blondel, "is helpful in understanding their activities in a comparative perspective but many more studies, both single-country and cross-national, are needed before we can become reasonably confident about the extent of activities and levels of influence corresponding to these legislatures in general."[15]

Delegated Legislation

Meaning and Nature : Delegated legislation (also known by the names of subordinate, executive and departmental legislation) is a term of constitutional significance employed to describe those statutory rules, regulations, orders, circulars, notifications, explanations, etc. which are issued by the executive departments at different intervals to supplement and amplify parliamentary legislation so that the 'parent act'does not fall short of its operation.[16] Of course, the work of legislation is a concern of the representatives of the people, but the law made by the legislature suffers from shortcomings when it is put into effect under the changing conditions and circumstances. The legislature does make an attempt to make the legislation comprehensive, as far as possible, yet there is a limit to human ingenuity. Hence, the legislature finds it not only desirable or expedient but essential to transmit through its statutes powers to the ministers and their administrative assistants to issue necessary orders to apply the provisions of the statute to the situation they are intended to regulate.

As a result, nowadays, a relatively small part of the total legislative output of the government is enacted by the legislature. Much more extensive in bulk than the statutes are the multitudinous rules and regulations issued by the subordinate executive authorities. The legislation of a modern democratic state is not confined to the pages of a statute book, rather it finds place in many official volumes as well where the copies of all such departmental rules and regulations are preserved. Hence, C.T. Carr, the Editor of the Statutory Rules and Orders in the United Kingdom, rightly says that the statute book "is not only incomplete but even misleading unless it be read with the delegated legislation which amplifies and amends it."[17] In this regard, Carr has rightly said thus : "The law of land besides the common law and statute law includes a great deal of what may be termed subordinate or delegated legislation. Few statutes form a complete code in themselves as to all the details relating to the subject with which they deal."

Delegated legislation is subordinate legislation made not by the legislature but by the executive departments in order to keep the wishes of the former in operation. The parliamentary legislation is the 'parent measure'; while the departmental legislation ensuing in the form of 'details' has the character of an offspring. There is a fundamental distinction between the two : while the authority of the legislature is original, inherent and unlimited (or limited by the terms of the constitution), the powers of the department are derivative and limited by the terms of the legislative statutes.

---

15. Jain, *op. cit.*, p. 372.
16. As a well-known English jurist, Sir John Salmond, says : "Legislation is either supreme or subordinate . . . Subordinate legislation is that which proceeds from any authority other than the sovereign power and is, therefore, dependent for its continued existence and validity on some superior or supreme authority." *Jurisprudence,* IX Ed., p. 210.
17. See G.B. Adams : *Constitutional History of England,* p. 674.

It follows that delegated legislation is secondary in character. As such, the legislature may review the departmental order and even make it void if its wishes are ignored by the executive authorities. However, in England, the striking point is the juristic fact of parliamentary sovereignty that has deprived the courts of the power of judicial review. The courts cannot question the legal validity of parliamentary legislation, though they can make a judicial review of delegated legislation unless the statute in very exceptional circumstances declares to the contrary. That is, the courts may scrutinise a departmental order, rule or regulation (unless forbidden by Parliament) and then pass a judgment on its constitutional propriety.

The derivative character of delegated legislation becomes clear when its continued existence depends upon the wishes of the legislature. The legislature does two things in this regard. First, it inserts a particular clause (in Britain called the Henry VIII clause) which provides that in the event of some ambiguity of parliamentary statute, the department may do the needful within the scope of the provisions of its law or wishes of the parliament. Sometimes, in the absence of such a clause, it is given to understand that the necessary details shall be filled in by the department concerned as per needs and situations in order to save parliamentary statute from being inoperative. From this point of view, parliamentary legislation has been characterised as 'blanket legislation', while the departmental legislation has been given the nickname of 'sub-legislation'. Second, particularly in Britain, in very exceptional cases, there is given a conclusive evidence clause which lays down that if the department adds anything in the course of application, it will *ipso facto* be taken as a part and parcel of the parliamentary statute. The object of this clause is to preclude the possibility of judicial intervention. The incorporation of this clause forbids the courts to entertain any suit or pass any judgment on the legal validity of a departmental order in view of the fact that in doing so the department has fully complied with the requirements of the will of the sovereign parliament. Adams thus points out: "Such a regulation issued for such purpose, would have to be treated by the courts as if it were the part of the act. It would seem that the object of a provision of this kind is to prevent the court from enquiring into the validity of the regulations. It has been laid down judicially, however, that it does not have this result; even if this formula is used in the act, a regulation will not be held valid by a court if it is inconsistent with the provisions of the act under which it is made or does not come within the scope of the powers conferred."[18]

However, it may by noted that delegated legislation does not cover that piece of legislation which the executive enacts by virtue of original power vested in it. An ordinance issued by the head of the state does not come within the ambit of delegated legislation. Likewise, in Britain orders-in-council (but not statutory orders) donot fall in this category, because they are made by virtue of original legislative authority vested in the Crown. In the same way, delegated legislation must not be confused with any other form of administrative action which is of an individual application like a particular command, license, inspection, remission of penality, etc. As delegated legislation refers to the delegation of law-making power of the parliament to the executive, it simply covers those executive orders, explanations, interpretations, notifications, etc. which are in the nature of subsidiary laws to keep the parliamentary law in operation.

Moreover, keeping in view the point of content and purpose, the nature of delegated legislation has three characteristics: Firstly, it is of a contingent nature and takes place where the legislature makes the applications of the main enactment dependent upon the existence of certain facts or conditions whose determination and (in accordance with them) the

18. Adams, *op. cit.*, pp. 577-78.

application of the statute is made the business of the department. Secondly, it is supplementary as it fills the details in the body of the parent measure passed in the shape of a skeleton by the parliament. Finally, it is interpretative as it clarifies and explains the provisions of the law to which it relates. On the whole, delegated legislation, by whatever name it may be called, is essentially subordinate legislation.[19]

Growth : Although delegated legislation appears to be of recent origin, its history "is not new."[20] Particularly in Britain, the Parliament delegated its powers to the departments for the sake of necessary supplementations and amplifications in its statutes even in the earlier centuries of the modern period. The only notable thing in this regard is that over the last one hundred years or so it has enormously increased. Keeping it in view, Sir Cecil Carr observes: "No one who looks at the collection of the annual output of delegated legislation can seriously propose that Parliament should now cancel the concession of legislative power and should undertake the future under its own direct authority all the legislative activities which at present are left to His Majesty-in-Council or to the various public departments."[21] The reasons for the inevitable growth of delegated legislation may be put as under:

In the first place, the growth has been effected by the expansion in the sphere of state activity. So long as the concept of *laissez faire* held sway, the political machinery looked for nothing more than the maintenance of internal peace and security. But when the schemes of social welfare and economic problems of a national and international character formed the concern of modern state, the province of state activity naturally increased. The provisions of social services like national health, social insurance, insurance against unemployment, urban and rural planning, etc. involved the making of detailed regulations to provide for individual benefits. All such schemes of social security undertaken in the name of welfare services signify that the modern state has accepted obligations "to meet certain department needs of the individual and of the family."[22]

The work of modern state is so complex that only experts can discharge it properly. As the legislative bodies consist of 'amateurs', the work of drafting the bills and filling details therein is left to the departmental experts. The legislators simply lay down the ins and outs of their policy, while the work of making contingent supplementations and interpretations is left to the executive departments. Sir Courtenay Ilbert rightly visualises that the increasing complexity of modern administration and the increasing difficulty of passing complicated measures through the ordeal of parliamentary discussion "have led to an increase in the practice of delegating legislative power to executive authorities."[23]

Another reason is the huge workload on the legislative bodies. Every parliamentary session witnesses a crop of bills. Moreover, the time of the legislature devoted to the questions and their answers, discussions, debates, etc. puts a further premium on the total amount of

19. In 1932 the Committee on Ministers' Powers (also known as the Donoughmore Committee) thus defined : "The word 'legislation' has grammatically two meanings—the operation of function of legislating; and the laws which result therefrom. So too 'delegated legislation' may mean either exercise by a subordinate authority, such as a Minister, of the legislative powers delegated to him by parliament; or the subsidiary laws themselves, passed by ministers in the shape of departmental regulations and other statutory rules or orders." The. Committee on Ministers' Powers defined it as "the exercise of minor legislative power by subordinate authorities and bodies in pursuance of statutory authority given by the Parliament itself." Dr M.P. Sharma aptly puts that delegated legislation means (1) the function of sub-legislation by the executive, and (2) the output of such activity." *Public Administration in Theory and Practice,* (Allahabad : Kitab Mahal, 1965), p. 630.
20. Laski : *Reflections on the Constitution,* p. 43.
21. Sir Cecil Carr : *Delegated Legislation,* p. 20.
22. Titmuss : *Essays on Welfare State,* p. 54.
23. Ilbert : *Legislative Methods and Forms,* p. 37.

time which remains for the discharge of legislative business. Naturally, resort to delegated legislation becomes indispensable. It relieves the pressure on parliamentary time by removing the details of administration from the legislative arena. It also enables the legislature to lay down broad and general principles without wasting time over the details. The Parliamentary Counsel to the Treasury in 1877, Lord Thring, thus viewed: "The province of Parliament is to decide material questions affecting the public interests, and the more the procedure and subordinate matters can be withdrawn from their cognisance, the greater will be the time afforded for the consideration of more serious questions involved in legislation."[24]

Then, there is the reason of expediency or law's march with the march of time. As the time changes, it brings new situations and circumstances. As a result, the parliamentary statute is bound to become obsolete in case fresh interpretations are not given by the courts and necessary supplementations and amplifications are not provided by the executive. The executive, unlike the legislature, always lives in session and as a measure to face the contingency, the legislature delegates its powers to the departments subject to its own scrutiny and control. In this regard, L.S. Amery has rightly viewed that much of social and economic legislation "covers so vast and detailed a field that no statute however cumbrous—and many of them are already cumbrous and unintelligible enough—could possibly provide for all contingencies."[25]

Finally, under the emergent conditions of modern age, delegated legislation provides the means by which the executive is armed with a power to take immediate action. It is essential that in order to face unforeseen contingencies, the executive department be armed with sufficient powers to meet the situation. It is owing to this that during the critical days of the Second World War, the British Parliament recognised delegated legislation as the only convenient and possible remedy. May's monumental work justifies it in these words: "Parliament is not always sitting; even when it is sitting, the law contained statutes can conveniently be supplemented by departmental rules and regulations and orders within prescribed limits and subject to parliamentary control. Details that are subsidiary to procedural matters can be worked out by departments without taking up time on the floor of the House."[26]

These are the reasons that have made the growth of delegated legislation inevitable; more so their cumulative effect has been to increase continuously and immensely the volume of subordinate legislation. It has now become an axiom of the theory and practice of constitutional law that if the legislature is not willing to delegate law-making power to the executive agencies, it would be unable to make the kind as well as the quantity of legislation as required by the people. Thanks to the infiltration of democracy into the realms of economics and sociology that the modern state has transformed itself from a mere police institution to an agency of public welfare and, as such, increased legislative delegation has become a valid phenomenon of modern positive state.[27]

Case of Britain : Delegated legislation is especially popular in the British constitutional

24. Refer to Amery : *Thoughts on the Constitution,* p. 50.
25. *ibid.*
26. Sir Edward Fellowes and T.G.B. Crocks (eds.) : *Sir Thomas Erskine May's Treatise on Law, Privileges, Proceedings and Usages of Parliament,* XVI Ed., p. 847.
27. It is now well realised that administrative agencies "offer the services of the expert and the better equipped for experimentation than legislatures." Refer to the *Encyclopaedia of Social Sciences* (New York), Vol. V, pp. 65-66. Hence, in Britain the Committee on Ministers' Powers held that without delegating its authority to the executive, the Parliament "would be unable to pass the kind and quantity of legislation which modern public opinion requires." It further held that delegated legislation "is both legitimate and constitutionally desirable for certain purposes, within certain limits, and under certain safeguards."

system. The reason should be traced in the centuries-old parliamentary model. As early as 1539, a legislative measure empowered the king to legislate by proclamation. Since then, a new term, called the Henry VIII Clause has come into circulation. Thus, any item which delegated legislative powers to amend the Acts of Parliament, either the Act under which the powers were delegated or other provisions of the same nature, was given the name of Henry VIII Clause. This system continued until the Donoughmore Committee insisted on its discontinuance in 1932.

The British Parliament gradually developed the tradition of its sovereign authority and delegated legislation developed as its necessary concomitant. The Parliament, contrary to the American practice, thought it sufficient to lay down an intelligent principle to guide the executive or administrative official. It was taken for granted that the work of filling in details into the body of parliamentary statutes is ministerial rather than legislative in character, even if considerable discretion is conferred upon the delegated authority. May's work on parliamentary practice thus recognises: "As this country does not accept the doctrine of the powers, i.e., the confinement of legislative power to the executive, and of judicial power to the judiciary, there is no constitutional impropriety in the practice of delegating legislative power to the executive. The practice, indeed is by no means a new development: it has been consistently adopted, with the encouragement of the legislature, by those responsible for the form of our statutes because of its obvious advantages in lightening the load otherwise to be borne by the legislative machine."[28]

As already pointed out, delegated legislation in Britain is not a new development. Taking the case of the present century, it may be said that in 1904 it was given that the orders and regulations then in force be published. They filled thirteen volumes. However, in view of the growing dissatisfaction of the members, the Lord Chancellor in 1924 set up a Special Order procedure whereby it was required that a sessional committee of the House of Lords would examine departmental rules and regulations. With the growth of social legislation, the scope of delegated legislation developed yet more and in 1927 the Parliament passed 43 Public Acts in which 26 contained a specific clause empowering the minister to issue orders (he deemed fit and necessary) having the force of law.

One important event in this regard is the appointment of the Committee on Ministers' Powers (under the chairmanship of Earl of Donoughmore) by the House of Commons in 1929. The Committee submitted very important recommendations in 1932 and although it regretted that the facilities afforded to Parliament to superintend or control the exercise of powers delegated to the ministers "are inadequate; there is a danger that the servant may be transformed into the master." It also expressed its conviction that delegated legislation "is inevitable and be subject to proper safeguard."[29] A little after, the valuable survey of this Committee was accepted by the House with appreciation. Yet, in order to keep the anxiety alive, the House in its sessions of 1943-44 appointed a Select Committee to scrutinise all statutory rules and orders (as well as other drafts so intended). It was also held that all departmental rules and regulations in this regard must be put before the House of Commons for an affirmation vote and be exposed to annulment if an address be carried through.

A similar Select Committee has been appointed by the House of Commons in its subsequent sessions from 1948 onwards. The Committee has worked with the help of the Speaker's Counsel. The order of reference shows that the House does not empower the committee to consider the merits or policy but enables

28. May, *op. cit.*, p. 847.
29. *ibid.*

them to draw the attention of the House towards provisions relating to the imposition of a charge on public revenues, making of provisions precluding judicial intervention, appearing to make some unusual or unexpected use of the powers conferred by the statute, purporting to have retrospective effect where the present statute does not provide, having been withheld from publication or from being laid before Parliament by unjustifiable delay, having not been notified in proper time to the Speaker in cases where they come into operation before being presented to the Parliament, or calling for elucidation of their form or purport.[30]

The Committee in its various reports also suggested improvement in departmental practices and the House of Commons in 1953 agreed that such a committee be set up early in each session to do the necessary work of scrutiny. The developments after the Second World War testify that the conclusions of the Committee on Ministers' Powers have been fully taken into account and the House of Commons has grown fully convinced of the inescapability of delegated legislation. May's great work thus admits: "Not needing to be fashioned to survive the processes of discussion and amendment to which a Bill is exposed, delegated legislation should be capable of more expansive and intelligent statement than a statute."[31]

Case of the US : Apparently the American Constitution forbids delegated legislation. Its basic feature of the separation of powers vests legislative authority in the Congress. The American constitutional system recognises the principle of *delegatus don-potest delegare.* It implies that 'the delegated cannot be redelegated.' That is, when the legislative authority has been delegated by the people to the Congress, it cannot be re-delegaied by the Congress to any other authority. The American system also attaches sanctity to *the principle of constitutional trust and implied prohibition* which holds that the trust reposed in one agency cannot be transmitted to another. Hence, in one of his judgments, Justice Cooley of the Supreme Court observed: "Where the sovereign power of the state has located the authority, there it must remain and by the constitutional agency alone the laws must be made until the constitutional agency itself is changed."[32]

But the conditions and circumstances forced the advent of delegated legislation in the United States though within certain limits. The Supreme Court in 1928 in the case of *Hampton A Co.* v. *U.S.* enunciated the new formula by holding that if the Congress "shall lay down by legislative act an intelligible principle to which the person or body authorised to fix such rates is directed to conform, such legislative action is not a forbidden delegation of legislative power."[33] Thus, within very limited scope permission was given to the delegation of legislative authority. However, the judiciary remained so sensitive that when the National Industrial Recovery Act of 1933 authorised the President to approve codes of fair competition for particular trades and industries, it was declared *ultra vires* of the Constitution on the plea that the delegation of power made to the President was virtually unlimited.

The existing position in the United States is in favour of forbidding excessive delegation of legislative authority to the executive agencies.[34] It appears that the courts have given allowance to the needs of the age and laid down certain conditions of valid delegation.

30. *ibid.,* p. 847.
31. *ibid.,* p. 856. The Committee on Ministers' Powers thus admitted : "In truth, whether good or bad, the development of the practice is inevitable. It is a natural reflection in the sphere of constitutional law, of changes in political, social and economic ideas, and of changes in the circumstances of our lives which have resulted from scientific discoveries."
32. Cf. N.B. Khare : "Delegated Legislation : A Legal Analysis" in A.B. Lal (ed.) : *The Indian Parliament,* p. 179.
33. See Avasthi and Maheshwari : *Public Administration,* p. 459.
34. Schwartz : *American Administrative Law,* p. 26.

They are: that while doing so the Congress must live within its constitutional competence; that the subject and scope of delegation must be properly defined; that the delegation must be in favour of public authorities only; that a finding must be obtained in case of a contingent delegation; and, that power to create offences or impose penalties must not be delegated. In this way, the compelling needs of the situation "have got over the constitutional difficulty by a subterfuge."[35]

Case of India : In this direction, India is no exception. The first striking instance is available of the year 1950 when the Speaker of the Lok Sabha in a Memorandum observed that the present control of Parliament over the delegated legislation was defective for two reasons, namely, that the members did not fully realise that the powers were being delegated to the executive so freely and that effective scrutiny of subordinate legislation had no longer been possible due to their quantity and complexity. These things had their effect so much so that the Speaker, on 1 December 1953, appointed a committee of ten members with H.V. Pataskar as Chairman. It received the help of the Lok Sabha Secretariat and in its deliberations it found that no bill (except one of Transfer of Evacuee Deposits Bills) had been given a clear memorandum of delegated authority.

The Pataskar Committee in 1954 strongly recommended that the memorandum should be accompanied with every bill which would clearly lay down the scope of executive authority so that there remained no confusion at the time of scrutiny. It also laid stress on the proper publicity of departmental rules and regulations through official gazettes and the press. It insisted that all such orders, rules and regulations be laid on the table of the House for a uniform and total period of thirty days before the date of their final publication. Finally, it reiterated that the rule-making authority of the department should never be left out of parliamentary purview or scrutiny.[36]

Yet it should be remembered that while India has adopted parliamentary system of government, her case is different from that of Britain to a great extent. The Indian Parliament is not a sovereign law-making body and its authority has been curbed by the constitutional provisions that guarantee federal system, fundamental rights and the judicial review. It appears that the courts in India have often made a serious review of legislative and sub-legislative measures and thus held those parts null and void that were taken to defeat the constitutional provisions. For instance, Justice Mukherjea in the case of *Jatindranath. State of Bihar* (1949) cited the view of Justice Cooley with approval and said that the authority "must remain where it is located and the power to which the prerogative has been entrusted cannot relieve itself of the responsibility of choosing other organs upon which it shall be devolved."[37]

The existing position is that while the delegation of legislative authority is not forbidden in India, it has been well settled that the legislature cannot delegate its essential legislative function in any case. It must lay down the legislative policy and principle and afford guidance for carrying out the said policy before it delegates subsidiary powers in that behalf. The Supreme Court in the case of *Harishankar Bagla and Another* v. *The State of Madhya Pradesh* thus observed: "The legislature cannot delegate its function of laying down legislative policy in respect of a measure and its formulation as a rule of conduct. The legislature must declare that policy of the law and the legal principles which are to control any given cases, and must provide a standard

35. M.P. Sharma, *op. cit.,* p. 636.
36. The Committee has really done a fine job by serving as the protector against what might be termed the New Despotism. An English writer Morris-Jones is of the view that it "has given an able and workman-like start to its important task." *Parliament in India,* p. 311.
37. See N.B. Khare, *op. cit.,* p. 179.

to guide the officials or the body in power to execute the law."[38]

Criticism: Although the points in favour of delegated legislation have already been incidentally discussed in the preceding sections, they may be summed up here under three heads—expediency, efficiency and flexibility. In the first place, it is pointed out that it relieves the pressure on the time of legislature by enabling it to concentrate on the general principles and issues of important policy. It rightly takes into view that the job of filling in the details can be done more effectively and usefully by the concerned departments. In this way, the legislature saves much of its valuable time and devotes it to the discussion of important matters of policy or principle. Secondly, it permits the utilisation of expert knowledge. Since the legislators are generally ignorant of the technicalities of modern administration and, as such, they are not competent to lay down the minute details, it is worthwhile that the details of a technical nature be worked out by the expert officials. Finally, it makes room for flexibility. The legislature can never be omniscient to foresee all possible contingencies. As the conditions and circumstances change, a corresponding change in the modes of implementation is required.

These benefits are not apparent but real and their proper appreciation by the constitutionalists is responsible for the inescapable growth of delegated legislation. It is indisputable that when the legislature does not remain in continuous session and when the executive departments have to deal with the matters as the conditions arise, it stands to reason that suitable powers should be given to them in anticipation. Hence, the Donoughmore Committee in its report emphasised that the system of delegated legislation permits of experiment being made and thus affords an opportunity, otherwise difficult to ensure, of utilising the lessons of experience.

In spite of the fact that the delegated legislation is inevitable and inescapable, critics have expressed serious fears and denounced it for the following reasons :

1. It diminishes parliamentary control over the business of legislation which falls within its inherent authority. By it the control of Parliament becomes a thing of nominal or theoretical significance. So many statutory instruments never, or hardly ever, come before the legislature for scrutiny; or when they come, they are carried through in a very casual way. An admirer of delegated legislation, Adams says : "Although the Parliament never desires to shake off its hold in *toto,* it sometimes happens that extraordinary powers are conferred on the departments which invest the executive with dangerous discretionary authority and constitute a distinct menace to the liberties of the people. Occasionally wide and ill-defined discretion is given to the minister so that he may make very important changes in policy matters."[39]
2. It enhances executive authority at the cost of parliamentary jurisdiction. Through this the legislature abdicates its own original authority in favour of the executive. As a

38. Refer to 1954 S.C.J. 637. Earlier, in a case Justice Mukherjea had observed : "The policy may be particularised in as few or many words as the legislature thinks proper and it is enough if intelligent guidance is given to the subordinate authority. The Court can interfere if no policy is discernible at all or the delegation is of such an indefinite character as to amount to abdication . . ." A.I.R. 1951, S.C. 332.
39. Adams, *op. cit.,* p. 578. He further says : "Ministers are principal recipients of delegated legislative power, though sometimes it is conferred on the King-in-Council or some other authority. But when power is given to the King-in-Council, it is really exercised by some minister, and the order-in-council is formed in the executive department concerned. The difference between statutory order-in-council and departmental regulations issued in the name of ministers is one of form, not of substance." *ibid.,* p. 574. John E. Kersell has thus aptly warned : "The government official like a good many other people in this imperfect world is to be watched most carefully when he is acting with the best intentions." *Parliamentary Supervision of Delegated Legislations,* p. 7.

result, the ever-expanding scope of government converts itself into an inconceivable regulation of people's life. The bureaucrats tend to exalt administrative convenience and national advantage at the cost of the individual and his freedom. The official in his zeal to achieve a desirable result may impose an unreasonable burden on the people. The power under a statute to make the rules gives him just the opportunity that he wants. In Nazi Germany Hitler used this device for the sake of his ambitious programmes. So, long before the fall of French democracy in 1940, the Government had been authorised to issue decrees by the French Parliament which thereafter scarcely ever met.

3. It adversely affects the area of judicial intervention. The delegated legislation often blunts the edge of the judicial weapon owing to the fact that the authority of the courts is limited by the provisions of parliamentary statutes. Not only this, in certain cases, a particular clause is added to preclude the possibility of any subsequent judicial intervention. This danger is more apparent in Britain where parliamentary sovereignty is a juristic fact and hence the courts are helpless when a parliamentary statute forfeits judicial authority in particular cases. The remarks of Lord Hewart of Bury in his well-known work, *The New Despotism*, give a bold assessment of this situation in these words : "There is in existence and in certain quarters in the ascendant, a genuine belief that parliamentary institutions and the rule of law have been tried and found wanting, and that the time has come for the departmental despot, who shall be at once scientific and benevolent, but above all a law to himself."[40]

It is pointed out by a protagonist that by publicity the dangers of delegated legislation may be removed. For instance, in Britain, the Statutory Instruments Act of 1946 has superseded the obsolete clauses of the Rules of Publication Act of 1893. In this regard, Hewitt thus observes : "The point of weakness is that even this Act does not make it mandatory that when the instrument comes before the House what method will be utilised—affirmative or negative. The only requirement is that it shall be laid before the House and if it takes no decision, it will continue in operation unless a clear decision is taken to the contrary. One obvious weakness is that there is no provision in the Statutory Instruments Act of 1946 determining the choice between procedure by affirmative resolution and procedure for annulment of rules and orders by an adverse prayer. If an affirmative resolution is required, it means that the House has complete control over the instrument; but if the instrument comes into effect, the House will hear nothing of it unless some active Member brings it to the notice of the House. It is most desirable that instruments imposing taxation or modifying the terms of the Act of Parliament should require an affirmative resolution of the House."[41]

Hence, it may be pointed out that in delegating its powers, the legislature acts in response to the immediate needs of the time or for the sake of administrative convenience with little appreciation of the significance or probable effects of its own action. It does not follow any general principle, and it is, therefore, not surprising that executive legislation should exhibit anomalies, inconsistencies and other fatal weaknesses. Much of these defects or dangers, as already pointed out, are certainly owing to the haphazard evolution of delegated legislation.

If the growth of delegated legislation is inescapable, the issue of suggesting proper

40. Cf. Adams, *op. cit.*, p. 581.
41. *ibid.*, p. 8.

safeguards is equally relevant. Lest the very object of delegated legislation be frustrated, the following safeguards may be suggested :

1. Delegated legislation must always be subject to well-defined limits. It must not be so vague, general or sweeping that its scope becomes indiscernible. Hence, the law-making power which the legislature desires to confer on the executive should always be explicitly defined by the statute, irrespective of the fact that the legislature is a sovereign body or not, the suggestion should be strictly followed.
2. Resort to delegated legislation should be made only for the sake of genuine necessity. That is, delegation of legislative authority should not ordinarily be made for the purposes which are 'unusual' or 'abnormal'. The duration must also be taken into view. In other words, the legislature should not delegate its power to the executive departments in a hasty, rash or ill-considered manner.
3. The legislature should be watchful. The departmental orders, rules and regulations should be placed before the legislature for scrutiny so that executive 'mischiefs' are easily eradicated. In Britain certain types of statutory instruments cannot come into force unless they have been approved by an affirmative vote of the Parliament. Herbert Morrison thus insists that although the practice of delegated legislation is correct, it "is well for the Parliament to keep a watchful and even jealous eye on it at all stages."[42]
4. There is the safeguard of adequate publicity. It should be held essential that all departmental rules and regulations going to supplement or amplify the provisions of parliamentary legislation shall be given proper publicity so that common people do not remain ignorant about them. In Britain the Statutory Instruments Act of 1946 thus superseded the rules of the Publication Act of 1893 and held that these instruments must be published in the official gazette of London, Edinburgh and Belfast. It further holds that within forty days of its publication, the instrument shall be placed before the Parliament and require an affirmative vote for its continuance.
5. The safeguard of judicial intervention may also be referred to. It implies that the courts have authority to question the legal validity of departmental orders and to pass a judgement declaring any such statute void to the extent that it goes against the spirit of parliamentary legislation. Even in a country like Britain, the courts may exercise power of judicial review in regard to delegated legislation save in very special cases where the parent act precludes it by the incorporation of the conclusive evidence clause. May's treatise fully endorses that if the exercise of rule-making power "should be *ultra vires*, i.e., beyond the powers authorised by the enabling Act, the validity of the rules and orders can be contested in the law courts."[43]
6. Finally, the safeguard of public scrutiny has its own importance. As the price of liberty is eternal vigilance, the people must keep a very vigilant attitude towards the executive and the rules framed by it must be challenged, if they go beyond the scope of delegation. The public scrutiny is a powerful factor in preventing the infection of official despotism. Laski rightly maintains that the protest against the growth of delegated legislation "collapses as soon as it is submitted to serious scrutiny."[44]

---

42. Morrison : *Government and Parliament,* p. 15.
43. May, *op. cit.,* p. 854.
44. Laski : *Parliamentary Government in England,* p. 350.

Committee System

Legislative bodies all over the world make use of the committee system for the sake of efficiency of work and economy of time. It is true that a legislative body is known by the committees it keeps.[45] These committees enable more and more members to be associated with the process of legislation and thereby facilitate the approval of many bills within the limited time at the disposal of a legislative body. As every legislature is faced with the crop of bills in the midst of its limited time, it becomes imperative to make committees for the detailed consideration of the proposed bills. In case all bills "have to be considered in all their stages by the whole House, it would prove a Herculian task."[46] As More suggests : "No legislature can function effectively without the aid of some committee. Discussion of details is impossible at a large meeting which is too unwieldy to debate anything but broad principles. For this reason all democratic legislatures elect smaller groups to discuss matters in detail and these bring the result of their discussion back to the larger body for decisions."[47]

Meaning and Nature : A committee may be defined as a body of persons chosen by a larger body to discuss a matter referred to it in detail and then submit its report to the mother body. In this direction, Wheare defines a committee thus: "It is important to have some idea of what is meant by a committee, if only because there are some bodies called committees which are not really such and there are many committees called by other names. The essence of a committee is that it is a body to which some task has been referred or committed by some other person or body. It may be asked to or required or permitted to carry out this task. But that is not all. The notion of a committee carries with it the idea of a body being in some manner or degree responsible or subordinate or answerable in the last resort to the body or person who set it up or committed a power or duty to it. It is difficult to state this position precisely. Suffice it to say that if a body or a person commits a power or duty completely to another body, and relinquishes this power entirely, surrendering full and final authority to this body, then this latter body is not a committee. There is inherent in the notion of a committee some idea of a derived or secondary or dependent status, in form at least; it lacks original jurisdiction. It acts on behalf of or with responsibility to another body. Any body which has a task committed to it in this way may be considered a committee, whether it calls itself a council, a commission or royal commission, a conference, a board, a bureau, a panel, or a working party. They are all committees and may be studied as such."[48]

It indicates that the definition of a committee has these important ingredients :

1. A committee is a body of persons. That is, it must have at least three members to discuss a matter referred to it and then decide by the majority of votes. At least two persons are needed to deliberate and at least one more is required to act as the chairman and cast his vote to break a tie if the other two differ. Hence, the idea of a one-man committee or a committee having less than three members is a contradiction in terms.
2. If the minimum number of a committee's strength can be earmarked, the maximum cannot. It can be said that the membership of a committee must not be too unwieldy to convert it into a public meeting. It is desirable that all members of a committee must be in a position to have direct and intimate touch with each other so that their deliberations are not of a haphazard nature and their views are fully and freely

45. W.H. Morris-Jones : *Parliament in India* (Philadelphia : University of Pennsylvania Press, 1957), p. 279.
46. B.B. Jena : *Parliamentary Committees in India* (Calcutta : Scientific Book Agency, 1966), p. 2.
47. S.S. More : *Practice and Procedure of Indian Parliament* (Bombay : Thacker & Co, 1960), p. 512.
48. K.C. Wheare : *Government by Committees* (Oxford : Clarendon Press, 1955), pp. 5-6.

expressed. It is possible only when the size of a committee is not in hundreds. Hence, the Committee of the Whole House (as in the House of Commons) is just a matter of conventional development and it may not be taken as a committee in the strict sense of the term even if the Speaker is not there and the rules of procedure are also liberalised.

3. A committee has a subordinate status. The mother body is entitled to accept or reject the report of its committee. Viewed thus, the Standing Committee of the National People's Congress of China is hardly a committee in the real sense of the term, for it has never shown its subordination to the Parliament and, as available evidence demonstrates, the mother-body is just like a constitutional rubber-stamp to put the mark of validity on the deliberations of its child. Such instances may be found in countries having a non-democratic pattern of government.
4. The job of a committee is to discuss matters referred to it and then take a decision. The members must have the freedom to express their views and the decision should be taken by means of votes. It depends upon the committee to hold its meetings *in camera* if the matter before it so requires; it also depends upon the nature of work to have meetings in public for some other considerations. Whether the committees do not allow public to take part in discussion as in Britain or France (unless so required in exceptional cases), or they hold their meetings in public as happens in the United States, the essential point is that the committee must meet in order to decide something. That is, the job of a committee is not to defer consideration to waste time or create undue delay for some extraneous purposes, but to submit its report within the allowed time whether it is a finding or a recommendation.
5. Mere decision-making is not enough; it is also needed that the report of the committee must be fair and plausible to the mother-body as much as possible. The committee must come to a good decision. The general body must not surrender its original authority to the committee to enhance the power of the subordinate agency to the extent of diminishing its own over-riding control, nor should the committee be asked to deal with a matter which does not properly come within its normal jurisdiction. For this it is essential that the membership of a committee should be given to those who are, as much as possible, specially interested in that problem and have some special knowledge and experience in that regard.

If a committee is a body of persons chosen by a bigger body to discuss some matter referred to it and then submit its report to the mother-body for final approval, it shows that a committee system of legislative bodies operates on some important grounds. These are:

1. A committee consists of different political parties in rough proportion to their strength in the legislative chamber even if their members are chosen by a selection committee of the political parties as in the United Kingdom, or they are appointed by the general body of the National Assembly as in France, or they are chosen by the House of Representatives by a formal resolution adopting the recommendations of the party caucus as in the United States. The provision is not applicable to a country having one-party system where all the members of the legislative body belong to the same political party.
2. A committee of the legislative chamber is usually, perhaps invariably, a body of laymen. There is lack of adequate number of experienced and specialised persons in every legislative body. The members of a legislative body are rank politicians who

are rather deeply interested in the politics of factionalism.

3. The chairmanship of a committee is held by a man either so designated by the Speaker (Chairman.) of the House or chosen by the members of the committee themselves. The office of the chairman is important as he conducts the meetings of the committee and, particularly in France, he frames the agenda and appoints staff for the working of the committee.
4. The main function of a committee is to expedite the legislative process by making possible the consideration of a number of legislative proposals and also to make possible a degree of specialisation, since a member of a particular committee, though not very competent at the time of his selection, may be expected to acquire some degree of proficiency by means of his services in the committee.
5. The committee must be so composed and it should be so allowed to work that its effectiveness is ensured. As the committee system affords the 'best hope of securing increased economy and efficiency in administration,'[49] the study of this subject "is best accomplished by a small group of individuals representing the major divisions of opinions of the larger house."[50]

However, for the sake of effectiveness, it is required that the composition of the committee and its working must be governed by certain important considerations. As Cripps says: "The effectiveness of the committee system would depend mainly upon three things: first, the bringing together within the committee of a sufficient number of members of all parties who would be prepared to take real interest in the subjects to be dealt with; secondly, ensuring a degree of continuity of membership and attendance as they would enable the members to gain that intimate and wide knowledge of their subjects which would give them power to control; and thirdly, building up an atmosphere of common endeavour in the committee based upon a desire to develop the best administration possible."[51]

Legislative and Non-Legislative Committees: It, however, does not imply that a legislative body has its committees just to expedite the process of legislation. True to say that the main function of the legislative committees is to discuss bills referred to them for a detailed consideration. But the legislative bodies may have a number of other non-legislative committees as well. The standing committees and select or sessional committees are undoubtedly the legislative committees of a legislature. In addition, legislative bodies have other committees as well. For instance, the investigating committees of the American Senate perform the work of making investigations into an alleged scandal and thus do practically nothing for the sake of legislative business. Such a committee may recommend the making of legislation in some important direction to cover a big loophole and the Congress may subsequently adopt a bill in that regard. The investigating committees of the Senate have enhanced their area of activity to the extent that they even assist the executive in matters of checking corruption in administration. They "are thus the buckle that binds the hyphen, that joins the legislature to the executive."[52]

Legislation is a very complex affair and the legislature may require the help of a committee for consultation purposes. The agency of consultation provides the means of access to all interests involved in the matter to approach the government. They get adequate opportunity to give an authoritative as well as representative exposition to their opinions and, at the same time, get an opportunity to learn and appreciate

49. Ramsay Muir : *How Britain is Governed,* IV Ed., p. 177.
50. John B. Moore and Z.S. Moore : *Essentials of Parliamentary Procedure* (New York : Harper & Bros., 1944), p. 44.
51. S. Cripps : *Democracy Uptodate* (London : Nelson, 1949), p. 11.
52. G.B. Galloway : "Investigating Functions of Congress" in *The American Political Science Review,* Vol. XXXI, No. 1.

the point of view of the government. It also makes possible for the representatives of the interests concerned to supply to the government authentic information on which the details of legislative measures may be constructed. As Laski says : "They form, in brief, a deposit of expertise upon the different aspects of policy which, effectively used, create an atmosphere of responsibility about governmental acts. If the minister acts upon their opinion, he is at least building upon a foundation of experience; if he rejects them, the creation of an opposition and, as a consequence, the discussion that is the life-blood of democratic governance is adequately assured."[53]

Legislative bodies also seek the assistance of advisory bodies. As such, advisory bodies are set up according to the laws made by the Parliament in the shape of boards and bureaus consisting of civil servants. These bodies are committees working under the rules and laws made by the Parliament without having its representatives. The legislative committees may seek their advice on some important matter before them, but the advice of these statutory committees is not at all binding upon the members of a parliamentary committee. Sometimes, committees of inquiry are also set up by the Parliament for making necessary findings. The general testimony is that departmental advisory committees "are rendering valuable services not only by bringing to the departments information and advice based on first-hand knowledge, but inspiring greater public confidence in administrative authorities as being guided by such information and advice rather by sheer theory of bureaucratic presupposition."[54]

A study of the working of modern government shows that the role of various committees covers the work of legislation, administration, negotiation, enquiry, scrutiny, advice, etc. Although the committees of legislative bodies play a very significant part in the construction of legislative measures, the services of professionals and experts in the statutory commissions cannot be ignored. As the successful operation of the government depends upon the harmonious cooperation of the laymen and the experts, it follows that the committees of departmental experts must be taken into consultation by the legislative committees in order to bring forth better measures of legislation. Bagehot said about a century and a half ago: "One of the most sure principles is that success depends on a due mixture of special and non-special minds which attend to the means and of minds which attend to the end."[55]

It, however, does not imply that the committees be associated with the work of policy-making. It is the 'prerogative' of the responsible executive alone to make policy and implement it and thus the area of concern of a committee must not go beyond consultation, advice or opinion in the form of report. As Wheare rightly warns that policy matters "should not be included in the terms of reference of such committees. If the terms of reference cannot be modified in the light of the aforestated considerations, it is probably time that the committee observes some self-denying ordinances to restrict the scope of its recommendations."[56]

Criticism : Although committee system is a matter of recent origin and, due to enormous increase in the amount of legislation, it has been accepted by the legislative bodies all over the world as inescapable as well as useful, it is not without some demerits of its own. A look at the working of committees (as in the American Congress) illustrates that the committees have become more important than the House. As a bill is first discussed in detail in the committee and not in the House as a whole, the fate of the proposed legislative measure is determined in

53. Laski : *A Grammar of Politics,* p. 133.
54. F.A. Ogg '.*European Governments and Politics,* p. 111.
55. Walter Bagehot : *English Constitution* (World Classic Edition) p. 174.
56. See R.N. Aggarwal : *Financial Committees of the Indian Parliament* (Delhi S. Chand & Co, 1966), p. 347.

the committee itself and it is seldom that the House adopts a resolution to call back a bill on the 'discharge' calendar. Second, the committees of the legislatures donot consist of 'experts' as required by the nature of work assigned to them. The members of the legislative bodies are generally 'laymen' and they deliberate without having full command over the business in hand. Moreover, the report of the committee is generally accepted as the wire-pulling of politics has its underground part in the working of the committee system. Faced with the shortage of time, the House normally adopts the report of the committee and many members are deprived of the chance of ventilating their views in detail as they desire. It is true to say that the report of a committee does not mean a condensed version of the views of the House as such. The work of the committee "is mostly done by the chairman and three or four other members who are more interested."[57] Wheare has rightly remarked that the Committee of the Whole House is a contradiction in terms, it is the general practice to keep a little section of its strength in the committee. A full-committee meeting "is notoriously wasteful of manpower."[58]

However, the committees have also a very useful role to play. They act as the watchdogs of the legislature over the government; they train a very large number of members of the committees in the ways of administration and familiarise them with various problems faced by the legislature and the executive in their day-to-day working. The committees also make up for the weak opposition in the Parliament. The reports of the committees have abundant educative value which inform the government about its failures and also warn it to change the course of its action. The committees sometimes go beyond their area of legislative concern and register their views on the working of the administration and thereby set up a link between the law-making and law-implementing organs of the government. By constantly decrying malpractices, the committees "act as a check and help the government to maintain high moral standards in administration."[59]

The enormous volume of work before a legislative body and the limited time at its disposal make it impossible that every matter should be considered at length in the chamber having all the members. If the work of legislation is to be done expeditiously and also with reasonable care and efficiency, some of the parliamentary burden of business "has to be entrusted to some other agency in which the whole House has its confidence."[60] This is the 'practical method"[61] to transmit much workload to the 'upstairs' (that is, committees sitting upstairs in the British Parliament) to which the House of Commons "has recourse for the despatch of its work."[62] While referring to the great services of the committees of the House of Commons, it has been commented that they are 'the eyes, the ears, the hands and often brains' of the Parliament. In many important cases, it has been noticed that the committees have judiciously counselled as to what course of action "should be taken."[63]

Of course, the study of committee system constitutes a very important and interesting subject where we deal with the conduct of parliamentary business through groups of people acting collectively. What Hicks said about the Estimates Committee is equally applicable to the useful role of other committees that the services of the committees "are conspicuous both for the range of their coverage and constructive criticism."[64] It, however, remains to be submitted that as the nature and

57. See Basil Chubb : *The Control of Public Expenditure* (London: OUP, 1952), p. 184.
58. *ibid.*, p. 213.
59. Aggarwal, *op. cit.*, p. 359.
60. Jena, *op. cit.*, p. 1.
61. Harvey Walker : *The Legislative Process*, p. 207.
62. Joseph Redlich : *The Procedure of the House of Commons*, Vol. II, p. 180.
63. H. Dodds : *Procedure in State Legislatures*, p. 101.
64. U.K. Hicks : *Public Finance Surveys : India* (UN 1951), p. 100.

merits of the committee system are not universally applicable, they differ from one constitutional system to another. Even in a representative system of government, the operation of committee system has its own characteristic features as we may notice in the cases of British and French Parliaments and American Congress. It is thus aptly remarked : "The lesson we learn from this is that in judging the work of the committees, in explaining and discussing them in terms of their functions, we must always take into account the institutional system to which they belong."[65]

Decline of Legislature

A critical examination of the functions and powers of the legislatures, in empirical terms, confirms this astonishing impression of some writers and commentators that the old distrust of the executive has been replaced by the new confidence in its leadership. The strong position of the cabinet working under the leadership of the Prime Minister in a parliamentary form of government, better known now as the Prime Ministerial Government, confirms the doctrine of Ramsay Muir that it "has to a remarkable extent diminished the power and position of Parliament, robbed its proceedings of significance, made it appear that Parliament exists mainly for the purpose of maintaining or of somewhat ineffectually criticising an all-good but omnipotent Cabinet and transferred the main discussion of political issues from Parliament to Platform and the members."[66] What is described about the British Parliament or any other legislature organised and based on the English model is applicable to the legislatures belonging to other varieties, though the nature of the executive control may differ for reasons of different constitutional systems or political setup. The American Congress has lost much of its legislative autonomy because of the Presidential check on the one hand and, more formidable than that, of the power of judicial review exercised by the federal judiciary on the other. The legislatures of communist countries donot have even that truncated area of authority, rather they are used as an agency for propaganda purposes. What Schapiro had said about the Supreme Soviet of the former USSR is equally true of all other legislatures of the Communist world that it "is a rubber stamp for decisions made elsewhere in the Russian political system."[67]

The charge of the decline, even demise, of the legislatures draws support from the following main points :

First, the area of authority originally belonging to the legislatures has been usurped by the executives. While confining our attention to the case of legislature in a country having parliamentary form of government, we find that it is the Cabinet that decides about many things like summoning and proroguing the session of the Parliament, writing the text of the inaugural address to be delivered by the head of state, preparing daily time-table of the session of the House or Houses, effecting initiation of debate on the bills and resolutions moved by it and doing a host of other things that constitute the stock of parliamentary business. In a country having presidential form of government like the United States, the legislature remains separate from the executive. The President vetoes the bills passed by the Congress as per his judgment and it is very seldom that the Congress readopts the same bill to over-ride the Presidential veto. Moreover, the President can send 'messages' to the Congress and through his 'friends' get certain kinds of bills passed. In a country having a queer mixture of the parliamentary and presidential forms like France, the President may even go to the extent of dissolving the legislature if he is dissatisfied with a decision taken by those who are called the representatives of the people. The right of making appeal to the nation is a powerful instrument in the hands of the executive to

65. Wheare, *op. cit.,* p. 3.
66. See Muir : *How Britain is Governed,* Ch. III.
67. L. Schapiro : *The Government and Politics of the Soviet Union* (London, 1959), pp. 109-10.

correct the erratic behaviour of the legislators. What Muir has written about the English Parliament is applicable to many other countries of the world : "When it (Parliament) deals with legislation, if it does not initiate, it does at least substantially alter the bill submitted to it, and often makes a mess of them. When it deals with the general policy of the Cabinet-..it debates even if not leading up to any definite resolution or decision, exercises a very important influence. But when it deals with the all-important subject, its own special subject, or finance, it seems to be almost impotent."[68]

Second, the power of the courts to look into the constitutional validity of a legislative measure has affected the authority of the legislatures. Though this factor does not apply to Britain, it does apply to others like the United States and Canada where federal judiciary has been given the power of judicial review. The Court may declare a law, or its part, *ultra vires* in case it finds that it is unconstitutional or, as the Americans say, it is against the due process of law. Numerous instances are available to show when the Supreme Court invalidated a law made by the Congress. Matters reached such a point in 1936 that President Roosevelt, in a mood of sheer irritation, called the Constitution 'a relic of horse and buggy days' and thought in terms of 'packing up the Court'. The same thing found its manifestation in our country in 1969-70 when the Supreme Court invalidated laws relating to the nationalisation of major banks and abolition of privy purses of the former rulers of the native states. Like the American President, the Indian Prime Minister (Indira Gandhi) thought in terms of restricting the scope of judicial review. It may be said that the factor of judicial review has no application in the Communist countries where the judges are elected by the legislatures and they are virtually accountable to them.

Third, what has also led to the attenuation of the authority of the modern legislatures is the role of party politics. The top leaders of the party keep the members under their strict control with the result that the latter have to toe the official line. The control of the whips is always there to deprive them of their 'autonomy'. The use of the whips in a rigorous manner and the frequent admonitions by the arch-leader or by his senior lieutenants compel most of the legislators to live and act like 'robots'. The result is that most of the legislators are hardly in a position to assert their independence to any noticeable degree whatsoever. What an eminent Indian figure has said about the position obtaining here, particularly in the ranks of the ruling party, is very much true about his counterparts in other countries of the world, excluding the United States, where strict party discipline is unknown, that "the price demanded by the Party bosses is too heavy : one must be prepared to forget one's self-respect, queue up for a ticket and forget such things as an independent judgment."[69]

One more cause may be traced in marvellous developments in the sphere of information and technology. Parliament was lauded as the 'committee of grievances' where high officers of the state were impeached. Now that role has been taken over by the critical press and vigilant agencies of mass communication. Not the Houses of Parliament or their committees, but the newspapers, radio and television are within the reach of a common man. The proceedings of the House may be secret or confidential inaccessible to an ordinary man, but information technology may expose any scandal from the Watergate in America to the Tehelka in India. Due importance should be given to the role of many non-governmental agencies like Amesty International of England, Human Rights Watch of America and Common Cause of India which may take the matter to the courts of the people and thereby tarnish the image of the Parliament whose crafty members do their best to conceal their misdoings.

---

68. Muir, *op. cit.,* p. 221.
69. B. Shiva Rao : "In India's Parliament" in *The Illustrated Weekly of India* (Bombay), August 30, 1970, p. 30.

Last, the patent reality cannot be overlooked that the number of such members of Parliament is constantly increasing who have hardly any knowledge of the laws, rules and regulations, and the norms of parliamentary behaviour. They often remain absent from the session and take pleasure in leaving the chamber after making a disorderly scene; sometimes they thump their desks when it is an occasion for shedding tears. The number of 'lay' ministers may be small, but the number of 'lay' legislators is quite large who serve sectional interests in the name of 'national interest' and who vitiate the working of the legislature without bothering for the fact that 'now their bright home is in the setting sun.'[70]

Though the decline of the powers and prestige of the legislatures cannot be denied, it cannot be identified with the situation of their 'demise'. Legislatures are working in all countries of the world with varying degrees of authority and influence. The charge of decline is a matter of controversy. Lowenberg emphatically asserts that the institution of legislature thus "seems to be one of the most enduring and widely applicable inventions of political man."[71] Blondel has pertinently argued : "While the 'decline of legislatures' may be apparent to some, the decline of assemblies as communicating mechanisms can scarcely be substantiated."[72] After a careful study of the legislatures in the countries of the Third World, it has been pointed out with a sense of confidence that it "is certain that the long-term trend is not towards the 'demise' or 'decline' of legislatures as has been made out by the earlier writers."[73] Though important decisions are taken 'elsewhere', the legislature is still treated as a formal centre of focus in every political system. Thus, it is well observed : "Decline is in the eye of the beholder and depends on his analytical perspectives."[74]

70. K.C. Wheare: *Legislatures* (London: Oxford University Press, 1968), p. 149.
71. Gerhard Lowenberg (ed) : *Modern Parliaments : Change or Decline* (Chicago : Aldine Athestor Inc., 1971), p. 19.
72. Blondel, *op, cit.,* p. 390.
73. R.B. Jain, *op. cit.,* p. 373.
74. Lowenberg, *op. cit.,* p. 15.

23

Representation

> The pure idea of democracy, according to its definition, is the government of the whole people by the whole people, equally represented. Democracy as commonly conceived and hitherto practised is the government of the whole people by a mere majority of the people, exclusively represented. The former is synonymous with equality of all citizens; but the latter, strangely confounded with it, is a government of privilege, in favour of the numerical majority, who alone possess practically any voice in the State. This is the inevitable consequence of the manner in which the votes are now taken to the complete disfranchisement of minorities.
>
> **—John Stuart Mill**[1]

All modern political systems claim to be based, though in varying degrees, on what Rousseau termed, 'the will of the people'. Since it is impossible for the people to meet and exercise the functions of government as a collective body in modern times on account of vast size of the state and wide enfranchisement of the people, this claim finds its implementation in some form of representation through which the rulers of a state are given the right to act for those who choose them. Thus, representation has come, as suggested by Lord Acton; as 'the vital invention of modern times'. A massive transformation has, however, occurred in the realm of representation so much so that classical theory, in this direction, coming from John Stuart Mill and A.V. Dicey, (implying that legitimate authority means political power flowing from the people to the parliament and from the parliament to the government) "is no longer true in an era when parliament is not necessarily the mediator between government and people and when the executive power may claim to be the embodiment of legitimacy, as does de Gaulle in France."[2]

Meaning, Nature and Typological Illustrations

The term 'representation' has its general as well as particular connotations. In general terms, it means that any corporate group, whether church, business concern, trade union, fraternal order or state, that is too large or too dispersed in membership to conduct its deliberations in an assembly of all its members is confronted with the problem of representation, if it purports to act in any degree in accord with the opinion of its members.[3] Such a definition of the term is too loose to be applied to a particular form of representation. We are here concerned with its particular meaning as applicable to the realm of politics. In this sense, representation "is the process through which the attitudes, preferences, viewpoints and desires of the entire citizenry or a part of them are, with their expressed approval, shaped into

1. Mill : *Considerations on Representative Government,* (Chicago : Reguers, 1962), originally published in 1861 in London by Parker Son and Brown, pp. 256-57.
2. Michael Curtis : *Comparative Government and Politics,* (New York : Harper and Row, 1968), p. 100.
3. Coker and Rodee in Seligman (ed.) : *Encyclopaedia of the Social Sciences* (New York : Macmillan, 1967), 16th Ptg., Vols 13-14, p. 302.

governmental action on their behalf by a smaller number among them, with binding effect upon those represented."[4] While in agreement with this definition of the term, in question, a German social theorist Robert von Mohl offers his unpretentious interpretation. According to him, representation "is the process through which the influence which the entire citizenry or a part of them have upon governmental action is with their expressed approval, exercised on their behalf by a small number among them. with binding effects upon those represented."[5]

The two definitions of representation, given above, deserve examination and comments. As Friedrich suggests, "we speak advisedly of *influence* rather than participation or control, since the large number of citizens is not very likely to participate in or effectively to control governmental action. We use the general expression 'governmental action' rather than legislation, because all kinds of governmental activities might be subjected to popular influence. By suggesting further, that influence of a part of citizenry, as well as the whole, may be represented, we recognise the representative quality of the American Senate. Group representation is more ancient than the representation of the whole people in any case. Finally, the most essential part of this descriptive definition is contained in the phrase: 'with the expressed approval'. This approval is expressed presumably in the constitutional provisions regarding representative institutions—the particular institutions of that constitutional order, as well as the general principle. In short, it is this phrase that we recognise as the constitutional setting of such representation. The authority of the representative is not only created by the constituent power, but it is subject to change by the amending power under the constitution."[6]

Curtis is of the view that the term 'representation' "is inherently ambiguous" and, for this reason, representative government "may have different meanings."[7] While carrying his point further, he says: "For some it is analogous to the activity of a lawyer acting on behalf of a client; for others it means that the representer approximates the characteristics of the represented. Some see the representers as embodying the declared interests of the represented; others view his function as acting on behalf of his constituents in the way he thinks most desirable."[8] The basic reason is that different attitudes on representation "mirror the various views on the relationship between the rulers and the ruled."[9] Samuel Beer has pointed out five typologies of views in this connection:[10]

1. The traditional conservative position based on the desirability of order, degree, authority and hierarchy holds that the common welfare is represented by a monarch or a government charged with formulating a political programme.
2. The traditional whig or aristocratic view is based on the idea of a balanced constitution symbolising the differences of rank in the society. Men of reason and judgment deliberate on affairs without the need for a mandate from an electorate to guide or

4. *Encyclopaedia Britannica,* Vol. 19, p. 135.
5. See Carl J. Friedrich : *Constitutional Government and Democracy* (Calcutta Oxford and IBH, 1966), p. 266.
6. *ibid.*
7. Curtis, *op. cit.,* p. 98.
8. *ibid.*
9. *ibid.*
10. *ibid.,* pp. 98-99. Prof. R.B. Jain is right in holding that undoubtedly, 'representation' has been an ill-defined concept that has acquired conflicting meanings through long use. It may be employed to denote any relationship between rulers and ruled, or it may connote responsiveness, authorisation, legitimation, or accountability. It may be used so broadly that any political institution performs representative functions or so narrowly that only an elected legislator can do so. *Comparative Legislative Behaviour : Research Explorations in Indian Perspective* (New Delhi : Uppal Pub. House, 1980), p. 53.

bind them, while an elected body like the house of Commons represents the common interest.

3. The liberal view sees national welfare and common good as represented by a parliamentary assembly made up of individuals rather than of corporate bodies, though under middle class domination, emphasising a property qualification for the franchise and based on approximate quality of electoral areas.
4. For men of radical view, representation is based on the unified will of the people binding individuals together. This will, regarded as the ultimate sovereign in the community, is in practice the will of the majority, expressed either directly or through interest groups.
5. Modern conservative democrats and modern socialist democrats see representation in terms of a government based on disciplined political parties with social classes as basic units, and also related to functional groups. The voters are thus faced with the situation of choosing either of the two parties (representing social classes) for the sake of their representation.

While we may agree with or differ from the five-fold categorisation of Beer, we may safely endorse the view of Prof. Ball that the theories of representation may be put into two broad categories— liberal-democratic and collectivist-socialist. The liberal-democratic theories of representation have these characteristics.[11]

1. Here is emphasis on the importance of individual rights, especially the inviolability of individual's property and the necessity of limiting the powers of government to protect these rights. Liberal-democracy implies not only an extension of the franchise but an equality of voting rights. The representative represents individuals, their opinions and their interests, and therefore he is elected according to geographically demarcated constituencies and not according to classes, occupational distinctions or distinct social interests.
2. Man is a rational being and he can identify his own opinions; he is also aware of the wider claims of the community. He will, therefore, use his vote in an intelligent manner and is consequently entitled to share in the selection of the representatives.
3. There should be universal adult franchise, secret ballot and fair and free periodic elections. Constituencies should be earmarked for the recruitment of the representatives acting according to the will of their electors; the business of the elected assembly is to protect the interests of its constituents against any encroachment made by the executive or by the majority acting in the name of 'general good'.

Opposed to this is the theory of representation as given by the socialists or collectivists whose salient features may be thus pointed out:

1. Emphasis should be laid not on the individual but on the class. The assemblies should represent not the individuals and their opinions but the majority class whose interests have been subordinated by middle-class parliaments.
2. Democracy means the presence of social equality and absence of economic exploitation. Representation should, thus, be governed by this important consideration.
3. There may be different parties and groups to represent social interests in the pre-socialist period; there must be only one party when the era of socialism is ushered in. The existence of the Communist party alone is justified on the ground of the absence of class conflicts.

---

11. A.R. Ball: *Modern Politics and Government* (London : Macmillan, 1971), pp. 123-26.

As claimed by the writers in the socialist countries, their representative system differs from a bourgeois system in matters of principle. They deprecate the bourgeois representative system as a process of growing emasculation and limitation and instead admire their own system as being dependent upon the line of popular self-government and self-administration the model of which can be seen in the Soviets of the former USSR and the communes of China. Socialist countries have also adopted a number of direct democratic devices and institutions such as method of recall, rural and town meetings, system of imperative mandate, role of social activists, popular initiative of legislation and the like so as to demonstrate that it "should be a distortion of the institution of socialist representation if all these existing traits were ignored in a study of the organs of state power, the representative institutions. It is thus maintained that socialist representation is a form of indirect democracy which is increasingly completed with a series of direct democratic institutions, and which is absorbing these institutions or part of them."[12]

Two important points strike us here from what we have discussed above. First, it is not easy to define the term 'representation' in a precise manner. Differences exist as to whether representatives are concerned with common needs and common values of the whole community or with particular needs of the individuals or special interests of the social class in conflict with each other. Acute differences in view also exist on the point as to which individuals, groups or parties are to be considered as genuine representatives and what kind of people ought to be chosen to act for others.[13] Second, the political representatives should in no sense be treated as 'duplicate of the average citizens.'[14]

Representation and Responsiveness: Role of the Representative and Doctrine of the Legislative Mandate

The way the subject of representation has been discussed by eminent writers has led to the rise and development of different theories. Keeping it in view, L.P. Baradat has referred to these important theories:[15]

1. ***Reactionary Theory*** **:** As given by Thomas Hobbes and Alexander Hamilton, it is based on the need for order and authority. The executive (preferably a strong monarch or a President) and a legislature subject to its authority serve public interest. While they should be open to popular input, being of superior knowledge and judgment, they should not be hindered by popular sentiment. It is the duty of the people to suppprt the state and accept governmental policies willingly in the confidence that the politicians have acted in the best interest of the people.
2. ***Elitist Theory*** **:** It stands on the assumption that the 'chosen best' are capable of representing people's interest. It is the element of merit that really counts. Elitists like Pareto, Mosca and Michels recognise no place for the role of popular control. The rule of the 'chosen few' is the best arrangement to serve public interest.
3. ***Conservative Theory*** **:** Supported by leaders like Edmund Burke and James Madison, it sanctions popular control without encouraging public participation in the governing process. In this variant, the people choose those who are to govern them from an elite group. Yet the people donot have the right to instruct their representatives or even, compel them to reflect a particular position on a given issue. If, however, the

12. R.B. Jain *op. cit.*, p. 67. For a detailed study see Otto Bihari : *Socialist Representative Institutions* (Budapest : Academini Kidor, 1971), pp. 103-4.
13. Curtis, *op. cit.*, p. 100.
14. *ibid.*
15. See L.P. Baradat : *Political Ideologies : Their Origins and Impact* (Englewood Cliffs, New Jersey : Prentice Hall, 1979), pp. 137-39.

officials do not satisfy the public, they may replace them by other members of the elite in the next election.

4. ***Liberal Theory :*** As given by thinkers like John Locke and Thomas Jefferson, it lays down that all people are essentially equal and, for this reason, capable of ruling. This mass-oriented theory requires the representative to act as a messenger for his constituents rather than as a policy-maker. Hence, the public officials are obliged to vote the way their constituents desire.
5. ***Radical Theory :*** As advanced by great democrats like Rousseau, it calls for the greatest amount of popular input. Rejecting the case of representative government altogether, it holds that only the people themselves are capable of representing their own views on important issues. In this way, this theory alone supports the case of pure democracy.

A comparative study of different theories on the subject of representation, as given above, leaves the impression that none but the liberal theory should be described as acceptable to most of the people in the present age of democracy.

The issue of 'representation' has also been studied through the analysis of 'responsiveness' of a system. For instance, Lowenberg and Kim have laid more emphasis on the 'responsive' aspect of the representation. According to them, from the vantage point of view of the members of parliament, responsiveness includes: a conceptualisation of the constituents who comprise their partners in relationship; the use of various channels of communication through which to listen and hear; and the propensity to consider and answer the demands of the constituents.[16] Reference should be made to the view of Eulau and Karps at this stage who have described four possible components of responsiveness in this manner:[17]

1. 'Policy responsiveness' where the target is the great public issues that agitate the political process.
2. 'Service responsiveness' which involves the efforts of the representative to secure particularised benefits for individuals or groups in his constituency.
3. 'Allocation responsiveness' that refers to the representative's effort to obtain benefits for his constituency through pork-barrel exchanges in the appropriations, process through administrative interventions.
4. 'Symbolic responsiveness' that involves public gestures of a sort that create a sense of trust and support in the relationship between the representative and his constituents.

The notable feature of the assertion of these two writers is that not one but all components should be taken into the representational nexus. In other words, it "is configuration of the component aspects of responsiveness that might yield a viable theory of representative government under modern conditions of social complexity."[18]

Political philosophers and writers have since long considered the problem of proper relationship between the rulers and the ruled. This issue has become of more immediate significance with the development of representative government. The question arises as to what is the proper function of a representative whom the people have chosen to act for them in matters of legislation. Garner points out three positions in this regard:[19]

1. The representative is regarded as a deputy, a delegate or an agent of the particular

16. Gerhard Lowenberg and Ching Lim Kim : "Comparing the Representativeness of Parliaments" in *Legislative Studies Quarterly*, Vol. 3, (1978), pp. 27ff.
17. See Heinz Eulau and D. Karps : "The Puzzle of Representation : Specifying Components of Representativeness" in *Legislative Studies Quarterly*, Vol. 3, 1977, pp. 233-54.
18. R.B. Jain, *op. cit.*, p. 65.
19. J.W. Garner : *Political Science and Government* (Calcutta : World Press, 1952), p. 665.

constituency which elects him, charged primarily with procuring legislation for the advancement of the local interests of his constituency, obtained appropriations of money for the constitution of public works therein, and of securing other favours which lie within the powers of the legislature or government to bestow.

2. He may be regarded as the representative of the whole state, elected to consult with other representatives and charged primarily with the case and advancement of the general interests, and only secondarily with the promotion of the particular interests of the immediate constituency.
3. He may be regarded as the mouthpiece or the spokesman of the political party which is in majority in the constituency from which he is elected and, as such, he is bound by the will of his party whatever may be his own personal views in regard to the expediency or wisdom of particular legislative policies.

John Wahlke has suggested a tripartite typology by which the role of a representative can be analysed:[20]

1. The *trustee-deputy role,* according to which a deputy can see himself as a delegate of his constituents and be willing to accept instructions, or can act as he thinks necessary without seeking their advice or consultation.
2. The *facilitator-neutral role,* according to which the representative consults interest groups and others to different degrees and attempting to perform some services for his constituents.
3. *The district-state or country role,* according to which the deputy decides whether the interests of his own area or that of the country as a whole should predominate in his actions

However, within the framework of legislative functioning, Joseph la Palombara divides the role of the legislators into these categories:[21]

1. ***The Ritualist*** **:** He is the law-maker *par excellence* whose expertise centres on the process of turning proposals into legislation. He regularly attends the sessions of the chamber as well as its committees and follows the intricacies of procedures very scrupulously.
2. ***The Opportunist*****:** He is not interested in the law-making function of the legislature but tries to raise his status for other purposes.
3. ***The Tribune*** **:** He is deeply involved in the articulation of interests, in the communication of demands, in the task of discovering what is desired by his constituents or the voters in general.
4. ***The Broker*****:** He tries to aggregate conflicting interests.
5. ***The Inventor*****:** He finds his major role in the creation of public policies that make of legislative outputs reasonably workable responses to many of the needs and requests that the legislature must confront.

We may say that the theory regarding the role of a representative has undergone serious transformation in modern times owing to new conditions and circumstances. The idea of the role of a representative in early stages of the

20. See John Wahlke and others : *The Legislative System* (New York, 1962).
21. See Joseph la Palombara : *Politics Within Nations* (Englewood Cliffs, New Jersey: Prentice—Hall, 1974), p. 181. Reference may also be made to the 'ambition theory* of J.A. Schlesinger. He says that the underlying assumption is that the 'ambition to obtain and hold a public office is universal.' *Ambition and Politics* (Chicago : Rand McNally, 1968). Developing the same theme, J.D. Barber divides the legislators into four categories—law makers, spectators, advertisers and reluctants. The 'law-maker' takes an active part in the legislative process and also desires to be re-elected. The 'spectator' is also interested in his re-election, but he is not equally interested in the legislative business. He tries to maintain his loyalty to the voters, the party and the constituency. The 'advertiser' has his interest in building up his image as a politician or a man of status. Finally, the 'reluctant' legislator plays a role for which decline of the legislative body is attributed. *The Law-maker* (New Haven, Connecticut : Yale Univ. Press, 1965).

development of a representative regime was to regard the deputy as the special agent of the class or estate, nobility, clergy, commons, peasantry or town population which chose him, that he was subject to its instructions, that he was immediately accountable to it, and that he could be recalled by it at any time. In short, his role "was more analogous to that of a diplomatic agent than that of a modern representative, who, according to the generally prevailing view, possesses the full power of legislation, freedom of deliberation and of voting, and is not subject to instruction or recall."[22] Different from this is the modern view that holds that the delegate should not be treated as the 'representative of a particular department' but of the entire nation and that no instruction should be given to him [23]

Of the merits of the three views in regard to the nature of the legislative mandate mentioned above, opinions of eminent leaders and statesmen differ, though they alike agree that the doctrine of taking a representative as a mere mouthpiece of the constituents is a vicious one. Such a view "not only subordinates the national or general interests to the assumed interests of particular localities, but it tends to narrow the horizon of the representative and thereby lower the level of character of the legislature, tends to deter men of large ability from serving in it, and accentuates the control of the political party over its representatives.[24] The classic statements of Edmund Burke is very important in this regard who (in his address to the constituents of Bristol in 1780) said : "The parliament is not a congress of ambassadors from different and hostile interests, which interests each must maintain as an agent and advocate against other agents and advocates. But parliament is a deliberative assembly of nation, with one interest that of the whole where not local purposes, not local prejudices, ought to guide, but the general good resulting from the general reason of the whole. You choose a member, indeed, but when you have chosen him, he is not a member of Bristol, but he is a member of Parliament."[25]

It is true that the representative ought not to sacrifice his opinion, his mature judgment, and his enlightened conscience to the whims and fancies of his constituents. The system of the recall of a legislator is a rank nuisance, for it is always amenable to its gross misuse and its incorporation in the law of the American states for example, may be described just as an instrument of political control exercisable by the party leadership rather than by the voters. We may not agree with the French doctrine of the *mandat imperatif* (imperative mandate) that reduces the representative to the role of a conduit pipe or a telephone wire through which the views and commands of the party are communicated to the legislature. As a matter of fact, a representative, though chosen by the people of a particular area, becomes the representative of the nation as a whole and not that of any group or corporation and the like. "This rule may, however, not apply so rigorously where the representative has pledged himself before the election to act in a certain manner, the question of his duty to obey instructions is somewhat simplified, for then a departure therefrom would be a breach of honour and of good faith such as no representative can afford to be guilty of."[26]

Varieties of Representation

Territorial Representation : The system of territorial or geographical representation implies that for the purpose of holding an election in a particular territory, the whole area should be divided into a number of electoral districts that

22. Garner, *op. cit.*, p. 666.
23. *ibid.*
24. *ibid.*, p. 667.
25. *ibid.*, p. 670 n 1.
26. *ibid.*, p. 672.

may, or may not, coincide with the administrative districts into which the country is divided. These electoral districts are termed 'constituencies.' The constituencies may be either single-member or multi-member. When the total area is divided into as many electoral districts as there are representatives to be elected and one representative is chosen from each constituency, it is called a single-member constituency. Different from this, when the whole area is divided into a small number of constituencies, and two or more representatives are elected from each of them, it constitutes the model of a 'multi-member' constituency.

Single-member constituencies are relatively small geographical areas, usually approximately equal in population to each other and sometimes identical with political divisions of the country as in a country like India, France, Norway and Switzerland. The usual method is that the candidate with the highest number of votes is declared successful. The result is decided by the majority of votes. This method has the virtue of being quite simple; it tends to limit the number of parties and occasionally fosters a two party system as in Britain or a single-dominant party system as hitherto in India. However, this system is inequitable. We may take note of the fact that in most of the cases, the successful candidate gets less than absolute majority of votes. In order to do away with this defect, either alternative vote system or run-off ballot system (also called the second ballot system) is adopted. It has its application (as in France) where the election is cancelled if no candidate gets absolute majority of votes and it is held again in which only two candidates (who had secured highest number of votes in the cancelled election) are allowed to contest. In Ireland single transferable vote system has been adopted for the same purpose.

In multi-member constituencies the most usual electoral system is some form of proportional representation, the chief advantage of which is to obtain a more accurate parliamentary representation of electoral opinion, ft may be that the country as a whole is reduced to a single constituency with as many seats as possible as we find in Israel, Monaco and the Netherlands. Here parliamentary representation is allocated to parties in proportion to votes received in the country as a whole. It may also be that the country as a whole is divided into certain groups, each group having as many seats as possible as we find 23, 28 and 32 parliamentary seats respectively in Denmark, Sweden and Italy.

Proportional Representation : The model of proportional representation stands on the principle that the votes should be 'weighed, not counted'. It has three ingredients: (i) there is a multi-member constituency; (ii) a candidate is elected not by gaining an absolute or relative majority but by obtaining a quota of votes that is equivalent to total number of votes cast and divided by the number of seats to be filled, and (iii) there is a mathematically exact, as far as possible, representation of the electorate in the legislature.

A question arises as to how proportional representation system can be put to application. For this sake, two methods have been evolved—single transferable vote system and list system. They may be discussed as under:

1. ***Single Transferable Vote System :*** It was first evolved by a Danish minister Carl Andrae in 1793 that was presented in a refined form by Thomas Hare in England in 1851. It is sometimes called the Hare System. Hare, however, could not make it free from the basic defect that has now been removed. According to this system, the voter is given a paper having names and symbols of all candidates on its left side and blank columns on its right side. He has to fill these blank columns with figures of 1, 2, 3 and so in order to mark his order of preferences. He may fill all the columns or some of them, but it is required that the marking of preferences should be done correctly, otherwise his ballot paper shall be declared invalid.

At the time of counting, all invalid papers are cancelled and the total number of valid ballot papers is divided by the number of seats to be filled up plus 1, and then the figure of 1 is added to the quotient. In case the remainder is more than half of the denominator, the figure of 1 is further added to the quotient. This is called electoral quota. This formula may be presented thus :

$$\text{Electoral Quota} = \frac{\textit{Total no. of valid votes}}{\textit{Total no. of seats}+1}+1$$

For instance, if there are 107 votes polled in an election and out of which 17 are declared invalid, then there remain 90 valid votes. If the total number of seats is 4, the electoral quota would be:

$$90 \div 5 = 18 + 1 = 19$$

After this, counting begins.

A candidate securing votes equal to or more than that of the quota is declared successful. If some seats remain vacant, the candidate having least number of votes is eliminated and his votes are transferred to other candidates according to the order of second preference marked by him. This process continues and votes are transferred according to subsequent preferences until all the seats are filled up, or only the required number of candidates remains in the field after the elimination of other candidates. In this way, only those candidates are declared elected who obtain the quota after the transfer of surplus votes or the votes of those candidates who have procured the least number of votes at the polls and are, therefore, progressively eliminated.

2. *List System :* Here the candidates are grouped in lists according to the labels of their political parties. Each party submits a list of its chosen candidates equal to the number of seats to be filled up or even less than that. The voter is asked to vote for a particular list that also means his preference to the candidates in the order given in that very list. It is a different thing that in some countries the voters are given extra freedom to show their individual preferences to the candidates as well. At the time of counting, election quota is determined in the same manner as given above. Then, it is seen which party has secured votes in what percentage and the seats are apportioned between or among them according to the same percentage. Suppose a party secures 50 per cent votes in an election for 20 seats in all, it has a title for inducting its 10 members in the legislature in the same order as given by it in the declared list. It may be that some parties either fail to have a clear-cut percentage entitling them for certain seats, or they may have to forego some of their percentage of votes. In such a situation, the party may take its surplus percentage to the adjoining or some other multi-member constituency and get its claim duly adjusted by capturing one seat or more by the accumulation of rump surpluses, or it may lend its surplus percentage to some other party so that a seat is obtained by them for a common candidate.

The system of proportional representation may be appreciated for several reasons. It is said that it is the best way to ensure representation to all sections of the people as far as possible. It gives political education to the masses and a sense of security to those people or parties that are in minority. It leads to the recognition of political parties in respect of their stands on social and economic problems. The independence of the voters is secured and an effective check on the practices of electoral corruption can be put. It recognises the nature of modern political parties as based not altogether on sectional divisions but on social and economic problems of national importance. As Lord Acton says : "It is profoundly democratic, for it increases the influence of thousands who would otherwise have no voice in the government and it brings men more near an equality by so contriving that no vote shall be wasted and that every voter shall contribute to bring into a parliament a member of his own."

It is true that the system of proportional representation provides a more accurate representation of electoral divisions and ensures some representation to minority groups, classes, races and their parties, it also inevitably creates or perpetuates a multi-party system with possible undesirable consequences for a stable or effective government. It may prevent the development of disciplined parties and encourage factional groups in the parties and frequent and temporary party alliances. France of the pre-1958 period had the worst experiments with the proportional representation system. It is rightly said that the success of the Nazi party of Hitler in the elections of 1932-33 was partly owing to the prevalence of this system in Germany. A French jurist Esmein expressed his vigorous opposition to the whole idea of proportional representation system in these words: "To establish the system of proportional representation is to convert the remedy supplied by the bicameral system into a veritable poison; it is to organise disorder and emasculate the legislative power; it is to render cabinets unstable, destroy their homogeneity, and make parliamentary government impossible."[27]

While appreciating the system of majority representation and finding fault with the system of proportional representation, Jean Blondel says ; 'The majority system has the great advantage of being simple to administer. It is also easy to understand: the candidate who wins the most votes is elected. In systems of proportional representation, rules are more complex, so much so that they may sometimes defeat their own purpose. It is not immediately clear who has been elected or why, and the process may be lengthy, if preferential votes have to be transferred . . . Quotas or quotients have to be calculated and the result, although fair, may not always seem to be so. There is also an often noted tendency to manipulate the system, for instance, by introducing candidates in order to split the vote so as to benefit from the mechanics of the quotient calculation. Proportional representation is not a panacea. It works well in many countries, but the majority system has achieved generally acceptable results in others."[28]

Minority Representation : The issue of minority representation is, indeed, a very delicate affair. While democracy means majority rule, it does not at all mean suppression of the minorities. We appreciate the classic statement of Mill that the minorities should be adequately represented as 'an essential part of democracy'. As he asserted : "Nothing is more certain than that the virtual blotting out of minority is no necessary or natural consequence of freedom, but instead is diametrically opposed to the first principle of democracy : representation in proportion to numbers."[29] Mill frankly admits that in a representative system of government, majority must rule and the minority yield to its will, but from this it does not follow that the minority should have no representation at all. As he says : "In any really equal democracy, every or any section would be represented, not disproportionately but proportionately. A majority of the electors would always have a majority of the representatives; but a minority of the electors would always have a minority of the representatives. Man for man they would be as fully represented as the majority, and unless they are, there is not equal government, but a government of inequality and privilege—contrary to all just government, but above all contrary to the principle of democracy which

27. Cited in Garner, *op. cit.*, p. 653.
28. Blondel : *Political Parties : A Genuine Case for Discontent* (London : Wild-wood House, 1978), p. 94. However, in appreciation of proportional representation system, Prof. C.A. Beard says that it "is a plan for the cooperation of all diverse interests of modern society in the solution of common problems and the management of common affairs ... It is the governmental institution through which a cooperative democracy can realise its ideals and accomplish its purposes." See C.G. Hoag and G.H. Hallet, Jr : *Proportional Representation* (New York : Macmillan, 1926), p. 98.
29. Mill, *op. cit.*, Ch 7.

professes equality as its very root and foundation."[30]

It is not an easy job to offer a standard and precise definition of the term 'minority,' because the very nature of this problem differs from place to place and from people to people. A minority means a group of persons numerically smaller than others. Such a simple definition fails to carry any definite sense for the obvious reason that it does not specify the actual condition or conditions relating to the factor of numerical dimension. Thus, a better definition of this term shall be to treat the minorities "as groups held together by the ties of common descent, language or religious faith and feeling themselves different in these respects from the majority of the inhabitants of a given political entity."[31] It is also stated . "The term 'minority' includes only those non-dominant groups in a population which possess and wish to preserve stable ethnic, religious or linguistic traditions or characteristics markedly different from those of the rest of the population."[32]

For the sake of convenience, in matters relating to the political study, one may say that a minority means a group of persons whose race, or language, or religion is different from that of the persons in majority. The factor of subjective consideration is inapplicable in this direction. Thus, a group of people feeling like a minority does not constitute a minority. There can be no factor like choice or will, though the factor of force (as in the case of the Negroes in the United States) cannot be entirely ruled out. It is necessary that the people in minority should be concerned with preserving their separate identity and thus not be willing to have their assimilation with the people in majority. For this reason, the depressed classes of India should not, and cannot, be taken as belonging to the minorities, since they donot wish to preserve their characteristics which are markedly different from those of the rest of the population. "Rather, they like to be assimilated with the majority, but are prevented from doing so by the opposition from within the ranks of the majority party."[33]

It is now widely believed that the minorities should be adequately represented. This is possible only when some special devices are adopted. We may refer to certain special methods evolved for the sake of minority representation :

1. ***Second Ballot System :*** Under this system, it is required that the successful candidate must secure more than 50 per cent of the votes polled. If no candidate secures absolute majority, the election is cancelled and only two candidates (who had secured highest votes in the cancelled election) are allowed to contest. The result is that the successful candidate wins absolute majority. Such a method slightly betters the position of the minorities inasmuch as they may have a political bargain with one of the candidates before giving their choice in his favour.
2. ***Alternative Vote System :*** It is also known as the contingent or preferential vote system. Here single transferable vote system is used whereby electoral quota is obtained by dividing the total number of valid votes by 1 + 1 =2 and then adding the figure of 1 to the quotient in order to see that the successful candidate gains absolute majority either in the first count or by the transfer of votes according to subsequent preferences of the voters. The voters are given a ballot paper having names and symbols of the candidates printed on the left side with blank columns on the right side. He has to show his order of preferences for candidates by putting the figures of 1, 2, 3, etc. in the blank columns. The candidate securing votes upto the figure of electoral quota or more than that is

30. *ibid.*
31. *Encyclopaedia Britannica,* Vol. 15, 1953 Ed., p. 542.
32. See Report of the United Nations Sub-Commission on Prevention of Discrimination and Protection of Minorities in *Year-Book on Human Rights for 1950.,* p. 490.
33. K..K. Wadhwa : *Minority Safeguards in India* (New Delhi : Thompson Press, 1975), pp. 3-4.

declared successful, otherwise the candidate with least number of votes is eliminated and his votes are transferred to other candidates in accordance with the order of preferences given in the ballot papers. This process continues until one candidate secures absolute majority, or until one candidate remains in the field after elimination of others having votes less than those of him. Here again, the minorities may have a political bargain with a particular candidate and thus reap the dividends of their floating votes.

3. ***Limited Vote System :*** It requires that there should be at least three seats in a multi-member constituency and the voter be given votes less than the number of seats; they should also not be allowed to cast more than one vote for a candidate. We may, for instance, say that a voter be. given two votes in a three-member constituency. In this situation the position of the minorities is improved a little and they may have a chance of capturing one seat if they are fairly large, united and well organised.
4. ***Single Vote System :*** It prevails in a multi-member constituency with one vote of each voter. The candidates are elected on the basis of the majority of votes. The position of the minorities is much improved in this system inasmuch as they may cast their votes for their own candidate, while the votes of the persons in majority are sure to be divided among different candidates.
5. ***Proxy System :*** Under it, a voter may cast his vote for one candidate in a multi-member constituency. A minimum number of votes is fixed and a candidate securing that point is declared elected. It is also provided that those who vote for a candidate who fails to be sucessful, may vote again for others so that the unfilled posts may be filled up. Obviously, this would require either a preferential ballot or one which is most secret.
6. ***Cumulative Vote System :*** Under this system, each voter has as many votes as there are seats and he is allowed to cast his votes either for different candidates, or he may give all votes to a particular candidate. It is obvious that the persons in minority may cast their all votes in favour of their own candidate. It is also known as plumping vote system.
7. ***Weightage :*** It means that the persons in minority may be given some extra benefits. That is, they may be entitled for more votes than those given to the persons in majority. For instance, in India the Muslims and Christians in pre-independence period were given two votes—one for the elections in general constituencies and one for the election of a candidate of their own community.
8. ***Reservations :*** There may be the system of reservation of seats or nominations by the head of the state. We may see that in our country seats are reserved for the Scheduled Castes and Scheduled Tribes at the time of elections, while some Anglo-Indians may be nominated as members in the Union and State legislatures.

Though we may not refute the wisdom of a great democrat like Mill who said that the minorities should be given adequate representation and some special arrangement should be made for this purpose so that some seats be shared by them, it should also be borne in mind that nothing should be done for the sake of appeasing them. It should also be carefully noted that the special benefits or favours given to them are not converted into vested interests harmful to the interests of the nation as a whole. Let the minorities have the right to preserve and protect their religion, language, race, culture, etc. and let the state afford them special safeguards for this purpose. However, let it also be carefully noted that these privileges are not misused for purely selfish purposes. What the Indian Supreme Court has ruled in the

Gujarat University Case of 1974 (that the state cannot interfere with the management of educational institutions established and run.by a minority community), for instance, opens the way for the perpetration and perpetuation of exploitation particularly in the academic field. If such a situation ever arises, suitable steps should be taken, including an amendment of the provisions of the fundamental law of the land, so that the minorities are not allowed to make mischief in the name of privileges given to them.

Functional Representation : The system of functional representation has been suggested by a good number of social and political theorists as a better and more efficacious alternative to the system of territorial representation. It desires that the basis of representation should not be the territorial distribution of seats or even the selection of the representatives on the basis of some proportion, rather it should be according to the occupational composition of the society. Thus, it is not only a reaction against the system of territorial representation, it is also against the systems of proportional and minority representations as discussed above. The keynote of this idea is that the social, economic and professional groups, having special interests of their own. should find a place in the national legislature. The so-called 'democratic' system of territorial representation should, thus, "be replaced by a system of professional, occupational or functional representation which would disregard territorial lines which are largely artificial and donot mark off precisely the boundaries which separate the real interests of the various classes of which modern societies are composed."[34]

The idea of functional representation derives inspiration from the social set up prevalent in the middle ages when community groups had their autonomous character. Thus, a section of the evolutionary socialists, known as the Guild Socialists, presented it in a revised form that sought to impart a new meaning to the idea of democracy. For instance, Duguit said that the general will could find proper expression through the representation of various groups. Well-known English Fabians like Sidney Webb and Mrs Beatrice Webb recommended a new constitution for the 'socialist commonwealth of Britain' based on the principle of functional representation. However, its best exponent is G.D.H. Cole who said : "All true and democratic representation is, therefore, functional representation... It follows that there must be in the society as many separately elected groups of representatives as there are distinct groups of functions to be performed".[35]

The idea of functional representation took a concrete form in the post-first World War period. The territorial system of representation was replaced in Russia by a system based on the vocational principle for the All-Russian Congress in which miners, iron workers, farmers, professional men and other classes were allowed to choose their own representatives without regard to territorial lines. The same idea found its application in Italy where the Senate was reorganised on the functional basis as desired by Mussolini's doctrine of a corporate state. Various social, industrial and cultural organisations were also given representation in the chamber of deputies. The Weimer constitution of 1919 also created a national economic council in Germany representing special interests of labour, capital and consumers. The constitutions of Yugoslavia and Poland provided for the establishment of advisory councils (consisting of functional representatives) to collaborate with the legislature in the formulation of projects of legislation in regard to social and economic problems. Its example could be seen in Indonesia (before 1965) when President Soekarno, in accordance with his plan of

34. Garner, *op. cit.,* p. 596.
35. Cole : *Guild Socialism Restated,* pp. 32-33.

'Guided Democracy,' reorganised his parliament in a way consisting of the representatives of the armed forces, women, local bodies and others. It was virtually a model of composite legislature in which the idea of functional democracy was applied to some extent. President Suharto revived it in his People's Consultative Assembly having 920 members out of which 460 constituted the parliament.

Though the idea of functional representation has an attraction of its own, its demerits far outweigh its merits. It makes the legislature an arena of conflicting functional groups with the result that sectional interests over-ride national interest. It is also a very tedious job to make a standard census of all social and economic occupations and then decide in terms of their adequate representation. Thus, it is rightly said that an equitable distribution of representation of various interests is impossible. It lays too much emphasis on the autonomy of the social groups that becomes a sort of potential challenge to the sovereign authority of the state. Prof. Herman Finer well visualises that this idea "does not proceed from the integration of the community and then tempers this with the representation of differences, but it proceeds at once from the postulate of integration into a large number of separate communities whose ultimate integration is thenceforward to be fabricated."[36] Coker and Rodee, while attacking the plan of representation on the basis of economic or occupational groups, point out that such groups "are indefinite and impermanent in their composition. Many essential occupations form no distinct interests in relation to fundamental political questions."[37]

Characteristic Representation : It may be taken as a little different form of functional representation. It is argued that the legislative chamber should be a microcosm of the social composition. As such, the representative drawn from a particular segment of the society alone can represent or articulate its interests. For instance, the women understand the problems and interests of the women and so they alone can represent the women folk. It cannot be appreciated in view of the fact that if representation is given to sectional groups on any basis whatsoever, then nobody will care for the public good or national interests. Indeed, it "may simply be a recipe for social division and conflict."[38]

Concluding Observations : Though proportional, minority and functional representation systems have merits of their own, it cannot be denied that their demerits far outweigh their merits. It is just for this reason that the system of territorial representation is considered to be the best one in the midst of other systems of representation in order to apply it to a democratic state. However, a successful operation of the territorial or geographical representation system needs taking of certain important steps that may be enumerated as under :

1. There should be universal adult franchise system. The formula of 'one person, one vote' should be scrupulously adhered to. Thus, any discrimination on artificial grounds like those of property in Portugal (where a minimum tax payment is required), or sex as in Saudi Arabia, San Marino and Paraguay (there is no female franchise), or standard of literacy as in Brazil (where illiterates are not given right to vote) etc., is a slur on the name of representative government.

---

36. Finer: *Theory and Practice of Modern Government,* Vol. II, p. 907.
37. See Seligman (ed.): *Encyclopaedia of the Social Sciences,* Vols 13-14, p. 309. In a true sense, representation "cannot mean that all occupational and educational categories will be found in legislatures in exact proportion to their members. Furthermore, it may be crucial to a nation's viability that ethnic, religious, racial or other sub-divisions of the population be given stronger guarantees of being represented. Representation thus is a special aspect of the broader problem of political participation." Jain, *op. cit..* p. 55.
38. Andrew Heywood: *Political Theory: An Introduction,* p. 239.

2. Representation should be given to the really competent and incorruptible people. The system of representative democracy demands from the representative the duty to devote himself to the cause of public service and this important function cannot be discharged unless the deputy chosen by the people is both competent and immune from the bonds of material temptations. It becomes the sacred duty cf the voters themselves to see that their choice goes for the really deserving politicians.
3. A concerted attempt should be made both by the constituents and their legislators chosen through the medium of political parties to strengthen the constitutional regime. Thus, parties going to either extremes, from rank rightism to rank leftism, should be discouraged. It is also needed that ultra-revolutionary parties should be banned.
4. The number of political parties should be controlled. Laws should be made for the regulation of party system. Statutory provisions can be made for granting recognition to political parties on the basis of election results as we have in our country. It is also necessary that some penalties should be imposed on the defeated candidates so that the field of elections remains confined to the really serious contestants. We in India have a statutory arrangement for the forfeiture of security deposit of a defeated candidate in case he does not get at least 1/6 of the total votes polled. In Germany, a candidate must get at least five percent of the votes polled to have state subsidy for his election expenses. If a party fails to secure at least five per cent of the total votes polled, it farfeits its claim to any seat in the national legislature.
5. The *raison d' etre* of a legislature is not only to reflect the opinion of the nation as a whole that ascribes to it the title of being the'mirror of the nation', but to maintain good government. Thus, schemes of electoral reforms should be adopted with a view to produce the best possible type of representatives.

Critical Appraisal

It should be remembered that the system of representation has no workable alternative of its own. The agencies of direct democracy like those of initiative and referendum (as operating in Switzerland) may hardly serve the really desired purpose. Historical experiences show that the real value of these agencies of direct participation is not as substantial as it seems to be on a theoretical plane. The device of referendum as it has been adopted in some countries (like France and Australia) to override a decision of the legislature on a matter of great constitutional importance has not been as fruitful as it is claimed to be. What is left for us is that the system of representation should be made as usefully workable in the prevailing conditions of the country as possible. As Strong suggests : "Schemes of electoral reform, whose object is to produce the best poss'ble type of legislature, may therefore have to sacrifice something of the ideal electorate. The reflection of the opinion of the electorate in the legislature is only partially feasible and not always desirable. Any conceivable system of election is at best an arbitary attempt to approximate to a correspondence between the electors and the elected body. Government must, after all, be relative to the conditions of the society it governs, and account must always be taken of the peculiarities of the people to which it in each case applies."[39]

Undeniable is the fact that the subject of representation has an importance of its own in the study of modern democratic system. As such, the 'responsiveness' of the deputy needs its proper examination in the light of social and economic conditions of the country. Besides, the proper role of a representative

---

39. C.F. Strong : *Political Constitutions* (London : Sidgwick & Jackson, 1966), p. 192.

Some Important Statements about Representation

A member of Parliament represents the people of the whole community, exercises his own judgment upon all measures, receives freely the communications of his constituents, and is not bound by their instructions, though liable to be dismissed by not being reflected in case the difference of opinion between him and them is irreconcilable and important.

— Lord Brougham

"The British Constitution" in his Works, *Vol. XI, p. 94.*

The representative should be a pillar of state, not a weatheroock on the top of the edifice exalted for his levity and versatility, and of no use but to indicate the shiftings of every fashionable gale.

— Edmund Burke

Bristol address of 1780 cited in Garner: Political Science and Government, *p. 670.*

In politics representation suggests that an individual or group somehow stands for, or on behalf of a larger collection of people. Political representation, therefore, acknowledges a link between two otherwise separate identities - government and the governed - and implies that through this link the people's views are articulated, or their interests are secured. The precise nature of this link is, nevertheless, a matter of deep disagreement, as is the capacity of representation ever to ensure democratic government.

— Andrew Heywood

Political Theory : An Introduction, p. 233.

should be examined in the context of different institutional and regional situations. Indeed, this subject is so complex that it, according to Prof. R.B. Jain, embraces these significant aspects : (a) his role perception, role expectation and role performance in different institutional contexts, (b) his socialisation process, (c) his constituency linkages, (d) his relationship with other representatives and the emerging collective behaviour, (e) his relationship with his own partymen in and outside the representative bodies, (f) his support-bases, and (g) his individual, ideological, sociological and psychological make-up which in actual reality compose his personal traits and condition his behaviour in the legislative bodies.[40] Important studies can be made in the sphere of comparative politics by keeping the above points in view.

The subject of 'representativeness' has not yet been properly discussed. It is also deplorable that the representatives of the people have also done a lot to devalue their own position by showing indifference to the norms of proper representation. Thus, Herman Finer regrets that "no particular profession or training offers the royal road to the proper legislator, but that any one is eligible who has involved immersion in the life of the society and has acquired rigorous reflection and the use of mind and his assertion that the more ample the variety in the legislature, then the better."[41]

40. Jain, *op. cit.*, pp. 74-75.
41. Finer: *The Theory and Practice of Modern Government* Vol.I (London : Methuen 1961). p. 386.

24

Rule-Application Department

> Along with the chief executives, their cabinets, or councils, have undergone considerable change. Their relationship both to the chief executive and to the elected representative assemblies has changed in accordance with the increasing emphasis upon executive leadership . . . It is, therefore, no wonder that the cabinet tends to occupy a somewhat independent position and is not ordinarily, as the phrase used to go, 'an executive committee of the parliament'. Cabinets today depend once again upon the chief executive, as they always have been in the United States. What is more, the old formulas about policy-making and policy-execution require extensive revision.
>
> **—Carl J. Friedrich**[1]

One of the astonishing features of modern political systems is that distrust in executive dominance has been replaced by a confidence in its leadership. The reason for this is that the political process has become a subtle interplay of public pressure and effective leadership. Vast extension of the scope of state activity has made the executive a much more important organ of the government with the result that the classical doctrine of 'the three organs of political organisation with equal powers' has been subjected to the need for a theoretical restatement. The leadership of the government in the hands of a Prime Minister or of a President controlling his followers through the mechanism of party system and the distribution of patronage has, to a very great extent, usurped the autonomy of the domain of the legislators. The pattern of modern politics keeping the large body of legislators confined in a dull and mechanical discipline has established a surprising degree of contrast between the creative force of the leader (executive) and the equalitarian mediocrity of the mass majority (legislature).[2] The strong position of a cabinet under a Prime Minister in a parliamentary form of government and so of a President in its opposite model makes it above board that the legislative-force model has become outmoded. What Greaves has said about the English model of government is largely applicable to the systems of other countries as well that the executive "has become in practice the first chamber in our law-making mechanism."[3]

Executive : Meanings and Varieties

We are living in an age in which the legislative-force model has been replaced by the executive-force model. It is owing to this irrefutable fact that the core of political power in modern political systems, both developed and developing, is said to lie in the executive organ of government.[4] The first question that arises at the very outset is as to what is meant by the

1. Friedrich : *Constitutional Government and Democracy* (Calcutta : Oxford and IBH, 1966), pp. 354-55.
2. *ibid.*, p. 355.
3. H.R.G. Greaves : *The British Constitution*, p. 31,
4. Michael Curtis : *Comparative Government and Politics* (New York : Harper and Row, 1968), p. 202.

term 'executive'. This term has its broad as well as narrow connotations. "In a broad and collective sense, the executive organ embraces the aggregate or totality of all the functionaries and agencies which are concerned with the execution of the will of the state as that will has been formulated and expressed in terms of law." In this sense, the term embraces not only the supreme head of the government—the chief of state, as he is called in the countries of Europe (president, king or emperor)—but also the ministers and the whole mass of subordinate executive and administrative functionaries who constitute what in Great Britain and the United States is known as the 'civil service'. Thus understood, it "comprehends the entire governmental organisation, with the exception of the legislature and the judiciary and possibly the diplomatic corps. Thus, tax collectors, inspectors, commissioners, policemen and perhaps officers of the army and navy are a part of the executive organisation."[5]

Though the term executive is understood both in broad and narrow senses, in the realm of the study of politics its narrow meaning is applied. It is the executive heads and their principal colleagues who run the machinery of government; they formulate national policy and see to it that it is carefully implemented. The large arrmy of administrators is there just to carry out the policies laid down by the top excutive authorities. It is for this purpose that a line of distinction is made between the executive and administrative departments. As Willoughby says : "The executive power or rather the function is that of representing the government as a whole and of seeing that all of its laws are properly complied with by its several parts. The administrative function is that of actually administering the law as declared by the legislative, and interpreted by the judicial branches of the government. This distinction is usually made by declaring the executive function to be essentially political in character; that is, one involving the exercise of judgment in its use; and the administrative function to be one concerned with putting into effect of policies and the carrying out of orders as determined or given by other organs."[6]

Though the term executive may be understood in a broad as well as a narrow sense, or it may be distinguished from the term 'administration', our purpose is limited to the study of the rule-application department that works under the 'leadership' of the real executive of the state. As we shall see, it is the position of the leader that counts above all whether it is a presidential model of the American type, or a parliamentary model of the English type. None but the real leader of the government counts in the rule-application department. An empirical study of modern governments shows that along with the chief executives, their cabinets or councils, have undergone considerable change. The relationship between the chief executive and the representative assemblies has changed in relation to the increasing emphasis upon executive leadership. It is, therefore, no wonder that the cabinets tend to occupy a somewhat independent position and are not to be taken ordinarily, as the classical statements used to be, like executive committees of the parliament, it is all on account of this irrefutable fact that the "crux of executive power is leadership."[7]

Whereas the term 'executive' can be used in both a wider and a narrower sense, its various types may be mentioned with the help of a tabular illustration:

---

5. J.W. Garner : *Political Science and Government* (Calcutta : World Press, 1952), p. 677.
6. W.W. Willoughby : *Principles of Public Administration* (Allahabad, 1952).
7. Friedrich, *op. cit.*, p. 355.

Kinds of Executive

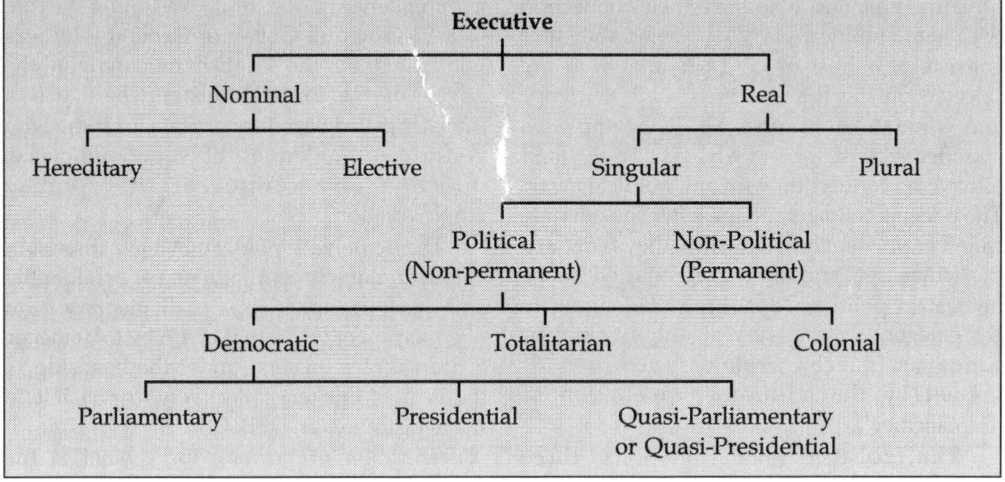

The difference between nominal and real executives obtains in a system where there is constitutional monarchy or parliamentary form of government. The monarch or the President is a constitutional figurehead with little or no real powers, though the entire administration is carried in his name. Its best example is afforded by the English monarch who, according to the established convention, 'can do no wrong'. In such a system, the real power is given to the Council of Ministers (headed by the Prime Minister) who are accountable to the legislature. The ministers constitute the real executive. Walter Bagehot designates the two as 'dignified', and 'efficient' executives respectively. The nominal executive may be of two types—hereditary and elective. That is, the monarch may assume his office by the law of hereditary succession; he may be elected by some direct or indirect process. In most of the monarchical systems the head of the state assumes his office by the law of hereditary succession as we still find in countries like Britain and Japan. History shows that in medieval times the kings were chosen by the people or by the lords and nobles of the land.

What actually matters is the real executive. It may have two types—singular or plural. A singular executive is one that is headed by a single leader who does not share his powers with others. The leadership of the President or that of the Prime Minister belongs to this category. Such an executive has only one leader endowed with real authority that is not shared by any other member of the government. Different from this is the case of plural executive where the directing authority is shared by a group of ministers. History shows several instances where the real authority of government has been shared by a team of leaders. Ancient Sparta was governed by two kings and ancient Rome by two Consuls. Its only instance in the modern world is found in Switzerland where the authority of the government is shared by seven ministers (called presidents) who are elected by the legislature for a term of four years. Its name is Federal Council. One of the seven presidents is formally designated as the 'President of the Confederation' who performs the ceremonial functions of the Head of the State. Moreover, this office goes by rotation annually with the result that every minister gets the chance on the basis of his seniority.

The real executive may, further, be divided into two varieties —political or non-permanent and non-political or permanent. While the former consists of the ministers headed by the

President or the Prime Minister who hold office for some time and who have their connection with some political party or parties, the latter consists of a host of civil servants who are selected on the basis of merit and efficiency and who remain in office till they complete a specified limit of age and who are also required to have no connection with any political party. The persons belonging to the latter category are called permanent officials, since they retire at a particular age and they are required to be neutral in politics. Top officers belonging to this category accumulate real authority in their hands and thereby create a system what is known by the notorious appellation of 'bureaucracy'.

The political executive has three categories—democratic, totalitarian and colonial. It is democratic when its members are chosen by the representatives of the people and remain accountable to their constituents. There is freedom of criticising and censuring the conduct of the ministers with the result that the real executive may go out of office in case a vote of no-confidence or a motion of impeachment is passed against it. The British cabinet may be removed by an adverse vote in the House of Commons, or the American President may be removed by the process of impeachment. These are the instances of a political executive belonging to the democratic category. In a totalitarian system the real executive cannot be removed by the people or their chosen representatives, since there is no freedom to criticise or censure the conduct of the government. The top leaders of a particular party or of a military junta run the government in a way that opposition means mutilation or death. A country having a fascist form of government or military rule or wedded to the ideology of Marxism-Leninism may be said to fall into this category. Finally, a colonial executive is one that acts under the superintendence, direction and control of the colonial government. It may be called 'nominated executive' as well, since the real rulers of a dependent country are nominated by the colonial power. For instance, in the pre-independence period, India was under the rule of a Viceroy and Governor-General who was nominated by the English monarch on the advice of the Prime Minister. There was a minister called Secretary of State for India who performed the duties of superintendence, direction and control of the Indian administration.

The democratic model may have three sub-varieties, namely, parliamentary, presidential and quasi-presidential. A parliamentary form of government is one that is run by a cabinet or a council of ministers (under the headship of the Prime Minister) collectively responsible to the legislature. It works on the principle of concentration of powers, for cabinet is the buckle that joins the legislative and executive departments. Different from this is the presidential executive. It works under the leadership of a President who is not accountable to the legislature, though he may be removed by it by the process of impeachment. This type of executive works on the principle of the separation of powers. In between these two is the model of French executive that may be designated as either quasi-parliamentary or quasi-presidential in view of the fact that here President is the real executive; the Prime Minister and the cabinet are under his control and, at the same time, they are accountable to the Parliament.

Functions of the Executive

If the classical theory of the three organs of government with 'equal' powers of each needs restatement anywhere, it is in the sphere of the executive. None can deny that it is the executive that has become the government in the real sense of the term. In order to have an understanding of this fact, we should have a look at the main functions of the rule-application department:

1. As its very name indicates, the first and foremost function of the executive is to run the administration of the country. The maintenance of internal peace and order is

the principal function for which the government is established. For this purpose, the executive keeps police force that acts under its command. It maintains external relations also. It also maintains defence forces to save the country against external aggressions. It makes appointments of high officers of the state. The formulation of national policy for domestic as well as external purposes is the concern of the executive. In short, making of treaties with foreign states, declaration of war and peace, mobilisation of troops, proclamation of emergency, valuation or devaluation of the currency, fixation of the prices of essential commodities, and the performance of a host of other activities pertaining to the maintenance and well-being of the state fall within the domain of the executive functions.

2. In recent times, executive has assumed the power of making legislation also. The Head of the State may promulgate an ordinance that has the force of law. The bills passed by the legislature are subject to the veto power of the Head of the State. In a cabinet form of government most of the bills passed by the parliament are official bills; even in a country like the United States, we find that the President manages to influence the legislative sphere by sending his 'messages' or having a bill passed by the Congress through his 'friends'. What has immensely contributed to the stock of executive powers in this regard is the rise and growth of delegated legislation. As no parliament can make a law that is complete in all respects, it is left to the executive departments to make necessary amplifications or supplementations in the parliamentary legislation by means of issuing circulars, notifications, etc. from time to time. Though it is true that these circulars and notifications should be in conformity with the wishes of the parliament or with the spirit of the parliamentary legislation, it generally happens that people donot bother about the nature and scope of departmental legislation with the result that they are passed by the legislature in a moment or so. All political scientists endorse this fact that delegated legislation has become an inescapable necessity.

3. Such a massive transformation has taken place in the sphere of public administration that executive departments have assumed judicial functions as well. In all countries the Head of the State is entrusted with the power of granting pardon, or reprieve, or amnesty to the offenders. This is called his prerogative of mercy. What engages our attention at this stage, however, is the subject of administrative adjudication. Administrative heads consitute tribunals for the settlement of departmental disputes in which the employees are involved. It is also possible that the ministers be given the power to act like appellate tribunals. In France there is a separate system of administrative law and courts. It is true that the administrative adjudication is subject to the control of the judicial process of the country as the decisions of the administrative courts may be challenged in the proper courts of the realm; nevertheless, it cannot be denied that the establishment of administrative courts prevents 'an inflexible dividing line being drawn between administrative and judicial structures'.[8]

4. The executive controls the 'purse of the nation'. The preparation of budget and its presentation to the legislature for its approval is the function of the executive. It is the executive that decides about the imposition or abolition of taxes, or the enhancement or reduction of the rate of taxation, or the sanction and realisation of loans, etc. Moreover, it is the function of the executive to see that the provisions of the

8. Ball, *op. cit.,* p. 203.

budget are implemented after they are passed by the parliament. For this, the executive has comptrolling and auditing agencies to act as the financial watchdog of the country.

The scope of the function of the executive as pointed out by Chester Bernard in his work titled *The Function of the Executive* relates 'with the determination of the objectives, the initiation of policy, the manipulation of means, control over the instruments of action, and stimulation of co-ordinated action'.[9] What, however, strikes us here is that representative democracy is replaced by, what may be termed, executive democracy, even (what R.H.S. Crossman has termed) 'bureaucratic democracy'.[10]

Parliamentary Government : Classical English Model

The parliamentary form of government that has in the United Kingdom its ancestral place and that has been adopted in the Commonwealth countries and also in several countries of Europe "is that system in which the real executive—the cabinet or ministry—is immediately and legally responsible to the legislature or one branch of it (usually the more popular chamber) for its political policies and acts, and mediately or ultimately responsible to the electorate, while the titular or nominal executive—the chief of state—occupies a position of irresponsibility."[11] This type of executive has the following essential features :

1. ***A Nominal Head :*** The first prerequisite of this government is the presence of the head of the state endowed with nominal authority. The entire administration is run in his name. All powers are formally vested in him that are exercised by his ministers accountable to the parliament. This titular head of the state appoints his Prime Minister—the head of the government. The nominal head administers the oaths of office and secrecy to his ministers and accepts their resignations. He signs communications relating to the change in ministerial porfolios and may even dimiss the Prime Minister in case he forfeits his 'pleasure'. Its best example can be found in the English monarch who is said to rule, but not to govern.
2. ***Leadership of the Prime Minister :*** The Prime Minister holds the real executive authority and, as such, he may be described as 'the real working head of the state' (Ramsay Muir). He is the chief spokesman of the government, keystone of the cabinet-arch, leader of the House and generalissimo of the national administration. It is on his advice that nominal head of the state acts in matters relating to the appointment or dismissal of the ministers, reshuffle in their portfolios, summoning and prorogation of the session of the parliament, proclamation of war and peace, making an appeal to the nation and the like. Thus, while the nominal head rules, the real head governs. "As chief executive, chief legislator and chief administrator, the Prime Minister is potentially a very powerful individual. Everything depends on the use which he chooses to make of his position, and the success with which he delegates some of his responsibilities."[12]
3. ***Political Homogeneity :*** The Prime Minister is the leader of the party enjoying clear majority in the parliament, in the popular house if there is a bi-cameral legislature. All ministers belong to the same party that has its leader in the Prime Minister. It may be possible that two or more parties join to form a coalition government when no party is in a position to have absolute majority in the parliament. The case of such a

9. See Curtis, *op. cit.*, p. 202.
10. Douglas V. Verney : *British Government and Politics* (New York : Harper and Row, 1966), p. 86.
11. Garner, *op. cit.*, p. 323.
12. Verney, *op. cit.*, p. 57.

government is an exception and not the rule. It is a different thing that the Prime Minister may have some ministers belonging to other parties even when his own party is in comfortable majority. Such a government, called 'national government', is formed during times of acute crisis. The normal practice is that the party in majority forms its government and other party forms or parties form the opposition. Practical experiences demonstrate that such a government cannot function smoothly unless there is political homogeneity.

4. ***Collective Responsibility :*** The most important feature of this government is the principle of responsibility of the ministers to the parliament. It means that they can live in office only so long as they enjoy confidence or pleasure of the parliament. The Prime Minister himself and all his ministers are the members of the parliament. According to a well-accepted convention, the Prime Minister must be a member of the lower house, if there are two houses in the legislature. In case a minister (including the Prime Minister) is not a member of the parliament, he is required to secure the membership within a period of next six months. It is for this reason that the ministers take part in the proceedings of the parliament. They speak in defence of the policies and activities of the government, place motions and resolutions for discussion and see that their wishes prevail; they introduce budget in the legislature and see to it that it is passed. The ministers also have the power to exercise their vote in the house of which they are the members. In case a vote of censure is passed, or the government is defeated in the house, it amounts to the defeat of all. In such a situation, all ministers have to resign. This is called collective responsibility. It shows that all ministers sink or swim together. The ministers are also bound by the rule of individual responsibility which means that the Prime Minister may ask any minister to resign in case he forefeits his pleasure. It is this basic principle of parliamentary government that is still in observance despite the fact that the control of the legislature over the executive has become too feeble. Keeping this fact in view, Verney has remarked that though the power of the Prime Minister "has been increasing, but so far there is no firm evidence that the basic assumption of cabinet government—its responsibility to the legislature—has been forgotten cither by the Cabinet or by the Parliament.'[13]

5. ***Sound and Effective Opposition :*** The last requirement of a parliamentary form of government is the existence of a sound and effective opposition that may exercise check on the government so as to prevent it from taking to a path basically opposed to the existence of a democratic political system. If one party gets absolute majority and forms government, there are other parties that form the opposition. It is, however, required that the opposition should be constructive what the English people call 'loyal'. It is for this reason that the opposition attacks the government for its acts of commission and omission and the Prime Minister advises the nominal head of the state to make 'an appeal to the electorate' in case a vote of no-confidence is passed against the government, or when he thinks in terms of adopting some revolutionary measure in accordance with the mandate of the people.

The parliamentary form of government, having its best form in the English political system, may be described as the rule of the majority party working under the leadership of the Prime Minister with the help and co-operation of his trusted colleagues having charge of important potfolios and in which all

13. *ibid.,* p. 63.

have their sense of responsibility to the parliament and ultimately to the people who are their real constituents. The essence of this executive system, in the last analysis, is that the Cabinet 'is a committee of Parliament, tending to be, with the advance of democracy, a committee of the House of Commons. . .This implies that the ultimate control is in the hands of the electorate."[14]

Cabinet Government : Recent English Model

Though the essential principles of parliamentary government continue to remain in observance, a great change has occurred in the sphere of relationship between the cabinet and the parliament so much so that the very name 'parliamentary government' has been replaced by a more popular one—'cabinet government'. The cabinet has become, as W.B. Munro said, the 'single-most important piece of mechanism in the constitutional structure' or as Ramsay Muir says, 'the steering wheel of the ship of the state'.[15] A great degree of difference has come to exist in theory and practice. "In theory, it (Cabinet) is dependent upon Parliament : in practice it is the master of Parliament, but its omnipotence is qualified by the fact that a small body of men cannot effectively wield such plenitude of powers as it possesses."[16]

The omnipotent position of the cabinet draws its sustenance from the following essential points:[17]

1. The cabinet defines the lines of national policy and decides how each problem at home or abroad is to be faced and dealt with. The Parliament is supposed to exercise its control over the cabinet in matters of formulation of national policy and its carrying out by the ministers concerned, but this control becomes unreal when the cabinet is in command of a majority of pledged supporters.
2. The cabinet is held responsible for every detail of the administrative work carried on by the vast administrative machinery. The cabinet refuses to allow any other body to interfere in it, even the House of Commons, for it commands majority.
3. The cabinet realises the need for legislation so as to run administration of the country well. For this, it prepares legislative proposals and submits them to Parliament. Since it has majority, it sees to it that official bills are passed and that too in substantially the same form as it desires. The result is that invariably all official bills are passed by the parliament.
4. The budget is prepared according to the policy of the cabinet and then introduced in the Parliament for having its approval.
5. The cabinet makes high appointments at home and abroad and the parliament has practically no right to interfere in this respect.
6. The cabinet decides, within fairly wide limits, what business shall be submitted to Parliament and how much time shall be allotted to discussion over it. It decides about the summoning and prorogation of the session, text of the inaugural address to be delivered by the titular head of the state, daily time table of the business of Parliament and, above all, dissolution of the House to seek a fresh verdict of the people.

These points show that the powers of the Parliament have been usurped by the cabinet. The responsibility of the cabinet has been converted into its mere responsiveness. The immensely increasing power of the cabinet cannot be denied and along with it one cannot disagree with the critical observation that

14. C.F. Strong : *Modern Political Constitutions* (London : Sidgwick and Jackson, 1966), pp. 240-41.
15. Muir : *How Britain is Governed* (Allahabad : Central Book Depot, 1951), p. 69.
16. *ibid.*, p. 68.
17. *ibid.*, pp. 66-68.

though nominally supreme, the House of Commons has virtually become subservient to the executive.

However, the powerful position of the cabinet should not be described as its 'dictatorship'. There is nothing like the 'dictatorship of the cabinet'in view of the fact that the cabinet makes use of its 'omnipotent'position in the midst of the attacks of the opposition. Refuting the label of 'dictatorship', Jennings observes: "The real difference between Britain and the dictatorship countries is that with us there is not one faction seeking to maintain itself in power by persuasion, fraud or force, but at least two factions each trying to achieve and maintain power by persuasion."[18] Likewise, Lord Herbert Morrison says: "The cabinet seeks to get its own way. That does not mean, however, that it can impose its will upon the Members of the House of Commons clumsily, in an arbitrary fashion. It must be persuasive. It must be respectful to the House of Commons."[19]

Prime Ministerial Government : Latest English and Indian Models

The most astonishing development in the sphere of the Westminster model of government should be discovered in the extremely powerful position of the Prime Minister calling for the rechristening of this form of political system as the 'Prime Ministerial Government'. The classical doctrines that the cabinet is accountable to the Parliament, and the Prime Minister 'is first among equals' stand thoroughly discredited if we closely examine the powers and position of the Prime Minister. Humphrey Berkeley, an independent-minded member of the English Parliament, expressed his astonishment in these words: "....after six and a half years in the House of Commons, I have been at sufficient close quarters to realise that almost every premise on which my knowledge of constitutional theory was based has turned out to be untrue. Parliament is not, in practice, sovereign.". Again, "The parliamentary democracy has now collapsed at Westminster... the basic defect in the British system of government is the supra-ministerial power of the Prime Minister."[20]

Though the Prime Minister comes from a particular constituency of the country, his election assumes the character of a general election. All eyes are set on his/her election and the image of his/her personality casts a great impact on the electoral behaviour of the people. One may refer to the case of India where the Lok Sabha polls of 1971 and 1977 became like a battle of the ballot box hinging on the crucial issue of'Save Indira'v.'Remove Indira'. "Elections largely radiate around the personalities of the Prime Minister and the Leader of the Opposition so that they largely become a plebiscite of which two individuals will head a government. In the 1964 and 1966 British elections the strategy and conduct of the Labour Party campaign was closely in the hands of Harold Wilson. This has almost created a quasi-presidential system in which the Prime Minister draws support from the people, and the real check on his behaviour is anxiety about the vote at the next election rather than the next vote in the House of Commons."[21]

The 'presidentialisation of the Prime Minister's office', finds place in the highly autocratic behaviour of the real working head of the state. The cabinet has ministers who are no longer the 'colleagues' of the Prime Minister as they are reduced to the status of his 'palace guards'. The Prime Minister may induct any number of ministers, make changes in their portfolios, or demand resignation from one who is in disagreement with him, or even get him dismissed by an order of the nominal head of the state. A strong Prime Minister like Harold Macmillan removed about a dozen ministers in

18. Ivor Jennings : *Parliament,* p. 504.
19. Morrison : *British Parliamentary Democracy,* p. 65.
20. Berkeley : *The Power of the Prime Minister,* p. 118.
21. Curtis, *op. cit.,* p. 216.

July, 1962 that ascribed to him the nickname of being the 'wielder of long knives'. Numerous instances may be given while we refer to the position of the Prime Minister of India (like Indira Gandhi) who pushed out the dissident ministers of her cabinet and invoked the plea of her discretionary powers in this regard.

The American President acts with the help of advisers who sometimes overshadow the authority of the ministers. For instance, President Nixon reposed so much confidence in his adviser Prof. Henry Kissinger that, for some time, he overshadowed the authority of his Secretary of State (Rogers). This type of behaviour can be seen in the case of Indian Prime Minister (Indira Gandhi) who often acted with the help of her most trusted advisers like D.P. Dhar and P.N. Haksar whose activities overshadowed the real areas of authority belonging to the ministers concerned.

A close study of the office of the Prime Minister, particularly of the United Kingdom and India, confirms the impression of some critics that the office of the Prime Minister has been 'presidentialised'. Aware of the new constitutional developments, R.H.S. Crossman affirms: "The postwar epoch has seen the transformation of the cabinet government into Prime Ministerial government. Under this system, the hyphen which joins and the buckle which fastens the legislative part to the executive part becomes one single man."[22]

Presidential Government : Models of USA, Brazil and South Africa

The presidential system of government is typified by the United States and other countries such as Brazil, Argentina, Mexico, Chile, Philippines, South Africa etc. It is based on the doctrine of the separation of powers. The chief executive is the real head of the state who is elected by the people, whether directly or indirectly, for a definite period and who is not accountable to the legislature, though he may be removed by the process of impeachment. Thus, what has been called presidential government, as contradistinguished from the cabinet or parliamentary government, "is that system in which the executive (including both the head of the state and his ministers) is constitutionally independent of the legislature in respect to the duration of his or their tenure and irresponsible to it for his or their political policies."[23]

The presidential system of government has the following essential features:

1. ***Real Authority of the President*** : The leadership of the executive is in the hands of the President who is elected by the people for a fixed period as of four years in the United States. The procedure of election may be either direct or indirect and the constitution may also specify as to the number of tenures a person may hold as of two terms in the United States. He appoints his ministers as his advisers who are not his colleagues but, what is called in the United States, his 'palace guards'. The body of the ministers is called the cabinet that is either like a 'family' of the President or a 'brains trust'. The President may change the portfolios of his ministers as per his will, or may dismiss any one of them in case he loses the confidence of the 'boss'. The President appoints a large number of high officers of the state whose proposals may be subject to ratification by some other agency as that of Senate in the United States. He formulates national policy, orders mobilisation of troops, declares state of emergency and takes necessary steps for the enforcement of laws and maintenance of order in the country. He, as is said about the American President, "is the final source of all executive decisions. He is the authoritative exponent of nation's foreign policy."[24]

22. Cited in Anthony King (ed.): *The British Prime Minister*, p. 163.
23. Garner, *op. cit.*, p. 340.
24. Laski : *The American Presidency*, p. 37.

2. ***Process of Impeachment :*** It is feared that the President may abuse his authority to the extent that his removal becomes a matter of necessity. For this purpose, the constitution provides the process of his impeachment. The President takes the oath of office whereby he swears that he will defend and protect the constitution of the country. In case he violates the sacred oath, he becomes liable for the charge of 'misbehaviour', or gross dereliction of duty, or for the breach of the constitution for which impeachment proceedings may be initiated. For instance, President Andrew Johnson of the United States was impeached in the Senate of the United States in 1868, though he was saved by a single vote. The process of impeachment is provided to keep a powerful deterrent that can be made use of in extraordinary circumstances to remove the head of the state in case he is guilty of the violation of the constitution.

3. ***Separation of the Legislature from the Executive :*** Instead of fusion, there is separation of powers in the presidential system of government. The President and his ministers cannot be the members of the legislature. In case the President appoints somebody as his minister who is also a member of the legislature, he will have to resign his legislative membership before accepting the ministerial assignment. It is for this reason that the ministers donot attend the sessions of the legislature and though they may go and also speak in the House, they cannot vote. The President may send his messages to the legislature and the latter may, and may not, act according to the wishes of the head of the state. The legislature cannot censure the conduct of the ministers, it can only initiate proceedings of impeachment against the President. The bills passed by the legislature are subject to the veto power of the President who may exercise this power in case of bills not pertaining to his choice. The budget prepared by the President is submitted to the legislature that may pass it, or cut it wherever it so chooses. It is due to this that a deadlock occurs when the executive and legislative departments are at loggerheads.

4. ***Checks and Balances :*** A system of checks and balances is devised to see that the three organs of government not only live within their respective spheres, rather they also act as a check against another so that the balance remains intact. There must be some inter-linking arrangement between the legislative and executive departments so that neither assumes the position of behaving like 'George III'. It is on account of the recognition of this fact that the doctrine of the separation of powers, as so elaborately formulated by Montesquieu, has been supplemented with the system of checks and balances so wisely devised by the American Founding Fathers. As a result, while the President can. make appointments and sign treaties with foreign states, they are subject to Senatorial ratification. Likewise, all bills passed by the Congress are subject to Presidential veto power and that the Congress may override the Presidential veto by re-adopting the same bill by 2/3 majority. The Supreme Court may invalidate an administrative action or Congressional legislation if it is repugnant to the provisions of the Constitution or the due process of law, while the Congress may make a law enhancing the number of judges to be appointed by the President and may remove a judge by the process of impeachment if found guilty of proved misbehaviour or incapacity. Mere separation of governmental organs will not do, separation supplemented with checks and balances makes the system work.

Brazil has presidential system established under the constitution of 1988. It is like as well as unlike the American system in certain respects. The President has enormous powers given to him by the provisions of the constitution and new dimensions have been added to them by the abusive deeds of the incumbents of the great office like Collor and Franco. The source of such a development may be traced in people's preference for presidentialism over parliamentarism and the untidy system of checks and balances established by the new constitution. His special powers may be thus enumerated:

1. He selects and dismisses his ministers. He selects ministers for the armed forces according to the merit system prevailing in their respective branches. He appoints other ministers from the groups of his life-time cronies and collaborators or from any of the existing parties. His vast powers of appointment are not subject to the control of any other institution the type of which we may see in the case of American Senate.
2. The President may enforce 'provisional measures' which must be approved by the two-thirds vote of both the houses of Parliament. Obviously, an ambitious President like Collor could abuse his powers by issuing 150 provisional measures during first year of his Presidency. Even the Supreme Tribunal felt helpless in exercising a check on the exercise of such powers by the President in a blatantly wrong manner.
3. Unlike the American President, the Brazilian President may exploit the situation by invoking the argument of bad state of affairs of the country in the political and economic spheres. People appreciate such extra-constitutional powers of the President in the name of his efforts to check inflation or to maintain national security.

Obviously, such a strong position of the President is reinforced not by the provisions of the constitution but by the prevailing conditions and beliefs of the people. "Support for the presidential system was based mainly on the view that decision-making functions should be centralised in the chief of the state. For many Brazilians, governmental effectiveness has historically been identified with presidential supremacy. Also for a large number of politicians, the presidential office became the ultimate distributor of clientelism, credits, public investments, and the arbiter among regional interests. For the popular sector it has been the focus for demand for improvement in living conditions and better wages. For the military the President is the very embodiment of national security."[25]

Peculiar is the case of South Africa whose system hovers between the presidential system of the United States and the quasi-presidential system of France. The President is elected by the National Assembly from amongst its members for a term of five years. He cannot have more than two terms like his American counterpart. Soon after his election, he ceases to be a member of the National Assembly. He can be removed by the process of impeachment on the charge of misconduct or violation of the constitution. A resolution to this effect must be passed by 2/3 majority of the members of the National Assembly present and voting. He has immense powers which may be enumerated as under:

1. He appoints his ministers and administers to them the oath of office. He may remove any minister. He presides over the meetings of the cabinet. Though he cannot appoint more than 27 ministers, he may appoint any number of deputy ministers.
2. The President and his ministers cannot be the members of the National Assembly, but he may nominate any minister to act as the leader of the government business in the National Assembly.
3. The President and his cabinet ministers are responsible to the Parliament. The National Assembly may pass a vote of no-confidence against the cabinet by simple majority of votes. In such a situation the President shall reconstitute his cabinet. The National Assembly may remove the President as well

25. Maria do Carmo Campello de Souza: "Brazil" in William A. Joseph, Mark Kasselman and Joel Krieger (eds.): *Third World Politics at the Crossroods* (Lexington: D.C. Heath and Company, 1996), p. 238.

by passing the motion of impeachment. In such a situation he and all members of the cabinet must resign.

4. The President summons the session of the Parliament. He may call its extraordinary session as well. He gives his assent to the bills passed by it. He may return a bill to the Parliament for reconsideration, or he may refer it to the Constitutional Court for ascertaining its view on its constitutional validity. He may also put a bill for national referendum.
5. He appoints his ambassadors for foreign countries and receives the ambassadors of other countries. He maintains foreign relations and signs treaties and agreements with other countries.
6. He appoints judges of the Constitutional Court, Supreme Court of Appeal and High Courts and members of the Commissions of Inquiry.
7. He may use his emergency powers to preserve peace, national unity and indivisibility of the republic.

It is clear that in the political system of South Africa the position of the President is weak compared to his American and French counterparts. He has to choose his ministers in proportion to the strength of the parties in the National Assembly. He cannot cross the ceiling on the size of the council of ministers. The process of his removal is not tedious as we may see in the case of the United States. Just by virtue of having special powers, he is the real head of the state as in USA and France.

The chief characteristic of the presidential form of government is the existence of a powerful executive (called the President) who enjoys a fixed term. His enormous powers virtually remain unchecked and his position remains unchallenged as the process of impeachment by which he can be removed is deliberately made very difficult. Aware of the tedious nature of the process of impeachment, the President acts like a 'dictator'. An ambitious President may also incorporate a penalty clause in the basic law of the land applicable to those who make an unsuccessful attempt to initiate process of impeachment. It is done to deter the possible opponents as was done by President Ayub Khan of Pakistan. (The Ayub Constitution of 1962 had provided that the members of the National Assembly would lose their seats and also be declared unqualified for holding any elective post for the next 10 years in case the move of impeachment initiated by them became unsuccessful.) A powerful President may manipulate to keep a big chunk of legislators in his group, or he may influence the public opinion in his favour with which, as is said about the American President, he "may sometimes prevail over the opposition even of an antipathetic Congress."[26]

Quasi-Presidential Government : The French and Russian Models

A peculiar mixture of the parliamentary and presidential models is visible in France that may be termed quasi-presidential or quasi-parliamentary. The de Gaulle Constitution of 1958 provides a powerful President endowed with real authority, elected for a term of five years and also removable by the process of impeachment. At the same time, it provides a Prime Minister and a cabinet accountable to the Parliament. It is stated that the President shall appoint the Prime Minister on whose proposal he shall appoint other members of the government (Art. 8) and that the government shall be responsible to the Parliament (Art. 20).

The elements of a presidential government are thus traceable in the constitution of the Fifth Republic of France. The President is the real executive head with wide powers of control over the legislature. In the event of a vote of censure passed by the Parliament against the government, the President can dissolve the National Assembly and call for a new election. The ministers are not allowed to be the members

26. Strong, *op. cit.*, p. 266.

Vital Political Powers of the French President

1. He names the Prime Minister and other Cabinet Ministers as well as high civil, military and judicial officials.
2. He presides over the meetings of the Council of Ministers.
3. He conducts foreign affairs, appoints ambassadors and receives ambassadors of foreign countries.
4. He commands and directs the armed forces.
5. He may dissolve the National Assembly and call for new elections. He cannot dissolve the new Assembly within first year of its tenure.
6. He appoints three of the nine members of the Constitutional Council, including its president, and refer bills passed by the Parliament to the Council to determine if they conform to the constitution.
7. He may sponsor a referendum, ratify proposed treaties as well as approve proposed changes in the constitutional powers of political institutions.
8. He may ensure by his arbitration, regular functioning of the governmental authorities as well as maintenance of the state.
9. With the concurrence of the Prime Minister he may propose constitutional amendment.
10. He may assume emergency powers when, in his judgment, the institutions or implementation of some international treaty or commitments are threatened.

of the legislature. The President may take drastic steps if there is a threat to the institutions of the republic, the independence of the nation, the integrity of its territory, or the execution of international obligations. Under these conditions, the governmental organisation of France "could perhaps be more properly described as a semi-presidential system, based on at least a partial separation of power."[27]

At the same time, the elements of a parliamentary form of government are traceable in the French constitution. It provides a Prime Minister with a council of ministers who are required to have the confidence of Parliament. The President is empowered to act with the help and co-operation of his Prime Minister and ministers. The members of the Parliament may ask questions from the ministers and censure the conduct of the government. The Prime Minister, though appointed by the President, is required to seek a vote of confidence in order to clear his position that he enjoys the confidence of the majority. The Parliament may also discuss the conduct of the President and remove him by the process of impeachment and criticise his 'high-handed' action as it did in 1962 when the President desired to change the method of his election. (President de Gaulle had desired that the new head of state be elected directly by the people without any participation of the members of the Parliament). The President put his revolutionary proposal to the referendum (invoking the provision of Art. 11) without first submitting it to the Parliament as required under Art. 89 of the Constitution. The National Assembly showed its resentment and passed a vote of censure against the government.

The powers of the President are immense and fuel is added to the fire if the same party controls the legislative and the executive wings of the French government. It shows that the French President "combines the independent powers of the US President—notably command of the executive establishment and independence from legislative control—with the

27. *ibid.*

powers that accrue to the government in a parliamentary regime—namely, control over parliament's agenda and its day-to-day activity, and the ability to dissolve parliament and force new legislative elections. Moreover, the government—usually under the direction of the president—controls parliament more tightly than other democratic regimes do. The result is a greater degree of executive dominance within the French political system than in virtually any other democractic nation. And the president occupies the office at the very top of the commanding edifice."[28]

Though it is true that the French model of government presents a queer blending of the English and American models, it is more of a quasi-presidential variety for the simple reason that the position of the President is too strong and that of the Parliament too weak. Let us also look at the political behaviour of Charles de Gaulle— the founder of the fifth Republic and the First President under the new constitutional dispensation. He exercised unquestioned control over matters such as foreign affairs, military and defence that fell within the domain of his reserved authority and that he intermittently concerned himself with social and economic affairs of the realm as well. On a number of occasions, he used the device of referendum to seek popular approval of his policy decisions. He interpreted the constitution in a highly personal fashion. In 1962 he refused to convene the emergency session of the Parliament on some specious grounds and went to the extent of dissolving the National Assembly that had passed a vote of censure against his government. The new National Assembly passed the amendment bill as desired by him (election of the President by universal suffrage) whereby he "finally achieved his purpose of transforming what had once been a Parliamentary Executive into a Plebiscitary Presidency."[29] It is rightly commented that the Fifth Republic, however, "is a regime in which the President, rather than the Prime Minister, has been the chief director of policy."[30]

The Russian constitution (adopted in December, 1993) shifts the balance of power decisively in the direction of the executive branch. The President is designated as the head of the state who acts like the President of France. He is elected directly for a term of four years and may not be eligible for re-election after having two terms consecutively. He may be removed by a very tedious process of impeachment. His very strong position is evident from his powers which may be enumerated as under:

1. He nominates the Prime Minister (head of the government) whose name is approved by the State Duma. If the Duma rejects such a nomination three times, he may dissolve it, appoint an interim Prime Minister, and call for parliamentary elections.
2. He presides over the meetings of the government.
3. In case the Duma passes a vote of no-confidence against the government, it must be repassed within three months. In the meantime he can call new parliamentary elections, even though by remaining in office.
4. He may issue 'decrees' having the force of law and may over-ride a resolution or decision of the Parliament.
5. He is chief of the armed forces and heads the Security Council that holds the charge of security matters.
6. The Prime Minister or his ministers may also issue decrees, but the President may over-ride them.
7. He gives his assent to the bills passed by the Parliament.

---

28. Mark Kesselman: "France" in Kasselman, Joel Krieger and William A. Joseph (ed): *Comparative Politics at the Crossroads* (Lexington: D.C. Heath and Company, 1996), p. 129.
29. *Strong, op.cit., p.266*
30. Curtis, *op. cit.*, p. 221.

8. He recommends names to the Federation Council for appointment of the judges of the Constitutional Court, Supreme Court and Supreme Arbitration Court.
9. He appoints ambassadors and receives ambassadors of other countries to maintain foreign relations.
10. He may issue a declaration of emergency covering the country as a whole or any of its parts.

"The structure embodied in the constitution resembles the French presidential system in many ways, but some critics in Russia call it an authoritarian constitution, becasue it places so much power in president's hands."[31]

Chancellor Government : The German Model

The structure of government in Germany pertains to the parliamentary and not to the presidential model, though it may be treated as a variant of the English model on account of the very strong position of the Chancellor. The Chancellor is the real working head of the state. His name is proposed by the President; he is elected by absolute majority of the Bundestag and is responsible to it. The Chancellor appoints the ministers individually who are responsible to him and not to the Parliament (Bundestag), though they are parliamentary deputies and they can be asked to resign by him. The Chancellor is removable only by a constructive vote of no-confidence which entails the election of a successor by absolute majority of the Bundestag. This is difficult to obtain under the present conditions. It is possible only when there is a serious spilt in the ruling party as happened in 1966 when Chancellor Ludwig Erhard was replaced by Kurt Kiesinger.[32]

The Chancellor may advise the President to dissolve the Parliament (Diet) or to issue a declaration of the state of 'legislative emergency' that for a period of six months can enable government bills to become law if the upper chamber (Bundesrat) had consented to them even if they had been rejected by the Bundestag. The Chancellor determines the general policy of the.government. The ministers are responsible for the conduct of their departments and they can make decisions on concrete individual matters. The relationship between the Chancellor and his ministers and the reconciliation of the sometimes conflicting principles of hierarchical powers placed in the Chancellor, collegial or cabinet decisions making, and ministerial autonomy have been a matter of empirical approach than conscious theory. The policy of the Chancellor is outlined in official instructions to ministers. He is assisted by a Chancellory of about 100 officials headed by a Secretary. This administrative wing has control over all ministers. The contact between the Chancellor and his ministers is maintained through the Chancellory.

The ministers can introduce legislative and budgetary proposals, they cannot take important decisions without the consent of the Chancellor. It shows that the office of a minister does not pertain to a powerful position. The constitution is not very clear so far as the principle of ministerial responsibility is concerned. It has been laid down that the Chancellor is accountable to the Bundestag, but the legislators may ask questions about the conduct of his ministers. As a matter of fact, the ministers are responsible to the Chancellor.

In spite of the fact that the German constitution places many limitations on the centralised executive power, the Chancellor may use his special powers in some situations.

1. As a leader of the majority party or a common leader of the coalition, he picks up members of his Cabinet who can best augment and support the executive branch.

---

31. Jean DeBourdeleben: "Russia" in Kasselman and others, *op. cit.*, p. 331.
32. Curtis, *op. cit.*, p. 224.

2. He relies on strong ministers in key posts, but he may assume ministerial responsibility himself in key areas such as economics and foreign policy.
3. He has considerable authority to govern by virtue of the power of the Federal Chancellory. It enables him to efficiently oversee the entire government as well as mediate conflicts among other ministers.
4. His position is strengthened by the 'constructive vote of no-confidence.' That is, he cannot be removed by the no-trust motion unless the Bundestag elects his successor. It cannot happen unless the opposition is well united.[33]

Council Government : The Swiss Model

A very peculiar form of executive obtains in Switzerland, the 'ancestral home of democracy' that, as remarked by Lord James Bryce, 'deserves the best study'. Though looking like a wonderful combination of the English and American models and at the same time fundamentally different from both, the Federal Council (Bundesrat) is a peculiarly Swiss institution. It is well observed : "No executive system in the world is so deserving as that of Switzerland, for the founders of the Swiss Constitutions of 1848 and 1874 would appear to have succeeded in a project which has baffled the ingenuity of all previous statesmanship, and especially that of France, namely, to combine the merits and exclude the defects of both the parliamentary and non-parliamentary executive systems."[34]

The Federal Council is a body of seven ministers (Presidents) who are elected by the Federal Parliament in its joint session for a period of four years. The Councillors hail from different provinces (cantons) of the Confederation, though convention requires that the three big cantons of Zurich, Berne and Vaud should be invariably represented. According to another well-established convention, the same Councillors are elected again and again until any one of them declines. The result is that Swiss ministers enjoy a very long tenure going upto three decades or so. In case the legislature is dissolved earlier, the Federal Council also stands dissolved. The new elections take place and the new Federal Parliament elects the Councillors again. Thus, the tenure of the Federal Councillors is linked to the tenure of the federal legislature. All ministerial departments are divided among these seven presidents.

One of the presidents of the Federal Council is formally designated by the Federal Parliament as the President of the Confederation for a year and one more as its Vice-President on the basis of seniority. The office of the President rotates as a result of which the Vice-President becomes the President after the year is over and he is succeeded by the Vice-President. The Councillor junior to him is designated as the Vice-President. Thus, the office of the President rotates among the seven Councillors and the same person may have it after every seventh year in case he continues to hold his position in the Federal Council. The Swiss President has no special powers. He is just a ceremonial head designated for a year. In short, the office of the President "has no true national significance. It confers no special privileges, nor even any particular influence."[35]

The members of the Federal Council take part in the deliberations of the Federal Assembly; they prepare budget and legislative proposals and get them passed by the legislature. They answer questions put to them by the members of the legislature, but they cannot vote. They cannot be removed by the vote of no-confidence or by the process of impeachment. They also belong to different political parties and yet they

33. Christopher S. Allen: "Germany" in Kasselman and others, *op. cit.,* p. 196.
34. Strong, *op. cit.,* p. 266. The new constitution of Switzerland came into effect on 1 January, 2000.
35. W.E. Rappard : *The Government of Switzerland,* p. 379.

never cultivate political differences that shows the peculiarly flexible character of the Swiss people. They cannot be the members of the Parliament also. The entire administration of the country is run by this Council which, on account of being a collegial body of seven presidents, is rightly called a 'plural executive'. It may be pointed out that though some points of resemblance may be discovered between the Swiss Federal Council on the one side and English or American cabinets on the other, it is peculiarly a Swiss institution that is not only a committee of the legislature, but it also lives and acts under it. As a leading Swiss writer says : "The theory of the Swiss constitution seems to be that the executive is not an independent or co-ordinate branch of government but the servant of the legislature."[36]

Critical Appraisal

The executive is the most important organ of the political organisation. As already pointed out, the classical theory of the three organs of the government having equal powers stands thoroughly discredited in modern political systems. The executive consists of the political leaders of the country who "emerge either by displaying outstanding ability or by showing themselves competent to carry out a necessary activity."[37] The days have gone when the legislature was known as the first and most powerful organ of the government. Curtis calls it'passing away of the golden age'. As Rodee remarks: "On the one hand, the earlier enthusiasm for the wisdom and competence of representative assemblies has declined; on the other, a century and more of experience with popularly elected (or popularly controlled) executive power has dissipated earlier suspicions and established confidence. Moreover, the rapidly multiplying problems and functions of democratic governments have virtually compelled the transfer of many powers from the legislature to the executive. The growing need for prompt governmental action in the fields of domestic and foreign policy has caused the modern legislature to delegate much legislative authority to the executive, subject as a rule to guiding principles and limitations set forth by the legislature."[38]

The need of the time is, however, not to wail at the decline of legislative authority but to think in terms of placing proper limits on the leadership of the executive. The authority of the rule-application department is integrally connected with the fact of political obligation. It is necessary that the people take the authority as 'legitimate'. The fate of the political system thus depends on the role of the political leaders who are said to be entrusted with three important functions, namely, founding, implementing and stabilising a regime.[39] What is thus needed is the imposition of proper checks on the authority of the executive so that it efficiently as well as properly performs its manifold functions that include the "creation of a welfare service, the extension of social welfare to the whole population, and the 'restoration of compassion', in Adlai Stevenson's words."[40]

---

36. Zurcher : "Switzerland" in Neumann (ed.) : *Governments of Continental Europe,* p. 994.
37. Curtis, *op. cit.,* p. 204.
38. Rodee and others : *Introduction to Political Science,* p. 123.
39. See Curtis, *op. cit.,* p. 205.
40. *ibid.,* p. 202.

25

Rule-Adjudication Department

> The political situation affecting the administration of justice at the state and local levels has particularly attracted the attention of political scientists, concerned with the allocation of justice (or the 'rationing of justice')—with why different members of the community are treated differentially by law enforcement officials. The topic is one which comes within the purview of public law mainly because those who have shown interest in it have been previously doing work in the public law field. The same is true with respect to the activities of the legal profession. While it is sociologists who have undertaken work on what can be called the 'ecology of the legal profession', that is the organisation and pattern of legal practice, political scientists have not been far behind, particularly in relating this structure to participation in politics.
>
> **—Stephen L. Wasby[1]**

Considering that one of the primary objects for which the political system is established is the protection of the rights of the individuals, the necessity of a judicial organ as the means through which this object is to be realised has been recognised from early times. If a society without a legislative organ "is conceivable and, indeed, fully developed legislative organs did not make their appearance in the life ol the state until modern times, but a civilised state without judicial organs and machinery is hardly conceivable."[2] However, the judicial department is not thoroughly immune from the effect of politics. It "is important to recognise that legal adjudication is not a process far removed from the world of politics, and that there is an interplay between the legal structure, the political culture and the political and social values of the judges, which all bring the legal system firmly into the arena of choice, priorities and conflicts."[3]

Judiciary : Meaning and Nature of Law and Political Process

Judiciary, in quite simple terms, may be defined as the third organ of government concerned with the job of doing justice. As its name indicates, it consists of the magistrates. and judges charged with the function of administration of justice. A pertinent question arises as to what is justice. According to earliest notion, it meant punishment to the wrong doer by one who was the aggrieved. The matter was related to the private offences as there was no executive machinery to effect the redressal of grievances. In course of time developed the idea of'king's peace'signifying that any offence that involved disorder or violence was an attack upon that peace to which the king could not be indifferent. Gradually, the notion of king's peace was extended to embrace offences such as theft, perjury and enforcement of contracts. It "marked

1. Wasby: *Political Science : The Discipline and Its Dimensions : An Introduction* (Calcutta : Scientific Book Agency, 1970), p. 479.
2. J.W. Garner : *Political Science and Government* (Calcutta : World Press, 1952), p. 750.
3. A.R. Ball : *Modern Politics and Government* (London : Macmillan, 1971), p. 204.

the beginning of the idea that crime was an offence not only against the individual victim but also against the state and that it belonged to the state to see that it was properly punished."[4]

In early times, the function of the administration of justice was done by some social association like church, guild and panchayat, or by influential landlords and nobles etc. over whose authority the state had hardly any over-riding jurisdiction. With the advent of sovereignty, the royal authority could deprive all such associations and feudal barons of exercising the power of administration of justice. Thus, in modern times, the transformation became complete, and the administration of justice became an exclusive function of the state. Not only this, administration of justice at the hands of the state assumed a sacrosanct character. It began to be felt as impossible to imagine any satisfactory substitute for the courts of justice. An American jurist Rawle comments : "It is indispensable that there should be a judicial department to ascertain and decide rights, to punish crimes, to administer justice, and to protect the innocent from injury to usurpation."[5]

The nature of law and political process finds its basically different forms in liberal-democratic and totalitarian systems. In a liberal-democratic system, the legal system is said to be characterised by such concepts as impartiality, consistency, openness, predictability and stability.[6] Rule of law signifies equality of all citizens in the eye of law and that a person is deemed as innocent unless he is convicted by a competent court. It is also required that the trial should be open and fair. It is based on this celebrated principle of jurisprudence: let a thousand culprits be acquitted, but not even a single innocent person be punished. It is a different thing that the powers of the courts are drastically cut during the days of emergency caused by the factors of external aggression or internal disturbances. It is also possible that severe restrictions are imposed during normal times in the name of 'interest of the state' that may be wide enough to give extra power to the police and confer increased jurisdiction on administrative tribunals. Despite this all, the judicial system and legal process of a liberal-democratic state remain basically different from that of a totalitarian state on account of the fact that there is no deliberate attempt on the part of the state to abrogate normal procedure and end of justice.

Opposed to this is the case of a totalitarian state where we find a basically different form of law and political process. Though some semblance of administration of justice may be given to civil cases in such countries, the elements of bias are very much present. The judicial process operates in a way that political opponents are punished by the courts without following the process of a free and open trial. Courts thus serve the purpose of the executive. The Communists, in particular, have no reservations in holding that they "see the legal system of liberal-democracies and non-Marxist totalitarian or autocratic states as instruments of class rule, and believe that the main functions of the courts in these systems are to legitimise and buttress the domination of the capitalist class."[7]

Recruitment and Functions of Judges

The judges may be nominated by the head of the state, or appointed by following a process of selection, or elected (whether directly or indirectly), or co-opted by the fellow judges. In a country like the United States, the judges are nominated by the President and their appointments are ratified by the Senate. In

4. Garner, *op. cit.,* p. 749.
5. *ibid.,* p. 750.
6. Ball, *op. cit.,* p. 205.
7. *ibid.,* p. 206.

India, only higher judges (those of the High Courts and Supreme Court) are appointed by the President who is required to act on the advice of his Council of Ministers. So far as the case of district judges and others serving under them is concerned, they are appointed after they are declared successful in written competitive examinations followed by personality tests. That is, here, the process of selection is at work. These judges get promotions from time to time on the basis of seniority and efficiency. However, the President has the power to appoint a distinguished jurist as a judge of the High Court or Supreme Court, while the Governor may nominate a renowned practising lawyer as a judge in a district court.

In Japan, the judges are designated by the Cabinet and their appointments are formally made by the monarch that are subsequently confirmed by the Diet. British judges, above magistrates, are selected from among the barristers. Germany and France provide the best examples of hierarchical career structures for judges. In both countries, the judges are appointed by the government after they acquire a university degree in law and then undergo a period of legal training following a stiff competitive examination. In a Communist country like China, the judges are elected by the legislature for a period of four years. The election of the judges for the lower courts takes place in some states of the United States of America.

Constitutional courts and courts which have the constitutional powers of adjudication as a part of their functions are even more involved in overt political considerations as regards the appointments of their judges. The Supreme Court of Canada, that was made the final court of appeal in 1949 when the jurisdiction of the Privy Council was abolished, invariably has three judges from the province of Quebec to ensure ethnic and religious balance. The 16 judges of the Federal Constitutional Court of Germany are elected by the Bundestag and Bundesrat (8 each) with 6 coming from the ranks of the career judges elected for life, and the other 10 being selected from the most important groups in the country such as political parties administration and other elite groups. These judges are recruited for a period of 12 years. The Constitutional Court of France, which may hardly be classified as a court in the strict sense of the term but which has the power to examine the constitutional validity of laws made by the Parliament has a different source of recruits from the regular and administrative courts. Its members are not professional judges, they are ex-Presidents of the republic with three judges appointed for 9 years each by the President, the National Assembly and the Senate.

The nature of the recruitment of judges is conditioned by the legal structures obtaining in a country. It also determines the character of the judiciary. For instance, there is a double system of courts in a federal country, but there is a single system in a country having unitary form of government. It may be possible that even in a federal state the two tiers of courts are integrated in a way that the judicial system of the provinces, in spite of being separated from that of the Centre, is somehow linked at the higher levels as we find in India. The High Courts, though looking like the third department of the State Governments, very much constitute a sub-department of the Supreme Court of India. Moreover, the powers of the High Court to hear appeals against the decisions of the district courts and their supervision over all subordinate courts speaks of the integrated nature of judiciary in the Indian federal system. Canada has only one system of courts, although it is a federal state. The Supreme Court of the Russian Federation stands at the top of a pyramid of the Supreme Courts of all the Union and Autonomous Republics with courts in area circuits and regions : at the lowest levels are people's courts in the town and rural areas.

There may be two types of courts to deal with ordinary and administrative laws as in France. There are administrative courts to deal with the cases of administrative law in France, while there is a single system of courts to deal with civil and administrative cases in other countries like Britain and India. Of course, there are separate courts in England to deal with civil and criminal cases at the higher level. For instance, the British House of Lords is the highest court of appeal in civil cases only. (It should be pointed out here that while the House of Lords sits as a Court, only 9 Law Lords take part in it.) The Judicial Committee of the Privy Council acts as a final court of appeal for some Commonwealth countries, or for any country that is under the colonial hold of the U.K. In Germany there are three types of courts—civil, criminal and constitutional —to try three types of cases.

The way judges are recruited has its effect on the character of judiciary. For instance, the British judges represent the upper middle class with conservative background, for they are recruited from among the barristers. Likewise, the judges in Germany and France represent the upper middle class. They have to choose a judicial career early in life. The methods of their recruitment and training mean that the recruits come from predominantly upper-middle class backgrounds. The nomination of the judges by the President in the United States and their subsequent ratifications by the Senate without any mention of their qualifications either in the Constitution or in the Acts of Judicature shows that only persons having high-class social background can have the appointments. It is only in countries having elected judges that the persons belonging to the lower class can have the chance to occupy the seats of justice. In a country having the process of selection of the judges by means of written competitive examinations (as in India) persons with lower middle class background may have chance of getting the posts of judges. It is obvious that the system of recruitment of judges very much affects the character of the judicial department.

The functions of the judiciary may be grouped under several heads with this remark that they differ from one political system to another :

1. The first and foremost function of the courts is administration of justice. The courts hear and decide cases—civil, criminal and constitutional—in which the parties involved in dispute present their arguments. The courts are called the defenders of the rights and liberties of the people. In countries having written constitutions, the courts are also entrusted with the power of interpreting the constitution. They are charged with the duty of upholding the constitution as the supreme law of the land and thus acting as the guardian of the constitution.
2. Though legislation is the work of the legislatures, the courts also legislate in a different way. What an American judge (Hughes) said is not a legal fiction but a fact that the 'judges do legislate'. Where a law is silent, or ambiguous, or appears to be inconsistent with some other law of the land, the courts decide what the law is and how it should prevail. In this respect, they are guided by the norms and rules of equity and judicial commonsense. The judicial precedents are thus laid down that are called case-laws.
3. In a federal system of government, the courts play the role of an independent and impartial umpire between the central and regional governments. They are charged with the work of interpreting the provisions of the constitution whenever there arises a dispute between the two 'co-ordinate' governments and their interpretation is regarded as the correct meaning of the terms of the fundamental law of the land. In this way, the courts of a federal country assume the status of a'constitutional court'. Though it is true that the decisions of the courts in most of the cases go in favour of the central government, it is not so in every case. Sometimes, the Supreme Court or the Constitutional Court does decide in favour

of the regional governments. As the movement in present times "has been towards stronger and more complex functions being given to national governments, constitutional courts as part of the political process have tended to reflect this movement."[8]

4. The courts are important agencies of legitimising the outputs of government. It is expected that the courts should keep themselves aware of the growing urges and aspirations of the people and, as Chief Justice P.B. Gajendragadkar of India once said, they should interpert the meaning of law dynamically in the light of obtaining situations. Thus, the courts should shun 'conservative' attitude no matter they, as the Canadian Supreme Court, may be accused by some traditionalists of having 'anti-civil liberties tendencies'. For this sake, the courts perform the task of contributing legitimacy to the decisions of the government. It is possible that an 'innovative' decision of the government is taken as unconstitutional by the people who challenge it in the court of law. It then becomes the job of the judges to examine the situation from a dynamic point of view and then deliver a judgment to give it the character of legitimacy. We may take note of the fact that even the American Supreme Court made a change in its outlook in 1937 when it ceased to regard economic regulations by the federal government as a serious threat to the basic structure of the constitution and that entailed an era of happy relationship between a strong executive and an equally strong, rather provoked to behave like a powerful judiciary. Such a great change in the behaviour of the American Supreme Court had its clear reflection in the *National Broadcasting Co. Case* of 1942 in regard to which Geoffery Marshall says: "The power of a Federal regulatory agency to make rules is justified by 'public convenience, interest or necessity', for example, might in earlier times have been struck down as an abdication of legislative responsibility, but is no longer so pictured."[9]

5. Allied with this is the function of the courts to stabilise and support the existing political system. The decisions of the court, as pointed out above, contribute the element of 'legitimacy' to the outputs of the government. It, thus, becomes essential (that the behaviour of the courts must not be obstructive or destructive so that the smooth running of the political organisation becomes a problem. The role of the political culture has its special importance in this direction. In the event of a confrontation between executive (or legislature) on the one hand and judiciary on the other, it is the attitude of the people that has a vital role to play. The political beliefs and convictions of the people alone can save the situation from reaching a point to the sheer detriment of any department of the government. If it becomes the function of the judiciary to see that no serious threat is posed to the stability and support of the political system, equally important is the function of the executive to see that no serious threat is posed to the independence and impartiality of those who are charged with the delicate task of administration of justice. The leading instance of the United States should once again be referred to. While the people supported the stand of the judges that the President should not be empowered to tamper with the composition of the Supreme Court (who had decided to 'pack up' the Supreme Court and a bill in this regard was moved in the Congress in 1937 that sought to extend the number of the judges from 9 to 15) and thus the controversial move was defeated, the Court,

8. Ball, *op. cit.*, p. 215.
9. Geoffery Marshall : *Constitutional Theory* (Oxford : Clarendon Press, 1971), p. 115.

on its part, "showed its political sensitivity by changing the policy that had given rise to the conflict."[10]

6. The most controversial function of the courts lies in their power of judicial review that signifies their authority to examine the validity of a legislative or administrative measure and then declare it, either in part or full, *'intra vires* or *ultra vires of the constitution'*. This unique power of the courts originated in the United States and has its best form there, though the case of India can be cited as the second best example in this regard. However, its weaker instances can be found in other countries also like Germany, Italy, Australia and South Africa. The exercise of this power by the courts often creates a situation of confrontation between the executive (including legislative) and judicial departments as we may find in the United States. It is possible that a strong political culture may exercise its weight to keep the two departments in their proper places, or in the case of its being too weak, the executive may transgress its authority to over-ride the onslaught of the judicial review as we find in the case of South Africa.

As already pointed out, the functions of the courts differ from one political system to another, though most of them, as given above, are common to all and which lay down the basic line of distinction between the executive, legislative and judicial spheres. Keeping such functions of the courts in view, it has been said that judicial power, according to one dictum, means "the power which every sovereign must of necessity have to decide controversies between itself and its subjects... (involving) some tribunal which has power to give a binding and authoritative decision (whether subject to appeal or not)".[11] Another dictum is that the holder of judicial power "investigates, declares, and enforces liabilities as they stand on present or past facts and under laws supposed already to exist."[12]

Judicial Review

Meaning and Essential Maxims : Judicial review may be defined as "the power of a court to hold unconstitutional any law or official action that it deems to be in conflict with the basic law, or the constitution."[13] Prof. Henry J. Abraham defines judicial review as "the power of any court to hold unconstitutional and hence unenforceable any law, any official action based upon it, and any illegal action by a public official that it deems to be in conflict with the basic law."[14] In other words, judicial review "is the power exercised by the courts of a country to examine the actions of the legislative, executive and administrative arms of government and to ensure that such actions conform to the provisions of the nation's constitution. Actions not so conforming are considered unconstitutional, *i.e.,* illegal and of no effect. The institution of judicial review is predicated upon the existence of a written constitution that is also rigid in the sense of being changeable only by some extraordinary process, usually requiring some special legislative or popular (referendal) majorities. Normally, though not invariably, judicial review is associated also with a federal constitution, involving division of legislative powers between a central government and member-states or provisions and with a bill of rights or some other system of fundamental limitations in law-making power."[15]

Judicial review is, therefore, a power in the hands of the courts to look into the constitutional validity of a legislative or

10. Ball, *op. cit.,* p. 215.
11. Marshall, *op. cit.,* p. 119.
12. *ibid.*
13. Ferguson and McHenry : *The American Federal Government,* (New York : McGraw Hill, 1969), p. 612.
14. Abraham : *The Judicial Process* (Fair Lawn, New Jersey : Oxford University Press, 1962), p. 251.
15. *Encyclopaedia Britannica,* Vol. 13, p. 121.

administrative measure and then give a judgment in regard to its being *intra vires* or *ultra vires* of the constitution either in full or in relation to a particular part. As exercised by the American federal judiciary, in particular, this unique power of judicial power stands on certain well-accepted maxims that may be enumerated as under :

1. Before the court will glance at a particular issue or dispute, a definite 'case' or 'controversy' of law or inequity between *bona fide* adversaries under the constitution must exist, involving the protection or enforcement of valuable legal rights, or the punishment, prevention, or redress of wrongs directly concerning the party or parties bringing the judicial suit.
2. The party or parties bringing a suit must have a standing.
3. The court does not render advisory opinions.
4. The court will not entertain generalities, it will deal with specific and particular issues.
5. The party bringing a suit must be a sufferer and not a gainer by the challenged statute.
6. All other remedies have been exhausted before coming to Supreme Court.
7. The question under study must be of a substantial and not of a trivial nature.
8. The question of fact, as distinct from a question of law, is not normally accepted as a proper basis for the exercise of judicial review.
9. The court may change its views from time to time.
10. The court will not entertain political controversies; it will be concerned with legal aspects only.
11. The court will begin with the presumption that the statute under challenge is valid.
12. The court will not ordinarily impute illegal motives to the law-makers.
13. The court may declare the whole law or its part as invalid.
14. The court is not to be used as a check against inept, unwise and unrepresentative legislators.
15. If the court finds that it must hold a law unconstitutional, it will usually try hard to confine the holding to that particular section of the statute which was successfully challenged on constitutional grounds.

Judicial Review in the United States : The American constitution, as written in 1787, did not explicitly provide for what came to be known as the judicial review, rather the doctrine "was read into the Constitution by the Supreme Court at an early date."[16] It is given in Art. VI: "This Constitution, and the laws of the United States which shall be made in pursuance thereof; and all Treaties made, or which shall be made, under the authority of the United States, shall be the supreme law of the land." Another relevant provision is Art. Ill, Sec. 2, which says: "The judicial power shall extend to all cases, in law and equity, arising under this Constitution, the laws of the United States, and treaties made, or which shall be made, under their authority."

The power of judicial review originated in the United States in the leading case of *Marbury* v. *Madison* (1803) in which Chief Justice Marshall made a biting indictment of Jefferson's administration for dishonouring the commission (made in favour of Marbury by the outgoing President Adams in 1800 as justice of peace for the district of Columbia) and held: "It is emphatically the province and duty of judicial department to say what the law is...If, then, the courts are to regard the Constitution, and the Constitution is superior to any ordinary act of the legislature, the Constitution and not such ordinary act must govern the case to which they both apply." The opinion of Marshall is based on the following assumptions:

1. The Constitution is a written document that clearly defines and limits the powers of government.

16. Ferguson and McHenry, *op. cit.*, p. 267.

2. The Constitution is a fundamental law and superior to ordinary enactments.
3. An act of the legislature contrary to the fundamental law is void and therefore cannot bind the courts.
4. The judicial power, together with oaths to uphold the Constitution that judges take, imposes an inescapable responsibility upon the courts to declare unconstitutional those acts of Congress which contravene the fundamental law.

Marshall served as the Chief Justice of the United States till 1835 and he repeated his ingeniously invented power of judicial review in the case of *McCulloch* v. *Maryland* (1819) and *Gibbon* v. *Ogden* (1824). His successor Roger B. Taney (also written as Tawney) declared an act of the Congress unconstitutional in the leading case of *Scott* v. *Stanford* (1857). Thus, the American federal judiciary assumed a power that grew more and more formidable in due course so much so that the outstretched authority of the courts covered even those legislative and administrative measures that were made by the State governments. It led to an increasing criticism of the behaviour of the federal courts.

Things reached a point in the 1930's that a sort of constitutional struggle erupted between a President determined to implement his New Deal programmes in order to meet the economic crisis on the one side and a Court equally determined to protect and defend the Constitution on the other. The invalidation of the National Recovery Act (1933) by the Supreme Court infuriated President Roosevelt so much so that he labelled the Constitution of the United States as'a relic of horse and buggy days' in a mood of sheer irritation and annoyance and thought in terms of 'packing up the Court'. The result was the introduction of a bill in the Congress in 1937 to enhance the strength of the Supreme Court from 9 to 15 judges that would make room for the nomination of 6 additional judges amounting to the infusion of new blood in the federal judiciary. The Supreme Court judges took it as a matter of serious challenge to their authority. They jumped into the arena of politics to see that the bill could not be adopted by the federal legislature. The eruption of the Second World War in 1939 pushed the issue into the background and the death of President Roosevelt in 1945 closed the matter for ever. The only result of this constitutional struggle was the making of a law in 1947. It provides for the voluntary retirement of a judge on attaining the age of 70 or after completing a service of 10 years with all emoluments and facilities available to a judge in office.

Judicial Review in India : The power of judicial review is clearly engrafted into the Constitution of India vide Art. 13 that says:

1. All laws in force in the territory of India immediately before the commencement of this Constitution, in so far as they are inconsistent with the provisions of this Part, shall, to the extent of such inconsistency, be void.
2. The State shall not make any law which takes away or abridges the rights conferred in this Part and any law made in contravention of this clause shall, to the extent of contravention, be void.
3. In this article, unless the context otherwise requires:—

(a) 'law' includes any ordinance, order, bye-law, rule, regulation, notification, custom or usage having in the territory of India the force of law;

(b) 'laws in force' includes laws passed or made by a Legislature or other competent authority in the territory of India before the commencement of this Constitution and not previously repealed, notwithstanding that any such law or any part thereof may not be then in operation either at all or in particular areas.

4. Nothing in this article shall apply to any amendment of the Constitution made under Art. 368.

The power of judicial review, specially given to the Supreme Court and High Courts, is of a limited nature when we compare it with that of the power of the American federal judiciary. The scope of judicial review in our country is confined to the examination of the impugned matter on two counts: (i) whether the law under challenge falls within the competence of the authority that has framed it, and (ii) whether it is consistent with Part III of the Constitution having Fundamental Rights. Thus, judiciary in India cannot make use of that powerful tool that is known by the name of 'due process of law' in the United States.

As the power of judicial review has been specifically incorported into the Constitution, the Courts have made use if it ever since matters of constitutional dispute arose after its inauguration in Jan., 1950. In the *Champakam Durairajan* v. *The State of Madras Case* (1950), the Supreme Court struck down an order of the. Madras Government wherein reservation of seats in the medical colleges was made in such a way that the backward classes could have a position of discriminatory weightage at the time of seeking admissions. The Supreme Court in another leading case of *Smt. Bela Bannerji and others* v. *The State of West Bengal* (1954) ruled that the determination of compensation must be made according to the prevailing market rate if it was to be 'adequate'. The most formidable instance was afforded by the *Golak Nath Case* (1967) in which it was held that henceforth Parliament had no right to make constitutional amendment so as to abridge the scope of fundamental rights. The Supreme Court invalidated the Bank Nationalisation Act of 1969 and, similarly, held the order of the President void in regard to the *en masse* derecognition of the former rulers (making them disentitled for privy purses and privileges) as *ultra vires* of the Constitution in 1970. In the *Fundamental Rights Case* of 1973, it laid down the doctrine of the 'Basic Framework of the Constitution'. If a comparative study of the American and Indian Supreme Courts is made in this direction, it will appear that the latter is not as powerful as the former, nor can it be, on account of these points:

1. Indian Constitution deliberately substitutes the phrase'due process of law'as obtaining in the United States by another one 'procedure established by law' on the pattern of Japanese Constitution. There is a world of difference between the two in the sense that whereas the former leaves unlimited power in the hands of the courts to define what is due or undue process of law, the latter makes the courts bound to follow the procedure laid down by law as made by the legislature.
2. The rule of the supremacy of the Parliament has been well established. The Parliament may make another law to do away with the lacuna discovered by the Court while invalidating a particular legislative measure, or it may go to the extent of making a change in the Constitution to deprive the Court of the power of looking into the constitutional validity of a particular law. For instance, the 25th Constitution Amendment Act put the word 'amount' in place of the word 'compensation' in Art. 31 and that it also laid down that the provisions of Art. 13 shall not apply to a constitutional amendment act. The 44th Amendment of 1978 deleted right to property from Part III of the Constitution.
3. Above all, there is the provision relating to the appointment, retirement and impeachment of the judges. The judges of the Supreme Court and High Courts do not enjoy a life term as in the United States. They retire at the age of 62 in the High Courts and at 65 in the Supreme Court. Their appointments are made by the President acting on the invisible recommendation of the Prime Minister. Naturally, the factor of social philosophy of the judges forms an integral part of the considerations that take place before the nomination of a judge. It is also possible

that a junior judge be appointed as the Chief Justice and in that situation the superseded one or ones may tender resignation (s) in protest that may facilitate the task of the executive in regard to the elimination of the judge or judges whose social philosophy is not conducive to the policies and programmes of the government.

The position of the courts in regard to the exercise of the power of judicial review, as it obtains in our country, is evident from the observations of Justice S.K. Das as given by him in the case of *A.K. Gopalan* v. *State of Madras* (1951): "In India, the function of the judiciary is somewhat between the courts in England and the United States. While in the main leaving our Parliament and State legislatures supreme in their respective legislative fields, our Constitution has, by some of its articles, put upon the Legislatures certain specified limitations...The point to be noted, however, is that in so far as there is any limitation on the legislative power, the Court must, on a complaint being made to it, scrutinise and ascertain whether such limitation has been transgressed and if there has been any transgression, the Court will courageously declare the law unconstitutional, for the Court is bound by its oath to uphold the Constitution. But outside the limitations imposed on the legislative power, our Parliament and State legislatures are supreme in their respective legislative fields and the Court has no authority to question the wisdom or policy of the law duly made by the appropriate legislature. Our Constitution, unlike the English Constitution, recognises the court's supremacy over legislative authority, but such supremacy is a very limited one, for it is confined to the field where the legislative power is circumscribed by the limitations upon it by the Constitution itself."

Judicial Review in Other Countries : The study of judicial review is mainly related to the two great democratic countries of the world, (America and India) having written constitutions and federal systems of government. There is no place for judicial review in Communist countries where the judges are elected by the legislatures and they are required to honour the'will of the people'as embodied in the decisions of the ruling party having complete control over the law-making and law-application departments of the government. We may refer to the process of judicial review in some other democratic countries of the world. First, we take up the case of Britain. It is said that there is no judicial review in Britain as the Parliament is a sovereign law-making body. This is true that the English courts cannot look into the constitutional validity of a legislative measure made by the sovereign Parliament. However, they may exercise the power of judicial review over delegated legislation. The courts may look into the constitutional validity of an executive order issued by a department to supplement or amplify a law made by the Parliament by virtue of power delegated to it. If an executive action contravenes the law of the Parliament, in letter or in spirit (unless the Parliament itself so authorises or it provides to the contrary), the courts may strike it down. Second, the Federal Court of Switzerland has the power of judicial review that it may exercise in relation to the laws made by the Cantonal legislatures only.

Last, we may refer to the case of Japan. Art. 81 empowers the Japanese Supreme Court to exercise the power of judicial review. However, such formidable checks have been imposed on the functioning of the judges that the Court has not been able to use this power effectively. Provisions relating to the designation of the Chief Justice and other 14 judges by the real executive and their formal nominations by the monarch, their impeachment by the Diet and, above all, a review of their activities by the people at every general election, and also after every 10 years, are instances of the fact that Japanese Supreme Court is 'both a subject and an object of checks and balances'.[17] Even in the

17. A.W. Burks : *The Government of Japan* (London : Methuen, 1964), p. 164.

most controversial *Sunakawa Case* of 1957 (a dispute arisen out of the government's decision to acquire land in the Sunakawa village for the construction of a large military base for the American forces), the Court gave its judgment in favour of the Government of Prime Minister Kishi and did not agree with the contention of the appellants that the purpose behind the acquisition of land was contrary to Art. 9 of the Constitution enjoining upon the State to adopt the course of renunciation of war as an instrument of national policy. It is also owing to this general feeling among the Japanese intelligentsia that judicial review "would violate the principle of the separation of powers and the doctrine of legislative supremacy."[18]

Criticism : The power of judicial review, as exercised by the American and Indian Supreme Courts, has been highly attacked as well as defended by the students of politics and constitutional law. It is said that judicial review opens scope for more and more judicial debates signifying a 'paradise' for the lawyers. It virtually leads to a hostile confrontation between the executive and judicial departments. It is also commented that judicial review becomes an effective instrument at the hands of the vested interests owing to a highly conservative attitude of the courts. Further, the courts, instead of giving stability to judicial thought, tamper with their shifty stands as a result of which uncertainty prevails in the realm of law and justice. Above all, it elevates the position of the courts to act like the 'third chamber' or the 'super-house of the legislature'. Thus, there occurs the politicisation of the judiciary that seriously undermines the authority of the chosen representatives of the people. For instance, Justice Felix Frankfurter rightly visualised that "the phrase of 'Supreme Court's being the Constitution' cannot be accepted unless it is taken for granted that some of the judges, at least, are keen politicians by training and are keen enough to yearn for the Presidency even after they have become Justices of the Supreme Court."[19]

Viewed in a different perspective, judicial review looks like an essential instrument in the hands of the judges to work as the protectors of a democratic system. It is by virtue of this power that the judiciary can save the people from the onslaughts of the executive or legislative despotism. What is really needed is that the just custodians of the Constitution must not exercise their power in a way that leads to the intrusion of their personal philosophy into the social philosophy of the state and thereby causes a sort of hostile confrontation between the two departments of the political organisation. As Chief Justice Patanjali Sastri observes: "In evaluating such elusive factors and forcing their own conceptions of what is reasonable in all the circumstances of a given case, it is inevitable that the social philosophy and the scale of values of the judges participating in the decision should play an important part and the limit to their interference with the legislative judgments in such cases only be dictated by their sense of responsibility and self-restraint and the sobering reflection that the Constitution is meant not only for the people of their way of thinking but for all, and that the majority of the elected representatives of the people have, in authorising the imposition of the restrictions considered them to be reasonable."[20]

Critical Appraisal

In order to make an evaluation of the real nature of the role of the rule-adjudication department, we should move from normative to empirical directions. According to classical or traditional point of view, judiciary is not only the last essential, but also the only sacrosanct, department of the government. Sir Francis Bacon said that 'there is no worse torture than the

18. J.M. Maki : *Government and Politics in Japan* (New York: Praeger, 1962), pp. 105-108.
19. Laski : *The American Presidency,* p. 68.
20. *V.G. Row v. The State of Madras,* 1952, SGJ, 253.

torture of laws'. Chancellor Kent said: "Where there is no judicial department to interpret and execute the law, to decide controversies, and to enforce rights, the government must either perish by its own imbecility, or the other department of government must usurp powers for the purpose of commanding obedience to the destruction of liberty." Its best representation is seen in the statement of Lord James Bryce who says: "There is no better test of excellence of a government than the efficiency of its judicial system, for nothing more nearly touches the welfare and security of the average citizen than his sense that he can rely on the certain and prompt administration of justice. Law is respected and supported when it is treated as the shield of innocence and the impartial guardian of every private civil rights. If the law be dishonestly administered, the salt has lost its flavour, if it be weakly or fitfully enforced, the guarantees of order fail...if the lamp of justice goes out in darkness, how great is the darkness."[21]

A different conclusion is arrived at when we examine the nature and role of judiciary from a purely empirical point of view. We find that politics pervades everywhere and judiciary remains no exception that can be discovered in three essential points. The very process of the recruitment of judges opens room for the politicisation of judiciary. The President exercises his power of nomination of the judges (as in the United States) from a political point of view and the same element can be traced in their ratification by the Senate. To take a concrete case, we can say that the nomination of Justice Fortas as the Chief Justice of the American Supreme Court (made by President Lyndon B. Johnson in 1968) was withdrawn as there was a lot of opposition to this proposal in the name of his (Fortas's) huge financial involvements. In a country like India where the nomination of a judge falls within the area of discretionary powers of the head of the state, the appointments are made on the recommendation of the Cabinet that is invariably guided by the considerations of politics. Thus, we find the cases of supersession of judges in the Supreme Court and High Courts. The very consideration of 'social philosophy' of the judges speaks of the fact that what really matters is 'political' consideration. So, in other countries where judges are appointed on the recommendation of the real executive, the factor of political consideration has its decisive part. One may discover a difference of degree, but not of kind, while comparing the methods of the appointment of judges in these countries. Nothing but politics counts, and that too in a quite naked form, when we study the method of the recruitment of judges in a Communist or an authoritarian country. Since the very recruitment of the judges is a political matter, they can hardly remain immune from the influence of this factor in an absolute sense.

What further adds to the stock of the politicisation of the judges is the offensive role of the executive and legislative departments. In most of the countries the executive heads deprecate the tendency of 'judicial autonomy' and they take it as a matter of challenge to their authority when the decisions of the courts go against their wishes. This lack of tolerance has its unfortunate part that may be checked by the existence and operation of a strong political culture only. New and still new laws are made or executive orders promulgated to see that the authority of the executive prevails over and against the will of the judges as they 'represent the will of the people'. The administrators and the legislators may go to the extreme stage of criticising the conduct of the judges or starting impeachment proceedings against any to create a sense of fear, even terror. We know that there was a faint move in India to impeach two judges of the Supreme Court who had delivered

21. Bryce : *Modern Democracies,* Vol. II, p. 422.

their judgment against the government in 1969 in the Bank Nationalisation Case on the plea that they had their shares in the nationalised banks. We may refer to the case of South Africa where in 1955 the government of Strijdom managed to set up a High Court of Parliament to over-ride the decisions of the Appeal Court and increased the number of judges in it to see that its ardently desired 'coloured voters legislation' was validated. Under such conditions, the judges have to jump into the arena of politics.

Finally, the judges live like conscientious citizens of the country. They read newspapers and books, listen radio commentaries and see telecasting programmes, attend important meetings etc. in order to keep themselves aware of the events going on in the country and abroad. Thus, they have their own inhibitions, reservations and value judgments that have their reflection on their judicial conduct. Their social backgrounds also have their own impact. The result is that the judges, in a peculiar way, come to reconcile their judicial independence with the judicial sensitivity to social, economic and political pressures. What Dahl has said about the American Supreme Court has its application to the higher judiciary of other countries also, though in varying degrees, that it "is inevitably a part of the dominant national alliance. As an element in the political leadership of the dominant alliance, the Court, of course, supports the major policies of the alliance."[22]

Viewed thus, we should say that the courts have their share in the political process of a country, though this varies with the nature of the political system and the political culture of the people. What is really desired is that the role of the courts should be appreciated and there should be no hostile confrontation between the real administrators and the honest adjudicators. Cooperation and conflict between the two should go together so that the political system is more and more developed, not decayed. All organs of the government must live in their places and a situation of happy interaction go on between them. It is well observed: "The courts are the part of the political process and one should stress cooperation as much as conflict. They interact with other parts of the political system, not as illegitimate outsiders but as part of the stable ruling political alliance."[23]

22. R.A. Dahl : *Pluralist Democracy in the United States* (Chicago, 1967), pp. 167-68.
23. Ball, *op. cit.*, p. 219.

26

Separation of Powers

> The co-ordinateness or equality of the legislative and other functions means simply that all are equally allotted their role by the constitution in the American style of separation of powers. None is supreme in allotting powers to the others. But it does not follow from this that they are equally entitled to exercise any particular function. Their functions and capacities are different and their impacts upon each other must be different in consequence. Adjudication must by definition have an impact upon everything in the system. The subjection of legislators, amongst others, to the law does not make the legislature an inferior branch, or detract from its co-ordinate status.
>
> — **Geoffrey Marshall[1]**

Government is the agency through which the will of the state is formulated, expressed and realised. The organisation of this agency of the state can be viewed either territorially, *i.e.,* government at the national, provincial or regional and local levels, or functionally, *i.e.,* government acting through its rule-making, rule-application and rule-adjudication departments. The theory of the separation of powers belongs to the functional aspect. It desires that the government should have three organs— executive, legislature and judiciary— and that the powers of all of them should be separated from each other. It is obvious that this doctrine rejects the 'duality theory' according to which the government has only two organs (legislature and executive as judiciary is not an independent but a sub organ of the executive); it accepts the trinity theory according to which government has three organs and further stresses that the powers of each department should be separated from the other if the liberty of the people is to be saved from the crushing authority of the state. It is a different matter that in modern times varying meanings have been given to the idea of the separation of powers and varying interpretations have been devised to present a restatement of this theory with a view to make its empirical character up-to-date with the result that the phrase separation of powers "has become one of the most confusing in the vocabulary of political and constitutional thought."[2]

Meaning : Classical and Modern Interpretations

As pointed out above, the doctrine of the separation of powers implies that there should be three separate organs of government with their separate sets of powers. In other words, it implies that the three organs of government should be kept apart from each other in the interest of individual liberty. The functions of the government should be differentiated and performed by distinct organs consisting of different bodies of persons so that each department is limited to its respective sphere of activity and not be able to encroach upon the

1. Marshall: *Constitutional Theory* (Oxford : Clarendon Press, 1971), p. 109.
2. *ibid.,* p. 97.

independence and jurisdiction of another. The whole idea is based on the maxim that power should be a check to power. Thus, the constitution should be so designed that no organ of government be made to do things to which it is not obliged or empowered.

A classical or 'pure' interpretation of the doctrine of separation of powers is thus given by M.J.C. Vile: "It is essential for the establishment and maintenance of political liberty that the government be divided into three branches or departments, the legislature, the executive and judiciary. To each of these three branches there is a corresponding identifiable function of government, legislative, executive or judicial. Each branch of the government must be confined to the exercise of its own function and not allowed to encroach upon the functions of other branches. Furthermore, the persons who compose these three agencies of government must be kept separate and distinct, no individual being allowed to be at the same time a member of more than one branch. In this way, each of the branches will be a check to others and no single group of people will be able to control the machinery of the state."[3]

Though keeping in his mind the special case of the American constitution, Prof. E.S. Corwin sums up the following propositions of the doctrine of separation of powers:[4]

1. There are three intrinsically distinct functions of government —the legislative, the executive and the judicial;
2. These distinct functions ought to be exercised respectively by three separately manned departments of government;
3. Which should be constitutionally equal and mutually independent; and
4. ...the legislature may not delegate its powers.

A modern interpretation of the theory of separation of powers has a wider connotation. It not merely hinges on the essential point of the 'separation' of powers, it also covers a cluster of over-lapping ideas as 'distribution', 'differentiation', 'isolation' and 'confrontation'. "Not all of these are synonymous and the implications of some are mutually inconsistent. At least the following may be distinguished:

1. The *differentiation* of the concepts 'legislative', 'executive' and 'judicial'.
2. The *legal incompatibility* of office holding as between members of one branch of government and those of another, with or without *physical separation* of persons.
3. The *isolation, immunity,* or *independence* of one branch of government from the actions or interference of another.
4. The *checking* or *balancing* of one branch of government by the action of another.
5. The *coordinate* status and lack of accountability of one branch to another.

Reference to the separation of powers may be references to any one or to any combination of these ideas."[5]

Main Exponents: Montesquieu's Classic Contribution for the Protection of Individual Liberty

The idea of the separation of powers has a long historical background, since it may be said to begin with those political thinkers who contributed to the trinity theory of the organs of government. Aristotle designated three parts of government as deliberative, executive and judicial. In the Roman period, Cicero and Polybius emphasised three organs of government, no matter they dwelt on the excellence of a mixed system of government. This idea became more popular in the modern age. Jean Bodin faintly touched this subject. It

3. M.C.J. Vile : *Constitutionalism and the Separation of Powers* (Oxford: Clarendon Press, 1967), p. 13.
4. Corwin: *Constitution of the United States of America: Analysis and Interpretation,* pp. 9-10.
5. Marshall, *op. cit.,* p. 100.

is Locke who gave a clear explanation when he discussed the forms and organs of government. He said that it "may be too great temptation to human frailty, apt to grasp at power for the same persons who have the power of making laws to have also in their hands the power to execute them, whereby they may exempt themselves from obedience to the laws they make."[6]

The best exposition of this doctrine is, however, contained in the work of Montesquieu who should be described as the worthy disciple of Locke in this regard. He says: "When the legislative and executive powers are united in the same person, or in the same body of magistrates, there can be no liberty; because apprehension may arise, lest the same monarch or Senate should enact tyrannical laws, and execute them in a tyrannical manner. Again, there is no liberty if the judiciary power be not separate from the legislative and the executive. Were it joined with the legislative, the life and liberty of the subjects would be exposed to arbitrary control, for the judge would then be legislator. Were it joined to the executive power, the judge might behave with violence and oppression. There would be an end of everything, were the same man or the same body, to exercise those three powers, that of enacting laws, that of executing the public resolutions, and of trying the cases of individuals."[7]

In this way, Montesquieu endeavours to establish that whoever has unrestrained power will abuse it. His chief contention is that individual liberty is certainly endangered when the two organs of government are combined. When the legislature and the executive are combined, the liberty of the people is jeopardised, because the makers and executors of law are the same. If the legislature and judiciary unite together, again liberty is destroyed inasmuch as law-makers become the interpreters and administrators of law as well. If the organs of executive and judiciary are aligned, the same agency becomes the prosecutor and interpreter of law with the result that the liberty is killed. The sum and substance of the whole analysis is that if the three organs of government are united in the same hands, then there would be 'an end of everything.'

Separation of Powers in the United States : Application of the Doctrine with the System of Checks and Balances

The theory of Montesquieu had its definite influence upon the Founding Fathers of the United States. A leading figure like James Madison thus wrote in the *Federalist* : "No political truth is certainly of greater intrinsic value, or is stamped with the authority of more enlightened patrons of liberty than that the accumulation and concentration of all powers—legislative, executive and judicial —in the same hands-.whether one, few or many and whether they are elected, appointed, nominated or hereditary...may justly be pronounced the very definition of tyranny." Montesquieu thus became the intellectual father of the American constitution-makers who vested executive power in the President, legislative power in the Congress, and judicial power in the Supreme Court and federal courts under it. As a result, no feature of the American governmental system "is more characteristic than the separation of powers, combined with precautionary checks and balances."[8]

The separation of powers thus constitutes the hallmark of the American constitutional

6. Locke : *Second Treatise of Civil Government,* Ch XII, Para 143.
7. Montesquieu : *Spirit of the Laws* (Eng. Trans. by Thomas Nugent and edited by Franz Neumann), Book VI, pp. 151-52.
8. Ogg and Ray : *Essentials of American Government,* p. 38. L.P. Baradat well observes that the "basic powers of three branches are, indeed, separate and unique; however, some of the powers of each branch overlap with those of the other two. These overlapping powers are called the *checks and balances*". *Political Ideologies : Their Origins and Impact* (Englewood Cliffs, New Jersey : Prentice-Hall, 1979), p. 119.

system. The American Supreme Court in the case of *Kilbourn* v. *Thomson* (1880) thus observed: "It is believed to be one of the chief merits of the American system of written constitutional law that all powers entrusted to government, whether state or national, are divided into three general departments, the executive, the legislative and the judicial. That the functions appropriate to each of these branches of government shall be vested in a separate body of public servants, and that the perfection of the system requires that the lines which separate and divide these departments shall be broadly and clearly defined. It is also essential to the successful working of the system that the persons entrusted with the power in any of these branches shall not be permitted to encroach upon the powers confided to others, but that each shall by the law of its creation be limited to the exercise of the powers appropriate to its own department and no other."[9]

The fundamental contribution of the American Founding Fathers should be seen in their design of checks and balances that they invented to make the system of separation of powers workable. What Locke and Montesquieu gave as the first half was supplemented with the second half at the Philadelphia Convention of 1787 with the result that the theoretical affirmation of the lovers of liberty became an empirical proposition. The American leaders were not only political theorists, they were natural scientists as well. Though they agreed with Montesquieu's idea of taking inspiration from the trilogy of the sun, the moon and the earth as three planets made by the nature, they also looked at the law of constellation whereby all the three planets are connected with each other. The theory of the separation of powers thus came to have a workable form at the hands of the American Founding Fathers. The practical proposal contained in the doctrine of separation of powers "requires that each of these powers be attributed to separate person or body of persons. It was, however, never proposed that the exercise of all of each power be entrusted to one person or one body. The doctrine of checks and balances requires, on the contrary, that after the main exercise has been attributed to one person or body, care should be taken to set up a minor participation of all in all, by way of budget and impeachment, judicial review of ordinances and laws and finally pardon."[10]

It is due to this that the three organs of the American government, though separated, are connected with each other by the system of checks and balances. Though executive authority is vested in the President, it is required that all appointments made and foreign treaties concluded by him be confirmed by the Senate. In case the President is found guilty of misbehaviour, or of violation of the constitution, he can be removed by the process of impeachment. The House of Representatives shall prepare a charge-sheet against the President and the Senate shall decide by two-thirds votes. Executive orders given by the President are subject to the power of judicial review. The President takes the oath of his office in the presence of the Chief Justice to defend and protect the constitution that smacks of the great moral check on his authority. In this way, the President is under the checks of the Congress as well as of the Supreme Court. The Congress is also under the check of both the President and the Supreme Court. All bills passed by the Congress are subject to the Presidential veto. In case the President abuses his veto power by rejecting a bill passed by the Congress, the Congress may over-ride Presidential veto by re-adopting the bill by two-thirds majority. The Supreme Court may declare a law, in part or full, null and void in case it is found to be against the constitution or the due process of law. Finally, the Supreme

9. See Carl J. Friedrich : "Separation of Powers" in E.A.R. Seligman (ed.) *Encyclopaedia of the Social Sciences* (New York : Macmillan, 1967), Vol. VI, p. 663.
10. *ibid.*, p. 666.

Court is under the checks of the President on the one side and of the Congress on the other. The judges are appointed by the President and Senate confirms their nominations. The Chief Justice takes the oath of his office in the presence of the President. The Congress may pass a bill to increase the strength of or confer more jurisdiction on the Court. In case of proved misbehaviour, incapacity or violation of the constitution, a judge may be removed by the process of impeachment.

Many important changes have taken place in the American constitutional system with the result that the 'basic feature of the constitution', as described by Charles A. Beard, has undergone serious transformation. The President has immensely enhanced his authority so much so that the Congressional check over his powers has become almost a matter of constitutional fiction. The Senate generally confirms the appointments made by him and the President often supersedes the requirement of Senatorial ratification of foreign treaties made by him in the name of their being 'executive agreements'. So tedious is the process of impeachment that a President rarely bothers for it. On the other extreme, the Supreme Court has immensely expanded its scope of authority in the name of its power of judicial review. The desired balance is hardly at work as the position of the Congress has become too weak as compared to the positions of the President in the executive and of the Supreme Court in the judicial spheres. As Marshall says: "In fact, American separation of powers theory seems a mixture of ideas about isolating, checking, balancing and interacting. These were sometimes brought into a sort of inconsistency by the argument that mutual checks and powers of interaction were necessary practical ways of protecting and preserving the original 'paper' separation or isolation."[11]

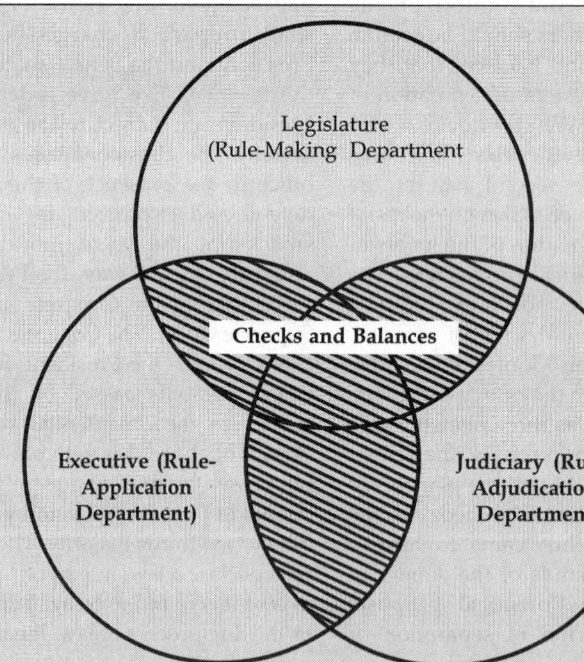

Separation of Powers: Checks and Balances

11. Marshall, *op. at.,* p. 103.

Critical Appraisal

The theory of the separation of powers has its shortcomings. Though it is true that the three organs of government should be kept apart, it should be remembered that their absolute separation is an impossibility. Montesquieu forgets that the government is an organic whole whose three organs are integrally connected and in the interest of responsibility and efficiency they cannot be separated. In the modern age of specialisation, it is true that the three organs of government correspond to three different modes of action, even then no organ can be left in complete isolation.[12] The theory also wrongly advocates that all departments are equal, because with the growth of democracy the responsibilities of the legislature have become much more than those of the executive and the judiciary. The idea of separation of powers does not apply to the political system of a totalitarian country. It is also argued that in modern welfare states, the functions of the executive have much widened. In brief, the separation of governmental functions would inevitably create frequent deadlocks as each department acting in defence of its own powers "would never lend its aid to other and the consequent loss in efficiency would outweigh all the possible advantages arising from independence."[13]

It is said that the main purpose behind the theory of separation of powers is the protection of individual liberty. One may say that the liberty of the individual can be protected even when there is no separation of powers as we find in Britain. Moreover, it may be that there is little protection of individual liberty in the midst of separation of powers obtaining in a country. What is really required is the existence of a strong public opinion, or a very developed political culture, as is said in the language of comparative politics, that can keep the government in its place. Keeping in mind the merit of the English constitutional system, where there is concentration instead of separation of powers, Laski says that the legislatures "would not fulfil their tasks unless they were able both to interfere in the execution of law, and also on occasion, to over-rule by statute the decisions of the judges the results of which are widely felt to be unsatisfactory."[14]

While dealing with the 'disutility' of this theory, Marshall says that it "seems to suffer from the following disabling deficiencies :

1. It is rarely clear whether, and in what sense, there is such a separation. The argument that legislative, executive, and judicial powers are constitutionally declared to be vested in particular persons or bodies is inconclusive.
2. If there is a separation of powers it is unclear what is that is separated, since the notions of'legislation', 'adjudication' and 'execution' have not proved capable of precise definition.
3. The concept of 'separation' itself has been used to cover the ideas of physical separation of persons, legal incompatibilities between rules or offices, differentiation of functions, isolation or immunity of agencies, and mutual checking, supervision, or policing of one branch by another.
4. In considering the mixing of governmental functions different treatment has been given to the division between legislative and executive functions from that accorded to the division between the judicial and other two functions. The doctrine provides no guidance as to whether this differing treatment is appropriate or necessary or whether voluntary transfers or partial delegations of function between branches of government are legitimate.

In short, the principle is infected with so much imprecision and inconsistency that it may be counted little more than a jumbled portmanteau of arguments for policies which

12. Ernest Barker : *Principles of Social and Political Theory,* p. 261.
13. See John Stuart Mill : *Considerations on the Representative Government.*
14. Laski : *An Introduction to Politics,* p. 63.

Some Important Statements about Separation of Powers

The purpose of the doctrine of separation of powers is to fragment government power in such a way as to defend liberty and keep tyranny at bay. In its formal sense, it demands *independence*, in that there should be no overlap of personnel between the branches. However, it also implies *interdependence* in the form of shared powers to ensure that there are checks and balances.

—Andrew Heywood
Politics, p. 315.

The feasibility of making a radical separation between legislation and the judicial process, or between the making of a policy and control over its execution, would hardly have commended itself in any age to a political realist.

— George H. Sabine
A History of Political Theory, p. 559.

Montesquieu was searching for means to limit the crown, to make a constitution, to build equals through which, but not over which, power should stream to create intermediary bodies, to check and balance probable despotism and yet he did not wish to fly to the extreme of democracy.

— Herman Finer
Theory and Practice of Modern Government, p. 98.

ought to be supported or rejected on other grounds."[15]

Despite certain points of criticism, as given above, we may highlight the importance of this theory by adding that it is one of those monumental doctrines of political theory whose purpose is to save the liberty of the individual from the arbitrary power of the state. Though Montesquieu made some misjudgments about the English constitutional system or the political developments of the United States have taken away much of what was really desired by the Founding Fathers, we cannot but appreciate the observation of Carl J. Friedrich that constitutional democracy "presupposed a balanced system of divided powers, for only within such a system could the citizens hope to enjoy a measure of independence and freedom through a guarantee of civil liberties"[16]

I5. Marshall, *op. cit.*, p. 124.
16. *Encyclopaedia Britannica,* Vol. 20, p. 227.

27

Political Elites

> Power shows many faces and takes many forms. It may be as visible as the policeman's badge or billy or as veiled as the politician's whisper in the back room. It may exist as an overwhelming presence or as a potential that can be drawn on at will. It may appear in the form of money, sex appeal, authority, administrative regulation, charisma, munitions, staff resources, instruments for torture. But all these resources must have this in common : they must be relevant to the motivations of the power recipients.
>
> **—James MacGregor Burns[1]**

The political process of a modern state involving participation of the people in it, as much as possible, seems to stand on a mythical assumption if the study of politics is made in the light of certain oligarchical elements obtaining invariably in every political system of the world, whether primitive or modern, developed or developing, democratic or totalitarian. In recent times, serious attempts have been made by a good number of social and political theorists to refute the normative interpretations of the democratic form of government as a rule of the people and by the will of the people. With a view to make an empirical study of politics, they have sought to prove the fact of limited political participation and thereby made a frontal attack on the operational dimension of the liberal-democratic system as conceived by the people of the world. Such a study revolves around the assumption that "however much one may try to be democratic in one's political system, there is a strong element of oligarchy in every organisation. The larger the organisation, so it is argued, the greater is the tendency towards oligarchy."[2] Ball puts the same in a better way when he adds: "But there is agreement that forms of representative government are merely disguises to cover minority control; the majority cannot control this ruling minority. There are problems of who actually constitute the political elite and whether it is defined narrowly or widely; also there are differences on the means of recruitment, but there is unanimity on the inevitability of the minority rule."[3]

Theory of Political Elites : Nature and Essential Implications

Political theory "always reflects on political practice and in many ways the political circumstances of the time favoured attempts to theorise about the nature of control and the role of leadership in society."[4] As a result, the study of political elites has become a part of modern political theory. Leading social theorists like Michels, Mosca, Pareto, Gasset, Burnham, C. Wright Mills and Lasswell have sought to prove that there "may exist in any society a minority

1. Burns : *Leadership* (New York : Harper & Row, 1978), p. 17.
2. Doughlas V. Verney : *An Analysis of Political Systems* (London : Routledge and Kegan Paul, 1959), p. 10.
3. A.R. Ball : *Modern Politics and Government* (London : Macmillan, 1976) p. 258.
4. Geraint Parry : *Political Elites* (London : George Allen and Unwin, 1969), p. 15.

of the population which takes the major decisions in the society."[5] Realisation of this political truth has led social and political scientists to write on the significance of the elite theory in contemporary political analysis. While highlighting the importance of this momentous subject, Lasswell adds : "By this time recognition is widespread that the world-inclusive study of power elites is indispensable to all serious inquiry into political processes. If inquiry is directed towards the past, to retrace the sequence of change, the omission of elite data is unthinkable. If the principal aim is to uncover key factors in the arena of power, there is no avoiding the study of elites. The inquirer who faces the future, seeking to estimate the locus and speed of political encounters, must perceive the salience of elite data."[6]

The political theory of 'elite rule' represents the repudiation of the sanctified norm of the 'rule of the general will'. Thus Maurice Duverger advises that the formula 'government of the people, by the people' must be replaced by another formula; 'government of the people *by an elite sprung from the people.*'[7] Obviously, elite theory stands on the classical doctrine of the natural inequality of mankind and thereby leads to the tendency of irresponsibilism and self-perpetuation of political absolutism in clear negation of the norm of general participation as conceived by the doctrine of a liberal-democratic state. It implies that even if all men are taken as equal according to the Biblical injunction of 'Fatherhood of God and Brotherhood of Man', some are more equal than others with the result that the few have a position of advantage over the many. Inequality is still a universal phenomenon making every polity 'oligarchical' in varying degrees and the recognition of this point has informed many philosophers and sociologists to subscribe to the maxim : 'every people is governed by an elite, by a chosen element of the population'.

This 'chosen element' constitutes a minor part of society and it enjoys an exalted position by virtue of ancient traditions, physical might, wealth, economic status, etc. That is, an elite, literally meaning a 'chosen element', consists of those persons who sit at the top of the society over others, lying at the bottom or in the middle strata, by virtue of having 'a silver spoon in their mouth'. This chosen class may exist in a big family, club, trade union, bureaucracy, armed forces, etc. to demonstrate a group "emerged to positions of leadership and influence at every social level."[8] Such a view of elite rule blurs the line of its distinction with an oligarchical or aristocratic system of government. Despite the fact that elite rule embodies within itself certain fundamental traits of an aristocratic or oligarchical system and informs a writer to use all terms interchangeably, the line of real distinction does not disappear altogether. Adherence to the protection and promotion of the vested interests is the *sine qua non* of an elite rule like that of an aristocratic or an oligarchical system.

However, the line of demarcation is traceable in the fact that elite rule lacks both traditional grandeur and tendency of self-perpetuation which are the hallmarks of the rule of the few known by the names of aristocracy or oligarchy. Verney warns against the wrong tendency of blurring the line of distinction by pointing out : "An elite appears to combine some of the characteristics of both an oligarchy (government by the few) and an aristocracy (government by the best) but is not to be confused with either. It is a minority, like an oligarchy, and consists of superior people, like an aristocracy, but there is neither the sense of self-perpetuation and selfishness which

5. *ibid.*, p. 30.
6. Harold D. Lasswell and Max Lerner (eds.): *World Revolutionary Elites : Studies in Coercive Ideological Movements* (Massachusetts : Massachusetts Institute of Technology, 1965), p. 4.
7. Maurice Duverger : *Political Parties* (London : Methuen, 1954), p. 425.
8. G.D.H. Cole : *Studies in Social Structures*, pp. 105-6.

surrounds the former nor the pomp and grandeur which often is associated with the latter."[9]

Owing to this line of demarcation, it is noticeable that the character of an elite changes from time to time and place to place. The stages of social development have their decisive impact upon the character of an elite. If free men constituted an elite in a slave society, the lords did the same in a feudal order. If white men constituted the political elite in South Africa, the same privilege became available to the negroes in this country now. It is due to the fact that, unlike in an aristocracy or an oligarchy, the elite "owes its peculiar position of privilege to the recognition and esteem accorded to it by the masses. Should a society change its standard of values, for example should the Age of Empire give way to the Age of Technology, a different set of men is awarded esteem and honours and forms the elite of a nation."[10]

It follows that the existence of an elite depends upon the foundation of social grace. The chosen persons invoke the instrument of popular appreciation to retain and justify their position of advantage. As traditional norms of inherent inequality of mankind and employment of brutal force to coerce the dissidents have outlived their usefulness, the class of the chosen few finds its best defence in the strategy of appeal to the ordinary man's recognition and appreciation of its 'qualities'. As modern societies, developed or developing, are becoming more critical of the traditional values, the elite has come to assume a broader complexion to include not only those who are at the top but also those who constitute the strata of society from which leaders usually emerge.[11] Many factors like superior education and training, physical and mental make-up and utilisation of better techniques not only facilitate the task of some people's going up on the social ladder, they also tend to create a status-symbol for a particular section of the people. This social composition has its bearing on the political process when we discover that even important activities like distribution of election tickets and formation of ministries are influenced by the norms of elite politics. The people "may think that they may participate in the political process but in reality, so the argument runs, their influence is largely confined to elections. At the centre of power there is in being a social elite which wields considerable influence."[12]

As the existence of an elite depends upon the factor of 'social visibility', change is inevitable whenever there is a reversal in the degree of social distinctions and values available to the men composing it. Elites thus change from time to time and place to place. Now the English peers are not important like their ancestors. Politics means struggle for power and thus a struggle for political existence is always existent in the compartmentalised character of society. If there is an elite, there are counter-elites as well. Interaction and interpenetration go on to make changes in the *status quo*. Hence, every disturbance in the existing order of things drifts the current from right to the left or *vice versa* "in order to push the governing elite and the membership it represents out of office and below the waterline, and to take its place. And the mere fact that such a push could have precisely this result tends to make the elites of the 'governing' segments anxious to minimise the purely sectional aspects of their own policies so as to discourage the counter-elites from the concerted effort to overthrow them."[13]

Elites grow and develop in every society and compete for power that creates data for a study of political culture. In such a situation sharing of power becomes unequal to substantiate the view of Lasswell that "most

9. Verney, *op. cit.*, p. 161.
10. *ibid.*, pp. 161-62.
11. See Harold Lasswell : *The Comparative Study of Elites*, p. 6.
12. Verney, *op. cit.*, p. 166.
13. S.E. Finer : *Comparative Government* (London : Allen Lane, The Penguin Press, 1970), p. 27.

influential are called elites; others are mid-elites and rank-and-file."[14] Finer illustrates this position by the simile of orange having slices as given below.[15] He thus explains: "This orange, with its skin representing the elite of society, floats in water; that portion of the skin that is above the water-line represents the governing elite, and the segments which it covers represents those associations in society which have succeeded in the competition to have their leadership participate or hold office in the government. All those segments under the water-line, however, represent those associations which have lost this competition, and whose policies are temporarily being subordinated to those of the victorious ones, and the portions of peel that cover them represent, for society as a whole, the counter-elite that seeks to displace the governing elite at any point of time."[16]

The doctrine of elite rule stands on the notion that men are inherently unequal and thus only a 'few' have a title to rule 'many'. In this respect, it looks like an aristocratic or oligarchical system on a highly restricted scale. However, the most pernicious aspect of elite politics is that it goes for justifying the existence of the 'qualified few' as a good thing. It stands on the maxim that if a man does what he preaches, then he is a poor preacher. It argues that while all men may be equal in the eye of God, they are not so in the eye of man. The members of the chosen element employ shrewd tactics to justify their position of advantage and often indulge in nefarious practices to make the people appreciate their system. Elite rule, for this reason, degenerates a democracy into a tyranny of the snobs. It may also happen that an obstinate political elite (like white regime of South Africa till 1996) may go to the inhuman extent of using brutal force to crush every opposition and thereby strive and struggle to perpetuate its undemocratic rule making it worse than a perverted oligarchy. As Verney says : "All elite theories conflict with the notion of general participation, but some find it more abhorrent than others."[17]

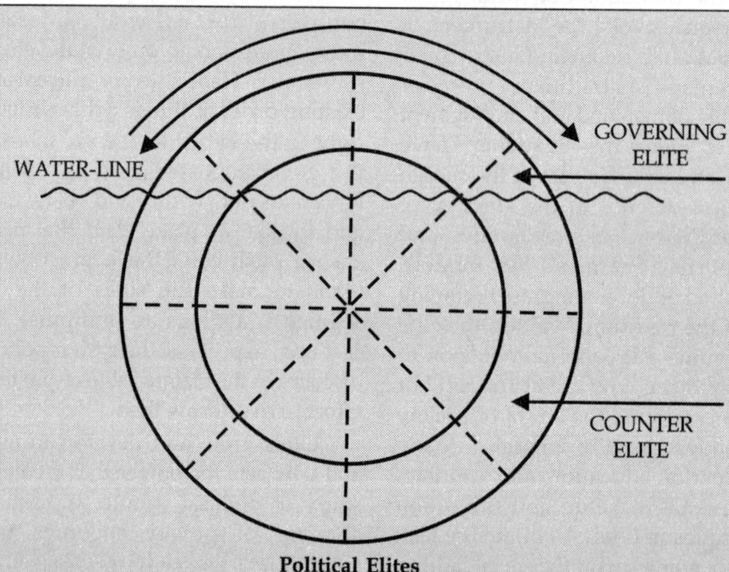

Finer's Model of Political Elites

14. Lasswell and Lerner, *op. cit.,* p. 5.
15. Finer, *op. cit.,* p. 26.
16. *ibid.,* p. 27.
17. Verney, *op. cit.,* p. 169.

Different Approaches : Kroese's Theory of Fulfilment of a Specific Mission by the Elites

If elites are so important in the decision-making process because of their influence and if they are the real controlling forces in a political community,[18] we may refer to the following important approaches adopted by leading social theorists to make an empirical study of the subject:[19]

1. ***Positional Approach :*** It signifies that the persons holding position of authority actually make key decisions. Lynds and Mills hold that the position of influence is gained by virtue of economic power, while Stouffer finds its source in top civil and political status of the person. Schulz and Blumberg spread their canvas to include all economic as well as non-economic factors. Subscribing to the same view, Jennings gives importance to government officials, civic staff as well as economic dominance. Thus, different writers have found the source of a person's high position in the decision-making process in different factors—economic, social and political.
2. ***Representational Approach :*** Basing their conclusions on Weber and Lasswell, writers like Warner, Hollingshed, Hunter and Angell pinpoint the role of very influential persons of the community who may be treated as its representatives by virtue of their understanding of the power structure and their role in it. In a way, it looks like another variant of the 'positional approach'. However, a point of difference between the two may be discovered in that while the former lays emphasis on the objective factors, the latter hits at the subjective aspect of the same. For this reason, while the former may be appreciated for being determinate, the latter is criticised for being indeterminate. Members of an elite have power, influence, authority and the like, but there may be some persons of repute in a community having no power or influence.
3. ***Issue-Participant Approach :*** Also known by the names of decision-making and event-analysis approaches, it lays emphasis on the role of real decision-makers for the reason they enjoy influence in the real life situations.

However, Kroese has sought to justify the elite system in his own way. He defines elite as a separate group which "has a specific mission to fulfil in society ."[20] In terms of historical development, it means a division of its emergence into three stages —the announcement of message, the carrying out of the plan set forth in the message, and the conservation of the order achieved by carrying out the plan. It may be asked as to what sort of circumstances are favourable to the development of an elite notion on the part of a group burdened with the preservation of the existing order. Four generalisations seem possible:[21]

1. The fact of having been an elite in a previous phase: If the ruling party has become an elite during the message-announcing phase or during the phase when the plan was being carried out, when

18. On this point, an eminent English writer like Percival Spear says: "It would seem that a line should be drawn between influence and control. An elite is a body which controls a particular sphere of life, though it may be influenced by other elites at other levels or in different departments of life." Refer to his paper "The Mughal Mansabdars'" in Edmund Leach and S.N. Mukherjee (eds.) : *Elites in South Asia* (London : Cambridge University Press, 1970), p. 1.
19. See S.K.. Lal : "Approaches to the Identification of the Elites" in Sachidanand .and A.K. Lal (eds.) : *Elite and Development* (New Delhi : Concept Pub, 1980), pp. 29-30. Also see CM. Bonjean and D.M. Olson : "Community Leadership : Direction of Research" in *Administrative Quariterly,* Vol. 9, No. 3, December, 1964, p. 282 and R.A. Dahl : *Who Governs?* (New Haven, Connecticut : Yale Univ. Press, 1961).
20. J.S. Banks (ed.) : *The Elite in the Welfare State,* written in Dutch by Stenfert Kroese and translated into English by J.E. Bingham (London : Faber and Faber, 1966), p. 80.
21. *ibid.,* pp. 80-81.

the third phase is reached, the characteristics of the difficult, or heroic, phase often linger on for a long time.

2. The state of tension between what is and what ought to be : It is true that the order-preserving group likes to take the view that this order is the outcome of a natural order. Therefore, the tension between what is and what ought to be is, in theory, done away with, yet they recognise that this is only so in theory. They are well aware that, as things are, certain groups are subjected to an order which has nothing to do with them. They claim emphatically that if they were to abdicate, the result would be that other groups, unemancipated or capable of being emancipated, would drift back to an earlier lower state, or indeed to a complete chaos.
3. The logical deduction from the statement is that the social situation is marked by a certain degree of alienation. There are sub-groups subjected to the order of things which the elite has designated as the obligatory form of society and which are, in one way or another, tainted with a different system of belief.
4. Even so, it all might happen that the group which has taken up the task of interpreting and preserving the mission entrusted to it, will not explicitly style itself an elite. They can be a set of representatives, elected by the majority exercising a tolerant attitude towards groups who think differently from them. However, this cannot be so...if the leading group should be a slender minority. For in that case, tolerance would lead to the overthrow of the established order by the dissident majority. So this final condition is, at the same time, the primary distinguishing feature of an elite which stands as a preserver of the existing order.

Leading Elite Theorists

The study of elites established itself as a significant element of political science in the late nineteenth and early twentieth centuries largely as a result of the contributions of two sociologists of Italy—Vilfredo Pareto and Gaetano Mosca. Others like Michels, Burnham and Wright Mills made their own contributions. Though there are underlying points of differences between them, the common thread running through the contributions of all is that every society "is ruled by a minority that possesses the qualities necessary for its succession to full social and political power. Those who get on the top are always the best. They are known as the elite. The elites consist of those successful persons who rise to the top in every occupation and stratum of society: there is an elite of lawyers, an elite of mechanics and even an elite of thieves and an elite of prostitutes."[22]

Let us briefly discuss the ideas of leading elite theorists in the light of the central theme of their contributions :

The elite theory of Pareto (1848-1923) is contained in his principal affirmation that 'history is a graveyard of aristocracies'. He develops his idea to the point that his theory of elite also becomes a theory of the circulation of the elites. According to him, in every society there is an increasing movement of individuals and elites from higher to lower levels and from lower to higher levels resulting in a considerable increase of the degenerate elements in the classes which still hold power and, on the other hand, in an increase of elements of superior quality in the subject classes. Psychological changes in the characteristics of the elites occur from time to time that lead to the changes in the composition and operation of different elites so much so that some elites are replaced by others that sometimes causes political instability. Pareto finds that elites make both logical or rational and illogical or irrational

22. S.P. Varma : *Modern Political Theory* (Delhi : Vikas, 1975), pp. 227-28.

Political Elite Theorists

Theorists	*Approaches*	*Contentions*
Gaetano Mosca	Organisational	In every society two classes of people exist—the rulers and the ruled—the former always less numerous, performs all political functions, monopolises power and enjoys advantages that follow, tries to find out a legal and moral basis for being in the citadels of powers.
Robert Michels	"	Who says organisation, says oligarchy, the fact of technical indispensability of leadership is always at work.
Wilfredo Pareto	"	History is the graveyard of aristocracies, elites remain in circulation, they rise and fall in spite of having special qualities (residues) which help a powerful position.
James Burnham	Economic	The power of elites has its source in the ownership of the means of production and distribution of goods, the privileged few manage to receive preferential treatment from the society and thereby prevent others from being in power.
C.W. Mills	Institutional	The elites are a product of the institutional landscape of society, power is an attribute not of classes but of institutions, all elites cannot be of equal significance as few may have access to the seats of power.

actions for the attainment of their ends. He, however, advises that the elites should have the qualities, what he calls 'residues', with which their members can rise up and maintain themselves in power. These residues are:[23]

1. combination—tendency to invent and embark on adventures;
2. persistence of preservation—tendency to consolidate and make secure;
3. expressiveness—tendency to make feelings manifest through symbolisation;
4. sociability—tendency to affiliate others;
5. integrity—tendency to maintain a good self-image; and
6. sex—tendency to see social events in erotic terms.

As a matter of fact, Pareto makes use of the first two residues and on that basis lays down his doctrine of 'innovation' and 'consolidation' what are the substitutes of his 'instinct for combination' and 'persistence of aggregates'. Apart from this, he refers to certain 'derivatives' (like assertion, appeals to authority, appeals to sentiments or principles, and verbal proofs) or the ways by which actions are made to assume the appearance of logical actions.

An imbalance between the elements of 'innovation' and 'consolidation' causes replacement of one elite by another. One ascends, another declines and thus goes on the continuous replacement or circulation of the elites. Sometimes it becomes like a revolution that may, however, be checked or avoided by an open recruitment into the elite. As he says: "Revolution comes about through accumulation in the higher strata of society—either because of a slowing down in class-circulation, or from other causes of decadent elements no longer possessing the residues suitable for keeping them in power, and shrinking from the use of force; while meantime in the lower strata of society elements of superior

23. See Pareto : *The Mind and Society : A Treatise on General Sociology* (New York : Dover, 1963), pp. 516-19. Originally written in the Italian in 1916, it has four volumes covering about 3,000 pages.

quality are coming to the fore possessing residues suitable for exercising the functions of government and willing enough to use force."[24]

Another leading exponent of the elite theory is G. Mosca (1858-1941) whose work *The Ruling Class* is considered as an independent contribution less on sociology but more on politics. His approach is contained in this portion of his classical work: "Among the constant facts and tendencies that are to be found in all political organisms, one is so obvious that it is apparent to the most casual eye. In all societies, two classes of people appear—a class that rules and a class that is ruled. The first class, always the less numerous, preforms all political functions, monopolises power and enjoys the advantages that follow, whereas the second, the more numerous class, is directed and controlled by the first, in a manner that is now more or less legal, now more or less arbitrary and violent and supplies the first, in appearance at least, with material means of subsistence and with the instrumentalities that are essential to the validity of the political organism."[25]

What is of special attention in Mosca's theory of two classes is that one class counts on the cooperation of another. While the ruling class needs the support of the ruled class, the latter provides protection to the former. The people can only act politically under the direction of a small group of leaders. A minority, Mosca affirms, 'has advantages simply because it is a minority'. A political class has two strata—higher and lower—the latter being more important as it consists of the real 'bosses' who direct party's electoral campaigns and thereby control the government. They are the 'grand electors'; they distribute tickets, launch canvassing campaigns and go to the final length of determining the range from which the electorate must exercise its supposedly 'free choice'. Mosca attaches a great deal of importance to his 'political formula' implying that the ruling class tries to find out a legal and moral basis for its being in the citadels of power and represents it as the logical and necessary consequence of doctrines and beliefs that are generally recognised and accepted. Mosca's ruling class "is a mere category of top people'.[26]

Mosca makes some interesting observations on the point of heredity when he says that political forces seem to possess a quality that in physics is known by the name of 'inertia'. It is evident from the fact that elites have a tendency to stabilise themselves, and yet the fact of their replacement cannot be denied. He forcefully asserts that "the whole history of civilised mankind comes down to a conflict between the tendency of dominant elements to monopolise political power and transmit possession of it by inheritance, and the tendency towards a dislocation of old forces and an emergence of new forces: and this conflict produces an unending ferment of endos-mosis and exomosis between the upper classes and certain portions of the lower."[27]

The organisational approach of Mosca has its repetition in the works of Robert Michels (1876-1936) who in his well-known work on political parties (1915) laid down his 'iron law of oligarchy' by emphatically affirming: 'Who says organisation, says oligarchy'. According to him, in every organisation of any size, leadership becomes necessary to its success and survival. The nature of organisation is such that it gives power and advantages to the group of leaders who cannot then be checked or held accountable by their followers. This is

---

24. *ibid.*, p. 1431. While keeping in view the contributions of this Italian sociologist, also known by the nickname of 'the Newton of the moral world', Parry characterises his great work as 'the grandest of all the classical doctrines, a garguantan retort to Marx' and 'a part of much more sociology in which social activity is explained by reference to certain fundamental psychological factors. *op. cit.*, p. 45.
25. Mosca : *The Ruling Class* (New York : McGraw Hill, 1939), p. 50.
26. Parry, *op. cit.*, p. 41.
27. Mosca, *op. cit.*, p. 65.

true despite the fact that where the leadership is elected, the leaders are supposedly the agents of those electing them. The factor of the 'technical indispensability of leadership' is always at work which informs that the control of the party passes into the hands of its leading politicians and its bureaucracy. Power breeds power and this forms the central tenet of elitism. The result is that the leaders are 'bourgeoisiefied', who are quite strangers to their class and the party hierarchy becomes an established career offering a rise in social status as well as income.[28] What really sustains this sort of power concentration in the hands of the ruling elite is the fact that the majority of people are indolent, apathetic and politically neutral. Michels calls it the 'mass mind'. The shrewd leaders influence the people by their oratory or flattery and the laws made to weaken their power are weakened by the political apathy of the people themselves. As he says: "The democratic currents of history resemble successive waves. They break ever on the same shoal."[29]

Ortega Y. Gasset (1883-1955) developed his theory of political elites on the basis of his superficial reverence to the dogma of the masses. It is the people who create the elites by reposing their faith in and by rendering their support to the chosen element. It shows the capacity of leading in very few and the capacity of being led by the very few in many. The masses "revolt when aristocracy becomes corrupt and inefficient, and the motive behind the revolt is not that they have objection to being ruled by aristocracy but would like to be ruled by a more competent aristocracy."[30] The fact of aristocratic rule thus cannot be lost sight of. The central concern of Gasset is to tell that when the masses "in a country believe that they can do without aristocracy, the nation inevitably declines. In their disillusionment the masses again turn to the new leadership, and a new aristocracy emerges."[31]

The political theory of elites finds place in the writings of two recent American social theorists as well—Burnham and C. Wright Mills. Burnham's is an economic approach that looks more or less analogous to the Marxian approach in certain respects. According to him, the basis of any elite's power lies in the control over the principal means of production and distribution. It is by virtue of this privileged position that the group in power manages to receive 'preferential treatment' from the society and it is because of this position that it manages to prevent others from gaining power. Thus, the easiest way "to discover what the ruling group is in any society is usually to see what group gets the biggest income."[32] However, Burnham should not be taken as a Marxist for the reason that his purpose is to justify and defend the present capitalist system. He takes nothing more from Marx than the significance of the control of means of production by an elite. He wants to reconcile the contradiction between managerial control of the state and state control of the economy by means of a new elite domination.

Finally, we may study the institutional approach of C. Wright Mills. In his view, an elite is the product of the 'institutional landscape' of the society. Power in modern society is institutionalised with the result that certain institutions and the uppermost ranks of the hierarchy in these institutions constitute the 'strategic command posts of the social structure'.[33] Power is then not an attribute of classes or persons but of institutions. The power elite consists of those 'in position to make

28. Robert Michels : *Political Parties : A Sociological Study of the Oligarchical Tendencies of Modern Democracy,* Translated from Italian into English by Eden and Cedar Paul (New York: Dover Pub, 1959), pp. 288-89.
29. *ibid.,* p. 408.
30. See Varma, *op. cit.,* p. 233.
31. *ibid.*
32. James Burnham : *The Managerial Revolution* (London : Putnam, 1942), p. 56.
33. Wright Mills : *The Power Elites* (London : Oxford University Press, 1959). p. 4.

decisions having major consequences...in command of the major hierarchies and organisations of modern society'.[34] The history-making power of the elite "is sufficient to overturn the *status quo,* call into question the existing social relationship and establish a new structure. The inner core of the elite is able, potentially, to determine the roles both it and others will play in society."[35]

Elite Theory and Different Political Systems

The political theory of elites, as discussed above, contradicts the basic assumption of democracy that government is in the hands of the people. To bring about reconciliation between the two thus becomes a matter of serious enquiry. The name of Karl Mannheim (1893-1947) is important in this direction who "could evolve a conception of democracy as a political system in which political parties compete for the votes of a mass electorate, the elites are relatively 'open' and recruited on the basis of merit, and the mass of population is able to participate in ruling the society at least in the sense that it may exercise a choice between the rival elites."[36] Mannheim asserts that though the actual shaping of policy is in the hands of the elites, it does not mean that the society is not democratic. It "is sufficient for democracy that the individual citizens though prevented from taking a direct part in the government all the time, have at least the possibility of making their aspirations felt at certain intervals . . . in a democracy the governed can always act to remove their leaders or to force them to take decisions in the interests of the many."[37]

A similar attempt has been made by two economists Schumpeter and Anthony Downs. Schumpeter has desired to have 'a new theory of democracy' in which the political theory of elites and classical theory of democracy have their reconciliation. Downs has likened political parties in a democracy with the entrepreneurs in a profit-seeking economy. The approach of these two important writers is thus summed up by an Indian writer: "As different groups of men look for different ways of obtaining support from the masses, different political parties are formed and enter into a competition with each other. This leads to a plurality of elites and a kind of system of checks and balances in the democratic societies, which are, on this account, often described as pluralistic societies. Associations of all kinds, professional as well as political, are formed and the government becomes a business of compromises."[38]

It is claimed by the exponents of a socialist system that in it there is no place for the rule of the elites, for there is the rule of the 'mass'. The dictatorship of the proletariat is thus the only alternative to the dictatorial rule of the elites. Some social theorists like Raymond Aron, and Djilas, however, disagree with such a contention. According to him, there is only one elite in power in a socialist society. Not the Communist Party but an elite of the same rules what is known as the dictatorship of the proletariat. What is worse is that "a classless society leaves the mass of the population without any possible means of defence against the elite."[39] The law of Max Weber has its application in every political system whether it is democratic or socialist. Picking up a thread from this Weberian interpretation, Milovan Djilas lays down his doctrine of the 'new class'. According to him, even a socialist system has an elite (called a class) made up of those who have special privileges and economic preferences because of the administrative monopoly they hold.

34. *ibid.*
35. Parry, *op. cit.,* p. 54.
36. Varma, *op. cit.,* p. 235.
37. Mannheim : *Ideology and Utopia : An Introduction to the Sociology of Knowledge,* English Translation by Louis, Wirth and Shils (New York : Harper, 1936), p. 119.
38. Varma, *op. cit.,* pp. 235-36.
39. Aron: "Social Structure and the Ruling Class" in *British Journal of Sociology,* Vol I,No. 2, 1950, p. 131.

The elitists have accepted much of the meaning of Marx; at the same time, they have given it a middle class bent so that the entire interpretation may be saved from exposure to a stimulus to working class revolutionary action. They have emphasised the point that it is political skill—or the lack of it—that determines who will rule and how power may change hands. The economic factors are really important, but it cannot be lost sight of that by political means an elite can control, accommodate or even counteract economic forces. It is thus obvious that even a socialist system cannot be taken as free from the prevalence of elite politics, or what Burnham calls, 'the political process of managerial revolution'. A change from a capitalist to a socialist system should be treated as a change in the engineers or the technological specialists or the 'keepers of the community's material welfare'.

Critical Appraisal

The political theory of elites has its weaknesses that may be enumerated as under:

1. Either the elitists lay too much stress on elite politics, or they have failed to offer a viable alternative to Marxian doctrine of the class war. It appears that the elitists seek to offer an ideology of their own in sharp reply to the Marxian ideology— 'a political theory of the middle class'.[40] By all means, such a political theory is a negation of the celebrated principle that democracy is a government of the people. Democracy implies political movement of the lower classes of society against the dominance of the aristocratic or wealthy classes. What the twentieth century theorists have done, rather arbitrarily, is to "identify democracy with a static political system in which elite rule is sanctioned by periodic elections."[41] Though we may say that the Marxian approach has its own shortcomings, it "would still be difficult to accept the theory of power elite as a satisfactory explanation of social change."[42]
2. The elitists take a wrong view of 'power'. In this respect, they blur the distinction between terms like power, authority and influence. The concept of legitimacy has its essential relationship with authority. The people may be coerced or terrorised by the display of power, but they accept only that amount of power that is legitimate and, for that reason, may be better designated as authority. If so, the arena of power is not open to a particular elite alone, rather it is open to several elites in so many forms. Keeping it in view, a critic like James MacGregor Burns says: "To define power not as a property or entity or possession but as a *relationship* in which two or more persons tap motivational bases in one another and bring varying resources to bear in the process is to perceive power as drawing a vast range of human behaviour into its orbit. The arena of power is no longer the exclusive preserve of a power elite or an establishment of persons clothed with legitimacy. Power is ubiquitous; it permeates human relationships. It exists whether or not it is questioned for. It is the glory and the burden of most of the humanity."[43]

---

40. Parry, *op. cit.*, p. 42. It is true that the elite theory, in its historical origins, stands in polar opposition to the Marxist theory of permanent struggle between fixed classes of owners and producers. In Marxist analysis, the emphasis is on the nature of political domination and its ultimate dependence on the control of strategic institutions with the economic infrastructure of society. However, in practice, the two types of theory are not necessarily mutually incompatible. Elitist analysis is concerned with how individuals are recruited into positions of personal influence as part of a political process." Refer to the "Introduction" by Leach and Mukherjee, *op. cit.*, p. ix.
41. Varma, *op. cit.*, p. 237.
42. *ibid.*, p. 243.
43. Burns, *op. cit.*, p. 15.

3. Elite theory justifies the existence and operation of the politics of secrecy and manipulation. Its understanding takes us very close to the appreciation of what Machiavelli and Hobbes said in the early modern period. In other words, it ignores the better and nobler aspect of politics as advocated by a great leader like Mahatma Gandhi. The moral and spiritual aspects of human life cannot be discarded in the realm of politics in all the cases. If elite politics is taken to be the only model of politics and its practice, there shall be no place for the norms of a good life in its operation. The history of the Indian freedom movement under the leadership of Gandhi is the glorious record of a clean, moral and open politics. As such, it cannot be explained with the tools of elite theory, though one may make use of it for explaining other great events of the world like Russian and Chinese revolutions. Gandhi could prove by his words and deeds that transforming leadership "ultimately becomes *moral* in that it raises the level of human conduct and ethical aspiration of both leader and led, and thus it has a transforming effect on both."[44]
4. The elite theory presents a wrong equation of the relationship between a leader holding power and the led who are his ardent and most trusted followers. It does not take into consideration the role of the factor of motivations that binds both the leader and his followers. It may be pointed out that certain concepts and techniques of the elitist school of power are indispensable in social and political analysis, but elitism is often used as a concept that presupposes the existence of the very degree and kind of power that is to be estimated and analysed. Such elite theorists commit the gross mistake of equating power and leadership with the assumed power bases of preconceived leaders and power holders, without considering the crucial role of *motivations* of leaders and followers. "Every good detective knows that one must look for the motive as well as the weapon."[45]
5. Above all, those who have all appreciation for the classical notion of democracy, cannot agree with the fundamental contention of the elitists that the will of a very small minority counts in all matters of decision-making and, for this reason. the most celebrated maxim of 'will of the people' is just a myth. They donot deny the existence and role of the elites. but they certainly refute the view that all importance should be attached to the will of the very few chosen persons only. Herbert Kaufman argues that in a democratic system choice of personnel should be open and subject to negotiation and bargaining among the various elements of the people.[46] Likewise, R.A. Dahl presents the concept of 'polyarchical democracy'. It "stresses the continuing responsiveness of the government to the preferences of its citizens."[47] John Plamenatz suggests that if the 'will of the people' is a myth, then the'will of the minority' also belongs to the same category.[48]

Despite these points of criticism, it cannot be denied that the elite theory has many points having a relevance of their own in the field of empirical political science. So many events of the world can be explained with the help of this theory for the reason that elite theories "refer to an observable and testable social phenomenon and successfully seek to explain social and political change. They are fertile and

44. *ibid.*, p. 20.
45. *ibid.*, pp. 22-23.
46. Kaufman : *Politics in State and Local Governments* (Englewood Cliffs, New Jersey : Prentice Hall, 1963), p. 89.
47. R.A. Dahl: *Polyarchy : Participation and Opposition* (New Haven, Connecticut : Yale Univ. Press, 1971), p. 1.
48. Plamenatz : *Democracy and Illusion* (London : Longman, 1973), p. 187.

suggestive enough for the construction of new theories." They are of particular relevance for the understanding of the politics of developing countries where economic, political and other developments are bringing about changes in social structure, that is, changes in the prestige and power of different social groups and consequently rise and fall of the elites. We can examine the social forces which are creating new elites as well as the activities of the elites themselves in the modernisation process of the developing societies.[49] Besides, this theory also informs us to examine "the relationship between economic structure, social structure and the structure of groups within the elites and the structures of the constitutional system."[50]

49. L.N. Sharma : "The Theories of Elites : Impact and Relevance" in the *Indian Journal of Political Science,* Vol. XXXVIII, No. I, January-March 1977, p. 79.
50. Raymond Aron : "Social Structure and the Ruling Class" in S.N. Eisenstadt (ed.) : *Political Sociology : A Reader* (New York : Basic Books, 1971), p. 420.

28

Oligarchy

> Each type of social order, without exception, must, if one wishes to evaluate it, be assessed according to which type of men it gives the opportunity to rise to a position of superiority through the operation of the various objective and subjective selective factors
>
> **—Max Weber**[1]

The discovery of the point of great disparity between an elaborate and formal democratic structure on the one hand and the realities of the residence and exercise of power on the other emphasising oligarchical element in every political system convincingly informs an empirical political theorist like Robert Michels to propound his 'iron law of oligarchy'. Like elite theory, as discussed in the preceding chapter, the 'iron law of oligarchy' amounts to the refutation of the normative assumptions of a liberal-democratic system. Once again, it may be seen, the interpretation of a representative democratic model is modified to reveal that it is more of an ideal than that of a reality. Whatever be the form of government, in a strict sense, it is the rule of the best few, call it by any name like aristocracy and oligarchy, for the obvious reason that both terms are usually employed "indiscriminately to describe any government in which only a small minority has the controlling power."[2]

Nature and Essential Implications : Its Distinction with Elite Rule

The word 'oligarchy' having its synonym in 'aristocracy' is quite old. Aristotle used these two terms as the 'rule of the few', though he characterised the former as the perverted form of the latter. Besides, he also distinguished oligarchy from democracy on the basis of wealth when he considered the former as a government of the rich few and the latter as the rule of the poor many.[3] Among modern writers, John Seeley described oligarchy as a 'deranged' or 'diseased' form of aristocracy.[4] A French writer Pradier-Fodere treated aristocracy as a government by a 'class' and oligarchy as a government by 'a small number of persons' who donot, strictly speaking, constitute a class. However, Lord James Bryce used the two terms interchangeably and prophesied that in future oligarchies would have to be either a mixture of plutocracy and bureaucracy, or else composed of the leaders of labour or trade union organisations.[5]

Call it by any name like aristocracy or oligarchy, it is the rule of the chosen few or of a very small section of the populace marked out by birth, wealth, talent, status and the like. It stands for the residence of power and its exercise by the few distinguished by superiority, ability and merit. As such, it has a conservative character. It tries to preserve what is best in the

1. Cited in David Beetham : *Max Weber and the Theory of Modern Politics* (London : George Allen and Unwin, 1974), p. 110.
2. J.W. Garner : *Political Science and Government* (Calcutta : World Press, 1952), II Indian Edition, p. 311.
3. *Politics,* Book III, Sections 6-7 (English translation by B. Jowett), p. 116.
4. Seeley : *Introduction to Political Science,* Lecture VI.
5. Bryce : *Modern Democracies,* Vol. II, (London : Macmillan, 1921), pp. 537ff.

traditions and institutions of the past. Moreover, it attempts to combine strength and efficiency, uniformity and stability in administration. In this way, it "tries to keep the people away from the stream of progress with a view to perpetuate its own class rule."[6]

Although the tendency of oligarchy, as claimed by modern empirical political theorists, is discernible in every political system, a line of distinction may be drawn between the rule of the elite and the rule of the oligarchs. The point of similarity lies in the affirmation of the 'rule of the few', while the element of differences lies in the way the chosen few come to hold and exercise power. Elite rule depends upon the appreciation of the masses, while rule of the oligarchs depends upon the apathy, ignorance or weak and meek attitude of the downtrodden people. As Verney explains : "In contrast to elite theories, where there is a psychological barrier to general participation owing to the existence of group of people whose superiority is acknowledged by the rest, the iron law of oligarchy does not depend primarily on the tacit approval of the masses. It results from their failure to assert themselves against their rulers and to challenge the 'never-ending audacity of the elected persons'. In both instances society is regarded as a pyramid, the few who rule being at the top and the many who are ruled at the base, but the relationship of the rulers and the ruled is intimate. Whereas elites especially celebrities and royal families tend to thrive on the interest of the masses in their doings, oligarchies flourish when people are apathetic about the democratic process and ignorant of the realities of political power."[7]

It follows that if the people are apathetic, ignorant or terror-stricken, there is a good ground for the existence and perpetuation of an oligarchical system. The rule of the Communist Party becomes oligarchical inasmuch as the elite consolidates its hold by playing and liquidating all possible opposition elements. Even in liberal-democratic systems the tendency towards oligarchy thrives when the head of the state exercises his patronage over a set of elected persons who concentrate their loyalty on the 'party boss' at the expense of their immense debt to the electors. The result is that in France a man like Charles de Gaulle had an army of 'official administrators' ready to do and die for him at his slightest behest. The accumulated support of these 'sworn loyalists' creates in the mind of the 'boss' the sentiment of Bonapartism : 'a leader who has owed his elevation to office to mass support may later imagine he is there by the grace of God."[8]

Operational Dimension

It is 'mistakenly' believed that oligarchical polities of the eighteenth century have now vanished in entirety in those states where the exercise of power has been taken away from the junker land-owning aristocrats together with other wealthy and bureaucratically-trained classes. Dynastic rule of the wealthy, the brave and the 'talented' have been swept away by the winds of 'popular sovereignty' not to be totally out of existence but to survive in a new guise, particularly in the 'backward' or 'developing' countries of the world. Their clandestine operation in a democratic polity makes the whole system like a 'facade' and it may be noticed that a series of feuds among the 'neo-oligarchs' suggest the rule of some autocratic power. As Finer puts : "Up to the end of the eighteenth century, the vast majority of states were dynastic autocracies or historic oligarchies : that is as much to say that they were governed by autocrats or oligarchs of lineage or wealth—or more usually—both together. But, with the French Revolution and the reception of its notion of popular sovereignty throughout the world, the autocrats and the oligarchs felt compelled bit by bit to bargain with this new political formula. Hence, the piecemeal introduction of liberal-

6. G.N. Singh : *Fundamentals of Political Science and Organisation* (Allahabad : Kitab Mahal, 1966), p. 163.
7. D.V. Verney : *An Analysis of Political Systems* (London : Routledge and Kegan Paul, 1959), pp. 174-75.
8. *ibid.*, p. 177.

democratic constitutions. But this by no means meant that the dynasts and the oligarchs had abdicated power. Far from it in most states, though not all, they continued to govern in spite of the new constitutional and popular order. So arose the facade-democracy. In this type of regime, historic oligarchies of lineage and wealth govern from behind a facade of liberal-democratic forms which serve as a cloak or screen to their oligarchical rule. But in this kind of regime also, the exercise sometimes proves too exacting or the oligarchs quarrel among themselves : in which case, for a space, "they yield to an autocrat, often a social upstart, and nearly always a military man."[9]

The study of some developing countries of the Latin-American, African and Asian regions illustrates the 'rule of the professionals of modernising and nationalist bent' who could achieve their status by virtue of their services and sacrifices for the cause of national liberation or development. They thus thrived on the popular support and their dominant party rule survived to stifle opposition until the people became well-conscious to shake off their traditional fallibility, or the military intervened to arrest the forces of corruption and demonetisation so rampant in the ranks of those leaders and their dominant party. The deteriorating situation converted even that 'facade-democracy' into a 'quasi-democracy' and ultimately contributed to the extinction of whatever remained to mark the existence of a liberal-democratic pattern. A line of distinction between the political developments of 'western advanced' and 'eastern developing' societies can be drawn here : while in the former countries, facade-democracy softened the passage of liberal-democracy with the extension of franchise and rise of stable and well-organised party system to run the government on the lines of a representative polity, in the latter the facade-democracy granted under the colonial or autocratic rule on an experimental basis could not mature to the desired extent and its failure led to the acceleration of the process of deterioration first towards quasi-democracy and eventually towards communist take-over or military dictatorship.

It, however, does not mean that such countries never had a liberal-democratic system of their own. The factual position illustrates that their liberal-democracy born out of facade-democracy witnessed the trend of regression. The new constitutional system envisaged after the advent of independence from a long colonial rule failed to strengthen the forces of liberty and self-rule. The pace of deterioration, ever more and never less, ultimately led to the 'murder of democracy'. When the neo-oligarchs sought to perpetuate their rule by the instruments of party purges, impassioned oratory, suppression of opposition, rigged and stuffed elections, even by the falsification of official records, the time did arrive when this facade-democracy "was overtaken by the changes in the social structure and the spread of a new political formula, both of them determining the old traditional deference without which the system could not work without an excess of coercion. Where it did rely on coercion, it found itself subordinated to the military, its instrument of violence. Where it still had roots and worked smoothly, it antagonised modernising elements among the officer corps, and they overthrew it."[10]

The above account suggests a line of distinction between facade and quasi-democracies. While the former has the desire and possibilities of a switch-over from immature to more and more mature conditions of a liberal-democratic system through the gradual and steady realisation of self-governing institutions, the latter is identifiable with the rule of a single dominant party or a junta allowing opposition only to the extent of its ineffective nature. Both have the ingredients of a democratic system in the sense that opposition is allowed and politics

9. S.E. Finer: *Comparative Government,* pp. 123-24.
10. *ibid.,* p. 460.

of electoral manipulation plays its part; likewise, both have an oligarchical character in the sense that the exercise of power is really in the hands of the few. As Finer holds : "Where the ruling group of the facade-democracy depends on its individual members who are important notables in their own right, the quasi-democracy is an oligarchy, but an oligarchy of a *new type.*"[11]

In order to make the point more clear, the same writer defines facade-democracy as 'a system where liberal-democratic institutions, processes and safeguards are established by law but are in practice so manipulated or violated by a historic oligarchy as to stay in office. The structure of the government is usually collegiate but for a time it may be superseded by an individual autocratic ruler using similar methods to perpetuate himself."[12] Different from this, "in quasi-democracies, the right to form political parties is usually confined to only one, official body, and if, as in a few cases, like Mexico's the right is extended, steps are taken to ensure that other parties are politically ineffectual.'"[13]

Iron Law of Oligarchy : Empirical Justification of Minority Rule

After studying the theory of political elites, as given in the preceding chapter, we may easily form an impression that the existence of minority rule in every political system can be verified by the facts. The critics of the democratic system suggest that the doctrine of the people's rule is nothing more than a celebrated myth. For instance, a critic like Lecky says that democracy has an inherent preference for an authoritarian solution of all important questions.[14] A distinguished English statesman like Gladstone affirms that the love of the English people for their liberties is equalled only by their love for the nobility.[15] A Russian anarchist like Bakunin asserts that in a society where the people, the mass of the wage-earners, are under the economic domination of a minority consisting of the possessors, the freest of electoral systems could be nothing more than an illusion.[16]

The elitists stress the same point. For instance, Pareto seeks to discover an elite within the socialist class and on this basis identifies the rule of the working class with a minority of the same class. Likewise. Mosca's ruling class is not a multitude as conceived by Marx and Engels, it is a very small group of the rulers. The substitution of power from one class to another really signifies the replacement of one clique by another. Sooner or later, the competition between the various cliques of the dominant classes ends in a reconciliation which is effected with the instinctive aim of retaining dominion over the masses by sharing it among themselves.[17]

While expressing his agreement with such affirmations, Robert Michels lays down his 'iron law of oligarchy'. It is evident from his interpretation : "Those who donot believe in the god of democracy are never weary of affirming that this god is the creation of a childlike mythopoeic faculty, and they contend that all phrases representing the idea of the rule of the masses, such terms as state, civic rights, popular representation, nation, are descriptive merely of a legal principle, and do not correspond to any actually existing facts. They contend that the eternal struggles between aristocracy and democracy of which we read in history have never been, anything more than struggles between an old minority, defending its actual predominance and a new and ambitious minority, intent upon the conquest

11. *ibid.,* p. 463.
12. *ibid.,* p. 441.
13. *ibid.,* p. 462.
14. W.E.H. Lecky : *Democracy and Liberty,* Vol. I, p. 267.
15. Cited in Robert Michels : *Political Parties : A Sociological Study of the Oligarchical Tendencies in Modern Democracy,* Translated into English by Eden and Cedar Paul (New York : Dover Pub, 1959), p. 378.
16. *ibid.,* p. 381.
17. *ibid.,* op. 378-79.

Iron Law of Oligarchy

Oligarchy is government or domination by the few. The iron law of oligarchy formulated by Robert Michels suggests that there is an inevitable tendency in political organisations, and by implication in all organisations, to be oligarchic. Participatory or democratic structures cannot check oligarchic tendencies, they can only disguise them. Arguments advanced in support of it are:

1. Elite groups result from the need for specialisation. Elite members have great expertise and better organisation skills than those possessed by ordinary members.
2. Leaders form cohesive groups because they recognise that it improves their chances of remaining in power.
3. Rank-and-file members of an organisation tend to be apathetic and are, therefore, generally disposed to accept subordination and venerate leaders.

Andrew Heywood: *Politics*, p. 256.

of power, desiring either to fuse with the former or to dethrone and replace it. On this theory, these class struggles consist merely of struggles between successively dominant minorities. The social classes which under our eyes engage in gigantic battles upon the scene of history, battles whose ultimate causes are to be found in economic antagonism, may thus be compared to two groups of dancers executing a *chasse croise* in a quadrille."[18]

Subscribing to the same thesis, a recent writer like Maurice Duverger has laid down the doctrine of 'inner circle leadership'. In every party there is a very small and also a very influential group into which it is difficult to penetrate. This 'clique' is the real decision-maker. The surprising feature of a democratic system is that while in theory all matters are settled by the votes of the many, it all occurs according to the will of the 'very few'. Even socialist and communist parties are no exception to it. As he says : 'In theory, the principle of election should prevent the formation of an oligarchy: in fact, it seems rather to favour it. The masses are naturally conservative; they become attached to their old leaders, they are suspicious of new faces. Socialist parties, in which the recruitment of leaders is more democratic than in others, find correspondingly greater difficulty in finding new leaders."[19]

Seen from a critical standpoint, it appears that the 'iron law of oligarchy' refutes the Marxian assumption of the'class rule'even after the overthrow of the bourgeois system. The 'dictatorship of the proletariat' is not at all a rule of the working class as conceived by Marx and Engels or of the Communist Party—the vanguard of the working class as stressed by Lenin— it is the rule of a very small band of professional revolutionaries who take every decision *in camera* and the bureaucracy working at their behest affords the example of a technocratic oligarchy. Though Lenin desired the support and cooperation of as many people of the working class as possible, he laid his hope on those who 'devote to the revolution not their free evenings but their whole life.' In his *What is to be Done* ?, he sought his reliance on those "whose profession is that of a revolutionary'.[20] If so, the leadership in a communist system is largely made up of the most trusted followers as a result of which there "is born an.authentic oligarchy which exercises power, retains it, and transmits it by means of co-option."[21]

18. *ibid.*, p. 377.
19. Maurice Duverger : *Political Parties : Their Organisation and Activity and the Modern State*, Translated from German into English by Barbara and Robert North, (London : Methuen, 1964), p. 151.
20. *ibid.*, p. 155.
21. *ibid.*

The tendency of making an entrenched leadership is not only confined to a communist or a fascist system; it is very much available even in a democratic country. The only point of difference is that the ruthlessness of the former is not possible in the case of the latter. The small class of real decision-makers does not like the idea of allowing others indiscriminately to swell the ranks of the organisation unless circumstances so force. The section of the most influential leaders also counts upon the conservation of the people who donot favour quick change in the position of those who happen to be at the helm of affairs. People belonging to this clique or caucus instinctively raise a barrier against those who seem to them likely to threaten their own position as leaders.[22]

Finally, it may be added in this connection that the oligarchical character of every party does not prevent it from pursuing democratic policies.[23] The real residence of power and its exercise may be in the hands of the 'chosen few', but every party seeks to have the label of a'democratic character'. Thus, national conventions of the party are held from time to time in which important policy decisions are taken and members of the higher party units with a president or a chairman at the top are elected. Even 'bourgeois' parties adopt some socialist programmes to have the stamp of wide acceptability. And it all occurs according to the will of the minority holding the real reins of power.

Critical Appraisal

If we start with the assumption that there is invariably in some form an iron law of oligarchy, and if we conclude that the most important questions which it raises for the would-be democrats are the replaceability and diffusion of the governing elite, then it "follows that we should think of revising some of the better-worn criteria for the appraisal of political systems."[24] It will certainly be desirable to rejuvenate the governing elite by replacing the old members if we cannot think in terms of replacing the ruling elite by another. Replacement of this kind "will be a problem under any system, authoritarian or democratic; there are as few constitutional bulwarks that can be built against gerontocracy as against oligarchy, for a principle of election is never by itself sufficient, as mass democracy has in practice made clear. Under any system of government—even where individual liberty is being sacrificed by either necessity or design—efficiency requires that those members of the elite may be replaced who have failed to further the interests of the governed on whose support or acquiescence any government ultimately rests."[25]

It remains to be observed that such a system of the oligarch's rule, whether old or new, reveals the residence of power and its exercise by a very few. Obviously, this type of rule is indicative of the limited political participation which, though a reality in its own way, negates the sanctified principle of a liberal-democratic order. In addition to it, its more sinister implication lies in the situation that accelerates the pace of deterioration more and more until even the truncated democracy is substituted by an autocratic rule of the communist, or fascist, or military oligarchs. Two correctives may be suggested to prevent the perversion of liberal-democratic system in this way—(i) a discriminating and vigilant attitude of the people, and (ii) a stable party system on democratic lines. "The sharp tendency towards oligarchy can be corrected provided the rank and file overcome their apathy and are prepared to demand that their leaders shall be responsible to them.... The tendency towards oligarchy is more easily corrected where there is a two or multi-party system in which opposition leaders keep those temporarily in power up to the mark."[26]

22. *ibid.*, p. 163.
23. See Martin Seliger ; *Ideology and Politics* (London : George Allen and Unwin, 1976), p. 71.
24. W.G. Runciman : *Social Sciences and Political Theory* (London : Macmillan, 1969), p. 80.
25. *ibid.*, p. 81.
26. Verney, *op. cit.*, p. 182.

29

Bureaucracy

> The general spirit of bureaucracy is secret, mystery, safeguarded inside itself by hierarchy and outside by its nature as a closed corporation. Thus, public political spirit and also political mentality appear to bureaucracy as a betrayal of its secret. The principle of its knowledge is, therefore, authority and its mentality is the idolatory of authority. But within bureaucracy the spiritualism turns into a crass materialism, the materialism of passive obedience, faith in authority, the mechanism of fixed and formal behaviour, fixed principles, attitudes, traditions.
>
> **—Karl Marx[1]**

The rise and growth of bureaucracy is integrally associated with the emergence of the 'capitalist' state in modern times. If the rise of a bourgeois system at the debris of a feudal order created a 'middle class', the same class swelled the ranks of a new type of executive that represented a switch-over from purely personal service of an absolute monarch to a public service of the state. In this way, the rise of capitalism not only brought about fundamental changes in the social and economic spheres, it brought with it similar transformation in the political (or administrative) sphere. A gradual but irresistible expansion of the sphere of state activity led to the development of an administrative class that not only served the new democrats, it also concentrated immense authority in its own hands with the result that eventually democracy or rule of the people degenerated into bureaucracy or the rule of public servants. Growing economic progress entailing from the success of the industrial revolution and new intellectual development "together dictated the necessity of reorganising the services on a principle and in a manner consistent with the requirements of a growing organisation rather than those of a static feudal state."[2]

Concept of Bureaucracy : Liberal and Marxist Interpretations

Obviously, bureaucracy suggests a middle-class concept as an essential consequence of the bourgeois system. However, it has been viewed differently by liberal and Marxist thinkers. While the former have appreciated it as at best a necessary evil, the latter have frankly denounced it and suggested its replacement by a new type of public services under people's bodies or 'Soviets'—a term used and popularised by Lenin. The leading liberal thinkers of England appreciated the new administrative class that witnessed its rapid growth with the democratisation of the House of Commons after the promulgation of the First Reform Act in 1832. Taking note of this important development, John Stuart Mill realised the necessity of the bureaucratic system in spite of the fact that it clashed with the principles of a representative government. Thus,

---

1. Cited in David McLellan : *Karl Marx : Early Texts* (Oxford, 1971), pp. 69-70.
2. B.B. Misra : *The Bureaucracy in India: A Historical Analysis of Development upto 1947* (Delhi : Oxford Univ. Press, 1977), p. 9.

in 1861 he wrote that the work of the government "has been in the hands of the governors by profession, which is the essence of bureaucracy"[3] and that a bureaucratic form of government "accumulates experience, acquires well-tried and well-experienced maxims, and makes provision for appropriate practical knowledge in those who have the actual conduct of affairs."[4]

However, a highly philosophical appreciation of the bureaucratic system found its expression at the hands of a German thinker—Hegel. In his *Philosophy of Right* (1821), he raised the concept of bureaucracy to 'abstract heights, a transcendental entity, a mind above individual minds'[5]. He defined it as 'state formalism', or 'state's will', or 'state's power' or a 'corporation'. Though only one social class, he considered bureaucracy to be the universal class, a synthesis uniting the particularism of civil society with the general interest of the state, the paradigm for meditation between the particular and the universal, between civil society and the state. The exercise of power, according to him, was a mission to be performed for God or society. Public officials shared in that mission by executing decisions made by the sovereign about the nature of 'general interest'."[6]

However, the best representation of the liberal view of bureaucracy is available in the works of a German sociologist Max Weber (1864-1920).[7] He laid down the theory of 'bureaucratic rationality' that includes his 'five beliefs' about the foundation and structure of bureaucracy and 'eight fundamental principles' of rational-legal authority. The set of 'five beliefs' includes:[8]

1. That a legal norm can be established either by agreement or by imposition with a claim to be obedience on the part of the members of a corporate group or organisation.
2. That the law is a system of abstract rules convincing all possible cases of conduct within the organisation, the administration of law being the application of these rules to particular cases.
3. The fundamental source of authority in the legal type is the authority to the impersonal order of an officer holding a specifically legitimised status under the rules with powers to issue commands.
4. That the person who obeys authority does so in his capacity as a member of the corporate group and what he obeys is only the law.
5. That the members of the corporate group, in so far as they obey a person in authority, do not owe this obedience to him as an individual but to the impersonal order. In other words, there is an obligation to obedience only within the sphere of the rationally delimited authority which, in terms of the order, has been conferred upon him.

The 'eight fundamental principles of rational-legal authority' include :[9]

---

3. Mill : *Considerations on Representative Government,* p. 113.
4. *ibid.,* p. 114.
5. Misra, *op. cit.,* p. 12.
6. *ibid.* It may, however, be added here that Hegel's attention is mostly confined to the model of Prussian bureaucracy that was adopted after 1806. In other words, he supplied a metaphysical tapestry to what was given in the Prussian code. As Misra says : "All that this super-structure aimed at was the subordination of bureaucrats to what he considered the universality of the states, thereby divesting them of their claim to being treated as an independent unit. In spite of its being a dominant class in society, Hegel did not conceive of bureaucracy as an element distinct from the state. Because of their identification, at least in theory, with 'general interest', both were to be treated as one and the same entity." *ibid.,* p. 13.
7. As David Beetham says : "Of all the features which Weber regarded as definitive of the modern state and its politics, his account of bureaucracy is the most familiar." *Max Weber and the Theory of Modern Politics* (London : George Allen and Unwin, 1974), p. 63.
8. Misra, *op. cit.,* p. 28.
9. *ibid.,* pp. 28-29.

1. organisation of official functions on a continuous rule-bound basis,
2. a specified sphere of competence and of distinct functions based on systematic divisions of labour,
3. principle of hierarchy with a lower office under the control and supervision of a higher one,
4. trained personnel for the conduct of business,
5. complete separation of members of the administrative staff from the ownership of the means of production or administration, with a clear separation likewise in principle of the property belonging to the organisation and controlled within the sphere of office and the personal property of the official available for private use,
6. a complete absence of appropriation of official position by the incumbent,
7. the formulation and recording in writing of all acts, decisions and rules, and
8. the ideal type being the purest form of legal authority or 'imperative coordination'.

Thus, the set of 'five beliefs' and 'eight fundamental principles of legal-rational authority' together constitute the 'ideal types' of bureaucracy applicable to all forms of modern corporate groups, whether political or not. Only such a system carries with it certain peculiar advantages like precision, speed, reliability, discipline, continuity, operational uniformity, discretion and provision for the reduction of friction.[10]

A denunciation of the bureaucractic rule and its replacement by another system of genuine public service under people's soviets or communes is contained in the Marxian view. Marx condemned modern state system as 'bourgeois' and deprecated the institution of bureaucracy as 'a middle class, bourgeois affair'. If the state is an 'executive committee of the bourgeois class', bureaucracy is its instrument. The bureaucrats sustain the bourgeois political system by holding the power of administration in their hands. Not only this, the bureaucrat identifies his own interest with that of the state and even subordinates the latter to the former. In his *Critique of Hegel's Philosophy* (1843), Marx says : "As far as the individual bureaucrat is concerned, the aim of the state becomes his private aim, in the form of a race for higher posts of careerism."[11] Elsewhere he says : "Bureaucracy identifies the interest of the state with particular private goals in such a way as to make the interests of the state into a particular private goal opposed to other private goals."[12]

The discredited bureaucratic system would find its termination in a classless society under the 'dictatorship of the proletariat'. In his *Civil War in France* (1871), Marx says that in a socialist society there would be no place for appointed officials, because the people would hold their power in their own hands and exercise it themselves. Lenin supports the same thesis in his *State and Revolution* (1917) when he says that with the establishment of the dictatorship of the proletariat, there would come to an end the rule of 'privileged persons divorced from the people and standing above the people."[13] The management of public affairs will be in the hands of free and voluntary associations of the people and all public servants will work under them. Moreover, it will be a sort of committed public service. Keeping it in view, Prof. Misra points out : "The communist bureaucracy is thus not only a bureaucracy of public service, but also of political life, an example of administration and politics being fused together, a committed bureaucracy but a bureaucracy none the less. It presupposes the

---

10. *ibid.,* p. 30.
11. See McLellan, *op. cit.,* p. 70.
12. Cited in Shlomo Avineri : *The Social and Political Thought of Karl Marx* (New Delhi : S. Chand & Co, 1979), p. 24.
13. Lenin : *Collected Works,* Vol. XXXV, pp. 486-87.

existence of a party state as an absolute condition."[14]

Bureaucracy : Nature and Essential Implications of the System

Although called by different names, good and bad, like civil service,[15] public service, government service, magistracy, officialdom, official despotism, departmental government, permanent executive, non-political executive etc., bureaucracy means a group of persons (not some mysterious, super-entity such as suggested by the word 'state') who "perform definite functions which the community at large considers worthwhile."[16] These persons enjoy a permanent tenure and get promotions on the basis of merit and seniority. They are expected to be strictly 'neutral' in matters of politics of the country. It may be emphasised that as an army of 'expert' and 'efficient' public servants is indispensable in every political system, there can be no government where there is no such agency of competent officials to manage and run the machinery of government. However, a government is said to be bureaucratic when it "is carried on largely by ministerial bureaus and in which important policies are determined and decisions rendered by the administrative chiefs of small bureaus. In a wider sense, it means any government, the administrative functionaries of which are professionally trained for the public service and who enjoy permanency of tenure, promotion within service being partly by seniority and partly by merit."[17]

In fact, the term 'bureaucracy' is used in broad as well as narrow senses and, for this reason, it lends itself to multiple usages. In a broad sense, it refers to the totality of personnel figuring on the payroll of the government from departmental secretaries at the top to clerks and peons at the bottom. Most of the common people are inclined to identify only those public servants with bureaucracy with whom they come in regular contact, because the top-ranking public servants sitting in the far away-offices of the secretariat are too remote from their world of comprehension. In a narrow sense, the term is applied to those important public servants who occupy policy-making and supervisory positions in the system of administration. In this way, a precise definition of this term would cover "those public personnel engaged in policy and supervisory responsibilities in public administration."[18]

While differentiating the term 'bureaucracy' from 'desk work'[19] and yet realising the element of that ambiguity in its real implications, a recent writer like F.M. Marx says that it implies the following:[20]

1. the type of organisation used by modern government for the conduct of its various specialised functions, embodied in the administrative system and personified more specifically by the civil service,
2. a mechanistic and formal approach in carrying out such functions, literal and 'inhuman', to the point of indifference towards the effects achieved,

---

14. Misra, *op. cit.*, p. 37.
15. Prof. Misra does not appreciate the way of identifying bureaucracy with 'civil service', because the latter conveys "a restricted legal sense and its use at times to signify public servants at a higher level only does not cover as full a range of public employees as does the term bureaucracy." *ibid.*, p. 1.
16. Carl J. Friedrich : *Constitutional Government and Democracy* (Calcutta : Oxford and IBH, 1966), p. 37.
17. J.W. Garner : *Political Science and Government* (Calcutta : World Press, 1952), p. 357.
18. S.R. Maheshwari : "Bureaucracy and Political Development in India" in *Indian Journal of Political Science*, Vol. XXXIX, No. 3, July-September 1978, p. 332.
19. While appreciating the term 'desk government', F.M. Marx says that obviously it is 'a phrase without a terror'. It suggests "forethought and planning, analysis of facts, considered decisions, direction, and co-ordination on a rational basis, predictability or performance, and assurance of results. It alludes to the constitution on the mind, highly esteemed in the era of science and technology. It carries a connotation of knowledge and even of insight." *The Administrative State : An Introduction to Bureaucracy* (Chicago : Chicago Univ. Press, 1957), pp. 19-20.
20. *ibid.*, pp. 20-21.

3. the kind of government that shoulders a large burden of responsibilities in support of the economic and social order or/as well as a political condition in which the executive branch plays a role increasingly more important in relation to the legislative and judicial branches as visible in a welfare state or social service states, and
4. a government subject to control not by the electorate but rather by a group of power-hungry visionary functionaries.

In short, bureaucracy is a government of permanent public officials who are neither elected by the people and nor, for this reason, responsible to them, but who play a very crucial part in the decision-making process of the country. They control the real levers of powers. As such, the narrow connotation of this term becomes really significant, because bureaucratic rule, in a political sense, becomes the rule of the elite. "Technically, a bureaucracy is an impermeable and complex hierarchy, its emphasis being on the principles of organisation, recruitment, education, training, conditions of service, rules of business, and so on. In other words, it deals with the machine and the whole structure of rules designed to keep the machine together. Politically, on the other hand, bureaucracy is a form of government with officials either acting as rulers themselves, or coexisting with elected executives, but connected conceptually in all cases with the exercise of authority as members of a class of power elites."[21]

Theories of Bureaucracy

Different views have been given by the writers on the theme of nature, working and influential position of bureaucracy out of which three main theories emerge which may be briefly put as under.[22]

1. **Rational-Administrative Model :** It has its expression in the analysis of Max Weber and its reinterpretations by the proponents of the convergence theory like James Burnham. According to Weber, bureaucracy is an 'ideal type' of rule based on a system of rational rules having their enforcement by the law of the state. So it is rational-legal. The salient characteristics are: (a) There is a firmly ordered hierarchy, which ensures that lower offices are supervised by specified higher ones within a chain of command. (b) Business is managed on the basis of written documents and a filing system. (c) The authority of officials is impersonal and stems entirely from the post they hold, not from personal status. (d) Bureaucratic rules are strict enough to minimise the scope of personal discretion. (e) Appointment and advancement within bureaucracy are based on professional criteria, such as training, expertise and administrative competence. In this perspective, the central feature of bureaucracy "is rationality, because bureaucratisation reflects the advance of a reliable, predictable and, above all, efficient means of a social organisation."[23] The rise of capitalism and the growth of democratisation are responsible for the expansion of bureaucracy and this process is irreversible in every industrialised society whether it is liberal-democratic or communist. Picking up a thread from such a version, Burnham in his *Managerial Revolution* observes that regardless of their ideological differences, all industrial societies "are governed by a class of managers, technocrats and state officials whose power is vested in their technical and administrative skills."[24]
2. **Power-bloc Model:** Contrary to Weber, Marx regards state as an 'executive committee of

---

21. Misra, *op. cit.*, p. 33.
22. Andrew Heywood: *Politics*, pp. 358-62.
23. *Ibid.*, p. 359.
24. *Ibid.*

the bourgeois class and bureaucracy as an instrument that protects it.' Bureaucracy is like an organisation that protects and promotes the interest of the capitalist class. In the words of Marx, bureaucracy is 'state's consciousness'. It is the corps of state officials, which extends its power capacity through secrecy and mastery.[25] It is a parasitic body on civil society and an autonomous source of political action. Lenin reiterates the same view when he says: "The bureaucracy and the standing army, direct products of class oppression, have to be smashed. The army would be replaced by armed workers and the bureaucrats by elected officials subject to recall."[26] Trotsky in his *The Revolution Betrayed* says about 'bureaucratic degeneration' and hopes that social stratum would be dismantled by a political revolution. So Milovan Djilas finds a close union between the clique of the Communist Party and the top civil servants who constitute a 'new class' that holds and exercises power in a 'state of the workers and peasants.' Among the neo-Marxists we may refer to Ralph Miliband who says that the top civil servants "are conservative in the sense that they are, within the allotted sphere, the conscious or unconscious allies of existing economic and social elites".[27]

3. **Bureaucratic Oversupply Model:** Different from the liberal model of Weber and the socialist model of Marx and his followers, the advocates of the 'new right' school like William Niskanen and Dunleavy study the whole case from the viewpoint of rational choice or public choice theories. Since individuals are rationally self-seeking creatures or utility maximisers, all senior bureaucrats, regardless of their image as public servants, are primarily motivated by career self-interest and thus seek an expansion of the agency in which they work and an increase in its budget. This is because bureaucratic growth guarantees job security, expands promotion prospects, improves salaries, and brings top officials greater power, patronage and prestige. Bureaucracies thus contain a powerful inner dynamic, leading to the growth of government and the expansion of public responsibilities.[28]

All the three theories, discussed above, have their inadequacy. The Weberian view is inadequate in the sense that it takes its 'ideal types' of bureaucracy as of universal application. Different political systems have their own way of operation and so the organisation and working of bureaucracy is bound to be different. The Marxian view is inadequate in the sense that it at first condemns bureaucracy as an instrument of capitalist domination and then integrates it with the rule of the Communist Party by making it 'committed' to the official ideology. So, the 'new right model' has its inadequacy in the fact that it scales down the significance of bureaucracy and desires its replacement by private sector management techniques in the age of liberalisation and globalisation.

The case of bureaucracy should be re-examined in the context of two new developments. First, liberalism has absorbed some of the traits of socialism and socialism has been softened by the touch of liberalism. This is known as the 'convergence thesis'. It implies that both the Communist and the Western states "are now obliged to adapt to the exigencies of the modern period, with increasing sophisticated industrial production and patterns of life."[29] Second, many states of the

25. Marx: *The Critique of Hegel's Philosophy of Right,* p. 46.
26. Lenin: *State and Revolution,* pp. 35-39.
27. Miliband: *The State in Capitalist Society,* p. 123.
28. Heywood, *op. cit.,* p. 361.
29. Adam Westoby: "The Anatomy of the Communist States" in Gregor McLellan, David Held and Stuart Hall (eds): *The Idea of the Modern State,* p. 144.

world have taken to the course of the rationalisation of their administration—a process that is known as 're-inventing government.'[30]

Organisation of Bureaucracy

It is a fact that bureaucracy has its unavoidable place in every political system of the world in spite of the fact that it is taken by the Marxists as an instrument of capitalist domination that degenerates the state. Djilas of Yugoslavia takes it as an ancillary wing of the communist clique in power making a 'new class' of its own. Confining their attention to England, Kellner and Crowther-Hunt take it as 'Britain's ruling class'. If the press is regarded as the fourth estate, bureaucracy should be regarded as the fourth branch of government. The European Union is a body of 27 states which has a large army of the bureaucrats working in the European Commission and who are called 'Eurocrats'.

The organisational patterns of bureaucracy range from the centralised model of China to the decentralised model of the United States with a mixture of the two in many other countries of the world. In China bureaucracy has no separate and independent status on account of the practice of *nomenklatura.* It is a system that controls the career of the millions of officials in the government and elsewhere including banks, hospitals and trade unions. "Any personnel decision involving appointments, promotions, transfers or dismissals that affects the position on this extensive list be approved by the Organisation Department of the Communist Party. Through this system the Communist Party tries to ensure that leading institutions throughout the country will exercise only the autonomy granted to them by the party."[31]

Though a liberal-democratic state, France is also said to have the model of centralised bureaucracy. The Napoleonic model of administration still prevails there. The Council of State is the supreme administrative body, which advises on legislative and administrative matters and acts as the highest administrative court. The bureaucracy enjoys unusually great autonomy, because the constitution severely restricts the number of fields in which Parliament can legislate and authorise the bureaucracy to issue binding relations in all other fields. Special mention should be made of ministerial cabinets, or personal staffs, who advise cabinet ministers on policy and partisan matters, and informally supervise the department of the minister in his name. Besides, most of the members of the cabinet are recruited from the ranks of the talented rising young administrators, who often return to the regular administration when they leave the cabinet. It shows that bureaucracy "has enormous power and autonomy, defining policy objectives behind closed doors and pursuing them with grand indifference to criticism."[32]

On the other side, the United States has the model of decentralised bureaucracy. Here bureaucracy works under the control of the President who is elected for a term of four years. The saying goes that 'if the President sneezes, bureaucrats catch cold'. The Centre is not very strong as there is a federal system and, moreover, the separation of powers prevents any branch of government to play the role of George III. Permanent civil servants are recruited through permanent competitive public examination and they are placed on one of the General Schedule grades, but there is a very large number of political appointees in the so called Schedule C posts who invariably show their loyalty to the administration. Different

30. Heywood, *op. cit.,* p.365.
31. W.A. Joseph: "China" in W.A. Joseph, Mark Kesselman and J. Krieger (eds.): *Third World Politics at the Crossroads,* p. 66.
32. Kesselman: "France" in Mark Kesselman, J. Krieger and W.A. Joseph (eds.): *Comparative Politics at the Crossroads,* p. 135.

from this the officers appointed by the Civil Service Commission remain more committed to the growth of their bureaus or the continuance of their services and programmes. So there remains tension between the two.[33]

But in some developed countries like Britain and Sweden, the bureaucracy has neither the centralised model of China and France nor a decentralised model of the United States. Here the situation looks like a blending of the two. Movements for reforming bureaucratic system are under way and the area of ministerial activity is also being cut short. The new trend is towards a curtailed welfare state. With the launching of the 'Next Steps Initiative', unified national administration is being dismantled by restricting ministries to their 'core' policy functions and handing over responsibility for implementation to executive agencies. This is providing a good basis for, what is now known as, 'new public management'. It is feared that this trend may cause 'democratic deficit' and may weaken the public service ethos.[34]

Functions and Role

It is generally taken for granted that civil servants merely act according to the wishes and the dictates of their political chiefs. But such a view is mistaken. The civil servants perform a number of important functions as under:

1. The civil servants not only carry out the orders of their political masters, they also advise them. They serve as the reservoirs of information with the help of which ministers make programmes or lay down policies. Being 'laymen', the ministers lack both the knowledge and the ability to conduct the work of the department; they have to depend upon the advice of the experienced departmental chiefs in dealing with many knotty problems. The civil servants put before their masters useful suggestions supported by convincing arguments and facts which they accept in most of the cases. The political heads have to answer questions in the Parliament and also outside as in press conferences; they have to give statements and explanations so as to clarify their position and mould public opinion in their favour. The fear of 'accountability' always hovers over their heads. As a result, they have to bank upon the cooperation and advice of their expert officials. Thus, bureaucracy thrives under the cloak of ministerial responsibility.[35]
2. Not only in the field of administration where the political chiefs in most of the cases sign on the dotted lines, this penetrating role of bureaucracy may also be seen in the field of legislation. The bills are passed by the legislature and after being assented to by the head of the state, are placed on the statue book. But the work of drafting a bill is done by the departmental chiefs. The ministers may give an outline, but the civil servants may incorporate much into the text of the provisions that they like. In a dexterous way, they may even change the real nature of legislation: with or without the knowledge and the consent of their political heads. More important than this is the role of the bureaucrats in the sphere of departmental or administrative legislation. They issue 'letters, circulars, regulations, notifications etc. from time to time so as to supplement the blank portions of the law made by the legislature. These rules and regulations (constituting the case of delegated legislation) are placed before the legislature for approval and, in most of the cases, they are passed within a couple of minutes, unless some conscientious member raises his objections and draws the attention of the House towards violation of its wishes in a particular manner. It shows that while the

33. Heywood. *op. cit.,* p. 366.
34. *Ibid.,* p. 367.
35. Ramsay Muir: *How Britain is Governed,* p. 44.

cabinet has usurped the powers of the parliament, the bureaucrats have, in their own way, usurped the powers of the political chiefs. As a result, bureaucracy behind the veil "wields so much of the reality of power."[36]

3. So in matters of finance the bureaucrats manage to incorporate their desires and decisions into the provisions of the budget. Whether the minister is a conservative or a progressive, a liberal or a socialist, he has to count upon the gracious advice and cooperation of his subordinate officials. When the budget is prepared, the expert administrators occupying their position in the departments of finance, taxation and planning, forcefully suggest that how much money is to be raised and how it is to be spent on various items. The framing of the budget is so technical a job that it can be handled only by the experts and, for this reason, the bureaucracy "not only spends the proceeds of taxation, it largely decides how much is to be raised and how it is to be raised."[37]
4. Modern democratic state is increasingly developing its corporatist character. Several non-state agencies are playing their part in the decision-making process in view of the fact that their representatives take part in the deliberations. Such groups behave like 'clients' and receive the benefit of political patronage. Thus, bureaucracy has its close interaction with such interest groups. It not only proctects the interests of certain groups, in some situations it itself plays the role of a pressure group. This makes the case of 'institutional pluralism'.
5. It is said that the ministers formulate the national policy. But policy-making is done on the basis of expert advice. The function of the civil servants is to run the administration of the country according to the dictates and directions of their political chiefs, but by virtue of being more knowledgeable and experienced in the field of public administration, top civil servants offer their 'advice' to the ministers covering possible options and highlighting the impact and consequences of different options or alternatives.
6. Particularly in the developing countries of the world, bureaucracy performs the function of maintaining political stability and achieving economic growth. The reason is that the political chiefs of such countries, in most of the cases, are like raw hands, while bureaucracy is operational there as a matter of colonial heritage. The foreign rulers established their 'good governance' in the dependent countries with the help of bureaucracy that was like a 'steel frame'. After the departure of the alien masters, native leaders came to power who had neither training nor experience of running the administration of the country. Thus, the democratic system established in such countries has been overshadowed by the traditional hold of the bureaucracy. This evil is haunting many countries of the Third World where civil servants may be seen enjoying power without accountability. It has led to the emergence of widespread corruption.

It well demonstrates the fact that bureaucracy has become a far more vital and potent element in a modern system of government than generally understood by the people. What Ramsay Muir has said about the English system of government applies to all democratic countries of the world that the power of bureaucracy has become enormously strong in the fields of administration, legislation and finance. "Under the cloak of ministerial responsibility and cabinet dictatorship, it has thriven and grown until like Frankenstein's

36. *Ibid.*, p. 49.
37. *Ibid.*, p. 58.

monster, it sometimes seems likely to devour its creator."[38]

The Power Concept : Elitism and Bureaucracy

A study of bureaucracy not in a technical but in a political sense provides much material to the concept of 'power'. Once again, we return to the doctrine of political elites and find that the 'iron law of oligarchy' stands substantiated. The rule of the bureaucrats provides evidence of the rule of the minority. Taking account of the actual power wielded by the bureaucrats (top policy-makers and decision-takers), we find that they constitute powerful elites in their own ways. Thus, Gaetano Mosca proceeds to divide all governments into two categories—feudal and bureaucratic. He defines the former as a government in which all executive functions of society—economic, judicial, administrative, military—are exercised simultaneously by the same individuals, the latter as a political organisation with an extensive number of public servants receiving their 'salaries' from the government for the performance of 'public duties' demanding a 'greater specialisation' of functions, 'a far greater discipline in all grades of political, administrative and military services'.[39] Though he "did not define the term 'bureaucracy' conceptually, he certainly identified it with a body of public officials who not only formed an integral part of the ruling class, but also defined the characteristic features of public administration in the modern state."[40]

Like Mosca, Robert Michels assumes that the immediate concern of bureaucracy is the exercise of power. In his view, bureaucracy is an instrument through which the dominant class exercises control over the rest of society. The peculiar thing about this writer is that he mixes up the concept of bureaucratic power with the organisation and functioning of political parties. The essential fact stands out : the rule of the oligarchy exists through the dominant political party. As he says : "The organisation of the state needs a numerous and complicated bureaucracy. This is an important factor in the complex of forces which the politically dominant classes avail themselves to secure their dominion and to enable themselves to keep their hands upon the rudder."[41] However, as every governmental system is managed or operated by the mechanism of party system, the role of bureaucracy, in a strict sense that of party bureaucracy, engages our attention. Thus, Michels asserts that the hold of bureaucracy in a state must be examined through the labyrinth of party bureaucracy. Even if a political party takes to the path of decentralisation in order to make its structure more and more democratic, the network of an oligarchical system gets more and more sustenance. In this way, an attempt to prevent the formation of a single gigantic oligarchy results merely in the creation of a number of smaller oligarchies, each of which is no less powerful within its own sphere. The dominance of oligarchy in party life remains unchallenged."[42]

Max Weber found that though in theory having an impersonal status, a bureaucracy forms at the same time a separate group within the state with its own special interests, values and power basis. Its separate interest "lay in the maintenance and extension of administrative positions and power; its distinctive outlook lay in a belief in its own superior objectivity in interpreting the national interest free from party bias; its power lay in its knowledge and experience in the cloak of

38. *Ibid.,* p. 51.
39. Mosca : *The Ruling Class,* p. 85.
40. Misra *op. cit.,* p. 20.
41. Michels : *Political Parties : A Sociological Study of the Oligarchical Tendencies of Modern Democracy,* Translated into English by Eden and Cedar Paul (New York : Dover Pub, 1959), p. 185.
42. *ibid.,* p. 201.

secrecy with which it concealed its operation."[43] As he says : "The power position of all officials rests . . . on *knowledge,* which is of two kinds : first, specialised knowledge gained through specialised training, which can be called 'technical' in the widest sense . . . secondly, official knowledge, that is concrete information relevant to his performance which is available only to the official through means of administrative apparatus."[44]

So confident is the bureaucracy of its power, asserts Weber, that in a mood of sheer arrogance, it treats its political masters like members of parliament as 'vain individuals' running a 'talking shop'. Besides a sense of duty to their office, the bureaucrats cultivate a belief in the superiority of their own qualifications as compared to those under whom they are required to work. All this is sustained by the instrument of 'official secret'. In his view, the most decisive means of power for officialdom "is the transposition of official knowledge into secret knowledge by means of the notorious concept of the 'official secret'. This is simply a way of securing the administration against external control".[45] Referring to the systems of Prussia and Russia, he further says that it is the bureaucracy and not monarchy that is in a position of actual command. "The monarch imagines it is he who is ruling, when in fact what he is doing is providing a screen, behind which the apparatus can enjoy the privilege of power without control of responsibility."[46]

In short, the whole concept of bureaucracy boils down to this fact that it is the real controller of power. And since it is a small circle of highly influential public servants, it is like a group or an elite that plays the most crucial part in the management of public affairs. Proceeding from the Marxian premise that the state is no more than a mere agent of the ruling class, Mosca, Michels, Weber and others emphasise that the iron rule of oligarchy is irrefutable. However, differing from Marx, they justify the power-elite concept both as essential and advantageous to the society. In this way, the start of Mosca and others from a Marxian premise is just like a superficial affair, rather at their hands the contradiction of the Marxian theory of class struggle culminating in the justification of the dictatorship of the working class is a fact. In brief, the power-elite concept of bureaucracy is an attempt to refute the basic premises of Marxism.

Bureaucracy and Military: Similarities and Differences in the Assumption of Power

From what we have said so far, it is clear that like the rule of the elite, bureaucratic government represents a system where participation in the decision-making process is denied to the people at large or to their chosen deputies. It is a body of permanent and expert officials who owe no accountability to the voters or to their representatives. Obviously, it contradicts the celebrated maxims of a liberal-democratic system. And yet this system is appreciated from the standpoints of spirit, methods and professional character of the administrative personnel. In this way, bureaucratic hold and military rule come to resemble each other in view of the fact that "among them develop the body of professional civil servants an *espirit de corps* and a spirit of discipline somewhat similar to those found in a regular army."[47]

Keeping such a point in view, a study of bureaucratic government looks like a corollary to the study of military rule in a certain perspective. Similarity between the two may be established on these grounds. First, both constitute the most literate, advanced and efficient sections of the public servants who

43. Beetham, *op. cit.,* p. 72.
44. *ibid.,* p. 74.
45. *ibid.*
46. *ibid.,* p. 75.
47. Garner, *op. cil.,* p. 357.

lead a developed and westernised pattern of life and thereby become a 'class' or 'caste by themselves.'[48] Their professionalised career and entire pattern of life makes them distinct from the life of the people at large. Second, both have a disciplined and an hierarchical organisation where the permanency of tenure is guaranteed or the promotions take place on the grounds of seniority or efficiency or both. Both are required to be strictly neutral and detached from political matters and to serve their political masters faithfully irrespective of their personal predilections. Last, both develop the tendency, even an obsession, to drag political heads under their influence and to do what the political chief have failed to secure in their judgment. That is, both constitute an elite of their own. It is owing to this that some writers on the subject of comparative politics "have pointed out that the army and the bureaucracy are the alternative elites, committed to growth, utility, stability, etc., and if the politicians cannot provide these, then one or both of the alternative elites must try."[49]

On the basis of empirical findings, it is asserted that military's motives and its disposition to intervene in the politics of a country either to dictate some policy or take over national administration are not very different from the motives and dispositions of other segments of the bureaucracy. In any political system, the military establishment "tends to develop its own corporate identity and orientation based on a particular mode of life, hierarchy and the traditions and rules under which it has developed and that regulate its behaviour. The sense of identity, and conceivably apartness from the rest of the body politic, may be reinforced by the unique social, cultural and economic backgrounds of its leaders. Finally, the army's orientation with respect to things political is likely to be shaped by the functional purpose and the attempt to adapt to the successful execution of its missions—in sum, by professionalism."[50]

If bureaucracy may influence the formulation of national policy, drafting of legislative measures, preparation of the budget and the like, the military may also be seen interested in demanding the stockpiling of strategic arms, prosecution or suspension of war activities, production of atomic weapons and the like. As specialists in their own field, the military leaders "may believe that they alone are competent to judge such matters as the size, organisation, recruitment, and equipment of the forces. In their professional capacity, they may be impelled to establish national security as they see it economically and socially as well as militarily, in the narrow sense of the word. They may seek to convince the civilian authorities that only in the context of certain policies can they guarantee victory. Such views are all consequences of professionalism, yet they have often led the military to try to intervene in politics."[51]

It is true that bureaucracy and military both may be described as elites in their own ways, at the same time a line of distinction may be drawn between the two. While military desires to keep aloof from the politics of the country as far as possible and its intervention is a consequence of certain compelling reasons, bureaucracy has an irresistible tendency to

48. While hitting at the character of the Indian Civil Service in 1945, Jawaharlal Nehru says : "In this land of caste the British and more specially the Indian Civil Service have built up a caste which is rigid and exclusive. Even the Indian members of the service donot really belong to that caste, though they wear the insignia and conform to its rule. That caste has developed something in the nature of a religious faith in its own paramount importance, and around that faith has grown an appropriate mythology which helps to maintain it. A combination of faith and vested interests is a powerful one, and and challenge to it arouses the deepest passions and fierce imagination." *The Discovery of India* (Calcutta : Signet Press, 1956), p. 312.

49. See the paper of J.S. Coleman in Johnson (ed.): *The Role of the Military in Under-Developed Countries,* pp. 398-405.

50. A.J. Groth : *Comparative Politics : A Distributive Approach* (New York :Macmillan, 1971), p. 243.

51. *ibid.*

wield power. Its hunger for a position of influence in the administration of the country can never be satisfied. In other words, while bureaucracy may be designated as the regular contender for power, military's contention for power is not a rule but an exception. It is, however, a different matter that the latter is in a very strong position to win the game of power. Under any alternative, the bureaucracy itself "is likely to become from time to time an open contender for supreme power in the system. This tendency is most likely to be expressed through the armed forces. The armed forces' virtual monopoly of the means of coercion gives them an advantage over other possible power claimants."[52]

Varieties of Bureaucratic Hold: Direct and Indirect, Democratic and Autocratic

Bureaucratic government has two principal dimensions—indirect or negative and direct or positive. In the former case, it exists and thrives under the cover of political or non-permanent executive. It happens when the ministers become tools in the hands of their subordinate officials. The ministers, on account of being like a'layman', depend upon the support and co-operation of their permanent officials who are 'experts' by virtue of their long education, training and administrative experience. Facts show that in most of the cases a person raised to the status of a minister, though an expert in matters of politics, hardly possesses qualities of exceptional grasp, courage and ability to keep the self-aggrandised permanent official under his thumb; in ninety nine out of hundred cases, he accepts the views of his subordinate officers and signs on the dotted lines.[53]

The direct or positive dimension of a bureaucratic government may be either independent or coalitional. It is independent where the bureaucrats know no masters over their heads. They are supreme authority; they formulate policies, take decisions and run the government. Even military works under their command. In such a system the chiefs of the bureaucratic set up are like a masterless man over the entire area under their jurisdiction. The whole army of subordinate public servants swears loyalty and observes accountability to them. This type of bureaucratic government is found in countries having the anti-thesis of a liberal-democratic order, whether it is a colonial country or one under a dictatorial regime. While throwing light on the role of 'white bureaucracy' in India during the British period, Nehru says: "The Viceroy speaks in a manner such as no Prime Minister of England or the President of the United States can adopt. The only possible parallel would be that of Hitler. And not the Viceroy only, but the British members of the Council, the Governors, and even the smaller fry who function as secretaries of departments or magistrates. They speak from a noble and unattainable height, secure not only in the conviction that what they say and do is right, but that it will have to be accepted as right whatever lesser mortals may imagine, for theirs is the power and glory."[54]

Viewed from a different standpoint, bureaucracy has two more important dimensions—democratic and autocratic. A democratic bureaucracy is one that is ultimately open to public challenge, criticism, scrutiny and the like. The people, the parties, the pressure groups and the press all may scrutinise the role of public servants and then guilty officials may be suitably punished. Although bureaucrats may enjoy the positions of anonymity and autonomy and their conduct may not be a subject of public debate, but in case some public official commits a wrong, his action must be open to public criticism. In other words, "democratic bureaucracies are controlled by and accountable to public officials,

52. *ibid.*, p. 242.
53. Ramsay Muir : *How Britain is Governed* (Allahabad : Central Book Depot, 1951). IV Indian Reprint, p. 42.
54. Nehru, *op. cit.*, p. 310.

but they are generally more thoroughly protected from direct personal reprisals by rulers, while their policies and procedures are more amenable to public pressures."[55]

Different from this is the case of an autocratic bureaucracy. Here bureaucracy is immune from public criticism. Its rule is so ruthless that opposition to its position of power is visited with severe tortures. The legislators, party leaders, journalists and the people in general have no right to criticise the conduct of the high public servants. Obviously, the direct dimension of a bureaucratic government finds its similar part in its autocratic counterpart. Groth is right in holding that autocratic bureaucracies "are subject to massive direct manipulation by the rulers but are far less sensitive to popular pressures from below."[56] In this way, the line of distinction between these two varieties of bureaucracy relates "not to efficiency or to technical competence but to accountability and control primarily."[57]

Bureaucracy as a Pressure Group in its Own Right

Although bureaucracies are primarily regarded as organisations which execute policies assigned to them by the society, they must also be treated as sources of influence upon social policies. The nature of this influence is basically two-fold. First, the members of bureaucracy can give shape to stated policies through the exercise of choice and judgment in administering them. Second, in attempting to affect the objectives and working conditions which the society will authorise for their organisations, members of bureaucracies necessarily engage themselves in pressure politics. Naturally, our attention **is** engaged by the associations of the bureaucrats that play a very important role in influencing the decision-making process of the government.

This fact was well assessed by Max Weber who says that bureaucracy moulds itself into a special group within the state as per its own interests. So strong is the affirmation of this German sociologist in this regard that he mentions two types of interests that the bureaucrats have relating to their prestige and power. Citing several instances from Prussian and Russian political systems, he suggests a variety of interests like those minimising the power and importance of the national legislature, by-passing parliament and co-operating directly with other organised groups, centralising the activities of local governmental institutions, maximising the secrecy of governmental operation, monopolising positions in government as posts for bureaucratic advancement, extending the influence and power of the state externally. All these were interests which the bureaucracy was able to pursue successfully. They are all involved in an interest in power, not merely as a means to improve administrative performance, but as an end in itself. Hence, the explanation for the rapid development of bureaucracy in modern society and state "lay not simply in its technical superiority, but also in the pressure exerted by officials in pursuit of their own special interests as a group."[58]

A good number of recent social and political theorists like D.B. Truman and V.O. Key, Jr. have accepted the contention of Weber and then come to hold the view that since bureaucracy is concerned with the special and limited aspects of public policy, it resembles a pressure group to a noticeable extent. It "is a congregating place for individuals concerned with the same objects. Some of these interested individuals become members of the administrative agencies, while others join groups which look to that organisation as a rallying point, and that agency takes a leading

55. Groth, *op. cit.*, p. 240.
56. *ibid.*
57. *ibid.*
58. See Bcetham. *op. cit.*, pp. 72-73.

part in representing their interests. In this representative process perhaps the bureaucracy's most important function is to promote the idea that its special area of concern is important—be it education, air power or mental health. The bureaucracy also promotes special solutions to policy problems in this area. Finally, it promotes objectives which are of particular interest to its members as bureaucrats. These are matters such as their working conditions, status and compensation, as well as the maintenance and survival of their organisation."[59]

This can be verified by looking at a few leading situations. For instance, in the United States, the role of bureaucracy as a pressure group can be visualised in the clandestine liaison of the departmental heads with important legislators and administrators. It can also be traced in their endeavours to mobilise support of their own clientele as well as of other similar groups. Countries like Britain, France and Italy are no exception to it. We may refer to several cases when the associations of the bureaucrats take up the issue with their ministers concerned whenever a disciplinary action is contemplated or initiated against a particular high-ranking civil servant. It may be discovered that the top bureaucrats strive to keep clandestine connections with important leaders of the leading political parties for no other reason than to maintain or grab the positions of influence in the administrative set up of the country.

What must be stated in clear-cut terms at this stage is that bureaucracy operates the levers of power in a democratic country in a very subtle and anonymous manner. The fraternity of a civil servant, whenever his colleague is entrapped in some disciplinary action, shows itself in every moment of crisis. It is on account of this fact that the civil servants "have interests, and self-projection of interests is undertaken by highly placed individual officials, and this self-projection of interests brings them into contact with the members of Parliament, especially those who can articulate their interests in the democratic system."[60] Again: "All organised groups have their political activity, bureaucracy can not be an exception."[61]

Politicisation of Bureaucracy: Debate on Neutrality Versus Commitment of Public Services

Making an attempt to deal with bureaucracy as a value-free as well as a value-laden instrument of political power is like having confrontation with a very sensitive issue. When studied from a normative standpoint, a student of this subject may tread the traditional path and say that the concept of neutrality of public services is a very noble affair that includes within itself anything like impartiality, anonymity, obscurity and political aloofness of the public servants. Viewed thus, bureaucracy is lauded for being a 'neutral' instrument of the power of modern state and, for this reason, one of the strongest bulwarks of democracy, essential to the system of parliamentary democracy where the political complexion of the ruling party is ever subject to periodic changes.[62] Opposed to this is the empirical observation of a good number of recent writers who have thrown light on the politicisation of the bureaucracy. The burden of their argument is that the classical norm of 'neutrality' of public services has broken down.[63]

The breakdown of the concept of neutrality of public services is sustained by the fact of their politicisation, no matter a critical student

59. J.L. Freeman : "The Bureaucracy in Pressure Politics" in *The Annals of the American Academy of Political and Social Sciences*, Vol. 319, September 1958, p. 11.
60. C.P. Bhambhri : *Bureaucracy and Politics in India* (Delhi : Vikas, 1971), p. 201.
61. *ibid.*
62. See Earl Attlee : "Civil Servants, Ministers, Parliament and the Public" in W.A. Robson (ed.) : *The Civil Service in Britain and France* (London : The Hogarth Press, 1956), p. 16.
63. See R.B. Jain : *Contemporary Issues in Indian Administration* (Delhi : Vishal Pub, 1976), Ch 5.

of this subject may discover variations in the degrees of their connection with the political leaders in different countries of the world. Everything depends upon the factor of their 'autonomy'. Relationship between the bureaucrats and their political heads is like a two-way traffic in view of the fact that both have and try to protect and promote their interests. Keeping it in view, Prof. R.B. Jain thus defines the term 'politicised bureaucracy': "The concept of a politicised bureaucracy is one which is involved or influences or is influenced to any degree, consciously or unconsciously, by overt or by implicit actions, in the streams of the politics of the day whether of the party in power or of the party/parties in opposition. Such an involvement may mean the bureaucratic promotion of special interests of political party at the expense of national objectives. In a more extended form, it may also be regarded as a type of bureaucracy which uses political parties in furtherance of their collective or individual objectives or which is used by political parties in the achievement of party objectives."[64]

The fact of the politicisation of bureaucracy in developed and developing countries of the world has forced us to redefine the related terms of its 'neutrality' and 'commitment'. While the notion of 'neutrality' implies "acceptance of the discipline of working without reservation—indeed with devotion—for the success of every government lawfully in power",[65] the concept of 'commitment' signifies that the progressive goals of a government "can not be realised effectively unless the civil servants are fully dedicated to them and to the political process through which they are formulated."[66] As a matter of fact, the classical notion of the 'neutrality' of public servants has now been overshadowed by the fact of their 'responsivism'. Besides, in the liberal-democratic countries the notion of their 'commitment' has taken a direction that is basically different from what we find in a totalitarian country. Thus, the modern view is that there cannot be anything like programme neutrality when gigantic welfare schemes are undertaken and no civil servant "can possibly take a neutral position between welfare and stagnation, between service and apathy, and between action and inaction."[67] If so, Prof. T.N. Chaturvedi is right in affirming: "Thus, the concept of neutrality, instead of being redundant, requires to be reinterpreted and reaffirmed in a positive perspective in a fast changing socio-political spectrum as well as obligations. As the administration must be in tune with the public opinion and changing needs of the society, the public servant has all along to be a student of public opinion, but no party politician."[68]

In simple terms, the concept of the commitment of public services in a liberal-democratic system implies a harmonious

---

64. *ibid.* p. 156. This writer quotes G.E. Caiden in his support who observes that "political leaders could not tell to what extent they were exercising political power without extensive feedback, ranging from personal spy systems to airing public grievances. Citizens approach public officials to intercede on their behalf before the political leaders and to seek an exercise of discretion in their favour. Public officials have never been seen as mere catalysts, ciphers or instruments whatever image they may have held of themselves. They are political actors and they are expected to be political actors. Political leaders use them for personal and party interests. Qualification for public office depends on compatibility with political leaders. In short the public bureaucracy is politicised." *The Dynamics of Public Administration : Guidelines to Current Transformations in Theory and Practice* (New York : Holt, Rinehart and Winston, 1971), p. 82.
65. F.M. Marx : "The Higher Services as Action Group" in Joseph la Palombara (ed.) : *Bureaucracy and Political Development* (Princeton : Princeton Univ. Press 1966), p. 93.
66. Haridwar Rai, S.P. Singh and M.K. Gour : "Neutrality Versus Commitment : A Futile Debate" in *Indian Journal of Political Science,* Delhi, Vol. XXXIX, No. 2, 1978, pp. 177-78. Also see. M.K. Chaturvedi : "Commitment in Civil Service" in *Indian Journal of Public Administration,* New Delhi, Vol. XVII, No. 1, 1971, p. 41.
67. M.K. Chaturvedi : "Commitment in Civil Service" in *Indian Journal of Public Administration,* New Delhi, Vol. XVII, No. 1, 1971, p. 41.
68. T.N. Chaturvedi : "Commitment in Public Service—Its Implication and Imperatives" in *Journal of Constitutional and Parliamentary Studies,* New Delhi, Vol. XI, No. 1, 1977, p. 23.

relationship between the political chiefs who try to fulfil their electoral promises with a view to contribute their might to realise the goals of a welfare state and the public servants who are expected to carry out the official policies with a zeal without involving themselves into the labyrinth of party politics. By all means, it is a very ideal position. It requires a new orientation to the attitude and functioning of the civil servants. One may say that it implies their dedication to the provisions of the constitution of the country. If the head of the state is under an oath to protect, preserve and defend the constitution of the country, so must be the case with all public servants. However, if the word 'commitment' is to be shunned, then a better name of 'political responsiveness' must be used instead.

Basically different is the case of a country having a totalitarian political system where public servants are required to follow the official ideology. Here 'commitment' carries a particular connotation. The party or the junta in power has its own official line and everyone has to follow it with a sense of full dedication. The 'detractors' and the 'deviationists' are 'purged'. In a communist country, for instance, a sort of new movement (called 'cultural revolution') takes place. All public servants are commanded to implement the official policies faithfully, otherwise they are removed from the service and tortured in different ways. The top leadership also instructs its lower cadres to adopt the new 'culture'. New courses are introduced and fresh instructions imparted that must be followed by all partymen as well as by government functionaries. Not only this, all important public offices are given to the 'faithful' elements with the result that the difference between the party cadres and government servants is virtually blurred. Those who excel in all such programmes, they constitute the supreme aristocracy of the party. "Obviously a system so highly organised is possible only under a single party regime when the selection of leaders for the party is tantamount to choosing the leading political strata of the state."[69]

Bureaucracy and the Third World Perspective

What we have said above, by and large, applies to the advanced countries of the West. A question arises as to what should be said about the undeveloped and developing countries of the Afro-Asian and Latin-American regions. If bureaucracy is ubiquitous in functional terms, no country of the world can be an exception to it. However, its study offers a new perspective when we compare the cases of the Third World countries with their developed counterparts in the Western world. The 'ideal types' of Max Weber hardly apply when we study the bureaucratic system of most of the backward countries of the world where bureaucracy is largely a gift of the colonial system and, as such, it is not prepared to change its ways after the advent of independence when authority has fallen into the hands of the native leaders chosen by the people.

The undeveloped and the developing countries of the world are faced with a dilemma: clash between the 'new culture' adopted by the political leaders so as to harbinge a new socio-economic revolution in the country under the aegis of a democratic constitution on the one hand and the 'old culture' represented by the obdurate bureaucracy not prepared to appreciate the light of change on the other. Not only this, bureaucrats strive to capitalise on the weak position of the party leaders. The fact of unstable governments is a god-send opportunity for them with the result that bureaucratic hold eats into the vitals of a democratic system.

69. Maurice Duverger : *Political Parties : Their Organisation and Activity in the Modern State,* Translated into English by Barbara and North (London : Methuen, 1954), p. 156. As Prof B.B. Misra says: "There is, in fact, no escape from bureaucracy as a part of a ruling class. Functionally, it is indispensable. Under a socialist system, or one party dictatorship its role tends to be all the more pervasive." *The Bureaucracy in India,* p. 22.

The result is an unholy alliance between bureaucracy and military in certain cases. The failure of democratic experiments in countries like Indonesia, Burma, (Myanmar), Pakistan and Bangladesh may be illustrated in this very regard. Prof. C.P. Bhambhri takes note of this fact when he says: "In all political systems, the various centres of power are involved in competition against each other, with a view to exercising more power than legally belongs to them All centres and sub-centres of political power are keen to extend their zones of influence in the corridors of the government. This kind of competition is very commonly found between the political leadership and bureaucracy.... If political leadership is weak or is uncertain about its base of support, under such circumstances, the bureaucracy becomes either a victim of indecision or arrogates more powers to itself than formally it is entitled to have. The hypothesis is that in a struggle for power between public bureaucracy and political leadership (elected representatives), the former thrives if the leadership authority is weak. Closely connected with it is also the hypothesis that the bureaucracy gets immobilised if political leadership is sharply fluctuating or unstable."[70]

Such a situation forced the democratically elected leaders of India to invoke the notorious appellation of the commitment of public services in the country. Prime Minister Mrs. Indira Gandhi criticised the character of the public services in the name of their obstructionist attitude towards ushering in a socialist order in the country. While addressing a meeting of the Congress Parliamentary Party on November 16, 1969, she desired that the public servants in our country must be committed to the ideals of democratic socialism as enshrined in the Directive Principles of State Policy incorporated into Part IV of the Constitution of India. She expressed the view that the country would fall into a rut if it followed the British system in which civil servants were not supposed to be concerned about which political party was in power, nor its ideology. Likewise, Jagjivan Ram, the President of the New Congress, in his address at the Bombay session of the Indian National Congress held in the following month repeated the call for a committed bureaucracy in the country. The implications of such utterances were widely criticised. However the real motives of the Prime Minister could be understood after some time when it became clear to all that her purpose was not at all to invoke the model of a communist country rather than to see a fundamental change in the attitude of the public servants in our country. It took some time when the people, in general, could understand the weight of this observation of Mrs. Gandhi that "only a committed bureaucracy in place of the old, indolent, passive, apathetic and political one could possibly bring about the desired change in the country."[71]

We may say that in all developing countries of the Third World, the constructive role of public services is ardently desired. If the trend of their 'politicisation' cannot be avoided, at least this much can be stressed that their role must be informed by a sense of dedication to the cause of the teeming millions. Keeping it in view, Prof. R.B. Jain has mentioned these important points:[72]

1. The processes of policy-decision making are no longer confined to the political executive; they spread over the entire fabric of government, resulting in inescapable delegation and zones of such policy, where the political executive does and need not come into the picture at all and yet the decisions presumably reflect the ethos of the party in power.
2. The leadership role of public bureaucracy is explicit in all political systems, but it is more pronounced in the setting of developed countries with a democratic constitution.

70. Bhambhri : "A Study of the Relationship between Prime Minister and Bureaucracy in India" in *Indian Journal of Public Administration*. New Delhi, Vol. 17, No. 3, 1971, p. 367.
71. *The Hindustan Times* (New Delhi), December 1,1969.
72. Jain, *op. cit.*, p. 154.

In the context of a large-scale welfare scheme programme undertaken by them as part of modernising process – neutrality is neither possible nor desirable. A certain commitment to the goals and objectives of the State policy is inescapable; neutrality cannot be allowed to degenerate into disinterestedness; nor political sterilisation be allowed to slip into political desensitisation.

3. In the sphere of policy advice and execution, modern bureaucracy cannot afford to remain aloof without involving itself in the prevailing politics. Quite often, as has been pointed out, practical and political considerations are indistinguishable. In the legislative sphere particularly, the area of demarcation between what is political and what is non-political becomes extremely tenuous.
4. At the top levels, even the performance appraisal of public bureaucracy is done by political heads and an element of political assessment is bound to creep into such rating.
5. As a human being, no civil servant can be psychologically neutral on issues and problems which confront him; he is a child of his time with a certain degree of subjective bias which simply cannot be eradicated from his judgements.

In short, in the developing countries of the Third World, the bureaucrats have to find "a reconciliation of a public office holder's dual roles of citizen and official."[73]

Controlling Bureaucracy

Bureacracy is now a necessary evil or an inescapable necessity. The administration of the modern state is so complex that it can be managed by the 'experts' alone. The 'political chiefs' are, in most of the cases, 'laymen' and for this reason, the bureaucracy has established itself in a very strong position. When the government of the people degenerates into the 'rule of the public servants,' the result is that the evils of corruption, maladministration and abuse of official power become the order of the day. So the issue arises as to what should be done to control bureaucracy. For this, some devices have been made in different countries of the world which have their strong and weak points. These are:

1. ***Accountability :*** The civil servants or the permanent public officials must be accountable to some department or institution of the government for their acts of commission and omission. It is wrong to say that, as in England, civil, service, like the king, can do no wrong. The committees of the cabinet may be formed to cross-examine civil servants as well as the ministers over their heads. The system of the communist countries that prevailed in the former USSR and still prevails in China may not be appreciated that the top leaders of the Communist Party should have the right to pick up senior civil servants and to transfer or remove them as per their 'pleasure'.
2. ***Ombudsman :*** As in Sweden, so in many other countries a top-ranking anti-corruption officer is appointed either by the head of the state or is elected by the Parliament. He hears grievances of the public, investigates the matter, and then recommends punishment to be awarded to the guilty officer. A Vigilance Commission having members appointed by the head of the state may serve the desired purpose.
3. ***Publicity :*** The press and the agencies of mass media like radio and television should have the freedom to catch the cases of scandals or maladministration so that due publicity may be given to the wrong actions of the public servants. Some well organised

73. See V. Merikoski: "The Politicisation of Public Administration" in *International Review of Administrative Sciences*, Brussels, Vol. 39, 1973, p. 213.

groups may also do the same job. For instance, the publicity given to the Watergate affair in America led to tighter oversight of the government agencies.

4. ***Counter-bureaucracies :*** Iron cuts iron and power checks power. Thus, the power of the bureaucracies should be checked by counter-bureaucracies. The leaders of the government should take the advice of their senior civil servants, they should also seek such advice from unofficial sources of 'outsiders' which may provide expertise as required by the minister. For instance, in 1970 Prime Minister Heath of Britain set up the Central Policy Review Staff (CPRS) and his successor Wilson created the Policy Unit in 1974.
5. ***Politicisation :*** The head of the state or of the government should have the power to appoint his staff as happened before the creation of the civil service commisions. It creates the 'spoils system'. If American President Jackson initiated it, it led to the assassination of President Garfield at the hands of a disgruntled public servant. In Germany the Berufsverbot system allows incoming ministers to discard unwanted officials by retiring them on full pay and appoint more sympathetic ones in their place. The political chief may adopt any possible tactic for this purpose. For instance, in 1981 Prime Minister Thatcher abolished the Civil Service Department and in 1983 she disbanded the CPRS. In India Mrs. Gandhi strengthened the Prime Minister's office by inducting officers of her choice. If Indira preferred Haksar, Vajpayee preferred Mishra. Such devices are practised in different countries of the world with different political systems and their success may be measured in varying degrees as well. It is well observed: "The perceived need to control bureaucracy reflects a wide range of concerns. Most importantly, unchecked bureaucratic power spells the demise of representative and responsible government. For political democracy to be meaningful, appointed officials must in some way be accountable to the politicians who, in turn, are accountable to the general public."[74]

Critical Appraisal

The liberal theory of bureaucracy as given by Weber and others derives inspiration from the philosophical interpretations of Hegel who takes this concept to abstract heights by making it a transcendental entity. In his *Philosophy of Right* (1821), he defines it as 'state formalism or state's will or state's power or corporation, a mind above individual minds'. Such a view is refuted by Marx who in his *Eighteenth Brumaire* (1853) condemns bureaucracy as an instrument of the sate that is the executive committee of the bourgeoisie. According to his harsh criticism, the executive power of the state with its enormous bureaucratic and military organisation is 'an appalling parasitic body'. Lenin argues that if bureaucracy sustains the hold of the bourgeoisie, it must likewise be 'committed' in a socialist state ruled by the Communist Party.

The Weberian interpretation is criticised not only by the Marxists, it is also attacked by contemporary sociologists. For instance, Anthony Giddens in his *Central Problems in Social Theory* (1979) says that Weber failed to disengage the impact of cultural, economic and technological forces on the growth of bureaucracy and to tell us as to what extent these were independent of capitalist development. His assertion that the development of bureaucracy leads to an increased power of those at the highest levels of administration leads him to neglect the ways in which those in subordinate positions may increase their power. Like a neo-pluralist, R.A. Dahl in his *Polyarchy* (1971) invokes the argument of 'participation and opposition' in a

74. Heywood, *op. cit.,* p. 371.

democratic system. Numerous interest groups fight for the protection and promotion of their specific interests. In this struggle for power some groups participate, directly or indirectly, in decision-making process, some other groups play the part of opposition. It puts an effective check on the hold and role of bureaucracy. Thus, in the operation of a democratic process, numerous groups compete with each other and individual government departments are sometimes conceived as just another kind of interest groups. G.A. Almond takes bureaucracy as an 'institutional pressure group'.

Ramsay Muir has criticised the system of bureaucracy for creating 'red-tapism' 'self-aggrandisement' and 'departmentalism'.[75] Justice Lord Hewart of Bury has condemend the hold of bureaucracy as 'new despotism'. These points of attack are valid. But equally valid is the argument that no government can function without the role of expert civil servants. The heads of the political executive are politicians who devote most of their time for party work or in political activities. They have very little time to spare for departmental work. Moreover they change quickly under the weight of political winds. It is the community of civil servants who run the administration of the country. It may be endorsed that policy is made by those who know the secret of mechanism: those who are in charge of daily administration tend to accumulate awe-inspiring knowledge, surround themselves with mystery, and assume operational control.[76]

Following critical impressions may be gathered from what we have discussed in the preceding sections:

1. A bureaucratic government is criticised for creating 'red-tapism' by maintaining punctilious exactitude in the observance of rules and regulations of the department, for developing tendency of 'self-aggrandisement' by feeling contempt for the 'amateurs' (ministers) who insist upon meddling in departmental affairs to the great chagrin of their permanent officials, and for sharpening the danger of 'departmentalism' by splitting up the work of each department into a number of isolated and self-dependent sections, each pursuing its own ends without any adequate correlation with the rest.[77] It all causes undue delay in the discharge of departmental functions and, at the same time, it strengthens the evils of corruption and maladministration.
2. The bureaucrats donot care for the liberties of the individuals. They remain concerned with the grabbing of power in their own hands. They want their own initiative in all matters of policy-making and decision-taking. The will of the people, as eulogised by Rousseau, thus stands dishonoured. "The dependence upon superior authorities characteristic of the average employee suppresses individuality and gives to the society in which employees predominate a narrow petty-bourgeois and philistine stamp. The bureaucratic spirit corrupts character and endangers moral poverty. In every bureaucracy we may observe place-hunting, a mania for promotion, and obsequiousness towards those upon whom promotion depends; there is arrogance towards inferiors and servility towards superiors."[78]
3. Bureaucratic government is a very sinister affair. However, more sinister than this is the government where we find a combination of bureaucratic and military rule. Here is a partnership of mutual give and take. The civil servants lack the capacity to rule; the military leaders need an expert and efficient steel-frame of administration run by loyal servants. When the two coincide, there comes a situation

75. Ramsay Muir, *op. cit.*, pp. 54-56.
76. Bernard E. Brown, *op. cit.*, pp. 49-50.
77. See Ramsay Muir. *op. cit.*, pp. 54-56.
78. Robert Michels, *op. cit.*, p. 189.

where political authority is shared by both, though the military oligarchs sit at the higher pedestal. As Dowse says : "The reason for this is simple. On the one hand, the army does not have the expertise or the numbers to run a country and if they did run it, it might cease to be an army. On the other hand, the bureaucracy cannot bring down a government : that is the army's task. But when the government has been displaced, the bureaucracy is still necessary and hence by no means powerless. There must be a coalition of sorts, and hence an accommodation between the partner; whatever the conditions of the coalition, the fact of its existence is a certainty."[79]

4. Both bureaucracy and military rule have an insecure range of life when they exist apart; they have a stable and secure duration of existence when they combine to make a coalitional adjustment in the political system. When this civilian-military coalition government comes into being, the bureaucracy remains not merely an instrumental agency but assumes a position what "may be called a power-situation in which it has to cast its influence and to generate processes of power on its own behalf and in which it is under pressure from different centres of power in the society which would control it."[80] So, the military leaders reap their part of the dividend. They have a steel-frame of administration to run the machinery of government as smoothly as it is done by a party in power on the mandate of the people. While referring to the peculiar case of Sudan, it is commented that experience "has shown that the authoritarian rule of the military, in conjunction with a civilian bureaucracy, is not necessarily the ephemeral arrangement; indeed, it may be a substitute for party government."[81]

It is a fact that a bureaucratic government creates red-tapism and it inculcates the feelings of self-aggrandisement in the minds of the permanent officials. It leads to official gangsterism called 'new despotism' by Justice Lord Hewart of Bury. However, if the bureaucratic government may be denounced for its self-aggrandisement, its weak and docile character like that of a stooge of the minister is equally condemnable. Both situations of extremes are 'unhealthy'either when the minister blindly defers to the views of his secretary, or when the secretary becomes a 'stooge' of the minister.[82] It is also very unfortunate when the civil service becomes the 'handmaid of the politicians'.[83] A pure bureaucratic government is a curse, a bureaucratic government in coalition with the rule of the military elite is a bigger curse. The civil service must operate within a liberal-democratic framework in sincere cooperation and harmony with the norms of a social welfare state. What Laski wrote about the parliamentary government of England is a workable ideal for others to emulate that most successful cabinets "have always been those in which a number of dynamic personalities have been balanced by secondary men of this kind."[84]

79. Robert E. Dowse : "The Military and Political Development" in *Politics and Change in Developing Countries* (London : Cambridge Univ. Press, 1969), pp. 231-32.
80. See S.N. Eisenstadt: "Bureaucracy and Debureaucratisation" in *Administrative Science Quarterly,* Vol. Ill, (December 1959), p. 307.
81. Coleman and Roseberg (eds.) : *Political Parties and National Integration in Tropical Africa* (Berkeley : Univ. of California Press, 1964), p. 678.
82. See *Morale in Public Services,* Indian Institute of Public Administration, New Delhi, 1969, p. 60.
83. Dwivedi and Bhargava : *Political Corruption in India* (Delhi : Allied, 1967), p. 17.
84. Laski: *Parliamentary Government in England* (London : George Allen and Unwin, 1954), p. 287.

30

Military Rule

> The armed forces have three massive political advantages over civilian organisations : a marked superiority in organisation, a highly emotionalised symbolic status, and a monopoly of arms. They form a prestigious corporation or Order, enjoying overwhelming superiority in the means of applying force. The wonder, therefore, is not why this rebels against its civilian masters, but why it ever obeys them.
>
> **—Samuel E. Finer[1]**

The subject of military and politics has engaged the attention of a fairly good number of social and political theorists in recent times. The momentous significance of such a study gets sustenance from the fact that now no country can be said to be absolutely free from the politics of military intervention, if it has to save itself from the disasters of domestic anarchy or foreign aggression. Historical facts amply demonstrate that although the poor and backward countries of the Third World are mainly affected by the emergence of this type of order, what Lasswell calls a 'garrison state',[2] even most of the developed countries of the Western world cannot be treated as an exception to this phenomenon in absolute terms. Whether it is the rule of the military leaders for a short time and for a specific purpose just to correct and consolidate the constitutional government, or it is a long-range arrangement born out of a coup, it is the rule of an elite unbound by constitutional restraints. As such, it is a clear violation of the principles of a democratic system, no matter the leaders in power loudly declare their commitment to the cause of protection and promotion of the legitimate interests of the governed by saving them from the imminent disasters of a crisis.[3]

Types of Military Rule : Search for Legitimacy and Distinction with Authoritarian Regimes

The military rule whether transitional for the sake of implementing some specific programme or a long-range arrangement established after the overthrow of a civilian government has two dimensions —direct and indirect. It is *direct* when there is no civilian government and the

1. Finer : *The Man on Horseback : The Role of the Military in Politics* (London : Pall Mall Press, 1962), p. 6.
2. An eminent political scientist of the United States like Prof. Harold D. Lasswell asserts that now the arena of politics is moving towards the domination of specialists on violence. The garrison-state construct "proposes a ' model in which the sequence marches from the relatively mixed elite pattern of the nineteenth century to military police dominance in the impending future". As he continues : "We formulate the fundamental conditions of a garrison system as follows : (1) the power elites value power enough to resort to large-scale coercion when they regard such coercive strategies as useful to the maintenance of their ascendancy; (2) the elites accept the expectation that the retention of power during at least the immediate and middle-range future depends upon capability and willingness to coerce external or internal challengers." Refer to his paper "The Garrison-State Hypothesis Today" in S.P. Huntington (ed.) : *Changing Patterns of Military Politics* (New York : Free Press of Glencoe, 1962), pp. 51, and 53.
3. See J.J. Johnson (ed.) : *The Role of Military in Under-Developed Countries* (Princeton : Princeton Univ. Press, 1962).

military leaders are the supreme decison-makers. However, it is *indirect* when the military leaders have a definite influence upon the civilian government and thereby mould its policy according to their will. Such a government may be termed either 'quasi-civilian' or 'quasi-military' inasmuch as the organised group of military leaders has its part behind the screen. In this case, the military leaders keep aloof from running governmental machinery but exercise 'incursions', now and then, either to block some official measures or to defend some others in accordance with their interests.

The indirect dimension of the military rule keeps the leaders of the armed forces in a safe situation and enables them to eat and keep their cake too. Any opposition to the strong, even overbearing, influence of the military leaders is seldom successful, for the civilian leaders (whether President or Prime Minister and his Ministers) are always there to defend the hidden hand of the men with the guns. However, direct dimension of the military rule exists in an undemocratic form and strives to justify its existence on the shrewd plea of having their hold as a short-term arrangement perforce brought about to implement some long over-due programme desired by the people. In addition, it seeks its gradual civilianisation by the purges of 'ambitious' military leaders, creation of a political party, sanction of universal adult suffrage, holding of elections, inauguration of a new constitution, etc. The military oligarchs take note of the 'market murmurs' and, instead of suppressing them, try "to translate them into political claims."[4]

A serious effort in the dtrection -of legitimising the hold of the military is made to liberalise the rule of the bayonets by converting right into might and forced obedience into willing dutifulness. Even the power-drunk military leaders cannot dismiss the view that a legitimate regime must secure genuine co-operation of the people at large. As Samuel E. Finer holds : "The junta that has taken control must assure itself of two things—the co-operation of key-civilian sectors of society (that is to say, technological wherewithal; and the legitimacy of its rule. Without the latter, it will rule by bayonets, whereas with legitimacy it will have converted rights into might and obedience into duty. Without the former it will prove inefficient in providing even essential services. Both these requirements—the technological and the moral—in some sense involve one another. A legitimate regime should have no difficulty in securing the cooperation of key sectors; and one that has the cooperation of the key sectors can smooth its way for legitimizing itself."[5]

When considered in relation to the principle of constitutionalism, military rule may be of two kinds—a short-term arrangement made on behalf of a constitutional government, or a long-term arrangement made on behalf of a totalitarian regime. In the former case, the rule of the military is not seen with abhorrence or resentment, for the people regard it as a mere makeshift arrangement just to tide over a grave national crisis. However, in the latter case, it marks the existence of an authoritarian rule implying the application of "terroristic secret police state techniques with their characteristic total disregard for basic human rights of all who are subject to their control."[6] It is a different matter, however, that such an autocratic government liberalises its control to allow some

4. See G.A. Almond: "Introduction" in Almond and Coleman (eds.): *The Politics of the Developing Areas* (Princeton: Princeton Univ. Press, 1960), p. 8.
5. S.E. Finer : *Comparative Government* (London : Allen Lane, The Penguin Press, 1970), pp. 554-56.
6. Carl J. Friedrich : *Constitutional Government and Democracy* (Calcutta : Oxford and IBH, 1966), First Indian Edition, p. 588. The same writer warns: " Military government needs to be distinguished clearly from martial rule, military law and civil affairs. For military government is the government by the military of the civil population of occupied enemy territory whereas the term 'civil affairs', properly speaking, is used to designate functions of liaison and supervisory direction in occupied territory belonging to friendly powers, while military law is the law applying to persons in the military forces, and martial rule consists in rule by the military of domestic territory and citizens." *ibid.*

trends of democratisation just for the sake of legitimising its despotic system. In such a situation, the concern of a military government expands so as to gradually include even those processes which are the prerequisites of a liberal-democratic state.

The process of democratisation in this context has a disputed connotation between the proponents of a liberal order on the one side and of a totalitarian one on the other. However, in spite of differences over the areas of comparative evaluation, the term 'process of democratisation' lays stress on a government's inclination to identify democracy with its particular institutions of 'truly' democratic views. In an effort to clarify the resulting situation and to guide the Germans who were approaching the task of formulating constitutions in three states of the American zone, the American military government issued a policy statement wihch "defined democratisation in terms of eight criteria which may be summed up thus : basic political power stems from the people, and those who exercise power must submit their programme and policies to frequent popular elections; such elections must be competitive between at least two parties; such parties must be democratic, voluntary association of citizens ;basic right of these citizens must be firmly guaranteed ; public opinion channels must be kept free of governmental domination; the rule of law must be recognised; and the excercise of governmental authority must be decentralised."[7]

A military government may, and also may not, be likened with an authoritarian regime irrespective of the fact that its character pertains to the variety of a totalitarian system. With a view to make a distinction between the two, it may be added that the authoritarian regimes in which a coalition, predominated but not exclusively controlled by army officers and bureaucrats, establishes control of government and excludes or includes other groups without commitment to specific ideology, acts pragmatically within the limits of their bureaucratic mentality, and neither creates nor allows a mass single party to play a dominant role are the most frequent sub-types. They may operate without the existence of any parties, but more frequent is the creation of an official government-sponsored single party which rather than aiming at a controlled mobilisation of the population, tends to reduce its participation in political life even in a manipulated form (to quote the expression of P.C. Schmitter) 'to occupy political access'. In quite a few such cases, such regimes "allow a multi-party system but make sure that the elections donot offer an opportunity. In a free competition for popular support, even among the limited range of parties allowed, an attempt is made by a variety of manipulations, going from co-option and corruption to repression, to assure the collaboration, subservience, or ineffectiveness of such parties."[8]

Forms of Military Intervention

The role of military in the politics of a country is visible to all in the event of a coup that may either usher in the form of a momentous change, or whose results may be hardly perceptible to a common man. An eminent American sociologist like S.P. Huntington mentions three forms of coup in this regard :[9]

1. ***Palace Revolution :*** It occurs where the leadership of the government is changed, but no significant change takes place in the social structure or in groups and institutions participating in politics and supporting the government. The transition from fourth to fifth republic in France in 1958 may be cited as an instance in this direction.

---

7. *ibid.,* pp. 591-92.
8. J.J. Linz : "Totalitarian and Authoritarian Regimes" in F.I. Greenstein and N.W. Polsby (eds.) : *Macropolitical Theory* (Massachusetts: Addison-Wesley Pub, 1975), Vol. 3, p. 285.
9. Huntington : "Patterns of Violence and World Politics" in Huntington, *op. cit.,* pp. 32-34.

Some Important Statements about Military Rule

Militarism : It can be used in two ways. First, it refers to the achievement of ends by the use of military force. Any attempt to solve problems by military means can be described as militarism in this sense. Second, and more commonly, militarism is a cultural or ideological phenomenon in which military priorities, ideals and values come to pervade the larger society. This typically includes the glorification of armed forces, a heightened sense of national patriotism, the recognition of war as a legitimate instrument of policy, and an atavistic belief in heroism and self-sacrifice. In some cases, but not all, militarism is characterised of the abuse by the military of its legitimate functions, and its usurpation of responsibilities normally according to civilian populations.

—Andrew Heywood
Politics, *p. 380.*

Praetorianism : Military supremacy in politics; a type of increased involvement by soldiers in politics when military officers threaten to use force to influence political decisions and outcomes. The term derives from the Praetorian Guards of the Roman Empire, who were established as a unit to protect the emperor but who abused their power to overthrow and select the emperor themselves.

—December Green and Laura Leuhramann
Comparative Politics of the Third World, *p. 479.*

Bureaucratic Authoritarianism : Military rule typically lacks a specific ideology, although sometimes military leaders espouse radical or reactionary political attitudes. Military rule also tends to lack any charismatic or traditional source of authority, meaning that if they seek legitimacy in the eyes of the people, they most often fall back on rational authority. One particular variant of military rule that reflects this logic is known as bureaucratic authoritarianism, a system in which the state bureaucracy and the military share a belief that a technocratic leadership focused on rational, objective, technical expertise, can solve the problems of the country as opposed to 'emotional' or 'irrational' ideologically based party politics. Public participation, in other words, is seen as an obstacle to effective and objective policy-making, and so is done away with.

—Patrick O'Neil
Essentials of Comparative Politics, p. 139.

Two Methods of Controlling Military

Liberal or Objective Method : There is a clear division between civil and military roles and responsibilities. Military is carefully kept out of politics. It is done through various mechanisms. First, military is formally subordinate to civilian leaders who are responsible to the legislature and through it to the people. Second, policy covering defence matters is made by the civilian leaders, though consultation may be had with army military officers. Third, the armed forces are instructed to remain strictly neutral in political matters and to be loyal to the government. It prevails in all liberal-democratic countries.

Subjective or Penetration Method : The civilian control over military is there of course, but the head of the state or government assumes full control over the armed forces which binds them to the civilian leadership by imbuing it with the values and ideals of leadership. That is, a civilian leader like Hitler in Germany, Stalin in Soviet Russia, or Mao in China places armed forces under his full control and thereby converts his country into a 'garrison state'.

—Andrew Heywood
Politics, pp. 384-85.

2. ***Revolutionary Coup :*** It brings about fundamental changes. However, it differs from a governmental coup not in the internal seizure of power but in the post-coup efforts to make basic social and economic change and to alter the underlying distribution of power within the political system by eliminating or subordinating some groups and adding or strengthening others. Col. Nasser's revolution in Egypt of July, 1952 immediately engages our attention. Here the old political system is no longer tolerated, nor does socio-economic structure remain intact. A coup that proceeds into a full-fledged revolutionary phase usually involves additional violence by the revolutionary government against the islands of social, political and military resistance within the society. Often the result is a civil war. While a revolutionary war is a revolution from outside, a revolutionary coup is a war of attrition against government and society; the revolutionary coup is a blitzkrieg against the government and a war of attrition by the government against society.
3. ***Reform Coup :*** It falls somewhere between the two types given above. A combination of military and civilian groups seizes power intending to make reforms in the political, economic and social structures. They usually do make some reforms, though they donot instigate a convulsive revolutionary process. Instead, the coalition responsible for the coup usually begins to disintegrate after a few years. New alignments are formed with opposition elements. The momentum of change slows down and in due course another coup takes place with a new coalition coming to power and dedicated to making different changes in the system.

This writer gives much importance to the category of a reform coup. It "tends to follow a dialectical process resembling swings in the political pendulum in a constitutional democracy. Residual reform coups are followed in a few years by conservative reform coups. The radical coups are usually led by army officers, middle class civilians, leaders of reformist political parties (where these exist) and possibly labour leaders. Military leaders usually have a crucial role in the radical group. The army is more exposed to Western influences than other groups in society; its officers usually include a high proportion of able, energetic, nationalistic and upwardly mobile individuals from middle-class background; it is the one social and political institution capable of unified, effective and disciplined action. . . The radical reformers are almost always highly nationalistic, progressive, authoritarian and development-minded. They also tend to be contemptuous of politics and the politician. In some cases, this is manifested in an apolitical, glorifying the uncorrupt admininistrator who stands above party and is devoted solely to the national good."[10]

Finally, the most interesting thing about a coup is that it brings in a new set of leaders. As each American election brings in a new administration, so each coup "usually produces a 'brief honeymoon' period in which the leaders of the coup enjoy a widespread popularity and support. This does not last long, however, for the coup arises expectations which cannot be satisfied; once the old government has been ousted, conflicts develop among the various elements which supported the change. The objectives of the coup are forced to be mutually contradictory, the expansion of the military forces conflicts with new social welfare programmes and the acquisition of weapons from foreign countries conflicts with efforts to achieve greater independence from them."[11]

10. *ibid.,* p. 34.
11. *ibid.,* pp. 34-35.

Causes of Military Intervention

That no state can remain absolutely free from the onslaught of military intervention is a fact, but the tragic event of military intervention culminating in the long-range arrangement of a totalitarian order is conditioned by two main factors—political and societal. In the first place, political conditions have their definite impact on intensifying the capacity and propensity of the military leaders to intervene in the politics of a country. If the constitutional provisions allow allocation of some ministerial assignments to the men of the armed forces, or when civilian government depends upon the support of the military either because of its weak power of decision-making or to suppress its opponents by the force of arms, the likelihood of military intervention naturally gathers more and more weight. In the second place, societal factors have their own part. The absence of a healthy and organised public opinion implying a minimal political culture coupled with civilian leaders' loss of popularity among the people sharpen the zeal of the military leaders to overthrow the corrupt and notorious civilian administration. Thus, the army "intervenes because other elites are absent, impotent or indifferent; it improvises and expands its role to carry the burden created by a modernisation crisis."[12]

According to S.E. Finer, the intervention of military in the politics of a country is governed by these pertinent causes :[13]

1. ***Professionalisation of the Officer Corps :*** The professionalised character of the army officers makes them well-disciplined and thus keeps them away from the domain of politics. At the same time, it impels them to intervene in the politics of the country if severe frustration impinges on their well-trained minds.
2. ***Nationalism and Nation-State :*** Nationalism provides military with a civic religion and an over-riding set of values, for they have a unique role to play as guardians of the national territory and ultimate repositories and custodians of national values. Where nationalism has gripped the masses, the armed forces tend to become the visible symbol and the pledge of nationhood and independence and to attract an esteem for that reason.
3. ***Defence of Popular Sovereignty :*** Democracy stands on the celebrated maxim : 'voice of the people is the voice of God'. Thus, any person or group, including the army, which succeeds in mustering a small semblance of popular support can claim to be the lawful government. By this token any faction can seize power and legitimise itself in the name of the sovereign people. Thus, the path is laid wider open for the military to intervene and supersede the civil war altogether on the plea that they embody the sovereignty of the people.
4. ***Emergence of an Insurrectionary Army :*** An army working for the liberation of the national territory or for the overthrow of the social order commands a great respect in the eyes of the people. The military officers of such an army have a sort of rudimentary ideology. They draw their strength from the public at large and pretend to be the representatives of the whole population. In them intellectuals, scholars, and national leaders transform themselves into fighting men and may show unexpected and unsuspected gifts of military skill, administrative ability and diplomacy. They may disband themselves after the establishment of a new order, but they may intervene any time in the politics of the country to save the rewards of their revolution.
5. ***Widespread Chaos in a State Emancipated from Colonial Subjection :*** Where the situation becomes very acute due to social, economic and political cleavages and

12. See A. Perlmutter : "The Israeli Army in Politics" in *World Politics* Vol. XX, July 1968.
13. Finer : *The Man on Horseback,* pp. 207-10.

tensions, army intervenes after invoking the dogmas of nationalism and popular sovereignty particularly in a state recently emancipated from colonial subjection. A sure invitation to military intervention takes place when passionate nationalism of the people of a newly independent country is mixed up with the desire for the establishment of a strong central government that the civilians fail to provide.

Apart from these five major causes, reference may be made to the prevalence of rampant corruption and inefficiency in the administration of the country, the examples of which may be seen in the emergence of military rule under Ayub Khan in Pakistan in 1958 and its recurrence there under Zia-ul-Haq in 1977, in Burma under Ne Win in 1959 and in Bangladesh under Zia-ur-Rahman in 1975.

As already pointed out, by all means the military rule affords the case of an authoritarian order. Our analysis of such a regime with a military component requires a perusal of some other factors as well. These are:[14]

1. Not all interventions are aimed at the creation of such regimes, nor do they all lead to their establishment.
2. It would be wrong to derive the motives of the officers and the circumstances leading to the overthrow of a democratic regime from the nature and politico-social functions of the regime, established with the military's help, ignoring 'internal' specifically military factors, the mentality of officers, institutional interests, organisational problems that shaped the military's response to the actions of political leaders. It is because of this that often it is difficult to predict the course to be followed in political, economic and social matters by a military junta after taking power.
3. We should not forget that more often than not it is the civilians who call at the barracks for support either to overthrow or defend a constitutional government and that in many societies the civilian and democratically elected constitutions attribute to the military a 'moderating power' that legitimises their intervention. Ultimately even weaker democratic governments in crisis situations become dependent on military support.
4. The role of the military in internal politics does not exhaust the topic of civilian-political-military relations, since there is the whole problem area of the role of military in international affairs and the pressures for military and political considerations and leadership in the conduct of war so brilliantly formulated by Karl von Clausewitz.

Obviously, it informs us to look into the pattern of civil-military relations. Its key components have thus been summarised by Stepan:[15]

1. All major political actors attempt to co-opt the military. Apoliticised military is the norm.
2. The military is politically heterogeneous, but it also seeks to maintain a degree of institutional unity.
3. The relevant political actors grant legitimacy to the military order under certain circumstances to act as moderators of the political process and to check or overthrow the executive or to avoid the breakdown of the system, especially one involving massive mobilisation of new groups previously excluded from participation in the political process
4. Approval given by civilian elites to the probably heterogeneous military to overthrow the executive greatly facilitates the construction of a winning coup coalition. Denial by civilians that the overthrow of the executive by the military is a legitimate act conversely hinders the formation of a winning coup coalition.

14. Linz, *op. cit.*, p. 301.
15. Alfred Stepan : *The Military in Politics : Changing Patterns in Brazil* (Princeton : Princeton Univ. Press, 1971), p. 64.

Levels and Methods of Military Intervention

Levels	*Methods*
1. Influence	The normal constitutional channels; Collusion or competition with the civilian authorities
2. Blackmail	Collusion or competition with the civilian authorities; Intimidation of the civilian authorities; Threat of non-cooperation with or violence towards the civilian authorities
3. Displacement	Threat of non-cooperation with or violence towards the civilian authorities; Failure to defend the civilian authorities against violence
4. Supplantment	Failure to defend the civilian authorities against violence; Violence

Source : Finer : *Man on Horseback*, p. 140.

5. There is a strong belief among civilian elites and military officers that while it is legitimate for the military to intervene in the political process and exercise temporary political power, it is illegitimate for the military to assume the direction of the political system for long periods of time.
6. This rough value congruence is the result of civilian and military socialisation via schools and literature. The military doctrine of development is also roughly congruent with that of parliamentary groups. The military officers' social and intellectual defence facilitates military cooption and continued civilian leadership.

Levels of Military Intervention

Viewed in a wider perspective, military intervention in the politics of a country may be found to have four levels—influence, blackmail, displacement and supplantment. The first level of 'influence' occurs when the military leaders overpower the minds of their civilian masters. Like other catalytic groups of a social order, military leaders have their own institutionalised agency to protect and promote their interests. They not only secrectly advise or send feelers to the civilian policy-makers, but may go to the extent of threatening the government to accommodate their choices, otherwise they would relinquish their posts. This form of exercising pressure amounts to the doing of a 'blackmail'. Then, 'displacement' means change in the position and relationships of players. The military leaders may succeed in creating cabinet reshuffle or transfer (even removal or compulsory retirement) of some civilian officers or any other similar thing in a way that their hold over the civilian administration outweighs the position of others who are in disagreement with or opposition to them. Finally, 'supplantment' means replacement of the civilian government by the rule of the military junta. The examination of all these, levels of intervention "does, therefore, suggest a clear progression in the extent to which the leader becomes involved and is able to influence both the decision and the choice of the decision-makers."[16]

In order to make a better study of the conditions favouring military intervention in the politics of a country, attention should be paid to three significant factors, namely, professionalisation of the military, legitimacy of the political system and general plausibility of the 'official' ideology. When the military is highly professionalised, it lives in isolation with the society at large and converts itself into

16. Jean Blondel : *An Introduction to Comparative Government* (London : Weidenfeld and Nicolson, 1969), p. 425.

a 'class' of its own having training and capacity to wrest power from the other party. In such a situation, its members develop a particular 'outlook' and emphasise it without making it in tune with the ideology of the civilian sections. A check on this tendency of professionalism can be imposed if armed personnel are recruited from different sections of the society and they are also arranged in different divisions and regiments. Thus, the'general law of sectionalism' prevents each professionalised section of the military to be powerful enough to impose ideology upon the civilian government.

Then, a regime which is 'unstable' and 'discredited' provides a ripe opportunity for the military leaders to join their hands and stage a coup which is often successful in not only overthrowing the political order which had forfeited its legitimacy but, more curiously, in winning popular appreciation as well making the roots of a new order strong within no time. Finally, the ideological factor has its part. If there is a clash between the views of the civilian administrators and those of the military leaders and if this point of divergence creates an unbridgeable hiatus, the matter is to be decided by the force of respective parties at their command. The policy of the civilian government unacceptable to the people at large puts more weight into the side of the military leaders and thereby enthuse them to bring about a new order according to their ideology.[17]

Critical Appraisal

Following impressions may be gathered from what we have discussed in the preceding sections:

1. Military rule provides the model of an elite rule irrespective of the fact that the military leaders try to accommodate some other important groups in the decision-making process. The character of a totalitarian order survives for the simple reason that the accommodation allowed to or sought by other groups and organisations is of a temporary nature. In this way, a military rule does not afford the case of pluralism by design, though it may be termed so by means of default. The real state of affairs is neither pluralistic nor singularistic, though it may be termed 'prismatic'. As such, by definition, these prismatic configurations of political forces are unstable and at best they "be conceived of as representing a transitional stage in the process of political change. The prismatic condition of polity may lead to a full-fledged totalitarianism, intra-party institutionalisation, a multi-party system, or further a complete disintegration, to maintain some of the possible alternatives."[18]
2. The military rule has no ideology of its own irrespective of the fact that the leaders in power may so claim in most of the cases. As a matter of fact, ideological orientations find their conflict in such a system. It is a different matter that the military leaders may take refuge in the world of some ideology just for tactical reasons. This fact stands out even when a military rule allows the existence of a political party in the form of its own offspring. As Janos says : "Thus, the emerging one party state will often be totalitarian in ideology and form, but not in reality. On the other hand, the precepts of the revolutionary ideology will militate against bargaining, compromise and reconciliation, and the development of institutional mechanisms for the resolution of conflict. In such political context-.-tension between ideology and state structure will

17. As Morris Janowitz points out : "An unpolitical ideology operates in the same direction; but in varying degrees the mixture of activism, ascetism, and pragmatism in its orientation predisposes the military at least to recognise the need for developing mass support." *The Military in Political Development of New Nations* (Chicago : The University of Chicago Press, 1964), p. 85.
18. A.C. Janos : "The One-Party State and Social Mobilisation : East Europe between the Wars" in S.P. Huntington and C. Moore (eds.) *Authoritarian Politics in Modern Society* (New York : Basic Books, 1970), p. 233.

Finer's Paradigm

Order of Political Culture	*Characteristics of the Order of Political Culture*	*Characteristic Levels to which military intervention is pushed*
I. Order Mature Political Culture	Legitimacy paramount and *unobtainable* by military	Influence
II. Order Developed Political Culture	Legitimacy important and resistive to military	Blackmail
III. Order Low Political Culture	Legitimacy of some importance but fluid	Displacement of Civilian Government
IV. Order Minimal Political Culture	Legitimacy *unimportant*	Supplantment of Civilian Regimes

Source : Finer : *Man on Horseback,* p. 139.

produce considerable randomness in the political process and may result in recurrent attempts by competing groups to eliminate one another from the political scene."[19]

3. Military rule is a curse and its curseness is not mitigated by the consideration that it aims at establishing a clean and an efficient administration. It may be found that even after the liquidation of a corrupt political order, there remain groups within the military hierarchy which strive to overthrow the new regime. Rather their mutual feuds create more unstable and insecure conditions. The remedy becomes worse than the disease. The result is a permanent danger to the life and liberty of the people. Even the admirers of a military rule return to the way of appreciating their old, though corrupt, order of a liberal-democratic model that was substituted by the military regime with the tacit, though injudicious, concurrence of most of the people in search of a desperate solution to their crying problems. As a matter of fact, military rule "rarely succeeds in producing legitimate leaders and never become, as such, legitimate. Military intervention is, thus, like a technocratic action, a problem for national governments but it does not provide more than, at best, transitional solutions.":[20]

In brief, call it by any name like a 'garrison-state' or a 'praetorian state'[21] or append with it the label of democracy (like Ayub Khan's 'basic democracy' in Pakistan, Nasser's 'presidential democracy' in Egypt, Franco's 'organismic democracy' and Stroessner's 'selective democracy' in Spain and, to some extent Soekarno's 'guided democracy' in Indonesia), the real character of a military rule cannot be

19. *ibid.*
20. Blondel, *op. cit.,* p. 432.
21. The term 'praetorian state' has different meanings. Originally, the Praetorian Guard was simply an elite military unit that Roman Emperor Augustus established to shield his person and government against domestic unrest. But now it has different meanings. It "refers to soldiers hired by a government to police an unruly poulation, but it also suggests that the loyalties of these soldiers are not fixed, for they often overturn governments they were hired to defend. The term, finally, is associated with venality, corruption, and military incapacity or cowardice. In effect, a praetorian state is one where private ambitions are rarely restrained by a sense of public authority or common purpose; the role of power, (i.e. wealth and force) is minimised." See D.C. Rapoport; "A Comparative Theory of Military and Political Types" in S.P. Huntington (ed.) : *Changing Patterns of Military Politics,* p. 72.

concealed, nor can it be justified with the canons of a liberal democratic system. By all means, it represents a state of affairs "where a group of military leaders takes over the functions of government in the name of the armed forces and then rules coercively through their support without a popular mandate."[22] It illuminates the potential influence of a military elite where a society's political traditions have not firmly established the respective roles of the civil and military leadership. Undeniable is the fact that military establishes a system by which political power "is translated into actual power in policy formulation and political action."[23]

22. Finer : *Comparative Government,* p. 551.
23. Geraint Parry : *Political Elites* (London : George Allen and Unwin, 1969), p. 76. Also see G.A. Craig : *The Politics of the Prussian Army* (New York : Oxford Univ. Press. 1964).

31

Democracy

> The twentieth century saw the developed world descend into a paraoxysm of ideological violence, as Liberalism contended first with the remnants of absolutism, that threatened to lead to the ultimate apocalypse of nuclear war. But the century that began with full of self-confidence in the ultimate triumph of Western liberal democracy seems at its close to be returning full circle to where it started: not to an 'end of ideology' or a convergence between socialism and capitalism, but to an unabashed victory of economic and political liberalism.
>
> **—Francis Fukuyama**[1]

Democracy is a form of government or a political system having its establishment and stabilisation in some advanced countries belonging to the 'first world', its perversion and eventual collapse in the communit countries belonging to the 'second world', and its frequent rise and fall in the under-developed and developing countries belonging to the 'third world'. Irrefutable is the fact that while all other forms of government failed in the laboratory tests, democracy alone could stand to scrutiny and, as such, is surviving in many countries of the world. Equally irrefutable is another fact that now all are 'democrats' in their own ways and so democracy has its numerous varieties and sub-varieties whose thorough study is both perpelexing and interesting to a student of comparative politics. "Liberals, conservatives, socialists, communists, anarchists and even fascists are eager to proclaim the virtues of democracy and to demonstrate their own democratic credentials. Indeed, as the major ideological systems shattered and collapsed in the late twentieth century, the flame of democracy appears to burn yet more strongly. As the attractions of socialism have faded, and the merits of capitalism have been called in question, democracy emerged as perhaps the only stable and enduring principle in the post-modern political landscape."[2]

Meaning and Forms

The word 'democracy' originates from two Greek words demos (people) and Kratia (rule). In a literal sense, it means 'rule of the people'. So the great Athenian leader (Pericles) defined it as 'a government in which people are powerful'. According to Abraham Lincoln, 'it is the government of the people, by the people, and for the people'. In the words of Sir John Seeley, "it is a government in which everyone has a share."[3] To Dicey, "it is a form of government in which the governing body is comparatively a large fraction of the entire nation."[4] Lord James Bryce affirms: "Since the times of Herodotus, the word 'democracy' has been used to denote that form of government in which the ruling power of a state is largely vested not in any particular class or classes,

1. Fukuyama: "End of History" in *National Interest* (Summer, 1989), pp. 3-18.
2. Andrew Heywood: *Politics* (Houndsmill, Basingstroke: Pelgrave Foundations, 2005), p. 67.
3. Seeley: *Introduction to Political Science*, p. 324.
4. A.V. Dicey: *Law and Opinion in England*, p. 350.

Some Important Statements

Democracy is a political method or an institutional arrangement for arriving at political, legislative and administrative decisions by vesting in certain individuals the power to decide on all matters as a consequence of their successful pursuit of the people's vote.

—**Joseph A. Schumpeter**

Liberalism is a doctrine about what the law ought to be; democracy is a doctrine about the manner of determining what the law will be.

—**F.A. Von Hayek**

I believe that the most defensible and attractive form of democracy is one in which citizens can participate in decision-making in a wide array of spheres.

—**David Held**

but in the members of the community as a whole."[5]

Democracy as a form of government existed in the city-states of ancient times. All public affairs were discussed and decided in the assembly of the free and adult males. Athens may be said to be its best example where the assembly decided to award death penalty to Socrates after declaring him guilty of treason. Now such a form of government is not possible in the large nation-states of the world. Surprisingly, it still exists in five cantons of Switzerland, where its two new devices in the form of initiative and referendum prevail in the country.[6] One more device known as 'recall' prevails in the states of America where the people may call back their elected governor. Also known as pure democracy, it "is one in which the will of the state is formulated or expressed directly and immediately through the people in a mass meeting or primary assembly, rather than through the medium of delegates or representatives chosen to act for them."[7]

A new form of democracy appeared in the modern age as a result of the Glorious Revolution in England (1688), American Declaration of Independence (1776) and the French Revolution (1789). It is known as 'representative government' in the words of John Stuart Mill. Sir Henry Maine in a sarcastic tone calls it 'popular government'. In it power is vested in the people, but its exercise is delegated to the representatives elected by the people who are accountable to their electorate. In such a system the will of the state is formulated and expressed through the agency of a relatively small and selected body of persons chosen by the people to act as their representatives. It is based on the idea that "while the people cannot be actually present in person at the seat of government, they are considered to be present by proxy."[8]

In terms of operation, democracy has its direct or pure and indirect or representative forms. In respect of its nature, it has three other forms-liberal democracy, social democracy, and socialist democracy. In a liberal democracy, power is vested in the people and its exercise is delegated to the elected representatives. For this sake, the principle of universal adult franchise is implemented and elections are held at regular intervals in a free and fair manner. There is multi-party system and a number of interest groups also operate. Thus, R.A. Dahl prefers to call it 'polyarchy'. The government is limited and accountable. It exists in the midst of a civil society. Right to dissent is respected

5. Bryce: *Modern Democracies,* Vol, I, p. 20.
6. These cantons are-Appanzell, Uri, Underwalden (Upper), Underwalden (Lower) and Glarus.
7. J.W. Garner: *Political Science and Government,* pp. 314-15.
8. Ford: *Representative Government,* p. 3.

Salient Features of Liberal Democracy

1. A liberal state is based on the principle of limited government, the idea that the individual should enjoy some measure of protection from the state.
2. Government is a necessary evil, always liable to become a tyranny against the individual if its power is not checked. It leads to support for devices designed to constrain government, such as a constitution, a bill of rights, an independent judiciary and a network of checks and balances among the institutions of government.
3. It respects the existence of a vigorous and healthy civil society based upon respect for civil liberties and property rights. It typically coexists with a capitalist economic order.
4. It is based on the idea of popular consent that is manifest in the system of free, fair and periodic elections. It respects the principle of political equality.
5. The core of the democratic process is the capacity of the people to call politicians to account.
6. Its attraction is its capacity to blend elite rule with a significant measure of popular participation.
7. Political pluralism, open competition between political philosophies, movements, parties and so on, constitute the essence of such democracy.

Andrew Heywood: *Political Theory: An Introduction* (Houndmills, Basingstroke: Pelgrave Macmillan, 1994), pp. 226-27.

Salient Features of Radical or Social Democracy

1. It is not a means for laying down framework within which individuals can go about their own business, but rather it is a general principle applicable to all areas of social existence.
2. People are seen as having a basic right to participate in the making of any decisions that affect their lives, with democracy simply being the collective process through which this is done.
3. This position is evident in socialist demand for the collectivisation of wealth and the introduction of workers' self-management, both of which are seen as ways of democratising economic life. It makes up the case of industrial democracy.
4. The feminists demand the democratisation of family life, entitling women to take part in public affairs.
5. From this perspective democracy is regarded as a friend of liberty, not as its enemy. Only when such principles are ignored, can oppression and tyranny flourish.

Andrew Heywood: *Politics* (Houndmills, Basingstroke: Pelgrave Foundation, 2005), p. 71.

and opposition has its honoured place. Independence of judiciary and press is also ensured. "In a liberal democracy the voter exercises the same power in the political market as the consumer does in the economic market."[9] Such democracies "are, therefore, described as pluralist democracies: within them political power is widely dispersed among a number of competing groups and interests, each of which has access to government."[10]

The case of social democracy is a bit different. It is like liberal democracy with this point of distinction that in it the interest of the individual is subordinated to the interest of the society. It may be said that while the model of liberal democracy stands on the foundation of classical or negative liberalism as advocated by Adam Smith, J.S. Mill, Herbert Spencer and Hayek, the model of radical democracy is based on the foundation of positive or modern

9. Andrew Heywood: *Political Theory: An Introduction*, p. 227.
10. *Ibid.*

Some Important Terms relating to Democracy

Consent: Democracy as popular power, it has been suggested, should be seen as a continuous process of interaction between government and society with a maximum involvement of the people in decision-making process at every level. A parody of this or pseudo-democracy occurs when the decision-makers put as a show of consulting those whom their decisions affect when, in fact, the crucial decisions have already been taken and the policies decided on. Consent, as Lindsay says, should not be manufactured.

—Anthony Arblaster
Democracy, pp. 91-92.

Participation: It is evident that the only government which can fully satisfy all the exigencies of the social state is one in which the whole people particpate; that any participation even in the smallest public function is useful; that the participation should everywhere be as great as the general degree of improvement of the community will allow; and that nothing less can be ultimately desirable than the admission of all to a share in the sovereign power of the state.

—John Stuart Mill
Utlitarianism, On Liberty, and Considerations on Representative Government, p. 217.

Accountability: A characteristic of democracy existing when government is held responsible for its actions; governments that are promoting accountability seek to control corruption not only by reducing the incentive to steal, but also by raising the costs and risks of official misconduct and demonstrating to the population that no one can violate the law with impunity. Accountability is of two types-horizontal and vertical. The former implies that democracy centres on the decentralisation of power. It desires separation of powers and checks and balances. By the latter is meant government's relationship with its citizens. The more responsive a government is to popular demands, the more satisfied people will be with the way government works and support it through hard times.

—December Green and Laura Luehrmann
Comparative Politics of the Third World, pp. 319.

liberalism as adocated by MacIver, Laski, Hobhouse and Tawney. People have the right to maintain their property, but the state has the right to impose reasonable restrictions on economic freedom of the indivduals so as to eliminate the evils of poverty and exploitation. It is for this reason that while liberal democracy takes inspiration from the philosophy of individualism, social or radical democracy seeks to harmonise individualism with socialism and thus assumes the name of democratic socialism. In other words, while liberal democracy desires a 'police state', social democracy desires a 'welfare state'. It "seeks an invented system of society that stresses the social as against the selfish, the cooperative as against the competitive, sociability as against individual self-sufficiency and self-interest, strict social controls on the accumulation and use of private property, and either economic equality or at least rewards according to merits or need."[11]

Fundamentally different from both is the case of socialist democracy that seeks to give a good name to the 'dictatorship of the proletariat.' As advocated by Marx, Engels, Lenin and their followers, it has its own model in which political democracy is sacrificed at the altar of what they proudly call social and economic democracy. The excellence of a discredited system of communism is justified in the name of social equality and eradication of great evils as poverty, exploitation, oppression and injustice which dominate the scene in a liberal

11. Bernard Crick: *Socialism* (Delhi: World View, 1998), p. 29.

Huntington on Three Waves of Democracy

First Wave: It began in the nineteenth century and culminated with the establishment of many new democracies after Allied victory in the First World War.

Second Wave: It occurred after World War II. It included many ex-colonial countries as well as the countries which became free from the hold of the fascist or authoritarian powers owing to their defeat in the war.

Third Wave: It occurred in the late 1980s when the authoritarian regimes lost their legitimacy. It appeared in a vivid form after the collapse of the Soviet Union and termination of the communist regimes in all countries of Eastern Europe.

democracy and what they denounce as 'bourgeois democracy'. Social equality is possible only in a classless society in which economic equality can be established by abolishing private property system. Only then the meaning of the term 'people' may be a reality and the government may be like 'rule of the people'. Lenin says that 'political democracy without social and economic democracy is a sham' and that' a socialist system is million times more democratic than a bourgeois democracy'. That is, democracy cannot exist unless there is a socialist system. Stalin made a distinction of its own type by arguing that a coalition government under the dominant hold of the Communists was a 'people's democracy', it became a 'socialist democracy' when the Communists alone were in power. After the Second World War, it occurred in many east European countries like Poland, Czechoslovakia, Hungary, Romania, Bulgaria, Albania and East Germany.

The model of socialist democracy has seen its 'grand failure' and now the post-communist states are in a state of quandary. All are being haunted by the spectre of democracy and the progress in this direction displays that different states have achieved success in varying degrees. "In some countries transition appears to be less from totalitarianism to democracy than from old to new dictatorship, but elsewhere democracies are becoming established."[12] The distinction between liberal and radical democracies has almost disappeared as refined liberalism has given a humane face to democracy. People have endorsed the view of Fukuyama that Communism has seen the 'end of history' and that universalisation of Western liberal democracy has become the final form of humane government the unabashed victory of economic and political liberalism.[13]

Democracy had its birth in Europe in the nineteenth century and then it gradually had its place in other countries of the world. The pace of the transition of democracy from few to many countries of the world has demonstrated its universalisation. It may be described as a major feature of world politics that began in Western Europe and then sailed across the Atlantic. It covered many countries of North and South Americas. After the Second World War, it saw its triumph in the ex-colonial countries of Asia and Africa. However, the startling feature is its penetration into the countries which were once under the hold of fascist, communist or some kind of authoritarian systems. Huntington defines this progress as the 'three waves' of democrcy.[14]

---

12. Richard Sakwa: *Post-Communism,* p. 67.
13. *Ibid.,* p. 98.
14. S.P. Huntington: *The Third Wave: Democratisation in the Late Twentieth Century* (Norman: University of Oklahoma Press, 1991).

Case of Developed Countries: 'First Wave of Democracy'

The political systems of the developed countries are known by the name of 'advanced democracies'. Here democracy may be seen in a well-established and stabilised form having these salient features:

1. ***Civic Republicanism:*** All such systems share in common a belief in participation, competition and liberties. Participation involves role of the people in the political process of the country that is evident in the exercise of franchise at the time of elections which are held regularly in a free and fair manner. It may also be seen in their involvement in the decision-making process at local, regional and national levels. Civic republicanism enjoins that the voters take active interest in the management of public affairs and support or criticise the government as they deem proper. Then, competition involves the role of many political parties and numerous interest groups which fight for the protection and promotion of their specific interests. It is necessary that all such organisations observe 'rules of the game' and thus carefully and invariably use peaceful or constitutional means for the achievement of their aims. Then, a democratic state stands on the pillars of liberty and equality. While liberty implies a bundle of rights available to a person with which he may have the best possible development of his personality, equality implies that such rights are available to all without any distinction on some artificial ground as that of religion, race, caste, creed, sex, wealth and the like.
2. ***Political Diversity:*** These democracies are politically diverse. All such systems guarantee participation, competition and liberties, but they differ in defining the contours of these boons and their practical application. Of course, freedom is a basic guarantee, but its content and form vary from one country to another. Democracy does not desire singularity or uniformity. Reasonable restrictions may be placed on the freedoms of the people. Britain has its 'rule of law', France has its 'administrative law'. The state may take 'affirmative action' in the United States for the welfare of the negro children. Other countries may allow facilities or extra benefits to the people belonging to poor or backward classes in the name of 'social justice'. Rule of law, not man, exists in all such countries, but variations in its implemenation may be noted. The courts may not have the power of judicial review as in Britain, they may go to the extent of exercising their supremacy over other organs of government as in the United States.
3. ***Economic Freedom:*** Such systems also share in common a similar approach to equality in matters relating to private property and a free market. Economy is either private or mixed and thereby it is by and large free from excessive state control. Anything like 'command economy' cannot be established in such countries. The state may have its exclusive control over some very important industries, or it may compete with private sector in some other fields, but it cannot dispense with private economy altogether. In an exceptional case, a private industry may be nationalised in the public interest, but it must be done by the authority of law and on the payment of reasonable compensation to the person whose property is taken over by the state.
4. ***Institutions of Liberty and Equality:*** Such democracies have a common set of basic institutions to reconcile liberty and equality. But the construction and operation of such institutions may be different. The entire paraphernalia of a democratic state exists in all such countries in the form of autonomous legislature, responsible executive and independent judiciary. Differences may, however, be seen in their compostion, operation, jurisdiction and their over-all place in the governmental

structure of the country. British Parliament is a sovereign law-making body, but the American Congress is not. The American Senate is a powerful upper chamber, but the French Senate is not. The devices of initiative and referendum have curtailed the authority of the Swiss national legislature, but the Bundesrat of Germany is much more than being merely the upper house of the national legislature. Unitary system prevails in France and Britain, but America, Canada and Germany have federal system. Not only this, while America and Switzerland are lauded for having a ' genuine' federal system, Germany's federal system is defined as 'vertical' and Canada is said to be 'quasi-federal'.

5. ***Political Modernism:*** All such systems are admired for being 'modern'. That is, they are secular, rationalist, materialistic, and technologically bureaucratic placing greater emphasis on individual liberty than on collective equality. A modern state is by all means a bureaucratic state. It has a vast army of public servants who are recruited on the basis of merit and promoted on the basis of efficiency of work and length of service. Their tenures are permanent and they are required to remain aloof from the politics of the country. It is known as uncommitted or 'neutral' bureaucracy. Of course, it thrives under the cloak of ministerial responsibility, but it has become, in the words of Laski, 'an inescapable necessity' in spite of the fact that it is ridden with the evils of conservatism, red tapism and self-aggrandisement.

6. ***Industrial Development:*** All such countries are economically developed and highly industrialised. What makes democracy strong and stable and so successful in these countries is the existence of a sound economy. The per capita income is very high and the evils of unemployment and poverty have a very little place. The groups of seven such states (G-7) formed in 1975 is its bold example.[15]

7. ***Political Integration:*** A new trend may be seen in the move of such countries towards political and economic integration. Integration is a process by which states pool their sovereignty by surrendering some individual powers in order to gain political, economic and social benefits in return. It blurs the distinction between countries by forging tight connections, common policies, and shared roles that bind them together. Its examples may be seen in the formation of the European Economic Community[16] (now European Union) and North America Free Trade Agreement.[17]

8. ***Trend towards Decentralisation:*** Surprisingly, such states have also taken to the way of decentralisation or devolution of powers. It is a process by which political power is 'sent down' to lower levels of government. It is intended to increase local participation, efficiency and flexibility as tasks once handled at the national level are managed by local authorities. Devolution is a process or a means to rebuild political participation by making people more directly responsible for policy-making. However, it may also undermine the capacity and autonomy of the central state especially if coupled with integration.

9. ***New Shape of State:*** Whether integration or devolution, in both cases the capacity, autonomy and sovereignty of the states are affected by influencing the relationship between freedom and equality. Although both may be found in varying degrees around the world, it is among the advanced democracies where such processes have

---

15. It included France, Britain, Italy, West Germany, America, Canada and Japan. Russia became its eighth member in 1992.
16. Originally, it had six members-Italy, France, West Germany, Belgium, Netherlands and Luxemburg. Now it has 27 members.
17. It includes United States, Canada and Mexico.

Essential Features of Democracy

1. Selections to the highest public offices shall be on the basis of free and fair elections; for an election to qualify as fair, votes must be counted accurately, with the winning candidates selected according to pre-existing rules that determine the kind of plurality or majority required to gain electoral victory.
2. All citizens possess civil and political rights-the right to participate and vote in elections, periodically held to select key state office holders-and civil liberties, that is the right of free assembly, conscience, privacy, and expression, including the right to criticise the government.
3. Political parties must be free to organise, present candidates for public office, and compete in elections.
4. The minority party or parties those not represented in government organise and criticise the incumbent government.
5. The elected government develops policy according to specified procedures that provide for due process and accountability of elected executives (at the next election, through judicial action, and in parliamentary systems to parliament).
6. The political system contains a judiciary with powers independent of the executive and legislatures charged with protecting citizens' civil rights and liberties from violation by government and other citizens, as well as with ensuring that government officials respect constitutionally specified procedures.

Mark Kesselman, Joel Krieger and William A. Joseph: *Democracies at the Crossroads* (Lexington: D.C. Heath and Company, 1996), p. 15.

Features of a Post-Communist State

1. End of Communist Party's monopoly over politics, economics and society.
2. Emergence of pluralistic societies but ones where interests are weakly defined and where the establishment of genuine polyarchy is usually poorly institutionalised.
3. Uneven introduction of elements of the market into a heavily bureaucratised economy, facilitating rent-seeking and encouraging the corruption of economic relationships.
4. Liberalisation of prices accompanied by the retention of monopolistic concerns.
5. Rapid changes in the class structure, with the emergence of a thoroughly monetised 'new' class enjoying the new-found wealth; equally rapid changes in the employment structure.
6. Radical orientation of foreign and typically security policy.
7. Proliferation of new institutions and practices often hybrids of the old yet oriented to very different purposes.
8. Tension between those who seek to draw a thick line under the past, and those who believe that the perpetrators of communist violence should be brought to book.
9. A generalised belief that the autarchic development strategies are no longer viable and that the only option is to enter the global economy.
10. Various facets of identity politics, including national, ethnic and cultural questions, accompanied by the tension 'nativist' trends and 'cosmopolitans' who define the transition in terms of 're-joining world civilisation'.

Richard Sakwa: *Post-Communism* (New Delhi: Viva Books, 2002, pp. 5-6.)

taken a most developed and profound form and it is there that they "are shaping the very future of the state."[18] It is a fact that devolutionary tendencies further the spread of small grass-roots organisations focused on local and regional issues. Opposed to it, the tendency of integration pushes the states towards globalisation in degrees.[19]

10. ***Post-Materialist Values:*** Above all, such systems subscribe to the values of the post-modern era characterised by a new set of norms centred on quality of life and post-materialist issues. They are more concerned with such high ideals than with material gains. The relevance of the welfare state has gone and even a leading country like Britain under Thatcher preferred to 'roll back' the welfare state. Thus, welfare state once established by Prime Minister Attlee in 1945 became a 'curtailed' welfare state under Thatcher and her successors after 1980.

All these features make a democracy basically different from an authoritarian system of any variety. It is well observed: "In democratic systems, competitive elections give citizens the chance to shape policy through their selection and rejection of key policy-makers. In large societies, competitive elections with full adult suffrage are a necessary condition for meaningful government by the people. In authoritarian regimes, on the other hand, the policy-makers are chosen by military councils, hereditary families, dominant political parties, and the like. Citizens are either ignored or pressed into symbolic assent to the government's choice."[20]

Case of Developing Countries: 'Second Wave of Democracy'

The profile of democracy in the developing countries is neither as good as it exists in some developed countries, nor is it as bad as we may notice in many post-communist countries of the world. The scenario is hovering between the poles of optimism and pessimism. In some countries it may be said to have its ups, in others it has its downs, while in many others the graph shows the figure of its intermittent ups and downs. In such countries democracy has been facing serious challenges from the side of leftism, fascism and religious fundamentalism having its sinister form in cross-border terrorism. Facts demonstrate that democratic transformation is not an easy or a smooth affair. Everywhere multiple changes move at different speeds promoting distortions and political instability. And yet the struggle for its establishment and preservation has been going on for the last more than fifty years. Dahrendorf similises it with the dilemma of 'three clocks'.[21]

Dahrendorf on the Dilemma of Three Clocks

1. 'In the hour of a lawyer':	Establishment of a constitutional and political order or framework that may take the duration of several months.
2. 'In the hour of an economist':	The rudiments of market economy are built on forces that may take five or six years.
3. 'In the hour of a citizen':	Social impulses of civil society are regenerated in a course of process that may inevitably take decades.

18. Patrick O'Neil: *Essentials of Comparative Politics,* p. 189.
19. *Ibid,* pp. 188-89.
20. G.A. Almond, G.B. Powell, Jr., Kaare Strom and R.J. Dalton: *Comparative Politics Today: A World View* (Singapore: Pearson Education, 2004), p. 103.
21. Ralf Dahrendorf: *Reflections on the Revolution in Europe* (London: Chatto and Windus, 1990), pp. 71-78.

The abnormal features of democracy in the developing countries may be noted as under:

1. ***Institutionalisation:*** Democracy in the developing countries looks like struggling for the sake of its survival. People in general donot understand as to what does it imply. The leaders opt for an 'imported' system that fails to operate in the absence of necessary traditions and the result is, as Apter says, 'institutional indigestion'. The problem stands as to how foreign system should be planted on the native soil. In the absence of anything like a national consensus, the leaders switch over from presidential to parliamentary system or to a queer mixture of both. The whole system is perverted and curiously the shrewd leaders coin terms to call their autocratic regimes as democracy of a novel type. It becomes 'guided democracy' in Indonesia under Sukarno, 'basic democracy' in Pakistan under Ayub Khan, 'Islamic democracy' in Iran under Khomeni.
2. ***Rapport with Political Culture:*** Each political system is sustained by the political culture of the people. That is, the beliefs and convictions of the people in a set of political values (as rights, liberty, equality, justice, rule of law, limited and accountable government etc.) coupled with their attitudes and orientations towards them constitute their political culture. From this standpoint, the case of developing countries is very weak, rather vulnerable. In general, the people lack a rational and critical outlook. They adhere to their centuries-old traditions and primordial loyalties and thus subscribe to the way of 'hero worship'. They worship some charismatic personality with a sense of deep devotion so much so that they do not want to hear anything against the leaders chosen or elected by them. Such a political culture weakens the case of democracy and at its cost strengthens the system of authoritarianism established by a leader like Jinnah in Pakistan Gaddafi in Libya, or Saddam Hussain in Iraq. The distinction between the party and the state and between the leader and the government is blurred so much so that the supreme leader becomes everything—the state, the government, the nation, the country. Democracy cannot exist where personality cult prevails spontaneously or is imposed by the force of arms as by Ayatollah Khomeini in Iran or by Mullah Omar in Afghanistan.
3. ***Vulnerability to Authoritarianism:*** Since foundations are weak, democratic system remains vulnerable to take-over by the military or the junta of any other type. The conditions of a failing democratic state instigate and enable an ambitious leader to take the benefit of the situation and capture power in a coup as was done by Kassem in Iraq and Daud Khan in Afghanistan. Movement for the restoration of democracy may also continue in a limping form as a result of which the garrison state is modified to satisfy liberal aspirations of the people. A democratic system in a truncated form may be restored, but after a short interval the situation takes an about turn. The government of Nawaz Sharif is replaced by the military dictatorship of Musharraf and then a democratic government under Zardari is restored in Pakistan. Civilian dictatorship or military rule may also come into existence at the debris of a democratic system as was done by Idi Amin in Uganda and Pinochet in Argentina.
4. ***Corruption and Maladministration:*** Democracy in most of such countries is ridden with the problem of rampant corruption and maladministration. Any political party may be outvoted or be given a chance to be in power by the helpless voters, but the situation remains the same. The heads of the state and government are accused of embezzling and misappropriating public funds like Robert Mugabe of Zambia and Narsimha Rao of India. Their misdoings have their impact

Types of Democracy in the Third World

	Radical Democracy	*Guided Democracy*	*Liberal Democracy*	*Socialist Democracy*	*Constitutional Democracy*
1. Objectives	enabling undifferentiated individuals to exercise their rights and protect their interests	Achievement of the general will	representation and protection of diverse interests	equality and social justice	consensus among diverse groups
2. Perception of Society	aggregation of the individuals	organic whole with common interests	aggregation of diverse individuals and groups autonomous from the state	potentially organic whole but requiring transformation through state action	aggregation of diverse groups, autonomous from the state
3. Role of the State	executor of the will of the majority	executor of the general will	referee	redistribution of resources and guide to action	referee
4. Political Process	provision of arena for the pursuit of individual interests	unchecked pursuit of objectives proclaimed by the ruling class	checks and balances to prevent tyranny of the majority, its representatives, or of the powerful minorities	all citizens are given an equal notice by redefining inequality of wealth and resources	recognition of the diversity of interests and identity of bringing leaders of all major groups into the governmental process
5. Citizens' Participation	active participation is encouraged and electoral contestation	mobilisation by ruling elite, no elections to key institutions, or only non-contested elections	permitted but not actively encouraged electoral contestation	popular participation to effect elite power, may involve mobilisation or coercion, electoral contestation possible, sometimes only intra-party	participation with constituent groups and by group leaders in the allocation of resources, electoral contestation
6. Citizens' Rights	individual interests are subordinated to the interests of the majority, but are protected by equality before law	individual interests are seen as synonymous with state interests, rulers decide the extent of equality	constitutional safeguards of individual rights, equality before law	attitude to civil rights ambiguous, objective of social equality	variables may be safeguarded by state or with constituent groups
7. Actual and Potential Problems	tyranny of the majority	tyranny of the elite	elite domination on account of unequal distribution of resources	extent of coercion required to achieve objectives	reinforcement of social divisions immobilism

Source: Robert Pinkney: *Democracy in the Third World* (New Delhi: Viva Books, 2004), pp. 8-9.

on persons serving at the lower levels. "At its worst, such a system declines into a *kleptocracy* (literally, rule by theft) where those in power seek only to further fill their own pockets and drain the state of assets and resources. As these resources dry up, clientelism loses its ability to provide the perks it once did and may quickly unravel."[22]

5. ***Impact of Political Instability:*** In most of the developing countries, democracy is ridden with the conditions of political instability. Political modernisation is yet to take place there. The forces of ethnicity, racialism and tribalism are so powerful that a man of Indian origin (M.M Chaudhary) was deprived of the office of the Prime Minister by the native junta of Speight in Fiji in spite of the fact that he had occupied it by constitutional means. It has a bolder sway in the countries of Africa where the head of the state is pushed out or assassinated if he belongs to a rival tribe. Curiously the name of democracy or civilian government is invoked by those who stage a coup. One authoritarian system is replaced by another such system in quick succession. In Nigeria the rule of Gen. Ibrahim Babingada established by means of a coup in 1985 was replaced by the rule of Gen. Sani Abacha in 1993 who announced that the civilian rule would be established within next three years. At frequent intervals such coups occur which destroy even the superficial marks of a civilian rule established by the dictators.

6. ***Effect of Neo-Colonialism:*** Imperialism or colonialism is now a relic of the past, but neo-colonialism has taken its place and its impact may be seen on many developing countries of the world. Politically as well as economically, many of these countries are so weak that they cannot stand on their legs. Local conditions compel the rulers of such states to live under the cover of some super-power. If Angola, Mozambique and Ethiopia were under the sway of the Soviet Union, other countries like Iran, Jordan and Saudi Arabia preferred to live under the sway of the United States. The Soviet influence is over, but the American influence is very much there. In the Gulf War of 1991 Muslim countries like Saudi Arabia and Jordan provided help to America and her allies against Iraq for the liberation of Kuwait. In 2003 such countries did not raise their voice against American invasion on Iraq. Foreign interference or influence has sapped the vitality of the political systems of such countries despite the fact that some of them have been the members of the non-aligned movement.

7. ***Menace of Cross-Border Terrorism:*** In recent times, the spurt of cross-border terrorism has appeared as the most powerful, rather unprecedented, challenge to the nascent democratic systems of the developing countries. The Taliban destroyed the democratic system of Afghanistan by capturing power in 1996. After the assassination of President Najibullah, Mullah Omar became the head of the state and he remained in power until his rule was thrown out by an invasion of America and her allies in 2001. Now these elements have their targets fixed at India and Pakistan. Militant outfits of another variety of terrorism are also at work like the Tamil Tigers in Sri Lanka and the Maoists in Nepal and India. All such organisations have their aim at subverting democratic system and replacing it by an authoritarian system of their choice.

---

22. Patrick O'Neil, *op. cit.*, p. 134. The rulers of such a so-called democratic state may adopt any number of shrewd tactics as clientelism and rent-seeking. Clientelism is the process whereby the state co-opts members of the public by providing specific benefits or favours to a single person or a small group in return for public support. Rent-seeking is a process in which political leaders essentially rent out parts of the state to their patrons, who as a result control public goods that would otherwise be distributed in a non-political matter. *Ibid.*, pp. 301. and 306.

Commonwealth of Independent States
Democratic Features of the Minsk Agreement signed on 8 December, 1991

Striving to build democratic law-governed states; intending to develop our relations on the basis of mutual recognition and respect for state sovereignty; the inalienable right of self-determination; the principle of equality and non-interference in internal affairs; repudiation of the use of force or of economic or any other method of coercion; settlement of contentious problems by means of mediation and other generally recognised principles and norms of international law. (Preamble)

The high contracting parties guarantee their citizens equal rights and freedoms regardless of nationality or other distinctions. Each of the high contracting parties guarantees the citizens of the other parties and also persons without citizenship that live on the territory, civil, political, social, economic and cultural rights and freedoms in accordance with generally recognised international norms of human rights regardless of national allegiance or other distinctions. (Art. 2)

Members of the CIS-Armenia, Azerbaijan, Belarus, Georgia, Kazakhastan, Kyrgzstan, Moldovia, Russia, Tajikistan, Turkmenistan, Ukraine and Uzbekistan.

A comparative study in this regard indicates a surprising level of complexity in seemingly simple fact of the rapid spread of democracy in the Third World as well as elsewhere. It, however, leaves three bold impressions. First, it clearly shows the growing global appeal of the democratic idea, the claim by citizens that they should exercise substantial control over the decisions made by the states and governments. Second, democracy may appeal to many people in authoritarian settings because democratic regimes often rank among the world's most stable, affluent, and cohesive countries. Another important pressure for democracy is the widespread popular desire for dignity and equality. Third, democratic transition is ridden with potential fragility. "The fact that popular movements and moderate factions within authoritarian regimes often overthrow undemocratic regimes and force the holding of elections does not mean that democratic institutions will endure. A wide gulf exists between a *transition* to democracy and the *consolidation* of democracy."[23]

Post-Communist States: 'Third Wave of Democracy'

The establishment of a communist system in any country of the world was an unfortunate event. Hence, its termination should be lauded as a fortunate event in spite of the fact that the feature of uniformity or similarity may not be noted in such developments of different countries of the world. Such a system has now no place in the countries of Europe and Africa. A student of comparative politics may hold that while such a system has been amply diluted in China, it is standing on its last legs in North Korea and Cuba. The flow of democracy has now become like a flood and hence Huntington's view should be taken with a reservation that "with a few exceptions the prospects for the extension of democracy to the other societies are not great."[24]

The trend of democratisation or 'anti-revolution', as it was sarcastically remarked, had its sway over many erstwhile communist countries. Its impact may be seen in these directions:

23. W.A. Joseph, Mark Kesselman and Joel Krieger: *Third World Politics at the Crossroads* (Lexington: D.C. Heath and Company, 1996), pp. 12-13.
24. S.P. Huntington: "Will More Countries Become Democratic?" in *Political Science Quarterly* (Summer, 1984), p. 218.

Some Important Statements about Socialist Democracy

Between 1974 and 1990 more than thirty countries in Southern Europe, Latin-America, East Asia and Eastern Europe shifted from authoritarian to democratic systems of government. This global 'democratic revolution' is probably the most important trend in the late twentieth century.

— S.P. Huntington

For us, therefore, socialism without democracy is unthinkable.We understand by modern socialism not merely social organisation of production, but democratic organisation of society as well. Accordingly, socialism is for us inseparably connected with democracy. No socialism without democracy. A government so strongly supported by the masses has not the least occasion to interfere with democracy.

—Karl Kautsky

From very different perspectives, Tocqueville and Marx in the mid-1800s predicted that sooner, rather than later, a democratic revolution would sweep away autocracy throughout the world and many nations would join the first wave of democratisation rooted in Western Europe and the United States in the late eighteenth and nineteenth centuries.

—Mark Kesselman, Joel Krieger and W.A. Joseph

Democracy should be seen in its institutional and cultural context and not imposed as a universal for humanity as a whole. From this perspective, post-communist democratisation becomes an over-determined super-ideological normative project.

—Richard Sakwa

1. ***Triumph of Liberalism:*** Now there is no place for any particular ideology to determine political, economic and social structure of the country. Ideology has either seen its 'end', or the new ideology of liberalism has established its firm sway at the debris of Marxism-Leninism. The people felt disillusioned. By having the knowledge of marvellous developments of advanced democratic countries through the press and electronic media they could think in terms of a 'detour' of the official ideology,[25] or about the 'long agony' of their great revolution.[26] The Solidarity Movement of Lech Walesa had its victory in Poland and Ceausescu's dictatiorial regime was thrown out in Romania. Similar points may be noted in the role of Civic Forum in Czechoslovakia and Citizens Against Violence in Slovakia in November, 1989.[27]
2. ***Reorganisation of State:*** In a communist system the state had lost its independent status by virtue of being a vassal of the ruling party. Superficially, it was very much there, but it was in a very ineffective and imbecile form. Now the party no longer enjoys its exclusive hold over all spheres of people's life. The state has regained its autonomy and capacity in carrying out vital reforms like establishment of the rule of law, multi-party system, free and fair elections, limited and accountable government and the like. Thus, supremacy of law has been established over supremacy of the party. The goal is yet to be realised in view of the fact that the new leaders are

25. Neil Harding: "The Marxist-Leninist Detour" in John Dunn (ed.): *Democracy: The Unfinished Journey, 508 B.C. to A.D. 1993* (Oxford: Oxford University Press, 1993), pp. 155-88.
26. Robert V. Daniels: *The End of the Communist Revolution,* pp. 98-116.
27. Fukuyama says the the total and manifest failure of communism forces to ask whether Marx's entire experiment was not a 150-year detour." *The Guardian,* 15 December, 1989.

hesitant in placing themselves under the rule of law as the new regime enjoins upon them. However, the problem of statehood remains to be solved in some new states which had never seen 'stateness', for they had been component parts of a federal system like the republics of the former Soviet Union.

3. ***Construction of a Democratic Regime:*** The old norms of authoritarianism have been replaced by the new standards of a popular rule. New constitutions have come into force with broad provisions of a secular and democratic system. The functions and powers of the organs of government have been separated and clearly demarcated. Essential freedoms or civil liberties of the people have been ensured and arrangements have been devised to check and control corruption and maladministration. Judicial bodies have been revamped with effective powers. However, the new regime is yet to have a stable postion. Some segments of the people are opposed to the new regime and so the crisis of legitimacy is very much there the examples of which may be seen in Yugoslavia and Russia. The constitution-making proved like a stupendous exercise. Russia could have a new constitution enforced in October, 1993, Ukraine in June 1996 and Poland in May 1997. Some countries like Belarus and Uzbekistan could not have a final decision in favour of a parliamentary or a presidential system. Despite this all, the remnants of authoritarianism still survive in such states.

4. ***Restructuring of government:*** With the inauguration of a new consitution all the institutions of a political system like legislature, executive and judiciary have become more or les autonomous in their respective domains. Duly elected representatives of the people have their berths in the national legislature. The executive, whether parliamentary or presidential, is responsible to the legislature and through it to the electorate. Independence of judiciary has also been recognised. However, all such attractive features pale into insignificance in the midst of what may be termed 'plebiscitary authoritarianism' having its marks in the fusion of public and private spheres, limited political pluralism, minimal popular mobilisation and little scope for legitimate opposition resulting in violent overthrow becoming the only way to remove the leader.[28]

5. ***Economic Transfarmation:*** Such a dramatic change in the economic sphere has its own importance. The trends of privatisation, liberalisation and marketisation demolished the pattern of 'command economy' and the system of centralised planning. Private property system saw its rebirth and so private initiative had its expression in the sphere of agricultural and industrial production. Communism had been obsessed with the question of property rights what Brzezinski dubbed 'grand over-simplification locating the origin of all evil in property.'[29] Liberalisation broke old economic structures to establish individual economic freedom that "underlies political freedom and helps keep the power of the state in check."[30]

6. ***Social Reinvention:*** Transformation in the economic sphere may be taken as significant, but such a transformation in the social sphere appears to be startling. The communist system had forcibly suppressed distinct identities of the people in respect of religion, race, ethnicity,

28. Juan Linz and Alfred Stepan: *Problems of Democratic Transition and Consolidation,* pp. 70-71.
29. Zbigniew Brzezinski: *The Grand Failure: The Birth and Death of Commiunism in the Twentieth Century* (London: Macdonald, 1989), pp. 1-2.
30. J.R. Blasi, Maya Kroumova and Doughlas Kruse: *Kremlin Capitalism: Privatising the Russian Economy* (Ithaca, New York; Cornell University Press, 1997), p. 187.

Communist Regimes in the 1980s

Europe	*Asia*	*Africa and the Middle East*	*Latin-America*
Albania	Afghanistan	Angola	Cuba
Bulgaria	Cambodia	Benin	
Czechoslovakia	China	Ethiopia	
East Germany	Laos	Mozambique	
Hungary	Mongolia	South Yemen	
Poland	Vietnam	North Korea	
Romania			
Soviet Union			
Yugoslavia			

Communist system still exists in China, North Korea and Cuba.

Main Features of a Communist State

1. The reigning ideology of Marxism-Leninism determines the structure of state, society and economy. It is a different matter that tactical twists or turns may be given to it by the crafty leaders like Lenin and Stalin in Russia, Tito in Yugoslavia, Mao and Deng in China, Kim in North Korea, Ho Chi Minh in Vietnam, Castro in Cuba and the like.
2. Power, rather than being contained in the state and government, rests with the ruling party under the iron hold of the supreme ruler. So it is known as the 'party-state'.
3. Since power resides with the party, it flows directly from the party to the state by passing governmental structures. Thus, leadership turn-over occurs not through popular elections but through struggles for power in which top-ranking leaders like Trotsky and Stalin in Russia are involved.
4. Institutions of a modern political system like legislature, ministry, bureaucracy and judiciary exist so as to demonstrate the trappings of a liberal democratic order, but they operate like rubber stamps and do everything at the behest of the Central Committees of the ruling party called politbureau.
5. The party has its powerful wing in the form of nomenklatura (as in China) that prepares a list of faithful persons and inducts them into important offices of the state. In this way, all politically sensitive or influential jobs in the political, economic and social spheres are staffed, rather stuffed, by the people picked up by the elites of the ruling party. The result is committed bureaucracy. Even judiciary and press are deprived of their independence.
6. Private enterprise is tabooed. The entire economy is controlled by the state. Planning is centralised. Thus, command economy system prevails.
7. Social and cultural identities are suppressed by force. The people are not allowed to preserve or protect their distinct social, racial, cultural, ethnic or linguistic identity. A sort of uniformity or singularity is established in the name of 'Russification' or 'Sinification' of the country.

> **Some Important Definitional Statements about Democracy**
>
> ***Political Participation:*** It is an activity by individuals formally intended to influence either who governs or the decisions taken by governments. Both the extent and forms of participation vary between types of regimes. Liberal democracies channelised by voluntary participation are more participatory than most authoritarian regimes.
>
> ***Political Exclusion:*** It refers to those people who through occupying a marginal position in society are effectively excluded from participation in collective decision -making. Migrant workers, criminals, drug addicts and those who donot speak the native language are the examples of groups which face the difficulty.
>
> ***Regimented Participation:*** It is elite controlled involvement in politics designed to express popular support for the notional attempt by the rulers to build a new society. Its purpose is to mobilise the masses behind the regime, not to influence the personnel or policies of the government.
>
> ***Party Identification:*** It is a long-term attachment to a particular party which anchors voters' interpretations of the remote world of politics. Party identification is often inherited through the family and reinforced by the electors' social milieu. It influences, but is different from, voting behaviour.
>
> ***Partisan De-alignment:*** It refers to the weakening of bond between (a) electors and parties, and (b) social groups (for example classes) and parties; in most consolidated democracies, such links have declined in strength, but they have not disappeared; electorates are de-aligning, not de-aligned.
>
> Hague, Harrop and Breslin: *Comparative Government and Politics: An Introduction* (London: Macmillan 1982), pp. 80, 83, 84, 107, 108.

language, culture etc. in order to establish a classless and closed social and political system. Religion, in the words of Marx, was deprecated as 'opium of the people' and nationalism was debunked as a 'bourgeois ideology'. Such distinct identities have their expression now in spite of the fact that the new leaders have different perceptions in this regard. For Vaclav Havel of Czechoslovakia, civil society represented the kernel of an alternative emancipatory social process, while Klaus of the new Czech Republic would have none of this kind and instead he lauded anonymous operations of the market. Such elements are crying for their distinct identity. It has created the issue of 'multiculturalism'. Conditions of civil war emerged in the form of Serbian Charistians killing Muslims in Kosovo and the Muslims of Russia agitating for a separate state of Chechnya. The politics of identity has proved a blessing as well as a curse in the post-communist states. "This has been a two-edged process, allowing on the one side the emergence of civil associations, entrepreneuralism, philanthropy, organised religion, media diversity and so on, but, on the other, allowing the luxuriant, flourishing of social morbidities, crime, corruption, poverty, drastic inequal racism and ethnic conflict. Both processes represent in different forms the revenge of society on the state."[31]

7. ***National Reconfiguration:*** "The collapse of the Soviet empire suddenly threw sovereignty into the ring, and the fruits of an independence that had hardly been desired, let alone fought for, fell to those already well placed when the music stopped."[32] The termination of the monolithic state control encouraged

31. Richard Sakwa, *op. cit.,* pp. 54-55.
32. Richard Sakwa, *op.cit.,* p. 59.

separate and distinct groups to cry for the recognition of their 'identity' as well as to demand much more than mere democracy in the form of administrative autonomy or protection of the civil rights of their members. They may even go to the final extent of demanding their existence as a separate and independent political community. Called 'ethnic nationalism', it showed its form in countries like Yugoslavia and Czechoslovakia in particular. Nationalism (or political nationalism) that came into prominence after the French revolution of 1789 now faced the challenge of ethnic nationalism at an unprecedentedly high level. Mere administrative autonomy was not enough inspite of the fact that it had democratic credentials to some extent. Instead, some ethnic communities desired independence first and democracy after. Stress is laid on the redemarcation of territorial boundaries so as to satisfy demands of ethnic nationalism. The South Ossetians of Georgia demand their amalgamation with Russia, while the Chechens donot want to live like a part of the Russian political community. The introduction of democracy in such countries has created the problem of nation-building. The reason is that the suddenly emancipated people are not trained in the discipline of a liberal-democratic order. Zakaria rightly remarks that "without a background in constitutional liberalism, the introduction of democracy in divided societies has actually fomented nationalism, ethnic conflict, and even war."[33]

8. ***International Reorientation:*** The introduction of democracy has had its impact on the global scenario as well. "The old Westphalian system is under re-arrangement, and a new system is emerging based on a new type of statehood where sovereignty is eroded by the expansion of the jurisdiction of normative processes, international courts, universal declarations, final acts and the like."[34] The new democracies donot look like a faithful replica of the liberal democracy inspite of their orientation towards it. Not a determination to emulate but an obsession to imitate the Western model so as to subserve their purpose somehow may be noted in the political behaviour of such states. Liberal democracies may harbinge the new world order, but these post-communist states are certainly contributing their share to the retention of the present world disorder. As Zakaria says: "In countries not grounded in constitutional liberalism, the rise of democracy often brings with it hyper-nationalism and war-mongering."[35]

Synonyms for Semi-Democracy

1. Authoritarian Democracy
2. Contested Democracy
3. Delegated Democrocy
4. Democratura (a)
5. Electoral Democracy
6. Facade Democracy
7. Guided Democracy
8. Illiberal Democracy
9. Limited Democracy
10. Low Intensity Democracy
11. Partial Democracy
12. Plebiscitary Democracy
13. Prenental Democracy
14. Restricted Democracy
15. Superseded Democracy
16. Tutelary Democracy (b)

(a) It implies rule of a strong national leader (usually called President) who is delegated through elections full power to act as guardian of the nation as in Brazil.

(b) It implies a mixture of democracy and dictatorship.

33. Fareed Zakaria: "The Rise of Illiberal Democracy" in *Foreign Affairs,* Vol. 76, No. 6, 1997, p. 38.
34. Sakwa, *op. cit.,* p. 63.
35. Fareed Zakaria, *op. cit.,* p. 38.

Varieties of Democracy

Liberal Democracies: Such democracies are based on the decentralisation of authority. The citizens take part in making the decisions of the government. More simply put, democracy is a system of governance in which citizens hold their leaders accountable for their public actions. Accountability is ensured through open competition for offices. Democracy institutionalises competition for power through elections that are free, fair and held on a regular basis. But another important part of competition is inclusiveness, which demands a high level of political participation in the selection of leaders and policies. Democracies that pass a more comprehensive test are commonly known as liberal democracies.

Delegative Democracies: They are neither liberal democracies nor full blown dictatorships. They are sometimes called democratic, because they have an outward appearance similar to that of their more democratic counterparts. However, they are led by elites whose commitment to democracy is contingent and instrumental, not routinised, internalised, and principled. Such systems are a peculiar form of democracy; through clean elections a majority empowers someone to become the embodiment and interpreter of the nation's interests.

Virtual or Semi-Democracies: It is a system in which formal democratic political institutions exist to mask the reality of authoritarianism. Leaders (like Hosni Mubarak of Egypt and Mugabe of Zimbabwe) do to deal with what they call 'crisis management'. Authoritarians must come up with new survival strategies, because the old ones are no longer viable. They cannot portray themselves as new democrats and meanwhile fall back on the old strategy of mass repression. They can no longer afford to coopt the opposition with pork barrel items because of Structural Adjustment Program requirements. Instead, they try to create new friends, mobilise old ones, and find new ways to channel and control participation.

Low-Intensity Democracies: It is a system in which there may be a great fanfare about the coming democratic reforms. A new constitution may be created, opposition parties may be legalised, and elections may be held but the reform process is itself hijacked. Elections are carefully calculated to produce the victory of the incumbents, who can then resist further change by claiming the popular mandate.

Socialist or Procedural Democracy: It prevails in a communist country like China where elections take place for local committees and congresses, but there is lack of separation between party and government in almost all public affairs. The Chinese leaders insist that their country is a socialist democracy in which the people are the masters whose will is expressed through the actions of the Chinese Communist Party. Politics has been de-personalised and in many senses political relations are increasingly institutionalised.

December Green and Laura Leuhrmann: *Comparative Politics of the Third World,* Chapters 15 and 16.

Digital Democracy: Relatively recent developments in information technology, particularly in terms of the increased opportunities for interactivity between political actors and the public have excited and alarmed many commentators. The notion that new technologies and new medias can facilitate both qualitative and quantitive changes in the nature and extent of mass communication and politics is being explored to commentators, policy-makers, politicians and activists.

Richard Huggins: "Democracy and Democratisation" in Hague, Harrp and Breslin, *op. cit.,* p. 186.

On the whole, it may be commented that the post-communist states are seriously involved in establishing liberal-democratic order in the midst of many serious problems and challenges. Mere tinkering with the old order will not do. What is really required is that the remnants of an authoritarian political order and a command economy are thoroughly liquidated. At the same time, it is required that the civil society should be built on the foundations of liberty and equality. In view of the typical conditions of every country, the paths may be different, but the goal should be the same. Not a patchwork but an entirely new construction based on the values of liberalism, secularism and modernism. "A dilapidated house has unsound structure and thus any act of renovation would be like making the situation worse."[36]

Critical Appraisal

A comparative study of the democratic systems of the developed, developing and post-communist countries of the world leaves following critical impressions:

1. Democracy is now the only popular form of government by virtue of being based on the consent of the people and so having no substitute of its own.[37] Irrefutable is the aphorism of Lord Bryce that there can be no better form of government than this. Even patently undemocratic forms of government seek to affix the label of democracy on their foreheads. The fact of world-wide spread of democracy cannot be overlooked or refuted. Variations in degrees, not of kinds, may be noted, but the label of democracy remains untarnished.
2. Democracy, though widely lauded as 'rule of the people', has many forms and so its any particular form cannot be standardised. If there can be an Anglo-American model of democracy, there can be other models of democracy as well, provided each model ensures participation, competition and opposition in the political process of the country. Struggle for the creation, preservation and conservation of democracy has been going on in the midst of serious threats and challenges so that the goal is ultimately realised. In Latin-American countries, the trend of *abertura* may be noticed.[38]
3. Manifold are the problems of democracy, manifold are the solutions as well. The merit of developed or advanced democracies is that when the problems arise, solutions are found without creating any menace to the system at all. In developing countries such problems often become insurmountable and thereby cause disintegration of the system itself. In the words of Huntington, the drama of political development and political decay are enacted simultaneously.
4. In its broadest sense, democracy is a form of state, a form of government, a form of society, and a way of life. All the four aspects exist in the developed democratic countries. In the developing and post-communist countries it exists as a form of state and government. The traditional social structure is so obolete that it cannot have its rapport with the structure of a modern democratic state. In the post-communist states, democracy may exist as a form of state in the provisions of the constitution and it may have its superficial existence in the actual operation of the system, it has no place as a form of society and a way of life. The democratic system is well established and stabilised in the developed countries of the First World, it is failing and flailing in the countries of the Third World, and the waves of its resurgence and reversal may be witnessed in the countries of the Second World.

---

36. Patrick O'Neil, *op. cit.*, pp. 243-44.
37. In a democracy consent of the people must be genuine, not manipulated or manufatured. For instance, the silence of most of the people of Czechoslovakia in the twenty years between the crushing of the Prague Spring in 1968 and the popular uprising of 1989, indicated not any kind of consent, but resignation, hopelessness and despair, all reinforced by the fear inspired by the Communist regime's relentless persecution of those who dared to oppose it. Anthony Arblaster: *Democracy* (Delhi: Viva Books, 1997), pp. 89-90.
38. Abertura is a Portuguese term borrowed from the Brazilian experience describing a political opening that may or may not lead to democratisation.

Some Important Statements about Democracy and Democratisation

To speak today of the defence of democracy, as if we are defending something which we know and had possessed for many decades and many centuries is self-deception and shame . . . . The criterion must be sought not in the survival of traditional institutions but in the question where power resides and how it is exercised. In this respect, democracy is a matter of degree. Some countries today are more democratic than others. But none is perhaps very democratic, if any high standard of democracy is applied. Mass democracy is a difficult and hitherto largely uncharted territory, and we should be nearer the mark, and should have a far more convincing slogan if we speak of the need, not to defend democracy but to create it.

—E.H. Carr

The New Society (London: Macmillan, 1951), p. 76.

There are, therefore, good reasons to think that those who try to define democracy not only in terms of present-day realities-a type of political system or culture which some societies possess and others donot-will find themselves left behind by history. Democracy is likely to remain not only a contestable concept, but also a 'critical' concept that is a norm or ideal by which reality is tested and found waning. There will always be some further extension or growth of democracy to be undertaken. That is not to say that perfect demoracy is in the end not attainable, any more than is perfect freedom or perfect justice. It is rather the idea and the ideal that is always likely to function as a corrective rather than as a prop to complacency.

—Anthony Arblaster

Democracy (Delhi: Viva Books, 1997), pp. 6-7.

Therefore, democratisation is something that should be understood as an ongoing, dynamic process instead of a singular achievement. Just as we recognise that some countries may come closer to fitting the democratic ideal than others, we must recognise that a similar continuum exists for their less than democratic counterparts. In the end, most governments fall somewhere in between the two poles of democracy and totalitarianism, which is an extreme form of authoritarianism. Many governments allow far more freedoms than do rigidly totalitarian regimes, but these freedoms are so few that such governments cannot adequately qualify as democracies.

—December Green and Laura Luehrmann

Comparative Politics of the Third World (Delhi: Viva Books, 2010), p. 304.

5. Last, democracy is no longer a national system, it has broadened itself to cover the whole world. If the twentieth century was the 'age of democracy', the present century marks the age of its 'universalisation'. A new model of democracy is emerging in the present age of globalisation and liberalisation that may ultimately assume the shape of, what David Held calls, 'cosmopolitan democracy'.[39]

Recent trends hopefully demonstrate that the authoritarian systems, whether rightist or leftist, have crumbled and so the world-wide spread of democracy from South Korea to South Africa and thereon to Chile and Mexico underlines the bold fact that

39. "Cosmopolitan democracy is a radical model for rethinking democracy and governance at the global, regional and national levels. It does not seek to do away with states, however their structures and power is to be considerably altered through the construction of new forms of political institutions and substantial changes in existing political structures. Such a democracy refers to democratic governance on a multiplicity of levels from the local to the global." Martin Griffiths: *Encyclopaedia of International Relations and Global Politics* (London: Routledge, 2005), pp. 138-39.

democracy "has ceased to be a matter of contention and has become a matter of convention."[40] The nemesis of Communism and the world-wide reverberations of the crash "must mark also the beginning of the global triumph of the democratic principle . . . . Right wing regimes have also crumbled."[41]

40. Albert Weale: *Democracy* (London: Macmillan, 1999), p. 1.
41. Anthony Arblaster: *Democracy* (New Delhi: Viva Books, 1997), pp. 52-53.

Bibliography

Abraham, H.J.: *The Judicial Process,* Fairlawn, New Jersey, Oxford Univ. Press, 1962.

Airan, J. W.: *The Nature of Leadership: A Political Approach,* Bombay, Lalwani, 1968.

Alker, H.R. Jr: *Mathematics and Politics,* New York, Macmillan, 1965.

Almond, G.A. and Coleman, G.B. (eds): *The Politics of Developing Areas,* Princeton, Princeton Univ. Press, I960.

Almond, G.A. and Powell, G.B.: *Comparative Politics: A Developmental Approach,* Boston, Little, Brown, 1966.

Almond, G.A. and Verba, S.: *The Civic Culture,* Princeton, Princeton Univ. Press, 1963.

Almond, G.A., Powell, G.B., Strom, K. and Dalton, R.J., *Comparative Politics Today; A World View,* Singapore, Pearson edition, 2001.

Apter, David E.: *The Politics of Modernisation,* Chicago, University of Chicago Press, 1965.

————: *Introduction to Political Analysis,* Delhi, Prentice Hall of India, 1978.

Avineri, S.: *The Social and Political Thought of Karl Marx,* Delhi, S. Chand, 1979.

Ball, A.R.: *Modern Politics and Government,* London. Macmillan, II Ed., 1976.

Baradat, L.P.: *Political Ideologies: Their Origin and Impact,* Englewood Cliffs, New Jersey, Prentice-Hall, 1979.

Barker, E.: *Political Thought in England, 1848-1914,* London, Oxford Univ. Press, 1951.

Banks, J.S. (ed): *The Elites in the Welfare State,* Translated from Dutch into English by J.E. Bingham, London, Faber and Faber, 1966.

Beetham, D.: *Max Weber and the Theory of Modern Politics,* London, George Allen and Unwin, 1974.

Beer, S.H. and Ulam, A.B.: *Patterns of Government,* New York, Random House, 1968.

Bell, D.. *The End of Ideology: On the Exhaustion of Political Ideas in the Fifties,* New York, Colliers, 1961.

Bentley, Arthur: *The Process of Government,* San Antonio, Principia Press of Trinity University, 1949.

Bhambhri, C.P.: *Bureaucracy and Politics in India,* Delhi, Vikas, 1971.

Binder, L.: *Crises and Sequences in Political Development,* Princeton, Princeton University Press, 1971.

Blondel, Jean: *An Introduction to Comparative Government,* London, Weidenfeld and Nicolson, 1969.

————:*Political Parties: A Genuine Case for Discontent,*London, Wildwood House, 1978.

————(ed): *Comparative Government,* London, Macmillan, 1969.

Bottomore, T.B.: *Elites and Society,* London, Penguin Books, 1964.

Brecht, Arnold: *Political Theory: The Foundation of Twentieth Century Political Thought,* Bombay, Times of India Press, 1970.

Brown, B.E.: *New Directions in Comparative Politics,* Bombay, Asia Pub., 1962.

Brzezinski, Z., *The Grand Failure, The Birth and Death of Communism in the Twentieth Century,* London, MacDonald, 1989.

Burns, J.M.: *Leadership,* New York, Harper and Row, 1978.

Chandhoke, Neera, *Understanding the Colonial World,* New Delhi, Sterling, 1994.

Cantori, L. J. and Ziegler, A. H. (ed.) : *Comparative Politics in the Post-Behavioural Era,* Boulder, Lynne Rienner, 1988.

Charlesworth, James C. (ed.): *Contemporary Political Analysis,* New York, Free Press of Glencoe, 1967.

Chilcote, R. H. : *Theories of Comparative Politics : The Search for Paradign Reconsidered,* Boulder : The Westview Press, 1994.

Curtis, M.: *Comparative Government and Politics,* New York, Harper and Row. 1968.

Dahl, Robert A.: *Modern Political Analysis,* Englewood Cliffs, New Jersey, Prentice Hall, 1963.

Dahrendorf, R., *Reflections on the Revolution in Europe,* London, Chatto and Windus, 1990.

Davies, M.R. and Lewis. R.A.: *Models of Political System,* Delhi, Vikas Publishing House, 1971.

Deutsch, K..: *The Nerves of Government,* New York, Free Press of Glencoe, 1963.

Dodd, C.H.: *Political Development,* London, Macmillan, 1972.

Dunn, J. (ed.), *Democracy, the Unfinished Journey,* Oxford, Oxford Univ. Press, 1993.

Duverger, M.: *Political Parties,* New York, Methuen, 1954.

Dyke, V.V.: *Political Science: A Philosophical Analystis,* Stanford, Stanford Univ. Press, 1962.

Easton, D.: *The Political System,* New York, Alfred A. Knopf, 1953.

————: *A Framework for Political Analysis,* Englewood Cliffs, New Jersey, Prentice Hall, 1965..

————:*A Systems Analysis of Political Life,* New York, John Wiley, 1965.

Eckstein, H.S.: *Pressure Group Politics,* Stanford, Stanford Univ. Press, 1960.

Eckstein, H. and Apter, D.E. (eds.): *Comparative Politics—A Reader,* New York, Free Press of Glencoe, 1963.

Eisenstadt, S.N.: *Modernisation: Protest and Change,* New Delhi, 1969.

Ehrman, H.W.: *Organised Business in France,* Princeton, Princeton University Press, 1957.

Epstein, L.B.: *Political Parties in Western Democracy,* New York, Praeger, 1967.

Eulau, H., Eldersveld, S.J. and Janowitz, M.: *Political Behaviour: A Reader,* New York, Free Press, 1956.

Finer, H.: *Theory and Practice of Modern Government,* New York, Methuen, 1962.

Finer, S.E.: *The Man on Horseback: The Role of Military in Politics,* London, Pall Mall, 1962.

————: *Comparative Government,* London, Allen Lane, 1970.

————: *The Anonymous Empire,* London, Pall Mall, 1966.

Frankel, C: *The Democratic Process,* New York, Harper and Row, 1962.

Friedrich, C.J.: *Constitutional Government and Democracy,* Oxford and IBH, Indian Edition, 1966.

————: *Trends of Federalism in Theory and Practice,* London, Pall Mall, 1968.

Friedrich, C.J. and Brzezinski, Z.K.: *Totalitarian Dictatorship and Autocracy,* New York, 1965.

Germino, D.: *Beyond Ideology: The Revival of Political Theory,* New York, Harper and Row, 1967.

Green, D. and Leuhramann, L., *Comparative Politics of the Third World,* Delhi, Viva Books, 2010.

Gould, J.A. and Thursby, V.V. (eds.): *Contemporary Political Thought: Issues in Scope, Value and Directions,* New York, Holt, Rinehart and Winston, 1969.

Gouldner, A.: *The Coming Crisis of Western Sociology,* Delhi, Heinemann, 1971.

Greenstein, F.I. and Polsby, N.W.: *Political Science: Scope and Theory,* California, Addison-Wesley, 1975, Vol. I.

————: *Macropolitical Theory,* Vol. III.

Groth, A.J.: *Comparative Politics: A Distributive Approach,* New York, Macmillan, 1971.

Haas, M.B. and Kariel, H.S. (eds): *Approaches to the Study of Political Science,* New York, Chandler, 1970.

Hague, Harrop and Breslin, *Comparative Government and Politics : An Introduction,* London, Macmillan, 1982.

Heckscher, G.: *The Study of Comparative Government and Politics,* London, George Allen and Unwin, I960.

Heywood, A., *Politics,* Houndsmill, Pelgrave Foundation, 2005.

– – – –:, *Political Theory : An Introduction,* New York, Macmillan Pelgrave, 2004.

Hitchner, D.G. and Levine: *Comparative Government and Politics,* New York, Dodd Mead & Co. 1967.

Hitchner, D.G. and Harbold, W.H.: *Modern Government: A Survey of Political Science,* New York, Dodd Mead, 1965.

Holtzman, A.: *Interest Groups and Lobbying,* London, Macmillan, 1966.

Huntington, S.P.: *Changing Patterns of Military Politics,* New York, Free Press of Glencoe, 1962.

– – – –: *The Third Wave Democratisation in the Late Twentieth Century,* Norman, University of Oklahoma Press, 1991.

Hyman, H.H.: *Political Socialisation: A Study in the Psychology of Political Behaviour,* New York, Free Press, 1959.

Janowitz, M.: *The Military in Political Development of New Nations,* Chicago, Chicago University Press, 1969.

Johnson, J.J. (ed): *The Role of Military in Underdeveloped Countries,* Princeton, Princeton University Press, 1962.

Jones, R.E.: *The Foundational Analysis of Politics,* London, Routledge and Kegan Paul, 1967.

Jupp, J.: *Political Parties,* London, Routledge and Kegan Paul, 1968.

Kavangh, D.: *Political Culture,* London, Macmillan, 1972.

Kesselman, M., Krieger, J. and Joseph, A.W. (eds.) *Third World Politics at the Crossroads,* Lexington, D.C. Heath and Company, 1996.

– – – –: *Comparative Politics at the Crossroads,* Lexington, D. C. Heath and Company, 1996.

Key, V.O. Jr.: *Politics, Parties and Pressure Groups,* New York, T.Y. Crowell & Co., 1964.

Krishna, Daya: *Political Development: A Critical Perspective,* New Delhi, Oxford University Press, 1979.

La Palombara, J. (ed.): *Bureaucracy and Political Development,* Princeton, Princeton Univ. Press, 1966.

Lo Palombara, J. and Weiner, M. (eds): *Political Parties and Political Development,* Princeton, Princeton University Press, 1966.

Langton, K.P.: *Political Socialisation,* New York, Oxford University Press, 1969.

Lawson, K.: *Political Parties and Linkage: A Comparative Perspective,* New Haven, Yale University Press, 1980.

Lane, R.E.: *Political Ideology,* New York Free Press of Glencoe, 1962.

Lasswell, H. and Kaplan, M.A.: *Power and Society,* New Haven, Yale University Press, 1950.

Latham, E.: *The Group Basis of Politics: A Study in Basing-Point Legislation,* Ithaca, New York, Cornell University Press, 1952.

Leach, E. and Mukherjee, S.N.: *Elites in South Asia,* London, Cambridge University Press, 1970.

Levy, Marion, Jr.: *The Structure of Society,* Princeton, Princeton University Press, 1952.

Leys, Colin (ed.): *Politics and Change in Developing Countries,* Cambridge, Cambridge University Press, 1969.

Lijphart, A., *Democracy in Plural Societies,* New Haven, Yale University Press, 1977.

Lipset, S.M. (ed.): *Politics and the Social Sciences,* New York, Oxford University Press, 1969.

Macridis, R.C.: *The Study of Comparative Government,* New York, Doubleday, 1955.

Macridis and Ward (eds.): *Modern Political Systems: Europe,* Englewood Cliffs, New Jersey, Prentice-Hall 1968.

McLellan, G., Held, D. and Hall, S. (eds.), *The Idea of the Modern State,* London, Polity Press, 1988.

Manheim, K.: *Ideology and Utopia: An Introduction to the Sociology of Knowledge,* Translated from German into English by Louis Wirth and Edward Shils, New York: Harcourt Brace, 1906.

Marshall, G.: *Constitutional Theory,* Oxford Univ. Press, 1971.

Mcllwain, C.H.: *Constitutionalism: Ancient and Modern,* Ithaca, New York, Cornell, 1947.

Maisel, L. and Cooper, J.: *Political Parties: Development and Decay,* London, Sage Pub., 1978.

Meehan, E.J.: *Contemporary Political Thought: A Critical Study,* Homewood, Illinois, The Dorsey Press, 1967.

————: *The Theory and Method of Political Analysis,* Homewood, Illinois, Dorsey Press, 1965.

Merriam, C: *Political Power,* New York, McGraw Hill, 1934.

Merton R.K.: *Social Theory and Social Structure,* Illinois, Free Press of Glencoe, 1959.

Michels, R.: *Political Parties,* New York, Free Press, 1949.

Mills, C.W.: *The Power Elites,* London, Oxford Univ. Press, 1959.

Miller, J.D.B.: *The Nature of Politics,* London, Gerald Duckworth, 1962.

Misra, B.B.: *The Bureaucracy in India,* New Delhi, Oxford Univ. Press, 1977.

Mosca, G.: *The Ruling Class,* New York, McGraw Hill, 1939.

Narain, Iqbal (ed.), *Development, Politics and Social Theory,* New Delhi, Sterling, 1989.

Neumann, S. (ed.): *Modern Political Parties: Approaches to Comparative Politics,* Chicago, Chicago Univ. Press, 1956.

Nettl, P.: *Political Mobilisation,* London, Faber and Faber, 1967.

Nolte, E.: *Three Faces of Fascism,* London, 1965.

O'Neil, P., *Essentials of Comparative Politics,* New York, W. W. Norton and Company, 2004.

Organski, A F.K.: *The Stages of Political Development,* New York, Alfred A. Knopf, 1965.

Pareto, W.: *The Mind and Society: A Treatise* **on** *General Sociology,* New York, Dover, 1963.

Parry, G.: *Political Elites,* London, George Allen and Unwin, 1969.

Parsons, T.: *The Social System,* New York, The Free Press of Glencoe, 1951.

Pinkney, R., *Democracy in the Third World,* New Delhi, Viva Books, 2004.

Pinney, E.L.: *Comparative Politics and Political Theory,* Univ. of North Carolina Press, 1966.

Pye, L.W.: *Aspects of Political Development,* Boston, Little, Brown, 1966.

Pye, L.W. (ed.): *Communication and Political Development,* Princeton, Princeton University Press, 1963.

Randall, V. and Theobald, R. : *Political Change and Under-Development : A Critical Introduction,* London, Macmillan, 1998.

Rostow, W.W.: *The Stages of Economic Growth,* London, Cambridge University Press, 1960.

Runciman, W.G.: *Social Sciences and Political Theory,* London, Macmillan, 1969.

Robertson, D., *A Dictionary of Modern Politics,* London, Europa Pub., 2002.

Robson, W.A.: *The Civil Service in Britain and France,* London, The Hogarth Press, 1956.

Rush, M. and Althoff, P.; *Introduction to Political Sociology,* London, Nelson, 1971.

Sakwa, R., *Post-Communism* New Delhi, Viva Books, 2002.

Sartori, G.: *Parties and Party Systems: A Framework for Analysis,* London, Cambridge Univ. Press, 1976.

Schattschneider, *Party Government,* New York, Holt, Rinehart and Winston, 1942.

Schwartz, D.C. and Schwartz, S.K..: *New Directions in Political Socialisation,* New York, Free Press, 1975.

Seliger, M.: *Ideology and Politics,* London, George Allen and Unwin, 1967.

Sergent, L.T.: *Contemporary Political Ideologies,* Homewood, Illinois, Dorsey Press, 1972.

Shils, E.: *Political Development in New States,* The Hague, Mounton & Co., 1962.

Snyder, R., Bruck, H.W. and Sapin, B.M.: *Decision-Making as an Approach to the Study of International Politics,* Princeton, Princeton Univ. Press, 1954.

Spragens, T., Jr.: *The Dilemma of Contemporary Political Theory,* New York, Dunellen, 1973.

Stepan, Alfredo: *The Military in Politics: Changing Patterns in Brazil,* Princeton, Princeton Univ. Press, 1971.

Strong, C.F.: *Modern Political Constitutions,* London, Sidgwick and Jackson, 1966.

Taylor, T. (ed.): *Approaches and Theory in International Relations,* London, Longman, 1978.

Thornston, T.P. : *The Third World in Soviet Perspective,* Princeton, Princeton Univ. Press, 1964.

Truman, D.B.: *The Governmental Process,* New York, Alfred A. Knopf, 1951.

Varma, S.P.: *Modern Political Theory,* Delhi, Vikas, 1975.

Verney, D.V.: *An Analysis of Political Systems,* London, Routledge and Kegan Paul, 1959.

Wasby, S.L.: *Political Science: The Discipline and Its Dimensions: An Introduction,* Calcutta, Scientific Book Agency, 1970.

Weber, Max.: *Theory of Social and Economic Change,* Translated from German into English by T. Parsons, London, William Hodge, 1947.

Wheare, K.C.: *Modern Constitutions,* London, Oxford Univ. Press, 1956.

– – – –: *Federal Government,* London, Oxford, Univ. Press, 1963.

– – – –: *Government by Committees,* London, Clarendon Press, 1955.

– – – –: *Legislature,* London, Oxford University Press, 1968.

Widenfield, J. (ed.): *Conflict Behaviour and Linkage Politics,* New York, David Mckay, 1973.

Wotton, G.: *Interest Groups,* Englewood Cliffs, New Jersey, Prentice-Hall, 1970.

Ybcma, S.P. : *Constitutionalism and Civil Liberties,* Leiden, Leiden Univ. Press, 1973.

Young, O.R.: *Systems of Political Science,* Englewood Cliffs, New Jersey, Prentice-Hall, 1968.

– – – –: (ed.): *Approaches to the Study of Politics,* Evanston, Illinois, North Western Univ. Press, 1950.

Zeigler, A.: *Interest Groups in American Society,* Englewood Cliffs, New Jersey, Prentice-Hall, 1964.

Index

Abertura-510
Almond, G.A.-8, 10, 16, 27, 29, 38, 45, 52, 53, on political system, 55-58, 60, 63, 64-65, 68, 69, 86, 87-89, 90, 99-101, 109-112, 139, on political development, 145-147, 151-152, 154, 163, 174, 183, 184, 185, 187, 189, on political culture, 192-198, 279, 283, 288, 291-292, 308, 317, 318, 319, 320, 321, 481.
Approaches-meaning and nature, 19-21; traditional approaches-philosophical, 21; historical, 22-25, institutional, 25, 36; legal, 25-26; modern approaches-sociological, 27, psychological, 27-28; economic, 28; quantitative, 28-29, simulation, 29-30; behavioural, 30-32; Marxist, 32-34; behaviouratism, 36, enmeshment of traditional and modern approaches, 34-35, concluding observations, 36-37.
Apter, David, 12, 19, 20-21, 34, 35-36, 39-40, on political system, 66-67, 73, 77, 80, 81, 83, 91, 93, 157, 163-165, 172, 173, 190, 191, 279-280.
Aristocracy- 442.
Aristotle- 7, 11, 12, 14, 22, 24, 36, 119, 209, 218, 319, 358, 433
Autocratic state – 146-47

Bandh (Bundh) – 334-35
Blondel, J – 1, 6, 9, 14, 16, 18, 23, 60, 65, 250, 265, 282, 310, 365, 394, 487, 489.
Bodin, Jean-22-25, 230, 432.
Bryce, Lord James – 7, 8, 11, 25, 26, 122, 224, 245, 269, 285, 452, 492.
Bureaucracy (civil service) as a pressure group-299-302, 343, concept (liberal and Marxist interpretations) – 459-461; nature and essential implications, 461-462; different theories, 462-464; organization, 464-465; functions and role, 465-467; and elitism, 467-468; and military rule, 468-470; varieties of bureaucratic hold, 470-471; as a pressure group, 471-472; neutrality versus commitment debate, 472-474; and Third World, 474-476; controlling bureaucracy, 476-477; critical appraisal, 477-479.
Burke, Edmund- 185-186, 188, 255, 267, 400.
Burnham, J- see preassure groups.

Civil society-11, 462.
Cole, G.D.H-348, 397, 440.
Communist Party-211, 225, 257, 263, 265, 271, 276, 277
Communism-28, 33, in the Soviet Union and Russia – 203, 237, 275.
Communism in China-203, National People's Congress, 58-59, 157, 231, 361, 365, 378.
Comparative Politics-meaning, nature and scope, 3-7; emergence as a science of politics, 6-7; growth of the discipline, 7-12; comparative politics and comparative government, 12-14; comparative method, 14-16; critical appraisal, 16-18.
Constitution and constitutionalism-214-217; development-217-223; Greek, 217-218; Roman, 218; middle ages, 218-219; renaissance period, 219-220; in England, 220; in France, 220-221; in USA, 221, after First World War, 221-224; after Second World War, 224; liberal concept, 226-228; latest perspective, 228-231.
Corporatist and Non-corporatist state-347-50.

de Gule, Charles- 146, 167.
Decision-making theory- 126-134.
Delegated legislation- 367-376.
Democracy- 10, 12, 92, 168-169, 171, 207, 212; meaning and forms, 491-495; case of developed countries, 496-499; case of developing countries, 499-503; post-communist states, 503-510; varieties of democracy, 509 critical appraisal, 510-512; cosmopolitan democracy – 514.
Deutsch, Karl – 1, 8, 30, 52, 107, 108, 112, neuropolitics, 113-118, 120, 128, 131, 140, 152.
Developmentalism- 36, see political development.
Dicey, A.V.- 25, 26, 235, 384, 491.
Dictatorship- 348.

Easton, David- 8, 10, 11, 26, 27, 29, 31, 37, 38, on systems analysis, 45-51, 52, 53, 54, on political system 60-62, 82-84; input-output approach, 94-98, 103, 127, 131, 177.
Executive- 74, 193, (Rule-Application Department) – meaning and varieties- 401-404, functions, 404-406; parliamentary government, 406-408; cabinet government, 408-409; prime ministerial government, 409-410; presidential government, 410-413; quasi-presidential government, 413-

416; chancellor government, 416-417; council government, 417-418; critical appraisal, 418.

Fascism-178, 199, 205-206, 208, 273, 345, 346, 352, 502.

Federalism- 229-230, 232; meaning and implications, 233-235; essential conditions, 236-237; unitarian federalism, 237-240; cooperative federalism, 240-242; inter-governmentalism and inter-federalism, 242-243; critical appraisal, 243-245.

Frank, A.G.- 153-156.

French revolution-188, 220

Friedrich, C.J.- 6, 216, 223, 323, 341-342, 343, 386, 401-402, 435, 481.

Fukuyama, Francis-491-504.

Game theory- 119-126.

Gandhi, M.K. (Gandhism) - 166, 263, 281, 286, 333, 336, 450.

Gherao (encirclement)- 335-337.

Glorious revolution- 220, 492.

Group theory of politics-see pressure groups.

Huntington, S.P.- 136, on political development and decay, 141-194, 151-152; on political modernisation- 161, 162-163, 482, 495, 503-504.

Ideology- 179, 191, 192; meaning and characteristics, 201-203; and political process, 203-208; end of ideology debate, 210-213; elitism v. Marxism, 208-211; decline, 211-213; critical appraisal, 213, 271, 275-276, 349, 490.

Indian National Congress- 211, 239, 240, 263, 271, 283.

Input-output approach- 10; implications and general characteristics, 95-97; in comparative politics, 97-100; and Easton, 97-99; key concepts, 100-104; critical appraisal, 104-106.

Judicial review- 424-429.

Judiciary- 74, 193; (Rule-Adjudication Department)- as a pressure group, 301-304; meaning and nature of law and political process, 419-420; recruitment and functions of judges, 421-424; judicial review, 424-429; critical appraisal, 429-431.

Kaplan, M.S.- 28, 39, 41, 52, 54, 87-89, 124, 256.

Laski, H.J.- 25, 223, 298, 309, 339, 356, 369, 376, 380, 410, 429, 437, 479.

Lasswell, H.D.- 2, 6, 8, 27, 28, 54, 131, 174, 182, 254, 295, 440-441, 442.

Legislature- 74, 193, (Rule-Making Department) – meaning and functions, 360-363; emergency role, 363-364; typological illustration, 364-367; delegated legislation, 367-376; committee system, 377-382; decline, 382-384.

Lenin, V.I. (Leninism)- 67, 180, 204-205, 225-226, 229, 257, 460, 463.

Lobbying- 325-329.

Locke, John- 22, 24, 25, 434-435.

Machiavelli, N.- 7, 14, 22, 24, 25, 27, 220.

MacIver, R.M.- 254, 353-354, 497.

Mao Zedong- 93, 203, 225, 229, 260.

Marx, Karl (Marxism) – 17, 24, 25, 28, approach, 32-34; 36, 93, 99, on political development, 152-153, 154, 158-160, on political culture, 188-189, on ideology, 204-205, 208-209, 211, 225, 229, on political party, 257-258, 348, on bureaucracy, 480-481, on democracy, 494-495.

Michels' iron law of Oligarchy- 208, 209, 249, 439, 447, 455-457, 467.

Mill, J.S.- 25, 28, 190, 201, 248, 340, 352, 357, 385, 394, 437, 459.

Mills, C.W.- 181, 208, 437.

Military rule-types- 480-482; forms of military intervention, 482-484; methods of controlling military, 483; causes of military intervention, 485-487; levels of military intervention 487-488; critical appraisal, 488-490.

Mosca, G.- see political elites.

Montesquieu- 14, 22, 120, 221, 434-335.

NATO- (North Atlantic Treaty Organisation)- 124, 242.

Nazism- (National Socialism of Germany)- 178.

Nehru, Jawaharlal- 181, 190, 211, 470-471.

Oligarchy-165-166, 169-171; nature and essential implications, 452-453; operational dimension, 453-455, iron law of Michels, 455-457; critical appraisal, 467.

Pareto, W. - see political elites.

Parsons, T.- 10, 46, 49, 50, 58, on functionalism, 77-82, 83, 86, 90, 138-139, 173, 190.

Party system-essential implications, 266-268; determinants and functions, 268-271; classification, 271-279; Western and non-Western paradigms, 279-282; operational dimensions, 282-284; critical appraisal, 284-287; partyless democracy, 287.

Plato - 11, 22, 24, 121, 123, 217-218, 338, 344.

Political communication-nature and meaning-105-109; functional aspects of the approach, 109-112; social cohesion and change, 112-113; neuropolitics of Karl Deutsch, 113-117; critical appraisal, 117-118.

Political culture- 59, 69, 143, concept of secularisation, 188-192; and stability and change, 192-194; and ideology, 194-195; and political systems, 195-199; critical appraisal, 200-203, 267.

Political development-129-130; development syndrome, 135-141; concept and theory, 141-144; implications and dimensions, 145-148; crises, 148-153; stages model, 148-151; Huntington's paradigm of development and decay, 151-152; Marxian model of development, 152-153, political under-development and dependency, 153-158; critical appraisal, 158-160.

Political elitism- 209; nature and essential implications, 439-442; different approaches, 443-444; leading theorists, 444-448; and different political systems, 448-449; critical appraisal, 449-451; and elitism, 470-471.

Political modernization- 85, 135, implications and dimensions, 161-163; Apter's paradigm, 163-165; and social change, 165-167; and political systems, 170-175; critical appraisal, 172-173.

Political parties and party politics-249-251; linkage concept, 251-254; meaning and nature of political party, 254-58; Duverger's thesis, 258-262; leadership, 262-264, critical appraisal, 264-265.

Political simulation- 119-134; game theory, 119-126; decision-making theory, 126-134.

Political socialization- 69, nature and essential implications, 174-176, development in open and closed societies, 176-180; major agents, 180-183; critical appraisal, 184.

Political system- implications and nature, 52-55, properties and characteristics, 55-58; variables, 58-60; functional aspects, 60-67; Easton's model, 61-62; Almond's model, 63-65; Blondel's model, 65-66; Apter's model, 66-67; structure and culture of political system, 67-69; critical appraisal, 69-71.

Post-communist states – 503-510.

Pressure (interest) groups-288; significance of study, 288-290; and political parties, 290-292; and electoral process, 293-295; and legislature 205-297; and executive, 297-299; and bureaucracy, 299-302; and judiciary, 302-304; and public opinion, 304-305; determinants, 305-309; critical appraisal, 309; group theory of politics, 310-314; meaning and nature, 314-318; existence and articulation of pressure groups, 318-321; critical appraisal, 322-324.

Public opinion- 69, 304-305.

Pye, L. W.- 135-141, 147-150, 151, 162, 174, 185-186, 199.

Representation-meaning and nature, 385-388; and responsiveness, 388-391; varietes, 391-399; territorial representation, 391-392; proportional representation, 392-394; minority representation, 394-397; functional representation, 397-398; characteristic representation, 398; critical appraisal, 399-400.

Separation of powers- 220, 223, 411-412, interpretations, 432-433, Montesquieu's theory, 433-434, checks and balances, 435-436; critical appraisal, 437-438.

Schelling's strategic conflict theory, 124-125.

Socialism-28,33.

Strike, 329-334.

Structural-functional approach-36, implications and assumptions, 72-75; functional analysis, 75-76; functionalism in political sociology, 77-82; in political science, 82-90.

Systems analysis in Political Science, 38-42; concepts and implications, 42-44; general systems theory in politics, 44-45; Easton's analysis, 44-49; critical appraisal, 49-51.

Third World-33, 86, 89, 149, 153, 163, 165, 184, 185, 226, 250, 350-351, 474-477, 480.

Tocqueville, A de- 7, 16, 36, 224, 254.

Totalitarianism (totalitarian system) – 7, 144, 170, 179, 197, 205, 223, 227, 230, 231, 262, 270, 272, 274, 278, 281-282, 321, 342-344, 345-346.

Typology of states-liberal-democratic state, 338-342, totalitarian state, 342-346, autocratic state, 346-347, corporatist and neo-corporatist state, 347-349, state in Third World countries, 349-351, welfare state, 351-359.

Wallerstein, I.- 155-158.

Weber, Max-7, 27, 53, 54, 74, 137, 452; on bureaucracy, 465-472.

Welfare state- 353-361, 497.

Wilson, Harold- 167, 279, 299, 411.

Wilson, Woodrow- 298.

World War I- 221, 223, 399.

World War II- 189, 220, 221-222, 227, 250, 264, 346, 372, 426.